Handbook on
Electronic Commerce

Springer-Verlag Berlin Heidelberg GmbH

Michael Shaw · Robert Blanning
Troy Strader · Andrew Whinston
(Editors)

Handbook on Electronic Commerce

With 112 Figures
and 43 Tables

Springer

Professor Michael Shaw
University of Illinois at Urbana-Champaign
The Beckman Institute for
Advanced Science and Technology
405 North Mathews Avenue
Urbana, IL 61801, USA

Professor Robert Blanning
Vanderbilt University
Owen Graduate School of Management
Nashville, TN 37203, USA

Assistant Professor Troy Strader
Iowa State University
Management Information Systems
300 Carver Hall
Ames, IA 50011, USA

Professor Andrew Whinston
The University of Texas at Austin
MSIS Dept. – CBA .202
College of Business Administration
Austin, TX 78712-1175, USA

Originally published in the series: International Handbooks on Information Systems

---

ISBN 978-3-540-67344-6

Library of Congress Cataloging-in-Publication Data
Die Deutsche Bibliothek – CIP-Einheitsaufnahme
Handbook on Electronic Commerce /ed.: Michael Shaw ... – Berlin; Heidelberg; New York; Barcelona; Hong Kong; London; Milan; Paris; Singapore; Tokyo: Springer, 2000

ISBN 978-3-540-67344-6   ISBN 978-3-642-58327-8 (eBook)
DOI 10.1007/978-3-642-58327-8

Springer-Verlag is a company in the specialist publishing group BertelsmannSpringer.
© Springer-Verlag Berlin Heidelberg 2000
Originally published by Springer-Verlag Berlin · Heidelberg 2000
Softcover reprint of the hardcover 1st edition 2000

Coverdesign: Erich Kirchner, Heidelberg

SPIN 10765856   42/2202-5 4 3 2 1 0 – Printed on acid-free paper

Foreword

The U.S. and other developed nations are undergoing a transition from a paper economy to a digital economy, not unlike the transition from an oral exchange economy to a physically recorded (clay, papyrus) exchange economy that took place several millennia ago. As with the earlier transition, a change in the medium for recording and reporting transactions (i.e., from oral to written, from written to electronic) is bringing about a significant change in the economic and social system in which they are imbedded.

The oral-to-written transition eventually gave us the concepts of property rights, commercial law, accounting standards, and financial transparency. What will the written-to-electronic transition give us? The answer is not clear, but we can expect that the economic system that follows this transition will differ substantially from the current system to which we are accustomed.

In this book we examine the electronic exchange mechanisms of the emerging digital economy. We do so by examining eight salient topics in electronic commerce (EC). Each of these topics is examined in detail in a separate section of this book. The first topic is the *New Era of EC*. Electronic Data Interchange (EDI) over Wide Area Networks is beginning to transform the economies of the developed nations. In addition, the Internet, and especially the World Wide Web, is contributing to this transformation in an important way. This will have an impact on certain types of transactions (e.g., auctions), consumer search for products and services, marketing efforts (e.g., advertising), product customization and pricing, producer and consumer decision support, market research, and the like. We (i.e., the authors of the chapters in this part of the book) examine the broad scale impact of digital technology on commerce.

The second topic is *Consumer EC*. Specialists in consumer marketing are especially concerned with theories and models of buyer behavior - for example, how purchasing decisions are made and how these decisions are affected by marketing efforts. This in turn requires that the specialists develop methods for measuring buyer behavior. We examine the ways in which these theories, models, and measurement methods as applied to Internet marketing will differ from those as applied to marketing that makes use of more conventional media.

The third topic is *Web-based Storefront Design and Development*. An important and growing component of EC is the use of the World Wide Web, sometimes along with electronic mail, to advertise products, provide detailed product and other (e.g., pricing, delivery) information, and execute sales transactions. The result is a virtual store, which has characteristics analogous to but different from physical stores (i.e., specialty stores, supermarkets, shopping malls, etc.). We examine the similarities and differences between traditional physical stores and the emerging electronic stores and offer suggestions for the design of Web-based electronic stores.

The fourth topic is *EC Technology and Infrastructure*. Five topics are investigated here. The first is online payment methods, which have many of the problems of more traditional payment methods and a few additional problems as well. The second is smart cards, some of which are memory cards and some of which contain their own internal processing capabilities (i.e., chips). The third is the assembly of EC systems from reusable and interoperable components. The fourth is the digital library as a component of an EC system. The fifth is the use of intelligent agents in EC networks.

The fifth topic is *Business-to-Business (B2B) EC*. Much of the "talk" (news reporting, empirical research, speculation, etc.) about EC concerns consumer marketing, especially as it relates to the Internet. But there is a growing use of EC in B2B activities. At present, much of this is due to EDI, but increasingly it also includes the use of Internet technology in the form of extranets. Both of these will contribute to the rise of mass customization of products and services and will make possible more effective supply chain management. We examine how this will come about and how the structure of B2B relationships is likely to change.

The sixth topic is *Enterprise Management for EC*. Three topics are investigated here. One is the growing internal use of Internet technology in the form of intranets. The second is the rise of virtual organizations and their associated extranets. The third is the distribution of existing information technology applications, such as data warehousing and decision support, across the World Wide Web. In each case, existing useful and powerful systems (i.e., internal information processing systems, interorganizational systems, and computer-based analytical tools) are enhanced when distributed across an EC network.

The seventh topic is *Information Services and Digital Products*. The Internet can be used not only as a market mechanism for traditional products and services, but also as the foundation of a market for information. When compared with traditional markets, the market for electronic information is similar in some respects but different in others. We examine this new market for digital products, with special attention to the production and sale of digital products and the role of information intermediaries that help to match information producers with information consumers.

The eighth topic is *Security, Privacy, and Legal issues*. The Internet is inherently an insecure network, although it is becoming more secure. However, the rise of EC on the Internet offers financial incentives to exploit its lack of security, both by interfering with transactions (i.e., reading, tampering, spoofing, and repudiating) and by gaining unauthorized access to organizational networks (i.e., intranets and extranets). EC also presents legal issues, including the nature of electronic contracts (e.g., one-to-many contracts), the use of electronic authentication in reducing fraud, and capital markets transactions (e.g., disclosure as it relates to securities purchases).

So far we have talked about the electronic exchange mechanisms of our emerging digital economy. But what about an eventual digital society and digital polity? If companies and customers can exchange products and services for money (and for each other) over digital networks, why cannot politicians and constituents exchange votes and elective office for government actions (e.g., statutes, regulations, and referenda) over the same or similar networks? This fascinating topic awaits further investigation.

Michael J.P. Shaw
Robert W. Blanning
Troy J. Strader
Andrew B. Whinston

Contents

Part V   Business-To-Business Electronic Commerce

Part VI   Enterprise Management

Part VII   Information Services and Digital Products

Part VIII   Security, Privacy, and Legal Issues

Part I
The New Era

CHAPTER 1
Electronic Commerce: State of the Art

Michael J. Shaw
Department of Business Administration, College of Commerce, University of Illinois at Urbana-Champaign, m–shaw2@uiuc.edu

There is a revolution transforming the global economy. Web technology is transforming all business activities into information-based. The rate of technological change is so rapid that emerging electronic commerce already is making fundamental changes in the economic landscape, affecting every aspect of how business is and will be conducted. The Web has extended the reach of corporations. New business opportunities are growing incrementally because of the vast amount of business information made available by the global Web, which helps bring together the information passed between businesses, between a business and its customers, and among different departments of a business. It will no longer be possible operationally or strategically to ignore the information-based virtual value chains for any business. This chapter reviews the scope, current applications, and the potentials of electronic commerce. It also develops a framework for identifying the significant opportunities and important research issues associated with electronic commerce. The emphasis is on taking an interdisciplinary view that integrates technology and business models.

Keywords: Electronic Commerce; Web Strategy

1 Introduction

We are witnessing a revolution in commerce and society primarily due to an explosion in information technology and the resulting rapid emergence of *electronic commerce (EC)*. Transaction based commercial activities such as information gathering, shopping, trading, brokering, banking, accounting, auditing, auctioning, financing, negotiating, collaborating, marketing, supplying, partnering, training, meeting, scheduling, manufacturing, distributing, servicing, and retailing are experiencing rapid change due to the adoption of new information technology. In short, much of what we know about the everyday conduct of business will continue to change. All companies, large and small, will face inevitable challenges brought about by these technologically enabled developments. Fortunately, this change creates both risks and opportunities. Electronic commerce is in many ways an uncharted new frontier. Carefully thought-out business execution, strategy development, and research become important to understand all the shifting rules and to identify rising opportunities to develop new competitive advantages.

The information revolution is drastically reshaping global society and pushing the world toward an information-based economy. This revolution is touted as the beginning of a new era in which the majority of the value-adding activities in the economy will be shifted to cyberspace through globally connected electronic networks. There are many optimistic forecasts on how fast the electronic commerce market will grow. Most, including one from the U.S. Department of Commerce (Margherio, 1998), predict that the EC market will grow to hundreds of billions of dollars by early next century. A frequently quoted figure is that the total volume of electronic commerce will reach $327 billion by 2003 (CyberStats, 1997; *Business Week*, 1998). According to new projections from Forrester Research Inc., worldwide Internet commerce will reach as high as $3.2 trillion in 2003, representing nearly 5% of the global sales (http://www.forrester.com/press/pressrel/981105.htm). These predictions paint a rosy picture for electronic commerce. However, even with all the optimism, how to capitalize on the full potential of electronic commerce is still an open question. With technology moving at a blazing pace, governments, businesses, and the general public all are struggling to catch up. On the other hand, the scope of electronic commerce is so broad and its reach so wide that efforts by the participants and the stakeholders need to be well coordinated. Multidisciplinary perspectives are therefore necessary to understand many of the issues involved.

The next section surveys the scope and the developments in electronic commerce along a host of dimensions, followed by a review of the critical issues, challenges, and opportunities involved. The objective is to lay out a framework for understanding the state and direction of the developments. Specifically, the following issues need to be addressed.

- The scope of electronic commerce, its components, and potential impacts.
- The consumer-oriented electronic commerce opportunities, the enhancement of electronic storefronts, and the development of new consumer processes.
- The strategy for developing online business and digital services.
- The transformation of business-to-business infrastructure and partnerships.
- The rising needs to address security, privacy, and legal concerns.
- The technology and infrastructure for EC, such as electronic payment systems.
- The Web strategy for coordinating channel partners and for streamlining their processes.

This chapter ends with a summary of the challenges and opportunities in electronic commerce.

2 Review of Practices, Scope, and Opportunities

Electronic commerce covers a wide variety of perspectives. The technological enabler is the Web, including the globally connected networks, the universal networking interface and transmitting standard (based on TCP/IP), and the World Wide Web infrastructure that facilitates information storage, browsing, and retrieval. Statistics and success stories about the growth of the Internet and electronic commerce abound (the following statistics are based on an annual information technology survey in *Business Week* (June 22, 1998) and a report published by the U.S. Department of Commerce (Margherio, 1998)).

- Fewer than 40 million people around the world were connected to the Internet during 1996. By the end of 1997, more than 100 million people were using it. Some experts believe that there may be one billion people connected to the Internet by 2005.
- The Internet is growing faster than all other technologies that have preceded it. Radio existed for 38 years before it had 50 million listeners and television took 13 years to reach that mark. The Internet crossed that line in just four years (since the wide distribution of World Wide Web browsers).
- Traffic on the Internet has been doubling every 100 days. In addition, according to the Internet Domain Survey (http://www.nw.com/zone/WWW/report.html), there were 1,776,000 host computers on the Internet in July 1993. By July 1998, the number was 36,739,000.
- In 1996, Amazon.com, the first Internet bookstore, recorded sales of less than $16 million. In 1997, it sold $148 million worth of books to Internet customers. Cisco Systems closed 1996 with just over $100 million in sales on the Internet. By the end of 1997, its Internet sales were running at a $3.2 billion in annual sales.
- In January 1997, Dell computer was selling less than $1 million of computers per day on the Internet. The company reported daily sales of $10 million in fall 1998, according to a CNN report. In the meantime, Dell has developed its global supply chains into one of the most efficient, with the inventories turned around several times faster than its competitors.
- Online sales are growing in every category of goods. Between 1997 to 2001, financial services will grow to $5 billion from $1.2 billion, travel will grow to $7.4 billion from $654 million, computer hardware and software will grow to $3.8 billion from $863 million, and books and music will grow to $1.1 billion from $156 million.
- Business-to-business (B2B) EC sales will grow from $8 billion in 1997 to $183 billion in 2001. It will account for 78% of the total spent on cyber transactions in 1998.
- EDI is used to exchange about $250 billion of worth of products in 1998, which is 14 times larger than business-to-business EC. But EDI is pricey and complex to use. Within five years, EDI and Web-based B2B EC markets will be about equal, at more than $450 billion annually. By 2003, more than 30% of EDI data is expected to traverse the Web.
- General Electric Co. brought $1 billion worth of supplies via the Web in 1997. That saved the company 20% on material costs. By 2000, GE expects to be buying $5 billion over the Web.

- By the end of 1997, the number of profitable Web sites – both for consumer and for inter-business transactions- jumped to 46%, ending three years of stagnation at 30%. And some 81% of the remainder expect to be profitable in a year or two (BusinessWeek, 1998, p.126).

Due to its broad scope, the focus of electronic commerce must be viewed from a number of perspectives to appreciate a particular functional emphasis fully. Several dimensional perspectives are explained in the following.

1. *Technology*. Electronic commerce is made possible by the global networks where business processes, inter-organization transactions, and market trading take place. The Internet is the major contributor, but other communications networks, such as value-adding networks for carrying out electronic data interchange, also play a role.
2. *Marketing and "new consumer processes"*. Electronic commerce is the new channel to connect with customers and a new media to promote products. EC expands the boundaries of enterprises to reach out directly to their customers.
3. *Economic*. Electronic commerce is a new economy that is information-based and shaped by new institutional and industrial organizations (Stigler, 1968). EC creates new markets and economic activities that are characterized by instant information flows, the delayering of value chains, the emergence of new intermediaries, and the shifting economic rules and market dynamics (Choi, et al., 1997). The fundamental valuation has been transformed by these changes, leading to needs for new strategies and business models.
4. *Electronic linkage*. Electronic commerce provides new linkages to achieve more efficient economic activities, including: (a) the interface between businesses to consumers; (b) the linking of a business to its channel; and (c) the coordination of different units within a business.
5. *Information value-adding*. Electronic commerce accelerates the separation of the information-based value chains from the physical value-adding chains. The information-based or the virtual value chains (Sviokla,1998), create new ways to compile, synthesize, package, distribute, and market information as products and services.
6. *Market-making*. The global networks supporting electronic commerce have provided opportunities to form electronic markets to match buyers and sellers (Strader & Shaw, 1997; Bakos, 1998). This new market space features real-time information transmission, interactive communication, wide reach and connectivity, and rich content. These characteristics potentially can form more efficient markets for exchanging goods, resource allocation, and trading.
7. *Service infrastructure*. Electronic commerce needs a variety of services to support all potential functions, activities, requirements, and applications. These services need a coherent infrastructure to ensure integrity, uniformity, efficiency, and effectiveness. Examples of the infrastructure include infrastructures for public-key, payment and banking, information services for organizing, searching, retrieving,

filtering, and summarizing information, and for processing business-to-business transactions, sharing supplier-catalog information, and supply-chain coordination.

8. *Legal, privacy, and public policy.* All the structural, institutional, process, and technological changes brought by electronic commerce necessitate a new framework for addressing the legal, privacy, and public policy needs. This is a difficult task due to the number and diversity of interest groups involved. Yet, this is the one dimension that needs to be taken into account early in the development of EC to protect the interest of the general public. Addressing the issues involved requires a balanced approach that takes into account the interests and potential conflicts among different parties.

The scope of electronic commerce is depicted in Figure 1 (Shaw, et al., 1997), where, in addition to linking with suppliers (EC5) and distributors (EC4), it also includes the interface with consumers (EC3), and the management within the enterprise (EC1). Finally, electronic commerce also addresses the infrastructure issues (EC2), such as payment systems, network security, human-computer interface, and the information infrastructure. Electronic commerce provides unprecedented opportunities to integrate various types of communication networks, including the three

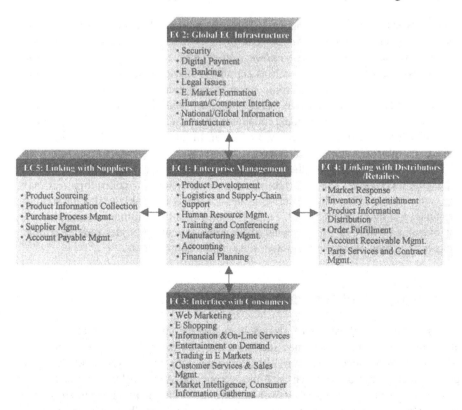

Fig. 1. The scope of electronic commerce

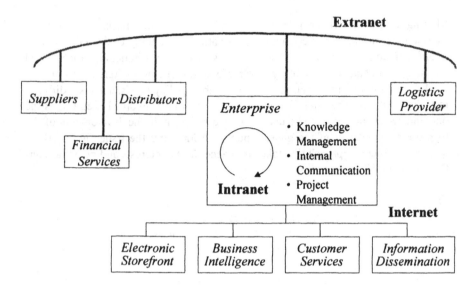

Fig. 2. The Web centric enterprise

primary types as depicted in Figure 2. These three types of networks have taken up their own specialization. (1) *The Intranet* for process, knowledge, and internal communication management, (2) *The Extranet* for external coordination and information sharing with channel partners such as suppliers, distributors, and dealers, and (3) *The Internet* for setting up electronic storefronts, providing customer services, and collecting market intelligence. In developing electronic commerce, there is a constant need for new business models suitable for the new products (e.g., digital ones), new industrial organizations (e.g., virtual organizations), and new economic structures (e.g., information intermediaries).

Figure 1 and Figure 2 together summarize well the major impacts of the Web on managing a company. The Web provides the infrastructure for collecting, distributing, and sharing information. It serves as new channels for making sales, promoting products, and delivering services. Finally, it integrates the information organization for managing activities on all levels of the company and provides new electronic links for reaching out to the customers and supply-chain partners.

3 Web Storefront and Consumer Interface

One of the first applications of electronic commerce involves the development of electronic storefronts. Companies such as Cisco (Clark, 1997) or Dell Computers (Hill, 1997) have developed their Web storefronts into major sales channels. High profile Internet companies such as Amazon.com and Auto-by-Tel have developed innovative business models using Web storefronts as their main channel. However, these early successes do not necessarily guarantee that the Web will become the dominant sales channel for every business. One of the critical aspects influencing the success of electronic commerce will be the effectiveness of the interface interacting with the consumers. To date, it is not clear what deciding factors will draw people to shop on the Web. What makes Internet shopping different from mail-order catalogues or TV shopping? There are a host of potential advantages associated with the use of Web storefront as the consumer interface. The Web can provide aggregate information and interactive transmission, for example, to make the presentation more interesting. It is especially good at achieving remote accessibility while delivering rich information content at the same time (Evans, and Wurster, 1997). However, there are still barriers against consumers using the Web for retail shopping. Yes, selling products such as books, music CDs, and computer equipment over the Web has been relatively successful, but the type of text-based interface design used by, say, Amazon.com may not be able to cope with products that have more variations. To make the Web the prime place for shopping, more efforts will be needed to make the Web a better interface for consumers.

Overcoming these barriers is essential. One enhancement to the human computer interface (HCII) incorporates virtual reality (VR) with 3D visual and audio displays to enrich the Web shopping experience. Some of the techniques and tools developed in this area can be useful in implementing virtual storefronts.

Imagine sitting in your living room browsing the Web from the VR Web TV. You search and retrieve a direct merchant's catalogue of winter clothing. Different styles of coats are displayed on a three-dimension digital model made to resemble your body. You can select the specific color combination and adjustment that fits your taste. While in this VR environment, you may also want to test the utility of the coat by walking around, getting into your car, and going to the office, to test its quality and suitability under various circumstances of use. In this way, a good VR interface could lead to the implementation of mass customization. You could interact with the VR display of the goods to select desirable features until you are satisfied and place the order through the Web to receive a highly customer specific product.

Although sales on the Internet through the electronic storefronts have met only limited successes to date, there are reasons for optimism. The bandwidth of the network infrastructure is improving to the extent that the information content presented in the Web storefront is getting richer. Statistics show that there is good potential for growth of this type of commerce. Each year about 55% of U.S. households purchase products from catalogs and about 7% purchase from TV (Burke, 1998). When the Web interface is better designed, catalog shoppers may be the first to consider electronic shopping.

Whether virtual-store shopping will take off or not certainly depends on more than the interface design. Users' acceptance of a new technology is always difficult to predict. Ease of use, prices, costs, sense of community, trust, search efforts needed, information richness, among other factors, will likely play a role. There are still plenty of uncertainties. For example, Proctor and Gamble, with a global advertising budget around $3 billion, is seriously developing interactive marketing through their Web storefront. Yet their advertising spending on the Web is only a

very tiny portion of the total advertising budget. Their executive for global advertising recently lamented that "the current state of Web advertising just isn't effective
enough to warrant any truly meaningful investment from us (Beausejour, 1998)."
Other than the technical constraints and the need for more reliable measurement, the
third reason he cited, which he emphasized was the major reason, was that marketing companies like Proctor & Gamble really don't know how to use the Web effectively yet. Questions on how to develop meaningful relationships with consumers,
whether brand name will play a significant role in the virtual shopping world, and
what the consumers' perception is about purchasing from virtual storefronts still are
mostly unanswered.

4 Online Business and Digital Interactive Services

The rapid adoption of personal computers and greater accessibility of Internet infrastructure continues to fuel the digitization of products (e.g. newspapers) and services
(e.g. voice communications) -- commonly referred to as digital interactive services
(DIS). Many companies in entertainment, creative content, news distribution, communications, computing, and financial services are seizing the DIS opportunity by
aligning capabilities and assets through mergers and acquisitions, resulting in the
consolidation of the information industries.

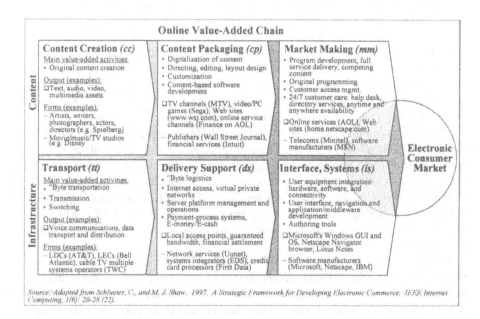

Fig. 3. The strategic framework for the digital interactive services

Consumer online services demand that diverse inputs must be combined to create and deliver value. No single industry alone has what it takes to get DIS off the ground. Success in DIS requires inputs from diverse industries that have only been peripherally related in the past. In order to seize the opportunity, a company from one of the related industries would have to exploit its own capabilities and make cooperative and collaborative arrangements with companies in complementary industries. Schlueter and Shaw (1997) provide a detailed representation of the value chain of digital interactive services. They describe the value-added stages of online industries and markets. As shown in Figure 3, the model consists of six core processes: (1) content direction, (2) content packaging, (3) market making, (4) transport, (5) delivery service, and (6) interface and systems. In electronic publishing, for example, strategic choices will evolve among online networks, community organizers, interactive studios, agencies, and platform providers. They are described in Figure 4.

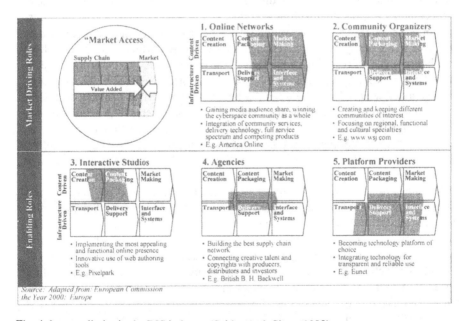

Fig. 4. Intermediaries in the DIS industry (Schlueter & Shaw, 1998)

5 Business-To-Business Electronic Commerce

Business-to-business (B2B) electronic commerce is projected to constitute the largest portion of the whole electronic commerce market for the next five years. Some estimates put B2B to be close to 78% of the overall EC market (Business Week, 98). It should not be difficult to understand why that is the case. While much media attention has been paid to buying books, music CDs, or flowers over the Web, behind the scenes companies are purchasing their computers, raw materials, and other supplies from one another as never before over the Web. For a multinational corporation such, purchases can easily reach billions of dollars annually.

There are two types of B2B EC markets. One is related to the management of material flows in production-oriented supply-chain networks. The other is related to the procurement of maintenance, repair, and operation (MRO) items, sometimes referred to as the *indirect* items. Purchases of direct items required in the production of an organization's products typically are planned well in advance and their procurement is under tight control. On the other hand, while the value of MRO items, or indirect items, is generally much smaller than that of direct items, the cost to process each order is roughly the same. Moreover, the procurement of indirect items can be improved more easily than production-related processes, which have already been greatly improved by reengineering efforts in the past decade. For either the direct or the indirect procurement processes, electronic data interchange (EDI) has been used to forge automated linkages between the buyer and supplier to transmit orders, receipts, and payments electronically. The indirect procurement process typically consists of selecting products and vendors, filling out requisition forms, getting approvals, sending out purchase orders, receiving the goods, checking the content, matching the invoices, and sending out the payment. This process has been carried out traditionally either manually with paper-based documents or electronically by EDI. Studies have shown that using EDI for linking with channel partners can help reduce processing cycle-time, improve accuracy, and create strategic value (Mukhopadhyay, 1998). But EDI requires the support of private lines or value-adding networks (VANs) and relies on software that still incorporates varying formats. It has not been easy for small companies to adopt the technology.

With the Web, major vendors have begun to put their product catalogs online. Buyers can thus conduct the procurement process directly through the Web. The Web-based electronic catalogs are fundamentally changing business-to-business procurement. Physical catalogs are cumbersome to use, require large storage areas, become dated soon after being published, and make searching and comparison very difficult. While putting catalogs on CD-ROM eliminates these problems, they too become obsolete soon after publication. Furthermore, CD-ROMs still require physical storage and either replication for each user or some means of remote access and control. The interactive possibilities of Web-based electronic catalogs remedy these deficiencies by eliminating the need for physical storage and making continuous updating effective and efficient. Web-based electronic catalogs also simplify comparison shopping, and keeping the catalogs up to date, while making it easier to locate and evaluate a supplier's goods.

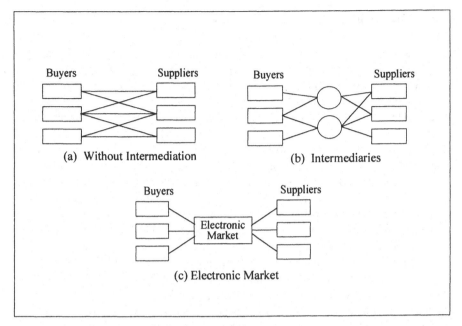

Fig. 5. Three types of buyer-supplier communication structure

Web-based procurement systems also create electronic links between suppliers and buyers, as does EDI (Choudhury and Konsynski, 1998; Kemerer, 1998; Sirini-vasan, 1994; Wang & Seidmann, 1995). These links can be organized in different ways. As shown in Figure 5, buyers and suppliers can either form direct connections without any intermediary (a), with intermediaries (b), or acquire the goods through electronic markets (Strader and Shaw, 1997) (c). Current EDI systems are mostly implemented in forms (a) and (b) through value added networks or private lines. Web-based catalog systems enable the buyers to check the online catalogs of a pool of (selected) suppliers and then submit purchase orders electronically. Therefore, Web-based systems tend to be more market oriented, which can translate into lower costs. It is interesting to note whether there are still opportunities for intermediaries, such as the integrated suppliers, to play a role in the supply chains.

Eventually, *interoperable electronic catalogs* will emerge and change the dynamics of the industry (CommerceNet, 1997). Buyers will be better served with inter-operable catalogs because they can then query multiple catalogs concurrently. Retailers and distributors will benefit because they can use interoperable electronic catalogs to reposition their products and services. For large manufacturers, the inter-operable electronic catalogs infrastructure provides them with direct links to reach out to more customers, although it is likely that they will lose some of their pricing power. Before B2B electronic commerce reaches that stage, however, there will have to be a standard for describing product and item classification.

6 Security, Privacy, and Legal Issues

Security is a critical issue in EC. Consumers demand secure systems if they are to use EC payment. Cryptography is used to ensure network and transactional security. While some experimentation with electronic banks and digital money has occurred, the most convenient payment method remains the credit card. However, just as everyone should be cautious about transmitting one's credit card number on an insecure phone line, the Internet is far from secure. The US government is concerned that the use of encryption will limit its ability to conduct electronic surveillance. In the name of national security, export restriction has been imposed on the more powerful encryption technology. By the same token, the current administration has adopted an encryption policy based on encryption key escrow with trusted third parties. For electronic commerce to develop its full potential, there must be a global encryption key management infrastructure to ensure the integrity of transactions concerning documents, digital signatures, payment, and certificates (Denning, 1997).

The era of electronic commerce will bring about greater use of electronic documents as the substitute for traditional paper-based documents. This shift requires the development of a new framework of legal precedent. In Illinois, for instance, there are thousands of statutory requirements for paper documents and signatures that do not pertain to electronic documents. The efforts to develop a new legal framework on the state, federal, and international levels need better coordination. In addition, the legal framework should directly address rules of engagement for EC participants. For example, when a company receives an electronic payment from a bank, the company needs to know what the rules and potential liability are. This issue becomes even more complicated when third parties, such as the verification agencies for digital signatures, are involved in the infrastructure.

Consumer polls have shown that privacy is overwhelmingly the most critical factor in deciding whether to purchase over the Web. Yet there are tensions between the interests of businesses, the government, and consumers in addressing issues related to privacy. For instance, large databases are increasingly available to companies for building consumer profiles, information on spending patterns and demand volumes and to enable companies to target their products and services much more effectively. To strike a balance between the openness of the Web and the privacy concerns of the general public, it is important that an agreed-upon practice or standard be adopted globally to govern information-collection in electronic commerce. The emerging framework is based on the concept of *notification* and *consent*. A company must notify individuals about their information-collection practices. Once they have obtained consent, companies would be free to use collected personal information for stated purposes. This approach should also allow the flexibility of having multiple levels of privacy for the individual.

An example of why there should be coordination internationally in moving electronic commerce forward is best illustrated by the recently issued European Union Data Directory, which went into effect in October 1998. The goal of the European law is to prohibit companies from collecting data, including through the Web, from their customers without their consent. The Directory can affect the electronic commerce effort in the U.S. because a key provision is that companies are prohibited to transmit data to countries that does not guarantee comparable data protection (http://www.privacy.org/). The U.S. on the other hand is taking a more voluntary system. It is essential for the U.S. and Europe to reach an agreement that guarantees privacy in cyberspace, so that global electronic commerce can progress without disruption.

7 Electronic Payment Systems

The payment transaction of electronic commerce – as opposed to cash, personal checks, credit cards, etc. used in the traditional forms of face-to-face transactions – is carried out by a form of digital financial instrument, such as electronic cash, (encrypted) credit information, prepaid smart cards, or electronic checks. These digital financial instruments are backed by a bank, an intermediary, or legal tender.

Currently, the most common means of payment is submission of credit card information through a secured Web transmission. While it is not new, there are several potential problems with this method. First, when purchasing over the Web a consumer rarely knows the merchant selling through an electronic storefront. Without a better financial instrument, this exposure of risks and the common perception of them can limit the growth of electronic commerce. Secondly, a substantial portion of electronic commerce involves digital products, which can be divided and repackaged in many nontraditional ways. A consumer may, for example, want to know the score for a particular professional ball game from a pay-per-view Web site. The charge for such online purchases may be very small. This type of so-called *micropayments* in electronic commerce is not economical for credit cards but needs new kind of digital financial instruments.

A third reason for new electronic payment systems is the lack of privacy because the consumer's behavior can be tracked through the credit card number. In the world of electronic commerce the consumer should have the option of using digital cash to pay for an online purchase without providing any personal information or leaving any record linking the transaction to the buyer. To meet their stated functional requirements, electronic payment systems must be (1) secure enough to fend off any fraudulent attempt to interfere with the Web system, (2) cost-effective for low-value transactions, (3) protective of the privacy of the users, and (4) convenient for Web purchasing. There are a number of commercial electronic payment systems developed to meet these requirements, such as First Virtual, CyberCash, Mondex, NetBill, NetCheque, and DigiCash (Chaum, 1988, Lynch and Lundquist, 1996; Medvinsky and Neuman, 1993). For Web-based credit processing, Visa and MasterCard have developed the Secure Electronic Transaction (SET) protocol. Although the volume of transactions is still relatively small, the projected rapid growth of EC will urgently require a more uniform standard for electronic payment systems to ensure the integrity, security, and effectiveness of the payment systems.

8 Enterprise Channel Integration and Mass Customization

Increasingly, network organizations of specialized units coordinated through electronic networks will replace the traditional hierarchical organization. Because of their agility, these network organizations can be configured and reconfigured rapidly to exploit small but profitable windows of business opportunity. The Web also provides new ways to coordinate workflow, manage documents, and enhance group work. Issues of inter-process coordination, client-server computing, and the design of firewalls are important.

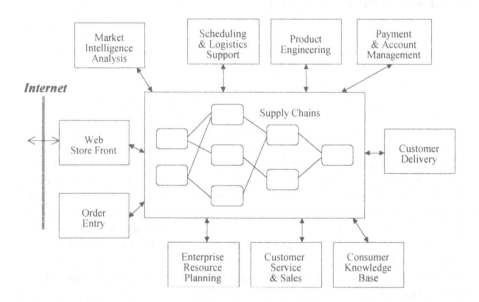

Fig. 6. Web-directed supply-chain network management

It is clear that through the combining of data mining technology with vastly improved data collection and communications capabilities, an enterprise-wide "sense and response" system for rapid deployment is emerging as the new paradigm for best utilizing new capabilities made possible by the availability of market data. The analytic outcomes will trigger the necessary product and process decisions. The ability of a company to develop a globally wired business network and its implementation as well as managerial components will determine its competitive position. This requires fully integrating the customer front-end with the supply-chain operations (Figure 6). Following this framework, the Web provides an additional channel for making sales and delivering services. Along with it comes the issue of having multiple channels competing with one another. The printed version of a magazine, for instance, may compete with its electronic edition. The Web site of a multinational manufacturing firm may provide services which are traditionally only pro-

vided by its dealers. What is needed is a coherent marketing strategy that best utilizes differentiating pricing, cross promotion, and the unique features of the media to
make them mutually enhancing. Moreover, in today's markets, where demand for a
product can suddenly shift, a manufacturer needs to be able to configure and recon-
figure a supply-chain network quickly to meet changing demand. This involves the
ability to integrate the underlying information infrastructure and business processes
quickly. This requires interoperability and adaptability.

With the Web providing the links for sharing information among channel partners
and the component technology providing the interoperability to integrate business
processes, companies will use more outsourcing in their business model. As a result,
companies will concentrate on their specialized products while working closely with
the suppliers. The ability to manage supply-chain networks will thus determine the
competitive advantage of a company. Supply-chain networks represent the emergent
behavior (Holland, 1995, Schlueter and Shaw, 1998) among a group of business
units working together to exploit the underlying adaptability, collective capabilities,
and market opportunities. The Web helps facilitate coordination among the units,
reducing the inventories and the cycle-times. The networked nature of the Web
forms a natural infrastructure to support and transform supply chains.

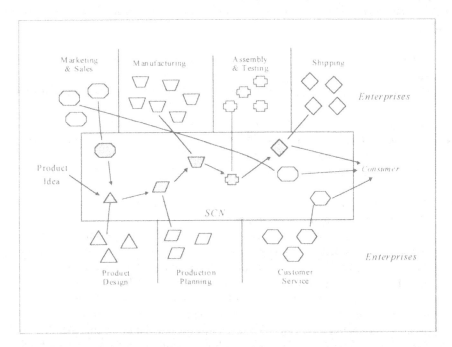

Fig. 7. Component-based supply-chain networks

The use of the component paradigm goes beyond software development. It has been applied to product design based on the concept of modularity (Baldwin and Clark, 1997). Increasingly, it will be applied to the design of business processes, and corporations. Most PC companies today, for example, do not make most components of their products. They organize the supply chains and deliver the final products to the customers. They not only share product and manufacturing information with their suppliers, they increasingly are letting the suppliers adopt parts of their business processes to enhance the coordination. If this trend continues, we will see more highly modularized companies with each unit specialized in its core competency but always prepared to link up with business partners (Figure 7).

9 Challenges Ahead

With all its promise, electronic commerce is still in its infancy. Whether it can fulfill its potential depends to a great extent on what happens over the next several years. The various issues addressed and their complexity help highlight the challenges ahead in bringing electronic commerce to its full potential. Often, these issues are complicated to resolve because of the broad scope of electronic commerce and the scale of the changes it brings. The following is a summary of the more prominent challenges.

1. Privacy - How to protect the privacy of consumers in executing Web-based transactions.
2. Valuation – How to evaluate effectively the potential values of investments on the Web.
3. Security - How to enforce the security of Web-based transactions.
4. Trust and authenticity – How to increase the level of trust and ensure the correctness of information distributed across the Web.
5. User acceptance - How to develop EC systems that are affordable and easy to use.
6. Pricing – How to price digital products and services, which seemingly follow different economic dynamics than traditional ones.
7. Legacy systems – How to integrate with and make the transition from corporate legacy systems when setting up EC systems.
8. Structural changes – How to implement and cope with structural changes brought by EC in organizations and in industrial value-adding chains.
9. Inter-operability – How to make different components of EC inter-operable (e.g., between suppliers' procurement systems and vendors' catalogs, or between a consumer's electronic payment software and that of the merchant).
10. Bandwidth limitation – How to get the breakthrough in communications bandwidth so multimedia information can be exchanged over the Web with greater ease and speed.

11. Information overload – How to cope with the vast amount of data generated (e.g., through data mining or intelligent agents).
12. Knowledge management – How to use the Web to enhance knowledge management in organizations.
13. User interface – How to design a better electronic commerce interface that can improve the effectiveness of EC.
14. Measurement – How to measure the effectiveness of commercial Web sites, electronic catalogs, and Internet Advertising.
15. Payment – How to establish a payment method with a comprehensive infrastructure that ensures security, privacy, and legal concerns.
16. Channel competition – How to make the Web and the traditional channels mutually enhancing rather than competing.
17. Legal framework – How to establish a legal framework to address new needs brought by EC.
18. Standards – How to establish standards on the presentation, transmission, and processing of EC transactions while coordinating the efforts of different participants.
19. Global coordination – How to promote global EC while reducing the conflicts between the efforts on the national level.
20. Changing business models - How to cope with shifting business models due to rapidly advancing technology.

10 Opportunities for Innovative Electronic Commerce Business Models

As with previous technological breakthroughs that have changed the social fabric and the life style of human beings – be it the telephone, the railroad, or electricity – electronic commerce has already led to many innovations and major transformations of the world economy. Although some of the changes in the economy have already taken place, this shift to electronic commerce is still in the beginning stage. The more significant business concepts used in electronic commerce include:

1. Integrated, ubiquitous consumer interface. The Web has expanded the reach of companies while distance has become less significant. At the same time, the Web makes it easy to present assembled information from different sources.
2. New channels for direct, interactive marketing. Through their electronic store-fronts, companies have new channels to reach out to their customers for product promotion, information distribution, and making the sale. The Web can also be the channel for collecting demographic information and customer feedback.
3. Plug-and-play inter-operability and modularity. As the economy moves toward mostly information based, the plug-and-play modularity (Baldwin and Clark, 1997) and interoperability of computer software will be applied to processes, systems, and organizations. The expertise, business processes, information sys-

tems, and even the supporting personnel of companies are increasingly modularized and ready to be integrated with those of other companies.

4. The "click here" economy. As consumers have access to more direct purchasing
channels at their fingertips, the increasing purchasing choices and lower search
costs give them more bargaining power. The same logic applies to business-to-
business transactions, where electronic catalogs and direct electronic links are
changing business procurement practices.

5. Virtual online communities and consumer participation. As the Web accumulates the critical mass of users, communities of focused interests began to
emerge. Advertisers have started to focus their efforts on these existing or potential virtual communities for product and service promotion (Armstrong and
Halel, 1996).

6. Agent-assisted Web services. While the Web has provided an unprecedented
amount of information, the sheer volume of it can become a problem. Software
agents (Genesereth and Ketchpel, 1994) are being developed to assist Web users
to search, navigate, retrieve, synthesize, and process information.

7. From data mining to Web mining. The difference between mining and searching
is that in data mining, there is less knowledge about what one is looking for. As
the Web becomes an important source for collecting business intelligence, data
mining techniques can be extended to Web mining to extract useful information.

8. Sense-and-respond as opposed to make-and-sell. The focus is to sense market
needs and to organize the enterprise for responding quickly to demand. This
strategy is in sharp contrast to the more traditional make-and-sell model (Bradley and Nolan, 1998).

9. Mass customization and digital personalization. With the digitization of product
information and interactive consumer interfaces, merchandise can now be sold
to each consumer to his or her exact specification, custom made.

10. Customer-centric, "friction-free' global supply-chains. With the connectivity of
the global Web and the manufacturing capacity available around the world,
components of most products can be made in different parts of the world,
quickly assembled and shipped to customers.

11. Rapidly deployed virtual organizations. Increased communication capabilities
make it possible to assemble an organization quickly from units possibly residing in different locations, to explore a window of business opportunities (Davidow and Malone, 1992).

12. Business-To-Business Partnership through channel integration and information
sharing. Companies in the same value-adding chains, i.e., channel partners, are
linking with one another to share information concerning demands, inventories,
production scheduling, shipments, etc., so that supply-chain activities can be
well integrated to keep the inventories low and the cycle-times down.

13. Web as a metaphor for intra- and inter-organizational structures. The Web is a
network of knowledge resources that are constructed through individual initiatives. Collectively it uses hyperlinks, universal interface, and a common transport standard to achieve great synergy. This has been used as a paradigm to or-

ganize and manage knowledge within an organization. By the same token, companies can be interconnected just like the individual nodes in the Web to achieve the same type of integration and synergy (Ware et al., 1998).

14. Unbundling of the physical and virtual value chains. Since companies started to connect with one another and process business transactions electronically, virtual value chains have arisen that provide new ways for value creation (Benjamin and Wigand, 1995).

15. Information assets treated as real estate, with access rights, designated portals, destination sites, and advertising space being charged at a premium. As the Web started to attract new businesses, the accessibility and amount of traffic visiting each site become a much-coveted competitive advantage. Search engines, online services, electronic markets, and browser tools all concentrate on building their sites up to attract as much traffic visiting their sites as possible.

16. Network economics and increasing returns of electronic commerce business. Network externalities and increasing returns characterize the dynamics of EC business. A viable explanation is that an EC business typically requires investing an infrastructure, building a user community, and climbing over a learning curve before successfully establishing product brands (Upshaw, 1995) and services.

17. Digital products, services, and their value chains. Digital products and services follow different economic rules. They change economies of scale, economies of scope, and are characterized by the infinite ability to divide into smaller units, reorganize content, transport to remote locations electronically, and duplicate into multiple copies. Business decisions involved in product pricing, property leasing, service delivery, payment collection, packaging, or shipping all need to be rethought.

18. Dynamic market making, brokering, and electronic auctioning. The Web can help form a market for any merchandise and sell it to the interested buyer. The simultaneous delivery of rich information and wide connectivity has resulted in more efficient markets in terms of the availability of market information and participation.

19. Specialized information vendors, intermediaries, and "trusted third parties." With all the delayering of the value chains, new segments are beginning to appear in the virtual, information-based value chains. An example is the Certificate Authority established for verifying the identity of EC users and authenticity of documents over the Web (Froomkin, 1996).

20. Component-based economy. Knowledge, business processes, enterprise systems, expertise, software, or any other type of digital products are broken down into components. Inter-operable interfaces and operational standards make it possible for these components to be assembled and integrated in different forms from different places.

11 Conclusion

Electronic commerce affects almost every aspect of how business is conducted. It fundamentally changes organizational and industrial infrastructure. While there are many challenges ahead, there is no question that it will very rapidly be operating globally. Companies are creating entirely new businesses and tapping markets not reachable to them before. Uncertainties in consumers' acceptance, the lack of adequate business models, and bandwidth limitations have limited the consumer electronic commerce. Whether electronic commerce will break those barriers depends on a host of factors. High on the list are issues such as privacy, costs, security, friendly consumer interface, and the social value it provides. Ultimately, the breakthroughs probably will come from the sheer creativity of some entrepreneurs who develop applications that everyone wants to use. Given the current momentum, there are plenty of reasons to be optimistic.

In the business-to-business area, fully realizing the potential of B2B electronic commerce still requires coordinated efforts among supply-chain partners, who usually have conflicting objectives. When successfully implemented, inter-operable electronic catalogs and more inter-organizational information sharing will make supply chains more efficient.

The Web provides the infrastructure for sharing and collecting information. What ought to be the focus of attention in this information revolution, as argued by Peter Drucker, is how to manage the information. That is, the emphasis should shift from the "T" in IT to the "I" (Drucker, 1998). The increasing importance of information value-adding activities will lead to drastic changes in industrial organizations. The emerging component-based economy will lead to more emphasis on specialization, modularity, and outsourcing. New intermediaries will arise to broker information, knowledge, and services.

The combination of more information, electronic links, and channels will give the buyers more choices, resulting in a shift of bargaining power to the buyers. Consequently business processes and supply-chains will increasingly focus more on the customers by putting the emphasis on capabilities such as efficient order fulfillment, high service level, and quickly responding to market demands. To that end, the key to a successful electronic commerce strategy is to realize those capabilities by integrating the Web with the supply chains.

References

Armstrong, A. and Halel, J., 3rd, "The Real Value of Online Communities," *Harvard Business Review*, (1996), 134-141.

Arthur, B., "Increasing Returns and the New World of Business," *Harvard Business Review*, (1996), 100-109.

Bakos, Y., "The Emerging Role of Electronic Marketplaces on the Internet," *Communications of the ACM*, 41, 8, Aug., (1998), 35-42.

Baldwin, C., and Clark, K., "Managing in an Age of Modularity," *Harvard Business Review*, Sept-Oct, (1997), 84-93.

Beausejour, D., "Branding and Bonding Beyond the Banner," http://www.pg.com/speech.html, 1998.

Benjamin, R. and Wigand, R., "Electronic Markets and Virtual Value Chains on the Information Superhighways," *Sloan Management Review*, (1995), 62-72.

Bradley, S. and Nolan, R., *Sense and Respond: Capturing Value in the Network Era*, Harvard Business School Press, Boston, MA, 1998.

Burke, R., "Real Shopping in a Virtual Store," in *Sense and Respond: Capturing Value in the Network Era*, Bradley, S. and Nolan, R. (Eds.), Harvard Business School Press, Boston, MA, 1998, 221-243.

Business Week, Information Technology Annual Report, Doing Business In the Internet Age, June 22, (1998), 121-194.

Chaum D. and Fiat, A., and Naor, N., "Untraceable Electronic Cash," *Proceedings of the Crypto '88*, 1988.

Choi, S.-Y., Dale, O. D., and Whinston, A., *The Economics of Electronic Commerce*, Macmillian Technical Publishing: Indianapolis, IN, 1997.

Choudhury, V. and Konsynski, B., "Inter-Organizational Information Systems and the Role of Intermediaries in Marketing Channels: A Study of Two Industries," in *Information Technology and Industrial Competitiveness: How IT Shapes Competition*, (C. Kemerer, Ed.), Kluwer Academic Publishers, Boston: MA, 1998, 67-90.

Clark, D., "Cisco Connect Online," *IEEE Internet Computing*, 1, 6, Dec. (1997), 55-61.

CommerceNet, "Catalogs for the Digital Marketplace," Research Report Note #97-03, March, 1997.
http://www.commercenet.com/research/freereport/97_03_r.html.

CyberStats, "How Online Transactions will be Carried out?" (Citing Forrester Research as the source of the statistics),
http://www.zdnet.com/icom/cyberstats/1997/11/, 1997.

Davidow, W. H. and Malone, M. S., *The Virtual Corporation*, (New York: Harper Collins), 1992.

Denning, D., "International Encryption Policy," in *Readings in Electronic Commerce*, (Edited by R. Kalakota and Whinston), Addison-Wesley, Reading Mass., 1997, 105-118.

Drucker, P., "The Next Information Revolution," *Forbes ASAP*, August 24, (1998), http://www.forbes,com/asap/98/0824/046.htm.

Evans, P. and Wurster, T., "Strategy and the New Economics of Information," *Harvard Business Review*, (1997), 71-82,.

Froomkin, A. M., "The Essential Role of Trusted Third Parties in Electronic Commerce," in *Readings in Electronic Commerce*, R. Kalakota and A. Whinston (Eds.), (Reading, MA: Addison Wesley), 1996, 119-178.

Genesereth, M. and Ketchpel, S., "Software Agents," *Communications of the ACM*, 37, 7, July, (1994).

Hill, K., "Electronic Marketing," in *Electronic Marketing and the Consumers*, R. Peterson, (Ed.), Sage Publications, 1997.

Holland, J., *Hidden Order: How Adaptation Builds Complexity*, Addison-Wesley, Reading, MA, 1995.

Kalakota, R. and Whinston, A., *Frontiers of Electronic Commerce*, Addison Wesley, Reading, MA, 1996.

Kemerer, C., *Information Technology and Industrial Competitiveness: How IT Shapes Competition*, (Ed.), Kluwer Academic Publishers, Boston: MA, 1998.

Lynch, D. and Lundquist, L., *Digital Money: The New Era of Internet Commerce*, John Wiley & Sons: N.Y., 1996.

Margherio, L., *The Emerging Digital Economy*, A report distributed by the U.S. Department of Commerce, Spring 1998, available at:
http://www.ecommerce.com

Medvinsky, G. and Neuman, B. C., "NetCash: A Design for Practical Electronic Currency on the Internet," *Proceedings of 1st ACM Conference on Computer Security*, Nov. 1993.

Mukhopadhyay, T, "How to Win with Electronic Data Interchange," in *Information Technology and Industrial Competitiveness: How IT Shapes Competition*, (C. Kemerer, Ed.), Kluwer Academic Publishers, Boston: MA, 1998, 91-106.

Schlueter, C. and Shaw, M. "A Strategic Framework for Developing Electronic Commerce," *IEEE Internet Computing*, 1, 6, December, (1997), 20-29.

Schlueter, C., and Shaw, M. "An Organizational Ecosystems Simulator Applied to Electronic Commerce," *Proceedings of INFORMS Conference on Information Systems and Technology*, Montreal, Canada, April, 1998.

Shaw, M., Gardner, D. and Thomas, H. "Research Opportunities in Electronic Commerce," *Decision Support Systems*, 21, (1997), 149-156.

Sirinivasan, K., Kekre, S., and Mukhopadhyay, T., "Impact of Electronic Data Interchange Technology on JIT Shipments," *Management Science*, 40, 10, (1994), 1291-1304.

Stigler, G., *The Organization of Industry*, The University of Chicago Press, Chicago, 1968.

Strader, T. & Shaw, M., "Characteristics of Electronic Markets," *Decision Support Systems*, 21, (1997), 185-198.

Sviokla, J., "Virtual Value and the Birth of Virtual Markets," in *Sense and Respond: Capturing Value in the Network Era*, Bradley, S. and Nolan, R. (Eds.), Harvard Business School Press, Boston, MA, 1998, 221-243.

Turban, E., "Auction and Bidding on the Internet: An Assessment," *Electronic Markets*, 7, 4, (1997), 7-11.

Upshaw, L., "The Keys to Building Cyberbrands," *Advertising Age*, May 29, (1995), 18.

Wang, E. and Seidmann, A., "Electronic Data Interchange: Competitive Externalities and Strategic Implementation Policies," *Management Science*, 41, 3, (1995), 401-418.

Ware, J., Gebauer, J., Hartman, A., and Rolden, M., *The Search for Digital Excellence*, McGraw-Hill, New York, NY, 1998.

CHAPTER 2
The Future of the Digital Economy

Soon-Yong Choi[1] *and Andrew B. Whinston*[2]
[1]Center for Research in Electronic Commerce, The University of Texas at Austin, Austin, TX, USA, soon@mail.utexas.edu
[2]Department of MSIS, Economics and Computer Science, The University of Texas at Austin, Austin, TX, USA, abw@uts.cc.utexas.edu

This chapter surveys effects of digital technologies on traditional economic research areas ranging from price negotiation to search activities, from product choice to monetary policy. The Internet and its commercial uses have stimulated a high level of interest but electronic commerce is often seen as an alternative marketing channel to existing physical media or markets. However, computer and networking technologies have the potential to transform not only the way we shop but also the way our economy operates. An economy characterized by these technologies is the digital economy where market agents behave differently under different sets of economic rules from the physical economy. We begin by discussing some economic implications of digital technologies. Then we examine major research issues in Internet infrastructure pricing, network effects, online auctions, advertising and consumer search, customized product and pricing, antitrust policies, fiscal and monetary issues and market globalization. Our goal is to demonstrate how fundamental are the economic transformations triggered by the use of technologies. We conclude by noting that computer and networking technologies not only improve efficiencies at the margin but also present a new type of market which might be a textbook example of a perfect market that requires a more vigorous reexamination of traditional economic assumptions and results.

Keywords: Digital Economy; Electronic Commerce; Networking; Auctions; Pricing; Customization; Price Discrimination; Advertising; Search; Taxation; Money Supply; Antitrust Policy

1 Introduction

The information technology (IT) industries–including computer hardware and software, communications equipment and services–accounted for 7.8% of the U.S. Gross Domestic Product and 12.4% of its nominal growth in 1997. While these statistics do attest to a growing economic importance of IT industries, a qualitative measurement of their economic impact derives from productivity and efficiency gains in the rest of the industries which use information technologies to streamline operations, lower labor and inventory costs, accelerate product development cycle and to implement responsive marketing and pricing. Firms invest in information technology equipment at a rapidly growing rate and now information processing equipment accounts for a third of the total business equipment in all nonfarm private industries. Major users of information technologies range from telecommunications, insurance to real estate industries (see Table 1).

Table 1. IT capital share of total equipment stock in top 15 industries, 1994

Industry	IT equipment stock In billions of dollars	Share of total percent
Telephone and telegraph	108.1	86.3
Insurance	1.7	86.0
Security and commodity brokers	2.7	80.7
Holding and other investment	5.2	79.6
Motion pictures	7.0	73.7
Insurance carriers	38.8	65.6
Radio and television	24.0	61.0
Miscellaneous services	14.8	57.2
Wholesale trade	95.0	56.1
Legal services	6.1	56.0
Educational services	0.4	55.3
Health services	18.8	53.1
Retail trade	98.1	46.2
Instruments and related products	10.4	45.4
Real estate	80.3	44.7

Source: Bureau of economic analysis, US department of commerce

Business spending on computers and communications equipment has been growing steadily since the early 1980s but reached a frenzied pace since the introduction of the commercial Internet. Internet's open communication standards offer what no other networking could: possibilities to transform networking into a seamless platform to run business applications, to conduct real time interactions with any virtually connected firms and individuals and to integrate raw computing power into every aspects of economic value creation from production to consumption. Internet technologies have changed the nature of IT investment that was geared toward business automation to a conscientious effort to innovate business organizations and processes. In this new world of digital economy, technologies are used to customize products to match consumer tastes, buyers search with the help of smart software agents, and prices are determined through an elaborate negotiation process or in a real-time auction. But what do all these changes mean when one is faced with a strategic choice of investing in the digital marketplace? Do technologies matter? Do conventional business models and economic wisdom apply to the electronic marketplace as well? To answer these questions, one must first understand how the digital economy differs from the physical economy. In this article, we evaluate how digital technologies affect conventional market processes and present a preliminary analysis of their economic consequences.

We begin by evaluating how computer and networking technologies affect the way we model economic institutions and interactions. Networked firms and consumers behave differently from their counterparts in the physical market as they have digital technologies to facilitate their market activities. As a result, conventional economic assumptions on market agents must be re-evaluated. In Section 2, we examine two issues related to networking: network usage pricing and network effects. Section 3 evaluates new market clearing mechanisms in the networked economy. Section 4 discusses online advertising and the viability of ad-supported business models in the digital economy. In Section 5, we analyze product choice and pricing strategies in the electronic marketplace. Antitrust and competition issues are discussed in Section 6. Section 7 surveys the thorny issue of taxing Internet transactions. Section 8 investigates the effects of digital currencies on macroeconomic policies. The global nature of the Internet is discussed in Section 9 and we conclude in Section 10.

2 Technologies of the Digital Economy

A number of Internet entrepreneurs observe that what works in the physical market should work in the electronic marketplace. To the extent that Internet technologies offer an alternative medium to existing business practices, conventional business models could be extended to the digital economy without major modifications. For instance, applications which improve and augment established operations and business relationship, such as intranets and extranets, have proven to be a winning strategy. Operational and transactional improvements, however, lead to new products and services, ultimately affecting institutional organization as well as consumer preferences. The open and interoperable networking allows market agents to interact as they do in physical market, but agents in the digital market are devoid of physical constraints and endowed with computing technologies which aid and influence their decisions. In this section, we investigate how these technologies affect the behaviors of firms and consumers.

2.1 Networked Firms and Consumers

The Internet protocol suite functions as a market infrastructure which combines the roles of the interstate highway system, telephone and postal networks and the media in the physical market. Unlike proprietary networks, the open Internet allows any user using TCP/IP protocol suite to communicate with others without the stringent requirements of building, maintaining and paying for networking. The networked market is in theory a global market with no artificial barriers or boundaries. And unlike private network standards, open TCP/IP protocols assure that communicating parties can exchange messages and products through interoperable software programs.

In physical markets, geographical distance and political boundaries hinder free movements of goods and people. Closed proprietary networks would separate virtual markets by establishing artificial barriers. The Internet on the other hand allows easy entry and exit into the market where a store located in a small tropical island can effectively reach global consumers and compete with multinational corporations. But the use of the Internet for marketing and customer interface is only part of electronic innovations that are changing the way firms do business (Chellappa et al., 1997). An indication of how the open Internet is altering the way networked enterprises are organized and managed today is the rapid growth of intranets and extranets. With Intranets, corporations distribute internal memos and announcements to their employees; need-based information finds those who need to be informed; and knowledge exchange and scheduling communications flow worldwide in a timely fashion. With direct connection to suppliers – i.e. an extended Intranet – the same technology is used for manufacturing and supply chain management. 3M, for example, expanded its EDI service to the Internet, allowing its 2,000 suppliers and business customers access to its EDI transactions via any way they choose–private value added networks, phones and faxes as well as the Internet.

Regardless of the terms used to describe today's corporate networks, the common thread in current business networking is the drive toward distributed computing. Open networking in turn brings firms in close contact with other firms and consumers in every stage of their operation. A value chain in a physical market typically consists of separate and distinct stages of, for example, market survey, product design, production, marketing, distribution and customer service. On the other hand, the value creating process in the networked market occurs through dynamic and real time interactions. A collaborative product research, for example, is continuously aided by feedback from production, marketing and consumption processes. This trend toward integration is evident in an effort to establish enterprise-wide database warehouses, where conventional distinctions among supply chain, order processing, payment, inventory and shipping databases are detrimental to integrated business solutions.

Consumers too will behave differently in a networked market. For example, access to product information via the network using sophisticated computer programs will certainly affect the way consumers compare prices. In turn, efficient shopping will affect product choices, pricing strategies, and competitive efforts among sellers. Business organizations and relationships will also be affected as the physical distance and geographical topology of a market are replaced with network architecture and preference-based market territories.

2.2 Computer-Mediated Processes

The network infrastructure is limited by the capabilities of the devices behind the network. For example, specifications of a telephone dictate what one can do with the telephone network. Thus, the ultimate advantages of the open Internet lie in the colossal amalgamation of computer hardware and software. Firms and consumers become virtual firms and virtual consumers indistinguishable from computers, peripheral equipment and software that not only provide a user interface to connect but also enhance user capability and productivity.

The advent of the Internet brought integration and versatility to the existing computer and network technologies, and thus opened up possibilities for widespread applications of these technologies to conduct commerce, provide entertainment and communication, filing and paying taxes, managing personal finance, research and education, etc. What characterizes the digital economy is the pervasiveness of technology in all types of market processes and products from Web-enabled automobiles and gas stations to online grocery shopping. Within an Internet-enabled firm, diverse activities—inventorying, supply chain management, product development, online marketing, consumer research—are tied to multi-user distributed computing applications in which data and objects flow through the entire economic processes. In short, the economic effect of these technologies is the ability to integrate existing practices and develop new business and market processes.

2.3 Market Implications of Technologies

Many efficiency and welfare results in economic models critically depend on assumptions about the sellers and buyers in the market. These assumptions often relate to some limitations observed in the physical world. Agents in a computer-mediated market, however, are free of many constraints encountered in a physical market. In such an environment, computer and network technologies affect economic efficiencies and welfare results in a significant way.

Computing Power and Bounded Rationality: The bounded rationality assumption postulates that consumers and other market agents have limited ability to process all necessary information. A buyer searching for a deal, for example, visits several stores gathering information about product specification, price and other attributes of a product. As the number of goods increases and visits are repeated over time, the amount of information one must remember and process quickly exceeds the rational boundary of human capability. For another example, a very complex negotiation procedure or a pricing structure increases costs so highly that it could not be implemented in the physical world. In the networked environment, however, Web surfers aided by intelligent agents can store and process a great deal of information (Maes, 1994). A complex set of procedure or market operations can be implemented as a computer-mediated market. As a result, the networked economy allows market participants to evaluate all feasible alternatives.

Gains from using computer and network technologies involve more than procedural efficiencies. Although economic agents are said to maximize utility, the maximization depends on a given set of choices available to them. In physical markets, many goods may not be available to purchase, for example due to geographical distance or the cost of obtaining and comparing product information. On the other hand, technologies of the digital economy not only reduce transaction costs but, more importantly, offer consumers and firms the possibility and the capability to access all available products and to explore various mechanisms for transaction. In this way, digital technologies expand the set of choices resulting in efficiency gains beyond marginal improvements.

Information on Products and Demand: Sellers depend on information about consumer demand for product development, pricing and marketing. Such demand information is assumed to be known in conventional economic models as we often prescribe standard utility or demand functions for certain goods. But as uncertainty models have shown, real markets seldom provide perfect information on demand due to many difficulties in observing and recording consumption behaviors. In a technology-enabled market, the cost of collecting such information is significantly lower. Cookies and web access logs observe and record all activities occurring in the digital marketplace. In physical markets, the cost to assemble an equivalent database about customers will be prohibitive.

The information gathered on the Internet is 'identifiable' meaning that the demand information is not aggregated or sampled but available at the individual level. Such detailed information has been the manifest goal of Nielson's television audience measurements. Even with sophisticated set-top boxes and enormous costs, however, measuring television audience for a specific program is hardly an exact science. In comparison, receivers of contents sent over the Internet are identifiable, and feedback loops enable senders to measure precisely who received what messages. While it is true that today's measurements of the Internet traffic are as varied as TV ratings, the Internet differs from one-way communications media such as the over-the-air broadcasting or print media.

An economic consequence of information proliferation is that sellers possessing individual demand information may be able to extract all consumer surplus, charging one's maximum willingness to pay. However, buyers do have access to information about products and to many sellers in the global market. While the amount and the truthfulness of information depend on sellers, consumers have ability to collect and process available information armed with search capabilities of computers and search agents. The value of having more and detailed information determines how active both consumers and firms will reveal information. If they benefit from perfectly matching products, prices and marketing, information will be plentiful. In other cases, private information remains private and the market is filled with problems associated with asymmetric information. Some technological aspects of the digital economy magnify this uncertainty problem.

The Uncertainty Problem: Only a few years ago, the Internet was hailed as a perfectly anonymous medium—"Nobody knows you are a dog on the Internet"—to be regarded now as an insecure network where no information is private. With little correspondence between online personalities and their counterparts in the physical world, the Internet sometimes appears to be an inadequate medium to conduct business. The virtual market is populated by products with unknown quality or lemons (Akerlof, 1970), sellers and buyers who can be anonymous, and transaction processes that are not as transparent as in the physical economy. Digital technologies do not provide an easy answer to the uncertainty problem but technologies and innovative market organizations may help solve the problem.

Digital signatures and certification authorities can provide technological solutions to the uncertainty problem (Froomkin, 1997). However, more fundamental reasons for uncertainty lie in the nature of digital products and the technological capability to conceal information. Pictures of a product can be viewed online, but cannot be touched and inspected as in a physical store, increasing the uncertainty. Information is experience goods for which no amount of information is sufficient to reveal its quality. For any legal and technical measure to make the market transparent, there are ways to defeat that purpose. Uncertainty, then, is more persistent in the digital economy than in physical markets.

The prevailing uncertainty indicates new roles of intermediaries in the digital economy. The need for an intermediary is often dismissed in the direct seller-to-buyer transaction model envisioned for electronic commerce. For example, the virtual market has little need for distributional intermediaries such as wholesalers and retailers who provide geographical coverage and access. Intermediaries who invest in product knowledge and testing will be unable to function as checking and guaranteeing the quality of millions of Web pages will be inefficient and ineffective. Nevertheless, uncertainties about product quality and identities of sellers and buyers can only be resolved by a trusted third party such as governments who issue digital identifications or by private profit-oriented intermediaries such as certification authorities. Certificates, however, are inadequate for resolving quality uncertainty for millions of products offered in the market. On the Internet, intermediaries must perform as a quality guarantor without incurring high transaction costs. But, how can an intermediary assure that its suppliers maintain high quality without continuously checking quality which raises costs so high as to make it unprofitable? Recent researches in contract theory have suggested that an electronic commerce intermediary can guarantee high quality at minimal costs by using short-term contracts under which suppliers are dismissed if the quality is found to be sub-standard (Taylor and Wiggins, 1998). A possible termination of contract acts as an effective punishment strategy for the long-run supply relationship to work (Bernheim and Whinston, 1998).

3 The New World of Networked Economy

Networks, both in physical sense of wired and wireless networks and economic sense—network effects—are dominant characteristics of the digital economy. For physical aspects of the network, researchers in telecommunications economics have focused on the issue of congestion and pricing of the Internet. For network effects, their implication on natural monopolization has drawn attention from antitrust economists, lawyers and policy makers. We briefly review and evaluate these two strands of network researches.

3.1 Network Infrastructure Pricing

The commercial Internet is still seen primarily as a new medium of communication, i.e. an open and interactive version of magazines, television, and telephone. If we were to consider only physical wires and cables, the Internet would be nearly indistinguishable from existing telecommunications networks. In fact, most of the Internet traffic is routed through the same pipelines that are used for voice, fax and data transmissions.

While technologies are perfected and more cables are strung, however, the key issue in managing this infrastructure and maximizing its utility remains a problem of efficient resource allocation in the face of congestion that turns the Internet into a tragedy of the commons (Gupta et al., 1996). The legacy of the Internet as a research project funded by public entities has resulted in the absence of an efficient pricing scheme to ensure a congestion-free infrastructure. The Internet infrastructure has experienced a cycle of congestion and network upgrades: from the 56 kbps backbone in 1986 to the 1.5 mbps T1 upgrade by 1989, and to 45 mbps T3 networks by the early 1990s. Now, each fiber-optic cable network, the latest upgrade, can carry twenty or thirty times more traffic than a T3 network can. Since many fiber-optic networks are built redundantly by laying several cables side by side, many predict an end to the bandwidth scarcity.

But congestion is a problem in the last mile, which represents the major portion of networking costs. For this reason, the last mile still consists of copper wires and coaxial cables. Even for fiber-optic backbones, what seems to be an unimaginably large bandwidth will cause severe bottlenecks in short time because of corresponding or outpacing growth in demand. Our experience with microprocessors amply demonstrates that possibility. Efficient pricing mechanisms can present effective solutions to problems of both congestion—by distributing traffic efficiently—and upgrades—by directing investments to where they can most effectively increase social welfare. The ideal economic solution is to charge optimal dynamic congestion tolls. However, private infrastructure owners, interested in profits rather than social benefits, are unlikely to voluntarily impose optimal congestion tolls. What the private market outcome will be is uncertain. More research is needed into how alternative public policies affect congestion, infrastructure investment and social benefits.

However, correct and efficient pricing is difficult to implement since the Internet is owned by multiple entities. Nevertheless, economic studies of the Internet infrastructure remain focused on traditional problems of wired telephone network where the economies of scale and regulatory efficiencies are of primary concern. Pricing regimes proposed for the Internet resembles those of telephone pricing based on access and usage charges such as multipart tariffs and other nonlinear pricing practices developed and practiced by firms with monopolistic market power.

In the digital marketplace, new forces are coming into play affecting the level of competition among telecommunication service providers. Foremost of these forces is the convergence in infrastructure, especially in the last mile where users gain access to the Internet, where a long list of companies—including telephone companies, cable system operators, Internet service providers, long-distance carriers, wireless operators, satellite systems and computer hardware and software vendors—face head-on competition due to the disappearing market boundaries. As a result, a monopolistic and insulated telephone industry is an inadequate basis to emulate Internet pricing. The focus of economic analysis should make a transition from regulatory economics and pricing to one of multiple infrastructure competition and related problems in resource allocation.

Finally, when pricing Internet usage, usage-based prices currently discussed often treat the content and the delivery aspects as one product. In this sense, network pricing is indistinguishable from content pricing. However, content and delivery prices must be separated. To use an analogy, take the example of a music CD being delivered via Federal Express. The price for the CD is determined separately from its shipping and handling charges, which may vary according to delivery schedules and preferences. When the same music is delivered via the Internet, its delivery charge is often subsumed under its product price. As the market for digital contents matures, content pricing must be considered independent of delivery pricing. In some cases, product prices may vary depending directly on delivery schedules, for example time-sensitive information. Even for these products, however, the time sensitivity and the product's value must be separated from the efficiency and the cost of delivery. Content pricing is discussed in Section 6 in more detail.

3.2 Network Effects

Many digital products have network externalities. Externalities are economic consequences that are not fully accounted for by price or market system. These could be either unaccounted benefits or harmful effects. Automobiles pollute air but its cost on environment is not reflected in the price of an automobile—an example of a negative externality. The value of an online discussion forum—e.g. offered by America Online—increases as more people join in the discussion, expanding the amount and the diversity of information offered. Such a positive externality is not reflected in the membership fee paid to America Online.

Software products prominent in the digital economy have network externalities since the value of a product increases as more people use the same software. The network externality may come directly from the increasing number of users, as in the case of the telephone or a computer game which is more enjoyable when there are more people to play with or against, or because more companies develop related programs. Network externalities are often reflected in product prices. For example, a popular operating system may command a monopoly price once it becomes a de facto standard. Its price then fully accounts for the external benefits to the buyers and the benefits are no longer economic externalities (Liebowitz and Margolis, 1995). The economic forces behind its dominance are now called network effects.

Network effects give credence to the argument that there is a natural tendency toward standardization and monopolization in the electronic marketplace where communications networks and software products abound. Furthermore, information and other digital products have low marginal costs so that extreme economies of scale are evident in these industries. When an industry has economies of scale, a natural monopolist may be the most efficient market structure, which eliminates unnecessary costs for duplicated production facilities that can never be recouped. Consequently, some fear that the digital economy by its nature would consist of a few firms with market power, raising prices and stifling competition and innovation.

Although the forces behind standardization and de facto monopolization may be explained by network effects or economies of scale, other factors have been largely ignored. First, the apparent dominance of some software products may be due to anticompetitive practices rather than to network externalities. When monopolistic prices reflect full benefits of network externalities, one product does not enjoy any advantage over another unless the former is priced at a predatory level. Secondly, digital products have non-zero marginal costs due to variable per copy copyright payments or quality differentiated prices for multiple versions and updates. Therefore, digital products cannot be priced at zero or given away freely without substantial costs. While the focus on network effects produced many insights on the digital product market, more research is needed to examine whether traditional economic concepts such as network externalities may be applied to the digital economy without considering its peculiarities. We discuss antitrust implications of network effects in Section 7 below.

Another effect of network externalities relates to copyright. Sharing of information, computer software, and other digital products is often encouraged by the fact that the gains from sharing are substantial due to network externalities and often exceed the potential copyright infringement fines if caught. The control over reproduction and sharing has been the primary objective of copyright protection. Copyright control has been effective as long as infringers are easy to locate. Copies of books and audio tapes, for example, are usually pirated by those who have access to mass production facilities. As the number of potential pirates is limited and the investment necessary for such an operation is relatively high, most serious copyright infringement by pirates has been by overseas publishers operating beyond the reach of territorial copyright enforcement (Gurnsey, 1995). However, digital products are highly vulnerable to copying by consumers who have the very same technology as the producers. The stake is raised even higher when we consider the possibility of pirate copies of digital currencies and electronic financial instruments.

Appropriate technologies and effective legal means must clearly be established to adapt to this new environment where pirated copies of a software program or an online news article can be circulated worldwide with a touch of a button. Despite this spectacular scenario, digital content providers have successfully established their presence in the electronic marketplace. The persistent network effects have helped firms formulate distinctive marketing strategies such as giving away free programs and charging for updates, personalization and services. In this regard, some market mechanisms may effectively substitute the need for legislation or a costly technological answers to digital copyright violations.

4 Interactive Markets

Computer-mediated online markets have introduced various marketwares to facilitate negotiation, brokering and market-making opportunities in the digital economy. In the networked economy where consumers interact with other consumers and firms online 24 hours a day, consumers and products are matched more efficiently than in physical markets where several factors—geographical distance, high transaction costs, low level of information and bounded rationality of market agents—leave unmatched products and unfulfilled needs. Interactive programs and online markets also allow agents a more elaborate negotiation process. In this section, we examine some implications of these efficient match making marketwares on prices and the optimality of market clearing.

4.1 Negotiated Prices

Interactive price determination may evolve into two types of pricing regimes. First, with technologies, sellers can vary prices as demand changes. Prices tend to be stable in physical markets despite changes in consumer tastes, costs or market environment. Even when changing demand information is available, menu costs are significant in physical markets. Furthermore, information must be incorporated with costs. For example, suppose that a soft drink vending machine operator wants to vary the price depending on the location, time of day or outdoor temperature. Unlike location or time-of-day pricing, temperature sensitive pricing requires smart and interactive vending machines that keep track of outside temperatures. Networked vending machine will be able to implement such a pricing more easily. This demand-based pricing, however, does not involve any interactions with consumers.

Secondly, prices may be settled either through individual negotiation or auction. Through product personalization and interactive negotiation processes, network and computing technologies affect more than transaction costs. Static economic models where a single optimal price is determined from an aggregated demand and marginal cost schedule is too static to describe the interactive markets in the digital economy. Posted prices are dominant in physical markets except a few cases, e.g. used car dealers. Posted price works well when there is a simple array of products sold to geographically dispersed customers as in consumer retailing. But unlike the retailing sector, quantity buyers in wholesale and industrial trade rely on negotiated prices. In commodity and stock trading floors, bidding and auction persist as they have been for many centuries.

Three factors facilitate a revival of negotiated prices in the digital economy. First, intelligent agents do comparison shopping to search for the best price in the virtual space. Then prices cease to provide a competitive edge in an efficient market. Product quality, customer service or other characteristics may be substituted for pricing strategies or prices will be personalized and negotiated. Secondly, computer and network technologies provide suitable means to engage in negotiation and auctioning. Thirdly, products and services are bundled and customized in the digital economy. As a result, one price does not fit all consumers. In personal services or insurance market, we observe no posted prices that are easily identified because goods and services differ across individuals. Digital products and services will not only be personalized but also "integrated" as a smart service to the extent that there is no standard product to speak of a standard price. For example, online travel arrangement may include airline tickets, lodging, rental cars, park admission fees and daily supplies. The price of a leased car may include not only the automobile but also its maintenance and service plans (net price varying according to consumption pattern), insurance, and other related services such as travel packages. Preferences for these bundled services differ among consumers and so are combinations of services and corresponding prices.

An economic concern is whether negotiated prices are more efficient than posted prices. Negotiated prices will be more responsive to demand changes as technologies allow sellers to avoid commonly observed price stickiness under posted price markets. Price negotiation will also enable different types of products and services to be produced for which consumer willingness to pay exceeds their costs. But, for example, are negotiated prices closer to marginal costs? To determine economic efficiency, the difficulty is in defining a relevant product or service market. When a product consists of several products (e.g. travel package), sellers can aggregate and allocate costs that are not revealed to buyers. It will be extremely difficult to analyze price efficiency of a bundled service if we focus on marginal costs. Nor can we easily determine demand characteristics for bundled products. More research is needed to clarify the effects of negotiated prices for many incidental combinations of goods and services that are possible in the electronic marketplace.

4.2 Online Auction Markets

When there are more than one buyer or a seller and the negotiation proceeds simultaneously, it is commonly considered to be an auction. In a typical auction, there may be multiple buyers but one seller or one buyer with multiple sellers. If there are multiple buyers and sellers at the same time, the auction is called a double auction where multiple units are sold in the same period and different prices are allowed. Technically, many of today's online auctions are double auctions.

Several types of online auction market exist. In a classic auction market, the auctioneer solicit bids from potential buyers. After a certain period, the market closes and the highest bidder wins. Most consumer-oriented online auctions such as Onsale.com follow this classic formula. In business-to-business auctions, the auction operator is often a market maker or a match maker, who searches products and bids and notifies potential sellers and buyers of the match. The matching process may be anonymous; price negotiation may or may not brokered by the auctioneer. In a new type of auction, buyers may place an order that consists of a bundle of products instead of repeating bidding for each individual product. A Java-based real time auction for bundles has been proposed by Fan, Stallaert and Whinston (1998).

Online auction markets are growing rapidly as they epitomize the allure of a real time, interactive global marketplace. Nevertheless, several economic issues remain unsolved. For example, auctions are employed to maximize prices or to extract the maximum willingness to pay as is observed in auctions for collectors' items. Auctions also reflect market demand correctly and tend to generate competitive outcomes if there are many sellers and buyers. These efficiency gains are the driving forces behind the proliferating online auctions. But for both sellers and buyers to benefit, artificial barriers such as monopsony or monopoly must not exist. If there are no such barriers, online auctions could produce the most efficient outcome akin to cooperative payoffs in the game of prisoner's dilemma. Another problem is to devise an effective punishment mechanism for cheating by fly-by-night operators on either side of buyers and sellers. Assuring quality of products and verifying every online participants can be extremely costly. One feasible punishment strategy is to maintain an interactive, long-run relationship with sellers and buyers (Bernheim and Whinston, 1997). As the loss of long-run profits outweigh the potential profit from one time cheating, an auction market may weed out low quality sellers without the need to check all goods offered at the auction as is practiced by Aucnet auto wholesaler. On the other hand, online auctioneers who do not guarantee product quality will be unable to sustain efficient outcomes in the long run.

Another issue is how to improve the match making process when products being auctioned or sought after are combinations of products (McAfee and McMillan, 1997; Brewer and Plott, 1995). In security markets, stocks are often purchased as a bundle. For airline tickets, a trip may require several tickets that may be offered by different airlines. An auction for these products must be able to bundle and unbundle several products to match disparate preferences of sellers and buyers. A dealer such as a mutual fund manager provides such a function, or an innovative software can offer a solution that does not rely on an intermediary (see for example, Srinivasan et al., 1998). Digital technologies present new opportunities to bundle products and to implement mechanisms to search and match complex preferences for these products. These examples demonstrate a clear need to apply economic research in understanding the strategic implications of the digital technologies.

5 Advertising and Consumer Search

The importance of advertising in the marketplace is evidenced in a large body of economic and business literature on that topic. The other side of the advertising is the process by which consumers search for product information in a digital world. In physical markets, consumer search activities include reading advertisements, calling vendors, and visiting stores. In a virtual marketplace, all these activities seem to converge into Web searches and Web browsing.

Not surprisingly, search services are the first market infrastructure to be built in the electronic marketplace, and have become the primary means of Internet advertising as well. Consumers of course need advertisements to find products they want. With an interactive media such as the Internet, advertisers and consumers can negotiate directly without the help of intermediary markets, where unrelated products—television programs, news and magazine articles, search services and email services—are exchanged just to convert consumers' attention into advertising dollars. Advertisers instead can offer consumers payments for viewing and responding to their ads. For example, Cybergold offers direct payments to consumers who read advertising messages. Nissan plans to pay about $1 to visitors to its Web pages. Micropayments using digital coins and coupons will make even smaller payments feasible. Advertisers will have a better way to evaluate the reach and effectiveness of their marketing effort, while consumers benefit from reduced search costs.

5.1 Selling and Pricing Advertisements

Many online services today do not go as far as selling advertisements to consumers. Currently, Internet advertising and marketing literature focuses on adapting traditional advertising framework to the peculiarities of the Internet as the Internet is seen as an alternative channel to traditional media such as newspapers, magazines, and television. The conventional wisdom is that advertisements can not be sold to consumers directly. They are intrusive eyesores but tolerated only if they lower costs of newspapers, TV programs or Internet services. The Extreme market valuations of Yahoo, Excite, Lycos and other search services reflect the conviction that online advertising provides the best profit opportunity in the digital marketplace although online advertising dollars are miniscule compared to revenues of the traditional media (see Table 2).

To draw visitors, popular Web sites offer several free services such as free e-mail and Web hosting service, duplicating the way television networks barter free programs in return for commercials. But advertising based on mass media is inefficient and ineffective. Broadcast and print advertisements are not targeted and often go unheeded by potential audience. Advertisers lack reliable means to verify reception or evaluate effectiveness of their marketing efforts. These means are available on the Internet, however. As a result, advertising revenues on the Internet must be justified not only by the number of visitors to an ad-sponsored Web site but also by whether visitors received the intended message. Search services must also be able to maximize traffic to their sites when, unlike television networks, they do not have the advantage of artificial monopoly over limited channels. Access points to the Internet is so diverse and uncontrollable that no one can deliver audience the size of a TV network to justify advertising charges common in mass media. The only feasible means to control Internet traffic is to control access by coupling Internet access service with a Web site. Such a trend is evident in mergers between Internet service providers and content providers.

The advertiser-supported business model arose out of necessity since TV networks cannot charge viewers directly for their programs. Ad-supported contents continue even with cable television where cable networks and operators do have means to bill consumers directly. This is partly because of the established preference for "free" programs or bundled programming. A more salient reason is a technological limitation for measuring and billing for individual programs. However, The Internet provides a means to sell advertisements directly to consumers as a commodity. Unlike over-the-air broadcasting or print media, digital transmitted contents leave a clear trail of information that can be verified by sellers and advertisers. A transparent market-based pricing for advertisements is an Internet-enabled practice uniquely fitted for the digital economy.

Table 2. Advertising expenditures, 1995

Industry segment	Expenditure, billions of dollars
Television	30.6
Cable and satellite TV	5.3
Radio	11.3
Newspaper	36.0
Magazine	14.5
Others	5.2
Internet	0.05
Total	102

Source: Veronis, suhler and associates (http://www.vsacomm.com/pr/prcif96.htm)

5.2 Consumer Searches and Economic Efficiency

A market is considered to be economically efficient when a product is sold at the lowest possible price or at the marginal cost of production for a given level of quality. For a homogeneous product produced by many firms using a common technology, an efficient price will be unique. In real markets, however, we seldom observe a uniform price since sellers and buyers have different information about the price and quality of a product. Bargain hunters must visit many stores to gather information on different prices and product specifications, and compare their records before deciding which offers the best deal. This search process clearly has costs associated with it. To obtain full information about prices and product qualities, consumers must incur unnecessarily high search expenses and duplicate the efforts of other consumers.

Similar to searches in physical markets, surfing through different Web stores is a sequential search with substantial costs. Internet innovations such as a database of prices or an agent-based search service offer tremendous advantages over physical market searches. Besides lowered costs in time and transportation, a computer-based search allows consumers to remember and compare information gathered from many stores. Furthermore, online searches enable consumers to process a wide range of information other than price—e.g. location and name of vendors, terms of sales, quality and performance variables, brand names, sizes and other product character-istics. Comparing prices alone will strain the capacity to process information in physical markets, especially if shopping involves many products. Online search technologies will automate this process and allow consumers to engage in more sophisticated and efficient searches.

The search and information transmission mechanisms used in the electronic mar-ketplace are too new for researchers to have determined their efficiency. In fact, there are contradicting predictions about what that will be. One view is that by using computer technologies such as search engines and intelligent software agents, con-sumers may be able to search the whole information space at little cost. However, there are some reasons why the electronic marketplace may not be so efficient. In the first place, sellers may not provide relevant information as they often provide information only if doing so increases profit (Lewis and Sappington, 1994). Sec-ondly, search algorithms or techniques may not be sufficient to gather all the rele-vant information. This may be because of access difficulties—as some Web sites do not allow access—or because all searches inevitably select and process information based on prescribed criteria which may not be efficient to begin with. Lastly, a non-zero search cost, however small it may be, results in noncompetitive pricing (Robert and Stahl, 1996). Using electronic media may reduce search costs to an arbitrarily small amount, but the cost may still be positive. As a result, it may be reasonable to assume that the problems associated with information will persist in electronic commerce as they do in physical markets.

Advertising and search process complement each other in electronic commerce and are essential in reducing the uncertainty about product quality and preventing a possible market failure. While search services on the Internet are very popular, con-sumers often have to access different search services who cover different sources. The sheer size of the Internet information often makes it impossible to compile an adequate level of information from all Web sites or the rapid changes on the Internet often render collected information outdated. Despite these drawbacks, search serv-ices are an essential tool in navigating the virtual marketplace. In the future, con-sumers themselves may send out automated intelligent agents to search the Web space according to the owner's specification. Instead of clogging the bandwidth with advertising, such bots or agents could be charged a minute amount of money to access certain metainformation of a Web page.

6 Product Choice and Pricing

Market processes of production, delivery, payment and consumption for digital products will be quite different from physical products. As pricing strategies are tied to these processes, it will be a folly to assume that existing economic models can simply be re-interpreted for electronic commerce. For instance, digital products are assumed to have zero or negligible marginal costs relative to their high initial fixed costs for first copy. If this were true, an efficient price for a digital product would be close to zero. However, at the very least, the marginal cost consists of a per-copy copyright payment. Thus an appropriate price for any product will be the amount due to the creator, which will most certainly be non-zero. In addition, the possibility of extreme product customization implies little duplication. In this sense, the marginal cost to consider is not that of distribution, but that of production quality of the first copy.

6.1 Product Customization

The computer-mediated market will accelerate the process of customization through its technologies. For example, travelers going through Korea or Hong Kong take the advantage by getting custom-tailored suits. Via 3D scanning and email, anyone may be able to order such suits from anywhere in the future. Through multimedia communications and electronic commerce, every computer becomes a commercial outlet for personalized products. Information products are highly customizable because of their transmutability. Changing contents may take only a few key strokes or a programmed routine. But even somewhat standardized physical products such as automobiles will be customized at the human-interface level. A physical product becomes a "smart product" when it has a digital interface that controls its functions. For example, functions of a smart automobile are controlled by a built-in, networked central computer whose operation and repairs will be done over the network via emails. Smart home appliances will have digital interfaces that allow users to change and control individual settings remotely. These operational settings are customized.

One might say that a toaster is a toaster even with a smart interface. However, in the information age, a toaster is not sold just as a manufactured piece of appliance. It serves certain functions: toasting your bread for breakfast. In the digital economy, those functions, not the manufactured physical goods, are the ones that produce most values. Instead of drawing revenues from one time sale, sellers provide customers with customized breakfasting service via online. It is an extension of software selling practice. Instead of selling an office suite on a CD, for example, software vendors sell applets that constantly monitor usage and report back. Instead of selling a car, an automobile dealers relies on leasing and renting a car that is networked to the dealer's computer. Prices for these smart products will depend on personalized usage, not on the cost of producing the physical unit.

Customized products raise important questions regarding the use of consumer information and the possibility of discriminatory pricing. For sellers to customize a product, customers must provide them with their preferences. For some products, consumers voluntarily reveal their needs and preferences. For others, reluctant consumers have raised the issues of anonymity and privacy in transactions. Faced with informational uncertainty, sellers want to know consumer's private information as much as buyers want to know the product quality. But a seller with consumer information may set prices according to an individual consumer's marginal valuation instead of the marginal cost of the product. Some sellers may even refuse to sell to certain 'identified' customers, and only profitable types of products are marketed excluding others. Although firms with better demand information may gain efficiency in production and marketing and provide products that match consumer tastes, the possibility of first-degree price discrimination based on consumer information has largely been ignored.

6.2 Personalized and Differentiated Prices

Unlike monopoly prices, discriminatory prices will generally increase market efficiency by expanding the market and allocating resources according to consumers' marginal willingness to pay. For example, a standard basic package in cable television, priced at $20, does not serve those with a minor taste who are willing to pay $10 for fewer number of channels. Various service tiers are offered to maximize subscribers and revenues, but the lack of a la carte options and billing choices does limit the maximum number of cable subscribers. In the electronic marketplace, sellers have the ability to offer individual choices and price their products and services according to individual willingness to pay without imposing a standard price for a standard product.

Personalized prices, however, mean perfect price discrimination. Economists pay scant attention to first degree price discrimination as conditions in physical markets often make it untenable. For example, in physical markets, products—and prices— are relatively standardized and informational needs and billing costs for individualized prices are substantial. However, new technologies such as XML and Hyperwave are being tested to customize and manage Web pages and other hyper documents. These technologies indicate a movement away from standardized content presentation on the Internet. Under perfect price discrimination, a firm sells its product by charging the maximum price each consumer is willing to pay. This may be socially efficient but consumers are seldom willing to pay the highest price without complaint. In individualized Web commerce, consumers may not discover what others are paying even for a very similar product when each makes a purchase on a personalized Web page for a personalized product paying an individual price.

Incentive-compatible prices—second degree price discrimination—sometimes minimize the need for demand information, and such differentiated prices are evident in a few industries such as airline and insurance. Even on the Internet, many predict that content sellers would be satisfied with second degree price discrimination—offering different types of bundles or subscription plans at set prices. Consumers seemed to prefer such simple arrangements as well over a pay-as-you-go pricing scheme. Nevertheless, technological developments—e.g. digitization, smart cards and micropayments—will ultimately affect the way goods and services are combined, delivered and consumed. A news article, for example, may be used for research, investment, education or entertainment. Each users has a different value for the same article depending on its ultimate application, and its value as well as price may be determined in relation to the total value of research, investment, education or entertainment. The implication is that the consumption pattern in the digital economy is so individualized that prices are personalized as well. Bundled products, integrated consumption and individualized prices all point toward a need to reexamine how sellers, who have the means to charge individually, implement discriminatory prices and influence market efficiency.

7 Market Structure and Competition

Regulatory policy choices for the new digital economy have become Scylla and Charypdis due to the apparent dominance by a few firms such as Intel and Microsoft and the desire to promote the emerging economic engine. The new economics of network effects and economies of scale seem to stifle innovations but regulatory and antitrust efforts have proven ineffective in physical markets, while the peculiarities of the market, e.g. its global nature, render local regulation unfeasible. Furthermore, the trend toward product customization implies that most firms will have a certain degree of market power but prices cannot be easily compared to discover anticompetitive practices. In this section, we examine how these aspects of the digital marketplace affect market structure and policy choices.

The new digital economy poses some serious questions regarding the validity and effectiveness of the conventional monopoly theory and its insights about economic efficiency. The economic sin of a monopolist is its restriction on output and the resulting increase in price. A monopolist produces less and charges more than a competitive, and therefore efficient, firm. The conundrum is that digital monopolists do not behave like physical monopolists. For example, Microsoft gives away a product for free and it seems to sell too many, not too few, products.

These unconventional results of low price and increased output of a software monopolist are explained by the new economics of network effects and scale economies. Monopolization is often a natural and necessary outcome when network effects favor one product over others. These are often products that were introduced early and achieved a certain threshold to become a de facto standard. The gravest sin of such a monopolist is the possibility of stifling innovation, a new source of economic inefficiency. For example, Microsoft is currently the de facto monopolist in the operating system (OS) software market for desktop computers. Its Windows OS covers more than 80% of the market.

Such a dominant market position, some argue, may lead to failures of new innovative OS products if the dominant player locks out any new entrants by its contractual relationship with hardware sellers or predatory pricing practices. Furthermore, its grip on the bottleneck (OS) may give it an unfair advantage over other vendors of application programs which must work on top of the dominant OS. Using one's monopoly power in one market to monopolize another market is clearly prohibited by most antitrust laws. Nevertheless, many attribute Microsoft's success in OS and other vertically related markets to its marketing savvy and the peculiarities of digital products such as network effects. The lack of conventional monopoly problems is an evidence that Microsoft is not a threat to economic efficiency. Conventional economic theories may not apply to the digital market.

However, although an OS is a software program that fits into the network economics, Microsoft's behaviors can still be explained by the conventional monopoly theory: its price for Windows OS may be too high and its output too low. The key is how we define the market that Microsoft has monopolized. The price that consumers pay for an OS is bundled with that of hardware. Since a desktop computer must have an OS and it is invariably a Windows OS, Microsoft effectively has monopoly over the desktop computer market. In Intel-Microsoft computing paradigm, the monopoly extends from computer hardware to OS and to applications. The most contentious issue between Microsoft and desktop computer manufacturers is whether one has a choice to install non-Windows OS. Through contracts and marketing practices, this choice is essentially eliminated. As a result, the price and the output one must examine are the combined price and output of a desktop computer with an OS. Although the computer industry may appear to be competitive because of the large number of hardware manufacturers, the monopoly profits accrue to Microsoft who controls the market via its control over OS. Despite exponential advances in computing power and lower component prices, desktop computers are still too expensive for average consumers. High price and low output of computers are clear indications that Intel and Microsoft have monopoly profits as conventional economic models predict.

Current focus on network effects and scale economies offers no clear guidance in understanding the nature of monopoly market power and available policy options. When Microsoft is considered as a common carrier who controls a bottleneck (i.e. OS), conventional economic theories still apply and appropriate regulatory and antitrust choices are available without embarking on constructing new economic models. While network effects and scale economies may appear very convincing on the surface, digital products and services may have conventional convex cost structure and network effects may not be the determining factor of success in markets (Choi et al., 1997). Regulatory policies based on conventional economic theories will suffice to tackle the new digital economy.

8 Fiscal Concerns

Taxing online sales has become a contentious issue between taxing authorities and Internet merchants and among different levels of governments. Online commercial transactions not only reduce transactional costs but also take away revenue sources from state and local governments. Many transactions that are now taxed migrate to the Internet, leaving governments with a reduced tax base. National governments may also suffer from reduced tariffs when goods move freely across national boundaries. The global Internet further complicates defining and collecting location-dependent income and corporate taxes. The specter of losing such services as education, transportation and parks funded by sales and use taxes have prompted taxing authorities to search for ways to draw revenues from the growing Internet commerce.

To at least maintain the current level of tax revenues, state and local governments need to figure out how to apply existing rules of taxation to electronic transactions. The initial efforts to tax Internet commercial activities by various governments have resulted in numerous instances where even the basic definitions of sales and use tax regulations have been found inadequate. Even the distinction between sales tax and income tax has become unclear when business is conducted on the Internet as many information products can be classified either as products or services (Erickson, 1996). But most of all, the fluidity of online entities makes it difficult to establish at any one time what is being taxed, who should be taxed and who can impose taxes.

8.1 How To Define a Digital Product

A heightened level of economic understanding on online taxation is critical in helping to resolve the dispute among governments and to clarify the effects of online sales taxation on local economies as well as on the future of Internet commerce. For example, the taxation issue is basically one of how to define digital products and transactions on the Internet. If we attempt to apply existing tax laws to electronic commerce, the first task at hand is to determine what digital products are taxable under which tax mechanisms—sales tax, income tax, royalty tax, etc. In the U.S., most state sales and use tax laws are based on the sale and sale price of some tangible personal property. A tangible personal property is defined as "personal property that can be seen, weighed, measured, felt, or touched or that is perceptible to the senses in any other manner" If we adhere to this definition, most digital products as well as many types of services will be excluded.

In order to extend taxation into the digital domain, some states specifically define computer programs and many types of services, e.g. information services, as taxable products and services. For each new type of service or product, governments need to redefine their tax laws. For instance, Internet service providers may be subject to sales tax if they are defined as a service liable for such tax (e.g. as information service providers), or to telecommunications tax, which is applied to communication service providers. Such a scenario is clearly impractical. Nevertheless, a clear definition of a commodity, a service or a product must first be established.

Digital files, although they all look similar, may indeed be fundamentally different products—for example, electronic house keys, digital currency, weather information, computer programs, concert tickets, medical advice, etc. In defining what a digital product is or what a digital service is, a further difficulty stems from the fact

that many of these products and services are 'portfolio' products, i.e. many dissoci-
ate products are combined and customized for sale. Ad hoc measures become infinitely haphazard as electronic commerce grows and a typical transaction includes a
wide range of products and services as a bundle. Clearly, an adequate solution will
entail simplifying existing tax laws instead of complicating them further by extending and applying them on an ad hoc basis.

8.2 Taxable Nexus in a Networked Market

Even when we agree on what to tax, the nature of the Internet network complicates
the task of identifying who should be taxed. In the U.S., businesses are required to
collect and pay sales taxes if they maintain a substantial presence in the taxing jurisdiction of a state. The U.S. Supreme Court set a guideline in its 1992 decision (Quill
v. North Dakota, 504 U.S. 298) that mail-order firms are not required to collect sales
taxes from customers in states where they have no physical presence—known as
taxable nexus. Therefore, if a mail-order firm in New York sells a product to a customer in Texas, the firm is not required to collect and pay sales taxes to the state of
Texas, unless substantial taxable nexus applies. What constitutes substantial nexus
differs from state to state, and depends on court interpretation. For example, a nexus
is established if an out-of-state business maintains an office or a representative—
either permanently or temporarily. Here too, the definition of a representative has to
be clearly determined. If a person lives in Oklahoma but commutes to his office in
Texas, does he have an in-state presence in Texas? If a Californian firm has a Web
site in an electronic mall served by an operator in Texas, does the firm have sufficient presence in Texas to be subject to Texas sales tax? Identifying proper taxing
jurisdiction is further complicated because a business may have no physical presence at all, but its virtual presence on the Internet may end up being interpreted as
"being present" in all locations. In this case, a Web business will be required to collect state and local taxes (including sales, use, excise, transportation, telecommunications and other taxes), all of whose rates differ from locality to locality.

A simple tax structure would be based on either the seller (originator of sale) or
the buyer (destination of sale). The U.S. Department of Treasury (1996), while discussing income taxes for the global electronic commerce, recognized the residence-
based (originator of sale) taxation as the preferred method as the residence of the
seller would be easier to identify and corresponds better to the economic activity.
Since the originator's residence simplifies the number of tax rates to be applied, it
would be simpler than to calculate different tax rates for its customers, who may
belong to different taxing jurisdictions. Complicated taxing schemes give sellers an
incentive to circumvent them altogether by using off-shore locations for business,
which will only involve establishing a computer server and managing remotely.
Others such as the Interactive Services Association (1996), whose members include
American Online, AT&T, CompuServe, IBM, and Microsoft Corporation, prefers
destination-based taxes. Under this scenario, as in the traditional mail-order business, out-of-state sales will not be subject to state sales tax. To simplify tax rates for

multi-state operators, ISA also advocates setting a single tax rate for each state and basing taxes on the state to which sales are billed—that is, to avoid thousands of different tax rates levied by local governments. Such a system might be implemented without much difficulty if Internet commerce is deemed to be subject to interstate commerce regulations of the federal government.

9 Digital Currency and Monetary Policy

Whether we are headed toward a cashless society or not is up for debate. However, more convenient forms of payment mechanisms have been adopted by modern economies as the number transactions increases and various credit-creating devices are introduced. Despite the popularity of checks and credit cards, coins are still in great demand to pay for low-value transactions. The future of digital coins will depend on their convenience, reliability and accountability over physical coins. Technologies and innovative processes—e.g. smart cards and micropayment options— are beginning to present digital monies as real alternatives to cash.

Besides technical and regulatory issues, digital currency payment systems have raised macroeconomic questions and concerns regarding their impact on the money supply and governments' control over monetary policy. In the U.S., research has shown, however, that the Federal Reserve system's control of the money supply can be adjusted to reflect the change in the money demand, and as such government officials consider the effect of digital currency on the monetary system to be minimal (Blinder, 1995). Nevertheless, proposed digital currency systems may affect the monetary system in two possible ways: they may influence the supply of money by changing the money multiplier, or they may change, in the long run, the velocity of money, affecting price levels and interest rates. The effect of digital currency on the money supply depends on how inside monies are created while its effect on the velocity of money is uncertain.

Electronic cash holdings will in general decrease the demand for cash as consumers hold less cash for transactions than they would normally do. Electronic cash such as Ecash is converted from a national currency (outside money) by an electronic bank such as Mark Twain Bank. If these banks are required to hold an equal amount of dollars to electronic cash they issue, the supply of money does not change as the same amount of cash has been withdrawn from the monetary system. If however Mark Twain Bank is allowed to lend this money as a regular bank, normal cash holdings have been converted into demand deposits and the money supply increases. If electronic currencies are not backed by national currencies at all, reduced cash holdings will significantly increase money supply. Overall, the use of digital currency tends to increase the supply of money.

U.S. monetary officials claim that changes in the money supply can be adequately met by the Federal Reserve System—through open market operations—whether or not digital currency is backed-up by fiat money. To reduce the supply of dollars, the Fed may engage in open market operations, i.e. selling government bonds to the public, thereby increasing its cash holding which goes out of circulation. Nevertheless, if the Fed wants to reduce money supply as the demand for dollars decreases, it needs to raise the interest rate to sell bonds. At the same time, people want to dispose of their cash by buying bonds, so that the increased demand for bonds will lower interest rates. The net effect of the Fed's open market operations and the citizen's demand for bonds may very well offset each other to produce stable interest rates. However, if the Fed's operations are out of sync, temporary instability will have a significant effect on the economy—as evidenced by the stock market response to a quarter point increase in the interest rate.

Another issue with more convenient forms of money is in the relationship between the velocity of money and inflation. The quantity theory of money equation shows that inflation would be increased if the stock of money or the velocity of money were to increase. However, if the money stock adjusts to compensate the change in the velocity of money, the price level will not be affected. Still the global nature of the Internet may add a significant instability to a nation's monetary system through mechanisms that are out of that government's control. For example, if offshore banks require no or lower cash reserves for deposits, this will effectively lower the reserve-deposit ratio. Also, if higher interests are offered by offshore banks, people will reduce their cash holding, depositing it at these banks, which lowers the currency-deposit ratio. As a result, the money multiplier will be larger. When there is a change in the monetary base, the larger money multiplier will produce a more volatile money supply, and possibly changes in price levels and fluctuations in the nominal Gross Domestic Product. Furthermore, if most people prefer to hold international electronic currency, open market operations by a central bank or the Fed may not be effective in controlling the amount of currency or interest rates. Like a small country whose exchange rate floats with dominant foreign currencies, domestic monetary policies may be rendered ineffective by a world-wide digital currency.

Finally, digital currencies, if they are not backed by national currencies, reduce government revenues from its right to print money—known as seigniorage. If digital currencies are to be backed by national currencies, governments retain the seigniorage and profits for the issuers of private money may come from either charging fees on electronic currency conversions or from usage fees for equipment used in transactions. These add transaction costs that may neutralize some benefits of electronic cash payment systems. On the other hand, the seigniorage—estimated to be in tens of billions of dollars in the U.S.—may be the source of profits in which case digital currencies may be traded without added costs at a par value with existing national currencies. Furthermore, an intense competition among private monies would have the effect of distributing the seigniorage to the consumers.

10 The Globalized Economy

Not many of the issues touched upon are local in the digital world. The internationalization of the Internet goes far beyond the expansion we witnessed in the last century. For most of the 20th century, corporations have operated as multinational entities "knowing no national boundaries." Free trade zones are springing up in North America, Europe, and around the Pacific Rim. While these large economic blocks of countries represent the most recent achievement in fostering the free movement of goods, the Internet was created without borders from its inception. For the goods and services that can be ordered and delivered over the network, the Internet is truly a global marketplace.

As political borders cease to be barriers to trade, the global electronic commerce has implications that reach far beyond mere economic gains from trading. For example, can nations control the movement of digital goods based on content or isolate themselves from the rest of the Internet? Can governments exercise their regulatory powers on the Internet? And how would the effort to set up a uniform legal and commercial environment for the global electronic commerce affect physical markets? It is easy enough to say that electronic commerce is global. The difficulty lies in identifying the effects of globalization on economic variables such as income levels, jobs and domestic prices. An interesting exercise in international trade and finance economics is to see how two previously closed economies are affected by subsequent interactions in human resources, materials, and capital.

For example, those concerned with ill effects of an open economy argue that cheap imports into the U.S. are a huge supply of cheap labor, which depresses the level of income for domestic low skilled workers and increases income inequality. Jobs moved overseas by multinational corporations further create an over-supply of unskilled labor and affects their income adversely. Those who advocate openness and free trade contends that competition from foreign labor is not the reason for the worsening income inequality but the introduction of high-technology, which raises the income level of skilled workers while non-technical workers do not gain. The flight of corporations abroad for cheap labor will not have a long-term effect since wages in those countries will eventually be driven up. Low productivity due to the low skill level of domestic workers is the primary reason why the income gap is worsening. For both sides, creating more jobs domestically will help to narrow the income gap. However, opponents to free trade argue that expanding job opportunities for low-skilled workers and perhaps encouraging more domestic investments by multinational corporations will raise wages for low-skilled workers. Advocates of free trade, on the other hand, argue that such policies will have no effect. Rather, the skill level and the productivity of low-wage earners have to be raised, perhaps through more job training and education, but not by restricting job exports by corporations.

The growth of global information infrastructure and its commercial use cuts through both of these arguments. Through electronic commerce, high-wage jobs—not just low-wage jobs—are being exported, i.e. high-value products are being imported. For example, software engineers in India work on projects via satellite networks linking directly with U.S. companies. High-skilled researchers and scientists in Eastern Europe can be linked via Internet for research purposes. This will depress wages for high-skilled laborers and should narrow income inequality. At the same time, education and training will become cheaper through electronic education services on the Internet, and technological skill and productivity in the electronic marketplace will level off among workers because the difference between high-tech and low-tech laborers is smaller than in physical markets. For these reasons, the income gap is expected to narrow as electronic commerce grows. The global nature of electronic commerce will make corporations more mobile enabling them to exploit even small differences in wages. In essence, this will result in more open economies worldwide and a possible convergence in income levels.

The global nature of the Internet is clearly one of its strengths, but a predictable international legal and commercial environment is lacking. Recent international agreements in telecommunication and information technology sectors negotiated by the World Trade Organization lay a solid foundation for global electronic commerce. However, a uniform import/export tax—such as no tax, making all Internet transactions duty-free—implies an open international economy which may result in the loss of policy control over domestic economy. Countries leverage tariffs and income tax policies to manipulate economic performance. Domestic industries are often protected by high tariffs, and a country's balance-of-payment position depends on selectively controlling exports and imports. Simple uniformity may not be acceptable to many countries if it means relinquishing this tool.

According to the U.S. and the European Union, the principal approach to achieve a healthy GII is to rely on the market itself. However, a uniform commercial environment can only be achieved through widespread international negotiation and cooperation, of which there has been scant evidence. Several exceptions exist in the areas of copyright, key encryption, and electronic contract standards. For example, it is imperative to achieve an interoperable encryption system since digital signatures, public-keys and encrypted digital currency are essential in providing identity, confidentiality, non-repudiation and other basic commercial requirements in the GII. However, policies regarding encryption technologies are first and foremost affected by national security interests while economic implications of a uniform encryption standard are largely ignored. Theorists in international trade and finance are only beginning to apply their knowledge to this innately global open economy.

11 Concluding Remarks

The digital marketplace is the first example of a market for which economic theories and models can be built and analyzed in a priori instead of traditional ex-post fashion economists are familiar with. In addition to stimulating new models and new insights on both physical and emerging digital markets, the use of computer and networking technologies by firms and consumers affects market conditions and behaviors to the degree that fundamental assumptions of a static economic model such as perfectly competitive market, perfectly informed consumers, and perfect price discrimination may no longer be considered as purely theoretical. In physical markets, the degree to which this perfectness can be expected is extremely low.

However, the digital marketplace comes close to actually being "perfect." On the surface, the technology-driven economy entails:

- a world wide market where all sellers and buyers meet to trade;
- full information about products and agents available instantaneously;
- market agents that have unbound capability to remember past purchase history and to compare and select among many offers;
- sellers that could individualize prices;
- externalities that can be priced through market mechanisms; and
- products that can match consumer preferences perfectly.

And even though some of these may not attain their predictions because of other non-transactional reasons such as quality uncertainty, the fact that there is such a potential warrants vigorous reexaminations of conventional economic assumptions. For example, first degree price discrimination can no longer be dismissed as a purely theoretical scenario. The availability of detailed demand information and the extreme customizability of digital products are compelling reasons to focus on pricing and competition strategies under product differentiation.

There are many obstacles for the digital markets to be perfect. Some may be artificial. For example, sellers may withhold product information or some sellers may prefer to standardize products. Access to private information may be significantly restricted due to legislation or technological means. Others may be due to the nature of the digital economy such as the uncertainty when digital identification is not persistent. Nevertheless, the digital economy will be 'smart' if not 'perfect'. In a smart economy, firms are organized to take advantage of virtual networks, consumers have access to any market any time, and products and services are integrated and interoperable. Market transactions are made smart with preference-matching products and bundles, flexible low-cost electronic payment systems and efficient negotiation and settlement processes. Clearly, Internet technologies enable these innovations, but to maximize the benefits of new technologies and ensure overall economic gains, technology developers as well as researchers must first understand market implications of these technologies.

References

Akerlof, G., "The Market for Lemons: Quality Uncertainty and the Market Mechanism." *Quarterly Journal of Economics*, 84, (1970), 488-500.

Bernheim, B.D., and M.D. Whinston, "Incomplete Contracts and Strategic Ambiguity." Forthcoming in *American Economic Review*, (1998).

Blinder, A., "Statements to the Congress." *Federal Reserve Bulletin*, 81(2), (1995), 1089-1093.

Brewer, P.J., and C.R. Plott, "A Binary Conflict Ascending Price (BICAP) Mechanism for the Decentralized Allocation of the Right to Use Railroad Tracks." *Social Science Working Paper*, #887, (1995), California Institute of Technology.

Chellappa, R., A. Barua and A.B. Whinston, "Intranets: Looking Beyond Internal Corporate Web Servers." In R. Kalakota and A.B. Whinston, eds., *Readings in Electronic Commerce*, pp. 311-321, Addison Wesley Longman, Reading, MA, 1997.

Choi, S.-Y., D. Stahl and A.B. Whinston, *Economics of Electronic Commerce*, Macmillan Technical Publishing, Indianapolis, IN, 1997.

Erickson, E., "Software Royalty Income from Licensing Software: Is It Rental or Sales Income?" *Hightech*, August, (1996).

Fan, M., J. Stallaert, and A.B. Whinston, "Creating Electronic Markets Using Java Applet and Middleware." *Dr. Dobb's Journal*, November, (1998).

Froomkin, A.M., 1997. "The Essential Role of Trusted Third Parties in Electronic Commerce." In R. Kalakota and A.B. Whinston, eds., *Readings in Electronic Commerce*, pp. 119-176, Addison Wesley Longman, Reading, MA, 1997.

Gupta, A., D.O. Stahl and A.B. Whinston, "An Economic Approach to Network Computing with Priority Classes." *Journal of Organizational Computing and Electronic Commerce*, 6, 1, 1996, 71-95.

Gurnsey, J., *Copyright Theft*, Aslib Gower, Aldershot, UK, 1995.

Interactive Services Association, "Logging on to Cyberspace." *Tax Policy White Paper*, 1996.

Lewis, T.R., and D.E. Sappington, "Supplying Information to Facilitate Price Discrimination." *International* Economic Review, 35, 2, (1994), 309-327.

Liebowitz, S.J., and S.E. Margolis, "Are Network Externalities a New Source of Market Failure?" *Research in Law and Economics*, 17, (1995), 1-22.

Maes, P., "Agents That Reduce Work and Information Overload." *Communications of the ACM*, 37, 7, (1994), 31-40.

McAfee, R.P., and J. McMillan, "Electronic Markets." In R. Kalakota and A.B. Whinston, eds., Readings in Electronic Commerce, pp. 119-176, Addison Wesley Longman, Reading, MA, 1997.

Robert, R., and D.O. Stahl, "Informative Price Advertising in a Sequential Search Model." *Econometrica*, 61, 3, (1993), 657-686.

Srinivasan, S., J. Stallaert, and A.B. Whinston, "Electronic Financial Trading Systems." *CREC Working Paper*, (1998).

Taylor, C.R., and S.N. Wiggins, "Competition or Compensation: Supplier Incentives under the American and Japanese Subcontracting Systems." Forthcoming in *American Economic Review*., (1998).

U.S. Department of Treasury, *Selected Tax Policy Implications of Global Electronic Commerce*, (1996), URL = http://ftp.fedworld.gov/pub/tel/internet.txt

CHAPTER 3

Decision Support Systems and Internet Commerce

Robert W. Blanning[1] and Tung X. Bui[2]

[1]Owen Graduate School of Management, Vanderbilt University, Nashville, TN 37203, bob.blanning@owen.vanderbilt.edu

[2]Decision Sciences, College of Business Administration, University of Hawaii at Manoa, Honululu, HI 96822, tbui@busadm.cba.hawaii.edu

With the increased competition in E-commerce, Internet-based business applications have migrated from being on-line and cost-saving transactions into full-service Internet Commerce. These systems are expected to provide increasing decision support functionalities to help traders optimize their business decisions. This chapter provides a broad overview of how Decision Support technology – an established area with a substantial literature and body of practice – can be incorporated into the design of IC. In particular, it provides examples that show the potentiality of applying Decision Support Systems (DSS) concepts to design a second generation of IC capable of assisting its trading partners in their decision making.

Keywords: decision support systems; electronic commerce; Internet commerce; electronic markets; negotiation support

1 Introduction: From Online Transactions to Business Decision Support

According to the money management firm Bessemer Trust, about seven million households made a purchase on-line during the second half of 1997. The technology research firm International Data Corp. (IDC) predicts that the value of online transactions will grow from $12.4 billion in 1997 to $32.4 billion this year, and would mushroom to $425 billion by 2002. In its 1998 Annual Technology Forecast, Price Waterhouse-Coopers also predicts a massive increase in business conducted via the Internet with a significant increase in business-to-business EC. By judging the value of the few publicly held companies practicing E-commerce, it is safe to argue that the Internet has provided a fundamentally less expensive and potentially more satisfying way to transact certain sectors of business. Well-noted examples include: Amazon.com (www.amazon.com) and Computer Literacy (www.cbooks.com) for selling books; CD Now (www.cdnow.com) and Music Boulevard (www.musicblvd. com) for selling music; E*Trade (www.etrade.com) and Charles Schwab (www.eschwab.com) for selling stocks; Preview Travel (www.previewtravel.com)

for selling travel; and Onsale (www.onsale.com) and Ebay (www.ebay. com) for auctioning just about everything. As such, Electronic Commerce (EC) can be seen as an opportunity to use information technology to compete effectively with existing companies in markets that are already well known as business people and consumers.

But recent technological innovations, e.g., online analytical processing (OLAP), multidimensional databases (MDD), visual information access and analysis (VIAA), data mining and warehousing, etc. – have elevated Internet commerce to a higher level. The recent success of Charles Schwab's E*trade is a prominent example. From an earlier generation of Web-based, on-line financial transaction systems that primarily sought to provide investors with a time-saving and convenient trading platform, E*trade has become a decision support tool helping investors search for stock performance, market studies, portfolio analysis and management. Charles Schwab Inc. has thus evolved from being a discount broker to a full-service IC-based investment corporation. According to a survey, sponsored by media and Internet companies Ziff-Davis and Yahoo! with consultants KPMG, business opportunities on the World Wide Web will not flourish until it becomes less daunting for new, less expert users. And the needs for decision support seem to concentrate on the use of decision making tools to optimize utilization of online and distributed information, and on the implementation of decisions through seamless Internet-based workflow automation and business process integration (Kalakota and Whinston, 1996).

As information technology becomes more widely applied to problems in industry and government, the resulting areas of applications are becoming increasingly specialized. We are concerned here with two applications of information technology that have attracted great interest in the business community. The first is decision support systems (DSS), which have become so well established that most people using them do not regard them as anything special. Examples are spreadsheet systems, interactive databases, and simulation models. The other area is Internet commerce (IC), which is a synthesis of the Internet and electronic commerce.

Although DSS and IC are each of interest in itself, they also bear an important relationship to each other, as exemplified by the success of E*trade. IC participants, both producers and consumers, are decision-makers. Not only must they make decisions about prices (offered or accepted), purchase quantities, and the like, but they must also search for information. Suppliers need to know about consumers and their needs, including their willingness to pay for certain types of goods and services. Consumers need to know about the availability of goods and services, including their prices, quality, delivery dates, and any other matters of interest. DSS technology, which has provided decision support to managers, can also support the decision processes of suppliers and consumers engaged in IC.

As a result, DSS and IC are coming together. There are four principal ways in which this is occurring. First, Internet technology is providing user interfaces to DSS. An example is the use of Web browsers as DSS front ends. Second, the Internet is being used as an IC knowledge base, with DSS technology facilitating intelligent user access to the Internet. An example is the use of intelligent agents by Internet shoppers. Third, the Internet can serve as a platform for distributed negotiation support tools. Fourth, the Internet can be designed as a market maker by providing a medium of communication for geographically dispersed actors engaging in commercial transactions.

We begin in the following section by examining the state of the art of DSS and especially the transformation of DSS to knowledge-based systems and to group support systems. Then we examine the state of the art of IC, emphasizing the transformation of the Internet from a research network to a commercial network. Finally, we examine the four relationships between DSS and IC mentioned above and give an example based on real-life IC application illustrating these relationships.

2 Decision Support Technology

The area of DSS arose during the 1970s from dissatisfaction with two existing areas of technology as applied to management. The first was operations research and management science (OR/MS), with its emphasis on the construction of decision models, such as linear programming and simulation models. The second was management information systems (MIS), with its emphasis on the development of management reporting systems (Keen and Scott-Morton, 1978).

DSS advocates argued that OR/MS people were attempting to replace managers with models, whereas they should be attempting to use information technology to support decision processes. OR/MS people did not see themselves in this light, but they did focus on the construction of sophisticated models, rather than on the interface between these models and their users. DSS advocates also argued that MIS were inflexible, since they were often based on large financial and logistical file processing systems. Thus, MIS were useful in supporting well-structured decision processes – ones in which objectives and courses of action were well understood – but they provided little assistance to managers facing semi-structured or ill-structured problems. Thus, DSS were intended to *assist* managers in addressing *semi-structured* problems (Keen and Scott Morton, 1978; Sprague, 1982).

The earliest DSS performed tasks that are now quite common, such as spreadsheet calculations and graphical presentation of retrieved data. Initially these tasks relied on mainframe computers, but increasingly they took advantage of the growing availability of minicomputers and microcomputers. DSS also began to incorporate two new technologies – machine intelligence and distributed systems – the former in the form of knowledge-based DSS and the latter in group DSS. DSS now perform a variety of functions, principally information organization and presentation, knowledge management, group decision and negotiation support (Blanning and King, 1992; Turban, 1995), and distributed intelligence using collaborative technology. As DSS methodology continues to adjust itself to technological progress, recent techniques in data warehousing, intelligent agents, and Web-enabled databases have made it possible to expand its impacts beyond the traditional boundaries, i.e., that of individual and corporate decision makers (Gray, 1997). In fact, until recently little has been done to explore the relationship of DSS to two dynamic areas of information technology – electronic commerce and the Internet.

3 Internet Commerce

Electronic commerce and the Internet arose in quite different ways. Electronic commerce began with efforts to facilitate financial and logistical transactions by providing electronic documentation of the transactions. Documentation of financial transactions is called electronic funds transfer (EFT), and documentation of logistical transactions is called electronic data interchange (EDI). Most EFT transactions (e.g., bank clearings) take place between financial institutions, and most EDI transactions (e.g., the transmission of invoices, waybills, or payment instructions) take place between commercial organizations or between commercial organizations and financial institutions. However, electronic commerce now includes consideration of issues in addition to the transaction-based issues of concern in EFT and EDI, including consumer information acquisition, electronic auctions, and online publishing (Kalakota and Whinston, 1996, 1997).

The Internet has a quite different history. Its predecessor, called ARPANET, was created by the U.S. Department of Defense to provide reliable communication among computers used by military organizations and defense contractors, many of them universities. The Internet, which emerged from ARPANET under the sponsorship of the U.S. National Science Foundation, was viewed as a communication network for university computers, and commercial transactions were forbidden. However, in 1990 the U.S. Federal Networking Council, which had required all subnetworks joining the Internet to be sponsored by a U.S. government agency, eliminated this requirement. Then in 1992 the National Science Foundation substantially relaxed its Acceptable Use Policy, which had forbidden most commercial uses of the Internet. This opened up the Internet to commercial exploitation (Lynch and Rose, 1993; Ellsworth and Moore, 1996).

The subsequent growth of Internet Commerce (IC) has been enormous (Cronin, 1995; Crocker, 1997), and this has given rise to many applications issues. Can the Internet, an insecure system initially developed for academic use, provide an acceptable level of security for commercial transactions? How can advertisers cost-effectively reach customers on the Internet? How can customers use the Internet to acquire information about available goods and services? How can suppliers of goods and services identify potential customers and gather information about competitors? More generally, what can IC offer that is not already being done or that is not being done very well?

Answers to these questions will not come quickly or easily. And those who find a correct answer will gain a significant competitive edge to IC. Trading partners in IC (e.g., producers, consumers, platform providers, and government regulators) will struggle with them for years to come. As they struggle, they will find that IC consists in part of decision processes in which producers, consumers, and other interested parties search for information, complete transactions, and continually reevaluate their procedures for performing these activities. They will also find that the technology of decision support, which has proven useful in managerial decision making, can be useful in IC decision making as well. In other words, just as DSS provide decision support to managers, they can also provide decision support to those engaged in commercial transactions. We will now examine the relationships between DSS and IC.

4 Decision Support in Internet Commerce

Probably the most adopted decision making model used as a foundation for building decision support systems is the one proposed by Simon (Simon, 1969). Simon postulates that a typical decision making process could be decomposed into three distinct phases: intelligence, design and choice. A good decision support system is one that would help its user be more effective in each of these three phases. Table 1 illustrates some examples of traders' decision making activities in IC according to Simon's three phases. We thus argue that the relationship between DSS and IC is to provide decision support to various decision making activities leading to Internet-based market transactions.

Table 1. Examples of DSS tools for online IC applications classified according to Simon's intelligence-design-choice

Intelligence	Interface Personalization: e.g., selection of search and mapping tools
	Cataloguing: e.g., customized databases, inter-sites, search for comparable products, search for complementary products
	Full online reports
Design	Interactive Problem Formulation: e.g., combining reusable software components, coordinating software agents (applets)
	Interactive Problem Analysis: e.g., price comparison, product comparison
	Systems Integration: e.g., linking I-Commerce solution to corporate MIS, accounting, stock control and customer service systems
Choice	Interactive Commerce: e.g., auctions and deal making
	Market Transaction: e.g., online payment with authentication

4.1 Design Approaches.

From a design point of view, there are four possible uses of DSS technology in IC. These concern (1) Internet technology as a user interface to DSS, (2) the Internet as an IC knowledge base, with DSS technology facilitating user access to the Internet, (3) the Internet as a platform for negotiation support, and (4) the Internet as a market maker that provides an interface between producers and consumers. We will examine and illustrate each of these relationships in a separate subsection below.

4.2 Internet Technology as User Interface

The first and most straightforward relationship between DSS and IC is that Internet technology may provide a user-friendly front end to DSS

The aspect of Internet technology that shows most promise in this regard is the World Wide Web. Components of a DSS may be viewed as separate information objects, each with a separate URL, and a Web browser would help the DSS user to navigate the objects in response to a decision problem or opportunity. The objects may be data relations, data analysis procedures, decision models, knowledge bases, text files, and the like. The front end (browser) would provide hypermedia support to the user navigating the modularized DSS. In addition, the front end might provide graphical or multimedia support for the user who is unfamiliar with some of the information objects and needs instructions on how to use them.

Researchers in the DSS field advocate that a friendly user interface should at least have the following features:

- Transparency and consistency to make the system easy to learn, use and remember for both novel and expert users
- User-control of the systems
- Conducive to effective usage and better decision-making
- Efficient use of resources.

In addition to these requirements, special considerations for browser-based interface should include flexible text input for browser interface and multiple Internet interface media.

As shown in Figure 1, Internet technology can be used in the form of a browser-based interface to the DSS located on a Web server. The browser provides a multi-platform and location-independent graphical user interface. The IC consumer is guided through the DSS process with each page. As such, the DSS allows for interoperability of computer-based decision making. With this technology, the seller expands his/her electronic market via Web servers to all traders who have access to the Internet via a browser.

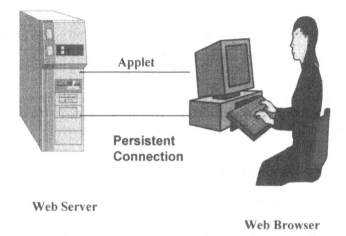

Applet

Persistent
Connection

Web Server

Web Browser

Fig. 1. Accessing DSS applications via Internet browsers

The design of the system is similar to that of a conventional DSS in terms of system architecture, because the model component and the main database component are centrally located in the server.

Since most of Internet transactions start with information search, browser interface for IC should be able to capture as accurate as possible the information request of the users. Techniques such as paraphrasing using conceptual indexing and dynamic passage retrieval, or algorithms to deal synonyms should be used. The paraphrase problem occurs when the user queries the system with a set of words that are different from, but conceptually related to, those described in the systems. In other words, while the query and the passage convey similar ideas, the wording of each is different.

In addition to the browser interface, other Internet-based communication technologies should be used whenever appropriate:

- Adding email correspondence between surfer and site support has become a common support to IC.
- To deal with a large number of typical queries, "chatbots" technology should be considered. A chatbot can be defined as an intelligent evolution of email. The chabot categorizes messages on the fly and provides answers to questions accordingly. As such, it can be used as a customer support tool.
- IP Telephony provides another support extension to IC. To establish telephony, real-time voice/text interactions require special installation.
- Real-time cameras that transmit online trading activities to provide IC traders with a feel of a lived-in office.
- The last DSS concept is to provide the true meaning of decision support to IC in adding a human support to customers to fully automated IC.

As Web technology brings DSS technology to IC decision makers, migration of a user interface to a Web-page medium requires little re-design effort, but does involve an initially steep learning curve of middleware to bridge the Web-based interface component with the model and database component of the DSS. However, once the technology is learned (for both data input and display), high migration productivity should occur and rapid deployment should be expected. Also, bandwidth capacity and reliability could become an issue in that slow access to the Internet is a major factor that would discourage decision makers from using this technology.

4.3 The Internet as IC Knowledge Base

The second relationship between DSS and IC is the complement of the first. In this case DSS technology is used in knowledge-based systems that help producers, consumers, and others to search the Internet for domain-dependent information and advice. Thus, we may have suppliers searching for information about customers or competitors, customers searching for information about suppliers or products, suppliers and customers searching for general information about the market, and government regulators searching for information about suspicious transactions and about unusual market behavior. An example of DSS use in IC is the Wired Digital Technology that offers a quick price-comparison feature in a search engine. Users can ask for a comparison and get back a list of products based on various specifications, including features and price.

Software agents – implemented as Web applets – are often the preferred choice for providing expert advice on the Internet. A software agent, intelligent or not, is a program that performs a specific task on behalf of a user, independently or with little guidance. Intelligent agents perform, reactively and/or proactively, interactive tasks tailored to a user's needs without humans or other agents telling it what to do. To accomplish these tasks, it should possess the following general characteristics of (Kalaota and Whinston, 1996):

- Independence
- Learning
- Cooperation
- Reasoning
- Intelligence.

Agents are the result of a paradigm shift in developing application software. Software is no longer regarded as a tool. Rather, it is considered as an autonomous assistant to the users – simulating a human relationship, hence the word "Personal Assistant" in the software engineering literature. In other words, the traditional approach to software development is a reactive one in that the computer is programmed to react to the user's instruction. Instead, the software agent approach is a proactive one, in that the user specifies what he/she wants the computer to accomplish, and the latter performs tasks on behalf of the users. By analogy, a software agent mimics the role of an intelligent, dedicated and competent personal assistant (e.g., a secretary of a busy executive, or a medical assistant of an engaged physician). In a network, an agent can be seen as a program that, once sent across the network, encapsulates the user's instructions and executes it with little guidance. Creating a new Internet-based agent involves simple steps (e.g., using Surfbot monitoring agent, www.surflogic.com):

- Identify working file location(s)
- Determine desired amount of information (volume and time frame)
- Select search extent (e.g., how many links)
- Choose presentation/report style.

Agents are typically used as a tool to gather, filter and interpret information. In addition to these functions, an intelligent software agent should be able to support various phases of the decision making and problem solving process, and serves as a:

- Problem analyzer
- Problem solver
- Implementation agent
- Monitoring agent
- Negotiating and conflict resolution agent.

More important and unlike routine tasks that can be automated, decision making involves complex set of tasks that requires integration of supporting agents. To work together, these agents should have behaviors to work in teams (e.g., O'Leary, 1996) with the ability to:

- Recall (the extent to which relevant information is retrieved)
- Execute tasks with precision (the extent to which gathered information matches decision tasks)
- Exhibit good citizenship (e.g., avoid unnecessary interaction with other entities/agents; report errors)

4.4 The Internet as Negotiation Support Tool

Negotiations take place in IC whenever matters of interest (prices, delivery dates, etc.) are not determined in the market but rather are arranged separately for each transaction. We assume that potential parties to a transaction have been identified and the problem is to decide whether the transaction will take place and if so to settle on prices, delivery dates, etc. The purpose of a negotiation support tool is to assist the parties to a negotiation in making these decisions. Such a tool may provide a common database containing information about current and previous negotiations, establish communication links between the parties, and help to identify areas of agreement and disagreement, presumably through mutual discussion and periodic voting on issues.

Negotiation support services are more difficult to provide when the parties are geographically distributed. The database may contain both centralized and dispersed components. Communication links are more difficult to establish when the parties are in different parts of the world, with different schedules in different time zones. Remote discussion and voting are also more difficult in a distributed environment than in a collocated environment. The Internet, with its worldwide reach, may facilitate distributed commercial negotiations. Software agents could be used to provide a distributed software architecture to provide negotiation support of IC traders.

4.5 The Internet as Market Maker

The fourth relationship between DSS and IC is a synthesis of the other three relationships: the making of an efficient market between producers and consumers. Development of electronic markets (EM) has recently gained much interest among both academics and practitioners. EM mechanisms are expected to increase market transparency, transaction speed and allocation efficiency while reducing biased decisions and time intensive routines. However, current EM can at best be described as an automated version of non-Internet-based market transactions with focus on information delivery (e.g., Web homepages as information centers) and on data transactions (e.g., Web browser-based ordering, sales auctions, and customer support). As such, current EM implementations fail to take advantage of the well-proven potential of decision support technology. Furthermore, existing EM are typically designed following a centralized clearinghouse approach with all transactions being performed at the server site with traders accessing the EM via remote clients.

An electronic market maker (EMM) combines DSS and IC to provide (1) individual decision support for producers and consumers and (2) collective decision support that helps producers and consumers to identify potential trading partners and to negotiate and complete a transaction. An EMM also attempts to identify market failures – for example an unusual concentration of pricing power in a few producers or consumers – and notifies appropriate regulatory authorities. Thus, an EMM serves three distinct groups of users: producers, consumers, and the market.

An EMM might also operate under conditions other than those found with isolated transactions in markets containing large numbers of producers and consumers. An example is an auction, in which the EMM serves as auctioneer and advises the seller as to the advantages and disadvantages of different types of auction. In addition, an EMM might participate in ongoing agency relationships – for example, when a firm is hiring contractors and rewards them on the basis of firm performance. In this case the EMM would suggest, implement, and monitor incentive systems used by the firm to reward and penalize contractors. In sum, we view electronic market as a dense network of electronic market mechanisms that seek to improve market efficiency via communications and decision support technologies (Figure 2).

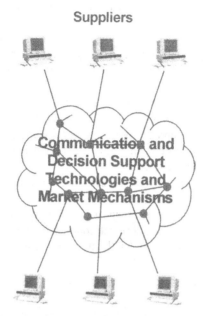

Fig. 2. Electronic markets

5 A Case Study: The Design of a DSS to Support Air Cargo Market Transactions in Electronic Markets.

The case study below illustrates in one single implementation the EMM concept. It relates to the design of a DSS to support air cargo market transactions via the Internet.

5.1 Toward an Electronic Market for Improving Market Efficiency

For many major airlines, cargo business has been insignificant compared to that of passenger transportation. One of the reasons for this lack of importance stems from the inherently weak approach to doing air cargo business. As communication by telephone and fax still dominates the coordination process between a forwarder and its airlines, only a very small choice of airlines are considered for a shipment. Consequently, forwarders tend to stick to airlines they know and have successfully done business with before. As such, preferences of officials of the requesting forwarder (ORF) dominate the choice of an airline transporter instead of the goal of finding an efficient fit between supply and demand. Thus, the reduced number of interaction relationships a forwarder can handle during one transaction is very small, resulting in potential loss of business.

However, the volume of goods to be shipped by air is predicted to double by the year 2000 with approximately 480 carriers worldwide. Airline companies have started to explore new computer-supported market mechanisms as a means to compete effectively in this market.

The need for a DSS stems from two causes. First, as the air cargo market is not a perfect market thus leaving room for efficiency improvement. The most important involved traders are airlines and forwarders; other stakeholders are typically banks, custom agencies, and airport companies. A DSS must adapt to their special needs, particularly those of the forwarders.

Second, the settlement phase in the air cargo market calls for decision support in dealing with bilateral negotiation between the forwarder and the air transport company. Last but not least, communications between market partners have been primarily done via telephone or fax. The introduction of the Internet as a seamless EMM platform is expected to be done without major infrastructure investments.

5.2 Design Considerations

A very special success factor of the cargo business is the ability of the forwarder always to know at any point in time where his shipment is located. This is currently achieved by telephone and fax calls. Time lags caused by phone tags, misunderstandings and double-checking should be eliminated.

In addition, integrated computerized support will prevent business partners from repeated data inputs that often cause errors. The idea of a virtual corporation connecting business partners guarantee the most efficient transaction has not been picked up in air cargo business. Yet, it is precisely this type of organization that is expected to improve service quality and – combined with modern IT – to minimize ineffective communication and coordination.

With this as a working assumption, and by focusing on the supplier-customer-relationship between airlines and forwarders, it is argued that smart and autonomous software programs called software agents can accomplish numerous routine tasks and, when needed, provide "intelligent" decision support as well. The implementation of these agents on the suppliers' and customers' sides is by far less expensive than the creation of a centralized clearinghouse.

5.3 A DSS architecture for supporting IC

Market transactions are typically divided into three main phases: information, nego-tiation and settlement. In the context of air cargo market, these phases can be broken down into a sequences of business processes, i.e., data input, market overview, offer collection, offer evaluation, auction, document dispatch, and tracking and tracing.

Figure 3 shows a high-level architecture of the electronic market maker. Software agents play the role of market makers linking various maker traders together, that is the official representing the forwarders and the airlines. Five types of software agents are identified: user agent as the "personal assistant", supervising agent, coor-dination agent, reply agent and retrieval agent. Their task assignments described below and summarized in Table 2 shows the allocation of business processes and tasks to various agents. Marks in parentheses denote agent support is not necessary but optional. An entire transaction with software agent support can be detailed into several steps, refining the activities (represented by columns in Table 2).

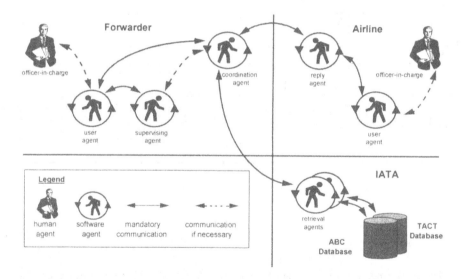

Fig. 3. Agents interaction in the air cargo market

Table 2. Mapping agents to market transactions tasks

	Data Input	Market Overview	Offer Collection	Offer Evaluation	Auction	Document Dispatch	Tracking & Tracing
FORWARDER							
Human agent	X				(X)	(X)	(X)
User agent	X				(X)	(X)	(X)
Supervising agent		X	X		X	X	X
Coordination agent		X	X	X	X	X	X
IATA							
Retrieval agent		X					
AIRLINE							
Reply agent			X		X	X	X
User agent					(X)	(X)	(X)
Human agent					(X)	(X)	(X)

Legend: X: necessary tasks, (X): agent's support is optional

Data Input

1. The forwarder received an order to send a shipment. As the ORF, he initiates the transaction by providing the *user agent* with shipment specifications (e.g., cargo size and weight, destination, time window of departure, time window of arrival, documents to be included, additional attributes like "live animals", "poisonous goods", etc) using a standardized form.
2. The user agent asks for the ORF's preferences. Preferences could be the exclusion of certain airlines, airports, routings, etc. In addition, qualitative requirements can be specified by weighing the needs for punctuality, reliability, minimization of reloads, etc. The ORF also specifies the deadline for offer collection.

3. The user agent initializes the *supervising agent* giving information on the offer deadline.

Market Overview

1. The user agent instructs the coordination agent to retrieve information about possible routings and corresponding airlines meeting the constraints of steps 2 and 3.
2. The *coordination agent* hands over the inquiry to the *retrieval agent*.
3. The retrieval agent selects appropriate routings from the ABC database located at IATA (International Air Transport Association), an independent agency, and returns routing and airline information to the *coordination agent*.

Offer Collection

1. The coordination agent sends the calls for offers to the reply agents of the selected airlines.
2. The *reply agents* automatically provide offers for standard shipments. In more complicated cases they return their offers after checking with the human officer-in-charge.
3. The supervising agent keeps an eye on the given deadline. In case of no reactions it causes the coordination agent to send reminders to the reply agents concerned.
4. The coordination agent sends reminders to the reply agents trying to get the required information.
5. The supervising agent collects the results from the coordination agent. As soon as all airlines answered the call for offers the information phase is terminated. If this goal cannot be achieved, the deadline introduced in Step 3 terminates this phase. The supervising agent informs the user agent about the offer collection results.
6. The *user agent* forwards the information to the officer-in-charge. Details included are the number of airlines asked for an offer and the number of airlines that answered the call for offers. In the same step, the officer-in-charge is requested to fix the deadline for the next auction.
7. The user agent forwards the deadline to the supervising agent.

Offer Evaluation

1. The user agent triggers the coordination agent to calculate net value prices for each offer considering quantitative and qualitative factors.
2. The coordination agent calculates net value prices and produces a ranking of the offers including information about the relative differences between the offers.

Auction

1. The coordination agent distributes this ranking to all of the airlines involved.
2. The airlines' reply agents receive the ranking and contact the user agent handing over this information.
3. The airline's user agent asks the officer-in-charge whether or how to adapt the offer to the market situation. The result is given back to the reply agent.
4. The coordination agent collects new offers from the reply agents and recalculates net value prices.
5. The supervising agent terminates the negotiation process and instructs subsequently the coordination agent not to accept any further offers.
6. The coordination agent delivers the final ranking to the user agent.
7. The user agent displays the results to the ORF and leaves him with the decision about selecting the market partner for this transaction

Document Dispatch

1. In the settlement phase the forwarder's user agent collects data for the necessary documents from the ORF and delivers them to the coordination agent.
2. The coordination agent transfers the documents to the recipients, e.g., airlines involved, custom agencies, or handling companies.
3. The documents are accepted by the partner's *reply agent.*
4. The entire process including the order of the documents is controlled by the *supervising agent.*

Tracking and Tracing

1. At the beginning of the actual transport process the *user agent* delivers the shipment milestones to the supervising agent. These data are fed into the system in step 1 of Document Dispatch when the decision of the routing is made.
2. According to these milestones the supervising agent triggers the coordination agent to request a status report from the airline.
3. The coordination agent demands this status report from the airline's reply agent and delivers it to the supervising agent.
4. If expected and actual status differ the supervising agent sends this information to the user agent, which reports this exception to the officer-in-charge and saves the information in the local quality database.
5. Once the last milestone verified by the coordination agent, the user agent informs the human agent about the closing of the transaction.

5.4 Implementation

The heterogeneity of the computer systems being used in air cargo led to the decision to use Smalltalk as a programming language in the ParcPlace© version of VisualWorks© 2.52 with compilers for many different platforms, including MS Windows© 3.x, 95 and NT, Sun Solaris©, OS/2© and AIX©. To pave the way for a rapid diffusion of decentralized market mechanisms, the communication system of choice is the Internet thanks to its interoperability. The gateway for information to be sent via Internet from the local VisualWorks© environment can be realized with VisualWave©. This tool produces html scripts from given data. Forms that need to be filled in are provided with the help of CGI (common gateway interface). To date, prototypes of user and coordination agents have been implemented with the tools mentioned (see Robra, 1996 and Wiesner, 1996).

Internet Technology as User Interface

To ensure user-friendliness of the interface, the implemented prototypes have adopted the common paper forms that have been used in the cargo business. Experience suggests that this requirement has been achieved. To assure access to all common databases, ParcPlace© offers various gateways so that existing software can easily be integrated.

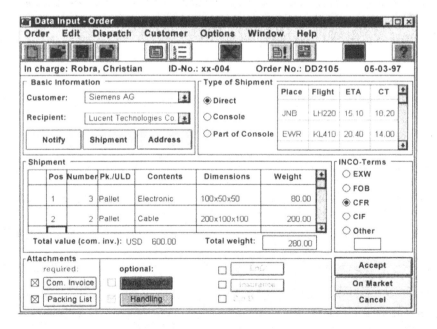

Fig. 4. Internet browser as DSS interface

As described earlier, when a forwarder receives an order from a client to send a shipment, he needs to feed the relevant data into the access system of the electronic air cargo market. The user agent leads him through this process. The interface for this task is shown in Figure 4. Screen buttons provide access to more detailed, specialized information. The button *On Market* allows this order be offered to other forwarders on a market with horizontal coordination structures. This may be necessary when the forwarder has no resources left to settle the order himself due to a lack of manpower or competence.

The Internet as IC Knowledge Base

The menu *Dispatch* leaves functions disabled which – according to the transaction process – are not yet next in line, to assure that a certain order is kept.

In the next step the ORF defines the special requirements of a shipment concerning place and time information for departure, destination and arrival (see Figure 5). The screen also offers access to more detailed specifications considering special qualitative issues (*Further Requirements*) and time restrictions for the coordination process (*Answer Time*) instructing the supervising agent to close offer acceptance at a certain time.

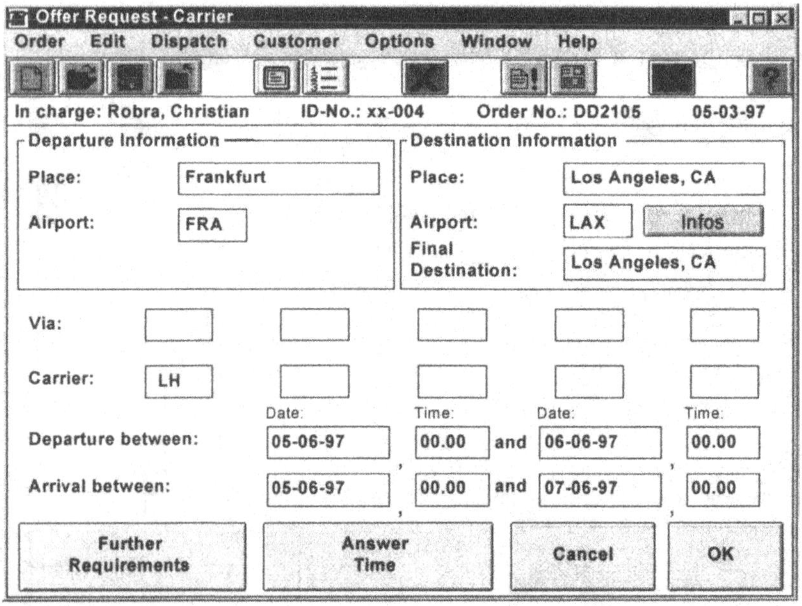

Fig. 5. Internet as knowledge base

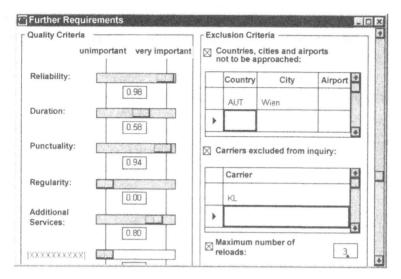

Fig. 6. Problem design with qualitative analysis

According to the special needs of a shipment, the forwarder can indicate his preferences for qualitative factors like punctuality, duration or reliability. Mandatory criteria about which countries, cities and airports to avoid, as well as which airlines not to consider can also be fixed here. Additionally, the number of reloads might be of importance for the choice of a market partner for a certain shipment. The system's supervisor can integrate additional quality criterion (the last scroll bar in Figure 6) as he sees fit.

The Internet as Negotiation Support Tool

When the user agent has received all necessary data from the ORF, he inquires basic routing information. The coordination agent forwards this information demand to the ABC database by communicating with the database retrieval agent. The coordination agent then contacts the airlines that could possibly handle the shipment and asks their reply agents for offers, thus initializing the auction during the negotiation process. This process continues until final offers from the airlines are accepted. This results in a final ranking which is delivered to the user agent and processed for the officer-in-charge. He is the one to finally decide which offer to pick.

The Internet as Market Maker

According to the milestones determined by the routing, supervising and coordination agents dispatch the documents to the places where and when they are needed. Only in special situation interference of the officer-in-charge is necessary. Tracking and tracing are performed autonomously as well, handing over exception reports to the officer-in-charge when necessary. All relevant data are stored in the quality database without any time expenditures on the side of the officer-in-charge. The results of the auction are shown on Figure 7.

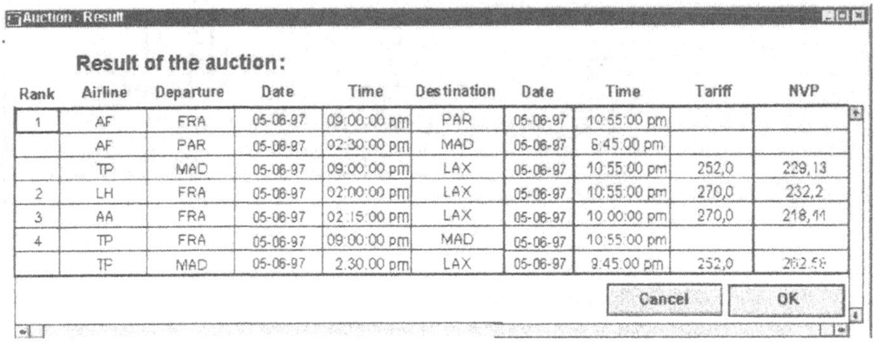

Auction - Result										

Result of the auction:

Rank	Airline	Departure	Date	Time	Destination	Date	Time	Tariff	NVP	
1	AF	FRA	05-06-97	09:00:00 pm	PAR	05-06-97	10:55:00 pm			
	AF	PAR	05-06-97	02:30:00 pm	MAD	05-06-97	6:45:00 pm			
	TP	MAD	05-06-97	09:00:00 pm	LAX	05-06-97	10:55:00 pm	252,0	229,13	
2	LH	FRA	05-06-97	02:00:00 pm	LAX	05-06-97	10:55:00 pm	270,0	232,2	
3	AA	FRA	05-06-97	02:15:00 pm	LAX	05-06-97	10:00:00 pm	270,0	218,11	
4	TP	FRA	05-06-97	09:00:00 pm	MAD	05-06-97	10:55:00 pm			
	TP	MAD	05-06-97	2:30:00 pm	LAX	05-06-97	9:45:00 pm	252,0	262,58	

Cancel   OK

Fig. 7. Results of the auction

5.5 Lessons Learned

The idea of an electronic market for the air cargo business was adopted quickly by all the parties involved. The decentralized design is perceived as an attractive concept for both the forwarders and the airlines. Of particular interest for all market agents is the integration of tracking and tracing capabilities, a very time consuming process in the actual communication between forwarders and airlines.

Impacts on Forwarders

The most apparent gain for the forwarders is the time reduction on telephone calls and fax messages. Transaction costs can be reduced as time can be saved for routine communication on information collection, negotiation and status requests. Additionally, cycle times for transactions are reduced through integration of the whole process and the ability of software agents to communicate with other agents much more efficiently compared to personal communication. Data, once put into the system, can be made available for all market partners, thus avoiding multiple data input. More importantly, the fact that communication can be simplified through the implementation of software agents allows expansion of market partners. The increase in market transparency also enlarges the choice for the forwarders, resulting in better matching of problem solutions and better prices due to increased competition.

Impacts on Airlines

On the airline's side, transaction costs are expected to decrease as well since repetitive data inputs can be avoided. This saves time and reduces the risk of input errors. Since most of the communication with forwarders takes place during the information exchange phase (offer inquiries) and during the settlement phase, the implementation of software agents that take over these tasks increases efficiency on the supplier side.

After a hesitant first reaction on the use of an electronic market, the airlines realized that an electronic market is a valuable tool for them. Market transparency enables airlines to better advertise their core competencies since qualitative issues like reliability or punctuality gain in importance compared to the status quo. In addition new markets can be developed and the presence in an electronic air cargo market will lead to competitive advantages when the added services are useful for the forwarders.

In summary, it is expected that the introduction of Internet commerce with decision support technology will decrease transaction costs while increasing transaction speed. Time consuming tasks can be moved from human to Web-enabled technology including software agents, saving time and decreasing biased decisions. Due to the distributed architecture, investments are minimal. The implementation of an electronic market in the air cargo business constitutes a radical change to existing structures, creating new opportunities for all traders without fundamentally changing business processes.

Research Opportunities

Internet Commerce offers an unprecedented opportunity for companies to redefine the relationship between buyers and sellers to better serve existing customers and to target new customers more profitably. Seizing this opportunity means embedding decision support technology into IC design. Examples of DSS use include promotion of advanced personalization, manageability and flexibility in performing decision-making processes. We have seen that DSS and IC are each important in themselves, but they also complement each other. The reason for the complementarity is that people engaging in IC are decision-makers, and DSS technology can provide decision support for IC participants, just as it currently provides decision support for managers. Thus, we may expect to see more instances in which Internet technology provides a user-friendly DSS interface, DSS provide an intelligent IC interface, the Internet provides a platform for DSS-based negotiation support, and the DSS and IC come together to serve as an EMM.

The emerging synthesis of DSS and IC will give rise to several fruitful areas of research. DSS researchers have studied how managers use information technology to acquire information, and they may also be able to offer insights into the ways in which potential purchasers can search a worldwide network of information sources in an attempt to locate a product or service that best satisfies their needs. In addition,

DSS researchers have studied how information technology can support financial, logistical, and marketing decisions. They should be well equipped to study methods of supporting these decisions when producers and consumers are linked in a world-wide network.

Acknowledgements. The authors would like to thank Professor Freimut Bodendorf and his research team for allowing the use of their prototype to illustrate the framework proposed in this chapter.

References

Blanning, R.W. and D.R. King, (eds.), *Current Research in Decision Support Technology*, IEEE Computer Society Press, Los Alamitos, 1992.

Bodendorf, F., T. Bui, and S. Rheimheimer, "A Software-Agent-Based DSS for Supporting Electronic Air Cargo Market", *Proceedings of the Fourth Conference of the International Society for Decision Support Systems*, University of Lausanne, Switzerland, July 21-22, 1997.

Crocker, D.H., "An Unaffiliated View of Internet Commerce," Chapter 1 of *Readings in Electronic Commerce*, Ed. by R. Kalakota and A. B. Whinston, Addison-Wesley, Reading, (1997), 3-27.

Cronin, M.J., *Doing More Business on the Internet: How the Electronic Highway is Transforming American Companies*, Van Nostrand Reinhold, New York, 1995.

Ellsworth, M.V. and M. Moore, "Forces Shaping the Internet," Chapter 3 of *The Internet Unleashed 1996*, Sams.net Publishing, Indianapolis, (1996), 23-32.

Gray, P., "The New DSS: Datawarehouses, OLAP, and Data Mining" *Proceedings of the Fourth Conference of the International Society for Decision Support Systems*, University of Lausanne, Switzerland, July 21-22, 1997.

Hinkkanen, A., R. Kakakota, P. Saengcharoenrat, J. Sallaert, and A.B. Whinston, "Distributed Decision Support Systems for Real-time Supply Chain Management Using Agent Technologies" *in Readings in Electronic Commerce*, R. Kalakota and A.B. Whinston, (Eds), Addison-Wesley, Readings, Massachusetts, 1997.

Kalakota, R. and A.B. Whinston, *Frontiers of Electronic Commerce*, Addison-Wesley, Reading, 1996.

Kalakota, R. and A.B. Whinston, *Electronic Commerce: A Manager's Guide*, Addison-Wesley, Reading, 1997.

Keen, P.G.W. and M.S. Scott Morton, *Decision Support Systems: An Organizational Perspective*, Addison-Wesley, Reading, 1978.

Lynch, D.C. and M.T. Rose, (eds.), *Internet System Handbook*, Addison-Wesley, Reading, 1993.

O'Leary, D.E., (1996) "AI and Navigation on the Internet and Intranet", *IEEE Expert*.

Robra, C., (1996) "Prototypische Entwicklung eines Zugangssystems für Speditionsbetriebe als Teil eines Elektronischen Marktes im Luftfrachtbereich", Master Thesis, University Erlangen-Nuremberg.

Schmid B.F. and M.A. Lindemann, "Elements of a Reference Model for Electronic Markets", *HICSS-31*, January 1998, Hawaii.

Simon, H., *The Sciences of the Artificial*, MIT Press, Cambridge, MA, 1969.

Sprague, R.H., Jr. and E.D. Carlson, *Building Effective Decision Support Systems*, Prentice-Hall, Englewood Cliffs, 1982.

Turban, E., *Decision Support and Expert Systems: Management Support Systems*, (4th ed.), Prentice Hall, Englewood Cliffs, 1995.

Wiesner, T., (1996) *Integration von Geschäftsprozessen einer Luftfrachtgesellschaft in einen unternehmensübergreifenden Elektronischen Markt und Modellierung zwischenbetrieblier Koordinationsmechanismen*, Master Thesis, University Erlangen-Nuremberg.

CHAPTER 4
Electronic Markets: Impact and Implications

Troy J. Strader[1] and Michael J. Shaw[2]

[1]Department of Management, Iowa State University, Ames, IA, USA, tstrader@iastate.edu

[2]Department of Business Administration, and Beckman Institute for Advanced Science and Technology, University of Illinois at Urbana–Champaign, Urbana, IL, USA, m–shaw@uiuc.edu

In this chapter we survey the economic impact of electronic markets (e-markets). We identify and analyze examples of e-markets, the impact of e-markets on the structure of industries, buyer and seller cost differences for traditional and electronic markets, revenue source implications for sellers and transaction intermediaries, and determinants of e-market success. The overall issue addressed is whether there are economic incentives for electronic markets, or are they just a passing fad?

Keywords: Electronic Markets; Transaction Cost Economics; Information Economics; Industry Structure; Consumer Behavior; Business Strategy)

1 Introduction

Commercial transactions have taken place for centuries, but currently there is a revolution taking place that is transforming the marketplace. This transformation is occurring because the relationship between organizations and consumers is increasingly being facilitated through electronic information technology (IT). This is generally referred to as electronic commerce (e-commerce), with a major component of e-commerce being electronic markets (e-markets). The number of products available on-line is growing steadily, but not enough is understood about this rapidly evolving phenomenon. In 1996 the number of losers exceeded the number of winners by 2 to 1 for Internet commercial ventures (Rebello et al., 1996). A question that arises from the current growth of electronic markets is whether there are economic incentives for buyers and sellers to participate in them, or whether they are a passing fad. The purpose of this chapter is to address this issue.

Past work has focused on the theoretical relationship, generally based on transaction cost economics analysis (Williamson, 1985), between IT and transaction governance (markets vs. hierarchies) (Bakos, 1991; Benjamin and Wigand, 1995; Gurbaxani and Whang, 1991; Malone et al., 1987; Malone et al., 1989; Malone and Rockart, 1991). Our study involves a cost-based economics analysis similar to previous work, but we compare traditional markets with electronic markets instead of markets with hierarchies. Williamson states that the economic institutions of capitalism (namely markets and hierarchies) have the main purpose and effect of economizing on transaction costs (Williamson, 1985). Our thesis is that, in many instances, electronic markets enjoy transaction cost advantages over traditional markets. Because of these transaction cost advantages we can expect a continued growth in online markets in many industries.

The following sections describe the findings of our study. In Section 2 we present some examples of electronic markets to provide background for the remaining sections. The remaining sections describe the impact of e-markets from three perspectives: buyers, sellers, and other organizations associated with commercial transactions. In Section 3 we identify the impacts that e-markets have on industry structures. We discuss traditional retail industry structure, industry structure for non-digital product e-markets, and industry structure for e-markets associated with digitized products. In Section 4 we evaluate the characteristics of traditional and electronic markets from a buyer perspective. We derive a number of revenue implications for sellers and other organizations from this analysis as well as the analysis from the previous section. In Section 5 we evaluate the cost-based differences between traditional and electronic markets from a seller perspective. In Section 6 we discuss the impact that e-markets have on revenue sources for product/service providers, transaction intermediaries, Internet service providers (ISPs), and state and federal government. Finally, in Section 7 we identify some factors affecting the success of e-markets, and in Section 8 we discuss our overall conclusions.

2 Electronic Markets: Description and Examples

The shift toward electronic commerce is revolutionary because it involves linking consumers to electronic marketplaces, not just electronically supporting hierarchical transactions within and between organizations (commonly referred to as the problem of enterprise integration). The involvement of consumers, in addition to product/service providers, dramatically increases the potential magnitude of change. A significant portion of the GDP is consumer transactions. As of the fourth quarter of 1997, more than 66% of the GDP was personal expenditures (Stat-USA, 1998). Past growth in enterprise integration systems missed these transactions. The revolutionary nature of electronic commerce provides adequate incentive to study electronic markets to increase our understanding of their impact on the market's participants, traditional and newly created industries, as well as the economy as a whole.

2.1 Electronic Market Description

Electronic markets are the foundation of electronic commerce. They potentially integrate advertising, product ordering, delivery of digitizable products, and payment systems. An electronic marketplace (or electronic market system) is an interorganizational information system that allows the participating buyers and sellers to exchange information about prices and product offerings. The firm operating the system is referred to as the intermediary, which may be a market participant - a buyer or seller, an independent third party, or a multi-firm consortium (Bakos, 1991). E-markets provide an electronic, or on-line, method to facilitate transactions between buyers and sellers that potentially provides support for all of the steps in the entire order fulfillment process. The business process model from a consumer's perspective consists of activities that can be grouped into three phases: prepurchase determination, purchase consummation, and postpurchase interaction (Kalakota and Whinston, 1996). Each of these phases can be supported electronically in a complete e-market, but e-markets today generally support only the prepurchase determination activities, although they are moving toward more purchase consummation.

2.2 Electronic Market Examples

A number of electronic markets are available to consumers to buy products ranging from music CDs to automobiles. The following are current examples of products and/or services that are available through electronic markets.

Flowers

Calyx & Corolla have used e-commerce to radically alter the way new cut-flowers are moved from the growers to the consumers. Traditionally, the value chain that supplied cut flowers involved a grower, jobber to transport to a wholesaler, and finally a florist. From a survey of Boston florists in July 1995, the price, including delivery charge and tax, for an example arrangement of flowers was $60. Calyx & Corolla are able to provide an electronic market to customers to buy directly from growers with the flowers being shipped using Federal Express. Their delivered price is $54 (Applegate et al., 1996). Much of this is due to the elimination of some of the intermediaries between the growers and the customers. The price paid to the firm providing the electronic market is generally lower than the profits made by the traditional wholesaler and retailer intermediaries.

Clothing

Similar to the cut-flower example, is an example in the shirt industry. The cost per high quality shirt in a value chain that includes a wholesaler and retailer is $52.72. The elimination of these intermediaries reduces the cost to $20.45, a reduction of 62% (Benjamin and Wigand, 1995).

Automobiles

Thanks to the World Wide Web, new car shoppers have more options, including access to valuable information, such as what a car really does cost a dealer. As a result, consumers are increasingly locking in better deals online. What's more, the trend has attracted the attention of some of the biggest car dealers, financial institutions and insurance companies. Electronic markets now exist than enable consumers to shop for and buy a new car, insure it and take delivery without ever setting foot in a dealership (Calem, 1996). A search of the directory of automobile dealers on Yahoo in late 1996 showed that 79 different dealers or locator services were listed (Yahoo).

Music

Jason and Matthew Olim founded CDnow Inc. from the basement of their Ambler, Pennsylvania home. Jason Olim, a jazz fan frustrated by skimpy selections in music shops, came up with the idea of a cyberstore that could offer every jazz album made in the U.S. and 20,000 imports. Shoppers place their orders with CDnow (cdnow.com), which, in turn, contacts distributors. Most disks are delivered to the customer's door in 24 hours. Add in advertising revenues, and CDnow expects to hit $6 million in sales in 1996, triple the previous year's revenue, with 18% operating margins (Rebello et al., 1996).

Books

Books are another product that consumers purchase on-line. One bookseller on the Web is Amazon.com Books. Their site advertises a spotlight book, book of the day, titles in the news, featured books, and books that are hot this week. Some of their books are discounted as much as 30%. By clicking on book titles, and some authors, more detailed information can be accessed (Amazon). It is no longer necessary to either go to a bookstore to buy a book or to find mail order bookstores through a print advertisement. Also, Web advertising is likely to be more current than print ads.

Electronic Magazines (E-zines)

With no printing or circulation costs, online magazines once held the promise of low overhead and quick profitability. Now most Web publishers have amended their business models and expect years of losses before turning a profit – a model much closer to print publications. Though analysts and publishers expect mainstream advertisers to up their antes in Web ads, most e-zines are exploring alternative ways of making money in the short term, including sponsorships, alliances and even subscriptions. Most online publishers have a rosy outlook now that the Internet has become a media focal point and mainstream advertisers better understand the Net. Jupiter Communications, a New York-based Internet research company, predicts that the total number of online consumers will jump from 13 million in 1996 to more than 35 million in 2000. Adam Schoenfeld, vice president and senior analyst at Jupiter, said that the universe of ad dollars online – both on the Web and on dedicated online services – would grow to $5.3 billion by 2000 (Glaser, 1996). A growing number of online consumers, as well as a growing amount of Net based ad money, provides an environment where electronic magazines with good content may flourish in the future.

Airline Tickets

Discount airfares you won't find anywhere else are popping up on the Internet. American Airlines and Cathay Pacific Airways are using their Web sites to reduce the thousands of seats that are unsold on flights every day. American began selling fares on 20 routes as much as 70% below the lowest fares consumers would be quoted through a travel agent or American's 800 number. Besides filling empty seats, airlines want to cut distribution costs by selling directly on the Internet instead of through travel agents (Rosato, 1996).

Stock and Securities

All of a sudden, innovations in technology, particularly the Internet, are bringing profound changes to Wall Street that hold a lot of promise, and a lot of peril, for the powerful firms that make their money in the securities business. For many people, the Internet could replace the functions of a broker. For example, almost a dozen small companies are trying to sell their stock directly to the public using Web sites like those run by Direct Stock Market and IPO Data Systems. And two small California companies, Real Goods Trading and Perfect Data, have set up electronic bulletin boards that allow their shareholders to trade stock without a broker, dealer or market maker. Because it allows traders to find each other easily, the Internet may ultimately make it possible to have a stock exchange that exists only in cyberspace, with no trading floor, directly open to every investor with a computer and a modem (Eaton, 1996).

Three sets of issues and research questions arise from an analysis of these examples. First, what is the impact that electronic markets have on the costs relevant to a consumer's choice between traditional retail markets and electronic markets? Second, what is the impact that electronic markets have on seller costs, as well as the structure of the value chains needed to provide products? And third, what impact do electronic markets have on other organizations involved in commercial market transactions? These three issues are addressed throughout the remainder of this chapter.

3 Impact of Electronic Markets on Industry Structure

It is apparent from the examples above that the diffusion of electronic markets in an industry has an impact on the structure of the value chain involved in supplying the products and/or services to the final consumers. This is mainly due to the disinter-mediating effect of information technology identified by Davenport in his research on business process reengineering (Davenport, 1993). Although, in some instances, intermediaries may be added to transactions facilitated through an electronic market. Based on the examples above we have identified two phases that industry structures potentially go through as electronic markets diffuse across the industry. The degree of change is determined by features of the industry and its products. This is dis-cussed in more detail at the end of this section.

An example of a traditional market is shown in Figure 1. The industry transfor-mation phases are described in relation to this example.

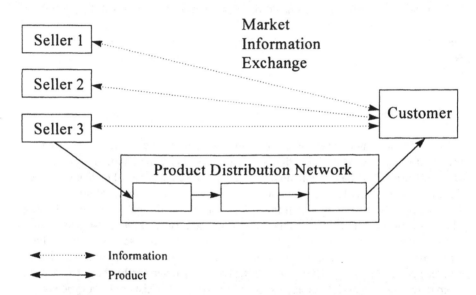

Fig. 1. Traditional market industry structure

In a traditional market (for a non-impulse purchase), the customer searches out information about the products available and their prices, quality and features. This information comes from a wide range of sources including advertising, traveling to retail stores, and so forth. At some point they stop their search because they realize further searching will probably not benefit them. Once the information gathered has been analyzed, the consumer decides where to buy the product. The product is then either purchased and transported home by the customer or is delivered to them through a distribution network.

Electronic markets affect the consumer purchase process. The first phase in the transformation of the structure of an industry is the digitization of the market mechanism. This is described in Figure 2.

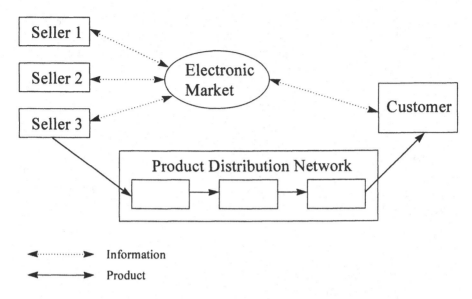

Fig. 2. Industry structure with an electronic market

An electronic market provides a mechanism for reducing the search costs (money, time and effort expended to gather product price, quality and feature information) for consumers. The phenomenon "search" can be described as a buyer canvassing various sellers to ascertain the most favorable price (Stigler, 1961). Search also reduces the likelihood that sellers will be able to charge significantly higher prices than their competitors because the consumer is unaware of the other prices (a form of regional oligopoly or monopoly). The result is that consumers can buy products for lower prices, intermediaries such as wholesalers are eliminated from the value chain, a new industry that provides access to electronic markets is created, and firms that produce products are able to maintain a profit margin comparable to the traditional markets.

The second phase in the transformation of the structure of an industry is the digitization of the product itself as well as its distribution. Examples of digitizable products include books, newspapers, magazines, computer software, movies and music. These products involve a cost structure with increasing returns and low marginal reproduction costs. Increasing returns accrue when a business incurs large up-front expenditures to develop a new product/service and the incremental cost of producing each new unit is minimal (Hagel and Armstrong, 1997). For example, if a consumer wants a new version of Navigator software from Netscape, the software can be downloaded from one of their sites on the Internet (Netscape). This eliminates the need for Netscape to maintain an inventory of software on CDs or diskettes that must be physically shipped to the consumer. Another example would be either evaluating or purchasing anti-virus software from McAfee (McAfee). If a software company charges for their software then they can receive payment before the software is allowed to be downloaded. This can be especially easy as electronic payment methods become more widely used in the future. This further transformed industry structure, that results from the digitization of products and their distribution, is described in Figure 3.

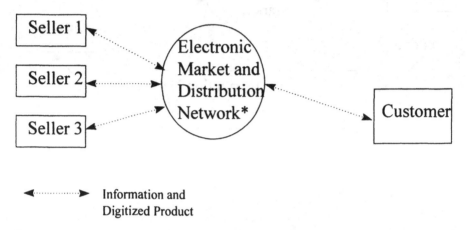

Fig. 3. Industry structure with an electronic market and distribution network

The electronic market and distribution network enables a wide range of seller and customer activities to converge into one place including marketing, order processing, distribution, payments and even product development processes that involve several separate firms. This makes these activities easier and more convenient while also reducing the costs involved. Value chain costs can be further reduced by digitizing the industry's product. Examples of digitizable products were given earlier. Digitization of the product reduces inventory and packaging costs. Digitized products can then be distributed electronically to the consumer which minimizes distribution costs which would otherwise be paid to the firms in the distribution network and passed on to the final consumer. These cost-based differences are discussed in more detail in Section 5. Beyond the cost benefits, cycle time for order fulfillment is minimized which may result in improved customer satisfaction. Digitized information can be distributed in minutes while shipping a product generally takes days (or longer to some parts of the world). The characteristics of the phases in the transformation of industry structures enabled by e-markets are summarized in Table 1.

Table 1. The phases of industry structure transformation enabled by electronic markets

	Traditional Market (example: retail store)	Electronic Market (Phase 1)	Electronic Market and Distribution (Phase 2)
Required industry characteristics	Transactions that do not require hierarchical governance	Accepted standards for describing the product through the electronic market	Description standards plus product that is feasibly digitized
Market digitized?	No	Yes	Yes
Product and distribution digitized?	No	No	Yes
Examples of intermediaries removed		Wholesalers and some forms of brokers (ones that simply gather and analyze information for consumers)	Phase 1 intermediaries plus firms in the physical distribution network
Examples of intermediaries added		Firms that provide access to the electronic market (ISPs or firms that operate electronic markets or electronic auctions) and possibly new forms of brokers (such as online better business bureaus)	Phase 1 intermediaries

The overall impact of electronic markets on industry structures is not strictly cost reduction and disintermediation. It is more complex than that. New intermediaries and costs may be added to a value chain, but in many instances the potential benefits outweigh these costs. In the next section we discuss a model that identifies costs relevant to differentiating between traditional and electronic markets from a buyer perspective.

4 Traditional and Electronic Markets: Buyer Cost Perspective

Electronic markets provide buyers with an additional sales channel through which they can buy products. Although there may be certain benefits derived by buyers in electronic markets (lower prices and search costs), it also increases the complexity of their decision process by adding another option to consider. It may also add new forms of consumer risk. In this section we describe a model to compare the cost-based differences between traditional markets (such as retail stores) and electronic markets.

4.1 Buyer Perspective Relevant Costs

From the consumer perspective (demand side of a transaction), the potentially relevant costs that we have identified include:

1. product price (P_B),
2. search costs (SC_B),
3. risk costs (RC_B),
4. distribution costs (DC_B),
5. sales tax (T_B), and
6. market costs (MC_B).

The product price is the sum of the production costs, coordination costs, and profits of the value chain that provides the product or service. Search costs include the time, effort and money involved in searching for a seller who has the product demanded at an acceptable price with acceptable product features and quality. The cost of the time and effort involved would be determined by the value the buyer places on their time and effort. Risk costs include the costs involved in minimizing transaction risk as well as the costs associated with losing value in a transaction. The risk dimensions typically considered are economic risk, performance risk, and personal risk (Simpson and Lakner, 1993). Economic risk stems from the possibility of monetary loss associated with buying a product. Performance risk represents the consumers' perception that a product or service may fail to meet expectations. Personal risk relates to the possibility of harm to the consumer resulting from either a product or the shopping process. An additional form of risk that is potentially important to Internet shoppers is privacy risk. Privacy risk reflects the degree to which consumers envisage a loss of privacy due to information collected about them as they shop (Jarvenpaa and Todd, 1997). Additional costs of concern include distribution costs, the costs associated with physically moving the product from the seller to the buyer, and sales tax. Market costs are the costs associated with participating in a market. Traditional markets are assumed to be costless to the buyer, while e-market costs may include fixed access costs and/or transaction (variable) costs paid to the firm(s) that operate the e-market.

4.2 Comparison of Buyer Costs in Traditional and Electronic Markets

Assuming rational decision making, the buyer's objective is to minimize the sum of the individual costs subject to the constraints that the product quality and features, including how soon the product can be received, must be acceptable. Figure 4 summarizes the findings of our evaluation of the costs relevant to a buyer's choice between traditional and electronic markets.

	Traditional Market	Electronic Market
P_B	○	●
SC_B	○	●
RC_B	●	○
DC_B	●	○
T_B	○	●
MC_B	●	○

Lower	●
Higher	○

Fig. 4. Comparison of buyer costs in traditional and electronic markets

Prices in electronic markets are generally lower than in traditional markets. If they were higher then there would be little incentive for consumers to switch to the newer e-markets. One explanation for why prices are lower is that search costs are lower. It is generally easier to gather relevant information, and compare a wider range of prices, in on-line environments. This is especially true as the number of products offered online increases. In traditional retail markets a buyer would have to either drive around town or call several sellers. This takes more time and costs more. Given this additional information in the e-market, buyers are likely to be able to find a price that is lower than in a traditional market. The question then is why aren't all products purchased in e-markets? One reason is that there are additional risks associated with buying online. It is apparent that buyers have incentives to participate in e-markets. These on-line markets provide access to specialized knowledge, fulfill the need to communicate with sellers, allow them to find and talk to other buyers with similar needs or experiences, enable access to multimedia information, allow participation at their convenience, integrate the consumer process, and enable sellers to tailor their products to individual needs (Champy et al., 1996). Given that there are incentives for buyers to participate in e-markets, the next issue is whether there are incentives for sellers to participate. Without any sellers in the e-market there would be no transactions.

5 Traditional and Electronic Markets: Seller Cost Perspective

Electronic markets provide sellers with an additional sales channel where they can market and sell their products. As with buyers, electronic markets provide sellers with certain benefits including reduced advertising costs (costs associated with seller's search for buyers), enhanced ability to target customers, greater ability to tailor products and services to their customers, lower overhead costs, broader geographic reach, and disintermediation potential (Hagel and Armstrong, 1997). But, it also increases the complexity of their operations by adding a new potential sales channel to evaluate which changes the way they may do business in the future. In this section we describe a model we developed to compare the cost-based differences between traditional markets (such as retail stores) and electronic markets from a seller perspective.

5.1 Seller Perspective Relevant Costs

From the seller perspective (supply side of a transaction), the potentially relevant costs that we have identified include:

1. marketing (advertising) costs (AC_S),
2. overheard costs (OC_S),
3. inventory costs (IC_S),
4. production costs (PC_S), and
5. distribution costs (DC_S).

Marketing costs are the costs associated with informing the consumer about the availability and features of a seller's products or services. Advertising channels in traditional markets include television, radio, newspapers, yellow pages, and so forth. Newer advertising channels include push-based methods (such as electronic mail), and pull-based methods (such as electronic bulletin boards and the Web) (Kalakota and Whinston, 1996). Overhead costs include the more fixed costs of the business including physical retail space and warehouses. Inventory costs include the costs to handle and hold inventory to deal with demand uncertainty for physical products. Production costs include the variable costs of producing a unit of a product including labor and materials. Distribution costs include the costs associated with moving the product from the seller to the buyer.

5.2 Comparison of Seller Costs in Traditional and Electronic Markets

Assuming rational decision making, the seller's objective is to minimize the sum of the individual costs subject to the constraints that they provide the products and services demanded by their customers. Figure 5 summarizes the findings of our evaluation of the costs relevant to a seller's choice between traditional markets. e-markets with non-digitized products, and e-markets with products that have been digitized.

	Traditional Market	E-Market (non-digital product)	E-Market (digital product)
AC_S	○	●	●
OC_S	○	●	●
IC_S	○	○	●
PC_S	○	○	●
DC_S	●	○	●

Lower	●
Higher	○

Fig. 5. Comparison of seller costs in traditional and electronic markets

Advertising costs are lower in e-markets than in traditional markets. For example, the advertising cost per consumer for a Web page is much lower than a television ad or a print ad (magazine or newspaper). This is true whether the product is digitized or not.

Overhead costs are similar to advertising costs. Traditional retail store markets require a seller to have a physical location they may either own or rent. In e-markets, a Web site may also serve as the storefront. This is especially true when the capability to order products electronically is integrated into the Web site. Inventory costs are more closely related to the product characteristics instead of the consumer interface. When products are digitized they require an inventory level of only one unit and the product is stored on a computer disk. The situation for production cost differences is similar to inventory costs. Physical products involve significant variable costs per unit for materials and labor. Reproduction of digitized products generally involves the copying of the computer file. Distribution cost differences are more complex. In an e-market with a digitized product, the product can be distributed electronically, perhaps through FTP, to the consumer. This is a very low cost distribution method. Traditional markets also have low distribution costs for sellers because the consumer comes to the store and transports the product to their home themselves. An electronic market with a non-digitized product still requires physical shipment of the product, for example through the USPS or Federal Express. This is the situation with the highest distribution cost to the seller.

6 Revenue Source Implications

A number of implications for business strategy (and potential sources of revenue) are apparent from our findings related to our e-market model and empirical study. These implications affect several entities: product/service providers, transaction brokers, Internet service providers (market makers), and also state and federal government. The buyer costs relevant to each of the entities (as potential sources of revenue) are marked in Figure 6.

	P_B	SC_B	RC_B	DC_B	T_B	MC_B
Product and Service Providers	X		X			
Transaction Intermediaries		X	X	X		
Interactive Service Providers		X				X
Government					X	

Fig. 6. Buyer transaction costs and entity revenue source implications

6.1 Product/Service Provider Implications

The revenue implications for product/ service providers in an e-market come from the price and risk cost components, P_B and RC_B, of our buyer cost model. Essentially, sellers can compete using a low cost producer strategy, and/or they can compete using a strategy by which they differentiate themselves from other sellers because they are less risky (more trusted) in the market. Competing based on reducing buyer risk costs, when the seller/buyer relationship is supported electronically, can be described as an *electronic virtual partnership*. This is described in Figure 7.

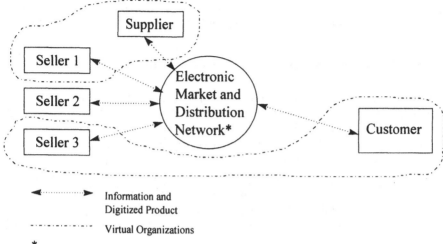

Fig. 7. Electronic market enabled virtual partnership

This is interesting because it describes how, over time, sub-markets may form within the overall electronic market because consumer knowledge is limited and there is still a cost to gather information about new sellers. Over time, there are reduced incentives for buyers to search the entire e-market for sellers of a product that has been purchased in the past. Unless a seller's price is significantly lower than prices from a trusted seller the switching cost will inhibit the consumer from buying from the unknown seller. Electronic markets also affect potential revenue sources for other organizations that support commercial transactions.

6.2 Transaction Intermediary Implications

The implications for transaction brokers (e.g. stock brokers, real estate agents, intelligent agent software developers, and so forth) in an e-market come from the search and risk cost components, SC_B and RC_B, of our model. In some situations buyers may be willing to pay someone to gather and/or analyze market information (a traditional broker role) related to their purchases, or they may pay for software that provides this same functionality (decision support software or more advanced intelligent agent software). They will pay for someone or some thing (such as an intelligent agent system) to do their searching. Also, consumers may be willing to pay for broker services such as risk assumption. For example, consumers may be willing to pay for a service such as an on-line better business bureau where they could check to see if there have been complaints against a certain seller. There are also implications for distribution companies (such as Federal Express) that arise from the distribution cost component, DC_B, of our model. Package shipment companies can expect continued growth in their business related to increased usage of e-markets, but, as more and more products are digitized, this growth may be reduced.

6.3 Internet Service Provider (Market Maker) Implications

The revenue implications for Internet service providers come from the market and search cost components, MC_B and SC_B, components of our model. Consumers may be willing to pay ISPs a portion of the money they save by buying products in an e-market versus a traditional market to gain access to the e-market. Consumers may also be willing to pay for access to systems because they provide much more than just e-market access, for example entertainment. The growth of ISPs clearly shows that consumers are willing to pay for these services. The fixed cost that consumers pay to ISPs varies, but it is common to pay about $20 per month.

6.4 Government Implications

Finally, the implications for state and federal government come from the tax component, T_B, of our model as well as organizational revenue generated through e-market transactions. As more transactions move from traditional markets to e-markets, it is likely that a smaller proportion of sales tax will be collected by state governments. Generally, laws exist that require the payment of sales taxes even on interstate commerce, but collection is a practical problem. This is especially likely since entry barriers into e-markets are low which increases the likelihood that there will be an increase in the number of sole proprietorships and small businesses that sell products online to buyers around the world. It is harder to track a large number of small sellers. It is also more difficult to track e-market transactions that involve buyers and sellers in different countries. For state and federal government there is also the problem of collecting tax from all of these sellers for taxable income generated from e-market transactions. As these problems increase with the growth of e-commerce, we can expect a greater effort on the part of government to collect the sales tax and income tax they are owed.

7 Determinants of Electronic Market Success

Based upon our analysis of a number of current examples of electronic markets, and the buyer and seller cost-based differences between traditional and electronic markets we have identified, we make several observations and conclusions. First, we discuss some factors that may inhibit the growth of electronic markets in the future. Second, we identify some factors that affect the level of impact that e-markets may have on industries.

7.1 Inhibitors to Electronic Market Success

Throughout this chapter we have assumed that the impact of certain factors that inhibit the future success of all e-markets, and e-commerce in general, will not sufficiently hinder their growth in the future. If this assumption is not true, then the study of electronic markets is moot given they may not exist in the future. It is important to acknowledge the existence of barriers to electronic market success. Four examples of inhibitors to electronic market success are discussed below.

Lack of IT Infrastructure

The lack of IT infrastructure in some world regions is a barrier to e-commerce participation by companies and consumers in these regions. In many countries consumers do not have the same level of access to the Internet, World Wide Web, and so forth that consumers in the United States have. This is a major barrier to electronic market diffusion because even if consumers wish to participate in e-markets, they are physically unable to. Even if access is available, an additional barrier may be poor physical telecommunications. However, the increasing recognition of the importance of telecommunications to national and business infrastructure has resulted in its proliferation to newly opened societies and markets, most notably Eastern Europe and the former Soviet Union, and to rapidly expanding markets such as Egypt and Iran (Goodman et al., 1994). We should expect a continuation in this trend toward greater access.

Computer Illiteracy

The level of computer illiteracy associated with the world's consumers that have access to IT infrastructure is a barrier to e-market success. Because of a lack of education about computers, or a lack of willingness to accept new technology, a certain proportion of consumers are unable or unwilling to participate in electronic markets. As more and more children are introduced to computers in school, the proportion of consumers who potentially may participate in electronics will increase in the future. Electronic markets are likely to be considered normal instead of novel for future generations of consumers.

Insufficient Security

Insufficient data and message security may inhibit some companies and consumers from participating in e-commerce because they feel the level of risk is unacceptable. Confidence, reliability, and protection of information against security threats is a crucial prerequisite for the functioning of electronic commerce (Kalakota and Whinston, 1996). Many initiatives are under way to improve security through improved data encryption and digital signatures. A specific example is S-HTTP, a more secure version of HTTP that is used in the World Wide Web. As the level of transaction security for e-commerce related information transfer improves, the expected level of e-market impact on industries, and the global economy in general, will increase.

Hierarchical Transaction Governance

An additional inhibitor to e-market success is the fact that a significant portion of all transactions are not market transactions, but are hierarchical transactions. Hierarchical transaction governance is often associated with transactions involving high asset specificity (Williamson, 1985). Asset specificity is the difference between the value of an asset (machine, employee and so forth) in its present use and its next best use. Transactions involving high asset specificity will continue to be governed by hierarchies because the firms involved generally need to maintain greater control over the transactions (perhaps through vertical integration or long term contracts) to minimize their overall risk.

These inhibitors, as well as other factors such as high market access costs, have resulted in the failure of some electronic markets. One example is an electronic market for real estate. The National Association of Realtors' widely publicized information network, created two years ago to provide extensive real-estate information on the World Wide Web, has run out of its $12.9 million in funding and is on the verge of collapse. Association officials and people in the industry say the network fell victim to overly ambitious goals, some free-spending ways and unexpected changes in technology that made it less attractive to its primary customers, real-estate agents. Funded from the national association's reserves, Realtors Information Network, or RIN, had lofty plans for keeping Realtors in control of real-estate transactions. The for-profit subsidiary would provide real-estate listings nationwide on the Web to consumers and would act as something of a proprietary America Online for real-estate agents. Agents who purchased the system would have access to information, chat rooms, real-estate vendors and e-mail. Along the way, network officials misjudged their audience.

Initially, the network tried charging $2 for each home listing on its Web site. But when competition charged less, it cut the price until it stopped charging for listings at all. Meanwhile, advertising for the site, which now has about 350,000 listings, never materialized. At the same time, the proprietary system for agents bombed. In New Jersey, a pilot state, fewer than 1,000 New Jersey Association of Realtors' 36,000 members chose to subscribe, says Michael Ford, the state group's president-elect and a national association director. Only four of the state's 18 multiple-listing services posted their listings on it (National Association of Realtors). This example highlights the need to understand the needs of both product/service providers as well as consumers in a market, especially when start up costs are in the millions. Market participants should not be charged anything to subscribe to a new electronic market until a large number of product/service providers and consumers are participating and both sides see the value of the e-market. With limited revenues at the beginning, new electronic markets need to tightly control their startup and operation costs.

7.2 Contributors to Electronic Market Success

It is also apparent, based on an analysis of the e-market examples previously discussed, that electronic markets will impact some industries more than others. The question then is what are some of the factors that determine this level of impact? We have identified six factors that each fall within one of four categories: product, industry, seller and consumer characteristics.

Product Characteristics

First, the form of the product is important. Digitizable products are particularly suited for electronic markets because they not only take advantage of the digitization of the market mechanism, but also the distribution mechanism, resulting in very low transaction costs. It also enables the order fulfillment cycle time to be minimized. Examples of digitizable products were described earlier.

Second, the magnitude of the product price may be an important determinant. The higher the product price, the greater the level of risk involved in the market transaction between buyers and sellers who are geographically separated and may have never dealt with each other before. Some of the most common items currently sold through e-markets are low priced items such as CDs and books.

Industry Characteristics

An industry factor that affects the impact of e-markets is the level of standards that exist in an industry for describing products. A lack of available standards that both the buyer and seller recognize is a barrier to consummating sales electronically. Current description standards would generally be textual, but future standards could include multimedia options. As multimedia capabilities such as video, audio, and perhaps virtual reality (enabled by the virtual reality markup language, VRML, in the WWW), are incorporated into electronic market interfaces it will become easier to describe products to potential consumers.

A second industry characteristic is the need for a transaction broker. Electronic markets are most useful when they are able to directly match buyers and sellers. Industries that require transaction brokers, or third parties, may be affected less by electronic markets than are industries where no brokers are required. Stock brokers, insurance agents, and travel agents may provide services that are still needed, but in some cases software may be able to replace the need for these brokers. This is particularly true as more intelligent systems that assist consumers become available.

Seller Characteristics

E-markets reduce search costs enabling consumers to find sellers offering lower prices. In the long run this reduces profit margins for sellers that compete in e-markets, although it may also increase the number of transactions that take place. If sellers in an industry are unwilling to participate in this environment, then the impact of e-markets may be reduced. In highly competitive industries, with low barriers to entry, sellers may not have a choice. But, in oligopolistic situations, sellers may determine the success of e-markets in an industry if they want to maintain an environment of lower volume, higher profit margin transactions.

Consumer Characteristics

Consumers can be classified as either impulse, patient or analytical. Impulse buyers purchase products quickly with little analysis, patient buyers purchase products after making some comparisons, and analytical buyers do substantial research before making the decision to purchase products or services (Kalakota and Whinston, 1996). Electronic markets may have little impact on industries where a sizable percentage of purchases are made by impulse buyers. An example of this is grocery store purchases. A high percentage of sales in these stores are impulsive. Because electronic markets require a certain degree of effort on the part of the consumer, these markets are more conducive to consumers who do some comparisons and analysis before buying (the patient or analytical buyers). Analytical buyers can use the facilities available to analyze a wide range of information before deciding where to buy.

The determinants discussed provide a framework for estimating the impact of e-markets on current or future industries. The more industry features (including product, industry, seller, and consumer characteristics) associated with higher e-market impact, the greater the expected impact of e-markets on that industry.

8 Conclusions

The main issue we addressed throughout this paper was: Are there economic incentives for electronic markets, or are they just a passing fad? In particular we looked at the impact of electronic markets on buyers, sellers, and other organizations that support commercial transactions. It is apparent that there are economic incentives for these entities to participate in e-markets although they may introduce new forms of transaction risk. The benefits that buyers receive from lower prices and search costs are in many instances more than enough to offset the potential additional risk, distribution and market costs. Sellers benefit from potential new sources for revenue as well as a reduction of many production and transaction oriented costs. The impact of e-markets on other organizations that support commercial transactions is more mixed. They reduce the need for certain types of intermediaries (such as wholesalers and retail stores) while increasing buyer demand for new intermediaries (ISPs, online better business bureaus, and so forth). They also have potential tax revenue collection implications for state and federal government.

Our overall conclusion is that there are economic incentives (both from reduction of costs as well as creation of new revenue sources) for electronic markets. It is not just a fad that will go away. Electronic markets are a new institution of capitalism and they are useful because they economize on transaction costs in many instances when compared with other available transaction governance mechanisms (such as traditional markets).

References

Amazon Books, "Welcome to Amazon.com Books!",
    URL = http://www.amazon.com/.
Applegate, L., F. W. McFarlan and J. L. McKenney, *Corporate Information Systems Management: Text and Cases*, Irwin, Chicago, 1996.
Bakos, J. Y., "A Strategic Analysis of Electronic Marketplaces," *MIS Quarterly*, 15, 3, (1991), 295-310.
Benjamin, R. and R. Wigand, "Electronic Markets and Virtual Value Chains on the Information Superhighway," *Sloan Management Journal*, 36, 2, (1995), 62-72.
Calem, R. E., "Auto Sales Are Booming on the Web," *The New York Times: CyberTimes*, October 17, (1996).
Champy, J., R. Buday and N. Nohria, "The Rise of the Electronic Community," *Information Week*, CSC Index, (1996),
    URL = http://techweb.cmp.com/iw/583/csc.htm.
Davenport, T. H., *Process Innovation: Reengineering Work through InformationTechnology*, Harvard Business School Press, Boston, 1993.
Eaton, L., "Slow Transition in Investing as Market Meets Internet," *The New York Times: CyberTimes*, November 11, (1996).
Glaser, M., "E-Zines Find Road to Profits Is Long, Bumpy and Winding," *The New York Times: CyberTimes*, October 18, (1996).
Goodman, S. E., L. I. Press, S. R. Ruth, and A. M. Rutkowski, "The Global Diffusion of the Internet: Patterns and Problems," *Communications of the ACM*, 37, 8, (1994), 27-31.
Gurbaxani, V. and S. Whang, "The Impact of Information Systems on Organizations and Markets," *Communications of the ACM*, 34, 1, (1991), 59-73.
Hagel, J. and A. G. Armstrong, *Net Gain*, Harvard Business School Press, Boston, MA, 1997.
Jarvenpaa, S. and P. A. Todd, "Consumer Reactions to Electronic Shopping on the World Wide Web," *International Journal of Electronic Commerce*, 1, 2, (1997).
Kalakota, R. and A. B. Whinston, *Frontiers of Electronic Commerce*, Addison-Wesley Publishing Company, Inc., Reading, MA, 1996.
Malone, T. W., J. Yates, and R. I. Benjamin, "Electronic Markets and Electronic Hierarchies," *Communications of the ACM*, 30, 6, (1987), 484-497.
Malone, T. W., J. Yates, and R. I. Benjamin, "The Logic of Electronic Markets," *Harvard Business Review*, May-June, (1989), 166-170.
Malone, T. W. and J. F. Rockart, "Computers, Networks and the Corporation," *Scientific American*, 265, 3, (1991), 128-136.
McAfee Associates, Inc., URL = http://www.mcafee.com/.
National Association of Realtors, "Realtors Information Network,"
    URL = http://www.realtor.com/.

Netscape Communications Corporation, URL = http://home.netscape.com/. Rebello, K., L. Armstrong, and A. Cortese, "Making Money on the Net," *Business Week*, September 23, (1996), 104-118.

Rosato, D., "Airlines Turn Internet into Discount Haven," *USA Today*, May 7, (1996), URL = http://www.usatoday.com/.

Simpson, L. and H. B. Lakner, "Perceived Risk and Mail Order Shopping for Apparel," *Journal of Consumer Studies and Home Economics*, 17, (1993), 377-398.

Stat-USA, "Real Gross Domestic Product and Related Measures: Level and Percent Change From Previous Period," (1998),
   URL = http://domino.stat-usa.gov/bea/gdp.bea.

Stigler, G., "The Economics of Information," *The Journal of Political Economy*, 69, (1961), 213-225.

Williamson, O. E. Williamson, *The Economic Insitutions of Capitalism*, Free Press, New York, 1985.

Yahoo. Business and Economy: Companies: Automotive: Internet Marketplaces: Dealer Directories,
   URL = http://www.yahoo.com/Business_and_Economy/Companies/Automotive/Internet_Marketplaces/Dealer_Directories.

Part II
Consumer Electronic Commerce

CHAPTER 5

Electronic Commerce: Markets and Users

Michael H. Dickey, Gabriele Piccoli, and Blake Ives
Center for Virtual Organization and Commerce, Louisiana State University, Baton Rouge,
LA, USA
mdickey@lsu.edu, gpiccol@unix1.sncc.lsu.edu, bives@lsu.edu

This chapter provides an analysis of electronic commerce markets and users. Here we describe the tools necessary to find, assess, select and interpret the wealth of available information that characterizes electronic markets and the Internet user population. We begin with an introduction to relevant Internet statistics as well as the quantitative and attitudinal measures commonly employed. Next, we portray the past, current, and future Internet user populations. Finally, the major advantages and disadvantages of different estimation techniques are highlighted, and the major producers of Internet statistics and forecasts are identified. Here our emphasis is on the reliability and trustworthiness of reported research results.

Keywords: Electronic Markets; Internet Statistics; Internet Demographics; Reliability of Research

1 Introduction

Electronic commerce appears to many as a promising opportunity for growing a business or for developing a new one. But how does one actually assess the promise of this emerging marketplace? The World Wide Web is an important resource for assessing the potential market as we will demonstrate in this chapter. But the sheer volume of information available on the Web is a source of confusion at best, and intimidation at worst. Even someone as experienced as John Murrell, senior editor of the online San Jose Mercury newspaper, laments:

> *"Whenever I despair of ever getting a handle on this wild and wacky world that I like to call the Internet, I click on over to Nua Internet Surveys, a clearinghouse site for studies and research into all facets of online usage. I don't come away with a clearer picture, but it makes me feel better to see that nobody else really knows what's going on either. I don't visit the Nua site looking for answers; I go for speculation fodder" (Nua, February 2, 1998).*

In this chapter we facilitate that "speculation" on electronic markets by providing an understanding of the statistics available on the Web that can be used for characterizing the Internet population and for evaluating its potential as a marketplace.

We first describe important measures of the Internet population and then discuss the evolution of the Internet population, and its current and projected characteristics. We then paint a portrait of the typical Internet user, past, present, and future. This is followed by a discussion of the reliability of Internet market statistics. The chapter concludes with a description and motivational assessment of those who compile Internet statistics.

2 Relevant Internet Statistics

There are certain statistics that anyone evaluating electronic commerce markets will find useful in assessing the likely efficiency and effectiveness of an e-commerce strategy -- for instance, target market population, growth rate, user demographics, user attitudes, and so on. Such statistics are publicly available and can be obtained relatively easily. The challenge is distinguishing reliable and scientific statistics from undependable and subjective ones, a problem we tackle later on in the chapter. The current section provides a guide to what statistics are useful in preparing an Internet market penetration strategy and why those measures are important. Two types of measures are identified: quantitative and attitudinal.

2.1 Quantitative Measures

Quantitative measures are used to estimate the number of users constituting the Internet population and to describe that population by various demographic and other objective attributes. The measures described here are: the total number of Internet users, demographic measures, purpose for using the Internet, location of Internet use, expectations of Internet use, and available access to Internet features.

Number of Users

The most important figure, the estimate of the total Internet marketplace, is the total number of people who have access to an Internet connection. The number of "netizens" - or net citizens - is the estimate of all potential customers who could be attracted to a particular site. Tracking changes in the Internet population also gives a good estimate of the emerging popularity of the medium and, therefore, its viability as a commercial channel. The total number of Internet users for an electronic commerce business might be roughly compared to the total number of residents in a particular subdivision for a traditional grocery store. It represents the maximum theoretical number of customers.

Demographics

A second set of statistics that has received a great deal of attention is the demographics of the Internet population. Demographic statistics are of great importance for assessing an electronic commerce business as they furnish information on the potential customer base which in turn indicates which products will prove to be appealing and marketable, and which will not. Gender, age, ethnic background, occupation, education, and income are the dimensions that are most useful in this regard. For instance, until fairly recently, the Internet was mainly populated by young white males adults located primarily in the U.S. This characterization, however, is rapidly changing. In the United States, for example, women now make up almost half of the on-line population.

Purpose for Using the Internet

Understanding why people connect to the Internet provides valuable insight to the marketer. Until relatively recently, the Internet was used primarily for academic research and knowledge sharing among professionals. With the opening of the Internet for commercial purposes in 1991 and, particularly, with the advent of the Mosaic browser in 1993, the Web became the place where anyone with access to a networked computer could retrieve or even publish information. Nowadays, people connect to the Internet and surf the World Wide Web for a variety of reasons, even though the Internet still remains primarily an information medium. According to the fifth annual Interactive Media Study, conducted for AdAge by Market Facts (Maddox, 1997), 87.8% of those surveyed connect to the Internet to gather information; 83.2% of users connect to send email; 80.5% to conduct research.

On-line users find information on companies and products, but they also look for news, weather, recipes, local events, the location of nearby tennis courts, and so on. The Internet is also increasingly becoming an entertainment medium. A poll of 5,800 Internet users by FutureScapes (NUA Surveys, January 16, 1998) concluded that television viewing decreased significantly as Internet usage increased. Netizens spent 60% more time surfing the Web than watching TV. Knowing your customers and what they look for in their Internet experience is extremely important in product positioning and in ensuring repeat visits to your site. So too is knowing what competitors or providers of similar products or services are offering to your customers.

Location that the Users Connect from

Users can connect to the Internet mainly from home, work or school. Often, an Internet connection is provided to employees at work, with many using their lunch hours for browsing and shopping. The RelevantKnowledge (1998) January of 1998 survey of U.S. Internet users found that 36% of Web users accessed the web from work. Cyber Dialogue (1998) reports that 71% of Web using adults used it predominantly for work. Office users who find the medium useful and interesting, and who can afford it, may request service from home through an Internet service provider (ISP). The connection location is one determinant of the amount of time users can spend searching and shopping and an indicator of the amount of privacy that they have. Generally, netizens that connect from home, will have more time to gather information, shop, search, and compare. This is especially true in the United States where the great majority of users have unlimited access (24 hours per day/7 days per week) and usage insensitive rates from their ISP and local phone companies. Home users may be more willing to explore, and more interested in sites that slowly entice them and provide an entertaining shopping experience. They also will likely have more privacy while surfing from home. On the other hand, home dial-up connections may be considerably slower than those available in the office and may need to be shared with other members of the family. And, in countries with regulated telephone markets, the expense will limit use.

Internet Experience Expectations [1]

This is a crucial and often understated piece of information. The marketer can use data on experience expectations to create an e-commerce strategy that offers the customer a satisfying experience that will encourage him/her to come back to the on-line business. Lately many research institutions and firms are focusing on trying to understand what the netizens are looking for in their on-line experience. One such example is the report: "What Makes Women Click?" (Hamilton, 1997), that concentrates on gaining an understanding of the characteristics of the on-line content and services that make women respond positively.

Experience expectations are themselves influenced by the user's own previous experience with the Internet. More experienced Internet users will look for the ability to try out products, particularly information-based products such as music, computer software, or books. They also may be expecting a more personalized experience, often based on a profile provided by the user, by the supplier's consumer databases, or by their previous experience with the site. An airline frequent flyer database, for instance, might allow a customer to look up their mileage balance, book a reservation, and then find a bulkhead seat for a tall customer.

---

[1] It is important to distinguish between the user's *purpose* (e.g., information retrieval or entertainment) from the user's *expectations* (e.g., task completion or enjoyment). For instance, two users may have the same purpose of retrieving information about farming. One user may be a student writing a paper on organic farming with the expectation of task completion. The other may be a hobbyist who has a small garden; that user's expectation is enjoyment.

Available Internet Features

To prepare an Internet strategy it is necessary to know what services the prospective clients can access. Often we tend to assume that Internet access means availability of all features, but many users will only have access to a limited number of Internet services. This is particularly true outside of the United States where many users can only access e-mail, still the most popular and easily obtainable Internet service. But even in the U.S. business designers must be careful in assuming full-featured access. According to a survey from Find/SVP (1998), there were 3.6 million users, 7.4% of the total 40.6 million users in the United States, who only accessed e-mail or commercial on-line services.

The technology available to the users is another potential constraint. Access to the World Wide Web, for instance, takes place through a browser, and the features available to users are constrained by that particular browser as well as the capability of the computer the browser is running on. If a web site uses graphical links, users with a textual interface will not be able to navigate the site. Or if bandwidth is constrained by a slow modem, users may choose to turn off image display in their browsers. Similarly, web sites that rely on large screen sizes may not be easily viewed on computers with smaller screens. If a web site uses JavaScript[2] to validate an order submission form, that form may not work with incompatible browsers. When creating an on-line storefront or envisioning an electronic business, the developer must take into account the volatile and inconsistent standards of the Internet and the technical platform(s) of the target audience.

2.2 Attitude Measures

Several recent surveys of the Internet population have assessed the confidence and trust that the public has in the Internet as a shopping channel. This research has been partially motivated by fears of privacy infringement through the use of technologies like cookies[3] and log analyzers[4] and concern regarding security of on-line credit card transactions. This section lists some of the more commonly used attitude measures.

Attitudes Toward Shopping and Purchasing on the Internet

Unfortunately for those envisioning a new electronic commerce operation, there is still considerable skepticism toward on-line purchasing. Netizens are still much more confident with looking for information about companies and their products on-

---

[2] Scripting language, developed by Netscape Corp., that needs to be interpreted by the browser.

[3] A cookie is a small piece of code that can retrieve and transmit information on the client's computer, navigation history through a site and other user supplied information.

[4] A log analyzer is server software that allows webmasters to analyze traffic through their sites and to, conceivably, identify the visiting clients.

line than they are with completing business transactions. Gauging consumer attitudes toward on-line purchasing is crucial because it provides insight on the short-term viability of a business-to-consumer electronic relationship but, even more importantly, it provides valuable information regarding consumers' concerns and fears that must be addressed before implementing a successful strategy.

Attitudes Toward On-Line Transaction Security

Security of the on-line transaction and transmission of credit card information over the public Internet still remains the primary customer concern and the main impediment to the explosion of the Internet as a distribution channel for business-to-consumer commerce.

Attitudes Toward Privacy On-Line

While concerns about the security of online transactions have begun to lessen, privacy concerns are increasing. The negative publicity surrounding the use of cookies and log analysis tools has contributed to increasing consumer anxiety about the potential loss of anonymity in the on-line environment. Often, fear is due to incomplete information, ignorance and quick judgment. It is important that existing research be evaluated to identify what consumers worry about and address these concerns quickly and directly.

3 The Internet Population

The Internet population has been surveyed, estimated, and analyzed by innumerable sources, with just as many different results. This section will discuss the various surveyors' definitions of Internet users and Web users. Then a synthesis of statistics from a variety of sources will portray the evolution of the Internet population over the past few years until the present. Finally, some projections about the future Internet population will be made.

Though the statistics vary from survey to survey, researchers collectively agree on one point: the Internet population is growing at an exponential rate.

The above paragraph is an illustration of how the plethora of Internet statistics can be used to advantage. An understanding of the Internet population is derived from ascertaining *overall trends*, and reviewing results across studies, and not necessarily from relying on specific figures, such as almost 10 million American Internet users have made online purchases (Wang, 1997).

Any statistics listed in this section are snapshots at particular points in time. They are not intended to be an accurate reflection of the Internet population at the time of this publication and readers are referred to the various online sources for the results from surveys reported since this work was completed. Users may also wish to subscribe to the free newsletter provided by Nua (1998) that provides regular briefings on recent Internet related market surveys. The statistics reported here, though current at this writing, are primarily intended to reveal trends.

3.1 Definitions: Internet User

Before a statement of how many people use the Internet can be made, it is necessary to see how various surveyors define an "Internet user." NUA Surveys (January 6, 1998) defines an Internet user as an adult or child who has accessed the Internet at least once in the prior three months. (Access to the Internet does not necessarily mean that the person has an account.) Nielsen, on the other hand, excludes users under the age of 16 and employs a narrower time period of use (one month vs. three) prior to an interview (NUA, January 6, 1998).

Other surveys are themselves conducted over the Web (GVU Surveys, 1994-98); thus the sample consists entirely of Internet users. In still other surveys (Find/SVP, 1998), Internet users are differentiated from Web users to provide further information on separate categories of users.

Interpreters of Internet demographic surveys must remember that the definition of "Internet user" will affect the statistical outcomes. Although these differences in definition alter the results, the trends will be consistent across surveys (Nielsen, 1998).

3.2 Total Size of the Internet Population

As of September 1998, the worldwide population of Internet users is estimated to be in excess of 147 million, with 87 million being residents of the United States and Canada (NUA, September, 1998). As stated earlier, the Internet population is growing rapidly. From 1995 to 1996, Nielsen estimated the number of users in the United States and Canada increased from 18 million to 34 million. Figure 1 shows the overall trend.

The most recent breakdown of Internet users worldwide is shown in Figure 2. Surveyors agree that worldwide usage will continue to rise; NUA Surveys (January 6, 1998) conservatively estimates that the number of users will top 150 million by the end of 1998, and suggest that 200 million is possible. Given the extreme growth of Internet usage, most researchers are not, at the time of this writing, forecasting beyond; however, a bold estimate of 707 million users by the year 2000 was derived by Matrix Information and Directory Services (*Computerworld*, 1998).

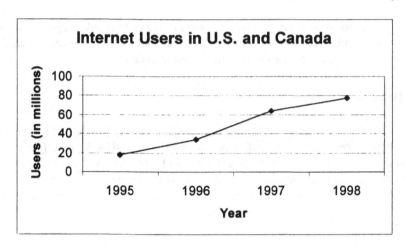

Fig. 1. Internet users in U.S. and Canada (*Source*: Nielsen Media Research, 1995-98)

Growth rates are high in many national markets. Estimates of the 1997 Internet population in Latin America ranged from 300,000 to 1 million. Those numbers represent a wide range and do not sound particularly large, but just as examples, the rates of growth in 1995 in Brazil and Chile were 360% and 600% respectively. Those users are largely English speaking, educated, cosmopolitan, and have "similar tastes to the developed world", and as such represent a significant growing market (Teveris, 1997).

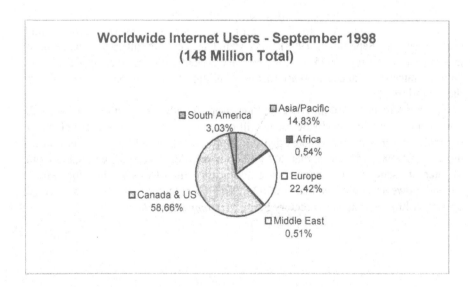

Fig. 2. Worldwide Internet users (*Source*: NUA surveys, 1998)

Likewise, the Asian and British markets are growing explosively. AT&T (Ullrich, 1997) announced winning a contract from China Telecom to provide fast Internet access. China Telecom predicts the number of Internet users in China to be between 3 and 4 million by the year 2000. Britain is reported to have seen a three-fold increase in WWW usage from December 1995 to June 1997 (NUA Surveys, 1996-97). British Internet usage is expected to grow to 9 million by mid-1998 (NOP, 1997).

3.3 Demographics

The total number of worldwide users or number of users in a given country is considered to be top-line data by many researchers. This information is readily attainable and often cited in the press. However, more detailed demographic data is difficult to obtain on a consistent basis from any given source without paying hefty content or subscriber fees.

Fortunately, Georgia Tech Research Corporation's Graphic, Visualization, & Usability (GVU) Center has conducted on-line surveys biannually for the past four years. Problems with on-line surveys will be discussed in the next major section. In spite of the problems, however, partial information gleaned from other sources is consistent with the GVU Survey results. (Specific examples are given within the measures discussed below.) Therefore, since we are confident that the GVU surveys represent a comprehensive, longitudinal resource, we used the surveys as a basis for describing the typical Internet user.

Gender

Historically, Internet users have been predominantly male. Over the past four years, the gender gap has been substantially reduced, particularly in the United States and Canada. For the GVU surveys, the percentage of females responding has increased from 5.1% in January 1994 to 38.7% in April 1998 as shown in Figure 3. The 1997 figure is consistent with the Jupiter Communications report that females represent 40% of the Internet population (Hamilton, 1997). In Europe, users continue to be primarily male (78% per the GVU survey).

This trend is being observed with great interest, since women account for up to 70% of all retail sales (Hamilton, 1997). Ostensibly, the more females that are connected, the greater the retail sales opportunity will be, since they are the primary household purchasers. The increase in the number of female netizens has implications for developers as well. Women like the Web because it is convenient, empowering and fun. Marketers that want to target the premier household purchaser must make their site interactive and personal, trying to serve useful content in an easy to access form (Hamilton, 1997).

Age

Beginning with the 4th GVU survey (October 1995) to October 1997, the average age of respondents increased from 32.7 to 35.7, with a slight decline in age for the most recent survey, in April of 1998 (see Figure 4). For the 7th survey, the researchers compared their numbers with that of Find/SVP, a marketing research firm. Find/SVP's average age was reported to be 36.5, and GVU's figure of 35.7 was within the margin of error reported by the firm. GVU consistently reports that the average age is constant across gender. Europeans are generally younger than their American counterparts (30.3 vs. 36.0).

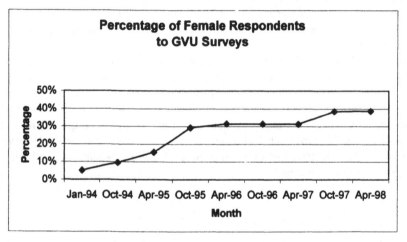

Fig. 3. Gender trend (*Source*: GVU surveys)

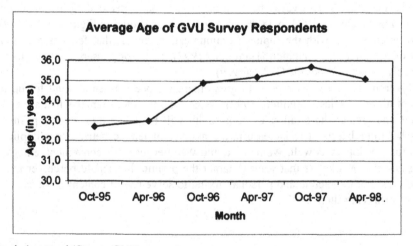

Fig. 4. Age trend (*Source*: GVU surveys)

The upward trend in the average age of netizens was partly due to the increasing number of third-agers coming on line. These new users connect mostly to keep in touch with family and develop relationships online. Marketers targeting this segment of the Internet population should make their sites simple to navigate, informative, and warm. The most recent survey shows a decline in average age, which perhaps reflects an increase in Internet usage among school age children.

Ethnic Background

GVU began collecting data on race for the 3rd survey (April 1995). Since that time, respondents have been overwhelmingly white with percentages ranging from 82-88%. All other groups have been reported consistently under 5%. No change in this ethnic distribution is expected.

Occupation

Since April 1995 (the 3rd survey), GVU respondents have been asked to classify their occupations into one of five categories: computer-related, education (including students), management, professional, and other. Managerial positions have hovered around 10-12%, and professional positions have remained around 20-22%. Educators and students initially rose as a percentage of respondents, but then, until the most recent survey, a gradual decline ensued. Until the April 1998 survey, a sharp increase in the percentage of respondents classifying their occupations as *other* occurred, with a corresponding sharp decrease in the percentage in computer-related fields (see Figure 5).

We suggest that those who are in computer fields have been using the Internet for some time, while those in other occupations are part of the usage growth. Thus, as the total population grows, the absolute number of people in computer-related fields will be more static than the number in other fields, resulting in the corresponding changes in the percentages.

The most recent survey results show an increase in education related occupations, which may also be explained by an increase in the number of school age children included as Internet users. As the percentage of users reporting education related occupations rose, the percentage reporting the *other* category dropped.

WWW site designers and Internet applications maker should develop intuitive and simple interfaces because they will no longer be able to "free-ride" on the experience and skills of users. For the above reason, marketers that intend to generate a critical mass of traffic to their Web sites must choose a location close to a successful portal[5].

---

[5] Portals are Web sites such as Yahoo! that provide an entry point to the wealth of information on the WWW. Portals also provide a categorization and search features. They are the preferred starting points of novice users when browsing the Web.

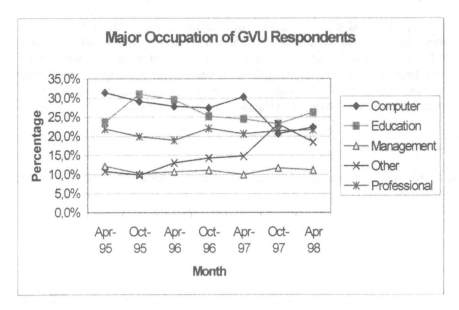

Fig. 5. Occupation trends (*Source*: GVU surveys)

Education

Typically the Internet user has been well educated; even today nearly 50% of the Internet population has obtained at least a bachelor's degree. However, Figure 6 shows a decline in percentages for GVU survey respondents who have bachelor, masters, and doctoral degrees. Conversely, increases in percentages are shown for those attaining high school diplomas and some college credit, except for the most recent survey. The April 1998 survey showed a slight decline in the percentage of respondents who were high school graduates and those with some college credit, with a corresponding slight increase in those attaining bachelor degrees.

Along the same lines as the occupational trends discussed above, we suggest that the well-educated contingent of the Internet population includes the more established users. Initially, the Internet developed as a communication medium for researchers in higher education institutions and was opened later for commercial use. So not unexpectedly, the high school graduates with or without some college credit would constitute a growing proportion of the Internet population. The most recent results showing a decline in the *high school* and *some college credit* categories as percentages were not large enough to suggest that this was a trend reversal. Perhaps the results of the next survey will shed more light on the expected future occupational composition of the Internet population.

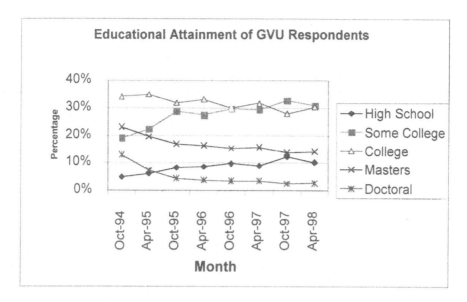

Fig. 6. Education trends (*Source*: GVU surveys)

Income

Historically, disposable income of Internet users has been significantly above the average of the general population. As mentioned in the preceding paragraph, the education level of netizens has always been significantly above average (since it was developed for the use of educators). Likewise, the income of Internet users has been traditionally higher than the average income of the general population.

There are barriers to obtaining Internet access that would suggest that the mean income of Internet users would remain above average. These barriers are of two kinds: monetary and technical. In order to connect to the Internet, most users still need a computer, a major expense for many households, as well as an account with an Internet service provider. Also, the perspective user needs to have a minimum proficiency level in computer usage. However the recent introduction of Web-TV products should lower both monetary and technical entry costs.

GVU surveys show that in the two years ending with the October 1997 survey, the average income reported by respondents had been steadily declining. Especially telling is Figure 7, which showed a steep increase in the percentage of respondents reporting income under $30,000 per year. This influx of users at lower income levels is also demonstrated in Figure 8. After declining as a percentage of the total for some time, in the most recent survey, use by affluent users has again begun to rise, perhaps reflecting the increased availability of web-based tools for managing personal finances.

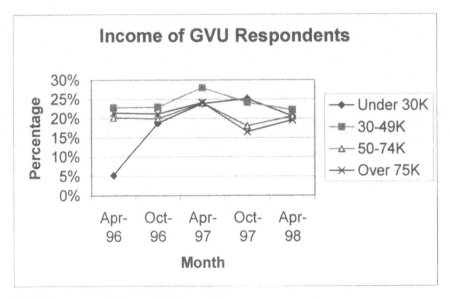

Fig. 7. Income trends (*Source:* GVU surveys)

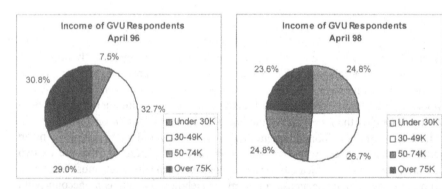

Fig. 8. Comparison of income brackets over time (*Source*: GVU surveys)

3.4 Picture of the Internet User of 1998 and Beyond

To summarize the previous discussion, it is expected that the typical Internet user of tomorrow will be either a white male or female, about the same age as today's user. Occupations will be more likely non-computer related than computer related. Education and income, though still skewed toward affluent individuals who hold a college degree of some sort, will over time tend toward the attributes of the general population. However, as the Internet population takes on the characteristics of the general population, those seeking to exploit this growing market will increasingly turn their attention towards segmenting that market. Because of the ability to tailor a marketing message to a single individual, segmentation or, more accurately, personalization, will become an increasingly powerful marketing tool.

4 Reliability of Internet Population Statistics

The number of Internet related statistics and companies that produce research on the subject has increased dramatically in the last two years. As is typical of the Internet, the amount of information available is enormous. Researching in such an environment, it is essential to be able to quickly identify reliable sources of information and dependable data. Also, when comparing different estimations and forecasts it is important to ascertain why they differ so dramatically. In this section we investigate the reason for such a lack of consensus and provide the reader with a guide to gauge the reliability of Internet statistics and the soundness of data sources.

The first problem with estimating Internet population is the difficulty in defining the Internet itself and the Internet user population. Many are the services available through the Internet: e-mail, the World Wide Web, Telnet, and Usenet just to name a few. Technically, users that can only send and receive e-mail with other users around the world are taking advantage of the Internet, but they are likely excluded from Internet census data and surveys that rely on web pages for their distribution. Can we compare an estimate based on a comprehensive definition of Internet and one that is based on a more restrictive definition? Which one is more accurate? Which one is more reliable?

Internet users can be defined as all the people who have, theoretically, the ability to connect. An example could be a student that has an account through the university and can access the Internet from a college lab. Or we could define users as all the people who have actually connected to the Internet in the past and had an experience with it. We could define users as the people who connect to the Internet on a regular basis, maybe monthly or weekly or even daily. Again, can we compare data that was gathered on a different basis? Which one is correct? Is there a better basis?

We can, at this point, break down the issue into two major categories: (1) reliability of survey data and historical statistics and (2) reliability of forecasts.

4.1 Reliability of Survey Data and Historical Statistics

To interpret data for the total number of Internet users requires avoiding a common mistake of interpretation. As the number of people on-line continues to grow, the rate of increase will tend to slow down in percentage terms. This is because the rate of increase is computed on the basis of previous term figures. For example, if in the year x there are 100 users and in the year x+1 there are 200 people on line the percentage increase is 100%. If the same number of people, 100, comes on line in the third year the percentage increase is halved to 50%.

There are also some compatibility problems among different statistics and survey methodologies that we need to pay attention to when interpreting the data. The first major compatibility problem among different estimations is that different techniques are used to survey Internet users and compute statistics. Among the most popular are: (1) estimation of the number of users as a function of hosts, (2) telephone polls, and (3) on-line surveys.

Number of Users as a Function of the Number of Hosts

This is a method that was primarily used in the earlier days of the Internet. A fairly precise estimation of the number of hosts can be obtained from DNS tables. This number is the minimum size of the Internet population because we can assume that there is at least one user per host. Then, the total number of users was estimated by multiplying the number of hosts by a constant representing the number of users per host. This method is clearly imprecise since small variations in the multiplication factor can lead to great estimation differences. Also, it is limited because no other information, such as demographic information, can be gathered through this method.

Telephone Polls

Random digit dialing can be used to select a random sample of the population. The surveyors can ask the people contacted if they connect to the Internet, and if they do, proceed with other questions. This seems to be the best method in finding a precise estimate of the number of Internet users as long the sample is randomly drawn, statistically significant, and that those agreeing to respond to the survey do not significantly differ from those who choose not to respond. RelevantKnowledge (1998) is one example of a firm specializing in telephone polling.

On-line Survey

This method is not used to estimate the on-line population, but rather to provide analysis of that population. The method pioneered and used by the Graphic, Visualization, & Usability Center (GVU) at Georgia Institute of Technology allows Internet users to fill out an on-line survey to capture demographic, technical, and opinion data. The method has problems as well as desirable features. Among the major problems are the self-selection bias of respondents and the fact that respondents tend to be more skewed toward experts and long time users. The advertising means chosen to publicize the on-line survey presents a further problem. Usually, on-line surveys are announced through links on frequently visited sites. The results of the survey can be greatly influenced by the choice of linking sites. For instance, if an objective of the survey is to evaluate users' browser preference, while the survey has a link from the Netscape site, it is clear the reliability of the results must be questioned. Similarly, surveys seeking to compare the technology platform preferred by web browsers are frequently biased by email messages sent to large lists encouraging fans of a particular platform (e.g., Apple Macintosh) to complete the survey. But, the on-line survey has some advantages compared to a random selection of respondents. As the survey is filled out on-line, respondents are by definition proficient Internet (or at least WWW) users and therefore represent a better sample of the population of "real" users.

Some surveyors have matched the data obtained through random digit dialing to conventional census data in order to compensate for response bias. Response bias may occur when the population of respondents is significantly different from the population that the researcher is trying to draw inference upon. To correct for the response bias, correction factors need to be applied to the data and the sample weighted until the best overall adjustment can be achieved. For example, if 35% of the resident population of United States lives in the Southeast, the data will be weighted so that roughly 35% of Internet users surveyed are residents of the Southeast region. Examples of weighting categories are census region, age and gender.

Attrition is another factor that may or may not be adequately considered in Internet surveys. A survey by Cyber Dialogue (1998) reported nearly 16 million U.S. adults had tried the Internet in the previous 12 months and were no longer users (over 25% of their estimate of the total U.S. Internet population).

When interpreting the results of an Internet survey, it is also important to take a look at the reward system and any incentives offered to the participants of the survey. It is not uncommon to see sweepstakes and prize drawings for the participants of on-line surveys. In fact it has been proven that an incentive, often in the form of a prize drawing, greatly increases the number of people taking part in the survey. What we need to pay attention to is the nature of the prize. Often the incentive for satisfactory completion of the survey is a cash payment. At times though, the reward may be of a less neutral nature. For example, the surveyor may offer a number of copies of a specific software package. In this case, we can assume that the choice of software will influence the results of the survey. If the software offered only runs on a Mac platform, we can expect that the results will be biased toward Mac users because they have a greater incentive to take part in the research than PC or Unix users.

Who sponsors the research? Who commissioned the research? These questions are more related to the usability and applicability of the research results to a specific environment than to the reliability of the data. Often times the research, especially if published by private research firms, has been commissioned by a particular organization or company or is targeted to the clients of a market research firm. Thus, it is important to identify the primary audience of the statistics gathering investigation. Depending on the sponsor of the research, many parameters may change such as the very definition of Internet and Internet user, the types of questions asked, the channels used to publicize the survey and the reward system. For example, a company that develops multimedia cartoons for children may not find the results of a survey sponsored by Ameritrade, an on-line stock trading service, to be at all useful; they may even be counterproductive if inaccurately interpreted. Clearly, when evaluating Internet research, attention must be given to the source of the study.

4.2 Reliability of Forecasts

Forecasting trends in the Internet environment is probably closer to an exercise in "black magic" than a scientific practice. Often the researcher will base the prediction merely on gut feeling and educated guesses. Evidence of the difficulty in forecasting Internet trends is the underestimation of future numbers by reputable researchers. For example, one recognized research firm reported that there were 9.5 million Internet users in May 1996, and forecasted that there would be 24.5 million by the year 2000 (*Advertising Age*, 1996), while estimates reported in Nua (1998) indicated that there were already 57 million users by February of 1997. But even in this very unstructured environment, there are some considerations that can help to identify more reliable estimates.

The Background and Prominence of the Researcher

The training and major areas of interest of the person publishing the estimates, along with his/her popularity and reputation in the field provides some basis for judging the credibility of the forecast. Being trained and actively participating in the area under evaluation provides the researcher a better appreciation of developing trends. Also, the greater the reputation and visibility of the person publishing the prediction, the greater the likelihood that this person will gather as much information as carefully as possible and will meticulously examine it so as to protect his/her status and reputation.

The Experience of the Researcher

Often estimation in a volatile environment like the Internet is more art than science. Considerable practice and trial and error are required to refine estimation skills. Therefore, early scholars of the Internet should have an advantage over researchers new to the field, and will be more likely to produce a reliable and credible set of predictions.

The Track Record of the Researcher

Just as we would examine the past accomplishments and precision of a financial broker before we trust him/her with our money, in the same way we want to know the researcher's past performance in forecasting Internet numbers.

4.3 Players in Internet Statistics Compilation

At this point, a picture of the Internet user population should be clearly drawn. Numerous sources have been cited, statistics have been presented, and cautions have been offered for interpreting those statistics. But who are the people who compile these statistics, what is their motivation for doing so, and why, if this information is valuable, are they willing to give it away? We will address these issues in this final section.

There are numerous "data collectors" attempting to answer an equally large number of questions, ranging from quantifying the number of Internet users in the entire world to learning about Web users' purchasing habits. These collectors fall into two main categories: educational institutions and market research firms.

Educational Institutions

Educational institutions compile Internet statistics to further their research efforts. A primary example is Georgia Institute of Technology's Graphic, Visualization, & Usability Center (GVU) which has conducted nine Internet surveys over the last four and a half years, and plans to continue its data collection with two surveys a year. These surveys were the foundation of our discussion of the Internet population. The data collected is provided free of charge as a public service to the Web community and, presumably, as an inducement for participation in the survey. The Center's stated objectives (GVU, 1997) in compiling the data are:

1. To "characterize WWW users" and their motivations for Web use.
2. To facilitate improvements in the development of Web related tools and technologies.
3. To demonstrate the effectiveness of Web based surveys.

Market Research Firms

By contrast, market research firms, which make up a substantial portion of the Internet "data collectors", have a profit motive. Their business model is to sell publications and consulting services. In general, a certain amount of information is available for free, either through a particular firm's Web site and/or in information given to the press for publication. This information, especially that published in the press, creates some brand awareness for the research being conducted by the firm and may draw potential clients to their web site. A firm will leverage its reputation for quality research (created by circulation of free material) and offer more detailed reports, bulletins, and/or newsletters for sale, more often than not, for very significant fees. In addition to the published content, these firms offer consulting services in the area of market research. Here's how one Internet consulting firm, NUA, justifies the survey data it provides in its weekly newsletter:

*"We provide you with quality information for free. We get our brand before
you. We establish credibility with you. We open up the opportunity of building
a relationship with you. Our end goal is two-fold: That you might talk or write
favorably about Nua, that one day you might become a Nua client" (Nua,
1998)*

Forrester, Intelliquest, and Jupiter Communications are examples of well known
market research firms involved in Internet surveys that are based in the United
States. Firms such as these are not exclusive to the U.S., but are found worldwide.
NOP Research Group and Paul Budde Communications, for instance, conduct similar research in British and Asian markets, respectively.

5 Conclusion

To facilitate the assessment of electronic commerce markets, we provided a guide to
interpreting and understanding the enormous wealth of on-line information on the
Internet user population, its demographics, and usage patterns. Some relevant quantitative methods for assessing the scope of the market were discussed, including the
total number of users, demographics, and purposes for using the Internet. Attitude
measures, such as attitudes toward shopping, security, and privacy (discussed in this
chapter), are also helpful in assessing not only markets but also the strategies necessary to infiltrate those markets.

We described the past, present, and likely future Internet populations. The user
population, historically typified by young, white, well-educated, affluent males, will
in the future consist of older, predominantly white, average (in terms of education,
occupation, and income) males and females.

We also analyzed the process of creating Internet survey data and statistics in an
effort to facilitate discernment between reliable and unreliable sources of information.

References

Advertising Age, "Survey Defines Internet Usage," (May 30, 1996),
     URL=http://adage.com/ns-search/interactive.
Computerworld, On-line News, (June 29, 1998), URL=
     http://www.idg.net/idg_frames/english/content.cgi?vc=docid_9-64453.html.
Cyber Dialogue, "American Internet User Survey finds more than 41.5 million U.S. adults are
     actively using the Internet," (January 27, 1998), URL=http://www.cyberdialogue.com.
Find/SVP, "The 1997 American Internet User Survey: Realities Beyond the Hype," (January,
     1998), URL=http://etrg.findsvp.com/internet/overview.html.
Hamilton, Annette, "What Makes Women Click?", ZDNet AnchorDesk, (October 6, '97),
     URL=http://www5.zdnet.com/anchordesk/story/story_1323.html.
GVU Surveys (1994-1998), URL=http://www.gvu.gatech.edu/user_surveys.

Kehoe, Colleen and James Pitkow, GVU's Seventh WWW User Survey, (April, 1997).

Kehoe, Colleen, James Pitkow, and Juan Rogers, GVU's Ninth WWW User Survey, (April, 1998).

Pitkow, James and Mimi Recker, GVU's First and Second WWW User Surveys, (January, 1994 and October, 1994).

Pitkow, James, Colleen Kehoe, and Laurie Hodges, GVU's Third and Fourth WWW User Surveys, (April, 1995 and October, 1995).

Pitkow, James and Colleen Kehoe, GVU's Fifth and Sixth WWW User Surveys, (April, 1996 and October, 1996).

Pitkow, James, Colleen Kehoe, Kimberly Morton, Li Zou, William Read, and Jarek Rossignac, GVU's Eighth WWW User Survey, (October, 1997).

Maddox, Kate, "Information Still Killer App on the Internet," Advertising Age, (October 6, 1997), URL=http://adage.com/ns-search/interactive/articles/ 19971006/article7.html?NS-search-set=/34d75/aaaa0007Ed759c3&NS-doc-off set=0&.

Nielsen Media Research, (1998),
URL=http://www.nielsenmedia.com/interactive/commercenet/grow.htm.

NOP Research Group, "One in Twenty Five British Households Now Linked to Internet -- with Significant Increase in Future Usage," (October 14, 1997),
URL=http://www.nopres.co.uk/internet/surveys/in07.htm.

NUA Internet Surveys, "NUA Analysis," (1996-97),
URL=http://www.nua.ie/surveys/analysis/graphs_charts.html.

NUA Internet Surveys, "Matrix Information and Directory Services: Internet Demographics," (February 18, 1997),
URL=http://www.nua.ie/surveys/index.cgi?service=view_survey&survey_number=108&rel=no.

NUA Internet Surveys, "1997 Internet Review - Part I," (January 6, 1998),
URL=http://www.nua.ie/surveys/analysis/yearinreview.html.

NUA Internet Surveys, "Activmedia Incorporated: Television Viewing Is Down Significantly," (January 16, 1998),
URL=http://www.nua.ie/surveys/index.cgi?service=view_survey&survey_number=566&rel=no.

NUA E-mail Newsletter, Vol 3, No 4 (February 2, 1998).

NUA Internet Surveys, "How Many Online?", (September 8, 1998),
URL=http://www.nua.ie/surveys/how_many_online.

RelevantKnowledge, Home Page, (1998),
URL=http://www.relevantknowledge.com.

Teveris, Edward H., "Accessing New Markets: The Latin American Internet," SRI Business Intelligence Program Article D96-2015, (1997),
URL=http://future.sri.com:8080/bip/dlss/dls2015.html.

Ullrich, Rita T., "AT&T Wins Contract to Boost China Telecom's Internet Service," AT&T News Release, (November 13, 1997),
URL=http://www.att.com/press/1197/971113.cia.html.

Wang, Nelson, "Nielsen Survey Finds 48M Net Users, Strong Growth in Online Purchasing," Webweek, (December 15, 1997),
URL = http://www.internetworld.com/print/1997/12/15/news/19971215-nielsen.html.

CHAPTER 6

The Internet as a New Marketplace: Implications for Consumer Behavior and Marketing Management

Gina Colarelli O'Connor[1] *and Robert O'Keefe*[2]

[1]Department of Management & Technology, Rensselaer Polytechnic Institute, Troy, NY, oconng@rpi.edu

[2]Department of Information Systems and Computing, Brunel University, Uxbridge, England, bob.okeefe@brunel.ac.uk

This chapter explores how the rising tide of interactive technologies will affect traditional marketing management practice and marketing strategy development. We focus on consumer behavior and marketing management, and how the two will interact via this new media. Clear trends are emerging, driven by information technology that directly links buyers and sellers. Based on the consideration of the model of buyer behavior, we draw insights for building a business that differ from traditional marketing methods. For example, we make clear that the use of the internet as simply another advertising medium grossly underutilizes its power to aid in building a strong business foundation. We take a futuristic approach, considering technologies that are under development but not yet perfected, such as electronic agents, as well as those currently in use.

Keywords: Marketing management; Customer relationships

1 Introduction

The marketplace continuously evolves as sellers seek new avenues of access to customers. Retail shops in the U.S. have given way to large chains and discount houses, and direct mail catalogs have enjoyed explosive growth since the 1970's. According to the "*Statistical Abstract of the United States*," sales activity ($millions) through catalog and mail order houses (SIC 5961) has been as follows: 1972: $4,528; 1977: $7, 555; 1982: $11,362 and 1987: $20,756. With the advent of home shopping, electronic media have become the most recent marketing vehicle (Marketing News, July 18, 1994); accounting for $2.5 billion of all U.S. retail sales dollars annually (Solomon, 1994). The question as to whether or not consumers would buy goods that, prior to purchase, they could neither touch nor try has been answered. The tide of activity in home shopping provides ample evidence that consumers are willing to buy under these circumstances, given the appropriate product and marketing mix elements.

Interactive and advanced multimedia technologies now allow for commercial activities that, until recently, have been unimaginable. The newest marketplace is the Internet, and, in particular, that portion of the Internet that provides for multimedia and interaction: the World Wide Web. The Internet looks like a seller's dream. It is a global and well-defined marketplace. Any company, irrespective of size, has instant access to a customer base that self-selects in its accesses to the firm's products, or that identifies its activities and interests via their participation in newsgroups and discussion groups. The cost of participation is minimal. Barriers to entry built on the need for heavy advertising expenditures may evaporate, and there is no longer the need for expensive retail outlets or point of sale presence.

But the changes are more profound than just the impact on selling. The Internet has the potential to become much more than an electronic catalog. Trends point to it fundamentally changing the way all of marketing management and business strategy are conducted. Traditional forms of marketing communication are being turned upside-down; the one-to-many model of marketing communication (the cornerstone of the advertising industry as we know it) is being replaced. Interactivity means that buyers have direct access to makers and sellers (Cronin, 1994; Hoffman and Novak, 1994), with profound implications for the management of the marketing function.

In this chapter we will consider the basics of marketing management and provide evidence of the changes that are beginning to occur. Our comments are informed by e-mail interviews with Internet vendors and the previous maintenance of a site that tracked new and interesting developments on the Web over a period of 2 years, plus observations of firms' home pages and Usenet discussion groups. What is striking is that nearly every component of the marketing manager's world is affected.

We present a classic model of consumer behavior, and illustrate how the Internet is going to severely impact each portion of the buying process. We then review the fundamental tasks of marketing management, and discuss how each will be altered for organizations that choose to operate with Internet technology. Finally, we discuss the diffusion of the Web as an innovation in and of itself, and briefly consider long term structural changes in industries that service the marketing management function under conventional marketing paradigms.

2 Consumer Behavior: The Place to Begin

A well-recognized buyer behavior model is shown in Figure 1. According to this model, a consumer's need is aroused or stimulated in one of a variety of ways. He searches out information on alternative solutions to his problem, evaluates competitive brands using some decision rule, chooses one, makes the purchase and then uses the product and evaluates it for future purchase decisions. A systematic consideration of the basic elements of this model reveals that classic avenues of behavior will be dismissed by consumers and replaced with new alternatives that the Internet's technology makes possible. These proposed changes are summarized in Table 1. We take these each in turn.

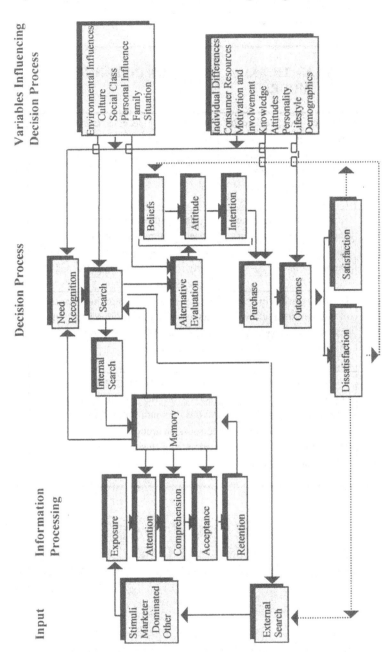

(Adapted from James F. Engel, Roger D. Blackwell and Paul W. Miniard, *Consumer Beavior*, Drydon Press, Orlando, FL, 1990)

Fig. 1. Model of buyer behavior

Table 1. Comparisons of consumer behavior

BEHAVIOR	TRADITIONAL MODEL	ON INTERNET
Need Recognition	Markets stimulate demand by creating awareness of problems via advertising that is presented in a strategically favorable manner.	Advertising is accessed at the discretion of the user.
Information Search	Risk levels for purchase and use of product determine amount of energy exerted.	Costs of information search are reduced or eliminated, making comparison shopping simplistic; third party referrals easily available via newsgroups.
Evaluation of Alternative	Use of heuristics in cases of info overload or low involvement products; trialability critical for high risk products.	Compensatory decision rules handled automatically; trialability becoming technologically feasible to reduce risk.
Purchase	Impacted by the service encounter.	Little interaction required; risks of service encounter reduced.
Post-Purchase Evaluation	Post purchase experience affects attitude toward brand, probability of repurchase, and word of mouth.	Word of mouth spreads rapidly over discussion groups, causing an accelarated diffusion curve.

2.1 Need Recognition

External sources of stimulation that are managed by the firm include advertising, point of purchase displays, and promotions. Others are not controllable by the firm. *A key difference with use of the Internet as a marketing medium is that the consumer has more control of the information.* Television commercials, for example, are aired at the discretion of the marketer, not at the discretion of the viewer. Home shopping TV stations currently choose the order in which they present products for viewers to see (Reilly, 1993). Catalogs present varieties of products on the same page to encourage crossover purchases.

Home pages on the Web, however, are accessed only at the discretion of the user. Unless he experiences a felt need, the consumer will not necessarily access various pages to learn about new products the way he may notice them on store shelves, or catch an ad on TV. Therefore, marketing tools traditionally used to arouse a sense of need or interest among consumers must be reconsidered.

2.2 Information Search

Under the traditional model, consumers exert varying levels of energy to seek out and process information as they learn about the products available from which they will ultimately choose. Risk levels (social and financial) play pre-eminent roles in how much energy consumers exert. They may visit a number of stores, read outside sources that rate brands, and talk to experts under conditions of high risk. For items requiring limited problem solving, consumers use proxies of information (brand name, price or past purchase history) as heuristics in their decision making process.

The Internet makes the information search portion of the decision-making process much easier. First, through the use of Usenet newsgroups, consumers gain full access to an interactive network and information exchange. Word-of-mouth plays a critical role in decision-making, particularly in purchases of high-risk products (Engel, Blackwell and Miniard, 1990). Postings to Usenet newsgroups can impact on buyers' decisions. Interested individuals now have access to a forum where people pool their knowledge by candidly discussing their experiences with products (Sherman, 1994). It is here that product referrals and negative experiences are relayed. This is third party information, considered the most credible by consumers, and many postings carry standard disclaimers proclaiming the writer's independence from the product's manufacturer. This form of information is completely out of the control of the marketer, except insofar as product and service offerings are delivering upon their promise. A careful monitoring of appropriate discussion groups may seem costly to marketers, but will become an important gateway for firms to learn about their markets. In the *comp.** hierarchy, for example, it is not unusual for hardware and software vendors to respond to criticisms or to suggest that concerns are being addressed.

Second, in contrast to the time and effort required to go to many physically located stores, visiting multiple sites on the Web requires minimal resource expenditure. Consumers will have nearly free access to all suppliers willing to pay a connection cost (Benjamin and Wigand, 1995). Hypertext allows for easy navigation from one firm's home page to any number of others, as designated by the page designer. When visiting a site, the user can click on any hypertext link and be drawn into another page that gives more detailed information. This nonlinear search method provides unlimited freedom of choice and greater control for the consumer, contrasted with the restrictive navigation options available in traditional media, such as television or print (Hoffman and Novak, 1994; Sherman, 1994). Directories and search engines are also increasingly available, allowing users to browse through comprehensive lists of vendors arranged by product and service, or to search for a vendor by name or page content.

Current research indicates that users believe that Web sites provide better purchase related information than traditional vendors (Gupta, 1995). Users seek factual information, and providers generally understand this. Puffery, deception, and profitmaking based on the costs of search will disappear:

> *Many companies want to treat (the Web)...like TV or print ads, just as a source of name and logo recognition...If this is all they do, they will fail. When I want a phone number for a company, I will look in a phone book. When I want to see the specials of the week for a local store, I will look in the newspaper. When I use the Web for shopping (which I have done), I want detailed product information, searching, cross-referencing ('You might also want to check out these related products'), up-to-the-minute in-stock information, and pricing...(Respondent on recent Web site previously maintained by one of the co-authors)*

Third, comparative shopping on price and product attributes becomes even easier, as all alternatives are presented in close proximity to one another. *Virtual malls* are presently composed of stores that sell varieties of products, modelled after physical malls. Yet the benefits of browsing a variety of products in one physical location are not needed by the Web shopper. The Web user can move from mall to mall with a few keystrokes or mouse-clicks. For this reason, virtual malls are moving toward specialization in their product and store offerings (O'Keefe, 1995). Thus, the CyberMusic mall includes stores devoted to the sales of CD's, tapes, and other products of interest to music lovers, and the Green Mall focuses on environmentally friendly products. Search costs are again reduced.

Fourth, and perhaps most importantly, *electronic agents* may eliminate the need for search altogether. "Two of the great ills of the information age are that there is too much useless information, and valuable information is too hard to find" (Hill, 1995). Electronic agents are software applications that can be programmed or trained to gather information or perform transactions and other tasks based on personal preferences. They'll search out products for consumers to buy, and will even complete a purchase transaction, based on programmed instructions regarding levels of key attributes that buyers desire (Donaton and Johnson, 1994; Kantor, 1994). To shop for a VCR, for example, a user will tap a list, probably supplied by a shopping service, fill in blanks identifying the kind of stores to be searched, the VCR model, the price range and the number of bids desired. The list will be sent to a directory on which stores have identified themselves as sellers of VCRs. Then the agent will "travel" to each virtual store and compare its data to the list of VCR models and prices in the store's own computer, until it exhausts the list or has the right number of matches. Then it will page or e-mail the user. If the user has provided a credit card number, the agent can even buy the VCR (Hill, 1995). The use of electronic agents lowers the cost of information search drastically. The only requirement of the shopper is the time required to enter the data on which the agent is to search. The implication is that cost and attribute-by-attribute comparisons can be made for product classes previously considered unworthy of such effort.

2.3 Alternative Evaluation

The theory of buyer behavior in Figure 1 describes alternative evaluation as the comparison of brands against standards and specifications set by consumers. For high-risk products, compensatory strategies are used to determine the most preferred brand (Engel, Blackwell, and Miniard, 1990). The Internet can make compensatory decision strategies automatic.

In the cases of too many brands to evaluate, information overload, or a low risk product, consumers normally use heuristics to inform choice. Brand names, price (used by consumers as a proxy for quality) and retail outlet are typical examples of heuristics used. The ease of compensatory decision-making afforded by the Internet may cause brand names to decline in importance (Rayport and Sviokla, 1994). Loyalty to a brand may be established based on delivery of value, but will be subject to re-evaluation as alternatives are introduced and are evaluated in a cost-free environment.

Trial is an important part of most evaluation processes, and serves to reduce consumers' risk. While the success of catalog orders, home shopping and direct mail purchases signals that consumers will try after they buy (as long as they can return goods with which they are displeased), marketers are aware of the importance of trial as a risk reducer. The Internet as a medium would seemingly inhibit trial; it is an information-defined transaction space, where information about products replaces products (Rayport and Sviokla, 1994).

Where products can be delivered over communications lines, however, the Internet can support trial. Many software vendors (for example, Oracle) allow users to download trial copies of software, and even full copies for a free (typically) 90-day trial period. Programs self-destruct after a trial period if payment is not made (Verity and Hof, 1994). There are also innovations developed specifically to aid trial. DealerNet, for example, is an online service that allows consumers to purchase cars without ever entering a dealership (Rechtin, 1995). Buyers collect information on various brands, and then e-mail local participating dealerships with requests to test drive certain models. Dealerships deliver the car to the customer's place of work for a test drive. Computer hardware buyers can log in to provider computers of various models and run programs on their own data to gauge the computer's effectiveness (Verity and Hof, 1994). Bookstores encourage shoppers to browse through specific offerings (Cronin, 1994), and music stores allow songs to be downloaded and heard. Finally, software is being developed that lets shoppers pick up a product and examine it in a virtual reality environment (Spethmann, 1994).

Senses of texture, taste and smell cannot yet be simulated, but motion, sight, sound and even fit can. To the extent that firms begin investing in mass customization manufacturing techniques (Pine, Peppers and Rogers, 1995) the trial problem may evaporate. For example, Textile/Clothing Technology corporation, a research consortium, is developing a body scanner that will allow people to have their clothing custom fit. The scan need only be taken once, and is then stored for all future orders (Lee, 1994).

2.4 Purchase

Many people view purchase and the rituals surrounding it with disdain. Waiting in line; rude, inept store clerks whose advice is oftentimes suspect; stockouts; and crowds are a few aspects of buying that many would gladly forgo (Gupta, 1995; Rechtin, 1995). Simply allocating the time to go to a store is a hardship for many. For these reasons, direct mail and catalog shopping have become extremely successful.

The Internet eases the purchase ritual even further. Once a book has been browsed, or a song heard (if trial is even necessary), the shopper fills out the order form (or simply clicks on the choices he's made) on the provider's home page. If he has questions, he can post them to the "inquiries" section of the home page and receive responses directly from the provider. Oftentimes, the provider is the manufacturer rather than a retailer, and thus offers more expertise in the responses. Orders are scanned, credit card limits are checked, inventory stock is verified and the customer is messaged regarding shipment date, past due balances, and/or other products in which he might be interested (Verity and Hof, 1994).

Goods are delivered to the consumer's door via some form of shipment method. Durables (computers), nondurables (clothing) and even perishables (groceries, flowers) are all currently being handled in this manner. Major advances in logistics stemming from the growth in catalog operations, where companies like Airborne Express will even store and manage a vendor's inventory, are aiding this process.

2.5 Post-Purchase Evaluation

The diffusion curve for new products will be drastically condensed as word of mouth spreads like rapidfire over discussion groups. Conventional wisdom is that a dissatisfied customer will tell nine of his closest friends of a negative experience. Now he may tell, for example, 10,000 or so enthusiasts worldwide. The speed with which knowledge about problems with the division operation in Intel's pentium chip was disseminated is a recent example. The warning that follows was posted to three newsgroups dedicated to the discussion of computer hardware:

**************DON'T BUY FROM EPS TECHNOLOGIES!!!!**************

This is a warning to any of you who may be thinking of buying a system from EPS Technologies of South Dakota. Don't be deceived by their 6 page ad beginning on page 26 of January's Computer Shopper. I ordered a 486-DX266 system from them on Nov. 23rd and have had **horrible problems** with my order! ...Among the problems I experienced:

   ** Their sales staff failed to answer technical questions regarding components and never called back with an answer as they said they would.
   ** They failed to answer any of my 11 messages over the course of a week regarding changes to my order.
   ** They have gone ten days over due (and counting) on the arrival date for my system.
   ** They never sent me an amended invoice to OK before shipment as is their policy.
   ** Hold times of over a half-hour on their 800 line.

***************DON'T BUY FROM EPS TECHNOLOGIES***************

The impact of this on marketing management is profound. Details about the service encounter, the purchase process and the tangible product together are given. Shoppers seeking advice about particular brands simply post the question to these groups, and receive detailed positive or negative accounts of others' past experiences.

An electronic market system that provides product and price information enables customers to locate suppliers that better match their needs. Producers may find that arenas of differentiation based on perception or heuristics fade quickly as consumers gain easy access to comparative information. Products are differentiated by quality, price and details of delivery, while selling becomes an auction. Markets are efficient in the economic sense, because the cost of information, in terms of search and availability, is minimized. Marketers will be concerned with ensuring that electronic agents have access to their offerings (Zachary, 1994). Convenience in ordering, payment and receipt of goods will be a major competitive factor. Responses to inquiries directly from the manufacturer will be viewed by customers as a key advantage to purchasing over the Web. Marketers may experience drastic and unexpected changes in sales as word of mouth spreads almost instantaneously to worldwide audiences.

3 Marketing Management Issues

Along with dramatic changes in buyer behavior, the technology of the Internet will allow for distinct differences in the conduct of marketing related business activities. We focus on market segmentation methods, the collection and use of market research data, and relationship management with customers and suppliers. Our discussion is summarized in Table 2.

Table 2 Marketing management issues

	CLASSICAL	**INTERNET**
Segmenting Schemes	Geodemographic and psycho-graphic criteria most often used due to measurement.	Benefit segmentation is possible.
Market Research	Scanner data is capable of connecting purchase data with demographic data.	Shopping behavior, both purchases and non-purchases, across stores, can be collected for an individual.
Relationship with Customers	Confined to customer service desk, and sales representatives.	All members of the firm become boundary spanners.

3.1 Segmentation and Target Marketing

Marketers typically use a number of segmentation schemes to divide the marketplace into groups that, theoretically, are homogeneous in their wants and needs with respect to the product category. The most typical scheme used is demographic segmentation, because it is simple to manage, easy to measure, and is intuitively appealing. Individuals belonging to the same age, income, and gender classifications are assumed similar with respect to attitudes and behaviors regarding brand and product choice. Demographic segmentation schemes, however, do not contribute significantly to the prediction of purchase behavior (Gupta and Chintagunta, 1994). Brand choice is best predicted by past purchase behavior. Yet marketers continuously spend money to understand psychographics, motives, life styles and usage patterns of their buying constituency so as to better tailor their messages and offerings to distinct segments of the market who are seeking the benefits that the product is positioned to offer.

The distinct advantage of the Internet as a marketplace is that it is so cleanly segmented in terms of interests and needs, particularly in the Usenet newsgroups. In today's environment, where marketers realize the importance of micro-marketing and niches, the Internet may be seen as an extremely efficient self-selecting segmentation mechanism. Verity and Hof (1994) have suggested that it may be nearly one-fourth less costly to perform direct marketing through the Internet than through conventional channels. Their rationale is that transaction costs are greatly reduced. While this is true, we believe that even greater efficiencies of marketing resources can be realized through the savvy use of the self-defined market segmentation scheme, built around interests and usage benefits, that Internet users have created.

Firms experiencing success on the Internet today are browsing appropriate newsgroups to understand their character and their tone. This is akin to direct observation of the market, without introducing observer or interviewer bias. The key is knowing who reads which discussion groups, and matching the distribution of announcements to the interests of a particular Internet list.

Business owners who view the Internet as access to a global mass market are setting themselves up for disappointment. Marketing in this medium requires a relinquishment of control to the consumer. Buyers seek out vendors; vendors cannot force consumers to be exposed to their messages the way merchants have in the past with mass media.

Virtual malls will have to organize for this effect if their stores are to have any success. There will have to be a mall dedicated to financial services, one for business applications software, and a third for music. As this occurs, consumers who are essentially prequalified, like those who inquire of a vendor based on finding him in a telephone directory, will seek out the appropriate places to shop.

In the end, directory lists may replace virtual malls (O'Keefe, 1995). The main benefit that malls provide is "Web presence" for small organizations, and that will become easier to obtain. Smaller companies may increasingly develop their own Web servers, and demand for virtual malls and third party marketers could diminish. Like word processing, Web tools will become easier to use and more seamless. Companies will be able to do more for themselves in terms of generating and updating home pages.

4 Market Research

The potential of interactive media to collect data about shopping behaviors at the level of the individual consumer, and to summarize data by individual product, signals an incredible change in marketing management. Purchase diaries and scanner data have given marketers access to actual purchase behavior within a single store, and have allowed them to relate it to richer consumer demographic data. Interactive media, however, allow not only for actual purchases to be monitored, but all shopping behavior across multiple outlets as well. Virtual stores are laboratories for observation and testing of consumer decision theory.

Web servers can provide access statistics by page (each access is commonly called a "hit"). Vendors who list each product or product line on a sub-page will be able to gauge how many shoppers are browsing each product. Further, many sites now require user registration where each visitor is given an account after providing some basic demographic information.

By tracking shoppers' paths, vendors can learn which products are getting the most attention. Data on browsing, inquiries, and interest in products that are eventually <u>not</u> chosen for purchase can all be collected. For all brands, the order in which pieces of data are accessed can be logged. This becomes an evaluation device for measuring the effectiveness of communications and merchandising programs. One can imagine new performance indicators emerging (such as the ratio of purchases to hits, or the number of times each day that a particular piece of explanatory information is consulted), that will determine whether or not a product needs different merchandising in a cyberstore, needs better explanation, or should be dropped from the virtual shelf. Search and purchase histories by individual buyers will also be available for vendors to analyze (Miller, 1995a). Vendors will be able to use their own electronic agents to monitor shoppers' behavior in their own and other stores.

5 Developing Relationships with Customers and Suppliers

Relationships with customers will be drastically different, and the differences reach far beyond the behavior tracking capabilities just discussed. The informality, ease of use and immediate access afforded by the Internet will promote bonds between provider and user and increase loyalty. The direct link between buyer and provider that was once reserved for business-to-business markets now will apply to consumer markets as well.

All employees of a provider firm with access to the Internet can interact with any customer that posts a question, either through the firm's home page, or through appropriate discussion groups. This concept of "intermarketing" (Cronin, 1994) serves to broaden the responsibility for keeping customers well informed and serviced to everyone in the provider organization. This takes Kohli and Jaworski's (1990) concept of Market Orientation to the limit. Employees in every department will hear and consider a response to user questions as soon as they are raised, rather than having them filtered through the sales or customer service organization. The marketing organization becomes extremely flat as every member of the firm becomes sensitized directly to the customer point of view and responds accordingly (see Figure 2).

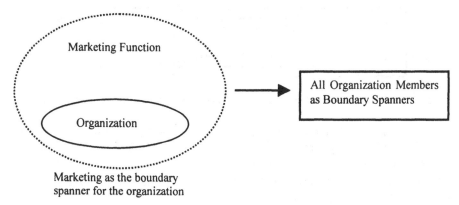

Marketing as the boundary
spanner for the organization

Fig. 2. Changes in roles of employees as a result of direct customer interaction capabilities

5.1 More Cross-Talk

Figure 3.a shows the typical link between provider and customer in a consumer products environment. Complaints are oftentimes registered with and serviced by retailers. Detailed inquiries or suggestions by customers are often met with poor or no response. Under almost no circumstance is there a direct channel of distribution for consumer products.

The Internet can provide a direct channel between customer and provider (Figure 3.b). Now customer training and support are handled directly. Any expert in the organization who knows the answer can be accessed. Appliance manufacturers might provide repair tips via video demonstration, as well as order forms for spare parts (Churbuck, 1994). Users of a new software package can log into the vendor's page and download information to help fix problems they encounter.

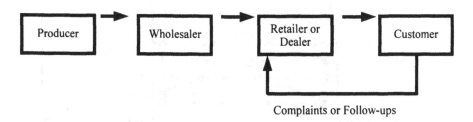

Complaints or Follow-ups

Fig. 3.a Typical customer-provider linkages for consumer products

Fig. 3.b Customer-provider linkages facilitated by the internet for consumer products

Typical customer contact points in business-to-business organizations are the sales force, service departments and, in the case of a complex buy, development engineers (see Figure 4.a). Although discussions have been direct between firms as a norm, and sometimes take place at multiple levels in organizations, they are, for the most part, dyadic (e.g., purchasing agent to sales representative, engineer to engineer). The Internet allows for increased efficiencies in cost, timeliness and breadth of distribution of information. Now anyone in one organization can easily communicate with anyone from the other (Figure 4.b). Usage demonstrations and diagnostic software can be made available by providers at almost no cost. Changes in product specifications and maintenance requirements can be made available as soon as they occur.

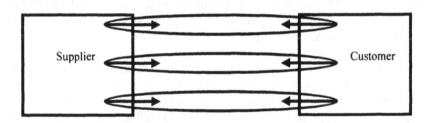

Fig. 4.a Typical customer-provider linkages for business-to-business products

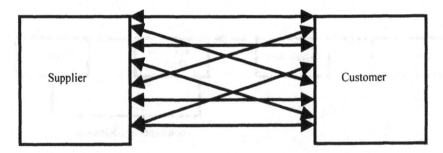

Fig. 4.b Business-to-business linkages facilitated by the internet

There will be a competitive advantage to firms who recognize and capitalize on this mechanism that serves to promote cross-functional integration both within the firm and across buyer-supplier organizational partners.

5.2 Managing the Customer Connection

Under these conditions, control over the messages that are sent under the firm's name can be lost. If several employees respond to a customer's inquiry, conflicting (or redundant) messages may easily result and serve to confuse or annoy. Formal management of the employee/customer interface will become necessary. An organizational role will need to develop to screen all responses to customer queries to ensure that they don't conflict with one another (or corporate policy) and don't raise expectations beyond what the company is willing or able to support.

6 Marketing Mix Elements

We now turn to the elements of the marketing mix and raise issues to be considered with each one as impacted by the Internet's potential.

6.1 Products: What will sell on the Internet?

Marketing academics typically categorize products by the consumer's degree of search effort and perceived risk. Murphy and Enis (1986) identify four such categories: convenience, preference, shopping and specialty products.

Convenience goods require minimal information search and processing effort and are perceived as the least risky purchases. They are commodity, impulse or unsought (emergency) items which are priced so low that the consumer will not spend much money or time in purchasing them. These include items like fresh produce, grocery staples and bandages.

Preference items are higher on the effort dimension and much higher on the risk dimension. They differ from convenience items through the marketer's efforts to position the product through advertising and branding. They exist primarily in consumer packaged goods (beer, soft drinks, toothpaste) but now even include produce (e.g. Dole bananas). *Shopping goods* require search effort and comparisons among brands on quality, price and style. Consumers will visit several stores before they choose.

Finally, *specialty products* are those for which consumers will accept no substitute brands. They involve a sizable investment of effort and are considered high in social and economic risk. Consumers are willing to wait for backordered models of a chosen product. Vintage wines, pianos and paintings by well-known artists are some examples.

The Web allows for comparison shopping on attributes that are easily defined. For convenience and preference goods, price, brand name and delivery systems are easily compared. To the extent that home delivery is valued and can be implemented for customers' convenience, these goods may succeed on the Internet. Peapods is an example of a highly successful net-based grocery service (Marsh, 1994). For a monthly fee, customers can have any amount of groceries delivered to their home.

Selection of items is handled through a forms interface. Some grocery chains, such as Price Chopper in Schenectady, New York, have followed this move to home shopping.

While the use of electronic agents seems most appropriate for shopping goods, since search effort is most extensive, consideration must be given to whether the attributes of the search may be easily defined. High technology products such as hardware or software, that are easily defined through technical specifications, or books and CD's, which are singularly identifiable by title, are likely to succeed, since the value of the product can be easily determined. If the products involve the sense of smell, feel, or finely detailed inspection, which the Internet cannot provide, they are unlikely to be bought via this medium.

Following this logic, certain specialty goods may be a natural fit for the Web. In situations where consumers have identified the brand and model they are seeking, and will accept nothing else, the Web is the best place to search out the most advantageous price. As noted, automobiles can already be ordered via the Internet, along with many other highly specialized products. Serviceability and delivery of these high-ticket items, for purposes of reducing perceived risk, will be the greatest challenges to their success. Conventionally, these issues have been handled through retail outlets, often exclusive dealerships. Consumers' ability to interact directly with the manufacturers of specialty goods via the Internet will add a dimension of risk reduction that they previously have not experienced.

6.2 Advertising

Hoffman, Novak and Chatterjee (1995) discuss several methods for developing a Web presence. These include storefronts, flat ads (image sites and information sites), content sites (fee-based or sponsored), yellow pages, and Web traffic controllers, which essentially behave as directories. Usenet advertisements are another method. *Any form of Web presence that a firm chooses must be considered an advertisement.* It establishes firm and brand identity, and can have powerful effects on consumers' perceptions of the business.

Advertising on the Internet is fundamentally different from conventional advertising. First, the trend toward information reduction required by conventional media is reversed. Conventional advertising is bound by space (for print) and time (for radio and television) constraints. Messages are short and fast-paced; their goal is to create a memorable perception rather than to deliver information. Hypertext linkages, however, allow consumers to probe deeper and deeper for more detailed information within a single on-line ad, at their own pace. The implication is that Internet advertisers must offer valuable information, allowing the browser to request more as his interest grows. Entire catalogs, detailed product specifications, product performance histories, examples of successful applications, usage demonstrations and anything else a company wishes to share with customers can be digitized and maintained at a relatively low cost. Advertisers who simply convert their print ads to the Internet are not capitalizing on the hypertext or multi-media capabilities that make the Internet a different and more interesting medium.

Second, the medium is interactive; as such, it allows consumers to actually engage in, and thereby customize, their own advertisements. Information is available whenever browsers need it, is tailored to their interests (since they choose which hypertext links to probe), and allows them to make comments or ask specific questions on-line. This attribute, termed *dynamic addressability,* makes Internet advertising resemble personal sales. Specific content can be sent to an individual based on that person's behavior.

Finally, the technological structure as well as the culture of the Internet community do not allow for intrusive, mass e-mail advertising. The choice to be involved in or to forego an advertisement is left completely up to the user. In one sense, advertising efficiency is maximized, because those who access the advertisement have self-selected and are therefore presumably interested, much as a potential customer accesses the business pages of a telephone directory due to a felt need.

On the other hand, intrusive advertising has a purpose, which is not accommodated on the Internet. How does the marketer get to potential customers who do not experience a felt need for the firm's offering but who might be interested if they were made aware? Current thinking is that ads must be designed to attract browsers via entertainment or other relevant information (e.g., Tide ads will have to help consumers understand how to remove stains) (Miller, 1994, 1995b; Spethmann, 1994). But what would cause a disinterested browser to search out the ad in the first place?

One alternative is to make browsers aware of the page by posting it's address in a relevant discussion group (O'Connell, 1995). The audience will be the narrowly focused target that already shares the interest in the advertiser's product. While this is efficient, it still does not gain the attention of those who do not yet share the interest. Secondly, the Internet address can be present in all other forms of advertising: TV and print ads, collateral material, packaging, even business cards and company letterhead. A number of companies, including Toyota and Magnavox, are now listing their URL's on some of their TV advertising.

A final, broader-scoped alternative, is to arrange for paid sponsorships of news content (Hoffman, Novak, and Chatterjee, 1995), or hypertext links to the ad from other pages that are accessed heavily. The word or phrase that is used as the link must be unusual enough to attract the browser's attention and cause him to want to link to the ad. It is this arena that poses the greatest challenge to advertisers on the Internet: enticing disinterested people to browse the product's home page. While it is true that this has been the challenge to advertising throughout most of its history, the Internet environment poses an extremely difficult dilemma that will require creative, workable solutions.

Once browsers are made aware of the page, advertisers must find ways to keep them returning regularly. Promotional games, contests, continuing stories, news updates and other material that is updated regularly and frequently maintain the page as an active site. Hoffman and Novak (1994) posit that the playfulness that the Internet encourages through its navigation tools serves to focus browsers' attention on the interaction. Irrelevant thoughts and perceptions are screened out, and information is processed rather than ignored as overstimulation. Higher levels of playfulness in human-computer interactions are correlated with higher levels of experimentation. Play, navigation, or "flow" is positively associated with expectations of future computer interactions. The implication is that hypertext environments that facilitate play are likely to experience repeat visits and longer times spent at each visit.

6.3 Tracking Ad Effectiveness

Tracking the effectiveness of advertising has always been a challenge to marketers. The advent of scanner data and cable television has greatly aided this effort. Still, those data are purchase-related only. Now technologies are available that allow marketers to track individuals' shopping behavior (search as well as purchase), across multiple shopping environments (Smith and King, 1993). The number of accesses to a Web site, the number of repeat accesses from a single visitor over time, the number of visitors that click from a home page into subpages and the amount of time spent by a visitor to any single sub-page are data that can all be captured. These statistics can be used to measure reach, frequency and depth of interest. It will also be easier to distinguish the effectiveness of the *ad* from the effectiveness of the *product* being offered. The number of accesses to fun or interesting sites means effective advertising, independent of whether or not a product is purchased.

Payment methods for advertising agencies will evolve as they become increasingly involved with their clients' Web presences. Commissions based on media billings are not relevant in the Internet environment, since the ad is accessible at any time. New systems for valuing ads are beginning to emerge (O'Connell, 1995). Given that ad effectiveness is easily tracked in this environment, and can be parsed out from product sales, a pay for performance system may arise. For example, agencies may be paid a commission each time the ad is accessed, and a higher commission rate each time a repeat visitor accesses the ad.

The question arises as to whether the need for ad agencies will be as great in the Internet environment (Rickard, 1994; Wells, 1994). Historically, an agent's original purpose was as a buying intermediary between the advertiser and various media. Media buying and scheduling are not necessary for the Internet. The primary skills required are those of the creative developers, graphics programmers and skilled information systems personnel. Some firms are handling all of this effort internally, and using ad agencies to develop strategies to maintain consistency among traditional media campaigns and the electronic marketing efforts. Today's agencies are struggling to adapt their skill bases to fit these emerging needs of their clients.

6.4 Distribution and Pricing

As customers and manufacturers grow more closely connected, and more individual orders are generated directly, conventional channels of distribution will be challenged. Some products and services (software, legal documents, financial analysis, language translation, music, movies) are suitable for actual distribution over the Internet. Other tangible items can be direct shipped via a physical distribution firm (such as Federal Express or UPS), and the growth in catalog sales has spurred a quiet revolution in distribution logistics. The need for services historically provided by intermediaries (storage, breaking bulk, accumulating complementary items, training, merchandising) is diminished. While this requires that manufacturers now take on the added tasks of bundling and shipping in smaller quantities, they no longer need to relinquish control of merchandising or advertising to wholesalers and retailers who may have other firms' products to consider as well.

The combined effect of convenience to the customer in the shopping effort, the abundance of price and stock availability information, the reduced need to inventory or merchandise goods, and the efficient market price will result in lower coordination costs throughout the value chain. The transactions costs of bringing goods from manufacturer to customer are greatly reduced. In the long run, this will likely result in lower prices. However, currently reduced prices are being resisted by most large firms who sell over the Internet (Rigdon, 1995). Besides the potential danger of using price as the key distinction among competing brands (a strategy most product managers prefer to avoid in the interest of quality perceptions), manufacturers who use other distribution and sales channels wish to avoid horizontal channel conflict, wherein customers can get the same good at two different prices. Ultimately, vendors will likely pass along the reductions in costs of doing business to customers, either as average price reductions across all channels, or selectively within the more efficient channels.

7 Diffusion of the Internet as a Mechanism of Exchange

There are several issues to consider with respect to how quickly this interactive medium will become widely used as a commercial marketplace. First is the investment required by firms and governments to make the technology usable and convenient, second is the lack of organization of the medium, and third is the human factors associated with the use of the technology.

7.1 Technology Deficiencies

The infrastructure required to provide on-demand interactive services demands the investment of billions of dollars and is not yet widely available. Telephone companies, computer (hardware and software) firms and cable companies are leaping into the competitive marketplace to deploy new technology without so much as a market test. Competitors consider test market results with current technological limitations to be unrealistic anyway (Cauley, 1994).

Transmission of data (especially graphical) is at present torturously slow. Hypertext leaps from one page to another can take so much time that the user becomes distracted. Sound and graphics are, on many personal computers, of poor enough quality to inhibit the attractiveness of any product requiring eye appeal, such as clothing or food.

Transmission of payments is currently a problem. Consumers are reluctant to transmit credit card numbers over the Internet. However, many solutions now exist, ranging from encryption of credit card numbers, to electronic and digital cash. Transaction management companies such as First Virtual are emerging to provide essentially a broker service between buyers and sellers to protect financial privacy of the buyer (Emery, 1995). A customer provides a vendor with a number that is then submitted to the customer's bank by the broker. The bank then has the customer confirm the purchase. Once confirmed, the customer's account is debited (or a credit charge is made), and funds are transferred to the vendor using secure methods such as Electronic Data Interchange (EDI).

7.2 Organization

The biggest problem for many current users is actually finding Web pages (Cringely, 1995; Rigdon, 1995). URL's are long, complex and non-intuitive. Barring a convenient, intuitive system of designating URL's, a listing of them sorted by company name, brand name, and product class will be necessary to promote ease of use for most shoppers. Currently, there are a number of such listings (Willmott, 1995), but like the rest of the Internet this is a free-for-all without clear established leaders.

For now, the firm's task is to make it's URL known. Increasingly, Web addresses are listed in print ads and on business cards and product literature. Hypertext linkages from other key Web pages are also critical. The system of payments between firms for allowing such linkages is as yet untried and undefined. Commercial services are racing to provide organizing frameworks (Knowles, 1995; Lewis, 1994) and search aids for subscribers.

While the use of electronic agents to search out particular products could defuse the problem or even mitigate the need for shoppers to find pages, retailers are refusing to allow early beta-test versions of agents into their stores (Rigdon, 1995). They claim that the competitive game is played completely on price under the electronic agent scenario (which is certainly true of the early prototypes), and are threatened by such a unidimensional strategy.

7.3 Human Factors

For most Americans, computers are associated with work. People with computers and modems are far more likely to use them for work and electronic mail than to read the news, play games or buy goods and services (Marketing News, 1994). Home shopping via TV may be more successful because television is associated with leisure. Online services sell a fraction of merchandise per year compared to the $2.5 billion that home shopping channels sell. The vast majority of online users are men, and most shopping dollars are spent by women (Buckley, 1993).

Some consumers go to physical retail stores for the entertainment and social aspects of shopping. Oftentimes, buying decisions are made in the store (e.g. meal planning is done in the grocery store). Many people like the combined physical activity, socialization and the sense of accomplishment of acquiring needed items (Bellinger and Korgaonkar, 1980). To some, sitting inactively while shopping is yet another move toward an Orwellian, isolationist society. The fun associated with impulse purchases and tangible handling of and learning about new products cannot be ignored.

As graphics quality improves, however, merchandising techniques in virtual reality will mimic those of the physical store, allowing for browsing and instantaneous decision-making. Technologies under development to promote trial, discussed above, allow for increasingly realistic settings. Many net surfers even testify to meeting their needs for socializing via the Internet's community-like atmosphere (Strangelove, 1995). Innovations like meeting places, message centers, libraries and town halls that some virtual malls are incorporating to deal with the social aspects of shopping, may further meet those needs.

8 Conclusion: Impending Changes in Market Structure

Communications technologies are moving us toward efficient markets, where information is nearly free and easily accessible. Competitive market structures will be affected as barriers to entry begin to erode. Small firms will compete against multinational giants on product attributes most important to prospective buyers. Advertising will be less intrusive and more informative.

Entire industries must reorient their skill sets and purposes, or risk severely diminished roles. Advertising agencies will hire more people skilled in computer graphics, and fewer media planners. Payment systems will undergo revisions as commissions based on media billings are supplanted by an agency's ability to maintain an active Web presence that generates sales. Market research suppliers must advance into the collection and summarization of Web activity data.

The future of channel intermediaries must also be considered as customers and suppliers increasingly deal directly with one another. Wholesaler functions, which have diminished in importance as retail chains have gained increasing power to purchase directly, will now suffer even at the hands of the small producer who provides product directly to consumers over the Internet instead of through small, non-chain retail outlets. Retailers, who have gained phenomenal power over producers in the last twenty years due to information systems- based infrastructures (which allowed chains to buy in volume and manage transportation logistics efficiently), will face erosion of power at the hands of the direct provider-supplier link. What will be demanded more and more heavily are third party transporters to funnel product from the producer's warehouse to the customer's home. Large suburban shopping malls may undergo transformation as buyers shop from their PCs. Perhaps they'll serve as catalogue showrooms, perhaps as social entertainment centers, but they'll not survive as holders and merchandisers of large volumes of inventory.

In the meantime, new types of intermediaries, *information intermediaries*, are emerging (Applegate and Gogan, 1995). Information brokers are specialists who serve as the source of information leads in particular categories, such as news, sports, and entertainment. Market brokers match buyers to sellers on the Internet. These, however, will only serve a medium-term function, until electronic agents establish themselves as easy and useful technologies.

A revolutionary change is occurring. It will impact marketing strategy and marketing management in firms, large and small, public and privately-held, across the globe. Marketing practitioners and academics alike must consider the future in light of the issues raised herein.

References

Applegate, L. M. and J. Gogan, "Paving the Information Superhighway: Introduction to the Internet," *Harvard Business School Publishing*, August, (1995).

Bellenger, D. and P. K. Korgaonkar, "Profiling the Recreational Shopper," *Journal of Retailing*, 56/3, (1980), 77-92.

Benjamin, R., and R. Wigand, "Electronic Markets and Virtual Value Chains on the Information Superhighway," *Sloan Management Review*, Winter, (1995), 62-72.

Buckley, W. M., "Online Shopping Fails to Fulfill Promise," *Wall Street Journal*, June 21, (1993), B6.

Cauley, L., "Pacific Telesis' Interactive Services to Skip Trial Stage," *Wall Street Journal*, August 17, (1994), B2.

Churbuck, D. C., "Dial-a-Catalog," *Forbes*, October 10, (1994) 126-130.

Cringely, R. X., "I-Way Potholes," *Forbes ASAP*, February, (1995), 88-89.

Cronin, M. J., *Doing Business on the Internet*, Van Nostrand Reinhold, New York, NY, 1994.

Donaton, S., and Johnson, B., "Diller Makes a Case for His Next Big Idea," *Advertising Age*, October 31, (1994), 16.

Emery, V., *How to Grow Your Business on the Internet*, Coriolis Group Books, Scottsdale, AZ, (1995).

Engel, J. F., R. D. Blackwell, and P. W. Miniard, *Consumer Behavior*, The Dryden Press, Orlando FL, 1990.

Gupta, S., "HERMES Project WWW Consumer Survey," March 6, (1995), URL = http://www.umich.edu/~sgupta/hermes.html.

Gupta, S. and P. K. Chintagunta, "On Using Demographic Variables to Determine Segment Membership in Logit Mixture Models,""*Journal of Marketing Research*, 31, February, (1994) 128-136.

Hill, G. C., "Electronic 'Agents' Bring Virtual Shopping a Bit Closer to Reality," *Wall Street Journal*, September 9, (1995), A1.

Hoffman, D. and T. P. Novak, "Marketing in Computer Mediated Environments: Conceptual Foundations," (1994), URL = http://colette.ogsm.vanderbilt.edu.

Hoffman, D., T. P. Novak, and P. Chatterjee, "Commercial Scenarios for the Web: Opportunities and Challenges," *Project 2000*, August 7, (1995),
URL = http://www2000.ogsm.vanderbilt.edu/.

Kantor, A., "Making On-Line Service Work for You," *PC Magazine*, March 15, (1994), 111-158.

Knowles, A., "Software Tracks Web Demographics," *PC Week*, April 10, (1995), 94.

Kohli, A. K. and B. Jaworski, "Market Orientation: The Construct, Research Propositions and Managerial Implications," *Journal of Marketing*, 54, April, (1990), 1-18.

Lee, L., "Garment Scanner Could Be a Perfect Fit," *Wall Street Journal*, September 20, (1994), B1.

Lewis, P. H., "Internet for Profit," *Computer Shopper*, November, (1994), 178-192.

Marsh, B., "Peapod's On-Line Grocery Service Checks Out Success," *Wall Street Journal*, June 30, (1994), B2.

Miller, C., "Advertisers Face an Interactive Future," *Marketing News*, July 4, (1994), 10.

Miller, C., "Concern raised Over Privacy on Infohighway," *Marketing News*, January 2, (1995a), 1.

Miller, C., "Marketers Find It's Hip to Be on the Internet," *Marketing News*, February 27, (1995b), 2.

Murphy, P. E. and B. M. Enis, "Classifying Products Strategically," *Journal of Marketing*, 50/3, July, (1986), 24-42.

O'Connell, G., "A New Pitch: Advertising on the World-Wide Web is a Whole New Ball Game," *Internet*, May, (1995), 54-56.

O'Keefe, R., "Cybershopping: Virtual Catalogs, Malls and Markets," *.net*, June, (1995), 34-39.

Marketing News, "Personal Computers Supplement Existing Media: Survey," July 18, (1994), 5.

Pine, B. J. II, D. Peppers, and M. Rogers, "Do You Want to Keep Your Customers Forever?" *Harvard Business Review*, March/April, (1995), 103-114.

Rayport, J. F. and J. J. Sviokla, "Managing in the Marketspace," *Harvard Business Review*, November/December, (1994), 141-150.

Rechtin, M., "Selling Autos Online," *Advertising Age*, April 3, (1995), S32.

Reilly, P., "QVC Ads Tout Network Over Retailers," *Wall Street Journal*, October, (1993), B8.

Rickard, L., "Blossoming Opportunities," *Advertising Age*, July 18, (1994), 24.

Rigdon, J. E., "A Trusting Oracle to Enter Market Via Internet," *Wall Street Journal*, January 4, (1995), B1.

Sherman, S., "Will the Information Superhighway be the Death of Retailing," *Fortune*, April 18, (1994), 98-110.

Smith, T. K. and T. R. King, "Madison Avenue, Slow to Grasp Interactivity, Could Be Left Behind," *Wall Street Journal*, December 7, (1993), A1.

Solomon, B., "TV Shopping Comes of Age," *Management Review*, September, (1994), 22-26.

Spethmann, B., "Closer and Closer to the Crowd," *Superbrands*, October 17, (1994), 24-27.

Statistical Abstract of the United States, U.S. Bureau of the Census, 102nd/107th/112th Editions.

Strangeglove, M., "The Walls Come Down: Net Age Advertising Empowers Consumers," *Internet*, May, (1995), 40-44.

Verity, J. W. and R.D. Hof, "The Internet: How It Will Change the Way You Do Business,"
    Business Week, November 14, (1994), 80-88.
Wells, M., "Desperately Seeking the Superhighway," *Advertising Age*, August 15, (1994), 15.
Willmott, D., "The World-Wide Web: A Guided Tour of 100 Hot Sites," *PC Magazine*, April
    11, (1995), 3-42.
Zachary, G. P., "Advertisers Anticipate Interactive Media As Ingenious Means to Court Con-
    sumers," *Wall Street Journal*, August 17, (1994), B1.

CHAPTER 7
Product Marketing on the Internet

Chandrasekar Subramaniam[1], Michael J. Shaw[2], and David M. Gardner[3]

[1]Department of Business Administration, University of Illinois at Urbana-Champaign, Urbana, IL, USA, csubrama@uiuc.edu

[2]Department of Business Administration, and Beckman Institute for Advanced Science and Technology, University of Illinois at Urbana-Champaign, Urbana, IL, USA, m-shaw2@uiuc.edu

[3]Department of Business Administration, University of Illinois at Urbana-Champaign, Urbana, IL, USA, dmgardne@uiuc.edu

In this chapter, we discuss product marketing using the Internet, particularly the use of Internet for product promotion and new consumer processes. Internet advertising, virtual storefronts, and virtual communities are explained with examples and our views. We then present new consumer processes on the Internet and show how they enhance the fulfillment of the consumer purchase needs and also support interactive marketing. We discuss the challenges of measuring Web advertisements and close the chapter with a summary of our views on Internet and marketing.

Keywords: Product marketing; Product promotion; Web Advertisements; Virtual Communities; Increasing Returns; Consumer Processes; Interactive Marketing

1 Introduction

Marketing, whether to consumers or to business, has a well defined purpose in most organizations. That purpose is to create exchanges that satisfy consumer and organizational goals (AMA, 1985). As marketing strategy is constructed to address a particular product/market, two tasks must be performed by elements of the marketing mix: the communications task and the operating task (Park et al., 1987).

The communication task can be thought of as "information" primarily conveyed through promotion, price, the product label and package. This information is used to position the product in the market and to inform and/or persuade present or potential customers. The operating task "is to remove barriers to transactions or exchanges so that customers who perceive the product as being capable of satisfying their needs and preferences can engage in a transaction with minimum effort" (Park et al., 1987). These barriers center around a) product accessibility, b) product availability, c) owning/using the product, d) correct perception and recall, and e) differential utility. The operating task has traditionally been implemented so that the transaction is enhanced by having the right product or service at the right place at the right time with the right service and the customer can take possession. A marketer, to execute these communication and operating tasks, uses one or more channels.

In this chapter, we examine the emergence of a new channel, the Internet, particularly its impact on consumer marketing and how it affects some of the marketing tasks. We discuss two important aspects of consumer marketing that the Internet is capable of transforming; (1) the communication process, and (2) the consumer need fulfillment through new consumer processes. We start with explaining the marketing functions and the effect of Internet on these functions. In section 3, we discuss the Internet communication model and advertising on the Internet. This is followed by a discussion on the use of virtual store-front and virtual communities as marketing channels. Section 6 introduces the new consumer processes on the Internet and the implications for marketing. We close the chapter by looking at the challenges of measuring the marketing efforts on the Internet.

2 The Marketing Functions and the Internet

The domain of marketing will, with rare exceptions, include at a minimum the following functions. These are the activities that need to take place to create exchanges that satisfy consumer and organizational goals. While there is no universal agreement on the exact designation of these activities, there is general agreement on the following as necessary (Churchill et al., 1995).

1. *buying* - ensuring that enough units of product are available to meet consumer demand
2. *selling* - using advertising, personal selling, and sales promotion to match goods and services to customer needs
3. *transporting* - moving goods from point of production to a location convenient to customers
4. *storing* - warehousing products until needed for sale
5. *standardization and grading* - ensuring that products meet established quality- and quantity-control standards or size, weight, and other variables
6. *financing* - providing credit for customers
7. *risk taking* - assuming the uncertainties that result from developing and distributing goods and services customers may purchase in the future
8. *information gathering* - collecting information about customers, competitors, and resellers to use in making marketing decisions.

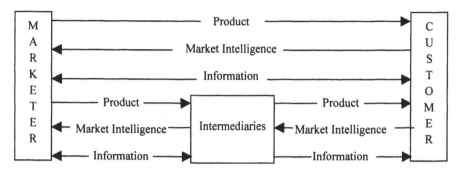

Fig. 1. Information and product flow between marketer and consumer

These functions are carried out by designing a marketing strategy to specifically target a customer segment. The strategy would combine in various ways the traditional elements of the marketing mix: price, product, promotion, distribution, service and customer sensitivity. The ultimate objective of all marketing efforts is to persuade the consumer to accept a product or service as the solution to her needs and then allow the consumer to take possession of the product or service.

The interactions between the marketer and the consumer thus involves the flow of products and information as shown by the simplified representation in Figure 1.

In the past, marketers have been, in most cases, constrained by the inadequacies of the traditional channels, particularly in the selling and information gathering functions. In figure 1, these are represented by the information flow and the market intelligence flow, both directly and through intermediaries. In this chapter, we show that the Internet has the potential to transform and enhance these flows, while having an impact on the material flow of certain categories of products like software and services like training. It is also our belief that the Internet does not change the ultimate objective of the marketer, but presents new opportunities to reach out more effectively to the consumer and to understand the consumer better.

One of the functions of the marketer is product promotion. Product promotion is defined as "the coordination of all seller-initiated efforts to set up channels of information and persuasion to facilitate the sale of a good or service, or the acceptance of an idea" (Cohen, 1988). And promotion includes, at a minimum, (1) advertising, (2) personal selling, (3) publicity, (4) sales promotion and (5) direct marketing. While serving as an additional media for promotion through advertising, the Internet allows marketers to use innovative channels such as virtual store-fronts and virtual communities. We start with an exploration of Internet advertising and follow it with a discussion on virtual store-fronts and virtual communities.

3 Internet Advertising

As the Internet was transformed in the 80s from a "research only network" to allow commercial activities, organizations realized that the sheer number of users connected to the network and the very low cost of reaching out to them, made the Internet an attractive medium for advertising. Almost all media planners now consider the Internet as a viable advertising vehicle and almost all marketers agree.

(IAB, 1997) cites the following reasons for considering the Internet in the media plan of the marketer.

1. Television audiences are migrating to the Internet and this trend is expected to continue. A Forrester Research Inc. (http://www.forrester.com) report in the summer of 1997 says that about 78% of PC users took time from television viewing to spend on computers.
2. The Internet is the fastest growing medium in history. The Web reached 50 million users in just four years, while it took the television 13 years and the radio 38 years to reach this milestone.
3. On-line advertisement revenues are expected to reach $9 billion by 2002.
4. The users of the Internet have the demographics which are a marketer's dream – young, well-educated, and earning high incomes.
5. The current younger generation, which is familiar with Internet technology, will be the future consumer generation, making the Internet an excellent communication medium.

Though most organizations are using the Web for advertising their products and services, the following categories are seen more on the Web.

1. Digital products: Products that can be delivered over the network like software packages and information packets.
2. Products where search costs can be reduced: Products such as cars and services such as travel, which require more information search prior to purchase.
3. Products with assured quality: Books and music CDs
4. Well known branded products: Visa credit cards
5. Products where time and location are crucial: Flowers

Surveys show that the profile of the Internet users is shifting towards that of average consumers. When this happens, the following product categories have the best potential for advertising over the Internet in the future:

1. Products where all related services can be brought together: Real estate, travel, hotel, medical and restaurant services
2. Products which can be customized by the consumer: Apparel, financial services, and software
3. Entertainment products: Movies and music on demand, events, leisure
4. Business-to-business marketing

Thus, the Internet is seen by marketers as a medium with very good potential as a promotional vehicle. In order to understand the characteristics of this new medium, we take up for discussion in the next section, the communication model of the Internet.

3.1 The Internet Communication Model.

The Internet can be viewed as a many-to-many communication medium, unlike the one-to-many model of the traditional mass media, as illustrated in Figure 2 (Hoffman et al., 1996). The model suggests that the primary relationship is between the consumer and the media on the one hand, and between the firm and the media on the other. Hence, the media becomes a major factor in determining what the consumer sees and how she sees it. In this model, the media does not just transmit the message from the sender to the receiver, but allows the environments to be created and experienced (Steuer, 1992). Thus new forms of interactions emerge between the consumer and the Internet, and between the firm and the Internet. From the consumer's perspective, we can describe some of the interactions as below:

1. Consumer can gather information about products and services, communicate with other consumers and firms for related products and services, and sometimes complete transactions. As the Internet session is a self selected environment of the consumer, the promotion message will be more effective. Internet is also capable of providing an experiential environment to the consumer through virtual reality interfaces thus allowing the consumer to experience some of the features of products before making the purchase decision.
2. Consumer can provide feedback content about the product, to the firm and to other consumers. A positive feedback becomes a good promotion for the marketer. A shrewd marketer can even exploit a negative feedback by solving the consumer's problem and showing the commitment of the organization to satisfying consumer needs.
3. Consumer can add "collective content" to the medium through discussion forums like the virtual communities. These discussion forums are rich sources of feedback about the organization and its products and should be closely monitored by the marketer to identify the needs of the consumers.

The Internet also provides capabilities to the firm to enhance the purchase process of the consumers and to understand the consumers better. Some of these interactions are:

1. Firm can interact with Internet for information, and knowledge about consumers and for communication with consumers, and other firms.
2. Firm can add content to the Internet by promoting its products or services on the online media.
3. Firm may provide "hyper-linked" content by bringing in links to other firms related to its product or service.

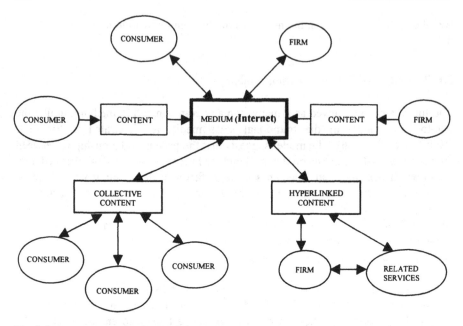

Fig. 2. Internet communication model

For example, a real estate firm may bring together other services like mortgage loans, schools, hospitals, shopping, entertainment and civic services, by providing hyperlinks in its Web page. Thus a consumer looking for real estate has access to all related information which is aggregated by one firm. Through the Internet, marketers can know much more about their consumers than through traditional channels. This knowledge about the consumers can be used to target the promotion messages for effective marketing.

3.2 Media Characteristics of the Internet

The Internet is unlike any other traditional media. The two-way communication capability and the information processing power of the connected computers makes the Internet an ideal medium for marketers to reach out and build interactive relationships with consumers on a global basis. The key characteristics of the Internet that aid in this process of relationship building are:

1. *Interactivity:* Internet is an interactive medium. The interface can be customized to continuously reflect the interests of the consumer and the appropriate choices offered by the firm. A consumer who sees an Internet advertisement can interact with the advertiser, seek more information, test the product and proceed to place order for the product. The consumer can also have access to the feedback of other consumers who had used the product, to make better informed decisions. Interactivity helps the marketer to establish a dialogue with each consumer.

2. *Rich and realistic experience:* Internet is a rich medium capable of text, image, audio and video content which can make the interaction experience of the consumer more engaging. With virtual reality, now beginning to be available on the Internet, experiential content like 3-dimensional viewing is also possible thus providing the most realistic experience to the consumer. Bandwidth is still a problem and currently limits this rich experience.

3. *Aggregation of services:* The Internet allows aggregation of different services, coordinated and hyper linked by the seller of the product or service. This gives the consumer access to all the necessary information to make a better purchase decision.

4. *Global access:* The Internet gives the firm a potentially global consumer base. But this feature could be a mixed blessing, as claims made on the Internet could now be challenged by virtually anyone from any corner of the globe. Marketers also need to be sensitive to the cultural and social characteristics of the target audience when trying to exploit the global accessibility of the Internet.

5. *Targetability:* Internet advertisers can focus on users from specific nations or geographical regions, computer platforms, as well as by time of day. Internet audience can be targeted based on demographics, psychographics (life-style characteristics) and technology demographics.

6. *Tracking:* Marketers can track how users interact with their brands and learn what is of interest to their customers.

7. *Deliverability and Flexibility:* Internet advertisement is delivered in real time 24 hours a day, and 7 days a week. Advertisements over the Internet can be launched, updated or canceled immediately. An advertiser can follow the progress of the response and make appropriate changes to the campaign.

Thus, unlike traditional media, the Internet is capable of providing an engaging experience for the consumer. Pine (1998) suggests that the future economy is experience economy, in which businesses must deliberately design and execute engaging experiences for their consumers. And, we feel that the Internet will emerge as the perfect vehicle to deliver this memorable experience. Having seen the media characteristics of the Internet, let us now discuss the different types of Internet advertisements.

3.3 Types of Internet Advertisements

An Internet advertisement is typically placed on the Web page of a Web site. Novak et al. (1996) classify Web advertisement sites into three major categories: (1) sponsored content site such as Hotwired and ZD Net, (2) sponsored search agents and directories such as Yahoo!, Excite and InfoSeek, and (3) entry portal sites such as Netscape and Microsoft. In 1996, the above three categories had 55%, 36% and 19% respectively of the total Web advertisements (Jupiter, 1996). From the advertiser's point of view, AOL is currently a very attractive Web site because of its very high membership. Increasingly, the Web pages of search engines and entry portals are becoming very popular Web advertisement spots. Web advertisements can be grouped into two major classes – the pull advertisements and the push advertisements which are discussed in the following sections.

3.3.1 Pull Advertisements

The pull advertisements are those which appear on Web pages selected by the Web user. While navigating a Web session, the user chooses the action to be taken on any advertisement that is displayed. Thus a user can choose to interact with the advertisement, click on the advertisement for further information or just ignore the advertisement. Following are some of the popular pull advertisements.

Banners

Banner ads are small, usually rectangular boxes that appear near the top of the Web pages (Figure 3). The messages are like the roadside billboards, but animated and interactive. Banner ads are primarily used for off-the-shelf products. Some banners, called "virtual tags", present offers to users and allow them to complete the buying process without having to leave the site of the publisher (Zeff et al., 1997).

Fig. 3. A banner advertisement

A modification of this allows users to play games in the banner area without forcing the user to change from the current Web site. An example of this was the AT&T's Olympic promotion advertisement. Banners are currently the most popular form of Web advertisement.

Buttons

Button ads are smaller than banner ads and are usually at the bottom of a Web page (Figure 4). Buttons contain only the name of a company or a brand. Clicking on the button takes the Web visitor to the corporate Web site of the company or brand. Buttons initially were from software companies and allowed Web users to freely download software by just clicking on the button. A popular button in this category is that of Netscape, the "Netscape Now" button. Buttons are simple and have been a great success in leading users to software developers' products. Buttons can be used to build brand awareness because of their constant presence on the Web pages (Zeff et al., 1997).

Fig. 4. Button advertisements

Advertorial

Advertorial is Web advertising designed to blend with the editorial content of the Web page publisher (Zeff et al., 1997). For example, the advertisement of the on-line bookstore, Amazon (http://www.amazon.com), appears on the review pages of Word (http://www.word.com). This is intended to attract the attention of the readers of the review if they prefer to order the reviewed book.

Keyword Ads

Advertisers can link a specific ad to a text or subject matter that is searched by a visitor. These ads are primarily found on Web search-engine sites. For example, the advertisement shown in Figure 5 is displayed when a search on keyword "college" is done on Yahoo!

A brighter future...

COMMUNITY COLLEGE DISTANCE LEARNING NETWORK

Fig. 5. Keyword search advertisement on Yahoo!

Interstitials

These ads are like television ads with video and audio. When users click on a specific topic at a site, a separate window pops up with the advertisement related to that topic. For example, clicking on "nutrition" at the health site Phys.com of Conde Nast, pops up an animated ad for Sunny Delight drink of Procter & Gamble. However, since consumer expectations are ill-formed with respect to intrusive advertisements, organizations should exercise caution while using this form.

Destination Sites

These ads create a new channel by using information and entertainment values to pull users in and bring them back again. For example, Metlife Insurance Company provides advice on parenting as well as various insurance products at its destination site (http://www.metlife.com).

3.3.2 Push Advertisements

There is now a new way of delivering information to the Web user using push technology. Push technology allows publishers to broadcast to the user (push) rather than wait for the user to initiate the session. This is also called Webcasting. A popular push vehicle is the e-mail, which is used to send promotional information to a list of users appearing on an address list. Since e-mail is text based, it's use as a promotional material is limited. Further, context, relevance and clutter will determine consumer reactions to unsolicited messages.

Now we have push systems that enable a Web user to sign up and receive broadcasts of news and information on her/his computer. These channels serve as new vehicles to carry Web advertisements. As the user provides personal information to subscribe to the push services, marketers can use the personal profile of the user to target advertisements.

PointCast (http://www.pointcast.com) is one such push service which delivers the updated news and information as screensaver. BackWeb (http://www.backweb.com) is another push service, and uses the network idle time for updating and delivering through a flash, running titles or as a screensaver.

Advertising, though popular, is not the only promotion strategy on the Internet. Organizations are building online store-fronts, also called the virtual store-fronts, to promote as well as sell the products on the Internet. In the following section, we will discuss the characteristics and the potential of virtual store-fronts for product promotion.

4 Virtual Store-front

A store is not just a place for commerce, but an appealing social environment experienced by the consumer. People like to walk by brilliantly lit display windows with artfully decorated product displays. Usually there is no immediate pressure to purchase, but just the curiosity to see and know about products. But recent surveys show that consumers may be spending less time visiting shops to learn about products. Catalogs are convenient, but in most cases, it may require a visit to the actual stores. This is where a virtual store-front comes in. With a few clicks of the mouse, an Internet user can visit a virtual store, find all that she needs about any product and make the purchase online.

4.1 Virtual Store-front Services

A virtual store-front is an online stores accessed through the Web or other online services. A virtual store has the potential to deliver both convenience and economy, the two major consumer benefits that have driven new retail formats (Burke, 1998). A typical store-front provides several services which can be categorized as follows:

1. *Product Display:* This service is provided by almost all the online stores. The products are categorized for convenience. For example, Peapod (http://www.pea pod.com) categorized the groceries as Deli, Bakeshop, Diary, General Groceries, etc. Each category may provide some sub categories. To be effective, the product display in an online store should be user-friendly for easy navigation and should be interesting to retain the attention of the consumer.

2. *Catalog Services:* The online catalog services provide a detailed booklet of products offered by well known catalog retailers and allow consumers to browse or order for the free catalog. Electronic catalogs are interactive and can be programmed to learn a consumer's preferences and provide a personalized catalog. Further, product demonstrations and manufacturer's responses to consumer's queries can be built into the catalogs to make them more effective.

3. *Search Engines:* The search service is a more advanced service offered on a virtual shop-front. This allows an online consumer to search for specific information related to the products or her needs. These services help consumers in their purchase decisions, but are more relevant for information intensive and customized products like insurance, financial services and travel. Travel agencies have long provided services to search for the best deal for a consumer travelling from one place to another. As more and more consumers demand products or services customized to their needs, search engines will be an integral part of all virtual stores.

4. *Transactions:* Transaction capability provides the most advanced of the services offered by online stores. This includes fulfillment and logistics services, and the mechanism for secure payment mechanisms. Though not many online stores have transaction services currently, we expect all stores to offer this facility soon as a convenient way for a consumer to fulfill the purchase needs.

5. *Customization:* This service allows consumers to tailor the product to their needs and tastes. Dell Computers (http://www.dell.com) provides one of the best examples of the customization capabilities available on the online stores. Here a consumer can build a computer online by choosing the processor, memory, disk storage and other accessories instead of just selecting one of the several computers already available for sale. Customization will be very relevant for services like financial products, insurance, clothing, travel and entertainment where the preferences of the consumers are varied and cannot be easily aggregated.

Online store such as Peopod and Amazon.com provide product display, search and transaction services. Other stores such as LL Bean (http://www.llbean.com) and Sears (http://www.sears.com) provide catalogs, product displays, and transactions. Dell provides product information, transaction and customization services in its online stores.

4.2 Promotion Strategies in a Virtual Store-front

A virtual store-front represents the product display window of an online stores. It can be considered an extension of online advertisements, in which the advertiser offers to provide all details of the products on display and to complete the purchase transactions, if needed. Some of the advantages of the online shelf space are:

1. Interactivity
2. Unlimited shelf space
3. 24 hour accessibility
4. Selector and aggregator of consumers
5. Potentially global audience

Marketers can follow a combination of the following strategies for promoting their products on virtual store-fronts.

1. Promotion through online product catalogs.
2. Exclusive advertising rights whenever specific products are accessed on other online store-fronts. For example, a snack food maker can have a banner for his brand of potato chips to appear whenever the snacks food category is accessed from an online grocery stores.
3. Advertising through banners or buttons on the free space of other online stores.
4. Providing hyperlinks to product sites from the results of the online store's search engines.
5. Creating own store-front with a combination of the services mentioned in section 4.1.

The real benefit of virtual stores to marketers is the ability to exploit the interactive capabilities of the Internet. Virtual store-front displays can be customized according to the preferences of the online shopper, thus providing a personal shopping experience for each shopper. As the marketer learns more about the consumer through the online interactions, a closer relationship can be established with the consumer, offering to fulfill more of the consumer needs, and strengthening the relationship further.

Internet advertising and virtual store-fronts are ways of exploiting the richness and interactivity of the new medium. Now, the Internet gives the marketers a new promotion tool in the form of virtual communities. Marketers are building virtual communities as a deliberate strategy to build a long-lasting and beneficial relationship with their consumers. In the following section we will take up for discussion the dynamics of these virtual communities and how they can be used as an innovative promotion channel.

5 Virtual Communities

A virtual community (or on-line community) is a group of Internet users who share a specific area of interest. The members of virtual communities exchange freely their ideas, experience and other information related to the specific topics of interest discussed in the community. The usual modes of exchange are discussion forums on specific topics, bulletin boards and chats. In the discussion forums, the community organizer provides the topics for discussion and members comment on the topic or ask questions to be answered by other members. Thus, members of the virtual community for cancer patients discuss and exchange their feelings, and how they are coping with the tragic disease. Members of the on-line bookstore Amazon.com ("Amazon.com Community") post their own reviews and are even offered prizes for the best book recommendation.

Virtual communities leverage the capabilities of the network to connect people with each other and to fulfill their specific needs for communication, information, and entertainment (Hagel et al., 1997). In fact, the very impersonal nature of the computers could have been a major reason for people to seek out companions in cyber space and at the same time use the capabilities of information collection of the computer. Though online services and private networks are all potential platforms for building virtual communities, the Web is by far the most popular place for these communities.

5.1 Characteristics of Virtual Communities

The virtual community is primarily a forum for members to freely exchange information, but it also provides commercial benefits to the members and the sponsors. It is important for the sponsor and other participating vendors to understand the characteristics of virtual communities to effectively exploit the potential of these communities. Some of the characteristics are described below:

Collective Knowledge

A virtual community represents the collective knowledge and information available to the members in the particular subject of charter of the community. Virtual community educates its members as well as allows exchange of views and ideas among members. Over time, the virtual community will emerge as the most authoritative and influential source of knowledge about the products and services related to the area of the community. For example, SeniorNet (http://www.seniornet.org) is a virtual community of senior citizens who would like to enhance their lives and share their knowledge and wisdom. This community may probably be the best source for information about "Retirement options", "Old Age Health Issues" and "Veterans". Citibank Channel, a virtual community sponsored by Citibank (http://www.citibank.com) may be one of the best sources to know about various financial products and services.

Economics of Increasing Returns

Virtual communities have economics of increasing returns, with a pattern of low revenues during the initial period, gradually increasing revenues as membership builds up and a sharp acceleration of revenues beyond a threshold level called the "critical mass" (Hagel et al., 1997). Though the initial investments are likely to be made in an environment of uncertainty and risk, as the membership builds and the credibility of the community gets established, the commercial benefits to be reaped are very attractive. Virtual communities display increasing returns due to marginal cost effect, learning curve effect and network externalities effect.

1. *Marginal Cost Effect*: An initial investment is needed to start the virtual community. Usually, this investment is for Web site development and allocation of site management resources. With each additional membership, the cost of adding and servicing the new member decreases. The cost of setting up additional communities also gets reduced as assets and other resources are shared. This effectively increases the returns from each additional member. The reduction in costs and the increase in revenues become significant beyond a threshold membership level.

2. *Learning Curve Effect:* The learning curve benefits start accruing when more members are added and the sponsor gains experience in maintaining the virtual community. The learning also reduces the cost of building additional communities, whereas the benefits increase.

3. *Network Externalities Effect:* In a network, or any group activity, the more units are aggregated and connected, the more valuable each additional unit becomes. Thus if there are n members in a community, a new member increases the interactions in the community by n, as each member can now interact with the new member. Thus the potential for creation of knowledge content increases proportional to the current size of the community. Further, each new member brings value to the community by

(a) having access to a larger knowledge base to generate content, and

(b) providing content to benefit a larger base of members, thus generating more content from their feedback.

5.2 Building Virtual Communities

Communities are built around what people care about. For example, Seniornet is built around the needs of senior citizens to live a quality life. Hagel et al. (1997) propose a four step process for building and nurturing virtual communities. Figure 6 presents the idea, but reflects our perception of it as a continuous process.

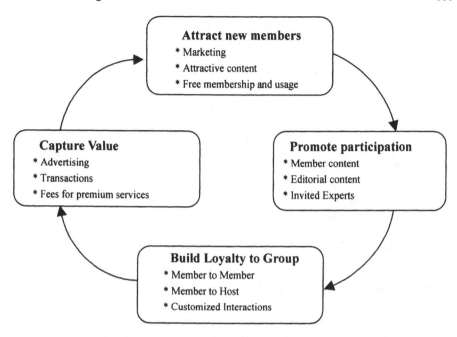

Fig. 6. Building virtual communities

Attract: The first step in this process is to attract visitors and encourage them to join the virtual community. Firms expanding into virtual communities from their primary lines of businesses, like Citibank, use their home pages and attract their primary users to register as members of the virtual communities. Exclusive virtual community organizers like SeniorNet set up sites and attract members by advertisements in Web or traditional media. Once people visit the site, they have to be provided incentives to register, like attractive discussion forums, free usage schemes and other incentives like Internet gifts. Members can be attracted by exploiting the capabilities of the Internet to provide a superior participating experience. For example, virtual reality can be used to give a member a sense of seeing and talking to other members of the community.

Promote: Once members have registered, the next step is to encourage the members to participate. As more and more members participate, the community can attract new members, accelerating its growth. The organizer may initiate discussions on interesting topics. For example, in SeniorNet, one way of encouraging participation is for the organizer to initiate a discussion on "After retirement options". As more members participate and provide feedback and suggestions for topics, new forums can be created. Inviting experts to discuss a topic of interest is another way to attract member participation.

Build: As members of a virtual community exchange ideas and information through the discussion forums, they are likely to develop loyalty to the community. The information available from the community becomes a major influencing factor in many of their decisions including purchase decisions. It is also possible for members to be loyal to the community and not to the organizer. In other words, members may not take the messages of the organizer as seriously as that of fellow members. It is important for the host to develop a relationship with the members by offering them helpful information and incentives and make each member feel special. The personal information provided by each member can be used to customize the environment for the member.

Capture: When the community has attained a critical mass in terms of the numbers and content aggregation, the host can offer the virtual community space for targeted advertising. For example, the Toyota forum on skiing can be offered advertising space for skiing equipment vendors. In addition, the host can sell products or services online to the members of the virtual community. For example, Citibank can promote and sell its financial products over its virtual community forums. Hosts can also capture value by charging a fee from members for premium services such as notification services.

5.3 Benefits of Virtual Communities

Though virtual communities are set up to provide a forum for communication among consumers, the very nature of these communities offers excellent commercial opportunities to the sponsor as well as other vendors who choose to participate in these communities.

Some of the benefits to consumer members are:
1. Ability to identify and interact with other members of similar interests without constraints of time and space and reduced search costs;
2. Access to a broad range of information about a product or service, including information from competing vendors, and thus better purchase decisions;
3. Economic benefits like special price, customized offers and better service; and
4. Being part of a powerful bargaining group that can influence important marketing decisions.

The benefits to sponsor organization are:
1. Aggregation of consumers, leading to reduced search costs and better targeting of products and services;
2. Building a positive frame of mind, in the member, towards the sponsor through content and editorial surrounding.
3. Community loyalty of members, which can be exploited to sell a range of products and services;
4. Disintermediation possibility because of direct contact with consumers; and
5. Global reach at much lower costs.

The benefits to vendors who participate in the virtual community are:

1. Target group with well known demographics and interests;
2. Effective response rate to any promotion efforts;
3. Reduced search cost of target customers; and
4. Global reach at much lower costs.

5.4 Product Promotion on Virtual Communities

Virtual communities present an excellent opportunity for marketers to exploit the "network externalities' effect. The key to promotion on the virtual community is the critical mass of members that can be reached. Marketers start by building a loyal constituency of consumers through advertisement on discussion forums, sponsorship of discussions, providing links to experts in specific areas for free consultation, and use of knowledge from other forums to honestly counsel community members. The well defined nature of the community then helps the product promoters to better target their messages.

Marketers may also open discussion forums to specifically attract new members with the profile of interest. For example, Toyota (http://www.toyota.com) sponsors a discussion forum on "Gardening" in its virtual community of car users. Through this forum, Toyota is probably hoping to attract members who are interested in gardening, and fit the profile suited to sell its "Family Vans". Related discussion forums are ways to increase the breadth of the discussion and thus attract members who may not be currently interested in the products, but may have the profile to be buyers in the future.

The real benefits of the Internet will be exploited when marketers use the interactive capabilities of the new medium and build a personal community environment for the consumer member, understand each consumer as an individual in addressing promotional messages, provide all related services at a single point, and make the virtual community a truly worthwhile place for the consumer to visit.

The Internet may have its greatest impact on the operating task of the marketing function and remove barriers to exchanges by fundamentally transforming the consumer need fulfillment process. In the following section, we will discuss how Internet changes these marketer-to-consumer relationships and its effects on interactive marketing.

6 Internet and New Consumer Processes

A consumer process is a collection of tasks or steps that a consumer goes through to achieve a goal, usually the satisfaction of a need. For example, the consumer process of buying a home may include visiting real estate agents, driving around neighborhood, obtaining a mortgage and homeowners insurance, and getting inspections. Most of the consumers, particularly those in a high involvement purchase, undergo a level of stress in this process as they engage in the tasks of information gathering, analysis, negotiations, purchase and post-puchase consumption or use. While under-going the purchase process, these consumers typically experience the following needs (Champy, 1997).

1. *Knowledge:* Having access to specialized information and feedback about the product or service.
2. *Interaction:* Fulfilling the need to communicate with the provider of goods or services.
3. *Networking:* Connecting to and interacting with other consumers with similar consumption needs or experiences.
4. *Sensory experiences:* Using sensory input such as sight and sound to arrive at a purchase decision.
5. *Ubiquity:* Having all that the consumer needs at the time and place of consumer's convenience (rather than at the provider's convenience)
6. *Aggregation:* Bringing together a number of related and required services at a convenient location.
7. *Customization:* Tailoring products to consumer's needs rather than adjusting needs to available product ranges.

In a traditional consumer process, a complex set of interactions are initiated among the consumer, the seller and the providers of services required to complete the purchase process. Depending on the time and other constraints, a few of the above needs are sacrificed by the consumer in order to complete the purchase process. Thus the consumer feels a lack of control over the purchase process, leading to post purchase dissonance. Marketers have long tried to reduce the stress level of consumers in the purchase process, particularly the high involvement purchases, by establishing communication links with the consumers and helping them have access to all information about the product and related services. The constraints of the traditional media stood in the way of achieving this objective fully. Now the marketer has the Internet to achieve this objective and build a trustful relationship with the consumer.

For example, let us suppose a consumer who wants to purchase a home. Using the Internet, the consumer can search for the real estate companies and visit their Web sites for detailed information. Using the search engines built in the real estate Web sites, the consumer looks for a home in a specified locality and a specified price range. The Web site can also allow her to design the features of her home according to her tastes and cost constraints. The interactive capability of the Internet can be used to make this session educative and informative, and can lead to the final design selected by the consumer to match her preferences and her financial capability. Using virtual reality, she can take a virtual tour of the neighborhood, using the computer keyboard to drive as she would in her car. This gives the consumer an experience of how living in that locality will be. She can then link to a bank's Web site for arranging a loan, an insurance agent's Web site to purchase insurance and to the utilities Web site. Thus, through the Internet, the consumer is actually able to complete the purchase process fulfilling all her needs satisfactorily.

The Internet interface, at the heart of the new process, provides the natural, user-friendly and platform independent environment for the consumer to enhance the purchase experience. Currently the Web browsers represent this interface, but we feel the interface will evolve independent of the browser, reflecting the demands of the new consumer processes. More functionality will be added to make the interface serve as a single window of interaction between the consumer and the marketer. Some of the functions that we expect the Internet interface to serve are:

1. *Communication interface* – to connect to other consumers on the Internet, to exchange ideas and information, and to communicate with business organizations and government agencies.
2. *Virtual Shopping interface* – to complete most of the shopping requirements on-line.
3. *Personal Management interface* – to obtain personal services like legal, medical financial, and career services, and to manage personal information.
4. *Education and Entertainment interface* – to satisfy all education and entertainment requirements like training, games, movies, music, etc.

The Internet interface and the new consumer processes benefit the consumer and provide excellent opportunities for the marketer to serve the consumers. To the consumer, some of the benefits provided by the new processes are as follows:
1. Access to all necessary information and feedback to make an informed and less stressful decision.
2. Access to all related services for completing the purchase process through a single interface.
3. Communication with fellow consumers for education and knowledge about products and services.
4. Sensory experience, through virtual reality, to feel the product without having to access the physical product.
5. Customization capability to tailor the product or service to suit individual's needs and preferences.

To the marketer, the opportunities created through the Internet interface are as follows:
1. Bring together providers of related services on a single interface so that the likelihood of purchase is increased.
2. Create a rich and realistic virtual environment for the consumer to experience and evaluate the product.
3. Build the loyalty and trust of the consumer so that the marketer is seen as an influential guide or counsellor in fulfilling the consumer needs.
4. Form on-line support groups, like virtual communities, that act as opinion builders for the products or services offered by the marketer.

6.1 Internet Interface and Virtual Reality

To the consumer, the entire purchase and fulfillment process is an experience. Marketers can make it memorable for the consumer by providing a personal and realistic experience in which to undergo the process. Virtual reality is one of the important technologies that has the capability to provide this rich experience to the consumer. Virtual shops equipped with virtual reality can enable consumers to "walk through virtual shopping aisles, examine and use the virtual product, and talk to virtual salespeople".

Virtual reality is currently available through the now widely accepted standard called VRML (Virtual Reality Markup Language). This standard is supported by both Netscape and Microsoft Internet browsers and provides 3-dimensional visualization on the Internet. More sensory capabilities are expected to be added in the future enabling the Internet to provide the full potential of virtual reality.

For the marketer, virtual reality is useful to design more effective Internet promotion campaigns as the product features can be presented more realistically. Consumers can have a better feel for the product and experience the effects of the product features. Virtual reality can also be used to educate and possibly train a consumer about how to use a product in order to experience the full potential of the product. An educated and knowledgeable consumer will be in a better position to appreciate the product features and thus will have a positive experience when using the product. This will invariably lead to favorable feedback from the consumer for the product.

6.2 Internet and Interactive Marketing

Interactive marketing is defined as the "process of being able to deal with customers by creating individual relationship, managing market size of one and addressing each in terms of its stage of development" (Blattberg et al., 1991). It has always been the dream of marketers to be able to establish a dialogue with each consumer and position the organization to serve the needs of the consumer. For effective relationship building, marketers have looked to several methods of collecting feedback about consumers and their buying habits. Most of these approaches have been indirect, expensive and rarely available at the level of individual consumer. Now, the Internet interface is capable of providing the marketer with just that kind of information useful in addressing each consumer personally in a most effective and inexpensive way.

6.2.1 Understanding the Consumer

The Internet provides various ways to collect information about consumers in order to know them better. Consumers frequently fill out forms on the Web to have access to Web site services. Further, during their on-line shopping, they provide several inputs regarding the products, quantities, and other preferences which can be captured and stored by the interface in files like the "cookies" and "session logs". These details can be used by the marketer to tailor the promotion message or product offering to the needs of the particular consumer. For example, a consumer who has recently asked for maternity benefits to be added to her health insurance, can be provided specific promotion and offers related to pre-natal care. In addition, the details of her location and family can be used to give her a specific deal at a nearby store. This consumer information can be constantly tracked to offer the benefits related to baby care in future.

As standards of consumer data capture and code of ethics are developed and accepted, personal details of the consumer and her purchase habits can be used by the marketer to benefit both the consumer and the business.

6.2.2 Data Mining for Understanding the Consumer

The large volume of data spread over the Web makes it a difficult job for the marketer to collect the data and extract information using traditional analysis tools. Data mining tools offer effective ways to search and extract useful patterns from these huge mass of Web data. *Data mining* is a non trivial process of searching and analyzing data in order to find implicit, but potentially useful, information (Frawley et al., 1992). It is a process of searching large databases using techniques like statistical analysis, visualization, decision trees, and neural networks to explore large amounts of data and discover interesting patterns that shed light on business problems.

Data mining on the Web is still at its infancy. As more understanding is gained about the structure of the data captured over the Web, we expect that specific data mining tools will be offered to extract consumer information from Web data. Armed with this knowledge about the consumer, the marketer can use the information processing capability of the computer to engage the consumer in an interactive dialogue, thus building a one-to-one relationship with the consumer.

6.3 New Consumer Processes and Product Marketing

The fundamentals of product marketing strategy suggest that the marketer should always start with the consumer, then the product and finally the communication and the distribution. Unfortunately, many attempts at product marketing on the Internet start with the communication process. The Internet is a channel that facilitates the consumer need fulfillment by removing some barriers present in traditional channels. For example, through the Internet, the marketer provides to the consumer easier access to product information, aggregation of services, convenient ordering procedures and delivery of some category of products. But this facilitation comes after the marketer has identified the customer and the product. The Internet does not substitute the strategic tasks of deciding who the consumer is and what product satisfies the needs of the consumer.

One of the other concerns of product marketing over the Internet is the lack of understanding on the part of marketers of the consumer perception of an innovation like the Internet. Robertson (1967) classified consumer reaction to innovation into three categories depending on the perception of the consumer – continuous, dynamically continuous and discontinuous. A consumer who perceives an innovation as continuous, and thus requiring little change in the existing behavior, is more likely to adapt the innovation than if the required behavior change is significant. When marketers focus on technology alone, they tend to create a threatening environment for consumers and the absence of a perceived match between the consumer needs and the marketing efforts further alienates the consumer.

Without the Internet, most consumers had to gather information, process information and complete purchases by involving more than one channel. The Internet allows consumers to access information, process information, and complete the purchase process all through a single and integrated channel. What marketers need to do is to understand the role of Internet in the consumer process and develop their marketing strategy so as to exploit the capabilities of the Internet and enhance the consumer's need fulfillment process.

7 Measurement of Internet Advertising

The ultimate effectiveness of any marketing channel can be measured by the extent to which the channel influences a consumer to purchase a product or service. For example, the effectiveness of the Internet as a promotion channel can be judged by how well the intended message and persuasion have been perceived by the consumer, as reflected in the consumer's response. The Web, as a marketing channel on the Internet, needs measures of advertising effectiveness in order to help managers plan their media investments. In fact, the successful Web sites all provide audience measurements, with many of the measurement data supported by third party sources (Fitzgerald, 1998).

Realizing the importance of audience measurement, research has recently turned towards development of new tools and methodologies to measure Web advertisements. Our focus in this section will be the discussion of some of the current measures, the challenges and the future trends in Web advertising measurement.

7.1 Web Advertising Measurement Terminology

The measurement typically used for traditional advertising is the cost of reaching an audience (cost per thousand, abbreviated as CPM), based on circulation for print media and projected viewing audience for television (Zeff et al., 1997). Being a new medium with new capabilities, the Web has spawned new measurement terms. We give below brief definitions of some of the popular terms used in Web advertising (Zeff et al., 1997; Novak et al., 1996).

Hit: A hit is a record of each time a file is requested from a server. If a Web page consists of eight graphics as well as text, nine hits would be recorded each time that Web page is requested.

Request: A request is a connection to an Internet site that successfully retrieves content.

Visit: A visit is a series of requests made by one user during a specified time period. If a user stops making request for a given period of time, the next request is counted as another visit.

Unique visitor: A visitor who could be identified by information provided through a registration form or some other identification system.

Exposure: It is the number of times a visitor to a site is exposed to a particular advertisement. An exposure is counted each time an advertisement is delivered by a Web server.

Reach: This is the total number of unique visitors exposed to a Web advertisement.

Click-through: This is a count of the mouse-clicks on a "hot-linked" advertisement such as a banner or button. This is also called as the "Page Information Requests".

7.2 Challenges in Web Advertisement Measurement

A number of Web sites use "hits" to indicate their popularity. Hits are not always valid measures of Web traffic as they are inherently non-comparable across Web sites (Novak et al., 1996). A request gives a more conservative estimate as it reflects only those requests satisfied by the server. 86% of Web publishers use CPM as the basis for Web advertisement pricing (IAB, 1997). Though exposure gives an estimate of the number of times the advertisement was shown to the consumer, it does not reflect the consumer controlled environment of the Web unlike traditional broadcast media like the television. Click-through measures the actual exposure and activation of an advertisement content by a consumer. But, Web publishers argue that click-through is not under publisher's control and depends on the creative nature of the advertisement. Some researchers point to the use of reach and frequency estimates if the goal is to engage in "brand building" (Leckenby, 1998). The complexity of the Internet and the innovative Web advertising models, like advertorials, add to the difficulty in measuring consumer response to Web advertisements.

Web advertisement viewership is also determined through ratings, i.e. the number of Web users exposed to a particular advertising site or advertisement. Ratings are done by Web rating companies like Media Metrix, Net Ratings, Relevant Knowledge and Nielsen Media Research. Lack of standard measures result in different media rating companies producing conflicting results. For example, the lists of the top 25 Web sites put together by Relevant Knowledge and Media Metrix shared only 19 names (Ratings, 1998), and even the shared names were not in the same order. A standard methodology is essential to understand the effectiveness of the Web and exploit its full potential. Some scholars recommend a set of metrics developed from considering the Web as a unique hybrid of direct response and traditional communication medium. We feel that some of the challenges to be addressed in Web advertisement measurement are:

1. Standardization of Web traffic measurement terminology;
2. Development of new models to understand and measure consumer response to interactive advertisements; and
3. Using resident programs like "cookies" or "session logs" to capture useful consumer information without duplicating the data and without violating consumer privacy rights.

7.3 Future Trends in Web Advertisement Measurement

Recently the Internet Advertising Bureau (IAB) and Digital Marketing Group (DMG) were reported to be close to agreeing common measurement standards for Internet advertising on an international level (Beyaztas, 1998). The agreement is backed by the Incorporated Society of British Advertisers and the Institute of Practitioners in Advertising. The standards are expected to create a common global language for buyers and sellers of Web advertising and thus go a long way in removing the current confusion. Third party auditors are also coming on the scene to verify and possibly certify Web advertisement statistics released by Web site publishers. Non-profit organizations and research institutions also have begun to contribute more to the measurement of Web traffic and Web consumers' online habits. It will require all players to come together to evolve standard measurement and reporting techniques, and to develop fully more credible Web advertisement measures as every one of them have a significant interest in realizing the full potential of the Web.

8 Summary and Discussion

In this chapter, we examined the capabilities of the Internet as a marketing channel and how this new channel can be exploited by marketers to effectively reach their message to the consumer. We also saw new consumer processes supported by the Internet and the challenges of measuring the effectiveness of this new channel.

The ultimate objective of all marketing efforts is to allow the consumer to take possession of the product or service that satisfies her/his needs. This includes the process of informing, persuading and removing all barriers for the consumer to possess the product or service. The Internet does not alter this ultimate objective. What the Internet does alter is the specific implementation of the various elements of the marketing mix directed toward the objective. While doing this, the Internet, as a computing network and an interactive two-way communication channel, provides marketers with new capabilities not available in traditional channels. These capabilities allow the marketers to (1) understand their consumers better, (2) communicate their message to the consumers more effectively, and (3) provide new services in fulfilling the needs of the consumers.

Having said this, it is to be noted that most organizations are still not clear of the impact of Internet strategies on their bottom line. As the organizations struggle with the changing consumer preferences, new technology, and the inadequacies of the traditional channels in achieving their objectives, the introduction of the Internet as a potential channel has created both excitement and anxiety among the marketers. For instance, the projected Web advertisement revenues of $9 billion by 2002 represents a tiny fraction of the overall advertisement revenues. A top executive of a leading consumer organization says that "the Web has the potential to be a dramatically more effective way for us to communicate with the people who buy and use our products" (Mand, 1998). While the same executive is concerned that the current state of the Web is not effective enough to really deliver the persuasive brand sell of other media, he also thinks that the eventual use of the Internet as an advertising medium is inevitable.

Brand building over the Internet is another area of concern for the marketers. While marketers like to capitalize on the reach and interactivity of the Internet to build online brands, the strategies that work in traditional media do not work so well on the Internet (Neuborne, 1998). According to a recent survey, banners, based on the billboard concept and the most popular Web advertising model used by market-ers, are "looked at" by only 9.1% of online users (Maddox, 1998). But marketers also know that there is enormous potential on the Internet, with the current genera-tion, which is comfortable with the technology, growing into the consumer genera-tion. Brand building efforts for this generation may have to consider, among other issues, consumer participation in the marketing efforts and replacement of the per-ception driven advertising models with experience driven interactive models. Also the Internet may be used with other marketing channels to build information flow and synergy among the product marketing efforts.

We can categorize the barriers to significant exploitation of the Internet as a mar-keting channel as follows:

1. Limitations of the Internet in its current state such as limited bandwidth, server capabilities and communication interface standards;
2. Lack of measurement standards that can give confidence to the marketers to shift to Internet; and
3. Absence of new business models that go beyond banner advertisement on the Web.

The communication capabilities of the Internet are being addressed by many gov-ernment, research and corporate agencies. The measurement issues are also expected to be addressed and standards established to enable marketers to evaluate the bene-fits of the new media. But, only a few organizations have shown the willingness to develop new business models for the Internet and even here most of the efforts have been in digital products such as software and services. We feel that marketers, while realizing that the Internet does not change their basic objective of serving the consumers, should evaluate their traditional consumer models and find new ways to establish a closer relationship with their consumers. We attempt to provide a framework to understand some of the ways in which the Internet can serve as a marketing channel. But, much more issues have to be addressed to develop and use new Internet marketing models as electronic commerce continues to advance and impact the marketing function.

9 Conclusion

The competitive advantage of any organization is derived from the long term relationship that it has built with its consumers. As consumers increasingly take control of their need fulfillment process, marketers should evaluate the value that they can add to this fulfillment process to benefit both the consumer and the organization. In this chapter, we show how the Internet can be used by marketers to build and manage this close relationship with their consumers.

References

AMA, American Marketing Association, *Marketing News*, March 1, (1985).

Batra, Rajeev, John G. Myers and A. David, *Advertising Management*, Prentice Hall, Inc., (1996).

Beyaztas, Binnur, "Industry measures up", *Marketing*, May 14, (1998), 13.

Blattberg, Robert C. and John Deighton, "Interactive Marketing: Exploiting the Age of Addressability," *Sloan Management Review*, Fall, (1991), 5-14.

Burke, Raymond R, "Real Shopping in a Virtual Store," *Sense and Respond*, Harvard Business School Press, (1998), Chapter 11, 245-260.

Champy, James, Robert Buday, and Nitin Nohria, "The rise of the Electronic Community," URL=http://techWeb.cmp.com/if/583/csc.htm, (1997).

Churchill , Gilbert A. and J. Paul Peter, *Marketing: Creating Value for Customers*, Richard Irwin, Homewood, (1995),15.

Cohen, Dorothy, *Advertising*, Scott, Foreman and Company, (1988).

Definitions, "Report of the Definitions Committee," *Journal of Marketing*, 13, 2, (1948).

Ducoffe, Robert H, "Advertising Value and Advertising on the Web," *Journal of Advertising Research*, September/October, (1996), 21-35.

Fitzgerald, Mark, "Measuring Web Site Traffic," *Editor & Publisher,*131, 7, (1998), 51.

Frawley, W.J., G. Piatetsky-Shapiro, and C.J. Matheus, "Knowledge Discovery in Databases: An Overview," *AI Magazine*, 13, 3, (1992), 57-70.

Graphic, Visualization & Usability Center, Georgia Institute of Technology, URL=http://www.gvu.gatech.edu/.

Hagel, John III and Arthur G. Armstrong, *Netgain*, Harvard Business School Press, (1997).

Hoffman, Donna L. and Thomas P. Novak, "Marketing in Hypermedia Computer-Mediated Environments: Conceptual Foundations," *Journal of Marketing*, 60, (1996), 50-68.

IAB, Internet Advertising Bureau, "Why Internet Advertising: The case for including the Internet in your media plan," *Media Week*, May 5, (1997), 9-10.

Jupiter Communication, "Web Ad Revenues Jump 83 Percent in Second Quarter," Press Release, URL = http://www.jup.com/jupiter/release/sept96/93adspend/, September 3, (1996).

Leckenby, John D. and Jongpil Hong, "Using Reach/Frequency for Web Media Planning," *Journal of Advertising Research*, January/February, (1998), 7-20.

Maddox, Kate, "Survey shows increase in online usage, shopping", *Advertising Age*, October 26, (1998), S-34.

Mand, Adrienne, "P&G to Hold Marketer Confab About Online Ads," *Adweek*, May 11, (1998), 39.

Neuborne Ellen and Robert D. Hof, "Branding on the Net", *Business Week*, November 9, (1998), 76-86.

Novak, Thomas P. and Donna L. Hoffman, "New Metrics for New Media: Toward the Development of Web Measurement Standards," Draft, (1996),
URL = http://www2000.ogsm.vanderbilt.edu/novak/Web.standards/Webstand.html/.

Park, C.W. and Gerald Zaltman, *Marketing Management*, The Dryden Press, Chicago, (1987),13-14.

Pine, B. Joseph II and James H. Gilmore, "Welcome to the Experience Economy," *Harvard Business Review*, July-August, (1998), 97-105.

Ratings, "The New Ratings Game," *Business Week*, April 27, (1998), 73-75.

Robertson, Thomas S, "The Process of Innovation and the Diffusion of Innovation," *Journal of Marketing*, 31, (1967), 14-19.

Steuer, Jonathan, "Defining Virtual Reality: Dimensions Determining Telepresence," *Journal of Communication*, 42, (1992), 73-93.

Zeff , Robbin and Brad Aronson, *Advertising on the Internet*, John Wiley & Sons, Inc., (1997).

CHAPTER 8

Internet Involvement: Instrument Development, Measurement and Implications for Electronic Commerce

A. F. Salam[1], H.R. Rao[2], and C. C. Pegels[2]

[1]Computer Information Systems, College of Business and Public Administration, University of Louisville, Kentucky 40292, USA, amsala01@homer.louisville.edu

[2]Management Science and Systems, School of Management, State University of New York at Buffalo, Buffalo, New York 14260, USA,

mgmtrao@acsu.buffalo.edu; cpegels@acsu.buffalo.edu

The concept of involvement underlying human behavior has been found to be a crucial construct in various disciplines. For example, a greater understanding of this construct has allowed marketing and consumer behavior researchers to develop insights into consumer search processes and strategies, audience involvement in advertising (Greenwald and Leavitt, 1984), temporal context of product involvement (Richins and Bloch, 1986), and advertising effectiveness (Petty, Cacioppo and Schumann, 1983). Similarly, a better understanding of the Internet involvement can allow researchers and business managers to develop better insights about consumer behavior in the context of electronic commerce. This study draws upon existing theories on involvement in multiple disciplines such as consumer behavior, information systems and economic psychology and adapts existing instruments (validated in past research), to develop a measure of internet involvement. The developed instrument is then used to investigate consumers' distinct behaviors regarding electronic commerce. The study provides evidence that high and low involved consumers differ in terms of their behaviors regarding the Internet.

Keywords: Electronic Commerce; Consumer Behavior; Internet Involvement; Marketing; Measurement

1 Introduction

The Internet is now presenting itself as an alternate marketing and advertising medium for corporations to reach potential customers. The Internet allows marketers to target and communicate with highly involved and interested consumers both domestic and global (Mehta, 1995).

The traditional advertising -TV, radio, and print-always operated on the broadcast model. One important difference between Television (TV) advertising and Web advertising is the motivation or curiosity of the viewer to view the advertising. The

Web viewer is going to be more homogeneous than the television audience, and as a result Web advertising may be more effective per viewer exposed to it. In addition, on the Web, businesses can obtain a more accurate exposure count per viewer, and that is quite valuable in terms of customizing product offerings and pricing mixes to suit the needs of individuals rather than an entire segment.

According to Brueckner (1996: pp. 60) "Right now too much of the Web's appeal is novelty (flashy graphics, labored Shockwave and Java animations, Real Audio, digital video) and too much of the Web marketers' time is spent trying to mimic television. When the novelty wears off, as it inevitably will, where will the value reside?"

To understand what constitutes 'value' for the consumer in using the Internet from an electronic commerce perspective, it is essential to discern what constitutes consumer involvement with the Internet. The concept of involvement has played a significant role in explaining consumer behavior in the marketing literature as well as in developing and formulating marketing strategies and policies.

The objectives of this research are two fold: one to draw on the current state of knowledge about the Involvement construct in various related disciplines and adapt existing instruments to measure "Internet Involvement" and two, to apply this instrument to discern certain consumer behaviors regarding electronic commerce. The fundamental focus is whether the adapted instrument is able to discriminate among consumers in a way that provides guidelines as to whether the consumers will engage in electronic commerce. We believe this research can provide a foundation for further investigation into consumer behavior related to electronic commerce as Involvement is recognized as a crucial construct underlying many consumer behaviors in marketing and consumer research literature.

2 Literature Review

In this section, we review the relevant research pertaining to the involvement construct from consumer behavior, social psychology, economic psychology and information systems literature. The objective is to develop a broad-based understanding of the involvement construct so that a meaningful investigation can be undertaken to understand the Internet Involvement construct.

2.1 The Involvement Construct

Conceptualizing and measuring involvement has been a consuming endeavor of consumer behavior researchers and social psychologists for more than twenty years (Higie and Feick, 1989). Additionally, a rich paradigm of research has also accumulated regarding "user involvement" in the information systems field (Barudi and Olson, 1985, Barki and Hartwick, 1989, 1991 and 1994; Kappelman and McLean, 1991, 1992 and 1994). As there are no known (to our knowledge) theoretical or empirical research papers regarding involvement as related to the internet, this paper builds on previous research in marketing, information systems, consumer research and economic psychology pertaining to the involvement construct.

Research on involvement dates back to Sherif and Cantril's (1947) early work. They expounded the concept of "ego involvement" to emphasize the personal and emotional nature of involvement. Though the involvement concept has been researched extensively over the past several decades, substantial ambiguity as to its nature exists (Gensch and Javalgi, 1987). The concept appears to be both multidimensional and multifaceted. The lack of agreement on what constitutes involvement is acknowledged throughout the literature (Arora, 1982; Engel and Blackwell, 1982; Laurent and Kapfirer, 1985; Ray 1985; Robertson, 1976). Lasvicka and Gardner (1979, pp. 48) state that there is "no clear statement or agreement on what this concept of involvement represents." Similarly, Tyebjee (1979, pp. 298) observed that "there is little agreement on what this concept of involvement represents." Muncy and Hunt (1981) summarized the literature on involvement and noted that the agreement on the nature of the involvement construct does not exist at present because involvement is defined variously depending upon the context. In their extensive review of the involvement concept, Chiseler, Collins, and Miller (1969) called it a potpourri concept which may encompass several independent elements. Rothschild (1979) concluded that no single indicator of involvement could satisfactorily describe, explain, or predict involvement.

A multitude of conceptualizations are available in the literature: enduring/situational involvement, cognitive/affective involvement, instrument/responsive involvement (Jain and Srinivasan, 1990). This diversity of views provides a very rich perspective of the construct. Much of the diversity in definitions adopted by researchers in the involvement area begins at the conceptual level. The following definitions of involvement have been proposed in the consumer research, marketing and economic psychology literature:

- Involvement is said to reflect the extent of personal relevance of the decision to the individual in terms of his/her basic values, goals, and self-concept (Eagel and Blackwell 1982, pp. 273).
- Zaichkowsky (1985) defined involvement as " a person's perceived relevance of the object based on inherent needs, values and interests."
- Greenwald and Leavitt (1984) conclude their literature review by stating that "there is consensus that high involvement means (approximately) personal relevance or importance."
- Involvement is an internal state variable that indicates the amount of arousal, interest, or drive evoked by a particular stimulus or situation (Mitchell 1979, 1981).
- Involvement is an unobservable state of motivation, arousal or interest. It is evoked by a particular stimulus or situation and has drive properties. It's consequences are types of searching, information processing and decision making (Rothschild, 1984).

- Involvement is 'a motivational state of mind with regard to an object or activity. It reveals itself as the level of interest in that object or activity' (Mittal, 1983).
- Involvement may be defined as a goal-directed arousal capacity (Park and Mittal, 1985)

Houston and Rothschild (1977) offered the concept of situational involvement as a covering term for the role of situational variables in determining involvement. Based in part on Howard and Sheth's (1969) conceptualization of importance of purchase, an important theme that has been developed is the role of product characteristics in determining involvement. The notion that involvement increases to the extent that products have salient distinguishing characteristics is also present in the work of Hupfer and Gardner (1971), Lastovicka and Gardner (1979), Ray et. al (1973) and Robertson (1976). Product characteristics can be treated either as a situational or as a personality determinant of involvement, depending upon whether one assumes these characteristics to elicit relatively fixed or, alternately, reactions that are conditioned by the unique characteristics of each consumer (Greenwald and Leavitt, 1984).

Krugman's (1965) distinction between two types of involvement (low and high involvement) and his assertion that both types can be associated with effective advertising have stood up remarkably well in light of subsequent research (Greenwald and Leavitt, 1984). Robertson (1976) noted that, even though low-involved consumers might not show much impact of advertising communications on beliefs, they might be induced more easily than highly involved consumers to try a new a product or brand. The consequences-consistent with Krugman's (1965) suggestion -is that, for low-involved consumers, attitude change should be more likely to occur after trial rather than being directly influenced by communication (Greenwals and Leavitt, 1984). The theme that different levels of involvement are associated with different sequences of impacts on the familiar attitude components of affect, behavior, and cognition has been developed most thoroughly by Ray et. al (1973) and has been elaborated even further by Calder (1979).

3 Involvement Measurement Research

Numerous research had been undertaken in consumer behavior, social psychology and economic psychology to develop measures for the involvement construct. This research adapts from and builds on previous research undertaken in these disciplines.

3.1 Involvement Measurement in Marketing and Consumer Behavior Research

A number of studies in marketing and consumer behavior literature have attempted to develop instruments for measuring the involvement construct. In the past a number of scales have been developed purporting to measure involvement and the dimensions underlying the construct (Jensen, Carlson and Tripp, 1989). Six basic and widely disseminated involvement scales have been developed in the marketing and consumer behavior literature (Bloch, 1981; Lastovick and Gardner, 1979; Laurent and Kepferer, 1985; Slams and Taschian, 1985; Traylor and Joseph, 1984; Zaichkowsky, 1985). With one exception, all of these scales have utilized Likert-type response formats from 6 (Traylor and Joseph, 1984) to 33 items (Slams and Taschian, 1985). Zaichkowsky (1985), on the other hand, argued that Likert scale items were problematic "because items that seemed to be appropriate for frequently purchased goods did not seem to apply to durable goods and vice versa (pp. 342). Hence, Zaichkowsky developed a 20 item semantic differential scale to measure involvement.

Laurent and Kepferer (1985) developed the Involvement Profile which they empirically established to be multidimensional. They have strongly argued that involvement should be thought of as a profile of several facets. They offered a 19-item profile of five dimensions: Importance, Pleasure, Sign-Value, Risk Probability and Risk Importance. However, the five dimensions collapsed into four factors during empirical testing, with Importance and Risk-Importance loading on the same dimension (Jain and Srinivasan, 1990). But the central problem with this instrument is whether *risk* (two of their five factors) has been properly conceptualized as a dimension of involvement or requires consideration as separate constructs (McQuire and Munson, 1992). Additionally, since the scale was developed using French items and has not been published in its entirety, the potential for its usage in the U.S. has been limited (Mittal and Lee, 1988).

The other stream of empirical research is largely based upon Zaichkowsky's 20 item Personal Involvement Inventory (PII). The PII appeared to capture one major factor-Relevance- and one minor factor which was not considered further. The major factor accounted for approximately 70% of the variance. The PII is appealing in its simple structure and the single score used to represent the degree of involvement. The scope of the PII was expanded by McQuarrie and Munson (1992), who concurred with Laurent and Kapfer's emphasis on a multidimensional involvement profile. Higie and Fieck (1989) in attempting to measure enduring involvement, also borrowed items from Zaichkowsky's Personal Involvement Inventory.

Hence, in the light of the theoretical development and empirical evidence related to the involvement construct in the marketing and consumer behavior literature, it is our contention that the Personal Involvement Inventory, developed by Zaichkowsky (1985) and later utilized and validated by numerous research, represents an instrument that can be adapted to develop a measure of Internet Involvement.

3.2 Involvement Measurement in Information Systems Literature

Interest in the "Involvement" construct in the information systems literature began with the work of Swanson (1974) with his assertion: "That management should be involved in MIS development is a popular wisdom... Unfortunately, what is meant by involvement is rarely clear, and nothing has been done to my knowledge to provide a rigorous foundation for its measurement" (pp. 178-179). A number of studies were subsequently conducted that investigated user involvement and its relationship to system success. Ives and Olson (1984) conducted a critical review to understand the relationship of user involvement and a number of indicants of information systems success and found the evidence to be inconclusive.

Barki and Hartwick (1989) reviewed and compared the "involvement" construct as used in the information systems literature with conceptualizations available in Psychology, Organizational Behavior and Marketing and Consumer Research literature. They recommended that "Consistent with work in other disciplines, the term "user involvement" should be used to refer to a subjective psychological state of the individual and defined as the importance and personal relevance that users attach either to a particular system or to information systems in general, depending on the users' focus." (pp. 59-60). They further recommended that "The context-free measure developed by Zaichkowsky (1985) in the field of marketing would seem to be a good starting point for (the development) of such a measure (of user involvement)" (pp. 59-60).

In summary, we find that conceptualization and measurement issues related to the involvement construct converges both in information systems literature and marketing and consumer behavior research. Our conceptualization and measurement of internet involvement is based upon previous research in these disciplines.

4 Internet Involvement

Due to the tremendous popularity and growth of the Internet specifically among consumers, it is important to develop an understanding of the Internet Involvement phenomenon. This study takes the first initiative (to the best of authors' knowledge) to define the construct based on past research and consuming development with the Internet.

4.1 Construct Definition

In conformance with researchers in economic psychology, information systems and marketing and consumer behavior literature, we view perceived personal relevance as an essential characteristic of the Internet Involvement construct (Petty and Cacioppo, 1981; Barki and Hartwick, 1989; Zaichkowsky, 1985). This conceptualization implies that a consumer's level of involvement with the Internet is determined by the degree to which he or she perceives the Internet to be personally relevant. We suggest that the Internet is personally relevant to the consumer to the extent that consumers perceive the Internet to be self-related or in some way instrumental in achieving their personal goals, values and objectives. To the extent that features of the Internet or the World Wide Web are associated with personal goals and values, the consumer will experience strong feelings of personal relevance or involvement with it. Hence in this study, we propose the following definition of Internet Involvement:

> *Internet involvement is an unobservable state of motivation of a person regarding the Internet or the World Wide Web and is his or her perceived relevance related to the Internet based on inherent needs, values, interests, goals and objectives.*

4.2 Scale Adaptation and Item Generation

Following the recommendations of Barky and Hartwick (1989) and based on our review of marketing and consumer behavior research, we have adapted the Personal Involvement Inventory (PII) developed and validated by Zaichkowsky (1985). The PII has been used in numerous research studies and was also adapted for use in information systems research.

The PII was developed as a semantic differential scale based on a initial list of 168 word pairs to represent the concept of involvement. Examples of those pairs are important-unimportant, interested-uninterested, and exciting-unexciting (Zaichkowsky, 1985). Through subsequent empirical research the final instrument was reduced to 20 bipolar items with Cronbach's alpha level of 0.95. In this study, we have adapted Zaichkowsky's (1985) 20 item bipolar scale to develop an instrument for measuring Internet Involvement. The entire Internet involvement instrument is presented in Appendix A. The reliability and validity of this instrument is discussed in the following sections.

4.3 Internal Scale Reliability

We proceed to test the reliability of the proposed instrument for measuring Internet Involvement following Nunnally and Bernstein's (1994: pp. 251) suggestion that "Because reliability is important to any measurement method, investigations of reliability should be made when new measures are developed." In order to test the reliability of the instrument, we conducted an initial study using undergraduate students enrolled in junior and senior level business courses at a large Northeastern University. Subsequently two other studies were conducted, one at the MBA level at the same Northeastern University and another at the undergraduate level at a large South Central University.

We concede that students are convenient subjects for academic research, they do not represent the general population. Additionally, Churchill and Peter (1984) hypothesized that college student samples should evince higher scale reliabilities than non-college student samples because students should be more experienced in completing questionnaires and perhaps more educated. But Peterson (1994) in his meta-analysis of Cronbach's Alpha Coefficient found that Churchill and Peter's hypothesis could not be supported. Peterson (1994: pp. 384) stated that "Given their (Churchill and Peter) findings and a lack of conceptual support for hypothesis of different alpha coefficients for different types of samples, type of sample was not expected to influence the size of an alpha coefficient." Hence, our use of student subjects in our samples do not limit our contribution to literature.

4.3.1 Study 1

In order to assess the reliability of the developed instrument, we administered the instrument to 71 undergraduate students enrolled in a core business course. The sample consisted of 70 percent male and 30 percent female subjects. Our initial scale reliability as measured by Cronbach's coefficient alpha with 20 items is 0.9582. The results of the reliability analysis are presented in Table 1.

Table 1. Reliability analysis – scale (alpha)

ITEMS In Instrument	Scale Mean if Item Deleted	Scale Variance if Item Deleted	Corrected Item-Total Correlatio	Squared Multiple Correlation	Alpha if Item Deleted
APPEALING	110.2254	250.3199	.8221	.8263	.9546
BENEFICIAL	110.1268	258.2551	.5466	.8008	.9591
OF CONCERN TO ME	110.0704	260.6378	.6555	.6851	.9569
DESIRABLE	110.0986	261.3187	.7747	.7715	.9557
ESSENTIAL	110.3803	256.9247	.7416	.8204	.9558
EXCITING	110.2394	251.2704	.8466	.9169	.9543
FASCINATING	110.3521	258.9171	.6674	.7111	.9567
FUNDMENTAL	110.7606	259.8990	.5423	.6137	.9589
IMPORTANT	110.0282	255.7992	.6627	.7495	.9570
INTERSTED	110.0423	255.0125	.7658	.8356	.9554
MATTERS TO ME	110.2958	254.8684	.7378	.8355	.9558
MEANS A LOT	110.5775	252.9618	.7504	.8199	.9557
NEEDED	109.9859	260.9569	.6924	.7063	.9565
RELEVANT	109.9014	256.9759	.8252	.8159	.9549
SIGNIFICANT	110.0141	257.1855	.8416	.8212	.9548
USEFUL	109.8732	253.7694	.8249	.8478	.9547
VALUABLE	109.9296	259.1235	.6729	.8432	.9567
VITAL	110.6338	259.3211	.6569	.7396	.9569
WANTED	110.0986	263.9759	.6534	.5915	.9570
INTERESTING	110.0986	255.9187	.7913	.9046	.9552

Acceptable level of Cronbach's Alpha is 0.7 (Nunnally, 1978).

Except for 'Beneficial' and 'Fundamental' items, which have item-total correlation of 0.5466 and 0.5423 respectively (see Table 1), all of the other items have very high item-total correlation. The corrected item-total correlation is the Pearson correlation coefficient between the score on the individual item and the sum of the scores on the remaining items. A high item-total correlation coefficient indicates that the item in question and the remaining items have a strong relationship indicating based on domain sampling theory that they belong and hence, are tapping the same common construct. As can be seen in Table 1, most of the items have very high item-total correlation indicating a strong relationship among the items in the instrument.

Table 2. Reliability analysis for study 2 – scale (alpha)

ITEMS In Instrument	Scale Mean if Item Deleted	Scale Variance if Item Deleted	Corrected Item-Total Correlation	Squared Multiple Correlation	Alpha if Item Deleted
APPEALING	113.9000	224.2462	.8385	.8493	.9428
BENEFICIAL	113.7250	226.4096	.6099	.8899	.9454
OF CONCERN TO ME	114.0500	223.9974	.4937	.6588	.9484
DESIRABLE	113.9500	220.8692	.8835	.9023	.9418
ESSENTIAL	114.2500	220.2436	.8582	.8987	.9419
EXCITING	113.9750	221.7686	.8380	.9236	.9424
FASCINATING	113.9000	225.3744	.6567	.8438	.9448
FUNDMENTAL	114.6250	221.0609	.4942	.5603	.9494
IMPORTANT	113.7500	221.5769	.6383	.8184	.9452
INTERSTED	113.7000	226.0103	.6351	.9200	.9451
MATTERS TO ME	113.7000	223.5487	.8669	.9390	.9424
MEANS A LOT	113.9000	223.9385	.7056	.8755	.9441
NEEDED	114.4000	221.9897	.5375	.6703	.9476
RELEVANT	113.6500	225.9769	.7546	.7958	.9437
SIGNIFICANT	113.7000	223.6513	.8325	.9142	.9427
USEFUL	113.7250	225.1276	.8115	.8383	.9431
VALUABLE	113.7750	219.4609	.6663	.7364	.9448
VITAL	113.6500	221.9769	.6378	.8736	.9451
WANTED	114.4250	222.2506	.5655	.5618	.9467
INTERESTING	113.8250	224.6609	.7138	.8190	.9440

Acceptable level of Cronbach's Alpha is 0.7 (Nunnally, 1978).

4.3.2 Study 2

The second study was carried out with MBA students enrolled in a core business course. The sample size was 40. Sixty-five percent of the students were male and 35 percent of the students were female. Our initial scale reliability as measured by

Cronbach's coefficient alpha (standardized) with 20 items is 0.9560. Except for the items OF CONCERN TO ME and FUNDAMENTAL, most of the items have a very high item-total correlation indicating that the items are tapping the same construct. The very high Cronbach's coefficient alpha in the second study again indicates a high internal consistency and reliability for the scale (see Table 2) .

4.3.3 Study 3

In the third study, the instrument was administered to 85 undergraduate students enrolled in a core business course in large south central university. The sample consisted of 32 female and 56 male students. The reliability analysis for the third study is shown in table 3. The Cronbach's alpha (standardized) coefficient in the third study is 0.9486 again indicating a high internal consistency and high reliability of the scale. Acceptable level of Cronbach's Alpha is 0.7 (Nunnally, 1978).

Table 3. Reliability analysis for study 3 – scale (alpha)

ITEMS In Instrument	Scale Mean if Item Deleted	Scale Variance if Item Deleted	Corrected Item- Total Correlation	Squared Multiple Correlation	Alpha ifItem Deleted
APPEALING	113.7765	177.8185	.6162	.6915	.9420
BENEFICIAL	113.6118	179.2880	.6498	.6030	.9418
OF CONCERN TO ME	114.0824	173.0289	.6192	.6342	.9420
DESIRABLE	113.9412	172.3894	.7212	.7314	.9402
ESSENTIAL	114.4000	172.8143	.5607	.6373	.9434
EXCITING	113.9294	171.8759	.7004	.7781	.9405
FASCINATING	113.9882	172.4165	.7306	.7192	.9401
FUNDMENTAL	114.7882	171.2403	.5173	.4221	.9453
IMPORTANT	113.5882	175.8403	.6888	.6429	.9409
INTERSTED	113.7647	171.6821	.7606	.7646	.9396
MATTERS TO ME	113.7529	173.1168	.6795	.8092	.9409
MEANS A LOT	114.0706	171.6854	.7613	.7592	.9396
NEEDED	114.2588	168.2894	.7683	.7539	.9393
RELEVANT	113.9059	175.3958	.5727	.6647	.9427
SIGNIFICANT	113.9059	175.3958	.5727	.6647	.9427
USEFUL	113.8471	174.7501	.6888	.7346	.9408
VALUABLE	113.5529	178.3454	.6903	.6939	.9413
VITAL	113.4941	178.4196	.6978	.7548	.9413
WANTED	114.5647	173.7725	.5416	.5286	.9437
INTERESTING	113.8706	170.6378	.7204	.6965	.9401

Acceptable level of Cronbach's Alpha is 0.7 (Nunnally, 1978).

In summary, in all of these three studies, the instrument has consistently shown high internal consistency and reliability as measured by Cronbach's coefficient alpha. This is quite promising for a new instrument as it well exceeds Nunnally's (1978) recommendation of 0.70 for coefficient alpha for preliminary research.

4.4 Scale Dimensionality

In this research, we conceptualize Internet Involvement to be multi-dimensional rather than unidimensional in line with the findings of Park and Mittal (1989). Two dimensions in particular are important: affective and cognitive involvement (Zaichkowsky,1994). Affective involvement stresses a person's feelings and achievements of certain emotional states and is used to describe all emotions, moods and feelings evoked by an object (McGuire, 1974). The object eliciting the affective involvement in our case is the Internet. On the other hand, cognitive involvement stresses the individual's informational processing activities and the achievement of idealization states.

Table 4. Result of factor analysis of Internet involvement-study 1

	Factor 1	Factor 2
Essential	0.82632	
Needed	0.76307	
Desirable	0.75972	
Exciting	0.75590	
Interesting	0.75536	
Vital	0.75406	
Significant	0.74614	
Fascinating	0.69443	
Important	0.68315	
Wanted	0.66872	
Of Concern to me	0.64305	
Relevant	0.60675	
Interested		0.87313
Valuable		0.83042
Beneficial		0.78261
Matters to me		0.76199
Useful		0.64752
Means a lot		0.64051
Appealing		0.61390

Unlike products or services that were the focus of study in the marketing or consumer behavior literature, it is our contention that the Internet represents the means to, as well as the ends with multiple objectives. Factor analysis suggests a multi-dimensional structure of the internet involvement construct implying that consumers may have a two dimensional involvement with the Internet: one dealing with flashy graphics, animations and fascinating aspects possibly representing the affective involvement, and the other dealing with value creating or rational aspects such as finding important information related to products, services or career or job opportunities etc.

The result of factor analysis with varimax rotation (Study 1 with N=71) supports the initial contention of two factors with the first factor (see Table 4) representing the affective component of the Internet involvement whereas the second factor representing the cognitive component of the construct.

In order to verify that both the number of factors and the pattern of loading of items on these factors, three more studies were carried out subsequently. The second study (N=45), consistent with the first study, also indicates a two factor model consistent with that of Zaichkowsky (1994).

Table 5. Result of factor analysis of Internet involvement-study 2

	Factor 1	Factor 2
ESSENTIAL	.82502	
VITAL	.79179	
INTERESTING	.78954	
NEEDED	.77873	
SIGNIFICANT	.76817	.43679
EXCITING	.75778	.45470
DESIRABLE	.71500	.41169
OF CONCERN TO ME	.67844	
IMPORTANT	.66286	
FASCINATING	.65063	
WANTED	.58238	
FUNDMENTAL	.42119	
VALUABLE		.83832
INTERSTED		.81725
BENEFICIAL		.77528
RELEVANT	.46229	.75527
USEFUL	.47001	.75424
MATTERS TO ME		.72643
APEALING	.53639	.68175

The third study (N=40) again shows two factor model of the internet involvement construct. Some of the items have changed their loading from one factor to the other. For example, APPEALING has loaded on to factor one (affective) in study three, consistent with Zaichkowsky (1994) item and factor loading pattern. Zaichkowsky (1994) had identified this item belonging to the affective component rather than the cognitive factor. Again ESSENTIAL has changed its loading from factor one to factor two (the cognitive component) which is also consistent with previous research.

Table 6. Result of factor analysis of Internet involvement-study 3

	Factor 1	Factor 2
INTERESTING	.81525	
FASCINATING	.80694	
APPEALING	.78220	
EXCITING	.72122	
DESIRABLE	.66968	.55537
WANTED	.66714	.57817
USEFUL	.65531	
BENEFICIAL	.63985	
VALUABLE	.63734	
OF CONCERN TO ME	.58269	.55926
FUNDAMENTAL	.48701	
ESSENTIAL		.93169
VITAL		.86164
SIGNIFICANT	.51244	.68562
RELEVANT		.67469
IMPORTNT	.50638	.66212
NEEDED	.50778	.65964
MATTERS TO ME	.59907	.63272
INTERESTED	.56743	.58298

In the fourth study (N=85), the pattern of loading of items on each factor has stabilized in the sense that those items that were identified by previous research (Zaichkowsky, 1985, 1994) to load on the affective component such as fascinating, exciting, interesting, appealing etc. has loaded on the affective factor. The other items such as relevant, essential, significant, important, matters to me, etc. has loaded on the cognitive factor. These items were also identified in the literature as belonging to the cognitive component of the Involvement construct.

Table 7. Result of factor analysis of Internet involvement-study 4

	Factor 1	Factor 2
INTERESTING	.90223	
EXCITING	.81726	
APPEALING	.80072	
FASCINATING	.77982	
DESIRABLE	.75749	
WANTED	.75287	
USEFUL	.59277	
VALUABLE	.58798	
INTERSTED	.58689	.52348
NEEDED		.75013
ESSENTIAL		.73408
SIGNIFICANT		.72837
VITAL		.67866
MATTERS		.66476
RELEVANT		.65914
IMPORTANT		.65851
OF CONCERN TO ME		.51874
BENEFICIAL		.50683

The fourth study (see Table 7) also shows a clear pattern and grouping of the items on each factor. Most of the items have a very high factor loading after varimax rotation. In summary, factor analysis of the data collected from students at two different Universities both at the graduate and undergraduate levels over a period of one year has lent strong support to the initial contention of two-factor model of the Internet Involvement construct. This two factor model of the Internet Involvement construct is also consistent with previous research in consumer behavior and economic psychology literature (Park and Mittal, 1985).

5. Latent Structure Analysis

In this section, latent structure analysis is carried out in order to confirm that the Internet involvement construct has a two-factor structure consisting of the affective and cognitive components rather than a one-factor structure. Based on the data collected in the preceding studies, the latent structure analysis can be carried out to determine the two-factor vs. the one-factor structure. The one-factor model has a Chi-square of 854.63 at 169 degrees of freedom and the two-factor model has a Chi-square of 732.049 at 168 degrees of freedom. The Chi-square change between the one and two factor models was 122.581 at 1 degrees of freedom (p<0.001). This indicates based on the significant (p<0.001) change in Chi-square value that the two-factor model has a better fit than the one-factor model confirming the original conceptualization that Internet Involvement has both an affective and cognitive components.

6. Discussion and Implication for Electronic Commerce

In this paper, we have attempted to develop an instrument for measuring the Internet involvement construct based on previous research in consumer behavior, information systems, and economic psychology literature. Based on several studies, we have established the reliability and internal consistency of the instrument as measured by the Cronbach's Alpha coefficient. The reliability and internal consistency of the instrument basically ensures that the instrument can be used to measure the Internet involvement at different times and under different conditions, but the instrument will measure the Internet involvement construct reliably under each of these situations. Thus, ensuring that the developed instrument provides a means to measure the degree of Internet involvement among consumers that can then be used to discern certain consumer behaviors as related to purchase situations involving the Internet.

In this research, we conceptualize Internet Involvement to be multi-dimensional rather than unidimensional. In our analyses using factor analysis with varimax rotation, we have established that the Internet involvement has a two dimensional structure. One of the two dimensions deals with the affective part of the Internet involvement construct and the other deals with the cognitive aspect.

Involvement is a motivational construct which partly relies on the antecedent factor of the person's values and needs. This definition does allow for an affective component, because self-reliance, per se, is affective. Affective involvement stresses a person's feelings and achievements of search and emotional state and is used to describe all emotions, moods and feelings evoked by an object (McGuire, 1974). Cognitive involvement, on the other hand, stresses the individual's informational processing activities and the achievement of idealization states. The affective component of the Internet involvement relates to the elicitation of emotional response among consumers when they come across flashy graphics, animations, etc. while visiting various company websites. Hence, a significant portion of most company web sites have flashy graphics, Shockwave and Java animations, Real Audio, digital video that have been designed to entice the visiting consumers to the particular web sites. Hence, the affective component of the Internet involvement relates to such items in the instrument as exciting, fascinating, interesting, etc.

On the other hand, the Internet is a medium for obtaining valuable product and service related information. Consumers can also find information related to job openings, education, training programs, etc. that create value for consumers visiting such web sites. Hence, we find that the internet also has an information processing component that appeals to the cognitive component of the Internet involvement construct. The cognitive involvement deals with how consumers process information. As information creates value in this age of information society, it is reasonable to expect that the Internet, being the largest and the most diverse information medium, will create and elicit cognitive involvement from consumers visiting various company web sites.

Hence, our establishment of the Internet involvement as having two distinct dimensions affective and cognitive has profound implications for managers developing strategies to incorporate the Internet as an integral component of their overall marketing and communications strategy. Findings of this research implies that flashy graphics, Shockwave and Java animations etc. relates only to one component of the Internet involvement. Companies developing and deploying web sites for electronic commerce that do not pay careful attention to the cognitive component of the Internet involvement are likely to create web sites that evoke emotion but which do not create value (through information) for the consumers as little or no cognitive involvement is evoked. This implies that web sites should have affective as well as a strong cognitive component so that consumers are emotionally touched and value creation is possible through concurrent cognitive involvement with the information made available for the visiting consumers.

Krugman (1965) in his seminal paper conceptualized two types of involvement: low involvement and high involvement. There is consensus that high involvement means approximately personal relevance or importance (Greenwald and Leavitt, 1984) and that communication impact for low involvement is different from that for high involvement. Additionally, Mitchell (1979) has conceptualized involvement as a high level of arousal or drive. In essence, these conceptualizations imply that at least consumers can be categorized into high involvement group and low involvement group with a suitable measuring instrument. This would then allow managers to distinguish between certain consumer behaviors that are of interest from an electronic commerce perspective.

Using data collected in our studies, the entire sample is divided into high Internet involvement group and low Internet involvement group. Following Zaichkowsky (1985), those scoring higher than the mean score (113) are grouped in the high Internet involvement group and those scoring below the mean are grouped in the low Internet involvement group. Based on literature review in marketing, consumer behavior research and economic psychology (Mittal and Lee, 1989,; Laurent and Kapferer, 1985; McQuarrie and Munson, 1992), certain external variables were identified that directly measure behaviors resulting from high Internet involvement. For example, under low Internet involvement condition, the literature identifies that there will be a relative lack of active information seeking about the Internet itself. There will be a relative lack of usage of the Internet. And there will be a relative lack of intention to buy product over the Internet.

The result of our one-way ANOVA analysis indicates that the developed Internet involvement instrument is able to distinguish between low Internet involvement subjects and high Internet involvement subjects as distinguished by these external response variables (Table 8).

Table 8. Analysis of variance

Difference between high Internet involvement group and low Internet involvement group in terms of external response variables

Construct validity and external response variable statements:

1) I often use the World Wide Web to find information related to products that I like to buy.

Source	D.F.	Sum of Squares	Mean Squares	F Ratio	F Prob.
Between groups	1	14.2277	14.2277	10.7076	.0014
Within groups	28	170.0800	1.3287		
Total	129	184.3077			

2) I use the Internet frequently.

Between groups	1	15.6182	15.6182	9.9779	.0021
Within groups	109	170.6160	1.5653		
Total	110	186.2342			

3) People often visit the web sites that I like and I suggest.

Between groups	1	10.4884	10.4884	6.9413	.0096
Within groups	109	164.7008	1.5110		
Total	110	175.1892			

The Internet involvement instrument is clearly able to distinguish among subjects with high Internet involvement and low Internet involvement. Additionally, the significant difference, among low Internet involvement and high Internet involvement groups, in responses to such consumer behaviors as actively seeking information over the Internet regarding products that they like to buy clearly demonstrates the construct validity and spells out the implication for electronic commerce. It is clear that highly involved consumers are more likely to engage in electronic commerce compared to low involved consumers.

Managers using this instrument in surveying consumers visiting their web sites will be able to distinguish among the high Internet involvement group from the low Internet involvement group. This will then enable the business managers to develop a more effective marketing and communications strategy specifically focusing on those consumers that are highly involved with the Internet. This will then allow businesses to develop a more customized approach toward consumers on the basis of the one to one marketing that the Internet affords.

7 Conclusion

This study has built upon existing theories on involvement in multiple disciplines such as consumer behavior, information systems and economic psychology and adapted existing instruments, validated by numerous past research, to measure "Internet Involvement". Involvement has been found to be a crucial construct in multiple disciplines to underlie human behavior. Similarly, a better understanding of the Internet involvement will allow researchers to develop better insights about consumer behavior in the context of electronic commerce.

The developed instrument was applied to discern whether low or high involved consumers exhibit distinct behaviors regarding electronic commerce. The study provides evidence that high and low involved consumers differ in terms of their behaviors regarding the Internet (in terms of usage) as well as in terms of their willingness to use the Internet for commercial activities.

Additionally, this study found two distinct dimensions of the Internet involvement construct. One dimension relates to the affective component and the other relates to the cognitive component of the Internet involvement construct. The affective component relates to the emotional part of consumer involvement with the Internet and is specifically evoked by flashy graphics, Java animations, digital audio and video, etc. The cognitive component deals with the information processing aspect of the involvement construct and specifically deals with the issue of value creating information available in various company web sites. The fundamental implication of these two dimensions is that company web sites need to address both the affective and cognitive components so that a greater value is created for the visiting consumer. If an web site pertains to one dimension or the other, it may loose the opportunity to engage certain group of consumers.

This study has also provided a foundation for future research incorporating the involvement construct to better understand consumer behavior in the context of electronic commerce. Further research needs to be carried out in terms of how consumer involvement with the Internet moderate the search for information over the Internet, how consumers process or evaluate information in a purchase situation in the context of electronic commerce and how Internet involvement might moderate the advertising effectiveness over the Web.

References (Abridged)

Barki, H. and J. Hartwick, "Rethinking the Concept of User Involvement", *MIS Quarterly*, March 1989, pp. 53-62.

Beatty, S.E. And Smith, S.M. (1987) "External Search Effort: An Investigation Across Several Product Categories", *Journal of Consumer Research*, Vol. 14, June, pp. 83-95

Bennett, P.D. And Mandell, R.M. (1969) "Prepurchase Information Seeking Behavior of New Car Purchasers--The Learning Hypothesis", *Journal of Marketing Research*, Vol. 6, November, pp. 430-33.

Bentler, M. *EQS Structural Equations Program Manual*, Multivariate Software Inc., 1995.

Bloch, P.H., Sherrell, D.L. And Ridegway, N.M. (1986) "Consumer Search: An Extended Framework", *Journal of Consumer Research*, Vol. 13, June, pp. 119-128.

Celsi, R. and J. Olson, "The Role of Involvement in Attention and Comprehension Processes", *Journal of Consumer Research*, Vol. 15, September 1985, pp. 210-224.

Churchil, G., "A Paradigm for Developing Better Measures of Marketing Constructs", *Journal of Marketing Research*, Vol. 16, February 1979, pp. 64-73.

Cortese, A., "A Way Out of the Web Maze", *BusinessWeek*, February 24, 1997, pp. 95-108.

Dunn, G., B. Everitt, and A. Pickles *Modeling Covariances And Latent Variables Using EQS*, Chapman and Hall: London, 1993.

Greenwald, A. and C. Leavitt, "Audience Involvement in Advertising: Four Levels", *Journal of Consumer Research*, Vol. 11, June 1984, pp. 581-592.

Guthrie, R. and L. Austin, "Competitive Implications of the Internet," *Information Systems Management*, Summer 1996, pp. 90-92.

Hagel III, Jan A. Armstrong *NetGain: Expanding Markets Through Virtual Communities*. HBS: Boston, MA. 1997.

Hawkins, S. and S. Hoch, "Low-Involvement Learning: Memory without Evaluation", *Journal of Consumer Research*, Vol. 19, September 1992, pp. 212-225.

Higie, R. and L. Feick, "Enduring Involvement: Conceptual and Measurement Issues", *Advances in Consumer Research*, Vol. 16, 1989, pp. 690-695.

Jan, K. and N. Srinivasan, "An Empirical Assessment of Multiple Operationalizations of Involvement", *Advance in Consumer Research*, Vol. 17, 1990, pp. 594-602.

Jensen, T., L. Carlson and C. Tripp, "The Dimensionality of Involvement: An Empirical Test", *Advances in Consumer Research*, Vol. 16, 1989, pp. 680-689.

Kalakota, R. and A. Whinston *Frontier of Electronic Commerce*. Addison-Wesley: New York. 1996.

Laurent, G. and J. Kapferer, "Measuring Consumer Involvement Profiles", *Journal of Marketing Research*, Vol. 22, February 1985, pp. 41-53.

Lynch, D. "Cashflow", *Internet World*, July 1996, pp. 75-80.

Martin, C. *The Digital Estate*. McGraw-Hill: New York. 1997.

Martin, J. *Cybercorp: The New Business Revolution*. AMACOM: New York. 1996

McQuarrie, E. and J. Munson, "A Revised Product Involvement Inventory: Improved Usability and Validity", *Advances in Consumer Research*, Vol. 19, 1992, pp. 108-115.

Middendrop, C. "On the conceptualization of theoretical constructs", *Quality and Quantity*, Vol. 25, 1991, pp. 235-252.

Midgley, D. and G. Dowling, "Innovativeness: The Concept and Its Measurement", *Journal of Consumer Research*, Vol. 4, March 1978, pp. 229-242.

Miniard, P., S. Bhalta, K. Lord, P. Dickson and H. Unnava, "Picture-based Persuasion Processes and Moderating Role of Involvement", *Journal Consumer Research*, Vol. 18, June 1991, pp. 92-107.

Mitchell, A. A. (1981) "The Dimensions of Advertising Involvement", in *Advances in Consumer Research*, (Ed) K.B. Monroe, Vol. 8, Ann Arbor, MI, Association for Consumer Research, pp. 25-30.

Mittal, B. and M. Lee, "A Causal Model of Consumer Involvement", *Journal of Economic Psychology*, Vol. 10, 1989, pp. 363-389.

Molenaar, N., "Recent methodological studies on survey questioning", *Quality and Quantity*, Vol. 25, 1991, pp. 167-187.

Noack D., "Planes, Trains and Cruise Lines", *Internet World*, July 1996, pp. 82-86.

Park, J. and M. Hastak, "Memory-based Product Judgments: Effects of Involvement at Encoding and Retrieval", *Journal of Consumer Research*, Vol. 21, December 1994, pp. 534-547.

Peterson, R., "A Meta-Analysis Of Cronbach's Coefficient Alpha", *Journal of Consumer Research*, Vol. 21, September 1994, pp. 381-391.

Petty, R., J. Cacioppo and D. Schumann, "Central and Peripheral Routes to Advertising Effectiveness: The Moderating Role of Involvement", *Journal of Consumer Research*, Vol. 10, September 1983, pp. 135-146.

Quelch, J. and L. Klein, "The Internet and International Marketing", *Sloan Management Review*, Spring 1996, pp. 60-75.

Robello, K., L. Armstrong and A. Cortese, "Making Money on the Net?", *BusinessWeek*, September 23, 1996, pp. 104-118.

Rowley, J. "Retailing and shopping on the Internet", *Internet Research: Electronic Networking Applications and Policy*, pp. 81-91.

Salam, A.F., "Three Essays on Electronic Commerce: WWW Information Content, Internet Involvement And Perceived Risk," *unpublished Doctoral Dissertation*, SUNY at Buffalo, June 1998.

Salam, A.F., H.R. Rao and C.C. Pegesl, "Content of Corporate Web Pages as Advertising Media," *Communications of the ACM*, Vol. 41, No.3, March 1998.

Salam, A.F., H.R. Rao, C.C. Pegels, "An Investigation of Consumer-Perceived Risk on Electronic Commerce Transactions: The Role of Institutional Trust and Economic Incentive In A Social Exchange Framework," in Proceedings of the *Association for Information Systems (AIS) Americas Conference*, (1998), 202-204.

Ubois, J., "Selling Delight", *Internet World*, September 1996, pp. 86-94.

Urbany, J., Dickinson P. R. and Wilkie, W.L., "Buyer Uncertainty & Information Search", *Journal of Consumer Research*, Vol. 16, September 1989, pp. 208-15.

Welz, G., "The Ad Game", Internet World, July 1996, pp. 50-57.

Zaichkowsky, J., "Measuring the Involvement Construct", *Journal of Consumer Research*, Vol. 12, December, 1985, pp. 341-352.

Zaichkowsky, J. (December 1994). "Research Notes: The Personal Involvement Inventory: Reduction, Revision, and Application to Advertising." *Journal of Advertising* 23(4): 58-70.

CHAPTER 9

Culture Clash in Internet Marketing: Implications for Marketing Practices

Ann Schlosser[1] and Alaina Kanfer[2]

[1]Owen Graduate School of Management, Vanderbilt University, Nashville, TN, USA,
ann.schlosser@owen.vandebilt.edu

[2]National Center for Supercomputing Applications, University of Illinois at Urbana-
Champaign, Urbana, IL, USA, alaina@ncsa.uiuc.edu

The history of the Internet and the tradition of marketing present an inherent culture clash in the emerging practices of Internet Marketing. In this chapter we describe how this culture clash developed, detailing the broadcast nature of traditional marketing messages, and differences between control of content and measuring effectiveness of Internet Marketing as compared with traditional marketing. Following the theme of culture clash, strategies for assimilation and accommodation to the Internet culture for effective Internet Marketing are presented. Current research results on consumer attitudes and reactions toward Internet Marketing provide support for strategies for commercial marketers to cope with the new culture, establish cultural competence, and finally, become a member of the Internet culture.

Keywords: Internet advertising; Internet Marketing; e-commerce; Web site strategy; interactive marketing; attitude toward advertising; integrated marketing communication; marketing strategies; attitudes; behavioral intentions; information intensive environments

1 Introduction

Marketing is currently in a state of forced transition. It has been argued that traditional marketing strategies do not apply well to interactive media such as the Internet (Hoffman and Novak, 1996; Rust and Oliver, 1994; Rust and Varki, 1996). However, current commercial Web sites contain primarily traditional marketing content, thereby ignoring the unique possibilities of interactive media such as engaging the consumer in role-playing (Schlosser and Kanfer, 1999a). That is, on-line marketers are caught in a pitfall common to intercultural relations (see Triandis, 1994): because the Internet has many similarities to traditional media (e.g., it has capabilities similar to that of television, radio, billboards, direct mail and print), it is common to respond in traditional/learned ways. However, although these responses may be appropriate in one's home culture (as applied here, traditional media), they are often unexpected and at worst, deemed inappropriate in the host culture (here, the Internet). Compounding this problem is that the history of the Internet is one of an open, egalitarian system rather than a "market/regulation regime" (King, Grinter and Pickering, 1997). Consequently, the Internet community has been primarily anti-commercial and in opposition to the traditional marketing culture

Research and theory has drawn upon historical Internet and/or marketing cultures to direct marketing in its transition into interactive media. From this, recommendations for Internet marketing (as well as the opportunities and challenges posed) have been made. In this paper, we review this clash between the Internet and marketing cultures on the current and future state of Internet Marketing as well as review recent survey and experimental research shedding light upon effective Internet Marketing. We begin by describing the development of the Internet and the traditional conceptualization of marketing. From this, we define Internet Marketing and highlight the potential culture clash inherent in the current practice of Internet Marketing. We also describe Internet users' attitudes toward Internet Marketing in its various forms and the factors contributing to such attitudes. We end by summarizing strategies for assimilating the marketing culture to the Internet culture and the opportunities such assimilation offers.

2 Development of Internet Culture

The Internet as we know it today began in 1969 as a U.S. Department of Defense research network connecting four sites. The U.S. National Science Foundation adopted the protocols developed by the Department of Defense in 1986 and the Internet grew to a research network of approximately 5,000 host computers (http://www.nw.com/zone/rfc1296.txt). With the development of a freely available integrated browser, NCSA Mosaic™, the Internet grew to nearly one and a half million host computers in early 1993. Approximately a year later, Netscape Communications Corporation was formed. In August, 1995, Netscape issued their initial public offering, Microsoft released Internet Explorer, and the browser wars began. At that time there were nearly seven million host computers on-line (Network Wizards, 1998) with an estimated on-line population in the US alone near 24 million adults (Layton and Kanfer, 1996). By June of 1998, estimates have grown to more than 29 million host computers on-line with 122.5 million Internet users world-wide (NUA, 1998).

Throughout most of this development, the purpose of the Internet was for research scientists to share computational resources, and not for marketing or advertising purposes. Indeed, commercial activities were banned from the network during most of the phenomenal growth of the Internet. It was not until April 1995 that the National Science Foundation transitioned the Internet to a competitively driven commercially managed network, where commercial transactions are legal. Thus, during most of its development, the Internet has been an academic rather than commercial environment with information freely (or relatively inexpensively) available (Hawkins, 1994; O'Leary, 1997ab), resulting in new concepts like "freeware" and "shareware." That is, the Internet environment has been such that resources are freely available and given rather than advertised and marketed (Oliva, 1997).

Another legacy of the Internet is the unexpected importance of email. Although the Internet was developed originally to allow researchers to share computational resources, those purposes were overshadowed by the exchange of electronic mail communications between researchers. Among the engineers building the original Internet, the ability to asynchronously communicate with colleagues around the world about anything from solving technical networking problems to finding lost personal items accounted for most of the early use of the Internet (Hafner and Lyon, 1996). Even today, while the Web holds great appeal as a marketing medium, electronic communications remain the most commonly used and most indispensable Internet feature for the general public (GVU, 1998; Miller and Clemente, 1997).

In addition to electronic mail, there are nearly 100,000 newsgroups and listservs that provide the ability for any member of a group to communicate directly with each of the others in the group (The Liszt). In other words, in addition to including expectations of free information, the Internet culture includes a great deal of two-way communications both one-to-one and many-to-many. Furthermore, the company is no longer the only one able to spread commercial content to many; the consumer has the ability to broadcast messages as well.[1]

3 The Culture of Marketing

In contrast to the emergent Internet culture, first and foremost, marketing is a commercial endeavor. Marketing has been defined as broadly as "[h]uman activity directed at satisfying needs and wants through exchange processes" (Kotler, 1980, G-4). More specifically centered on business processes, the American Marketing Association (1960) defines marketing as "the performance of business activities that direct the flow of goods and services to consumer or user" (American Marketing

---

[1] One might argue that as the population of the Internet becomes more representative of the U.S. population and/or when Internet access transitions from computers to traditional advertising media (e.g., Web TV), such cultural differences between the Internet and marketing community will dissipate. However, we argue that the Internet culture is not entirely a manifestation of the medium (or the people initially drawn to the medium) but rather a result of the information intensiveness of this new environment. Indeed, it has been argued that information intensive environments themselves require a change in the marketing approach: "....whereas traditional physical-based commodities (which are appropriable, scarce and have decreasing returns to use) lead to concerns with boundaries, ownership, and allocation, *information* (which is nonappropriable, nonscarce, and has increasing returns to use) *results in the breaking down of boundaries and leads to issues of access, sharing, and creating opportunities for use,*" resulting in such changes as shifting the focus away from a competitive to a cooperative strategy (Glazer, 1991, pp. 7, 13).

Association, 1960). Thus marketing includes product development, promotion, pricing, distributing, selling and customer service.

Another common component of marketing is advertising. Generally considered as communication from the company to the consumer, advertising has been defined as "any paid form of non-personal communication about an organization, product, service, or idea by an identified sponsor" (Belch and Belch, 1993, p. G-1). An additional characteristic of traditional advertising (whether the media is radio, print or video) is that most tends to be broadcast in nature. That is, rather than developing a two-way communication with potential consumers, most companies employ advertising that is a one-directional, one-to-many broadcast communication. Such tactics, however, are unlikely to thrive in such interactive environments as the Internet (Rust and Oliver, 1994).

4 What is Internet Marketing?

The definitions of advertising and marketing are not quite as clear when applied to the Internet rather than traditional marketing media. Contributing to this difficulty is that the line between what is marketing versus advertising has become blurred on-line. For instance, nearly all content with any commercial ties has been considered Internet advertising on-line. In a study of advertising on the Web, Ducoffe (1996) found that over three-fourths of on-line consumers in his sample considered shopper guides, on-line catalogs, graphical displays of products and free trial offers to be advertising. Furthermore, over half of the sample considered simply having a Web site to be advertising if it is commercially owned.

Given this broad conception of advertising and marketing on the Internet, in this paper we consider Internet Marketing (IM) to subsume Internet advertising, and define IM as *any form of commercial content available on the Internet*. This includes commercial content on the Web as well as using communication tools to serve Internet advertising purposes such as promoting products and services via email, listservs and newsgroups.

5 Internet and Marketing: The Clash of Cultures

While IM is considered to include all forms of commercial content on-line, the very idea of commercial content is inconsistent with the culture of the Internet, where software, information and services have been shared freely. Perhaps most evident of the clash between these cultures is the rising number of legal disputes regarding the Internet, among which include conflicts regarding (1) ownership of a domain name that matches a registered trademark of another company, (2) non-consensual linking between two sites, and (3) the delivery of junk email (Davis and Loundy, 1997). Indeed, many elements of the Internet (such as hyperlinks and frames) pose problems when applied to the commercial domain -- problems such as trademark dilution and infringements.

Moreover, the history of the Internet as an academic resource providing "free" goods likely contributes in large part to Internet users' unwillingness to pay for commercial content on-line – even if such exchange involves only divulging information on a registration form before viewing the commercial site (Hoffman and Novak, forthcoming) or spending time screening unsolicited commercial content (Wright and Bolfing, forthcoming). Supporting the notion that Internet users prefer to retain ownership of their personal information (rather than viewing it as a fair exchange for viewing a site), only 6% of respondents in a recent GVU study reported always registering with on-line sites, meaning they provide personal information to the company in exchange for access to information. Nearly 60% of the respondents say they do not register because they do not trust the entity collecting data (GVU, 1998).

Traditional marketing clashes with the Internet culture in form as well as in content. This clash is mainly evidenced by the broadcast nature, control and effectiveness metrics of traditional marketing strategies, each of which is reviewed below.

5.1 Broadcasting Messages

Traditional marketers are used to broadcasting their messages in a one-to-many format (see Hoffman and Novak, 1996, forthcoming for comparison of marketing models). Yet, the Internet is a many-to-many communication vehicle: consumers can (and expect to be able to) easily respond to the company as well as communicate with other consumers about the product. Indeed, many consumers have already established their own commercial newsgroups and Web sites for discussion of particular products (e.g., alt.cereal, the "Coffee Expert's Group" at http://www.island net.com/coffee/) or brands (e.g., alt.autos.saab, rec.toys.lego, the "Down with Snapple" page at http:// www.fas.harvard.edu/ ~ziniti/snapple.html). Moreover, recent survey results suggest that human interaction via the Internet is required by over half (63%) of Internet users before they are willing to buy on-line (Hof, Browder and Elstrom, 1997).

Currently, however, on-line marketers appear to be designing their commercial content according to traditional marketing strategies. In a systematic study of commercial Web sites actively promoted in advertisements appearing in popular magazines in 1996, it was found that most commercial Web sites primarily broadcast information, leaving little opportunity for communication with the customer or for the customer to interact with information available at the site (Schlosser and Kanfer, 1999a). Nearly all of the sites examined included information traditionally appearing in advertisements and product brochures such as information about the product (89%) and brand information (100%).

In terms of communication between the company and the consumer, most Web sites (68%) encouraged asynchronous communication with the consumer by listing an email address. This is similar to listing a postal address that the consumer can send their inquiries to without knowing when their message will be answered (or even if the message was received). Far fewer sites encouraged interactive on-going dialogues with the consumer (and between consumers) via a newsgroup, listserv (35%) or discussion page (20%) where the consumer's questions and comments are shared with the company and other consumers. Although organizations might view such on-line public forums (moderated or unmoderated) to be a risky venture, there are unique advantages to be considered. For instance, it would allow the organization to inexpensively tap consumers' concerns as well as address the appropriate audience with the organization's response to these concerns.

5.2 Controlling Exposure, Form and Content

Another common element of traditional advertising is its "push" nature. Push marketing is uninvited, thrust upon the consumer's attention while the consumer is completing other tasks. This is a method common in traditional advertising in such non-interactive media as television, radio, print and billboard. The audience of such one-way communication messages is a passive agent, the only choice being whether to absorb or ignore the commercial information as it is presented. Email, banner advertisements and other unsolicited commercial content are considered push marketing, as well.

Unlike non-interactive media, the Internet (particularly the Web) has the capabilities to let the consumer become an active participant in the construction of the commercial message by choosing what to see, when to see it and how often. One manner in which the consumer can control what is seen and when is through the use of navigational tools such as search engines or site indexes. The availability of such navigational tools shifts control to the consumer from the marketer (Hoffman and Novak, 1996). Recent research suggests that the most common navigational tools available at commercial Web sites are home and section icons (69% of sites had them; Schlosser and Kanfer, 1999a), which give consumers the option to "flip" between pages. Fewer sites had a site overview (31%) and/or a site search engine (34%) – features that would assist consumers in truly tailoring their Web site experience to meet their own needs. The lack of such search tools may partially explain why only slightly less than half of Internet users find what they are looking for most of the time (49%; GVU 1998).

The Internet is also capable of presenting information in interactive or dynamic (i.e., video, audio) as well as in passive or static (i.e., text, graphics) form (Hoffman and Novak, 1996), thereby allowing the consumer to select the form in which information is presented. However, in addition to the lack of such interactive features as search engines, few Web sites had dynamic content (less than 20% of the sites). Rather, most of the information was presented in a passive manner: textually (94%) and/or graphically (77%).

Adding interactive content to a Web site could be an invaluable asset. It appears that interactive or dynamic content strongly affects visitors' impressions of the site and the information it presents. For instance, in a recent study, participants were asked to evaluate a number of pages that differed only in whether the content was presented in an interactive or passive manner. The results revealed a strong relationship between interactivity and perceptions of how entertaining or fun the pages were (r = .83 and .84 respectively; Schlosser and Kanfer, 1999b). In fact, even though participants in this study considered the interactive and passive pages to be equally informative (an accurate perception because the content of the pages was nearly identical), people found the interactive pages to contain more interesting ideas than the passive pages.

In summary, it appears that most commercial Web sites lack two components that are uncommon among traditional advertising practices (communicability and interactivity). Moreover, research suggests that interactive features play a crucial role in consumers' satisfaction with on-line commercial content, especially for those browsing the commercial site. Thus, the culture clash inherent in Internet Marketing has resulted not only with distrust of commercial Web sites, but dissatisfaction with commercial Web sites which, by design, might not meet the on-line population's needs and expectations.

5.3 Measuring Effectiveness

Current metrics of Web site success are based upon traditional measures of advertising and marketing effectiveness – metrics that do not fully capture the benefits of Internet Marketing. For instance, some corporations assess Web site effectiveness in terms of the revenues that could be attributed solely to the Web site (Oliva, 1997). Such a metric is likely to undervalue a Web site's effectiveness, especially given consumers' concerns regarding the security of on-line sales transactions (Gupta, 1995; GVU, 1997; Katz, 1998), which might cause them to make off-line purchases after reading Internet advertising. Indeed, few sites include features that would assist in tying off-line purchases to the Web site, such as an on-line order form that could be printed and faxed/mailed to the company (20%) or by providing coupons via the Internet that are redeemable at retail outlets (2%; Schlosser and Kanfer, 1999a). By lacking such features, counts of offline sales driven by Internet advertising exposure are likely to be underestimated.

Another common metric for measuring advertising effectiveness has been counts of the number of visitors to a site or the number of "hits." Such a metric is ingrained in traditional advertising effectiveness models, which base success in terms of circulation statistics (Hoffman and Novak, forthcoming). This metric only captures the success of the advertisement in generating awareness and getting the consumer to react by clicking on the link or typing the URL. Such reach and frequency models are likely inadequate for assessing IM effectiveness (Ephron, 1997; Rust and Oliver, 1994). Rather, the effectiveness of a site might best be established by assessing whether the consumer seeks additional information at the site (i.e., loads additional pages) and/or revisits (Berthon, Pitt and Watson, 1996; Ephron, 1997).

Although traditional marketing practices might be effective in persuading people to visit a site once (e.g., the product trial problem), such practices provide little information about how to encourage repeat visits (Hoffman and Novak, 1996). Research suggests that one important variable affecting revisit intentions is navigational ease (Rice, 1997; Schlosser and Kanfer, 1999a; 1999b). Empirical research has demonstrated that the perceived amount of navigational tools available at the site (i.e., *navigational availability*) was positively related to visitors' attitudes toward the site, in turn increasing visitors' intentions to revisit the site in the future (Schlosser and Kanfer, 1999a). What's more, it appears that navigational availability is related to Web site impressions for both browsers and searchers of the site due to the affective experiences evoked. For browsers, the greater the navigational availability, the more entertaining were their experiences at the site and the higher their web site attitudes and intentions to revisit. Thus, it appears that navigation availability enhances (or at least, does not hinder) browsers' level of experienced entertainment. For searchers, navigational availability was positively related to entertaining experiences (i.e., positive affect) *and* negatively related to irritation (i.e., negative affect). That is, for those with task-oriented, utilitarian goals, the more navigational tools perceived to be available, the more positive (and less negative) were their affective experiences. This is likely because searchers are not only interested in finding information suiting their goals (and being intrigued/entertained by such findings), but doing so in an efficient manner. In other words, the lack of navigational tools available (and consequently, the inability to find the sought information in an efficient manner) likely not only reduces their level of entertainment but also increases their feelings of irritation. Thus, one metric of Web site effectiveness might include measurements of the site's navigational availability and capabilities (e.g., accuracy, usability, speed, comprehensiveness).

In addition to generating awareness and increasing sales, there are also indirect benefits to be gained by having an effective commercial Web site, such as those gained through productivity, marketing and sales savings (Hoffman, Novak and Chatterjee, 1995). For instance, by providing product information on-line, the company can save in costs attributed to brochure or catalog printing and mailing – including those costs incurred due to changes in printed documents. Furthermore, by having database information on-line, consumers can access the database to answer their own query, thereby lowering the demand for toll-free customer service. For instance, at any time of day, the consumer can find out if an item has been shipped (e.g., www.fedex.com) or find out their most recent loan balance (e.g., www.salliemae.com). Likewise, consumers can place their own orders by filling out on-line forms, thereby reducing the company's costs associated with order taking.

Thus, using traditional advertising and marketing metrics to assess Web site success will likely ignore many of the unique contributions of a Web site to customer satisfaction, thereby undervaluing the importance of including a Web site as part of a marketing strategy. Instead, companies venturing on-line should measure Web site effectiveness by employing metrics applicable to the Internet such as users' navigational satisfaction, the number of brochure requests made on-line and the usage of coupons that are traceable to the Web site.

6 Consumer Attitudes Toward Internet Advertising

With such great potential for culture clash in IM, it is especially important to monitor consumer attitudes toward marketing in the new medium. Recent research suggests that Internet users hold slightly favorable but mostly neutral opinions of Internet advertising (Ducoffe, 1996; Schlosser, Shavitt and Kanfer, 1999). Yet, compared to a matched sample's judgments of advertising in general, fewer Internet users liked Internet advertising (38% vs. 46%; Schlosser, Shavitt and Kanfer, 1999). In order to gauge why Internet advertising is liked by fewer people than advertising in general is, a closer examination of the components comprising these attitudes is needed.

Although theory and research suggest that informativeness and entertainment are both necessary to include when designing an effective Web site (Ducoffe, 1996; Eighmey, 1997), a recent large sample of randomly selected American households of Internet users suggests that the most influential factor on attitudes toward Internet (and general) advertising was entertainment value (Schlosser, Shavitt and Kanfer, 1999). Whether experienced or novice, most users believe that the Internet has the potential to provide entertainment (Diaz, Hammond and McWilliam, 1996). Yet, consistent across multiple studies, Internet users consider Internet advertising to be more informative than entertaining (Ducoffe, 1996; Schlosser, Shavitt and Kanfer, 1999). In fact, significantly fewer people enjoy looking at Internet advertising than a similar population enjoys looking at advertising in general (38% vs. 50%; Schlosser, Shavitt and Kanfer, 1999). Thus, the adherence to treating marketing on the Web (in particular, commercial Web sites) as broadcasted, non-interactive print media (i.e., informative but not engaging) may result in continued perception of IM as not entertaining and, consequently, less positive attitudes toward Internet advertising than advertising in general.

Marketing via email and newsgroups has been perceived unfavorably as well, even if commercial information communicated to a newsgroup is customized to the interests of the group (Mehta and Sivadas, 1995). Uninvited commercial messages sent via electronic mail are known as "spam" and often elicit negative consumer responses (Mehta and Sivadas, 1995; Wright and Bolfing, forthcoming). In fact, the Coalition Against Unsolicited Commercial Email (CAUCE) argues that spam burdens the consumer rather than the advertiser with advertising costs. In retaliation, this coalition seeks to outlaw unsolicited commercial messages and has compiled resources for fighting spam (such as a blacklist of Internet advertisers; CAUCE, 1998). While there are some companies such as Cyber Promotions whose services are only spam, (Kornblum, 1998), it is not an easy business and many Internet

Service Providers choose to simply block all incoming email from known spammers.

Clearly the rules that apply to traditional advertising do not apply directly to online advertising. For instance, consumers accept seeing (and may even expect to see) the same advertisement in different magazines, newspapers, radio and television programs. However, they appear to be less tolerant of reading the same advertising message across multiple newgroups or listservs (an equally unfavorable tactic as spam known as "velveeta", Boydt, 1998). Likely contributing to consumers' unfavorable judgements of on-line unsolicited advertisements (whether targeted or not) is the potential for experiencing email overload (Kanfer and Riphagen, 1997). Although a variety of agent and filtering systems have been proposed to help manage the potentially overwhelming amount of information exchanged via email (Balter, 1997; Boydt, 1998; Kanfer, Sweet and Schlosser, 1997; Maes, 1994; Mehta and Sivadas, 1995; Rust, forthcoming), it is clear that there is a fine line between consumer expectations for two-way communications in IM and consumer irritation with communication-based IM.

7 Assimilation and Accommodation to the Internet Culture

On the Internet, marketers and advertisers appear to be experiencing culture shock. As with the phases of adjustment to another culture (see Triandis, 1994), on-line businesses began with a sense of optimism about the commercial possibilities of the Web. However, when traditional marketing practices clashed with the Internet culture's practices, businesses became disillusioned, claiming that the marketing implications of the Web were simply hype.

At this crossroads between proceeding with Internet marketing or abandoning it, on-line marketers are currently posed with the challenge of adjusting successfully to the Internet environment. As with the successful emigration to another culture (Triandis, 1994), an on-line business needs to first learn to cope with the new culture, then establish "cultural competence" and finally become a member. Next we describe each stage toward successful assimilation into the Internet culture.

7.1 Coping with the New Culture

An initial step in transitioning successfully to the new culture involves adjusting to the new culture, i.e., finding ways to cope with the experienced cultural differences. We have discussed a number of ways in which traditional marketing strategies clash with the Internet culture, one of which was employing "push" tactics. It has been argued that consumers' dislike for marketing messages being delivered via email is related to the distinction between "push" and "pull" tactics (Rust, forthcoming). With "pull" tactics, consumers are invited to seek commercial content rather than having it thrust upon their attention. Hence, one method of coping with the Internet population's displeasure with "pushed" advertisements is to employ "pull" tactics.

There are a number of ways to transform on-line communication-based marketing from a push tactic to pull.

One recommended technique for avoiding spam while still benefiting from the advantages of email marketing is to send messages only to those who have directly requested such commercial content either from the company itself or through a mediator who compiles lists of email users requesting commercial information on specific topics (Leung, 1998; Wright and Bolfing, forthcoming). When sending invited communication messages to newsgroups or listservs, the marketer should observe the culture of the specific environment before participating. When participating, the marketer should deliver a subtle advertising message and, following proper "netiquette" (i.e., Internet etiquette), offer information that is of value to the audience (Sadikin, 1995; Wright and Bolfing, forthcoming). Furthermore, the marketer must discard traditional mass marketing messages in favor of more individualized messages. One way to start is to design the *solicited* message such that it is tailored to the interests of the newsgroup or listserv, such as relating the message to the specific request for information or to past archived lists of the group's frequently asked questions.

Another option would be to target on-line promotions to consumers who have embraced direct marketing. It appears that consumers who have responded positively to such direct marketing methods as home shopping and mail-order catalogs are more accepting of Internet marketing. For instance, Mehta and Sivadas (1995) found that those with favorable attitudes toward direct marketing also hold more favorable attitudes toward targeted email and newsgroup advertising than those with unfavorable attitudes toward direct marketing. Furthermore, exposure to Internet advertising is more related to exposure to catalogs ($r = .50$) than exposure to advertising in other media such as newspaper ads, radio ads, direct mail, television ads and sales calls ($.05 < r < .19$; Schlosser, Shavitt and Kanfer, 1999). Perhaps consumers viewing catalogs are those who are already comfortable gathering purchase information via text, without having physical contact with the merchandise. Thus, the transition from using catalogs to conducting consumer activities via the Internet may be a natural one. How the marketer can take advantage of these complimentary marketing strategies are discussed below in the section "Becoming a Member."

7.2 Establishing Cultural Competence

Another step in adjusting to the new culture includes "cultural competence" or developing skills that will help the company thrive in the new culture. Consider for example Volvo, who shortly after launching its Web site, became overwhelmed with a variety of types of email messages, regarding both the site and the products. Unable to meet the demand, they coped with the situation by removing their email address from their Web site (http://www.volvocars.com). Although Volvo's Web site includes a good deal of interactivity, removing communication from the marketing strategy was not an optimal response to entering a culture where email is prevalent. One method of establishing cultural competence is to develop a method of effectively routing messages to the appropriate person, either electronically or through "email" operators. For instance, the Microsoft Web site allows visitors to send comments to the company only after reporting details about the nature of the message. Other examples of establishing cultural competence include developing useful navigational tools, secure on-line shopping transactions, innovative role-playing devices and accessible databases.

In establishing cultural competence in these areas, the on-line marketer needs to keep in mind that the inclusion of such interactivity in IM has its challenges. Consumer reactions to interactivity on Web sites depend upon task motivation and the attitude or behavior targeted for change. In a recent study, attitudes toward products, the company, the Web site, and purchase intentions were assessed from respondents randomly assigned to view a commercial Web site with either a hedonic (browsing) or a utilitarian (searching) goal (Schlosser and Kanfer, 1999b). The perceived amount of interactive features at the site was positively related to attitudes toward the company, its products and intentions to buy the company's products for those browsing but was negatively related to such judgments for those searching. In contrast, the perceived amount of traditional marketing information (e.g., purchase information, product and brand information) was positively related to web site impressions (e.g., attitudes toward the site and intentions to revisit) and off-line corporate impressions (e.g., attitudes toward the company and intentions to buy) for those searching but was negatively related to such judgments for those browsing. It appears that interactive versus traditional marketing features have a positive effect on judgments of those whose goals are compatible with such features (browsing versus searching, respectively) and a negative effect when the features are incompatible with the visitors' goals. Therefore, a successful IM strategy would include interactive features of a Web site to increase its entertainment value for browsers, but not at the expense of traditional marketing content, particularly if the site is also frequented by searchers.

In a follow up study (Schlosser and Kanfer, 1999b), the delivery of information was manipulated in addition to manipulating respondents' task goals. In this study, each respondent was randomly assigned to either browse or search a site that contained information presented either interactively/dynamically or passively/statically. The interactive/dynamic site contained features allowing the consumer to have direct "virtual" experience with the product (e.g., on-line product demonstrations). The passive/static site contained features that allowed the consumer to have indirect experience with the product (e.g., textual lists of product specifications). It was expected that browsers would hold more favorable judgments toward the company and its Internet presence after viewing the dynamic rather than passive site. In contrast, searchers were expected to hold more favorable judgments after viewing the passive rather than dynamic site. Consistent with these hypotheses, those browsing the dynamic site held higher web site and corporate impressions than did those browsing the passive site. This appears to be largely due to the entertainment provided by dynamic site but lacking from passive site. Moreover, browsers of the passive site held lower product, company and web site attitudes as well as intentions to revisit the site than did searchers of the passive site.

Surprisingly, however, there was little difference between the judgments of those searching the interactive versus passive sites with two exceptions. Those searching the passive site held higher product attitudes than did those searching the interactive site. Despite this, those searching the interactive site reported a higher likelihood of buying the company's products either off- or on-line than did those searching the passive site. In fact, searchers of the interactive site were the only ones who stated a likelihood of buying on-line. There are a couple elements that likely contributed to these unexpected findings. One is that attitudes derived from direct experience with the attitude object are more predictive of behavior than those derived from indirect experience (Fazio & Zanna, 1981). Consequently, perhaps the highly favorable attitudes of searchers of the passive site (i.e., those with indirect product experience) were less likely to translate into purchase intentions than the moderately favorable attitudes of searchers of the interactive site (i.e., those with direct product experience). Furthermore, perhaps the interactive content implies technical competence – an important impression to deliver when ensuring secure Internet sales transactions. Thus, designing a Web site with an understanding of the type of audience visiting the site (or creating sites or sections of sites for those who identify themselves as browsers versus searchers) as well as the attitude targeted for change would be one way in which to establish cultural competence.

7.3 Becoming a Member

The final phase in adjusting to a new culture involves becoming a member of the culture and assuming the new roles that this entails. This involves following the norms of appropriate behavior and speaking the language of the culture. Such norms include offering free goods and allowing the consumer to have control over the presentation of information. One indication that a company has become a member of the Internet culture is the adoption of integrated marketing communication along with adaptive marketing and relationship marketing, where IM is coordinated with other marketing efforts. This approach is a departure from traditional marketing practices (Rust and Oliver, 1994) and signifies a level of commitment to marketing in the new medium.

Integrated marketing communication is defined as "[a]n approach to promotional strategy that involves the coordination and integration of the various marketing and promotional programs by which an organization communicates with its consumers" (Belch and Belch, 1993, p. G-8). Clearly, integration is needed between advertising and marketing efforts across media, especially when references are made across media.

An example of such referencing is using traditional advertisements to invite the consumer to seek additional information at the company's Web site. Although most people discover Web sites by following links, one survey reported that over 60% of the respondents use magazines to find Web sites (Gupta, 1995). On-line businesses appear to be embracing this tactic as well: the number of company addresses (or URLs) appearing in print advertisement appears to be increasing at a nearly exponential rate (Huffenberger, Kanfer and Schlosser, 1998). Merely presenting the URL of the company's homepage in the advertisement will likely be insufficient in satisfying consumers' expectations, however, unless the homepage provides clear links to those pages that contain product information that is being actively promoted in other media (Hansen, 1998; Schlosser and Kanfer, 1999a). In fact, for over half (59%) of commercial Web sites actively promoted in magazines in 1996, it was difficult to find the advertised product on the Web site, and for nearly a tenth of the sites (9%), the product advertised in the print ad could not be found anywhere at the Web site (Schlosser and Kanfer, 1999a). Thus, advertisements in traditional advertising media that refer to a Web site should make sure that (a) the URL listed in the ad links directly to the page upon which the advertised product can be found, (b) the URL is accompanied by directions in the ad of which links to follow in order to find the advertised information or (c) if the URL links to the homepage, the homepage links directly to products being actively promoted.

Another useful media cross-referencing technique would be tying together the sister marketing strategies: direct marketing and Internet marketing. Because those who have adopted direct marketing might be most likely to embrace Internet marketing, marketing tactics in both media could make direct references to and supplement each other. Up-to-date information about what is in-stock and when an item has been shipped as well as electronic coupons and discounts for buying on-line are just a few examples of how a commercial Web site could supplement direct marketing efforts. All of these tactics, however, require coordination between advertising and marketing sections within an organization.

Additional adjustments to the new culture may require employing adaptive marketing and relationship marketing – both of which are based upon an individually-customized marketing approach (Rust and Oliver, 1994). Adaptive marketing involves making product revisions to meet consumer demands. Such flexibility could be offered on-line by allowing customers to build and order customized products on-line. Not only would this meet individualized consumer needs, but also provide valuable product development information for the marketer.

Relationship marketing involves building relationships between the buyer and seller. Examples include providing 24-hour personalized customer service. Another example is to establish a mutually beneficial relationship with the consumer by buying market research information directly from consumers (Hoffman & Novak, forthcoming). This would be a resolution to another clash between marketing and the Internet: the perception that on-line information should be freely available rather than contingent upon registration to a site. Web site registration has been one tactic employed by on-line organizations to inexpensively assess audience characteristics. When employing this tactic, on-line marketers need to be aware that most Internet users believe privacy to be the most important issue facing the Internet (GVU, 1997). Furthermore, 82% of the respondents in this GVU survey disagreed that content providers have the right to sell user information. Indeed, such efforts to gain audience information ignore the Internet's capabilities to decentralize the marketing process, allowing the consumer to be an active participant (Hoffman and Novak, forthcoming). Thus, a way of resolving this cultural difference is for the on-line site to offer to buy consumers' personal information rather than "steal" information through the use of cookies (i.e., the retrieval of an identification string unique to an individual consumer which is stored on the consumer's computer upon visiting the commercial site, see Riphagen and Kanfer, 1997 for a review) or buying the information from a third party.

8 Conclusions

The outlook for IM is not necessarily bleak. Indeed, in a 1996 survey, it was found that more Internet users perceive Internet advertising to be trustworthy and appropriate than a similar sample finds advertising in general to be (Schlosser, Shavitt and Kanfer, 1999). Furthermore, few believe that Internet advertising increases product prices (28%). This is in sharp contrast to the majority of a similar sample's perceptions that advertising in general increases product prices (73%).

We stand at a pivotal point, with great opportunity to make commercial content on the Internet entertaining and likeable, while retaining its informative characteristics. Our hope is that companies will include all elements of interactivity and customer-company communication in addition to providing rich product information, and that consumers will respond by liking IM more, finding it more informative and trustworthy and equally if not more entertaining than advertising in general.

References

American Marketing Association, *Marketing Definitions: A Glossary of Marketing Terms*, Committee on Definitions, American Marketing Association., Chicago, IL, 1960.

Balter, O. "Strategies For Organizing Email," in *People and Computers XII: Proceedings of the HCI'97*, (1997), T. Thimbleby et al. (Editors), London, Springer.

Belch, G. E. and M. A. Belch, *Introduction to Advertising and Promotion: An Integrated Marketing Communications Perspective*, Irwin, Homewood, IL, 1993.

Berthon, P., L. F. Pitt and R. T. Watson, "The World Wide Web as an Advertising Medium: Toward and Understanding of Conversion Efficiency," *Journal of Advertising Research*, (1996), 43-54.

Boydt, A., "Blacklist of Internet Advertisers," (1998),
URL = http://math-www.uni-paderborn.de/~axel/BL/.

CAUCE, "The Coalition Against Unsolicited Commercial E-mail," (1998),
URL = http://www.cauce.org/.

Davis, C. W. and D. J. Loundry, "Surge in Online Disputes Won't Be Suppressed in '98: Net Prophets," *Chicago Daily Law Bulletin*, 143, December 30, (1997).

Ducoffe, R. H., "Advertising Value and Advertising on the Web," *Journal of Advertising Research*, (1996), 21-35.

Eighmey, J., "Profiling User Responses to Commercial Web sites," *Journal of Advertising Research*, 37, May/June, (1997), 59-66.

Ephron, E., "Or is it an Elephant? Stretching our Minds For a New Web Pricing Model," *Journal of Advertising Research*, April, (1997), 96-98.

Fazio, R. H. And Zanna, M. P. , "Direct Experience and Attitude-Behavior Consistency," in *Advances in Experimental Social Psychology*, Vol. 14, L. Berkowitz, ed. New York: Academic Press Inc., (1981), 161-202.

Glazer, R. "Marketing in an Information-Intensive Environment: Strategic Implications of Knowledge as an Asset," *Journal of Marketing*, 55, (October, 1991), 1-19.

Gupta, S., "HERMES: A research project on the commercial uses of the World Wide Web," (1995), URL = http://www.umich.edu/~sgupta/hermes.

GVU, "GVU's WWW User Surveys: General Bulleted List," (1997), URL = http://www.cc.gatech.edu/gvu/user_surveys/survey-1997-04/bulleted/general_bullets.html

Hansen, G., "Smaller May Be Better For Web Marketing," *Marketing News*, 32, January 19, (1998), 10, 13.

Hawkins, D. T., "Electronic Advertising: On Online Information Systems," *Online*, March, (1994), 26-39.

Hof, R. D., S. Browder and P. Elstrom, "Internet Communities: Forget Surfers. A New Class of Netizen is Settling Right In," *BusinessWeek*, May 5, (1997), URL = http://www.businessweek.com.

Hoffman, D. L. and T. P. Novak, "A New Marketing Paradigm for Electronic Commerce," *The Information Society, Special Issue on Electronic Commerce*, (forthcoming).

Hoffman, D. L. and T. P. Novak, "Marketing in Hypermedia Computer-Mediated Environments: Conceptual Foundations," *Journal of Marketing*, 60, July, (1996), 50-68.

Hoffman, D. L., T. P. Novak, and P. Chatterjee, "Commercial scenarios for the web: Opportunities and challenges," *Journal of Computer-Mediated Communication*, (1995), URL = http://shum.huji.ac.il/jcmc/vol1/issue3/hoffman.html

Huffenberger, K., A. Kanfer and A. Schlosser, "The Growth of the URL in Magazine Advertising," (1998), URL = http://www.ncsa.uiuc.edu/edu/trg/urlgrowth.

Kanfer, A., J. Sweet, and A. Schlosser, "Humanizing the Net: Social Navigation with a "Know-who" Email Agent," Paper presented at the annual meeting of Human Factors and the Web, (1997).

Kanfer, A. and J. Riphagen, "How Does Email Affect Our Lives? Initial results from the 1997 NCSA Communication Study", (1997), URL = http://www.ncsa.uiuc.edu/edu/trg/email.

Katz, J., "The Digital Citizen," (1998), URL = http://www.hotwired.com/special/citizen

King, J., R. E. Grinter and J. M. Pickering, "The Rise and Fall of Netville: The Saga of a Cyberspace Construction Boomtown in the Great Divide," in *Culture on the Internet*, S. Kiesler (ed.), Lawrence Erlbaum Associates, Mahway, NJ, 1998.

Kornblum, J., "Spam King Retires," C|Net News, April 13, (1998), URL = http://www.news.com.

Kotler, P., *Principles of Marketing*,Prentice-Hall, Englewood Cliffs, NJ, 1980.

Leung, K., "Marketing With Electronic Mail Without Spam," *Marketing News*, 32, January. 19, (1998), 11.

Maes, P., "Agents that Reduce Work and Information Overload," *Communications of the ACM*,. 37, 7, (1994).

McDonald, S. C., "The Once and Future Web: Scenarios for Advertisers," *Journal of Advertising Research*, April, (1997), 21-28.

Mehta, R. and E. Sivadas, "Direct Marketing on the Internet: An Empirical Assessment of Consumer Attitudes," *Journal of Direct Marketing*, 9, Summer, (1995), 21-32.

Murphy, I. P., "On-line ads effective? Who knows for sure?," *Marketing News*, 30, September 23, (1996), 1, 38.

Network Wizards, "Internet Domain Survey, January 1998," (1998), URL = http://www.nw.com/zone/WWW/report.html.

NUA, "How Many Online?," (1998), URL = http://www.nua.ie/surveys/how_many_online/index.html.

O'Leary, M., "Consumer Online in the Age of the Net," *Online*, January/February, (1997a), 61-62.

O'Leary, M., "Web Succeeds Consumer Services as Consumer Online Medium," *Online* (July/August), (1997b), 67-69.

Oliva, R. A., "Harnessing an Unpredictable Tool," *Marketing Management*, 6, (1997), 34-36.

Pratkanis, A., and E. Aronson, "Self-sell," in *Age of propaganda: The everyday use and abuse of persuasion*, Freeman, New York, 1991.

Rice, M., "What makes users revisit a web site?," *Marketing News*, 31, March 17, (1997), 12.

Riphagen, J. and A. Kanfer "In Search of the Elusive User: Gathering Information on Web Server Access," (1997), URL = http://www.ncsa.uiuc.edu/edu/trg/webstats/.

Rust, R., "The Dawn of Computer Behavior," *Marketing Management*, (forthcoming).

Rust, R. and R. W. Oliver, "Notes and Comments: The Death of Advertising," *Journal of Advertising*, 4, December, (1994), 71-77.

Sadikin, P., "Advertising on the Internet: When can it bring leverage to the business?," (1995), URL = http//web.city.ac.uk/~dd559/int-adv.html

Schlosser, A. and A. Kanfer, "Current Advertising on the Internet: The Benefits and Usage of Mixed-Media Advertising Strategies," in D. Schumann and E. Thorson (Eds.), *Advertising and The Internet*, Lawrence Erlbaum Associates, Hillsdale, NJ, (1999a).

Schlosser, A. and A. Kanfer, "Interactivity in Commercial WebSites: Implications for WebSite Effectiveness," working paper, University of Illinois at Urbana-Champaign, (1999b).

Schlosser, A., S. Shavitt and A. Kanfer, "Survey of Attitudes Toward Internet Advertising," *Journal of Interactive Marketing*, 13, 3 (1999), 1-21.

Triandis, H. C., *Culture and Social Behavior*, McGraw-Hill, New York, 1994.

Wright, N. D. and C. P. Bolfing, "Marketing Via Email: Maximizing Its Effectiveness Without Resorting to Spam," *COTIM Conference Proceedings*, (forthcoming).

Part III
Web-Based Storefront Design and Development

CHAPTER 10
Design of Electronic Stores

Ting-Peng Liang and Nian-Shin Chen
Department of Information Management, National Sun Yat-sen University, Kaohsiung,
Taiwan, liang@mis.nsysu.edu.tw; nschen@mis.nsysu.edu.tw

The number of electronic stores is increasing in an unprecedented speed. A recent study indicates that store design may affect customer's decisions on whether to buy electronically. This
chapter covers various issues involved in designing an electronic store. We first examine the
perspectives of the seller and the buyer. Then, requirements and procedures for building a
store are presented. Tools available for building the store are also introduced.

Keywords: Electronic Stores; Store Design; Design Tools; Guidelines

1 Introduction

The introduction of Internet, coupled with the rapid proliferation of world wide web
(WWW), has created a challenging arena for electronic commerce. More than sixty
million computers are now hooked up to the Internet. More than 30 thousand companies are using Internet to do business. It is estimated that the number of on-line
users will increase to more than 550 million (about one-tenth of the world's population) and the value of business transactions executed on the Internet will be more
than 100 billion dollars by the year of 2000 (Hoffman, 1997; Hamilton, 1997). This
indicates that Internet provides an important channel for electronic transactions in
the future.

An electronic store (or called a virtual store) is a web address at which its homepages provide information about its products or services and support of basic transactional processes (Yesil, 1997). There are at least two types of electronic stores:
single store and *electronic mall*. A single store has its web address to sell certain
products or services. For instance, Amazon is an Internet bookstore that sells books.
The store's web page must provide advertising, ordering, payment, security, customer services, and other necessary functions. An electronic mall is a web address
that combines many electronic stores to create a synergy. The mall provides common functions such as advertising, ordering and payment for its stores. By putting
the stores together, the mall intends to be more attractive due to its diversity and
integrated marketing.

The product offered in electronic stores can be *digital* or *physical*. Digital products such as computer software and data services can be ordered and delivered

through Internet, whereas physical products such as computer hardware or printed books can be ordered electronically but must be delivered through regular channels.

There are several advantages for running a electronic store. For the owner, the operating cost is lower than that of a traditional store in most cases. For instance, the warehouse can be located in a suburban area to reduce its rental cost. An electronic store also provides an inexpensive and effective way to access on-line users. For consumers, they have more flexibility in collecting and comparing product information electronically. Therefore, the widespread of electronic stores may create new business styles, affect current distribution channels, change consumer purchase behaviors and government legal regulations. In other words, electronic stores may change our living styles in the future and are full of challenges and business opportunities.

Among the existing electronic stores, some are very successful, whereas others may be disappointing. Many factors may affect their successful operations, such as product characteristics, store design, pricing, and promotion. A recent study indicates that store design can affect customer's decision on whether to buy electronically (Liang and Lai, 1998). A well-designed electronic store can better attract customers to visit and increase their willingness to purchase.

The purpose of this chapter is to present guidelines for designing a good electronic store. In general, a good store design must take into account customer requirements and functions necessary for transaction processing and store management. In the remainder of this article, Section 2 examines requirements for a good electronic stores from the perspectives of both the seller and the consumer. Section 3 describes guidelines for designing a good electronic store. Sections 4 and 5 present the procedures and development tools for building electronic stores. Finally, sample stores are discussed.

2 Requirement Analysis

Requirement analysis is a procedure for determining functional requirements of a store. Since the seller and buyer are two major stakeholders of an electronic store, both must be taken into consideration.

2.1 Perspective of the Seller

From the seller's perspective, an electronic store is a channel for marketing. There are four major concerns in marketing (generally called 4P): product, price, place and promotion. Therefore, designing an electronic store must take these 4P into account.

Product

What a store sells is sometimes more important than how it sells. Therefore, the first thing to consider is to choose products or services that are suitable for web marketing. These products can be digital or physical. In general, information-rich products are more suitable for the Internet market. A recent research found customers would buy electronically if the product involves less uncertainty and needs more effort to search in traditional channels (Liang and Huang, 1998).

Price

Electronic media has great flexibility in dynamic pricing. Products or services may be priced differently at different time, for different customers, or in different geographical areas. A good electronic store must support dynamic pricing.

Place

Where to locate an electronic store may affect its cost and performance. A major limitation of the web is its bandwidth. Therefore, running an electronic store must choose a proper server and, when necessary, setup mirror sites properly to increase the performance of information dissemination. Selecting proper mirror sites is similar to selecting a store location in traditional businesses. It is also necessary to use different languages to fit various local markets.

Promotion

In addition to traditional promotion techniques, the web technology provides an interactive media with strong analytical capabilities. New promotion techniques such as interactive and database marketing can be used more effectively.

Given the marketing concerns, design of an electronic store needs to take care of web page design, shelf layout, transaction process, and operational management.

Web Page Design

Since electronic stores may not have physical stores accessible to on-line customers, the web pages are the stores perceived by their customers. Therefore, designing attractive web pages so that on-line customers are willing to visit more often and stay longer is important.

Shelf Layout

Shelf management is important for traditional stores. In electronic stores, product indexing and organization are the perceived shelf layout to customers. It is, therefore, important to design a friendly and well-organized product shelf.

Transaction Process

Selling products must go through a transaction process, which includes ordering, payment, product delivery, and processing returned goods. It is necessary that the process is secure, reliable, flexibility and friendly to customers.

2.2 Perspective of the Customer

The requirement of the consumer can be analyzed by examining the purchasing process. A store with good support of the process is more likely to be attractive to consumers. There are several different consumer choice models. In this article, we adopt the popular EKB model to define the needs of consumers (Engel, et al., 1982).

The EKB Model divides the consumer decision process into five stages: *problem recognition, search for information, evaluation of alternatives, choice,* and *outcome evaluation.* When a problem is recognized, demand for certain products that can eliminate the recognized problem is derived. Product information is collected and alternative products are proposed and evaluated. Once an alternative is chosen, the consumer evaluates the outcome and saves the experience for the future.

The requirements for electronic commerce at each stage can be derived as follows:

Problem recognition: It is helpful if the system can identify consumer needs, stimulate demand, and generate an environment for them to recognize problems.

Information collection: The store needs to help consumers collect useful information during their decision process. This information can help them evaluate products and influence their decision criteria.

Alternative evaluation: It is useful to have functions that help consumers evaluate alternatives based on collected information.

Choice: At the choice stage, the consumer often has to make tradeoffs among various criteria. It is necessary to have functions that help them make a decision.

Transaction and post-sales services: The friendliness of the transaction process, post-sales services and other functions that make the transaction easier are also important for attracting customers.

3 Guidelines from the Consumer's Perspective

When people purchase at an electronic store, they may have different considerations at different decision stages. A good design must support customer needs. In this section, we examine guidelines derived from the process of consumer choice.

3.1 Problem Recognition

Major factors that affect problem recognition include environmental stimulation, individual experience, and inner motivation of the consumer. Although it is hard to provide support of individual experience and inner motivation, it is possible to develop a stimulating environment. The following are a few guidelines.

Designing stores properly: Consumers often prefer well-designed sites. A good store should have uniform user interface and well-organized contents.

(1) *Uniform interface styles*: Since customers often visit one shop at a time, it is helpful to design stores in the same style. This reduces the cognitive load of the consumer.

(2) *Hierarchical product organization*: Since it is impossible to view or touch products in an electronic store, as customers usually do in a traditional one, products must be organized in a creative way to stimulate customer imagination. Using the virtual reality technology may also be helpful.

Guiding shopping routes: An electronic store may have many different product items, it is necessary to have a good shopping guide and search engines. Customers need them to find proper products. There are a few guidelines for designing good shopping guides, as follows:

(1) *Proper use of special effects*: Special effects can attract immediate attention to a particular product. For instance, a moving banner can be used to show what is on sale.

(2) *Carefully designed hyperlinks*: In the traditional store, shelfe management is very important. For the same reason, the hyperlinks that lead customers through different shopping routes must be designed carefully to maximize sales potential. Since customers may get lost in numerous hyperlinks, an electronic store should help customers find where they are, and provide convenient ways to traverse.

Stimulating desire of purchase: Actions may be taken to stimulate consumer's desire to purchase. Popular activities include:

(1) *Using POP*: Traditional shopping malls often adopt POP (Point of Purchase) to get attention from customers. This can also be adopted in an electronic store. In fact, it is pretty easy to use POP on electronic media, such as labeling *NEW!* or *On Sale!*. It is also helpful to use sound and animation to present certain products.

(2) *On-line broadcasting*: Adding on-line broadcasting of music or other sound may help stimulate the desire of purchase. A periodical broadcasting may improve the usually quiet purchasing environment.

(3) *Adding auction mechanism*: Adding an auction square that allows people to bid for certain merchandise may help attract customers.

Providing reference groups: Consumers sometimes rely on their friends or other consumers for opinions. For example, people tend to go to popular stores that have more visitors. However, customers shopping on the web cannot see other shoppers. Without feeling the existence of other shoppers, consumers may lose some fun. So, we may use two approaches to help consumers know the existence of their peers.

(1) *Showing the number of current visitors*: The number of current visitors is an index of current shopping atmosphere. Showing the number and frequency of visits give information about the popularity of the store.

(2) *Providing chat rooms*: Chat room is an important tool that allows consumers to exchange their opinions on products or other issues.

3.2 Search for Information

Before making a purchase, search for relevant information is critical. Certain functions that support information search are important.

Allowing fast product search: An electronic store may have thousands of product items. Therefore, a good mechanism for finding a particular product rapidly is important. In addition to a proper organization of products, it is important to have a built-in search engine. Customers use the engine to find what they need.

Providing value-added information: One advantage of electronic stores over traditional ones is their ability in offering value-added information. This information, such as the best sellers, headline news, trend of fashion, or announcement of activities, can be useful information for consumers.

Providing customer information: Another advantage of electronic stores is its ability in data recording. The system can easily record and analyze sales data and the behavior of consumers. This information is useful for more effective marketing.

3.3 Evaluation of Alternatives

After collecting adequate information, customers will generate and evaluate which product to buy and whether to buy electronically. Therefore, an electronic store may provide functions that support evaluation of products and channels.

Supporting functions for product evaluation: When evaluating products, customers often compare candidate attributes, inquire information from staff, and bargain with the staff for a better price (Baty and Lee, 1995). It helps if an electronic store provides:

(1) *Price and other comparisons*: Price is a key attribute most consumers consider when they purchase. By comparing prices between electronic stores and traditional ones, it may be easier for customers to make decision.

(2) *On-line Customer Support*: Consumers often seek opinions from their friends or other consumers during decision making. An electronic store can provide online interaction with customers through the network. Consumers may also talk to each other.

Building trust in an electronic environment: For customers who are not used to electronic purchasing, it is important to build up their confidence. Possible guidelines include:

(1) *Guaranteeing Security of transactions*: Since the seller and buyer do not meet with each other in the virtual market, credit cards are popular for payment. Security is often a major concern in this case. Critical information such as credit data may be stolen from the network during transmission. Therefore, adopting proper security mechanisms such as authentication and making proper announcements about the security of the transaction are useful.

(2) *Offering the VIP system*: The VIP system that focuses on a small group of special customers can increase the royalty of the customer and make member authentication easier. This may reduce transaction costs and enhance the security of transactions.

(3) *Providing phone numbers for services*: To reduce the feeling of uncertainty at purchasing, it is helpful if service phone lines and other contact information are available. Although customers may not need to use them, these numbers do have psychological effects.

3.4 Choice

While making the final choice, consumers need tools to aggregate information and make a selection. An electronic store can provide support during the decision process and recommend for more purchases.

Providing shopping carts for continuous purchase: In a traditional store, consumers often use shopping barrows or carts to carry their merchandise. In the electronic environment, it is helpful to provide electronic shopping barrows for convenience. Tools may also be provided to counts the total amount of purchase for budget control.

Offering suggestions and substituting products, if necessary: The system may help customers choose proper products by offering choice models. Sometimes, customers may be constrained by their budgets. In this case, tools that recommend substitute products or more choices may be helpful.

Using online salespersons: It is common to bargain prices in some markets. It would be interesting if the system provides on-line salespersons or agents to deal with customers who are willing in bargaining. Online salespersons are people who promote their products to the client via the network. Their main responsibility is to interact with customers, observe consumer's reaction, and promote their products properly.

3.5 Transaction and Post-Sales Services

After making a choice, the transaction process as well as post-sales services becomes important. Customers may need support in the following aspects.

Supporting the transaction process. An empirical study shows that convenience in the transaction process is the most important factor affecting consumers to purchase in electronic stores (Liang and Lai, 1998). Therefore, attentions must be paid to the functions available to support the transactional process.

(1)*Placing an order*: on-line ordering is essential.

(2)*Delivering products*: customers ordering electronically may want the product to be delivered in different ways. Therefore, multiple alternatives for delivery such as surface mail and express mail are necessary.

(3) *Paying for the product*: It is common that customers pay by their credit cards. In this case, network security is critical. An alternative way is to pay by money orders. This is also popular in some countries because it is safer.

Post-sales services: Common functions include the following.

(1) *Inquiring and tracking product deliveries*: Customers often would like to know the status of their order. Providing support to product tracking makes customers feel more comfortable with their orders.

(2) *Allowing product returns*: Support of product returns is also necessary.

(3) *Organizing buyer clubs*: A buyer club provides a channel through which buyers can exchange their opinions and share their experiences. This kind of support may increase customer loyalty.

4 Procedures for Building an Electronic Store

The process for building a successful store is still more of an art. There is no guarantee that stores built following certain procedures will be successful in operation. Nonetheless, good practices that takes various issues into consideration can reduce the likelihood of failure, minimize development time and costs, and increase the competitiveness of the store. In this section, an approach that includes the following six steps is presented: (1) Choose products suitable for an Internet store, (2) Form a plan for running the store, (3) Locate the store properly, (4) Set up the store, (5) Promote the store, and (6) Manage store operations. Figure 1 shows the major issues in each of the steps.

4.1 Choose Products Suitable for an Internet Store

Internet stores are not for all products. Some are more appropriate than others. Therefore, the first thing to do is to determine what you would like to sell and whether it is suitable for electronic markets. Products available in electronic markets include *physical products*, *digital products*, and *on-line services*. Recent data indicate that books and computer-related products are often ranked high on the best-selling list of physical products. A study of Liang and Huang (1998) found that product uncertainty and asset specificity determine whether a product is suitable for selling in electronic markets. Products that need detail examination or trial before purchase (such as shoes) and a higher degree of post-sales services (such as micro

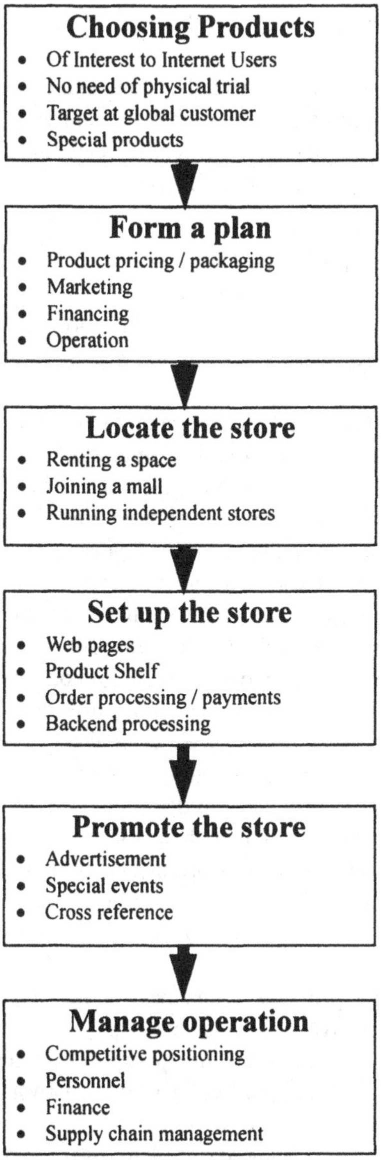

Choosing Products
- Of Interest to Internet Users
- No need of physical trial
- Target at global customer
- Special products

Form a plan
- Product pricing / packaging
- Marketing
- Financing
- Operation

Locate the store
- Renting a space
- Joining a mall
- Running independent stores

Set up the store
- Web pages
- Product Shelf
- Order processing / payments
- Backend processing

Promote the store
- Advertisement
- Special events
- Cross reference

Manage operation
- Competitive positioning
- Personnel
- Finance
- Supply chain management

Fig. 1. Procedures for building an electronic store

wave ovens) are less appropriate for electronic markets. General guidelines for choosing appropriate products include the following.

1. Of interest to Internet users, who are usually young and computer-literate.
2. Do not need physical trial or can be examined electronically.
3. Simple purchasing processes that need no complicated considerations.
4. Special products not easily found in other markets.

4.2 Form a Plan for Running the Store

Once products are determined, a plan for running the store must be formed. The plan should include realistic goals, product pricing and packaging, marketing, operating, and financial plans of the store.

Realistic goals: Although Internet stores sound flying high, you must have clear and realistic idea about where your store is going. Your store is competing with other Internet stores and all kinds of conventional stores. The electronic store can be an independent one or a supplementary one to your traditional store. For an independent store, you need to set up realistic goals of sales and profits for the next few years. If you want to supplement your current store, you need to know whether you want the electronic store to cut your costs or to make more sales, and to what extent can the current business benefit from the Internet exposure.

Product pricing and packaging: Most products sold on Internet are priced lower than those in traditional markets. The primary reason is that consumers feel more uncertain when they purchase electronically. Electronic stores may also have a lower operating cost because they can save operating costs by not renting an expensive business office or hiring fewer employees to deal with customers. Another reason is that electronic markets are more efficient than traditional markets in information dissemination. Consumers can easily compare prices offered at different stores and purchase from the cheapest one. This makes over-pricing very hard to sustain. Product packaging is another issue. Products may need to be redesigned to attract consumers in electronic markets.

Marketing plan: Internet provides a channel for merchandise transaction, but products won't sell by themselves. A good marketing plan is necessary. The marketing plan must take into consideration the specific characteristics of Internet. It also needs to integrate with traditional media such as newspapers, magazines, or radio programs.

Operating plan: For a store to operate, a plan covers merchandise demonstration, order processing, payment, delivery, and post-sales services is necessary. The plan must be tailored to the products to be sold. For instance, the plan for selling automobiles is usually very different from that of selling books.

Financial plan: A financial plan secures the financial resources necessary for running an electronic store. In general, three kinds of costs must be estimated and planned: installation, promotional, and operating costs. The installation costs are the costs necessary for building the store and connecting it with the Internet. They include hardware, software, and setup costs. Hardware costs cover web servers, mass storage and telecommunication devices. Software costs cover database, security management, and other related software. Setup costs include personnel and other costs occurred at the setup stage.

Promotional costs are necessary for informing potential customers of the existence of the store. In addition to advertising in traditional media, promotion can be done by cross-referencing with other stores on the web, advertising at search engines, and launching special promotional events. Operating costs include personnel, homepage update and maintenance, customer services, and other costs related to the daily operation of the store.

4.3 Locate the Store Properly

Location is the critical success factor of a traditional store. Although Internet has overcome the geographical barrier, it is still necessary to decide how you would like your electronic store to be located. An electronic store contains web pages through which customers find what it sells and order merchandise. Therefore, the location issue is about where the web page is installed. There are three generic approaches: renting a server space, joining an Internet mall, or running the company's own server.

Renting a server space: Renting a server space is the cheapest way to run an electronic store. Many ISP have space available for renting. In this case, the owner does not need to worry about the hardware and software environment. The focus is how to build a friendly customer interface. The guidelines introduced in Section 3 are helpful.

Joining an Internet mall: An Internet mall is a collection of many Internet stores. A mall often offers common operational functions such as ordering process, payment, security, and customer services. Stores in the mall can share these functions. The advantages of joining a mall, instead of running an independent store, are (a) certain costs such as marketing and customer services can be shared by the stores in the mall, (b) synergy can be created by integrating products and services available in different stores, and (c) the location may be more attractive to customers due to the product variety. Major drawbacks include that (a) the store may loss some control due to the necessity of more coordination among stores, and (b) the store does not have the identity it would have as an independent store.

Running the company's own server: Running its own server for a store is the third and the most expensive strategy. The store has the complete control over the operation of the store, has a clear identity, but costs more to run, and can take less advantage of complementary products. It also needs much effort to put all operations together, from order processing, customer management to payment and security systems.

4.4 Setup the Store

After choosing a proper strategy for location, the store needs to be actually installed. This includes designing web pages, managing the product shelf, processing customer orders, payments, customer services, and backend accounting and management information.

Designing the web page: The web page of the electronic store is the interface between the store and its customers. They must be very user friendly and can demonstrate the strengths of the store to attract customers. The web page also needs to be integrated with all operations and databases for easy management. Web pages may be designed by internal teams or be outsourced to professional designers.

Managing the product shelf: Managing the product shelf is another important issue. For electronic stores, product information must be stored in a database so that it can be shown effectively on web pages. Similar to traditional stores, the key is to organize products in a way that maximizes their exposure to customers. General guidelines include providing efficient functions to support product search and tailoring product presentation to seasonal, individual, and other contingent factors.

Processing orders, payments, and customer services: Customer orders, payments, and service requests must be processed by information systems integrated with the web page. These systems also need to be integrated with an efficient delivery system. The major tradeoff at this stage is balancing security and convenience.

Backend accounting and management information systems: Since transactions are processed on-line, it is easy to build accounting and other information systems for management support.

4.5 Promote the Store

The name is the most important asset of the store. When people need a web site, they go to Yahoo. When they want to buy books, the Amazon comes up to their mind. Therefore, promoting the store in the virtual world is more important than anything else. There are several ways to promote an electronic store. The store must be registered at popular search engines such as Yahoo. Internet users often rely on search engine providers to find new information. It is also helpful to have strategic alliance with complementary sites that cross-list each other's products. Advertisement can also be put through advertising agencies in the interactive world, such as the CKS Interactive of Cupertino, California, and Poppe Tyson of Mountain View, California.

A good promotion plan must include activities to attract new customers and those for retaining returning customers. It is critical that you create a homepage, i.e. the first page, that draws the visitor into your site to become the customer. You need to make your message clear and loud to tell visitors your specific features and their benefits from purchasing from you.

4.6 Manage for High Performance

Once a store is set up, the management team needs to determine its competitive position, hire proper personnel, finance the operation, and manage the supply chain and customer relationships. Although some traditional management rules still apply, the management team needs to pay special attention to the nature of the Internet environment that may affect the competition and operational efficiency. For instance, it is easy for an Internet store to run business internationally. Unless the store is positioned strictly for domestic operation, it must be able to handle transnational orders.

Overall, designing an electronic store has to consider both technical and managerial issues. Technically, the store must be designed to meet the requirements of both the seller and the buyer. Managerially, the store must be competitive internally and on the market.

5 Development Tools

There are two approaches to construct an electronic store. One is to use software packages tailored for EC development and the other is to use generic development tools such as Java or Java Script. The first approach is fast and convenient. The developer does not need to have a very strong technical background. The second approach has more flexibility and allows for including more customized functions, but the developer must be more knowledgeable in computer programming.

If you would like to use the first approach, a few software packages are available in the market. Popular ones include Netscape Merchant of Netscape, Inc., Easy Merchant and Net Commerce of IBM, Microsoft Merchant Server, Electronic Commerce Suite of iCat, Intershop of Netconsult Comm., Merchant Builder of Internet Factory, OM-Transact of Open Market. In most cases, these packages include major modules necessary for running an electronic store. The developer specifies what functions are necessary and install them.

In addition to using customized packages, it is also common to use generic tools in developing electronic stores. Since an electronic store is composed of a front-end, a backend and their interconnections, different tools are often used for building different modules. The front-end contains what the consumer sees on their screen. Therefore, tools used for designing the front-end must have good user interface functions. The backend provides database and other supports on the server. The SQL server and database software are the focus. The following are some of the commonly used tools.

5.1 Front-end Tools

The front-end offers the user interface for the user to view through a browser. In other words, it is the face of the store. The foundation is the HyperText Markup

Language (HTML). HTML is the language used to present web documents. Although HTML can be written in virtually any word processor, there are more and more WYSIWYG (What You See Is What You Get) tools for building web pages, such as FrontPage, Netscape Composer, Java Script and so forth.

FrontPage: Frontpage is a product of Microsoft. Its newest version, FrontPage 98, is a friendly tool for building and managing homepages. It is very user friendly and powerful. The user can easily build a home page through drag-and-drop. It supports FRAME and dynamic homepage design. It also has a built-in Active Server Page (ASP) Database Region Wizard that supports dynamic database search.

Netscape Composer: Netscape Composer is a homepage editor built in the Netscape 4.x browser. It also has WYSIWYG functions, but is not as powerful as FrontPage. Nonetheless, it comes with the browser and is free.

Java Script: Java Script is a script language developed by Netscape and Sun Microsystems. It allows the builder to write programs that can be inserted into an HTML document to perform certain functions. Special effects such as moving banners seen on web pages are often coded in Java Script.

VB Script: VB Script is similar to Java Script, except that it was offered by Microsoft and the syntax is compatible to Visual Basic. Because it is a product of microsoft, the Netscape browser does not support it. Similarly, Microsoft's Internet Explorer does not support Java Script.

Java: Java is an object-oriented language developed by Sun Microsystems. Its syntax is pretty similar to C/C++ and provides applets that can be executed at the Client site to reduce the load from the server. It is very powerful in processing sounds, images, and tables. Two tools are useful: (1) JDK: It is a Java development tool developed by Sun Microsystems. It compiles Java programs into byte-code and has debugging functions. (2) Visual J++: It is a product of Microsoft for fast development of cross-platform Java applets.

ActiveX: ActiveX is an OLE-based flexible technique. Its control object integrates desktop and web technology to generate more powerful capabilities in dynamic linkages. Plenty of tools support the development of ActiveX, such as Visual Basic, Visual C++, Delphi, Powerbuilder, etc.

VRML: VRML stands for Virtual Reality Modeling Language. It allows a homepage to have three dimensional effects. The homepage developed in VRML can only be viewed through browsers that support VRML.

5.2 Back-end Tools

The backend of an electronic store needs to have database and email supports. It may also need functions for information management. The following are ommonly used databases.

Microsoft SQL Server: SQL server is an engine for managing data retrieval. SQL Server 6.5, for instance, is capable of distributing data to web pages on the Internet. It has a distributed transaction coordinator that can manage transactions across multiple servers.

Oracle Database: The recent version of Oracle 8 supports Internet. It is able to manage a large amount of data in different formats and support multiple computing platforms, such as DEC, Solaris, Windows NT, OS/2, and so on.

IBM DB2: The recent version of DB2 Universal Database 5.0 is a multimedia, Internet-enabled database. It can integrate databases from different vendors and support many different computing platforms.

5.3 Interconnection Tools

The front-end and backend modules are integrated through a gateway. A commonly used standard is called CGI (Common gateway Interface). Its major function is to process message passing between the browser and the server to allow interactive uses of web pages. Tools used for writing CGI programs include Perl, C/C++, Visual Basic, and Tcl. Perl is the most popular CGI language. It is very portable and easy to use. C/C++ is more complex but its compiled program is more efficient in execution. Visual Basic is easy to learn and use, but is appropriate for Windows environment only. Tcl is similar to Perl but available on Unix only.

Since database access is essential to electronic commerce, tools in this regard are necessary. Although the developer can write CGI programs to manage data, the development and maintenance costs are higher than those of using customized database tools. The following are a few tools for database access.

Microsoft ASP and ADO: It is designed for accessing databases that supports ODBC, and is suitable for Internet servers running IIS3.0 or higher.

Microsoft ADC: It provides an active control that is operated at the client site. It is suitable for frequent data search and retrieval. The browser at the client site must support ActiveX.

Netscape LiveWire: This product comes with Netscape Enterprise Server. It supports ODBC and databases such as Oracle, Sybase, and Informix.

Oracle Web Application Server: It supports ODBC and has NT and Unix versions.

IBM Net.data: It can connect many different databases such as DB2, Oracle, and Sybase.

In addition to individual functions, there are tools that can integrate various modules. A typical one is the Microsoft Active Server Page (ASP). ASP is a script environment installed on the server to integrate HTML and the script language. It also supports CGI and database connections. Visual InterDev is a tool that can be used to develop ASP. It allows powerful and dynamic electronic stores to be developed. Net.Data is a similar product offered by IBM.

The alternatives and tools mentioned above are not necessarily the best for a particular store. The developer needs to know their advantages and drawbacks when choosing development tools.

6 Sample Stores

A good way to have a sense of electronic store design is to review existing stores on the Internet. In this section, two popular stores are described.

6.1 Amazon – http://www.amazon.com/

Amazon is arguably the largest bookstore on the web. It offers over a million book titles for on-line search. Most books sold here are heavily discounted. The store has a search engine that allows the customer to search books by author, title, subject, and key words. Once a book of interest is found, the customer can place the order electronically. The ordered book may be delivered by regular or express mail. Books are often paid by credit cards.

After an order is received, the store uses email to inform the customer the status of the order. From time to time, the customer may also receive emails that recommend books of potential interest to him. The store also offers information about best-selling books, book reviews, and other useful information. Figure 2 shows the homepage of Amazon.

Fig. 2. Homepage design of amazon

6.2 AcerMall – http://mall.acer.net/

AcerMall is an electronic mall in Taiwan, which integrates many complementary stores. The stores in the mall offer books, flowers, CD, gifts, electronic equipment, computer software and hardware, and credit data. The homepage uses a two-frame design: the left frame shows a menu of different stores, whereas the right one shows the content of special event and advertising banners. The mall handles order processing, payments, promotion, and interaction with the consumer. Once an order is received, the mall forwards it to the proper store for merchandise delivery. Figure 3 shows the homepage of AcerMall, whose design style is different from Amazon shown in Figure 2.

Fig. 3. Homepage of acerMall

7 Conclusions

Designing an electronic store is a complicated job. We need to consider both technical and managerial issues. In this chapter, we have discussed the requirements for an
electronic store from the perspective of both the seller and the buyer. Functional
guidelines and procedures for building a store were then presented. Finally, software
tools for designing homepages and two sample stores have also been presented.
Although following our guidelines may not guarantee profitability, it can help avoid
some mistakes. Since running an electronic store is still more of an art, it is also
useful to obtain more sense by reviewing the design of successful stores.

References

Baty, B.J. and Lee, R.M., "InterShop: Enhancing the Vendor/Customer Dialectic in Electronic
    Shopping," *Journal of MIS*, 11:4, (1995), pp. 9-31.
Engel, J.F., Blackwell, R.D. and Kollat, D.T., *Consumer Behavior*, 4th Edition, Rinehart and
    Winston, New York, 1982.
Hamilton, S., "E-Commerce for the 21st Century," *Computer*, 30:5, (1997), pp. 44-47.
Hoffman, D.L., et al., "Commercial Scenarios for the Web: Opportunities and Challenges," in
    R. Kalakota ad A.B. Whinston (eds.), *Readings in Electronic Commerce*, Addison-Wesley,
    Reading, MA, pp. 29-53, 1997.
Liang, T.P. and Lai, H.J., "Development of Electronic Shopping Malls in Taiwan," *Proceed-
    ings of the APEC Conference on Computer Literacy*, Tokyo, Japan, (1997).
Liang, T.P. and Lai, H.J., "Consumer-centered Design of Electronic Stores: Guidelines and
    Empirical Study," Working paper, Department of Information Management, National Sun
    Yat-sen University, (1998).
Liang, T.P. and Huang, J.S., "An Empirical Study on Consumer Acceptance of Products in
    Electronic Markets: A Transaction Cost Model," *Decision Support Systems*, 21, (1998),
    pp. 61-73.
Yesil, M., *Creating the Virtual Store*, New York, NY; John Wiley & Sons, 1997.

CHAPTER 11
Web Development and Management: Using the Cohort Model

Claire R. McInerney[1] and Kai R. T. Larsen[2]

[1]University of Oklahoma, School of Library and Information Studies, Norman, OK 73019-0528, USA, cmcinerney@ou.edu

[2]Information Science Ph. D. Program, University at Albany/S.U.N.Y., Albany, NY, USA, klarsen@acm.org

Organizing technology work in teams that meet in a larger group called a "cohort" can create a learning organization that uses time and energy effectively. Developing and maintaining World Wide Websites for information storage, dissemination, and for business transactions in a cohort is one way to reorganize work processes, but it requires learning and adaptation. An organizational cohort can allow members to learn from each other, thereby expanding the knowledge base and accomplishing tasks more quickly than working in isolation. This chapter demonstrates how a cohort is used to develop Websites and policies by profiling one case – The Center for Technology in Government's Internet Testbed Project. Practical tools, such as stakeholder analysis, best practices research, strategic framework, prototyping, and a cost performance analysis are highlighted and explained as part of a successful cohort undertaking. A discussion of effective means of developing policy and managing a Website is also included.

Keywords: Network Organization; Virtual Organization; Web Development Training; Internet Policy; Interorganizational Training; World Wide Web; Government Technology; Group Decision Support

1 The Cohort Model

"A cohort is any group of individuals linked as a group in some way – usually by age...or modes...or class" (Glenn, 1977). Most often cohorts are established for learning, for engineering change, or to experience an event. Originally conceived as a configuration of soldiers in a military organization, 'cohort' models today are commonly used in education where a group of students enters a program together, takes the same courses during a semester, and matriculates at the same time. The cohort creates a learning community where information is shared willingly and openly.

Most organizations develop Websites for information dissemination and service transactions, but they do so in isolation. A Webmaster or service agency designs the

Website, loads information, and implements it use. Another model of Web implementation – the cohort model – was developed by the Center for Technology in Government (CTG), an applied research arm of the University at Albany in New York. The Center traditionally partners with private sector and state and local government organizations to solve problems through the use of information and communication technology, so its *modus operandi* is collaborative projects. Because the Internet Testbed project involved so many state and local agencies, CTG chose the cohort model as a practical matter, but in the final analysis, this method proved more valuable than originally envisioned.

The cohort model required participants from seven different organizations (state and local governments) to work together to learn about assembling the Web team, gathering of ideas, setting service objectives, design principles, implementation, ongoing management, and evaluation of Web services. (See Figure 1) It was clear from the beginning that the purpose was not only to get Websites up and running, but that good processes needed to be established for continual development and ongoing Web use. Other organizations would want to come aboard the Web train as soon as the early Website adopters had their sites available to the public and to staff.

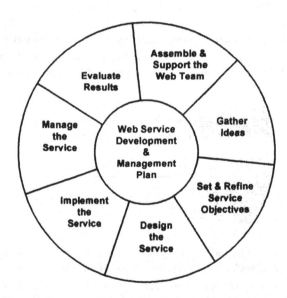

Fig. 1. The cohort model content (Dawes et al. 1996)

Concentrating on the service and management aspects in addition to the technology necessary for a Website, CTG provided the structure and led the teams in learning about practices and policy issues. Each team came together in the cohort model to attend seminars, workshops, and planning sessions. Some teams had done preliminary work in creating Websites, whereas others were complete beginners. The cohort model accommodates various levels of experience and expertise. The experienced Web developers were an asset to the project, often providing sophisticated examples of Web applications. The teams themselves shared information at each meeting, teaching each other about software, hardware, and choosing other tools for attractive and workable sites. In a cost analysis, groups helped each other estimate the costs of organizational readiness, end user support, and the necessary maintenance and infrastructure needed in addition to the human resources required. Based on processes observed, CTG created a methodology to supplement traditional information system methods.

Throughout the nine-month project, Web teams from the seven organizations came together to plan for Websites that would provide strategic advantages. The teams gave presentations of their work throughout the project, and they received feedback from others in the cohort. Subsequent to the presentations, they used suggestions and recommendations to refine ideas and make improvements. Though the project teams were governmental, the model could have been used with representatives of non-governmental organizations or businesses.

Teams were also able to see how others in the cohort were proceeding, and this gave them different ideas and also provided information about time expectations in the development process. The Web cohort all used the same textbooks and other materials, and they learned about electronic resources that provided tutorials and style guides for Web page creation. The cumulative knowledge gained by all the teams together minimized the effort needed to seek out information and apply it. The learning was shared in person and through e-mail as well as electronic discussion groups. The electronic discussion groups were facilitated through a Web discussion forum, and were set up to facilitate sharing of ideas and files, in addition to announcements. A review of the use of discussion groups, however, found that it took too much time to constantly check for messages. Email and distribution lists then filled the need for discussions. The announcements and dissemination of "homework" was then taken over by a combination of email, phone, and facsimile.

Working in a cohort meant that teams were motivated to meet timelines and to finish each phase of the process. There was a "pride factor" operating that was part competitive, part professional self-esteem that led the groups to produce according to the timeline. The creativity and synergy of ideas that developed by working together enhanced the Web service project, and lessened the frustration and feeling of isolation. If a team was "stuck" using its own resources, its members could ask for help from others. See Figure 2 for the sequential process CTG organized for the cohort.

The cohort model assumes that an expert or expert group takes responsibility for managing the process. Our concept of an expert is similar to the concept of a facilitator in the Group Decision Support Systems (GDSS) literature. A facilitator is viewed as a person who serves as the director and tracker of the group's discussions, deliberations, and process. This person does his or her best to remain neutral. He or she is not involved in the content discussion of the group. This person is, however, a deliberate manipulator of the process and flow of the group's work (More and Feldt, 1993, p. xviii).

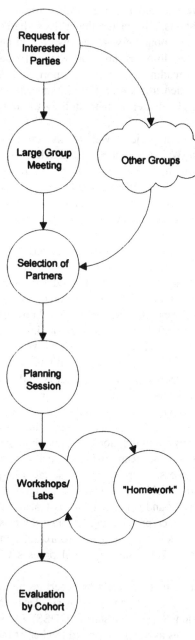

Fig. 2. The cohort model process

In a similar vein Bostrom et al. point out that "a facilitator, by his or her actions, attempts to influence three general targets: meeting *process, relationships,* and *task outcomes*" (1993, p. 156). By expert, we refer to an individual or a group of facilitators who in addition to supporting the process, relationships and task outcomes, also educates or brings in educators to support the three areas.

The cohort model needs contrasting to the existing research stream of GDSS. Vogel and Nunamaker (1990) broadly define GDSS as an application of information technology to support the work of groups. In short, the cohort model does not rely on information technology to support groups; instead, it relies on a set of knowledgeable facilitators. The focus is on supporting a *set of groups*, each of which supports each other on content issues.

In the cohort model a new endeavor starts with the experts, in this case, CTG, choosing a project in which several organizations could benefit. The experts could just as easily have been a consulting firm or an information technology department of a large organization. In this case the Center for Technology in Government had experience and skill in organizing collaborative projects and the technical skill and partnerships to provide guidance. The first step in the process, as CTG designed it, is to disseminate a general request for interested parties, and to hold a large group meting to present the information, raise awareness about a new technology, and demonstrate how it can be used. A cohort is then selected among potential partners on the basis of their interest level and their common need for the same technology.

At the planning session teams of between three and five people from each selected organization meet for the first time. Each organization is encouraged to select people with different skill sets and backgrounds. During the first session, the managers or experts present the preliminary plan for the whole project leaving time for questions, discussions, and revision suggestions from any of the participating teams.

The cohort teams learn together in workshops held at scheduled intervals during the course of the project. The teams assemble in preplanned workshops or labs, where they learn several methods and tools for accomplishing their goals. The concept of learning together, learning from each other, and sharing applications from the learning sessions is key to the cohort model. Between workshop sessions the teams go back to their respective organizations, and do "homework." During this applied work time, they fit the methods and tools to their specific organization. Iteration between workshops/labs and homework is where much of the practical work is accomplished.

When the teams meet again, they present the results they attained while working on their own. The teams who have confronted obstacles in the project talk about the problems and pitfalls to the group, generating discussion about solutions and alternatives. The synergy resulting from the discussions and the group problem-solving is one of the chief advantages of the cohort model. The teams return to their organizations with new ideas and solutions.

The process repeats itself until goals are accomplished and the project ends. There is no guarantee that every organization will complete its goals, but the cohort method allows substantial support, assistance, and encouragement. Sometimes the team is too close to the project to be able to look at their own product objectively and creatively. One advantage of working in the cohort is that others working within a similar framework, can provide constructive ideas for improvement or changes that the "home" team can not generate themselves.

2 Interorganizational Cooperation

The cohort model depends on a relationship based on the trust, risk, equity, and respect, all qualities of cooperative relationships (Sharma & Yetton, 1996). As Sharma and Yetton state "Interorganizational cooperative relationships offer the potential to develop high quality, low cost information systems" (1996, p. 122). Quality and cost effectiveness are just what working with a cohort is all about. Although competitors can certainly join together to develop a Website or other information system, it is the cooperative quality of the cohort that allows the benefits of sharing ideas, knowledge, and experience.[1] A cohort may come together for any of the traditional reasons that motivate interorganizational cooperation. Oliver indicates that these motivators include: necessity, asymmetry, reciprocity, efficiency, stability, and legitimacy (Oliver, 1990). Government groups, professional societies, business alliances, educational consortia, and community organizations in a cohort can depend on or need each other, can share reciprocal information, can work effectively through expanded expertise and information, and can establish stable and legitimate structures in which to transact business and exchange information. It is unlikely that the cooperative organizations attracted to the cohort are motivated by 'asymmetry,' another common interorganizational motivator, which Oliver describes as the "potential to exercise power or control over another organization or its resources" (p. 243). A cohort achieves power through alliance not power over another, and the power can be channeled through the management tools available for system development.

3 Policy Development

Whereas there are many benefits of the cohort model in designing and creating Websites, it is especially beneficial in the area of policy development. Though policies, by nature, can be hard to conceptualize and develop, interorganizational exchange of ideas and knowledge enables the participating organizations to create high quality policies that are enforceable. The cohort model is useful when dealing with uncertainties and innovative practices. Participants are able to discuss the number and

---

[1]   Cavaye (1997) does show how competitors can join together to develop systems for the purpose of creating standards, creating a stable environment, entering new markets, sharing research and development, and exploiting economies of scale. The focus of the cohort model discussed here, however, is on a cohort of cooperative members.

kind of policies they hope to establish, and best practices research can be conducted on Web policies from other organizations. Information is shared and policies are formulated with the advice and ideas from cohort members. Participation in effective planning and service design requires thoughtful policy development, organizational buy-in, and emphasis on the information and functions that will service customers most appropriately.

Before developing internal Internet policies, a best practice review has the potential of providing a great deal of useful information. Several Internet policies that have been made public on organizational Websites can be examined. These policies have been developed primarily by state governments, and belong within four different areas:

- Sanctioned uses of the Internet
- Web site design criteria
- Security policies
- Employee rights and responsibilities

Sanctioned uses of the Internet looks at the reasons for connecting the organization to the Internet, both when creating Websites and when giving employees access to the Web and email. While many organizations make these decisions without thinking in terms of advantages and disadvantages, this section of an Internet policy ensures that the organization makes Internet decisions based on good reasons. Education and research seem to be the most common reasons for giving employees access to the Web. Whereas the decision to create an organizational Website is often built on non-rational reasons, we expect organizations that analyze the reasons and incorporate them into their policies to enjoy a higher success rate those who do not. An organization can implement a Website and provide employee access to the Internet without any linkage between the two activities. However, organizations that coordinate Website implementation with employee access to the Web enjoy a higher degree of success.[2] This coordination may be especially important in organizations with strong departmental divisions.

Web site design criteria ensure a consistent "look and feel" across the organization's Web pages. This is especially important in distributed organizations and where there is more then one Webmaster. However, even an individual Webmaster may find it hard to be consistent over time unless templates are applied. This section of an Internet policy also regulates which features should be offered on a Website.

Security policies are probably the most "practical" of the policy sections. These policies consider the values of an organization's Internet linkages and lays out the security measures to be taken to protect these values. Though most organizations may think through the physical security issues of their computers, many do not have the internal expertise to secure their Websites and networks properly. Depending on their profile, organizations must take different steps to ensure that their systems are

---

[2] Cursory evidence supporting this was found in interviews conducted with the cohort.

safe. Though no definitive numbers exist of break-ins through the Internet, every organization should be aware of the possible consequences. Hackers have broken into several organizational Websites, and changed each site's contents. It may not come as a surprise that organizations such as Valujet, UNICEF, Kriegsman Fur, and East Timor have had their Websites hacked into and altered. However, even organizations known for their security experts and knowledge have not been spared the embarrassment. This goes for organizations such as the CIA, Department of Justice, NASA, and the United States Air Force (2600: The Hacker Quarterly, 1998). The failure of these organizations aside, being in good company is hardly a conciliation when the organizations' customers have received images better suited for adult magazines than a professional Website.

There are certain inherent risks in having a Website, and these risks are no less for any network that is connected to the Internet for purposes of electronic commerce. In May 1997, a hacker was arrested at San Francisco Airport after trying to sell a diskette with personal data on more than 100,000 credit card accounts ("Man Tried to Sell Credit Data, FBI Says," 1997). This data had been collected by examining packets going in and out of a major Internet Service Provider, and by breaking into several organizations' networks.

Employee rights and responsibilities is the section stipulating behavioral guidelines for the employees. The use of the organization's Internet connection for illegal activities, personal gain, or copyright infringements are regulated in addition to activities such as games and "surfing." There is now software available that some organizations use to enforce their policies in this area. The software monitors the employees' activities and compares them with lists of allowed and disallowed activities.

The four general areas of policies can be helpful at a conceptual level, but when getting down to implementing a policy, they do not provide enough detail to be really useful. The following Internet Policy matrix may help organizations working on their policies, by providing reminders for policy areas that need to be addressed (See Table 1).

Table 1 divides the different policies that an organization may create into six different types. Information dissemination, marketing, personnel, budgeting, security, and implementation policies. For each of these policies there are a number of issues to consider. The issues are legal, ethical, enforcement, obstacles, and measures of the policies. Though some examples of issues to think about within each policy are provided, these are far from complete. The table should be considered merely a checklist for policy development.

Table 1. Internet policy matrix

		ISSUES				
		Legal	Ethical	Enforcement	Obstacles	Measures
POLICY TYPES	Information Dissemination Policies	Specify original source	Accuracy, Quality, Access for disabled	Regular Review, Ownership, Editorial Board	Time, Money, Centralization, Lack of coordination	Volume, Feedback, Surveys
	Marketing Policies	Sponsorship, Links	Netiquette	Feedback loop (new service notification)	Social Embededness, Inexperience, Limited resources	External recognition (additional % of stakeholders reached), Server statistics
	Personnel Policies	Roles & responsibilities (handbook, newsletter, etc.)	Opportunities for personal growth, Enough staff for viable site	Exception, Monitoring, Severity	Rapid change, Inadequate training, Lack of communication	Staff morale
	Budgeting Policies	Contract law, Tax law, Generally Accepted Accounting Principles	Budget REAL costs for Internet service, Work included in job description	Auditing, Budget review process	Costs difficult to determine	Cost/Benefit analysis, Value analysis, Cost worksheet
	Security Policies	Privacy laws	Privacy, Confidentiality, Balance access with proprietary information	Monitoring, Software, Passwords, Encryption, Oversight	Rapid change, Complexity, "Weakest link"	Number of problems times severity
	Implementation Policies	Copyright, Trademarks, Software licensing	Choice of formats	Education & training, Standards	Rapid change, Better technology could preclude some users	Percent of users who can access Website, Focus groups

4 Tools for Website and Policy Development

The cohort along with the Center for Technology in Government staff developed and adapted a number of tools that are useful for Web development and management (Galvin, 1996). These tools, such as the stakeholder analysis, may be familiar to policy makers and information systems personnel from other contexts, but taken together to create Websites and policies, they form a solid foundation on which to base discussions and make decisions. For effective use, however, members of the cohort must work together harmoniously. Interorganizational cooperation is so critical to any cohort that the overall goals, no matter how noble or how well articulated, may never be realized if the spirit of cooperation is missing.

A **Best Practices Review** gives the cohort members an overview of an information technology's state of the art and, in the case of Web development, it can produce sites that have similar objectives, sites with pleasing screen designs, as well as useful features for customer service and transactions. Best practices provides learning and experience from others outside of the cohort. It is usually conducted during the startup phase of a project and can take the form of literature reviews, interviews, focus group sessions, site visits, demonstrations, or through scanning the Internet and other electronic sources. A well-organized and in-depth best practices effort can help a team truly understand a problem and the possible solutions that have been tried and proven successful. Although organizations outside the cohort may be reluctant to talk about system project failures, carefully focused best practices research will uncover practical solutions and critical success factors. A cohort can multiply the usual amount of best practices research undertaken in a project by a factor equal to the number of cohorts participating. In other words, a cohort increases the possibility of completing a comprehensive best practices review.

The **Stakeholder Analysis,** a structured way of identifying people who will be affected by a new system or other technology implementation, is a crucial tool for considering the human factors inherent in any new venture. The public nature of a Website widens the potential pool of stakeholders, and understanding who they are will influence the ultimate design of the site. Once stakeholders are identified, specific features of the site that will benefit that stakeholder group and any negative effects that will accrue are recorded in a formal way. Quantitative and qualitative impact estimates can be described and calculated, and eventually should be written into a narrative summary that can be used to adjust service objectives.

The cohort model allows all team members to participate in the thoughtful planning process that can result in a carefully designed Website. Another of the planning tools available is the **Strategic Framework**. The framework is a structured method to consider customers as the stakeholder analysis does, but it also helps identify resources, innovations, and internal and external forces that may affect a project. The heart of the framework focuses on the Website's individual service objectives and examines how needed resources, partners, customers (internal and external), and innovative products and services will relate to each objectives. In examining each objective, one at a time, teams should ask questions about potential partners, customer access issues, and the ability to secure resources. The aim is to reach clarity and consensus on the responses for each objective.

Of course, cohort teams will want to focus discussions on the information that will comprise the content of their organization's Internet presence as well as on other aspects of the Website. Once the information is defined, teams will find it helpful to map the categories in a graphic **Information Structure** hierarchy. Just as the information in a book is organized by a table of contents, a graphic representation or organization chart for the Website can help the design team envision the way users will be able to access their information. The graphic can also help to indicate the kind and number of links that will be necessary. Although the full complexity of the site does not need to be mapped at the design stage, a preliminary "menu" of the available information will be a tangible tool in the ongoing management of the site. It will show where updated information needs to be added and will identify material that should be removed or revised.

Any new information technology project relies on a clear delineation of roles and responsibilities to ensure smooth transitions from startup to implementation and to eventual support and management. Accountability for editorial content control, security, maintaining the Website and Web server, user support and training, etc. needs to be spelled out and clarified. An **Organizational Questionnaire** can help the individual cohort teams assess the personnel available or positions that must be added to make a viable and quality Website. The questionnaire used in the cohort delineated the necessary responsibility areas and provided an opportunity for team members to name the organizational units and the individual names or positions that would assume a specific responsibility. Naming roles and responsibilities has implications for budget planning, the level of service that can be offered, expanding the site beyond the initial implementation, and many other ongoing issues that ensure growth and improvement as the site becomes a routine part of the way daily business is conducted. The organizational questionnaire can also be an aid in policy development since some policies (e.g., personnel, procedure, security) are based on roles and responsibilities.

The cohort model is close to an ideal environment for **Prototyping,** a tool used in developing a new technology application like a Website. In the cohort, standard html development tools were used to develop the prototype. Prototyping, using rapid application development tools such as Visual Basic is a fast way to demonstrate the first version of a new technology. Prototyping does not require full implementation or exhaustive and complete design, and it allows for quick feedback from others. In a cohort, teams can try out each other's prototype and provide feedback within an atmosphere of trust and learning. Some of the cohort teams not only demonstrated the prototype for other cohort members, but they also presented the prototype to members of their own organizations. The simple matter of going public and scheduling a presentation date was a sufficient motivator to prepare the best possible prototype in time for the presentation.

Prototyping allows design teams to remain flexible, make changes, and add value to the original version without the risks of implementing a full system. Prototyping can be used as an iterative process along with phased implementation, so that new features can be tested along the way before introducing the Website to all internal or external customers. It decreases uncertainties about the system, thereby increasing the confidence of those who will implement and champion the system and train others to use it. Prototyping is a user-centered tool that allows the user to have direct involvement in defining requirements and giving suggestions for a system that will meet user needs and desires. Jenkins summarizes the time and efficiency advantages of prototyping in this way:

Table 1 divides the different policies that an organization may create into six different types. Information dissemination, marketing, personnel, budgeting, security, and implementation policies. For each of these policies there are a number of issues to consider. The issues are legal, ethical, enforcement, obstacles, and measures of the policies. Though some examples of issues to think about within each policy are provided, these are far from complete. The table should be considered merely a checklist for policy development.

The saying "strike while the iron is hot" applies here. The hotter the iron is the easier it is to work. The longer a project is stretched-out the less chance it has to succeed. It could even be turned into a can of worms.
(Jenkins, 1997, p. 3-23)

5 Cost and Performance Issues

While most organizations traditionally have created their Web services without thought to cost and performance issues, this may not be a good idea for organizations contemplating the implementation of a Web service today. Where the early innovators had the advantage of a wide open market, today's market is quite different. Organizations contemplating a Web service, be that a full-fledged distribution channel or an organizational Website, must consider the cost and performance issues of doing so.

Though an organization's purpose and strategic intent will dictate part of the solution, an organization must still consider the level of investment in the Web service. One research organization claims that organizations that created their Web services in the mid-nineties, would only be profitable after the turn of the century (Vonder Haar 1996). For these organizations the question is how long they are able to exist while losing money. For organizations creating Web services later, the question will be how to compete with those organizations that did start early, and had the resources to stay afloat until they turned profitable.

To help organizations that are thinking of creating organizational Websites, a cost and performance framework was developed. By explicitly specifying the expected costs and comparing these to the expected benefits at three levels of investment, the framework can help the organization think about the appropriate level of investment. Because the cost part of the framework may help organizations think more explicitly about the investment, some of its elements are reviewed here. These elements may be used as a checklist or a guideline.

The costs of developing a Web service should be thought of as a multi-year proposal. Specifying the costs for first year and subsequent years is one way to examine the needed resources. During the research on costs, five categories were found to contain significant costs. These are 'organizational readiness,' 'access for staff and other users,' 'end user support,' 'content development and maintenance,' and 'host of site-infrastructure.' Each area was again found to contain several sub-categories of costs. They are listed below in Table 2.

Obviously, not all costs apply to each project. Cohorts can use the list to ensure that all areas are covered when discussing costs. Because it is often difficult to visualize costs and especially hard to specify what will be offered by a Web service, the use of prototyping is encouraged.

Table 2. Cost and performance checklist

Category	Sub-category
Organizational readiness	Training for technology awareness
	Planning for Internet presence
Access for staff and other users	Hardware for end users
	Software for end users
	Network and Internet access for end users
	Other vendor services
	Start-up processes for equipment procurement
	Management of vendor and ISP contracts
End user support	Vendor services
	Management of vendor contracts
	Development and delivery of user training
	User time in training
	Help desk for users
Content development and maintenance	Hardware for content developers
	Software for content developers
	Network and Internet access for content developers
	Other vendor services
	Start-up processes for equipment procurement
	Management of vendor contracts
	Development and delivery of staff training
	Staff time in training
	Webmaster
	Editorial review
	Content creation and coordination
	Web site design and development
	Staff support for service
	Programming support
	Database administration
	Other management support
	Other clerical support
Host of site infrastructure	Hardware
	Software
	Network and Internet access
	Other vendor services
	Front-end research and technical evaluation
	Start-up processes for equipment procurement
	Management of vendor and ISP contracts
	Development and delivery of staff training
	Staff time in training
	Network and systems administration
	Web server management
	Operations support
	Clerical support

6 Conclusion

The cohort model is an effective means for learning about and developing a new technology application. In the model teams from various organizations or divisions of a single organization come together to share expertise, knowledge, and new learning within a larger context. Web site development, policy formation, and ongoing management are areas where the cohort model has proven successful. We have described particular tools that team members can employ to facilitate discussion and organizational planning. Website design and creation can take many forms, but experience has shown that organizations that cooperate enjoy the advantages and benefits of information synergy. Interorganizational cooperation may sometimes rely too heavily on individual partners for its success. The cohort model, however, is built as a loose network, and is less likely to suffer damage with the loss of one or more partners. Peer collaboration in the cohort benefits all members by providing skills and knowledge that otherwise would be unavailable to the individual organization.

References

2600 The Hacker Quarterly, www.hack2600.com/.

Bostrom, R., R. Anson, and V. Clawson, "Group facilitation and group support systems," in L. M. Jessup and J.S. Valacich (Eds.), Group Support Systems: New perspectives, Macmillian, NY, 1993.

Cavaye, A. L. M., "IS Collaboration Among Competitors," in Proceedings of the 8th Australian Conference on Information Systems, (1997), 1-12.

Dawes, S. S., T. Pardo, P. Bloniarz, A. DiCaterino, D. Berlin, and D. Connelly, Developing & Delivering Government Services on the World Wide Web: Recommended Practices for New York State, The Center for Technology in Government, Albany, NY, 1996.

Galvin, T. J., (Ed.), Making Smart IT Choices: a Handbook, The Center for Technology in Government, Albany, NY, 1996.

Glenn, N. D. Cohort Analysis, Sage Publications, Beverly Hills, CA, 1977.

Jenkins, G., Information Systems: Policies and Procedures Manual, Prentice Hall, Englewood Cliffs, NJ, 1997.

Larsen, K. R. and P. A. Bloniarz, Evaluating a Cost and Performance Model for Assessing Web Service Investments. Pre-ICIS SIM Workshop on Practice Oriented Research, Atlanta, GA., December 13, (1997).

"Man Tried to Sell Credit Data, FBI Says," San Francisco Chronicle, May 22, (1997), A25.

Moore, A. B. and J. A. Feldt, Facilitating Community and Decision-Making Groups, Krieger Publishing Company, Malabar, FL, 1993.

Oliver, C., "Determinants of Interorganizational Relationships: Integration and Future Directions," Academy of Management Review, 15, 2, (1990), 241-265.

Sharma, R. and P. Yetton, "Interorganizational Cooperation to Develop Information Systems," in Proceedings of the Seventeenth International Conference on Information Systems, (1996), 122-132.

Vogel, D. and J. Nunamaker , "Group Decision Support System Impact: Multi-methodological Exploration," Information & Management, 18, (1990), 15-28.

Vonder Haar, S., "Hold On: Web Sites Won't Turn Profit Until 2000," Interactive Week, June 17, (1996).

CHAPTER 12
A Framework for Garment Shopping over the Internet

Nebojša Jojić, Yong Rui, Yueting Zhuang, and Thomas Huang
Beckman Institute for Advanced Science and Technology, and Department of Electrical and Computer Engineering, University of Illinois at Urbana-Champaign, Urbana, IL, USA
{jojic, yrui, yzhuang, huang}@ifp.uiuc.edu

In this chapter, we propose a framework for integrated design, advertisement and retailing of garments over the Internet. This on-line shopping framework would make use of the latest research in computer graphics, image processing, computer vision and artificial intelligence. We describe these technologies in more detail, and explain how they can be used to build a visually attractive and easy to use interface to an intelligent integrated system that fulfils most of the functions of the traditional production chain, while allowing for mass-customization.

Keywords: 3D Body Modeling/Reconstruction; Advertisement; Case-Based Reasoning; Content-Based Image Retrieval; Garment Design; Knowledge-Based Design; On-line Shopping; Physics-Based Modeling; Virtual Agents; Virtual Reality

1 Introduction

The modern computer and telecommunication technologies have had an enormous effect on design, manufacturing and marketing in most of the existing industries. Computer aided design (CAD) systems have become indispensable tools for the designers of almost any type of products. The developed designs and the raw materials are the input to the next component in the chain, the highly automated manufacturing processes based on computer aided manufacturing (CAM) tools. The final products are delivered to distributors and retailers, but also advertized through attractively designed video commercials or images presented to the targeted group of users through different media.

Computers are also essential for administration, and in modern companies most of the relevant information, such as product and advertisement designs, market analysis results, raw material and final product orders, memos, e-mails, company presentations, etc. are processed, stored and communicated electronically. Therefore, it is not surprising that many industries have gone through a process of integration of the designers, suppliers, manufacturers, marketing infrastructure, etc. into global networks that can develop and market products in a much faster and more inexpensive manner than before. Most of the companies acknowledge the importance of the interaction among different parts of the company and/or the external partners, and work on improving it.

On the other hand the communication with the target of the whole system, the customers, is not nearly at the same level of interactivity. The information given to the customers may be carefully presented through impressive advertisement, but it is still mainly pipelined through the classical media: television, radio, newspapers/magazines, catalogs, etc. While different media require different strategy and technology in advertisement design, one feature of the modern marketing on classical media remains the same. The only feedback about their needs the customer gives by making a choice among the available final prooducts. This information comes back to the manufacturers through the market statistics. Of course, there are other attempts to get the customer feedback, through complaint records, customer satisfaction polls, etc., but these require additional mechanisms for acquiring and processing such information, and still result in some statistical data as the feedback to the manufacturer. The situation is somewhat remedied by a natural increase in the number of manufacturers and products with the aim of satisfying all possible needs. The problem is then transferred to the problem of markets cluttered with products and indecisive customers.

Instead of spending a lot of time browsing through the abundance of the available products (and meeting with variable success), many people find it appealing to sometimes shop for an item by specifying the features they need and having the appropriate product made exclusively for them. However, for this luxury, the customer usually has to go back to the small custom fit shops (tailors, custom fit carpenters, etc.) and give up the speed of delivery and the low prices inherent to the mass production.

In this chapter, we intend to demonstrate how the modern technology is going to further affect all the components in the production chain and make the whole system more accessible to the customers through the more interactive medium, the Internet, bringing them faster access to the product information and possibility of shaping the products before ordering them. We concentrate on the garment industry and study a possible design, manufacturing, distribution and advertising scenario using the Internet and the latest research results in computer graphics, image processing, computer vision and artificial intelligence. Many, if not all of the major technological components used in this scenario, can be, or already are successfully applied in the traditional approaches to garment design and advertising, or have been developed and used for other purposes. Before outlying the on-line garment shopping scenario and the involved computer technologies, we give a brief survey of interesting existing examples of the application of modern computer technology in the garment industry.

1.1 Existing Computer Technologies in Garment Design and Advertising

Several software companies specialize in the CAD software for garment design. The most popular are the tools used in the design of sewn garments, knitted and woven fabrics, and textile-prints.

For the purposes of sewn garment design, the software usually allows the designer to create patterns from basic sloper shapes (A sloper is a basic garment shape, also known as a body glove or a body block). The designer can then modify the patterns, insert darts and create seam allowances. The garment (always consisting of several patterns) can be parameterized by several size parameters to allow for better size customization in the mass production. The patterns can be viewed in the fabric layouts in which the designer can align the patterns, make the measurements, create markers etc. The final design can be printed in the form of a technical drawing. Also, the designs on paper can typically be digitized and then edited in such software.

Another type of CAD tools in garment industry is the software for knitted-fabric design. For example, the designer can choose stitches from the library of stitch groups and arrange them on a grid. Such software often interfaces directly to the computer controlled knitting equipment.

The tools for coloring the woven fabrics also exist. The designer can construct different weaves and colorways, or choose from the existing designs in the database, and apply the woven fabric pattern on a surface.

In textile-print design, the CAD tools are used for creating and manipulating tonal or flat-color designs, or processing arbitrary digital images and creating corresponding spot or tonal manufacturable prints. This type of software usually includes some basic image processing tools, and stores the designs in a database, just like all other types of CAD software.

These databases are searched in a traditional manner: by a combination of textual queries and browsing through the list of hits. For example, the user can ask for all floral print-fabric designs in the database, or specify a specific type of slopers (skirts for example), and retrieve several hits. The databases are typically annotated by hand.

Most of the CAD software developers also offer the tools for visualization of the designs for catalogs. These tools are based on operator-assisted texture mapping. The user manually defines a 2-D or a 3-D mesh over the garment in a photograph of a mannequin. Usually, the mannequin wears a garment of uniform color, so that the light-dependent shading in the photograph can be extracted. The woven, knitted or print-fabric designs are than mapped on the mesh and the shading from the photograph is applied. This process, often referred to as re-imaging (Computer Design Inc.), allows the user to create several images of a mannequin wearing different designs, all from a single photograph. Further more, some of the methods that we will cover later in this chapter, also allow for building an advertisement by changing the layout of the photo, adding text, etc.

The re-imaging method obviously does not take into account the topology of the garment, as specified by the patterns and sewing lines in the sewn garment design, for example. The correctness of the final image depends on the user's knowledge of the garment topology, their perception of depth in the given photograph and their ability to transform this perception into a good mesh for texture mapping. An alternative, a physics-based simulation of the complex garment's drape over the given three-dimensional geometry of a mannequin, often produces computer graphics-like images, i.e., it lacks realism.

With the growing popularity of the Internet, the CAD software in garment industry is slowly becoming "Internet friendly", but the network oriented capabilities usually offer a little more than an easy access to e-mail.

Another important technological development for textile industry is body scanning systems, usually based on laser scanners, photometric stereo or structured light assisted stereo systems. These systems can be used for automatic body measurements, and custom-fit shops based on these systems already exist. The customer chooses one of the offered garment styles, and then their body measurements are acquired automatically by the scanning system. These measurements are used to determine several size parameters of the garment, and the order is placed. The garment can still be manufactured on a regular manufacturing line.

1.2 The New Computer Technologies and a Scenario for Shopping over the Internet

There are several advancements in computer technology that have not yet been fully used in the garment industry. Here we propose a scenario for shopping over the Internet that is based on an integration of the existing and novel computer technologies (Figure 1).

In this scenario, the customer visits the virtual shop on the Internet. There, customer browses through different designs, and even uses a simplified CAD tool to change them. The customer can search the database for desired colorways, knitted or woven designs, print designs and/or different types of fabrics for sewn garments. In the case of the print designs, the customer could even submit the digital image that they want printed on their garment. Also, the customer should be able to specify images and shapes as the database query instead of simple text. The modern image processing techniques allow for image retrieval based on content. The computer can return images similar to the query image in color, texture or shape. This method can be applied to retrieval of print designs, woven design textures, or pattern shapes in sewn garment.

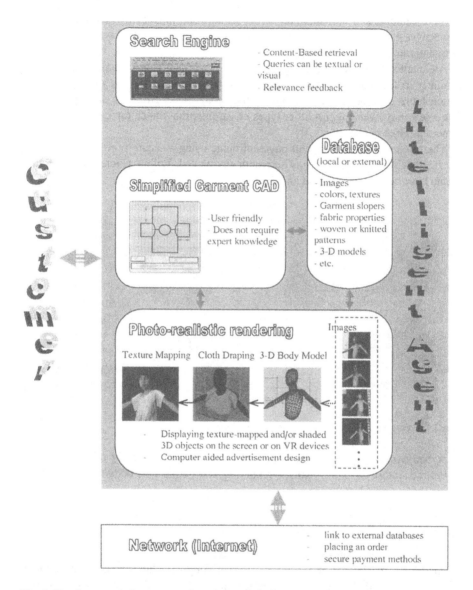

Fig. 1. The framework for garment shopping over the Internet

The customer's body has already been scanned, in one of the available scanning centers nearby, and they "brought" the electronic form of their body geometry with them to the Internet site. The selected garment can be shown to the customer draped directly over their body model, using the physics-based simulation and image-based rendering to increase the realism. In the future, with the increase of the computational power of personal computers, it will be possible for the customers to use one or more cameras and the computer screen as a virtual mirror in which they can see themselves just as in the real mirror, except that on the screen they are dressed into a virtual garment that they want to try on.

An intelligent virtual agent can assist the customer. This virtual salesman acts similarly to the real sales personnel. It uses its experience and the observations of the customer's actions to help in making the choices or to guide the database search. The agent may even suggest other types of garment that match the garment the customer has already chosen.

The sale can be finalized and payment made using a secure protocol directly on the Internet site, and the order is automatically placed. Within several days the garments have been manufactured and delivered.

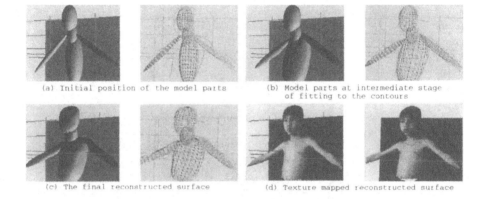

(a) Initial position of the model parts

(b) Model parts at intermediate stage of fitting to the contours

(c) The final reconstructed surface

(d) Texture mapped reconstructed surface

Fig. 2. Several stages of 3-D reconstruction of a human body

A body scanning system that efficiently reconstructs the body of the user, acquires the texture for photo-realistic rendering, and extracts the body measurements.

- A cloth draping algorithm based on physics-based simulation.
- Visualization tools and devices (from the computer screen to the immersive virtual reality devices).
- Databases with image-based retrieval capability.
- Artificial intelligence of the whole system simplifies the access to the system capabilities and also makes the interface more natural to the human, as it consists of an intelligent communication with a virtual agent.
- Simplified and easy-to-use CAD tools for increased customization.
- The Internet as the medium for integrated design, marketing and retailing.

In the rest of the chapter we will present the research performed by the authors and others, mainly in the first five computer technologies on this list.

2 3-D Body Modeling Using Images of a Real Person

While the traditional garment CAD systems work almost exclusively with two-dimensional data, as described in the introduction, some recent additions to the rich family of CAD software in textile industry are meant to allow the designer to work directly on a 3D model of a human body, making measurements, defining the darts, seam lines, etc directly on the model, and then visualizing the final design draped over it.

Apart from a potentially much easier way of designing garment using a user-friendly 3D interface, and perhaps 3D displays such as the stereoscopic devices, the advantage of modeling the human models, garment design and draping effect in three dimensions is in the possibility of photorealistic rendering of real people wearing the garment that is still in a design stage. This could replace the re-imaging procedures described in the previous section, that are very demanding in terms of human assistance.

There are several devices for capturing the 3D geometry of a human body, mostly based on relatively expensive laser scanning technology. However, several algorithms for reconstruction of 3D bodies using cheaper equipment (such as regular cameras and possibly overhead projectors) have recently been developed (Kakadiaris and Metaxas, 1995; Jojic et al., 1998a; Jojic et al., 1999).

There are several important issues in the problem of building 3-D models using visual information. One is the camera calibration and accuracy of triangulation techniques in stereo reconstruction. This problem has been extensively studied and several calibration techniques were developed (Tsai, 1987). Another problem is that a human body, being a complex multi-part object exhibits serious self-occlusions in images taken from almost any angle of view. Finally, there is a trade-off between stereo reconstruction accuracy that increases with the stereo pair baseline (distance between two cameras) and the ambiguity problems in stereo matching that become more serious when the baseline is increased.

Recently, there have been several approaches to 3-D reconstruction using occluding contours of objects in the images (Wang and Aggarwal, 1989; Kakadiaris and Metaxas, 1995; Jojic et al., 1998a; Jojic et al., 1999). The occluding contours from several views provide information about spatial extent of the imaged objects. When the properties of the class of objects that are being reconstructed are known, it is possible to incorporate these properties in a prior model of the reconstructed object, and then use occluding contours to build a rather good reconstruction. For example, if we know that the imaged objects are polyhedral, the occluding contours may even be sufficient for correct reconstruction. In the case of the human bodies, we can use a model consisting of smooth parts, such as deformable superquadrics, to build an imperfect, but still quite realistic reconstruction (Kakadiaris and Metaxas, 1995; Jojic et al., 1998a; Jojic et al., 1999).

Moreover, the reconstruction based on occluding contours has been shown to help guide the stereo matching process in wide baseline stereo. In other words, the parts of the body surface that were not estimated completely correctly using occluding contour constraints, are still sufficiently well estimated to give a stereo matching algorithm an idea where the 3D point resulting from triangulation should be. Stereo helps refine the surface further, and the combination of occluding contours and stereo has been shown to be more complete than pure stereo reconstruction, and more precise than occluding contours based reconstruction (Wang and Aggarwal, 1989; Jojic et al., 1998a; Jojic et al., 1999).

From the reconstructed body, the measurements necessary for garment design can be extracted automatically (Jojic et al., 1998a). Furthermore, the 3D reconstruction can be observed from arbitrary angle and the garment can be visualized draped over it.

For realistic rendering, the image information could also be used for texture mapping, i.e., pixel intensities from available images could be mapped onto the reconstructed surface in 3D (Jojic et al., 1999). As an example of 3-D reconstruction of a human body, in Figure 2 we show several steps in deforming the initial crude model to fit the image information.

3 Physics-Based Cloth Modeling

A number of physics-based cloth modeling techniques have been developed over the last decade or so. These techniques are based on simplified models of flexible materials that can drape under the influence of simulated gravity. These models typically have several stretching, bending and shear parameters that define the behavior of the cloth. For example, in Figure 3, the effect of bending constants is demonstrated in the case of the particle-based cloth model in (Jojic et al., 1998b).

$k_{bh} = k_{bv} = 0$ $k_{bh} = k_{bv} = 0.01$ $k_{bh} = k_{bv} = 0.02$

Fig. 3. 100x100 particle systems with different bending constants

Most of the research in cloth modeling has been done by two groups of researchers - computer scientists and textile engineers. While the research in computer graphics was until recently mainly concerned with the qualitative visual effect, textile engineers studied low-level mechanical properties of cloth such as Young's modulus, bending modulus and Poisson ratio (Chu et al., 1950; Skelton, 1976; Shanahan et al., 1978), and relationships between these properties and the parameters of the models they were constructing (Collier et al., 1991).

Fig. 4. Examples of dressing a human into virtual garment

A good survey of cloth modeling techniques is available in a recent special issue on cloth modeling of IEEE Computer Graphics and Applications (Ng and Grimsdale, 1996). While the first cloth models were geometrical, today most attention is focused on physics-based models, and to a certain extent on hybrid techniques. The two main approaches in physics-based modeling of cloth are either to treat the cloth as a continuum, utilizing finite-element or finite-difference techniques (Terzopoulos et al., 1987; Carignan et al., 1992; Collier et al., 1991), or to represent the cloth object as a large set of particles with prescribed interactions between them (Breen et al., 1994; Eberhardt et al., 1993; Ng et al., 1995).

Using the mechanical measurements of cloth properties, the cloth models can be tuned to represent real cloths. Another approach to tuning the physics-based cloth models to represent real cloths is based on a vision technique (Jojic et al., 1998b). The 3-D geometry of a real cloth drape is studied to recover optimal modeling parameters. The optimization algorithm is also capable of finding the contact points between the cloth and the object over which it was draped, by studying the given 3-D drape geometry. This has a potential to be used in analysis of the 3-D scans of dressed humans. In fact, by fitting garment models to the 3-D data acquired from images and estimating the contact points between the garment and the body, the detailed dressed human model can be built from images. This 3-D model can then be used in the re-imaging procedures described in the introduction, and not only for texture mapping of the new garment patterns, but also for creating new views at the model, and even for animating it.

In Figure 4, we show an example of dressing a reconstructed and texture-mapped body from Figure 2 into virtual garment. This garment exists only in the computer, as a set of definitions - topological (CAD design), physical (fabric properties for cloth draping simulation), textural (textile print design, or a woven pattern), and yet it can be realistically rendered on the computer screen or in the virtual reality, so that the customer in the virtual garment shop can decide if they want to order it. After the order is made, the garment can be manufactured and delivered.

4 Image Databases with Content-Based Retrieval Abilities

The usage of databases can be traced back to 1961, the year the first generalized Database Management System (DBMS) - GE's Integrated Data Store (IDDS) - was released. In the 1990's, the spread of the Internet and progress of multimedia processing techniques brought databases to all the fields of our society. Banks use databases to manage the accounts; universities uses databases to keep track of each student's performance; even an elementary school kid uses ``Databank" to maintain his or her friends' phone numbers. Databases are becoming a part of our everyday life in an ever increase rate.

Most of the existing databases use text as the searching mechanism directly or indirectly. That is, even in image databases, most of the existing databases search images by their titles and key words. As we will discuss in Subsection 4.1, this mechanism encounters many difficulties in today's databases.

Searching images over multimedia databases has great impact on today's garment industry. First, the design process involves the selection of colorways, knitted or woven patterns, and print graphics. In addition, a visual browsing and retrieval tool will be greatly appreciated by a garment customer as well.

The remainder of this section is dedicated to the content-based image retrieval techniques required by modern garment industry. In Subsection 4.1, we give a brief review of the history of image databases and the motivation of content-based retrieval for images. Subsection 4.2 describes what are the tractable visual contents of an image and how they can be extracted. The retrieval process and possible applications in garment industry are explained in Subsection 4.3.

4.1 Brief History of Image Retrieval

How can we search for an image in an image database? Research on this topic can be traced back to the late 1970's. A very popular paradigm for image retrieval then was to first annotate the images by text and then use text-based DBMS to perform image retrieval. Representatives of this approach are (Chang and Fu, 1980; Chang, 1981; Chang, 1988). Many advances, such as data modeling, multi-dimensional indexing, query evaluation, etc., have been made. However, there exist two major difficulties with this text-annotation approach. One is the vast amount of labor required in manual image annotation. The other difficulty, which is more essential, results from the rich content in the images and the difficulty of describing the content. This is particularly acute in the garment industry. For example, for a particular knitted pattern or a print design, two people, more often than not, may come up with two different sets of textual descriptions. This makes the future retrieval of this pattern almost impossible.

In the early 90's, because of the emergence of large-scale image collections from various fields including geographical information systems (GIS), museum archiving, garment design, etc, the two difficulties faced by the manual annotation approach became even more acute. To overcome these difficulties, content-based image retrieval was proposed as an alternative. That is, instead of being manually annotated by text-based keywords, images would be indexed by their own visual content, such as color, texture, shape, etc. Since then, many techniques in this research direction have been developed and many retrieval systems built, including QBIC (Niblack et al., 1994), Virage (Jeffrey et al., 1996), VisualSEEk (Smith and Chang, 1996a), MARS (Ortega et al. 1998).

The key techniques such as how to extract the visual content from images and how to search images efficiently will be discussed in the next two subsections.

4.2 Extracting Visual Contents

Color, texture, and shape are the most widely used image content features in the content-based image retrieval. These are also well suited for representing the ``raw information'' (such as colorways, knitted or woven designs, print designs, etc.) used in the garment industry. For example, colorways can be captured by the color feature; woven patterns can be captured by texture feature; and prints can be captured by the combination of color, texture and shape features.

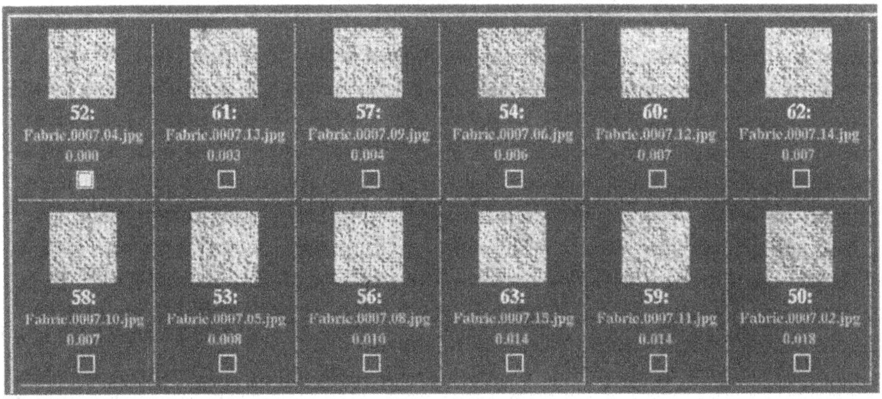

Fig. 5. Texture-based image retrieval results after relevance feedback

Since human perception of image content is subjective (different people may perceive the same image content differently), for a given feature, various representations have been developed to model the feature from different perspectives. For example, we can use both color histogram and color moments to represent the color feature, but with different emphasis. We next briefly describe various representations for the color, texture and shape features.

Color Feature: This is one of the most widely used visual features in image retrieval. It is relatively robust to background complication and independent of image size and orientation. It is useful in garment industry in characterizing the colorways of garment. Many color representations exist, out of which the Color Histogram is the most commonly used. Statistically, it denotes the joint probability of the intensities of the three color channels. Besides Color Histogram, several other color feature representations have been applied in image retrieval, including Color Moments (Stricker and Orengo, 1995) and Color Sets (Smith and Chang, 1995). The mathematical foundation of Color Moments approach is that any color distribution can be characterized by its moments. A Color Set is defined as a selection of the colors from the quantized color space. Color Set feature vectors are binary, which allows the use of binary search trees for fast search.

Texture Feature: Texture refers to the visual patterns that have properties of homogeneity that do not result from the presence of only a single color or intensity. It is an innate property of virtually all surfaces, including clouds, trees, bricks, hair, fabric, etc. It contains important information about the structural arrangement of surfaces and their relationship to the surrounding environment (Haralick et al., 1973). This is an important visual feature for characterizing garment's knitted and woven patterns. The most widely used texture representations are the co-occurrence matrix representation of texture (Haralick et al., 1973), Tamura texture representation (Tamura et al., 1978), and Wavelet transform based texture representation (Smith and Chang, 1996b). The co-occurrence matrix approach explores the gray level spatial dependence of texture. The motivation for the Tamura texture representation is based on psychological studies in human visual perception of texture. These studies helped the development of computational approximations to the essential visual texture properties. The six visual texture properties were *coarseness, contrast, directionality, linelikeness, regularity*, and *roughness*. Finally, the Wavelet transform based approach makes use of this transform's compact support of signal at both spatial and frequency domains. Experimental results show that Wavelet transform is very effective in capturing the texture feature (Smith and Chang, 1996b).

Shape Feature: The shape of the objects in an image is a very important feature in various applications including garment industry. For example, the slopers can be characterized by their shape feature. In general, an important criterion for shape feature representation is its invariance to translation, rotation, and scaling, since human beings tend to ignore such variations for recognition and retrieval purpose. The shape representations can be divided into two categories: boundary-based and region-based. The former uses only the outer boundary of the shape while the latter uses the entire shape region (Rui et al. 1996). The most successful representatives for these two categories are Fourier Descriptor (Persoon and Fu, 1977; Rui et al. 1996) and Moment Invariants (Jain, 1995).

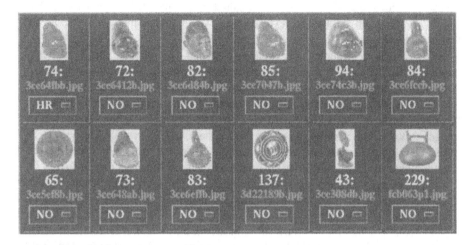

Fig. 6. Image retrieval based on shape similarity

4.3 Retrieval Process and Applications to Garment Industry

After the features have been extracted from the images, they are stored and indexed into the database. With these features, the retrieval system can then support content-based queries. A typical retrieval process can be summarized as follows:

- The user browses through the database. Once he finds an image of interest, he can submit this image as the query image. Alternatively, a query image can be generated outside the database, or even sketched by the user using a simple drawing interface.
- Based on the set of visual features supported by the database, the image retrieval system finds the best matches to the query image.

In advanced image retrieval systems (Rui et al., 1998), there is a third step called *Relevance Feedback*. By having this additional step, the retrieval system can interact with the user and refine user's query intention. This relevance feedback process can be considered as controlled by an intelligent agent as illustrated in Figure 1. In plain words, the intelligent agent uses the fed-back information from the user to dynamically refine user's query intention and intelligently provide the answers (Rui et al., 1998).

The described retrieval system is well suited for garment CAD applications. Two examples are given below for texture-based woven/knitted pattern retrieval and textile prints retrieval.

Imagine that a designer, or even a customer, is looking for a particular woven/knitted pattern. It is normally difficult to express such an image pattern in words, especially for a non-expert customer. The content-based image retrieval system offers a natural alternative. Figure 5 demonstrates the performance of the content-based retrieval for a knitted pattern. The top left image is the sample (query image) that the user submits to the retrieval system and the rest are the best 11 returns. The selected texture pattern can then be forwarded to the photorealistic rendering module and used as the pattern on the garment, as shown in Figure 4 (b).

In the design of textile prints (for example for T-shirts), all visual features can be important to the user. In Figure 6, an example of the retrieval for a print design is demonstrated. The top left images is the sample (query image) and the rest are the best 11 returns. This time the retrieval is based on all the color, texture, and shape features. The retrieved image 3 is what a user is looking for and then used as the print of a T-shirt, as shown in Figure 4 (a). Of course, the best result can be enhanced by using relevance feedback during which the system learns what the user preferences are, for example if the user is more likely to prefer similarity in texture, or color, or shape.

5 Artificial Intelligence in Garment and Advertisement Design

In the garment industry, several Artificial Intelligence (AI) techniques (Russell and Norving, 1995) have been used in applications such as the knowledge-based technology in the complex mechatronic systems (Czarnecki, 1995), intelligent textile machines and systems (Acar, 1994), and the "smart" garment that heats or cools in response to temperature changes (Davis and Botkin, 1994). In comparison, AI has been much less used in garment or advertisement design. The primary reason for this is that garment design is a very flexible and creative process, and it is often regarded as something that possesses too few rules that can be traced. But with the development of AI, design methodology, as well as other related areas, the application of AI techniques is becoming much wider.

In this section, we will focus on these new AI applications in garment design and advertisement. We first introduce knowledge-based and case-based design approaches in the first two subsections. We then describe knowledge embedded interactive garment design system. Finally, we discuss the intelligent agent and how it can be used in consultation for garment selection and design.

5.1 Knowledge-Based Pattern (Textile Print) Design

Here, *pattern* denotes any figure that is printed on cloth, T-shirt or other garment. Knowledge-based approach was introduced into the pattern design (Pan and He, 1986) to relieve designer from tedious work by automatically creating new patterns.

A *pattern* is defined as the combination of primitive elements, which can be flowers (e.g. rose), animals (e.g. cat, dog), or other patterns. Thus a pattern is regarded as the root of a tree. Each node of the tree represents one of its components, and each leaf node represents the primitive element.

The designer's knowledge is extracted to form the design knowledge base, which can be categorized into three types:

- *Pattern layout knowledge* defines how the components (either primitive elements or generated patterns) are arranged in the drawing space through a set of the basic layout rules. For example, one piece of the knowledge *is Four Corner Continuity (FCC)* which has been widely used in carpet pattern design. The following simple example shows how *FCC* is applied so that whenerver the element (a) is displayed in the middle, the pattern (b) is applied at the corners, so that the continuity is preserved.

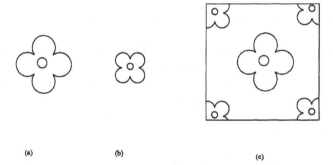

(a)   (b)   (c)

- *Element grouping knowledge* defines the grouping of elements, for example, the element *A (e.g. fish)* usually comes along with element *B (e.g. water)*. This type of knowledge ensures the selection and importantly, the harmonization of selected elements.
- *Element transformation knowledge* defines the possible element transformations such as translation, rotation, scaling, shearing, or concatenation of the above transformation sequences.

It has been estimated that if 30 pieces of knowledge and 30 elements are provided, the system has the capacity of designing more than $6.561*10^{18}$ different patterns simply through the combinatorial explosion.

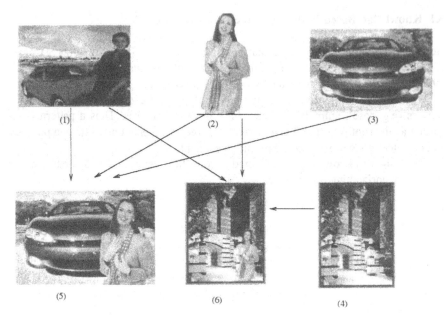

Fig. 7. An example of case-based advertisement design

5.2 Case-based Garment/Advertisement Design

An experienced garment or advertisement designer usually refers to some former design cases while creating a new design. When this is mimicked in AI, it is called case-based reasoning (CBR) (Mott, 1993). Compared with other design approaches, case-based reasoning provides a much more natural way to follow. No matter how difficult the current design problem is, the designer will always find some idea in a large collection of cases. In this way, a novice designer can utilize the knowledge of others. Figure 7 shows one example where (1) is an advertisement case, (2) is the fashion needed to be advertised, (3) and (4) are images taken from the image database, (5) and (6) are the design results by adapting (1)'a layout.

Garment advertisement is aimed at promoting the garment sale by attracting the customer's visual attention. In the past, advertisement was made fully by a human designer without any help from computer. But with the development of computer graphics and image processing techniques, computer-aided advertisement design systems came into being and had quickly started to dominate the design domain (Adobe, 1991; Corel, 1993). Furthermore, the case-based reasoning technique can be combined with the existing CAD systems to design advertisement automatically (Zhuang and Pan, 1995). The kernel of case-based reasoning consists of:

- *Case representation.* A case in CBR has two parts:
- *idea path,* which embodies the mapping of synthesis process from multiple design sources to the current design. The idea path is represented by a semantic network.
- *configuration* of the picture, represented as a list of 4-tuples (picture-element, position, content, composite-mode).
- *Case selection.* Cases in the case base are indexed and retrieved by a combination of keywords and content features. An ads case is more than a plain image. The design process starts with the user requirements, which are in return transformed into design constraints. Using the design constrains to look into the case bases, a set of candidate cases are retrieved.
- *Case adaptation and new design.* Case adaptation requires expertise, acquired from the design expert beforehand and stored into a knowledge base in the *if-then* form. After a candidate case has been chosen, rule based reasoning is applied to do the case adaptation.
- *User's final decision.* The right to make the final decision is always left to the user. If the new design scheme is not satisfying, the user can modify it directly or have the system run again. The user can also insert the appropriate knowledge into the system in order to make the system smarter.

5.3 Knowledge Embedded Interactive Garment Design Systems

In some garment design systems, the design knowledge and the design reasoning are directly embedded in the system. These systems usually provide a friendly user interface that guides the user through the design steps. For example, by providing the garment category and selection menus, it energizes the outfit design experience. Example categories are undergarments, shirts, pants, skirts, dresses, jump suits, jackets, socks, shoes, sunglasses, and backgrounds. Each category provides a list of selections and so on. These kinds of garment design software are easy to use either for professional designers or general customers. For example, Flash'N Fashion (Media Motion Publications) is a commercial product designed to bring the world of sewing to children. In (Tukaptrn), the TUKAdesign system makes it faster and more accurate to create various types of notches, darts, pleats, seams, drills holes, and internal contours.

Another example of knowledge embedding can be found in the systems capable of fulfilling a certain task using AI techniques. For example, some systems include features for intelligent trapping of adjacent colors, automatic join lines with protective masking, batch separations, and output file format support to connect with the leading production machinery (CAD Cut).

5.4 Intelligent Agent: Consultation for Garment Selection and/or Design

To make the whole system in Figure 1 attractive to a wide range of customers, intelligence and simplification in the design process and the user interface may not be sufficient. For example, the great advantage of physical garment shops is its human personnel that assists the customers, while the advantage of a human tailor is an easy access to his expertise.

For making the Internet-based virtual custom-fit garment shop closer to this, an intelligent agent that integrates all the intelligent functions discussed in this section is necessary. In addition, this intelligent virtual agent (that may even has its graphical representation, for example an animated human-like figure, or a talking head (Capin, 1997)), should also be capable of learning the customer's preferences and giving the suggestions based on its expertise and the learned customer's profile.

For example, the system should be able to suggest garments based on the customer's characteristics, such as the weight, height, skin and hair color, and even 3D model as a pre-stored record, and his/her preferences. The agent could also help the customer make the alternation on the basic design (using a knowledge-embedded interactive CAD utility, for example), or help him choose the color or the textile print design using the relevance feedback technique in the content based image retrieval. After a customer has selected one piece of garment, say a shirt, the intelligent agent may act as a virtual salesman and suggest a matching tie, or assist the customer in creating a whole outfit.

In the on-line shopping system, this consultation service can be realized either as an expert system or an intelligent agent that works between the clients and the server. The knowledge base is divided into two types: general (or user independent) knowledge and user-specific knowledge. General knowledge is generally applicable to a wide range of customers or to a category of customers and includes, for example, some general aesthetics standards, such as color harmonization. User specific knowledge describes learned individual aesthetics standards, for example the user's subjective preferences about garment matching.

6 Conclusions

In this chapter we described the computer technologies that can be used in the Internet-based garment-shopping network. With the increase of its bandwidth, the Internet will become a perfect medium for on-line shopping. It will give the potential customers fast access to the remote resources, such as the databases and computational resources. Furthermore, it already provides easy and relatively secure payment possibilities. This will allow making the computer technologies described in this chapter available to everyone, directly from their homes.

Most of the described systems are up and running in our lab, though some of them were not strictly applied to the garment industry applications. To build the whole Internet-based garment shopping system of the kind described here, the major effort would be invested in the integration of the described components and the refinement of the virtual intelligent agent, but the preliminary systems are fairly easy to construct. It is our belief that the commercial CAD Garment systems will evolve in the direction that we have described.

The major technologies descirbed in this chapter but which are not yet used in the existing computer systems in the garment industry are:

- the texture-mapped 3-D models of real humans, which can be combined with physics-based cloth draping simulations
- the image databases with content-based retrieval capability and relevance-feedback mechanism that learns the user's visual associations
- the automatic advertisement design using case-based knowledge

We have shown how these contributions can be used together, for example to allow the customer to search for the garment design, and the woven or print design on the selected garment, and finally see their selection on their own body, whose geometry and texture were acquired using a cheap computer vision technique Figure 4. This is an example of integration of the several separate components of the garment industry today: design, advertisement and retailing of customized garment are all done at one place. By allowing the customers to see themselves (instead of a model) wearing the selected designs and in different settings using animation and/or the described case-based advertisement design, the power of advertisement becomes considerably greater than in the case of the catalogs, for example.

In conclusion, we expect that the development of such integrated Internet-based systems will significantly reduce costs of advertisement and retailing, while still allowing mass-customization.

References

Adobe Systems Incorporated, *Adobe Photoshop User Guide*, (1991).

Acar, M., ``Advancements and Applications of Mechatronic Design in Textile Engineering'', in Proceedings of *the NATO Advanced Study Institute*, (1994).

Bach, J. R., C. Fuller, A. Gupta, A. Hampapur, B. Horowitz, R. Humphrey, R. Jain, C. Shu, "The Virage Image Search Engine: An open framework for image management, in Proc. *of SPIE Conf on Storage and Retrieval for Image and Video Databases*, (1996)

Breen, D. E., D. H. House and M. J. Wozny, "Predicting the drape of woven cloth using interacting particles", in Proc. of *SIGGRAPH*, (1994), 365-372. CAD Cut, URL=http://www.cadcut.com/optitex.html

Capin, T. K. et al, "Virtual human representation and communication in VLNet", *IEEE Computer Graphics and Applications*, 17, 2, (1997), 42-53.

Carignan, M., Y. Yang, N. M. Thalmann and D. Thalmann, "Dressing animated synthetic actors with complex deformable clothes", in Proc. of *SIGGRAPH*, (1992), 99-104.

Chang, N. S. and K. S. Fu, "Query-by Pictorial-Example", *IEEE Trans. on Software Engineering*, SE-6, 6, (1980).

Chang, S. K., "Pictorial Data-Base Systems", *IEEE Computer*, Nov. (1981).

Chang, S. K., C. W. Yan, D. C. Dimitroff and T. Arndt, "An Intelligent Image Database System", *IEEE Trans. on Software Engineering*, 14, 5, (1988).

Chu, C. C., C. L. Cummings and N. A. Teixeira, "Mechanics of elastic performance of textile materials, part V: A study of factors affecting the drape of fabrics - the development of a drape meter", *Textile Research Journal*, (1950), 539-548.

Collier, J. R., B. J. Collier, G. O'Toole and S. M. Sargand, "Drape prediction by means of finite element analysis", *Journal of the Textile Institute*, 82, 1, (1991), 96-107.

Computer Design Inc., URL=http://www.cdi-u4ia.com/

Corel Corporation, *CorelDraw User's Manual-version4.0*, (1993).

Czarnecki, C. A., "Integrating the cutting and sewing room of garment manufacture using mechatronic techniques", *Mechatronics* (UK), 5, 2, (1995), 295-308.

Davis, S. and J. Botkin, "The coming of knowledge-based business, *Harvard Business Review*, 75, 5, (1994), 165-179.

Eberhardt, B., A. Weber and W. Strasser, "A fast, flexible particle-system model for cloth draping", *IEEE Computer Graphics and Applications*, 16, 5, (1996), 52-59.

Fukuda, M., M. Katsumoto and Y. Shibata, "Perceptual Link Method based on Dynamic Hypermedia System for Design Image Database System", in Proc. of *the 29th Annual Hawaii International Conference on System Sciences*, (1996)

Haralick, R. M., K. Shanmugam and I. Dinstein, "Texture Features for Image Classification", *IEEE Trans. on Sys, Man, and Cyb*, SMC-3, 6, (1973).

Jain, A. K., *Fundamentals of digital image processing*, Prentice-Hall of India Private Limited, (1995)

Jojic, N., J. Gu, T. S. Huang and H. Shen, "Computer Modeling, Analysis and Synthesis of Dressed Humans", to appear in *IEEE Trans. On Circuits and Systems for Video Technology*, Special Issue on SNHC, (1999).

Jojic, N., J. Gu, I. Mak, H. Shen and T. S. Huang, "Computer Modeling, Analysis and Synthesis of Dressed Humans", in Proc. *of IEEE Conf. on Computer Vision and Pattern Recognition*, (1998)

Jojic, N. and T. S. Huang, "On analysis of the range data of cloth drapes", in Proc. of *3rd Asian Conference on Computer Vision*, (1998)

Kakadiaris, I. A. and D. Metaxas, "3D Human Body Model Acquisition from Multiple views", in Proc. of *the Fifth International Conference on Computer Vision*, (1995), 618-623.

Media Motion Publications, URL=http://www.media-motion.com

Mott, S., "Case-based reasoning: market, applications and fit with other technologies", *Expert Systems with applications*, 6, (1993).

Ng, H. N., R. L. Grimsdale, "Computer graphics techniques for modeling cloth", *IEEE Computer Graphics and Applications*, 16, 5, (1996), 28-41.

Ng, H. N., R. L. Grimsdale and W. G. Allen, "A system for modeling and visualization of cloth material", *Computer Graphics*, 19, 3, (1995), 423-430.

Niblack, W., R. Barber et al., "The QBIC Project: Querying images by content using color, texture and shape", in Proc. *of SPIE Conf on Storage and Retrieval for Image and Video Databases*, (1994).

Ortega, M., Y. Rui, K. Chakrabarti, A. Warshavsky, S. Mehrotra, and T. S. Huang, Supporting Ranked Boolean Similarity Queries in MARS, to appear *in IEEE Tran on Knowledge and Data Engineering*, 1998

Pan, Y. and Z. He, "A system to create computer-aided art patterns, knowledge engineering and computer modeling in CAD", in Proc. of *CAD*, (1986).

Persoon, E. and K. S. Fu, "Shape Discrimination Using Fourier Descriptors, *IEEE Trans. Sys. Man, Cyb.*, SMC-7, (1977), 170-179.

Rui, Y., T. S. Huang and S. Mehrotra, "Content-based Image Retrieval with Relevance Feedback in MARS, in Proc. *of IEEE Conf on Image Processing*, (1997).

Rui, Y., T. S. Huang, M. Ortega, and S. Mehrotra, Relevance Feedback: "A Power Tool in Interactive Content-Based Image Retrieval*", IEEE Tran on Circuits and Systems for Video Technology*, Sept, (1998).

Rui, Y., A. C. She and T. S. Huang, "Modified Fourier Descriptors for Shape Representation - - A Practical Approach", in Proc. of *First International Workshop on Image Databases and Multi Media Search*, (1996).

Russell, S. and P. Norvig, *Artificial Intelligence: A Modern Approach, Prentice-Hall*, (1995).

Shanahan, W. J., D. W. Lloyd and J. W. S. Hearle, "Characterizing the elastic behavior of textile fabrics in complex deformations*", Textile Research Journal*, (1978), 495-505.

Skelton, J., "Fundamentals of fabric shear*", Textile Research Journal*, (1976), 862-869.

Smith, J. R. and S.-F. Chang, "Tools and Techniques for Color Image Retrieval", in Proc. of *IS&T/SPIE Conf. on Storage & Retrieval for Image and Video Databases*, (1995).

Smith, J. R. and S.-F. Chang, "Intelligent Multimedia Information Retrieval", *Querying by Color Regions Using the VisualSEEk Content-Based Visual Query System*, edited by Mark T. Maybury, 1996.

Smith, J. R. and S.-F. Chang, "Automated Binary Texture Feature Sets for Image Retrieval", in Proc. *of IEEE Conf on Acoust., Speech, and Signal Processing*, (1996)

Stricker, M., and M. Orengo, "Similarity of Color Images", in Proc. *of SPIE Conf on Storage and Retrieval for Image and Video Databases*, (1995), 381-392.

Tamura, H., S. Mori and T. Yamawaki, "Texture Features Corresponding to Visual Perception*", IEEE Trans. on Sys, Man, and Cyb*, SMC-8, 6, (1978).

Terzopoulos, D., J. Platt, A. Barr and K. Fleischer, "Elastically deformable models", in Proc. of *SIGGRAPH*, (1987), 205-214.

Tsai, R.Y., "A Versatile Camera Calibration Technique for High-Accuracy 3D Machine Vision Metrology Using Off-the-Shelf TV Cameras and Lenses*", IEEE Journal of Robotics and Automation*, 3,4, (1987), 323-44.

Tukaptrn, Inc., URL=http://www.tukatech.com/tukaptrn.html

Volino, P. and N. M. Thalmann, "Efficient self-collision detection on smoothly discretized surface animations using geometrical shape regularity*", Computer Graphics Forum (EuroGraphics Proc.)*, 13, 3, (1994), 155-166.

Wang, Y. F. and J. K > Aggarwal, "Integration of active and passive sensing techniques for representing three-dimensional objects*", IEEE Trans on Robotics and Automation*, 5, 4, (1989), 460-471.

Weszka, J., Charles Dyer and Azeril Rosenfeld, "A comparative Study of Texture Measures for Terrain Classification, *IEEE Trans. on Sys, Man, and Cyb*, SMC-6, 4, (1976).

Yang, Y. and N. M. Thalmann, "An improved algorithm for collision detection in cloth animation with human body", *Computer Graphics and Applications (Pacific Graphics Proceedings)*, (1993), 237-251.

Zhuang, Y.and Y. Pan, "Case-based synthesis in automatic advertising creation system", in Proc. of *Inter. Conf. on Intelligent Manufacturing.*

Part IV
Technology and Infrastructure

CHAPTER 13
Consumer Mass Market Online Payment Solutions

Christoph Schlueter Langdon[1], Fabrice Roghé[2], and Michael J. Shaw[3]

[1]Department of Economics, Darmstadt University of Technology, and Beckman Institute for Advanced Science and Technology, University of Illinois at Urbana-Champaign, Urbana, IL, USA, cschlutr@uiuc.edu

[2]Department of Economics, Darmstadt University of Technology, Darmstadt, Germany, roghe@hotmail.com

[3]Department of Business Administration, and Beckman Institute for Advenced Science and Technology, University of Illinois at Urbana-Champaign, Urbana, IL, USA, m-shaw@uiuc.edu

We provide an overview of online payment solutions targeted at consumer mass markets. Starting with a categorization and description of systems and services, the survey is focused on two specific implementations: An SET-based online credit card application and an electronic cash trial have been chosen to illustrate important processes, systems architecture and infrastructure issues. We close with a discussion of strategic implications of online payment solutions.

Keywords: Electronic Payment Systems; Electronic Cash; Business Strategy

1 Introduction

One of the most essential ingredients for a continued strong growth of electronic commerce are online payment (OP) solutions. An OP solution is defined as an OP technology/system enabled service. As of mid-1997, both OP systems and services are significantly less developed and mature than, for example, Internet transmission/routing technology or Internet access services. The absence of ubiquitous, trustworthy, flexible and fail safe OP solutions has become one of the most severe inhibitors of electronic commerce growth. Absence of payment solutions even turns the notion of commerce *ad absurdum*. Most importantly, a lack of OP solutions severely constrains the choice of viable business models, thus limiting the scale and scope of digital interactive service (DIS) offerings. Making data available "just-in-time," on demand and anywhere is less problematic than collecting revenue for these data and related online services. Most Web-based content providers and interactive television trials reveal that advertising revenues will neither cover platform and application investments nor operating costs. New sources of revenues such as transaction fees are crucial for making DIS markets profitable. Therefore, OP solutions are required to address a wide range of payment needs from big-ticket item purchases to pocket-change bargain deals. The latter, in particular, appears to be in strong need. Small money, or micro-payments, would make possible *a-la-carte* pricing, which in turn could be more economically efficient than flat-fee bundles, thus increasing overall consumer welfare.

Providing OP solutions represents a new business opportunity in itself. OP solutions require the support of an entire platform composed of communication network infrastructure, middleware, and applications. All of these components have to be developed and organized into a service. Many ventures have positioned themselves to take advantage of the OP technology and service business opportunities such as CyberCash or DigiCash. The credit card companies, MasterCard and Visa, for example, have been collaborating with leading software vendors (Netscape, Microsoft and IBM) on a standard called SET (Secure Electronic Transaction), which is designed to extend the use of traditional credit cards on the Internet (European Commission and Andersen Consulting 1996, pp. 208–210). Large banks such as CitiCorp or Deutsche Bank are at the forefront of exploring electronic cash services targeted at a consumer mass-market audience.

These OP pioneers have many examples to look at to avoid the pitfalls of DIS development. Current success stories such as consumer online service provider America Online or failures like the numerous interactive television trials of the early 1990s, provide some important lessons. Instead of pushing technology systems, the more successful solutions have been thoroughly market-driven–easy to use, affordable, and cost efficient–by leveraging on existing infrastructure or platform assets.

This chapter surveys consumer mass-market OP systems and services. Furthermore, it describes, in greater detail, an SET system and a small money/micropayment solution. It concludes with a discussion of the overall strategic implications of the OP development.

2 Categorization and Review of Major Electronic Commerce Payment Solutions

Figure 1 provides an overview of the three broad categories of electronic payment systems (Kalakota and Whinston 1996, p. 298):

Banking and financial payments: This category covers electronic data interchange (EDI) for inter-organizational commerce. Using EDI, banks and other organizations exchange trading information electronically. The spectrum of EDI covers large-scale bank-to-bank transfers and wholesale payments as well as small-scale payments via automated teller machines (ATMs).

Retailing payments: This group of payment solutions describes a wide array of credit, debit and charge cards. The few large credit card companies—Visa, MasterCard and American Express—operate worldwide systems for electronic authorization and settlement of card-based payments. With the emergence of electronic commerce, both the technology used in the electronic clearing and the global clearing network infrastructure provided by these card system operators have evolved as valuable assets for extending the business into OP solutions.

Online electronic commerce payments: The last category covers all different payment solutions designed for electronic commerce transactions. OPs can be split into (1) credit or postpaid, (2) debit or prepaid and (3) token-based payments (Furche and Wrightson 1996, pp. 25-35; Kalakota and Whinston 1996, pp. 296-299). Electronic token can be viewed as the digital analog of traditional forms of money backed by authorized financial institutions (Kalakota and Whinston 1996, p. 299). Online debit and credit payment systems usually rely on a payer's conventional account such as a credit card or checking account. Therefore, these payment solutions are also referred to as access products (Bibow and Wichmann 1998, p. 4).

This chapter focuses only on the latter category–consumer mass market OP solutions. The following sections discuss some general characteristics of OP systems and services before introducing three broad categories of OP solutions.

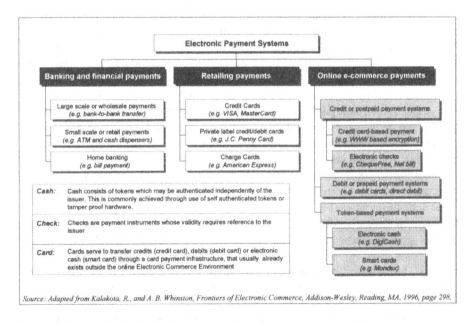

Source: Adapted from Kalakota, R., and A. B. Whinston, Frontiers of Electronic Commerce, Addison-Wesley, Reading, MA, 1996, page 298.

Fig. 1. Categories of electronic payment systems

2.1 OP Systems Characteristics and Services Features

An OP solution is comprised of hardware and software systems as well as technology-enabled service operations. The components of a payment system should include, for example, human computer interface and access software, secure transmission protocols and encryption methods. The service-specific elements relate to the way a particular system is operated. This includes customer care procedures (e.g. call centers routines, FAQ board maintenance) as well as marketing mix issues such as the pricing and bundling of OP solutions with other financial services products.

Developers and vendors of OP system technology are mostly non-banks such as DigiCash, Cybercash or Brokat. Even First Virtual is not a bank in the traditional sense. Operators so far are usually banks (e.g. Citicorp or Deutsche Bank) or other financial service organizations such as transaction processing companies (e.g. First Data Corp.).

System Technology-Specific Characteristics: The following criteria are used for comparing the numerous OP system technologies (Furche and Wrightson 1996, pp. 7-25; Kalakota and Whinston 1996, pp. 296-299).

Security features: A secure payment transaction requires correct authentication of both merchant and customer and the integrity of order and payment information. The crucial integrity requirement can be further broken down into the widely used ACID criteria – i.e., atomicity, consistency, isolation and durability (Gray and Reuter 1993). Atomicity implies that a transaction either occurs completely, e.g. on both the accounts of the payer and the payee, or it does not occur at all. Consistency means that all relevant parties agree on critical facts of the transaction, e.g. on the amount and on the payment conditions. Isolation requires that different transactions do not interfere with each other. Finally, durability refers to the ability to recover a transaction, e.g. after a computer has crashed.

Privacy protection measures: How is information in different types of transactions disclosed and to whom? The transaction traceability refers to the buyer's and seller's identities as well as the amount, date and time. Wyhen a payer's identity is hidden, then the transaction is said to be anonymous. DigiCash, for example, incorporates specially designed mechanisms to ensure the anonymity of the payment transactions. Data surveillance as well as abuse is an issue with electronic payment systems. Due to the digital nature of transactions each transactions creates traces and machine-readable records. There is a danger that data may be aggregated, misused or disclosured over open electronic networks (Hochwald 1993, pp. 62-63).

Authentication and settlement methods: Depending on whether an electronic payment system is based on account transfer (access products such as checks, credit and debit cards) or on circulating electronic cash token, the means of settlement differs significantly, implying tradeoffs between security, privacy, financial risks and cost. Account transfers raise authentication and verification problems, while tokens have to be protected against any attempt of forgery.

Interoperability: First, a payment solution should work for as many participants as possible–customers, merchants, financial institutions, and trading partners. Ubiquitous acceptance or reach is one of the critical success factors for traditional credit cards, for example. Second, a particular payment system has to be compatible with an online merchant's legacy system and architecture. While the latter might be achieved with costly systems integration efforts, the former issue requires widely accepted technology standards. Such standards can be official agreements among technology vendors and banks (e.g. SET) or may be set by international standard setting bodies.

Nature of transaction (average transaction value, frequency): What is the "target market"? Systems can be designed for small money/micro-payments or large payments. Furthermore, there might be special purpose payments such as value token that are issued and accepted by only one or a few merchants or smart cards that can only be used for certain applications (e.g. phone calls or public transportation).

Cost: Payment systems involve fixed cost such as software licensing fees, and expenses for application/database design, system development, and systems integration. Furthermore, payment systems cause variable cost for transaction processing, authentication and payment processing as well as system maintenance.

Security and privacy protection are two of the most critical aspects of OP solutions. How can the parties involved be securely identified, the integrity of the transaction be assured and privacy be protected at the same time? The solution lies in the application of encryption technology, the conversion of a message into a form unreadable to anyone without the secret code or algorithm to unlock it. Software encryption is at the heart of electronic payment systems. It can be distributed and updated economically over the Internet or bundled with applications.

There are two different types of software encryption methods: secret-key and public-key (Kalakota and Whinston 1996, pp. 195–213; SET Specifications 1997, pp. 14-16). Secret-key cryptography, also known as symmetric cryptography, relies on the use of the same key for both encryption by the transmitter and decryption by the receiver. A well known example is Data Encryption Standard (DES), which is used by financial institutions to encrypt PINs (Personal Identification Numbers). Secret-key cryptography creates distribution problems on large networks because each merchant would have to use a distinct key with each customer. Public-key cryptography, also known as asymmetric cryptography, solves this transmission problem. Each participant creates a pair of matching keys, a public key, which is published, and a private key, which is kept secret. One of the keys is used to encrypt the message, the other one alone is able to decrypt the message again. For example, a merchant could create a public/private key pair and publish the public key, allowing any customer to send a secure message to that merchant. One of the best-known public key systems is RSA, developed in 1977 by Ron Rivest, Adi Shamir and Leonard Adleman. Digital signatures, like conventional signatures used as a means of authentication, are usually based on public-key cryptography.

System-Enabled and Market-Driven Service Features: Users usually do not pay for a particular piece of technology but for technology-enabled utility. Therefore, the development of services is crucial for the success of any OP solutions. The OP service provider challenge is to avoid being pushed by technology but to be market-driven. The young history of digital interactive services, for example, is littered with failures due to technological push. One of the most prominent disappointments is the wave of interactive television trials throughout the first half of the 1990's. Driven by advances in digital transmission technology and regulatory incentives, many US phone and cable TV companies started to experiment with video dial tone networks or broadband, interactive transmission plants. When more and more technology components had to be built from scratch (e.g. set boxes with workstation motherboards or video servers), cost by far exceeded user utility thus willingness to pay. Finally, even the most ambitious and well-backed efforts such as Time Warner Cable's and US West's Full Service Network trial in Orlando, Florida was cancelled. Instead of interactive television over video dial tone networks, consumer online services (e.g. America Online) and web-based content providers such as The Wall Street Journal Interactive have created a vibrant digital interactive services industry on the Internet.

The lessons learned from the initial ITV failure and success of DIS pioneers can readily be applied to the development of OP solutions. First, it is more rewarding to leverage existing infrastructure installations to the greatest extent possible than to create entire platforms and applications from scratch. In the case of OP solutions, this clearly favors credit card companies, traditional retail banks, and transaction processors but also providers of personal finance management software with a significant installed base of user interfaces and applications (e.g. Intuit's Quicken). Second, addressing customer needs has to become a top priority. In particular, America Online gives valuable lessons on how to provide affordable online utility and services while creating a positive user experience. Critical success factors are ease of use, accessibility, convenience and affordability.

As with credit cards and, to some extent, with online services, OP solutions face a dual diffusion problem; consumers as well as merchants have to subscribe or support a particular service. Without a critical mass of accepting merchants there is little incentive for consumers to use an OP solution. In turn, without the prospect of a substantial market, merchants will not be enticed to invest in an OP solution.

2.2 Selected Types of Consumer OP Solutions

Credit or Postpaid Payments: All credit payments have in common that there is a significant time delay between initial transaction and the actual transfer of money. Thus, there is a credit risk involved. Postpaid OP solutions are per se access products, allowing the payee to access funds from a payer's account. They can further be broken down into two subcategories: electronic checks and credit card-based online payments.

Electronic checks are electronic notional money systems, which work in much the same way as conventional paper checks, authorizing the exchange of money from one account to another. An electronic check bears an encrypted digital signature, which authenticates the payer. The electronic check also carries the name of the payer, the name of the financial institution, the payer's account number, the name of the payee and value. Before a check can be paid, it will need to be endorsed by the payee, who uses a different digital signature. Checks can then be electronically exchanged between financial institutions through electronic clearinghouses that settle the accounts. Electronic check transactions usually conform to the criteria described by ACID. Electronic checks have the disadvantage of imposing a significant credit risk for the payee (checks might bounce) and a low degree of privacy (high traceability).

Examples of payment systems based on electronic checks are NetCheque and, to some extend, NetBill (Camp, Sirbu, and Tygar 1996, pp. 6-14). Systems by Cybercash and Checkfree also include check-like payment instruments. (Schoeter and Willmer 1997, pp. 18-21). NetBill is especially designed to facilitate the purchase of information goods. The online delivery is monitored by the NetBill gateway. Both NetCheque and NetBill use secret key-based Kerberos tickets to authenticate the user. Kerberos was developed in the 1980's at the MIT (Kalakota and Whinston 1996, pp. 205-206).

Credit-card based online payments have characteristics similar to those of electronic checks, e.g. creating similar records. While electronic checks require an online authentication and settlement network, which is separate from the paper check clearing process, credit card-based OP solutions can utilize much of the existing clearing networks for conventional credit card transactions.

OPs raise the problem of card authorization (Is the user also the owner?), data protection (How to protect the card number and expiration date?) and integrity of the amount charged. Solutions include: (1) Encryption of credit card and transaction data and (2) use of trusted intermediaries who will not pass credit card details to the payee.

In the first option, the payer has to trust the payee on two accounts. First, that the mutually agreed upon amount has been charged. Second, data are properly protected in the payee's database. As the payer has no written evidence of the transaction, it may be difficult to monitor and to protest an online transaction (Kossel and Wronsky 1997, p. 66). Secure online credit card payments of this kind are usually based on secure protocols such as SHTTP on the Internet.

The second option requires a standard to assure the interoperability of intermediaries as well as an infrastructure for verification and settlement. To that end, a standard has been established recently in the form of the Secure Electronic Transaction standard (SET). SET increases security and privacy for all parties involved. However, since SET involves numerous encryption and decryption cycles, plus some intermediaries (e.g. trust centers and payment gateway operators) it is too expensive for micro-payment applications on the Web. The SET standard has been widely discussed, including technical specifications, interfaces and current enhancements.

In addition to credit card payments, SET is conceived to be employed for debit and smart card-based solutions (http://www.setco.com).

Debit or Prepaid Payments. In general, with debit OP solutions, the payer has already deposited money before the payment transaction is initiated. Two subtypes have to be considered, the debit card, with the option of direct debit payments, and the value storage card.

The *debit card* works in a similar manner as electronic checks and credit cards, except that settlement (the actual payment) takes place immediately and online. The debit card is another typical access product. The debit card carries the bank account address of the payer. Usually, the card works with a PIN, which identifies the card user as the legal proprietor of the card. The use of debit cards in the electronic commerce environment works much like conventional "Electronic Fund Transfer at Point of Sale" (EFTPOS) systems. Once debit card data and PIN are transmitted, the payee asks the card emitting institution to authorize the payment online. The emitting institution checks the availability of funds and credits the payee while debiting the payer immediately. These transactions are fully atomic and do not involve credit or liquidity risk.

An example of a debit card is the EC-card, which is very popular in Germany and other European countries. Deutsche Bank is currently testing a direct online fund transfers solution with PIN verification and based on SET (Payment per "Lastschrift" on the Internet; Deutsche Bank 1997 a, p. 1).

Another prepaid instrument is the *value storage card*. Traditionally, such cards have been used in closed systems. Thus, the issuer of the card is the only one to accept payment with the card. Originally, cards were not rechargeable and the value of the card was paid at the time of purchase (pre-payment). Typical examples of such value storage cards are telephone cards. When it comes to electronic commerce, value storage cards can function as wallets for electronic cash. Cards carrying electronic cash are called smart cards (Furche and Whrigtson 1996, pp. 65-79). The term "smart" refers to chip-embedded software, placed on the card. Smart card-based systems are token systems rather than prepaid access products. A typical example is Mondex (Schoeter and Willmer 1997, pp. 36-38). Due to an unmatched service versatility and very lucrative bundling, co-branding, and cross-marketing opportunities and therefore ease of diffusion, smart cards might evolve as a major mid-term OP solution.

Payments with Electronic Value Tokens: Information technology has created a genuinely new form of money called electronic cash, representing a profound innovation rather than a modification of conventional payment instruments (such as electronic checks, credit and debit cards) (Bibow and Wichmann 1998, p. 1). The new electronic currency differs from other currencies in that it is not backed by a central bank. Success of electronic cash or electronic value tokens as money relies on the assumption that a token will not lose value and will be accepted in the future. While an electronic check might bounce just as a regular check—an event that can occur despite strict security measures—an electronic token will never lose its value, no matter where it circulates, unless the whole value token service collapses. Hence, concerns with electronic tokens are less with who is paying with the currency. Rather, one needs to be concerned with the token issuer and with how token can be protected against forgery. Token payments could generally be anonymous. As user authentication becomes obsolete cost savings could allow for small money or micropayments.

So far, some large banks have bought electronic cash systems and invested in middleware and application development to fashion an infrastructure to issue electronic cash, verify tokens and maintain electronic cash accounts (as opposed to notional money accounts). As commercial banks offer their own electronic cash systems, there could be an emerging market for branded electronic currencies. However, widespread and convenient use might require interoperability, which in turn would appear as yet another opportunity to set standards.

Figure 2 summarizes key findings of section two in a comprehensive comparison of the aforementioned OP solutions.

	System Name/Invention	Intro-duction	Concept	Cost	Largest trans-actions	Hardware/Software	Traceability	Transfer-ability	Divisi-bility	Online/Offline (On/Off)	Requirements for Customers	Advantages/Disadvantages
Credit	NetCheque, USC	NA	Account transfer	◐	◑	SW	Un-conditional	No	Yes	On	Checking account	- Credit risk of payee, no privacy / + Secure and fast authentication via Kerberos
	NetBill	NA	Account transfer	◐	◑	SW	Conditional	No	Yes	On	Account at Netbill server	+ Suitable for information goods because system verifies correct online delivery / - Requirement of having Netbill accounts
	CyberCash	NA	Account transfer	◐	◑	SW	Conditional	No	Yes	On	Credit card	+ Effective encryption of data (1024-bit RSA) / + No disclosure of credit card number / - May become superfluous because of SET
	SET (Secure Electronic Transaction), Mastercard/VISA	Feb. 1996	Account transfer	●	◑	SW	User-controlled	No	Yes	On	Credit card, certificate from trust center	+ MC/VISA support / + SET-standard published, worldwide available / - Banks (issuers of credit cards) have to provide services, e.g. issuing certificates / - Too expensive for low value transactions / - Diff. implementations, compatibility issue
Debit	Direct debit, (Girokonto, Telecash)	NA	Account transfer	◐	◑	SW	Conditional	No	Yes	On	Registered checking account	+ Authorization and settlement in real-time / + Use of existing settlement structures (Girokonto); - Java-wallet
	Geldkarte, Telecash	NA	Smart-card	◑	◑	HW	User-controlled	No	Yes	Off	Smartcard + reader	+ Low transaction cost / + Immediate credit for merchant / - Hardware required
	Mondex	July 1995	Smart-card	◑	◑	HW	Untraceable	Yes	Yes	Off	Smartcard + reader	+ Low transaction cost / + Immediate credit for merchant / - Hardware required
Token	Millicent, Digital	1997	Multi-use token	◑	○	SW	Conditional	Yes	No	Off/On	Broker account, software to store token	+ Very low transaction cost / + Payments of fractions of a cent / - Relatively low degree of security, encryption
	NetCash, USC	NA	Multi-use token	◑	○	SW	Conditional (traceable by bank)	Yes	No	Off/On	Account for elect. currency at issuing bank	+ Multi-layer authentication system / + Efficient tracking of double spending / - Traceability
	ecash, DigiCash	Oct. 1994	Single-use token	◑	◑	SW	Untraceable	Yes (token verified by issuer)	No	On	ecash-account, wallet software installed	+ Anonymity (blind signatures) / + High level of security (via token verification) / - So far no interoperability between different issuers (single-use)

Source: Http://www.schlueterresearch.com.

● High ○ Low
NA Not available

Fig. 2. Comparison of electronic commerce payment solutions

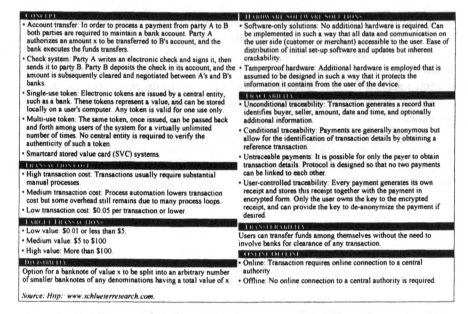

CONCEPT	HARDWARE SOFTWARE SOLUTIONS
• Account transfer: In order to process a payment from party A to B both parties are required to maintain a bank account. Party A authorizes an amount x to be transferred to B's account, and the bank executes the funds transfers.	• Software-only solutions: No additional hardware is required. Can be implemented in such a way that all data and communication on the user side (customer or merchant) accessible to the user. Ease of distribution of initial set-up software and updates but inherent crackability.
• Check system: Party A writes an electronic check and signs it, then sends it to party B. Party B deposits the check in its account, and the amount is subsequently cleared and negotiated between A's and B's banks.	• Tamperproof hardware: Additional hardware is employed that is assumed to be designed in such a way that it protects the information it contains from the user of the device.
• Single-use token: Electronic tokens are issued by a central entity, such as a bank. These tokens represent a value, and can be stored locally on a user's computer. Any token is valid for one use only.	TRACEABILITY
• Multi-use token: The same token, once issued, can be passed back and forth among users of the system for a virtually unlimited number of times. No central entity is required to verify the authenticity of such a token.	• Unconditional traceability: Transaction generates a record that identifies buyer, seller, amount, date and time, and optionally additional information.
• Smartcard stored value card (SVC) systems.	• Conditional traceability: Payments are generally anonymous but allow for the identification of transaction details by obtaining a reference transaction.
TRANSACTION COST	• Untraceable payments: It is possible for only the payer to obtain transaction details. Protocol is designed so that no two payments can be linked to each other.
• High transaction cost: Transactions usually require substantial manual processes.	
• Medium transaction cost: Process automation lowers transaction cost but some overhead still remains due to many process loops.	• User-controlled traceability: Every payment generates its own receipt and stores this receipt together with the payment in encrypted form. Only the user owns the key to the encrypted receipt, and can provide the key to de-anonymize the payment if desired.
• Low transaction cost: $0.05 per transaction or lower.	
TARGET TRANSACTIONS	TRANSFERABILITY
• Low value: $0.01 or less than $5.	Users can transfer funds among themselves without the need to involve banks for clearance of any transaction.
• Medium value: $5 to $100.	
• High value: More than $100.	ONLINE OFFLINE
DIVISIBILITY	• Online: Transaction requires online connection to a central authority.
Option for a banknote of value x to be split into an arbitrary number of smaller banknotes of any denominations having a total value of x.	• Offline: No online connection to a central authority is required.

Source: Http: www.schlueterresearch.com.

Fig. 2 continued

3 Examples of OP Solutions: Processes, Architecture and Infrastructure Requirements

After discussing general features and categories of OP systems and services some pioneering examples will be described in more detail: SET-based implementation by Brokat (X-Pay) and DigiCash's ecash system in a service with the same name developed and operated by Deutsche Bank. Furthermore, we compare the ecash solution with Digital's Millicent micro-payment product.

3.1 Secure Electronic Transaction Standard – The Example of Brokat's X-Pay System

In 1996, after an intense struggle for control, credit card processors (VISA, Master-Card) and software vendors (Netscape, Microsoft, IBM) have defined SET as standard for secure electronic transactions (Kossel and Wronsky 1997, p. 66).

SET is a complex protocol that aims to cover every aspect of online commercial transactions from the initial registration of the payer to the actual details of the payment process. The centerpiece of SET is authentication through certificates issued by an official trust center. The certificate, a message containing a customer's name and public key, is digitally signed by the certificate authority, which issues the certificate after verifying customer's identity. Certificates are verified through a hierarchy of trust. Each certificate is linked to the signature certificate of the entity that signed it digitally. By tracing it back to a known trusted party, one can be assured that the certificate is valid (SET 1997, pp. 14-29). At present, the hierarchy is still in an embryonic state - only the root certificate authority from Visa and MasterCard has been realized.

Figure 3 provides an overview of the processes and interfaces in an X-Pay-based SET implementation (as simplified in SET 1997, pp. 30-60). Each message exchange involves several complex encryption and decryption cycles.

Brokat Systems, a German technology vendor, offers X-Pay, a system that allows for the integration of online payment methods on the basis of SET. X-Pay at present supports credit card payments, electronic direct debit, payments with cash cards like the German ZKA (Zentraler Kredit Ausschuß) Geldkarte and with X-Pay coins. X-Pay coins is a token-based payment system similar to the Cybercoin system intended for micropayments. X-Pay payment solutions are based on Brokat Twister which provides an Internet platform to integrate online banking and traditional payment services. According to Brokat, the Twister platform at present is being used by approximately 30 banks, including Deutsche Bank (Brokat 1998).

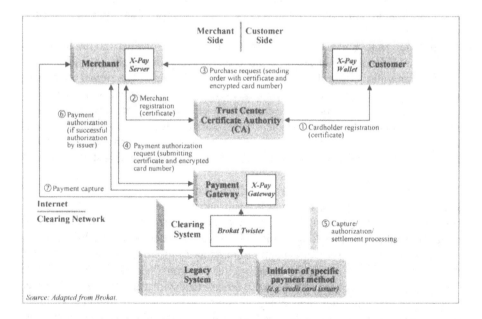

Fig. 3. SET interfaces and processes – the example of Brokat's X-Pay system

The core components of the X-Pay architecture include the Java-based X-Pay Wallet for the consumer, the X-Pay Server for the merchant, and the X-Pay Gateway for the system operator, as shown in Figure 3. The X-Pay Wallet is a Java-based application, which is automatically downloaded from the operator site during the payment phase. It handles the actual payment information exchange between customer, merchant, gateway and the Trust Center, including the SET routines for authentication and transaction processing. The X-Pay Gateway connects the whole system to the Brokat Twister platform and the legacy system for the actual settlement. With X-Pay, a merchant can offer a choice of payment methods to customers, either merchant operated or bundled from different operators and resold.

3.2 DigiCash's and Deutsche Bank's Ecash Solution

David Chaum founded DigiCash and developed the ecash system, which was first tested in October 1994. Mark Twain bank in the USA is the first financial service organization to issue digital cash based on Chaum's technology. As of early 1998, five other banks have joined the community of ecash issuers, including Deutsche Bank (DigiCash 1998 a, p. 1). Despite being based on the same technology, the ecash services are not interoperable yet due to the absence of an interbank clearing system and convertibility.

Deutsche Bank launched its ecash service trial on the Internet in October 1997 with a limited audience of about 1,500 users and approximately 35 online merchants. It provides a central server to act as electronic bank. The server issues and validates ecash and has access to the ecash-accounts of all participating customers and merchants. Customers and merchants have electronic wallet software installed on their computers. These electronic wallets store ecash tokens on the computer's hard drive that can be spent online. To join Deutsche Bank's ecash service, customers of the bank have to open an ecash account, download and install Deutsche Bank's electronic wallet software locally.

The processes of ecash withdrawal and payment evolve as follows: First of all, ecash has to be exchanged for conventional money. Therefore, a Deutsche Bank customer would have to transfer funds from a checking account to the ecash account using the bank's online banking service. However, in order to use ecash it must be withdrawn from the ecash account and be stored in the electronic wallet on the hard disk of the customer's computer. Therefore, the electronic bank server issues value tokens with serial numbers and different denominations that are transmitted to the customer as a message including strings of digits corresponding to digital coins. The ecash software automatically manages the purse of digital coins and keeps plenty of "small change" in the electronic wallet. Now that ecash is in the electronic wallet, the customer can spend it online. In case of a payment request, the ecash software chooses coins with the desired total value from the electronic wallet, removes them and sends them over the network to the payee. Before accepting the payment, the payee's software sends them to the electronic bank server for validation. If the server approves the coins, they are cashed in and their value is credited on the payee's ecash account. The serial number of each coin used is recorded. Every coin can be used just once. For validation, the bank server checks the serial number of the coins and compares it to the record of numbers of previously used coins. If a number is identical to a previously used serial number, then the bank server assumes double spending of an eventually counterfeit coin and refuses the coin. Thus, after each payment, the bank server has to be contacted for verification, and the ecash coins received by the payee return to the bank server. (DigiCash 1998 b, p. 2)

Figure 4 provides an abstraction of major processes and interfaces between in the ecash service (Deutsche Bank 1997 b, p. 2).

The DigiCash system features "one side anonymity": when clearing a transaction, the bank identifies the payee, but the payer remains anonymous, unless the payer chooses to reveal its identity. In order to avoid the traceability of coins issued, Chaum has developed the concept of "blind signatures" preventing the issuer from recognizing particular coins. The DigiCash payment system for ensuring anonymity is depicted in Figure 5.

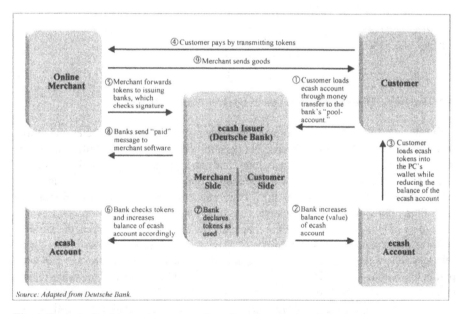

Fig. 4. Deutsche Bank's ecash system and service – interfaces and processes

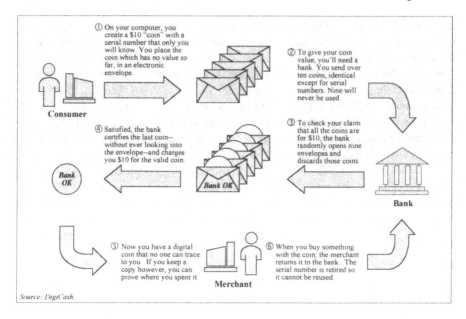

Fig. 5. Ecash's blind signature mechanism

3.3 Digital's Millicent Micropayment System and Service

Millicent is a token-based micro-payment system from Digital (Schoeter and Willmer 1997, p. 33). A main difference between the ecash system and Millicent is that the latter uses *scrip*, a token that is only valid at a particular vendor for a limited time. Hence, there is no need for the vendor to dial into the issuer's server and call for validation (as opposed to ecash). This reduces network traffic and eliminates cost, thus, allowing smaller payments (e.g. fractions of a cent). In order to avoid customers having to maintain different accounts with individual vendors, the system requires brokers to act as intermediaries. They are supposed to maintain long-term relationships to their customers and manage the exchange of their broker *scrip* and particular vendor *scrip*. This should relieve customers from worrying which token to use with a particular vendor.

Another important aspect of Millicent is the relatively low level of encryption, resulting in lower transaction costs. The group justifies this security risk with the low value of the *scrip*. The customer is not anonymous in that the broker saves account details. The system is offline to the extent that no connection to a central server is required.

4 Outlook and Strategic Implications

According to New York based market researchers Datamonitor (Datamonitor 1997, p. 1), by the year 2002, 95% of the payments for US online shopping and 75% of the European payments for online shopping will be settled online using credit/debit cards (the US and European consumer online markets are estimated to be worth US $ 12.5 billion and US $ 3.5 billion respectively). Furthermore, for the same year, Datamonitor predicts that micro-payment systems will account for up to 12% of online transactions in the US, and 8% in Europe. With such rosy forecasts, firms from various industries maneuver to take advantage of the emerging business opportunities. Two key questions are: (1) What is required to seize the various OP system/services as well as standard setting opportunities in terms of assets and skills? and (2) Who is best positioned to take advantage of a particular business in terms of strategic fit and learning curve experience?

As online retailing and financial services value chains are just being formed many firms are jockeying for attractive positions. Similar to the more mature electronic commerce market segments such as electronic publishing (e.g. The Wall Street Journal Interactive) and online retailing (e.g. Amazon.com), the quest appears to be the struggle for control over the customer connection.

Many integration activities are emerging. Equipment vendors buy assets and skills in payment industries. Examples include workstation maker Hewlett-Packard's US $ 1.18 billion acquisition of VeriFone (a provider of credit-card readers and related services used by merchants to verify credit-card purchases) in April 1997, and MSFDS, a joint venture company equally held by Microsoft and First Data Corp. After its 1995 merger with rival First Financial Management, First Data Corp. became the largest third-party processor of credit card transactions in the U.S.A., providing transaction reporting and billing services to financial institutions, oil companies, and retailers. In 1996, it processed 5.9 billion total card transactions for 500,000 merchants representing US $ 214 billion in merchant dollar volume. Other First Data business units include Western Union (one of the largest cash transfer agents in the world) and Telecheck (a leading check authorization service). Together with Microsoft, First Data aims at offering new electronic bill presentment and payment services to billers, banks, and consumers.

Software manufacturers together with financial service operators might be well positioned to leverage an installed base of human computer interfaces as well as application and middleware development skills and systems integration capabilities to set dominant system standards.

Commercial banks could leverage key assets such as an existing customer base, brand recognition (trust factor) and computer network infrastructure. Existing customers could be introduced economically to new solutions through product bundling to quickly create momentum and build critical mass for a particular OP solution.

Other potential OP solution providers might be online merchants. As typical intermediaries they are interested to secure positions by increasing value-added. OP capabilities and in particular scoring competence would complement current key strengths in merchandising and fulfillment to solidify positions in electronic commerce value chains.

In this chapter an overview of mass market online payment solutions has been provided. We started with a categorization of OP solutions and a description of system characteristics and services features to focus on specific implementations. The examples of Brokat's SET-based X-Pay and DigiCash's/Deutsche Bank's ecash solution were chosen to illustrate important infrastructure and implementation issues.

References

Bibow, J. and T. Wichmann, Elektronisches Geld: Funktionsweise und wirtschaftspolitische Konsequenzen, Berlecon Research, Berlin, Germany, 1998.
Brokat, "Brokat X-Pay—product information," Brokat Homepage, (1998),
     URL = http://www.brokat.com.
Camp, L. J., M. Sirbu and J.D. Tygar, "Token and notional money in electronic commerce," (1998), URL = http://www.cs.cmu.edu/~tygar/publications.html.
Deutsche Bank, 1997 a, "Die Deutsche Bank erprobt Zahlungen per Lastschrift und mit Kreditkarte im Internet gemäß SET-Standard," Deutsche Bank Homepage, December 12, (1997), URL = http://info.deutsche-bank.de/deuba/db/db.
Deutsche Bank, 1997 b, "Informationen zum e-cash Pilotversuch der Deutschen Bank," Deutsche Bank Homepage, February 27, (1998),
     URL = http://www.deutsche-bank.de/wwwforum/ecash.
Datamonitor, "Global online digital payments 1997-2002—a market ready to boom," (1997);
     URL = http://www.datamonitor.com/dmhtml/tc/tcwtsnew.htm.
DigiCash, 1998 a, "Current ecash issuers", Digicash Homepage, (1998),
     URL = http://www.digicash.com/ecash/issuers.
DigiCash, 1998 b, "Information to the ecash system", Digicash Homepage, (1998), URL = http://www.digicash.com/publish/ecash_intro.
European Commission, and Andersen Consulting, Strategic developments for the European publishing industry towards the year 2000: Europe's multimedia challenge, Brussels-Luxembourg, 1996.
Furche, A. and G. Wrightson, Computer money—a systematic overview of electronic payment systems, dpunkt Verlag für digitale Technologie, Heidelberg, Germany, 1996.
Gray, J., and A. Reuter, Transaction processing, concepts and techniques, Morgan Kaufmann Publishers, San Francisco, CA, 1993.
Hochwald, L., "The privacy keepers", Folio: The Magazine for Magazine Management, Vol 22, No.12, (1993), 62-63.
Kalakota, R., and A. B. Whinston, Frontiers of electronic commerce, Addison-Wesley Publishing Company, Inc., Reading, MA, 1996.
Kossel, A., and H. J. Wronsky, "Bare bytes," c't, Vol. 16, No. 16, (1997) 66-96.
Schoeter, A., and R. Willmer. Digital money online—a review of some existing technologies, Intertrader Ltd., Edinburgh, UK, 1997.
SET, "SET information homepage," (1998), URL = http://www.setco.com.
SET, Specifications, book 1: Business description, (1997); URL = http://www.setco.com.

CHAPTER 14

Smart Cards

Debbie McElroy[1] and Efraim Turban[2]
[1]Healtheon Corp., Los Angeles, CA, USA, dcmcel@ad.com
[2]California State University at Long Beach, California, and City University of Hongkong, eturban@csulb.edu

---

Smart cards have been in use for over two decades, primarily for storing small amounts of money for specialized purposes. People carry them to pay for telephone calls, transportation, photocopying in libraries and the like. These cards have become very popular in Europe and Asia. Recently, the use of smart cards has expanded considerably through the use of micro-processor chips. For example, in several countries smart cards are used as identification cards which include information ranging from health status and insurance to retirement benefits.

The latest development in smart cards technology is its Internet related applications, which are mostly related to the support of electronic commerce payment systems and security. There are many benefits in using smart cards that will ultimately translate into savings for businesses and consumers.

---

1 What are Smart Cards?

Two types of cards are classified under the generic term "smart card". The first is a **memory card**, typically built with a magnetic stripe. The second type of card is an **intelligent smart card** which contains a memory chip. Both are usually a standard-sized plastic card that looks similar to a credit card.

Conventional smart cards, or memory cards, have been in use for over two dec-ades, and have gained widespread acceptance in Europe and Asia. A Frenchman named Roland Moreno, who patented the technology, developed the first cards in 1974. Memory cards are basically information storage cards that contain stored monetary value which the user can "spend" in pay phones, retail vending, transpor-tation, or related transactions. Smart cards have matured over the last twenty years and today's smart cards are not only used to store data but can process it as well.

In 1998, it is estimated that almost 1 billion smart cards will be produced world-wide still with high concentrated use in Europe and Asia. Since smart cards origi-nated in France, the Europeans have been the primary adopters of this technology. Currently Western Europe holds approximately 70% of the world market of smart cards.[1] (See Table 1) By the year 2000, Data Monitor predicts that several billion cards will be in circulation, with over 15% of the total in use in the United States and Canada. These will be mainly intelligent smart cards.

Table 1. Where smart cards are used

Region	1996	2000
North America	3%	12%
South America	11%	10%
Western Europe	70%	40%
Asia	10%	30%
Rest of the World	6%	8%

The intelligent smart card is a card embedded with either a microprocessor/memory chip combination or only a memory chip with non-programmable logic. The microprocessor-card can add, delete, and otherwise manipulate information on the card, while a memory-chip card can only undertake a pre-defined operation. The integrated circuit chip makes a smart card much more versatile than the memory cards. By adding the chip, the smart card has the ability to serve many different uses since it has the ability to store and secure information, offers a "read / write" capability, and can be used to make decisions as required by the card issuer's specific application needs. This allows smart card applications to be built to include transactional elements that can be used later for further processing. Many industries are adopting the use of smart cards for the benefit of their customers for a variety of applications due to the versatility of the cards. In 1996, approximately 805 million smart cards were issues with an estimated 2.8 billion to be distributed in 2000.[2] (See Table 2).

The intelligence of the integrated circuit chip allows protection of the information being stored from damage or theft. For this reason, newer smart cards are much more secure than the magnetic stripe cards, which carry information on the outside of the card and can be easily copied or have information erased. Smart cards are an effective way of ensuring secure access to open interactive systems, such as encryption key mobility, secure single sign-ons and electronic digital signatures. As an access-control device, smart cards make personal and business data available only to the appropriate users.[3] These benefits are what will drive the triple digit growth of these cards in certain markets.

Table 2. Areas where smart cards are used

Card Application	1996 (000)	2000 (000)	Avg. Annual Growth
Pay Phone	605	1,500	29%
GSM	20	45	25%
Health Care	70	120	14%
Banking	40	250	105%
Identity / Access	20	300	280%
Transportation	15	200	247%
Pay TV	15	75	80%
Gaming	5	200	780%
Metering / Vending	10	80	140%
Retail / Loyalty	5	75	280%

2 Smart Card Standards

The size of a smart card is determined by an international standard (ISO 7816). This standard also defines the physical characteristics of the plastic such as temperature tolerance and flexibility, the position of the electrical contacts and their functions, and how the integrated circuit communicates with the outside world. Since this standard does not address smart card applications, initial application and service providers from the banking and finance, telecommunications, and health care industries have developed their own, open business-related specifications. Most prominent among them are the EMV Specifications, a de-facto standard for electronic payment systems. Developed by Europay, Visa, and MasterCard, the aim of these specifications is to ensure that all smart cards operate across all card terminals and related devices, regardless of location, financial institution, or manufacturer. CEN 726 is a set of European standards for the telecommunications use of smart cards defining a security framework, application-independent requirements for card and card terminals, payment methods, and telecommunications features.

There are several types of plastic used for smart cards. The main types are PCV (Polyvinyl Chloride) and ABS (Acrylonitrite Butadiene Styrene). PVC can be embossed but is not recyclable. ABS cannot be embossed but is recyclable.

Standards are required to ensure that cards and card-accepting devices are built to uniform specifications. This ensures that cards manufactured and issued by one industry sector in one part of the world can be accepted by a device and unrelated industry in another part of the world. The goal is for these cards and devices to support many different types of industries. For example, payment cards may be accepted in card-accepting devices at gas stations while the same card will be used by the owner to secure cellular phone services in another unrelated application.

3 Categories of Smart Cards

The three categories of intelligent smart cards are:

- Integrated Circuit (IC) Microprocessor Cards are microprocessor cards that are generally referred to as "chip cards". These cards offer greater memory storage and security of data than a traditional magnetic stripe card. Chip cards can also process data on the card. The 1998/99 generation of chip cards has an eight-bit processor, 16KB read-only memory, and 512 bytes of random-access memory. This gives the card the equivalent processing power of the original IBM-XT computer, except it has slightly less memory capacity. These cards are used for a variety of applications and have been the main platform for cards that hold a secure digital identity. Examples include: cards that hold money or monetary equivalents, cards that provide secure access to a network, and cards that secure cellular phones from fraud.[4]
- Integrated Circuit (IC) Memory Cards, or IC memory cards, can hold up to 1-4 Kb of data, but have no processor on the card with which to manipulate it. Thus, they are dependent on the card reader (also known as the card-accepting device) for their processing and are suitable for uses where the card performs a fixed operation. Memory cards represent the bulk of the cards sold in 1996, and were primarily used for pre-paid, disposable-card applications like pre-paid phone cards. Memory cards are popular as high-security alternatives to magnetic stripe cards.[5]
- Optical Memory Cards look like a card with a piece of a CD glued on top, which is basically what they are. Optical memory cards can store up to 4 megabytes of data, but once written, the data cannot be changed or removed. Thus, this type of card is ideal for record keeping. Examples include: medical files, driving records, or travel information. Today, these cards have no processor in them. While the cards are comparable in price to chip cards, the readers use non-standard protocols and are expensive.[6]

Smart cards can be classified also as "contact" cards or "contactless" cards. The contact smart card requires that the smart card be used in conjunction with a card reader. Once in the reader, the contact with the electrical connectors transfers data to and from the chip. The contactless smart card includes an antenna coil inside which allows it to communicate with a remote receiver / transmitter. Contactless smart cards are used when transactions must be processed quickly, as in mass-transit toll collection. These cards can be sub-divided into two groups; proximity cards and short-distance radio frequency cards. Proximity cards can be read from up to distances of 1 foot and are used for applications like building security, transportation payment, and in a newer credit-card tied application developed for gasoline payment. The radio-frequency cards are also used in transportation applications like toll-road payment systems, which are also tied to credit card payment systems. There is also a "combicard" which functions both as a contact and contactless card.

4 When Will Intelligent Smart Cards be in Wide Use?

The important thing about smart cards is that they are everyday objects that people can carry in their pockets, yet they have the capacity to retain and protect critical information stored in electronic form.

Modern society needs an enormous amount of information to function. Computers give us the means to process this information. Smart cards give us a way of individualizing the handling and control of this information.

Internationally accepted smart cards, such as those being developed by Visa and its member financial institutions, will be increasingly available over the next several years. In fact, many parts of the world already use them. Eventually smart cards have the potential to influence the way that we shop, see the doctor, use the telephone, and enjoy leisure activities. The use of smart cards technology will benefit the individual and increase the quality of life.

Some of the areas where smart card applications are being used today include:

- **Education**: Smart cards are being used on university campuses to link students with their schools by personalizing the student's administrative data and managing all student services on campus like grades, fees, library, sports, healthcare.
- **Transit**: Create secure and easy-to-use ticketing and payment methods for public transportation (trains, buses, taxis, ferries), plane tickets, parking meters, and toll roads.
- **Access Control**: Control and limit access to restricted areas: buildings, offices, doorways, computers, networks, software applications, and confidential data files.
- **Community Services**: Improve the interaction between individuals and their community services: library cards, tickets, local taxes, water usage fees, driving licenses.
- **Electronic Payment**: Offer an ideal solution for a myriad of applications: electronic purses, public telephone phone cards, payment coupons, customer clubs, electronic shopping, vending machines, and Pay-TV.

Most of these types of applications require a stored value type smart card. These cards are used for a variety of transactions and can be purchased with a pre-set value, which is then debited at each transaction. This is the case with the education and transit type cards. Many large banks are exploring the use of smart card technology for electronic payments. These cards are capable of being loaded with cash values from ATM machines or even home computers. Banks are now escalating their trials of digital cash and smart-money cards, so soon consumers will be able to use them in many businesses such as restaurants and hotels. [7]

Before wide-scale public usage of smart cards is possible, the public and private sectors must reach a consensus on creating a technological standard that can be adopted for use by consumers and merchants everywhere. Even though there are hundreds of smart card pilots in existence around the world, users may not take a card from one country or scheme and use it in another. In order to accelerate the widespread acceptance of multiple-application smart card technology, interoperability, compatibility between cards and card-reading devices, and applications must be achieved. To do this, the industry must examine the business and technical issues surrounding the need for standardized interfaces between cards, terminals, and slots, which is the key to securing dramatic growth for the industry. [8]

Second, industry and government players face the challenge of charting a technology migration path that will allow smart card technology to co-exist with established technology investments, such as the original "smart card", the magnetic stripe card.

Today there are about 1 billion credit cards in circulation, with the primary technology employed being magnetic stripe. A hybrid card may be developed to contain both an embedded microprocessor chip along with a mag stripe. This card would be able to access different hardware systems such as merchant card readers, ATM machines and bar code applications. Major uses will include providing enhances financial services, healthcare applications, and access control / security applications.

In addition, smart cards are expected to be used in 95 percent of the digital wireless phone services offered worldwide. Asia, Latin America and North America are areas believed to be of greatest potential during the next three years.

5 Smart Cards Adoption: The United States vs. Europe and Asia

Compared with European and Asian countries, adoption and use of smart cards within the United States has been rather slow. Recently there have been a number of pilot projects with one of the biggest occurring in Atlanta during the 1996 summer Olympic games. On the other hand, as shown in Table 3, smart cards in some European and Asian countries are more prevalent. The question for the future of smart cards in the USA is how to overcome various structural problems to make multi-application smart cards, with all of their advantages a commonplace.

One industry in the U.S. that has a lot to gain by the use of smart cards is the banking industry. To digress a little, let's look at the finance side of banking. Since

1966, its asset base has grown from $400 billion to $2 trillion - a five-fold increase. Yet, total deposits have dropped from 38% to 24%. In addition, computerized systems expenses for the U.S. banking industry have grown from less than $1 billion in 1966 to over $20 billion in 1996. Banks have high fixed overhead to support, yet have substantially fewer dollars to work with. [9] This is leading the banking industry to use home banking and new electronic payment mechanisms, which are significantly cheaper, and which may involve smart cards.

In Europe, the banking industry is dominated by very large institutions that can adopt new programs easily by foreclosing consumer choices. This has made it relatively easy to form large consortia of banks, merchants, telecommunications companies and governments to launch new technologies such as smart card programs. [10] The United States, on the other hand was built on Adam Smith's laissez-faire principles, and people were raised to think and act in their own interests. The results on the macro side include fragmented banking, merchandising and telecommunications systems, not to mention competing credit card programs. Industry observers point out that Americans like to think they control their own checking accounts. Europeans on the other hand are used to having their utility bills, for instance, paid directly out of their accounts to the billing authority.[11] Since many smart card programs work as debit cards, it may take some selling to convince Americans that smart cards are a smart move for them. Another reason is the size of the countries involved, and the centralized control of health services, driver's licenses, and insurance which are natural areas for smart cards. Therefore, it may take five to seven years before smart card technology in the US will catch up with that of Europe and Asia.

Table 3 Smart cards usage worldwide: A sample.

Program (location)	The players	No. of cards / Status	Date begun / Description
Mondex (worldwide)	Shares in Mondex International held by MasterCard (51%) and major banks on five continents	50,000 in various pilots around the world	1992: anonymous cash scheme which allows peer-to-peer transfers and handles up to six currencies; was launched by NatWest, two-tier ownership, with international and country licenses established in 1996.
Danmont (Denmark)	Danmont, major banks, Danish phone company	1,000,000 in continuous operation	1993: the first broad-scale electronic purse system uses disposable cards, but a reloadable function is planned.

Table 3. continued

Proton, Cash, ChipKnip (worldwide)	Belgian, Canadian, Swiss, Dutch, and other banks, plus American Express	2,000,000 in 1996; 12,000,000 in 1997	1994: system designed this year by Belgium banks and has since been licensed to banks in Switzerland, Holland, Brazil, Australia, Sweden, and Canada for their programs, but under different names in each country; American Express licensed for worldwide use.
Visa Cash (worldwide)	Visa member banks	2,000,000 in several parts of the world	1996: pilot at Atlanta Olympic Games, programs are being initiated in over a dozen nations using disposable and reloadable cards.
Clip (pan-European)	Europay member banks	50,000 in pilot	1996: pilots for Clip, Europay's electronic purse scheme, began in Austria, Iceland, and the Czech Republic, with other existing national programs announcing intent to incorporate Clip.
New York City pilot	Chase Manhattan and Citibank	50,000 pilot launch in late 1997	1997: program will be the first to accept both Visa Cash (Citibank) and Mondex (Chase Manhattan) stored-value schemes at same terminals
Group Carte Bancaire (France)	Major French banks	24,000,000 ongoing	1992: since this year, every bank-card in France has contained a chip for cardholder ID and transaction authorization.
Taiwan Financial Services Card	14 Taiwanese banks and Financial Information service center	700,000 in 1995	1993: system uses smart cards and point-of-sale terminals to deliver financial services to banking customers nationwide.
Zolotaya Korana (Russia)	Over 100 Russian banks	150,000 at roll-out; 400,000 now	1994-95: debit / credit smart cards for use with automatic teller machines (ATMs) and terminals, support varied banking applications, including electronic purse.
U.S. Treasury Electronic Certification Program	U.S. Treasury	5000 ongoing	Early 90s: smart card identifies disbursing officers at Federal agencies that send payment information to Treasury Financial Centers that execute transactions.

Source: Ben Miller, Card Tech / Secur Tech Inc.

6 Smart Card Application Examples

6.1 Making Payphones Convenient

France Telecom implemented the prepaid smart phone card in the early 1980's in response to the lack of security and high cost of the public phone system. The smart card is purchased in various denominations. When inserted in the telephone, the cost of the phone call is displayed and deducted from the total balance remaining on the smart card. Table 4 compares what happened when using payphones before and after use of smart cards.

Table 4. Smart cards in payphones

Before the smart card	With the smart card
Hassle of having exact change	No need to carry coins
Public phone vandalism	Reduces theft and phone maintenance
High maintenance cost	Faster transaction

The same benefits can be found in many other applications where coin-operated machines have suffered from the increased costs and loss of service from vandalism, coin collection, and low reliability. Examples include: toll booths, parking lots, arcade games, and laundry-mats.[12] Phone cards are also used as an advertising tool and as a collector's item, just like stamps.

6.2 Replacing Cash

In Singapore, the CashCard is a smart card which acts as an electronic purse; one that holds electronic money. In fact, it is replacing coins and bank notes for everyday purchases such as movies, parking, museums, gas, telephones, vending machines, retail outlets, and fast food restaurants. The CashCard is available in several different initial values of $20, $50, and $100 and can be reloaded.

People will use "electronic money" for several reasons like:
- Convenience - there is not more fumbling for that last coin in your pocket. People can just check the total amount on the register and insert their smart card for payment.
- Reduction in the Cost of Cash Handling - there will be no counting and balancing of cash receipts. Sales terminals can automatically count the daily receipts and wire deposits direct to the bank.
- Fraud Protection - electronic money is an effective weapon against payment fraud and against counterfeit money. [13]

6.3 Streamlining Healthcare Services

Smart cards are increasing the quality of service in healthcare and reducing its cost by improving the efficiency of handling medical and administrative information. They are useful in a wide range of situations on the medical field. Advantages are outlined in Table 5.

Table 5. Advantages of using smart cards in healthcare

Medical cards	Advantages
Health insurance card	• Reduces routine paperwork • Eliminates error and fraud • Speeds up payment and claim processes • Inexpensive equipment setup
Medical file access card	• Patient controls doctors' access to information • Patient's medical history readily available using a single process • Pharmacist has access to prescription information only • Allows automatic check for medication incompatibility.

In the United States, Oklahoma City has a smart card system called MediCard, available since 1994. Designed by healthcare professionals, this smart card is able to selectively control access to a patient's medical history that is recorded on his/her MediCard. However, essential information, including family physician and close relative contact, is available to emergency personnel in extreme circumstances.

Smart card readers are installed at hospitals, pharmacies, ambulance services, physician's offices, and even with the fire department, allowing the MediCard to be used in both ordinary and emergency circumstances. [14]

6.4 Smart Commerce, Japan

A consortium of Visa International and other companies sponsored by the Japanese government, introduced the world's most sophisticated integrated circuit (chip) card and electronic commerce programs in October 1997. Nearly 30,000 Visa cardholders in Kobe have received some of the world's most advanced chip cards which harness new technologies expected to revolutionize the way consumers use payment cards. Through the power of the chip, these multi-application cards enable consumers to access more information from more locations and become their key to a wide range of financial and non-financial services.

The launch of Smart Commerce Japan marked the successful completion of key milestones and a series of "firsts" in the development of emerging chip card and electronic commerce technologies. These "firsts" include:

- The first public implementation of the most secure technology available - public key cryptography - in a stored-value program. (Visa Cash is a fast, easy, and convenient method to pay for everyday purchases using monetary value stored in the card's chip).
- The first time credit and stored-value have been integrated and controlled by a single chip on a multi-application bankcard.
- The first use of chip cards for making purchases over the Internet through the SET Secure Electronic Transaction[TM] protocol.
- The first program of its kind in Asia, and one of the firsts in the world using stored-value cards for Internet purchases.
- The world's largest launch of Visa chip-based credit cards.

Smart Commerce Japan is a large-scale project established by Japan's Ministry of International Trade and Industry to develop new payment services based on the most advanced technology available. Participating cardholders have the opportunity to use a chip-based multi-application bankcard that combines Visa credit and "reloadable" Visa Cash stored-value functions. This is the first time in the world that credit and stored-value applications have been integrated into a single chip. It gives cardholders the first practical experience of the multi-function capability of chip cards. The added memory and processing capabilities of the chip card will enable financial institutions to offer more services to their cardholders, with increased convenience, flexibility, and security.

Smart Commerce Japan enables consumers to shop with their Visa chip cards in both the physical world at a wide variety of merchant locations and on the Internet through personal computers and special public kiosks offering Internet access. Cardholders, at their option, may choose to use either the credit function or the Visa Cash stored-value function on their Visa chip cards.

All transactions are processed through Visa systems, which have been developed in conjunction with technology partners Oasis Technology Ltd. and Integrated Financial Services Inc. [15]

7 Access Controls and Security Mechansims

There are different types of security mechanisms used in smart cards. Those necessary for a memory-only card are less sophisticated than those for a microprocessor card. Access to the information contained in a smart card is controlled two ways:

- Who can access the information (everybody, the card holder, or a specific third party)
- How can the information be accessed (read only, added to, modified, or erased)
WHO can access the information:

- Everybody - some smart cards require no password. Anyone holding the card can have access. For example, the patient's name and blood type on a MediCard can be read without the use of a password.
- Card Holder Only - the most common form of password for card holders in a PIN (Personal Identification Number), or a 4 or 5 digit number that is typed in on a key pad. Therefore, if an unauthorized individual tries to use the card, it will lockup after 3 unsuccessful attempts to present the PIN code. More advanced types of passwords are being developed.
- Third Party Only - some smart cards can only be accessed by the party who issued the card. For example, an electronic purse can only be reloaded by the issuing bank.

HOW the information can be accessed

Information on a smart card can be divided into several sections:

- Information which is read only
- Information which is added and/or deleted only
- Information which is updated only
- Information with no access available (i.e. computer application access only)

The smart card and applications using it must determine what and how to divide the information among these categories of access.

7.1 When Passwords are not enough

A smart card can restrict the use of information to an authorized person with a password. However, if this information is then transmitted by radio or telephone, additional protection is necessary.

One form of protection is ciphering, which is like translating the information into some unknown foreign language. Some smart cards are capable of ciphering and deciphering (translating back to an easily understood form) so the stored information can be transmitted without compromising confidentiality.

Smart cards can cipher into many foreign languages, and choose a different language randomly every time they communicate. This authentication process ensures only genuine cards and computers are used and makes electronic eavesdropping difficult. [16]

8 Smart Cards and the Internet

According to a report by International Data Corporation (Framingham, Mass.), the growth in the number of online buyers and the amount of the average transaction will drive e-commerce up almost a hundredfold from $2.6 billion in 1996 to more than $220 billion in 2001. This report also predicts that by 2001 over 300 million Web access devices will be in use. Today, Internet payments can be made by electronic checks, electronic credit cards, electronic cash or electronic debit cards. All of which have advantages and limitations. Some of these limitations can be removed by using smart cards.

Therefore, several companies are developing smart cards that can be used for shopping over the Internet. These cards slip into a smart-card reader that is a stand-alone unit, or installed in the PC and have been dubbed "Plug and Pay." In the UK for example, Visa is testing its "electronic purse" card for Internet purchases. And in France, the Banque Nationale de Paris, Gemplus, and various other organizations are working together to develop a secured way to purchase goods and services over the Internet by using smart cards. In the United States, Verifone demonstrated in mid 1997 its Personal ATM system, which is designed to support downloading of virtual cash from your bank account into a smart card that you slip into a card reader. [17]

Smart card readers are inexpensive, low-power devices that can be easily added to existing computers. The additional cost of building them into future computers or peripherals is extremely low. Many computer manufacturers are planning to include these devices as standard equipment in the near future.

The recently debuted WebTV includes a smart card reader in its hardware. WebTV is an Internet service provider that aims to capture a large part of what its management hopes will be the mass-market future of the Internet, including bank-originated electronic commerce.

As smart card technology and applications develop and mature, Internet users will see more sophisticated methods of connecting smart cards to Internet applications. In May 1996, five major companies in the computing industry (IBM, Apple, Oracle, Netscape, and Sun) have proposed a standard for a new form of computer called the Network Computer. The Network Computers are designed to interface directly with the Internet and have the ability to use smart cards. Also in 1996, the Alliance between Hewlett Packard, Informix, and Gemplus was launched to develop and promote the use of smart cards for payment and security on all open networks.

In future smart-card applications, in addition to using smart cards for payment over the Internet, the possibilities will seem endless. You will be able to easily carry your favorite addresses from one computer to another or very easily download your airline ticket and boarding pass and take it to the airport with you electronically. This development would add new meaning to the airlines' E-Ticket terminology.

9 Smart Cards Application Benefits

Those who advocate the use of smart cards contend substantial advantages like cheaper administration, better fraud protection, support of multiple financial services through the electronic channel, better prospects of data mining and, in their stored-value incarnation, an interest-free loan to the bank from the cardholder. These all represent good enough reasons for card issuers to adopt smart cards.[18] Such benefits can be observed in the following applications:

9.1 Cash Cards

The technological limitations of the magnetic-stripe card are recognized by many, including the large credit card issuers such as VISA and MasterCard. These cards have limited storage capacity and are passive devices without built-in logic for security control. With the power and capacity of integrated circuit chips growing rapidly, coupled with falling costs, the intelligent smart card is increasingly being acknowledged as the most likely alternative for the magnetic stripe.

While credit cards are commonplace in developed countries, especially the United States, they remain uncommon in other countries, particularly those with undeveloped credit markets and developing economies. But, even with credit cards, cash transactions have consistently accounted for more than half of total global personal expenditures. In 1993 alone, cash transactions accounted for $8.1 trillion of $14 trillion in global personal spending. [19] The new system of digitized commerce can be seen as market expansion for credit card companies. People who use only cash by choice, or cannot qualify for a credit card because they have yet to build a credit history, are ideal candidates for smart cards.

9.2 Transaction Savings

Smart cards enable customers to make payments without requiring communication between the merchants and a centralized credit card information network or ATM clearing system. They also avoid the high costs of physical check clearing and, unlike checks, entail no credit risk. As such, smart cards offer the convenience of cash without collection risks.

Another advantage is that like checks but unlike cash, smart cards could pay interest on account balances. Since the chip within the card costlessly keeps track of the timing and amounts of transfers, smart card banks could share several financial benefits with cardholders. These would include the cost savings from avoiding cleared-check processing and interest earned on the money while "stored" on the card.

9.3 Security Applications

Smart cards have advantages over software implementations for security by providing tamper-proof devices that users can carry with them to protect corporate data and communications. On a corporate level, it looks to be somewhat simpler to add smart cards to a security system than with consumer-banking-type applications. Smart cards are the attractive option for remote corporate users because private cryptographic keys, certificates, profiles, and other user data are held apart from the enabling device, and if a computer is lost or stolen, encrypted files and data will be protected.

9.4 Fraud Protection

The best way to appeal to the user's mind, say experts, is to appeal to his (her) common-sense self-interest, and stress smart cards' strong fraud protection. Since preventing fraud is in everyone's best interest, offering it should prove a strong selling proposition.

With credit card fraud topping over $1 billion annually in the United States alone, the need for enhanced authentication mechanisms are the main catalyst of the search for alternative solutions. In France, for example the Cartes Bancaires program reduced credit card fraud from about .27 percent when it was introduced in 1987, to nearly zero in 1996. Another study showed that in France, the use of smart cards with a personal identity number, cut the costs of fraud from around $4 - $5 per card per card in 1992 to almost nothing in 1996. [20]

9.5 Cash Error Handling

Similar in nature to fraud is cash pilferage from industries like restaurants, hotels, parking lots, and tolls. Traditional cash-management practices attempt to reduce pilferage, shortages, and overages, which inevitably occur with currency in cash handling with the help of a physical and perpetual inventory of cash. With smart cards, and their digital cash transactions, these problems should be eliminated along with the time-consuming accounting, auditing, and adjustment activities. [21]

The ability to store and in some cases to process data in a small wallet sized card is the primary strength of smart card technology. This strength translates into reduced loads over telecommunication networks, since there is no need for authentication and authorization from remote banks or certifying institutions. Also, there is a more efficient service delivery due to automated data access. The automation of previously manual processes through the use of smart cards results in an overall reduced cost of service delivery. Because of their relatively large data capacity, more elaborate security measures can be incorporated into smart cards. Digitized pictures or thumbprints would prevent theft and reuse. Proprietary encryption schemes can also be employed to prevent forgery.

10 Implementation Issues

In the on-going use of smart cards in future applications there are a number of issues which need to be addressed. Some of these include:

10.1 Encryption

The U.S. Congress once again faces a crucial though somewhat esoteric issue - U.S. encryption policy. Three bills have recently been introduced that would liberalize current export restrictions and derail some of the Clinton administration's attempts to guarantee access to encrypted communications. The results of the debate will have profound implications on electronic commerce. At the heart of the issues is how the law should be updated to account for changes in technology and the global political environment. Electronic commerce and the security of electronic messages rely on the encryption. Traditionally encryption was used by spies and governments during the Cold War to keep secrets. With this in mind, encryption hardware and software, certain technical data and discussions of the higher math that form the basis of cryptography, have been treated by the U.S. as munitions. Nowadays however, much stronger forms of encryption than those used during the World War II are used to protect a $5 smart card you can use to buy a Slurpee at the local 7-Eleven. Nonetheless, the law has not changed to match the evolving role of the technology, or the environment in which that technology is used. A manufacturer of security software offered a reward to the first person who would crack the strongest level of encryption that would be readily allowed for export under the administration's liberalized policy - it took a college student only 3 1/2 hours to collect. The currently exportable standard of encryption does not provide adequate protection for particularly sensitive data. [22]

10.2 General Security

In a report released in February 1997, the Computer Security Institute (CSI) and the FBI revealed that 47% of the 563 U.S. organizations surveyed had been attacked through the Internet, up from 37% reported in a 1996 CSI-FBI survey. The survey also contradicts the conventional wisdom that the vast majority of attacks come from within the organizations. While 43% of respondents reported attacks from within, 47% said they experienced external attacks. Smart cards are tools that, if used properly, can provide a high level of security. Hewlett-Packard broadens its security offerings in May 1997, with two smart-card solutions that include the cards, readers to scan the information stored on the processor embedded in the cards, and a management system. Also included is a developer's toolkit to let third-party vendors build hooks into applications that can then use the smart-card authentication capability.

10.3 Infrastructure and Standards

Lack of established smart card standards are a primary weakness of the technology. Until technology standards are developed it will be difficult and ill advised to implement large-scale smart card applications. The lack of a nationwide infrastructure to support smart card based transactions limits the wide spread use of stored value smart cards,[23] but widespread usage is only waiting for the availability of card readers integrated with computers. The cost of readers is relatively small, although the installation and support could be high[24].

Furthermore, the PC/SC Workgroup, a consortium of PC and smart-card vendors led by Microsoft, is ironing out the standards for interfacing smart cards and card readers with PCs. The specifications will insure interoperability among smart cards and readers and provide high-level APIs for application developers. HP is developing a keyboard with a built-in reader device, and Verifone is introducing low-cost readers attached to PCs. Currently plug-in devices that read smart cards are available for disk drives and PC card slots

10.4 Securing Privacy

One of the unknown elements in smart card technology is how much data mining will be built into smart card applications. Most people are very protective about privacy and issues relating to their rights to privacy. In fact, this quote was recently made: "Since privacy is such an evident value in our society, where technology threatens the value, entrepreneurs can be counted on to seek means to defend it," (Chairman of the USA Federal Reserve System's Board of Governors, Alan Greenspan). If we wish to foster innovation, we must be careful not to impose rules that inhibit it. To develop new forms of payment, the private sector will need the flexibility to experiment without broad interference by the government.

Alan Westin, a Columbia University researcher of privacy issues, cited a 1996 Louis Harris & Associates survey that found 83% of consumers believe they have lost control of how information about them is gathered and used. That figure was up from 80 percent only a year earlier. If smart cards are going to become ubiquitous in our society, consumers are going to demand that the issues of privacy be addressed right up front.

10.5 Legal Issues

As scores of banks and businesses charge onto the Internet, cyber-commerce and electronic cash (dubbed e-cash) transactions are creating a swamp of untested legal issues. One urgent issue: Is e-cash really cash and legally recognized currency? After months of study and debate, lawyers from Silicon Valley to Capitol Hill seem to be saying that e-cash is not a legal tender, like paper money and coins.[25] That conclusion will have vast implications for future consumer protection and banking regulations. E-cash is not real cash but an obligation that an issuer has created to pay a monetary amount at some future date. Unlike cash, which by law a merchant is obligated to accept, a merchant can refuse a payment from a stored-value card. Transactions conducted with real money are overseen by a range of state and federal laws and government agencies. Bank deposits, for example, are federally insured up to $100,000. What about insuring e-cash contacted on a stored-value smart card?

Other related legal issues include: who is liable if a smart card is lost or stolen? What kind of contract is best for all parties, including banks, merchants, and consumers? Will e-cash be affected by state civil and criminal laws on the Internet? Should e-cash be regulated by federal laws and policies? Or should the federal government let the cybermarket police itself?[26]

11 The Next Steps

11.1 Smart Card Incentives

Since cash has been a perfectly good medium of exchange for thousand of years, many smart card experts are aware that the adoption process for smart cards may not be so easy. So, in order to "jump start" this process, there is talk of offering incentive programs to induce consumers to change to the new technology. The vendors realize that convenience is not enough. The 1996 Olympic Games in Atlanta was a test-bed for smart cards. The depleted cards were saved as collectibles, so more people were motivated to use smart cards.

Wells Fargo is developing and testing a number of financial and technology incentive programs for paying for fast food. To find out how much incentive it will take to wean consumers off cash about 900 Wells Fargo employees are using the cards with 22 selected merchants near their downtown San Francisco headquarters.[27]

11.2 Banking and Stock Trading

Web users who bank, shop, and trade stocks on-line via the Internet are able to use cryptography-enabled smart cards as of 1998 for authentication, to access restricted areas, and to sign documents. Several pilot tests of cryptographic smart cards are under way in the corporate environment, and applications for intranets and business-to-business networks are expected to begin rolling out soon[28]. The advantages to stock traders in using smart cards relates to security. If you have the card and know what that encrypted password on the card is, a more secured environment can be created.

11.3 Digital Signatures

Smart cards are more secure, more portable, and more useful than software-based digital certificates. Public key certificates also called digital certificates, digital IDs, and certificates of authentication, are crucial for electronic commerce. Most Web experts expect the certificates to become as ubiquitous as driver's licenses. But as software, digital certificates are vulnerable to viruses and to tampering with the hard drive. They cannot be easily transferred among computers that many workers need to use at the office, at home, and on the road. A cryptographic smart card, can be taken anywhere where there is a card reader. In 1997, the reader's price was $100 - 300, therefore the price needs to come down a bit for wide-range acceptance and use.

Digital signatures can be used in other areas of electronic commerce, especially in business-to-business trading where you want to ensure that the person placing electronic orders is the person authorized to perform that function. In today's markets where competing on time is critical, an additional piece of security can expedite trades and facilitate electronic commerce tremendously.

11.4 Multi-application Cards

Although most current smart cards can only handle basic cryptographic processing, which is primarily used to verify digital signatures, future versions will be able to hold and process multiple applications. Sun Microsystems Inc. introduced in 1996 the Java Card APIs, and Gemplus and Schlumberger have licensed the APIs for use in developing an interoperable smart-card Operating System. The Java APIs are expected to allow multiple applications to be loaded and upgraded in a single card. Schlumberger introduced a Java-based smart card in May 1997 called CyberFlex, which includes support for Secure Electronic Transaction.

Spyrus, a San Jose-based smart-card developer, developed a smart card, in June 1997, that supports multiple encryption algorithms and key management capabilities for verifying digital certificates. With the introduction of Web Wallet certificates in mid 1997, Spyrus smart cards are able to process security, financial, and other applications on one card.[29]

However, early adopters should beware. Until smart-card solutions are widely available, it may be difficult to piece together best-of-breed and standards-based cards, applications, and software infrastructure. It's like the chicken and the egg, the standards won't be established until enough people start to deploy the technology. But, multi-application capability is seen as necessary for the widespread adoption of smart card technology. Otherwise we will be walking around with 15 cards.[30] A typical smart card should be able to handle cash, access to financial services, mass transit, medical information, and also provide credit card capabilities.

11.5 Infomediaries

Consumers are realizing that they get very little in exchange for the information they divulge so freely through their commercial transactions and survey responses. Now technologies such as smart cards, Web browsers, and personal financial management software are allowing consumers to view comprehensive profiles of their commercial activities, and then choose whether or not to release that information to companies. Smart cards could easily be enhanced to capture and store the names of vendors and transaction amounts. The smart card user then could routinely download this information into a PC to produce an integrated profile of his or her purchases. What would the value of this information be? Advertisers might be willing to pay handsomely for it. Such easily collected profiles would provide explicit measures of how advertising drives purchasing activities. People can chose whether or not they want to participate in programs like these. If they do not wish to reveal information, the technology makes denial possible.

These infomediaries would in fact play a very traditional role. When ownership of information shifts to the consumer, a new form of supply is created. By connecting information supply with information demand and by helping both parties involved to determine the value of that information, infomediaries would be building a new kind of information supply chain.

12 Summary and Conclusion

In looking at the information available on smart cards, it is apparent that there are compelling reasons to use this technology to provide new solutions to some electronic payment problems. Smart cards offer a clear advantage to card issuers, merchants and customers. They reduce cash handling expenses, reduce losses due to fraud, expedite customer transactions and enhance customer safety and convenience. In addition, new services will begin to evolve, or payment mechanisms for existing services will start to change. For example, through the use of smart cards, software could be paid for on a per use basis instead of through a license fee. Journalism could be bought by the article much more easily than today. Many companies would be able to set-up an on-line business and begin to receive revenue.[31]

Managers need to take a close look at their markets and their products to determine what their best strategy are regarding electronic card systems. In the long run, you can count on mass acceptance of electronic card payment systems. However, managers need to ask themselves many questions. Does our current payment handling system offer the level of service our customers expect? Is the electronic card payment industry heading in a direction that best suite our business? If not, should we get involved in the standardization effort to ensure our interests are considered? Would it be advantages to implement our own electronic payment system before a multifunctional card is widely accepted? If we develop our own electronic payment handling system, do we adhere to the developing standard? The answer to such questions can help companies in the development of smart cards strategy.

13 Appendix I: Major Smart Card Vendors and Products

MasterCard is a major player in the Internet business. It's gross dollars have been growing at a consistent 15 - 20% annually. And there was a recent acquisition of

51% ownership of Mondex International, the smart-card-based electronic cash venture started by the National Westminster Bank of London.

In a move to hasten the acceptance of on-line transactions, AT&T said in May 1997 it plans to use the Mondex electronic cash system to let consumers buy items such as music, published articles and games on the Internet. Hewlett-Packard and OpenMarket Inc. are working with AT&T to provide hardware and software for the system.

Microsoft, Hewlett-Packard and Oracle are developing smart-card support in operating systems, keyboards, servers and network computers, and a bevy of card-based applications is emerging as well. By 1998 the infrastructure should be in place to deploy smart-card systems that allow secure access from browsers, network computers, and other devices into servers, operating systems, databases, and other network resources.[32]

HP is working with Informix and Gemplus on its ImagineCard, a single-sign-on smart-card system that will provide secure access to network resources and a mechanism for secure transactions over the Internet. The system, which includes cards, readers, databases, servers, and software, will accommodate either passwords or stronger digital-signature-based authentication procedures in combination with smart cards. In the future, the ImagineCard may incorporate biometrics, nonrepudiation, and the capability to write Java applets to the cards improve Intranet convenience and security.

New processors such as Motorola's fast crypto chip used in Visa cash cards and Certicom's elliptic-curve cryptographic engine, which is embedded in Schlumberger's Multiflex smart card, are some of the first to enable fast processing of digital signatures at a low cost. Depending on capabilities, intelligent smart cards cost anywhere from $3 to $30 in their first generation, with varying memory and processor configurations. The real issue has been that although smart cards are ideal for security, they haven't been able to get public-key cryptography done fast enough and at a low-enough cost, like in the $3 or $4 range.

Netscape and Microsoft are also developing APIs - Crypto API and Security Native API to link cryptographic functions to existing network operating system. Browsers, servers, and applications, and Windows NT 5.0 will support smart-card integration. With NT directory support, IS administrators will be able to add cryptographic, key-based authentication's to existing password-based systems for network-access functions. Microsoft will also release standard driver kits to link smart-card-enabled applications and devices to PCs. Toolkits to build such applications are currently available from smart-card developers such as Schlumberger, Certicom, and SCM Microsystems.

Fischer International Systems Corp. developed a way for banks to use personal computers to read smart cards without waiting for PC manufacturers to add special readers. The company developed the Smarty, a smart card reader in the form of a floppy disk. The device can help banks with network security and other smart card applications. The user slips a smart card into a slot on the Smarty, then slips the device into a computer's ordinary floppy disk drive. The Smarty translates the information on the card's chip into a magnetic signal that the floppy drive can read. In addition, the Smarty can write new information on the card, under the computer's direction. This device is selling for around $60. Two commercial banks are testing Fischer International's technology. Wells Fargo is using the Smarty in several pilot programs, including an Internet banking application and its test of Mondex. Finally, Bank of America is developing a smart card that combines security as well as commercial applications

Visa is working with financial institutions in 30 countries to implement more than 70 payment programs using new technologies. These innovative programs are as diverse as a secure Visa Smart Debit system in Russia and a smart card-based loyalty program in Taiwan. A sampling of the 70 payment programs being implemented worldwide includes:

- Argentina - Visa Smart Debit and Visa Cash on a single card was introduced in January 1996. Today, Visa Cash can be used to pay for meals at McDonald's fast food outlets and at other merchants, such as video rental stores, newsstands, gas stations, and convenience stores.
- Hong Kong - Consumers are using Visa Cash enthusiastically as a replacement for cash. It's accepted in a wide variety of merchant locations, and it's one of the fastest growing Visa Cash programs.
- New York - Consumers are using Visa Cash on the Upper West Side. This is the first interoperability test in the U.S.
- Russia - Consumers are using a version of the Visa Smart Debit and Visa Smart Credit card, adapted for parts of the world where telecommunications may be limited, yet a secure method of transaction authorization is required.
- Spain - Consumers in Spain are using Visa Cash, and it's so popular that it's used and accepted throughout the country in telephones and mass transit.
- United Kingdom - Consumers are using Visa Smart Debit and Visa Smart Credit in the same way that they used their magnetic stripe cards. They are also using Visa Cash as a replacement for cash.[33]

References

1. "SCIA FAQ", www.scia.com
2. Ibid.
3. "What is a Smart Card?", www.smartcrd.com
4. "Smart Card Overview", www.sun.com
5. Ibid.
6. Ibid.
7. Sheel, Atul: Levever, Michael. "The Implications of Digital Cash for Hotels and Restaurants". *Cornell Hotel Restaurant Administration Quarterly*, December 1996, pg. 92
8. Future Banking section, "The U.S Smart Card Debate Rages On", *The American Banker*, March 17, 1997

9. Coleman, Arthur, "Java Commerce, A Business Perspective",
    http://java.sun.com/products/commerce/bizper.html

10. Future Banking section, "The U.S Smart Card Debate Rages on", *The American Banker*,
    March 17, 1997 pg. 10A

11. "The Role of Smart Cards in Today's World", www.gemplus.fr

12. Ibid.

13. Ibid.

14. "Smart Commerce, Japan", www.visa.com

15. "The Role of Smart Cards in Today's World", www.gemplus.fr

16. "Plug and Pay Up", *PC Magazine*, April 8, 1997, pg. 10

17. Future Banking section, "The U.S Smart Card Debate Rages On", *The American Banker*,
    March 17, 1997 pg. 10A

18. Sheel, Atul and Levever, Michael. "The implications of digital cash for hotels and restaurants", *Cornell Hotel and Restaurant Administration Quarterly*, December 1996, pg. 92

19. Smart Cards: A technology whose time has come", *Financial Times*, October 2, 1996,
    pg. 1.

20. Sheel, Atul and Levever, Michael. "The implications of digital cash for hotels and restaurants", *Cornell Hotel and Restaurant Administration Quarterly*, December 1996, pg. 92

21. Loundy, David, "Congress scrambles to address encryption", *Chicago Daily Law Bulletin*, March 1997, pg. 5.

22. Smart Cards, The State of Maryland Information Systems Technology Plan,
    www.mec.state.md/us/mec/mdplan/apdx-dsm.htm

23. Jones, Chris, "Special News Report; Sizing up Smart Cards", *Info World*, March 10,
    1997, pg. 1

24. Iwata, Edward, "Invisible Cash" *The San Francisco Examiner*, March 7, 1997, pg. B1.

25. Ibid.

26. Winkler, Connie, "Wells Fargo stakes out new frontiers", *Computerworld*, November 1,
    1996, pg. F14.

27. Roberts, Bill, "Internet gives smart cards whole new life", *Computing Canada*, March 3,
    1997, pg. 14.

28. Jones, Chris, "Special News Report; Sizing up Smart Cards", *Info World* March 10, 1997,
    pg. 1

29. Mead, Wendy, "Device Lets Ordinary PC Disk Drives Read Smart Cards", *The American Banker*, March 4, 1997, pg. 17.

30. Hagel, John III and Rayport, Jeffrey, "The Coming Battle for Customer Information",
    Harvard Business Review, January/February 1997, pg. 53.

31. Fox, Justin, "Cyberbunk: What's New About Digital Cash", *Fortune*, September 30,
    1996, pg. 50

32. Jones, Chris, "Special News Report; Sizing up Smart Cards", *Info World*, March 10,
    1997, pg. 1

33. www.visa.com

CHAPTER 15
Component-based Electronic Commerce

Arie Segev and Martin Bichler
Fisher Center for Management and Information Technology, Haas School of Business,
University of California at Berkeley, CA, USA, {segev, bichler}@haas.berkeley.edu

In this chapter we focus on system architectures for electronic commerce applications. The chapter surveys the impact of new software engineering concepts like object frameworks, distributed object computing and component-based programming on the development of electronic commerce applications. We outline limitations of current systems and show how these new techniques help in achieving increased interoperability and reusability of electronic commerce systems. As high-level interoperability between the systems of different participants is a critical enabler for many new applications in electronic commerce, the appendix gives an overview of upcoming approaches to document-centric electronic commerce standards.

Keywords: Component-oriented Programming; Distributed Systems; Object Frameworks; Interoperability Standards; Electronic Catalogs

"Software engineers should take a look at the hardware industry and establish a software component sub-industry. The produced software components should not be tailored to specific needs but be reusable in many software systems."
(Doug McIlroy, NATO Conference on Software Engineering, Germany, 1968)

1 Introduction

The past few years have seen several major information technologies come together to produce viable electronic commerce systems. EDI, WWW, cryptography, database servers, Java applets and distributed object standards form a bewildering mix of techniques and standards for the development of electronic commerce applications. Development of such applications is considered expensive and risky.

During the past few years, component-based software development started to strongly influence this area. Components are chunks of software with a contractually specified interface. They can be deployed independently of each other and are subject to composition by third parties. The vision is to assemble applications from reusable components of competing vendors. Component oriented programming has remarkable success in the development of desktop applications. Software components like Microsoft's Visual Basic Controls lead to an enormous progress in the productivity of and time-to-market for software developers. This trend can also be observed in enterprise software. Instead of delivering a system as a prepackaged monolith containing any conceivable feature, modern systems consist of a light-weight kernel to which new features can be added in the form of components. The procedure is very similar to other mature fields of engineering like electrical engi-neering and mechanical engineering, where prefabricated and tested building blocks, such as switches or integrated circuits are combined into new products.

This chapter investigates this new trend and shows how it is related to the devel-opment of electronic commerce applications. It should serve as a guideline for tech-nically oriented readers, as well as an overview for non-technical readers. After a brief discussion of the barriers for Internet commerce in section 2, we focus on two major concepts: object frameworks and Componentware. In section 3 we deal with the development and deployment of electronic commerce object frameworks and present a case study of the McKesson's InfoLink information system to illustrate the ideas. Section 4 investigates the trend towards black-box software components and section 5 concludes with some examples of business component frameworks from industry leaders like Oracle, SAP and Sun. The Appendix provides an overview of important interoperability standards for electronic commerce applications and how they interrelate with component standards.

2 Barriers to Internet Commerce

Currently, electronic commerce is mainly supported by EDI and Web-based elec-tronic catalogs. EDI has been in use for over 20 years, mostly running on proprietary networks between large companies (Sokol, 1995). A newer emerging technology, made possible by the Internet and WWW, is the electronic catalog. There is no stan-dard definition for the electronic catalog and the functionality is rapidly evolving, but at a minimum it should support listings of products and/or services, price infor-mation and transactions. Electronic catalogs are especially adept at using database and WWW technology to provide sophisticated search and retrieval functionality (Segev et al., 1995).

One of the most obvious problems of Web-based electronic catalogs is the lack of interoperability. Interoperability at the level of a common business language is a critical enabler for widespread electronic commerce. EDI standards like ANSI X.12 or UN/EDIFACT are only targeted at longstanding relationships between businesses and do not address the characteristics of Internet commerce. Web-based electronic catalogs format their CGI requests and HTML outputs in vastly different and often changing ways, each of which must be processed differently. Virtual catalogs (Keller, 1995) that aggregate information of underlying electronic catalogs are hard to implement. They have to keep track of all the various queries and parse the re-sulting HTML files. Moreover, these formats are likely to change quite often. The same problem is true for electronic negotiations and electronic contracting. There are simply no widely accepted high-level interoperability standards for ad-hoc trad-ing on the Internet. Some newer electronic procurement systems use proprietary protocols in order to support a wider range of tasks from search to payment. However, this approach only works, if both the supplier and the customer use the software of the same vendor. Currently, there are several approaches to standardize high-level protocols for Internet commerce; however, none of them has gained critical mass adoption so far (see the Appendix for an overview).

Another barrier for wide-spread adoption of Internet commerce are the high implementation costs for electronic commerce systems. A large proportion of today's electronic commerce applications is custom developed. Custom development is risky and expensive. There is little or no reuse even for very generic functionality like order entry modules or payment servers as many software modules are developed to run with a certain Web server or database server and cannot simply be "plugged" into another environment. Meanwhile, there is at least a market for packaged electronic catalog software. Nearly every big software vendor developed solutions to facilitate search in a product database, order entry and payment via credit card. Compared to custom development, packaged software is cheap. But these products have proprietary APIs and it can be quite challenging to extend their functionality by new modules or customize them in order to work with legacy systems. New techniques can force the user to upgrade the whole system. Reusable electronic commerce components could lead to lower deployment costs and a shorter time to market. This would make electronic commerce affordable for a much broader range of companies like small and medium sized enterprises.

In summary, the lack of reusability in current electronic commerce applications and the lack of interoperability standards are some of the greatest obstacles to widespread electronic commerce today. In the next sections we investigate new software engineering concepts that are designed to overcome these problems.

3 Object Frameworks for Electronic Commerce Applications

Distributed object technology provides standards for easy interoperability of software components in heterogeneous environments. Moreover, object technology provides several concepts for the reuse of software. This section covers an overview of distributed object frameworks and their use for electronic commerce applications. It concludes with a case study of McKessons InfoLink system. InfoLink is a sales information system using Web and distributed object technology. It is a good example of how distributed objects are used in commercial applications and illustrates the architecture of modern business applications.

3.1 Object Frameworks

Newer software engineering technologies are based on the principle of making the expression of ideas simpler and more compact. Especially the renewed popularity of object-oriented programming concepts like encapsulation, information hiding and polymorphism in the early 80s raised the level of abstraction in problem formulation. But merely programming with objects did not ensure software reuse. With the use of class libraries, reuse began to take serious shape. Domain specific libraries provided related classes, which one could use as is or could specialize via inheritance to solve a problem. Object frameworks are one step ahead as they also reuse designs for specific problems. An *object framework* is a collection of cooperating objects that provide an integrated solution (customizable by the developer) within an application or technology. The components of an object framework are not intended to work alone. The distinguishing feature from a class library is that when the library is an object framework the flow of control is bi-directional between the application and the library. This feature is achieved by the dynamic binding in object-oriented languages where an operation can be defined in a library class but implemented in a subclass in the application. Because of the bi-directional flow of control the object framework enables significantly more functionality than a traditional library, and also provides large-scale reuse.

A fundamental principle of object-oriented programming is that, due to the features of inheritance and dynamic binding, a new class can be implemented by specifying only the difference relative to an existing class. With object frameworks the same principle is applied to whole applications or sub-systems, allowing the highest common abstraction level among a number of similar applications to be captured in a generic design that can be instantiated for each application in the future. Each product is an instantiation of the object framework and the amount of unique code is proportional to the specific features of the product.

Of course, that is easier said than done and the established development methods offer little support for object framework design so far. In framework development, design reuse is more important than mere code reuse. Creating a new design requires knowledge of an application domain, experience with other designs and a flair for recognizing and inventing patterns. Framework design is an iterative process, which can take long time.

3.2 Distributed Object Standards

Distributed objects that operate in a concurrent and active way have been a research topic in the OO community for a long time because the metaphor of communicating objects is very well suited for distribution (Moessenboeck, 1996). Distributed systems standards like OMG's CORBA or Microsoft's DCOM strongly influence the object frameworks field (see also Lewandowski, 1998). The Common Object Request Broker Architecture (CORBA) is the Object Management Group's answer to the need for interoperability among the growing number of hardware and software products available today. CORBA allows applications to communicate with one another no matter where they are located or who has designed them. CORBA 1.1 was introduced in 1991 by Object Management Group (OMG) and defined the Interface Definition Language (IDL) and the Application Programming Interfaces (API) that enable client/server object interaction within a specific implementation of an Object Request Broker (ORB). CORBA 2.0, adopted in December of 1994, defines true interoperability by specifying how ORBs from different vendors can interoperate. (Microsoft's COM and DCOM are discussed in section 4.2.)

Object frameworks benefit from distributed object standards in several ways. First they gain high-level language bindings. CORBA separates the interface of an object from its implementation and provides language-neutral data types that make it possible to call objects across language and operating system boundaries. So it doesn't matter what language server objects are written in. Second, an ORB can broker inter-object calls within a single process or multiple processes across networks and operating system boundaries. The programmer doesn't have to be concerned with these differences, as CORBA makes it transparent. CORBA also provides introspection capabilities, as it is possible to query at runtime information describing the functionality of a server object. This allows the discovery of new services and their binding at runtime (Orfali and Harkey, 1997).

Besides the Object Request Broker (ORB) component the Object Management Architecture specifies three categories of object interfaces. These interface specifications represent functionality needed for a component economy:

- *Object Services* are interfaces for general services that are likely to be used by any program based on distributed objects. They are collections of system-level services like Persistence, Naming, Query, Transaction or Security Services.
- *Common Facilities* are interfaces for horizontal end-user-oriented facilities applicable to most application domains. They should provide semantically higher level services than the Object Services. The Common Facilities currently under construction include mobile agents, data interchange and the business object framework.
- *Domain Interfaces* are application domain-specific interfaces. Domain Task Forces focus on application domains such as Finance, Healthcare, Manufacturing, Telecom, Electronic Commerce or Transportation.

An object framework in the Object Management Architecture (OMA) is defined as a hierarchy of application, domain, common facility, and object service frameworks that are compositions of application, domain, common facility, and object service objects. So one can easily exchange the component of a vendor with the product of its competitor, as long as it adheres to the OMG interface standard. The payment, shipping or inventory components of an electronic commerce system can be taken from various vendors and compiled to an application.

3.3 Electronic Commerce Frameworks

In the past, frameworks were popular in the area of graphical user interfaces, but other domains are coming up as well. There are several vendors and research projects developing object frameworks for electronic commerce applications. OSM (Open Service Markets) (McConnel, 1997), an EU ACTS project, is developing tools to enable an open electronic trading market based on the OMG OMA. Besides there are a couple of different vendors like IBM, Microsoft, Oracle, Sun and Tandem trying to come up with various electronic commerce solutions for security, payment or catalogs.

OMG's Electronic Commerce Domain Task Force (ECDTF) tries to standardize electronic commerce facilities in the OMA. The current draft of the *ECDTF Reference Model* gives a good overview about facilities needed in electronic commerce applications. The architecture is composed into three principal groups, namely low level electronic commerce services including profile, selection, payment and certificate services; commerce facilities supporting service management, contract and related desktop facilities; and finally, market infrastructure facilities covering catalogs, brokerage and agency facility (see Figure 1).

The following is a brief description of the various parts of the architecture. The OMG is exploring technology for a *Payment Facility* that will support and allow the implementation of a variety of electronic payment protocols in a CORBA environment. The *Selection Facility* is an object service that provides support for configuration of supporting services across a set of domains. It includes the ability to issue and receive specification of requirements and the ability for multiple participants to negotiate on specification content. The *Profile Facility* provides a common structure for the semantic data describing products, services, content and assets. The *Service Facility* describes requirements for an object framework in which commercial services can be presented with declarative interface for consumers, providers and third-parties. The requirement specification includes details concerning life-cycle and policy management. *Contract Facilities* extend the service specification to include specific requirements related to commercial contracts. The *Object Browser Facility* provides the desktop facilities in a service management marketplace.

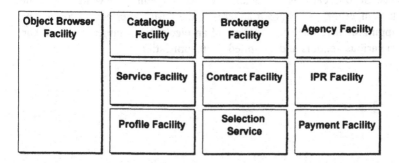

Fig. 1. OMG ECDTF reference model

Catalogue Facilities provide a framework for portable data stores in which service and contracts can be passed between participants. The *Brokerage Facility* requirement specification designates two primary interfaces, namely forwarding and recruiting. Requirements of a forwarding interface include the support for the "advertising" or "distribution" of profiles describing electronic commerce artifacts. A recruiting interface meets requirements "discovery", i.e., requests for "searches" for content matching a certain criteria. Finally the *Agency Facility* supports general requirements for the standardization of a point of presence in a marketplace.

The Reference Model helps identify the planned and future Electronic Commerce Domain Facilities of the OMG OMA. The work provides an overall framework of required electronic commerce components, but it is still in its early stages. So far there have been submissions for an Electronic Payment RFP (Request for Proposals) and for a second RFP on a Negotiation and Selection Facility. Little work has been done in higher levels like electronic catalogs, brokerage or electronic contracting so far (Bichler et al., 1998).

3.4 InfoLink: A Case Study on Web Object Technology

This section presents an example of an innovative use of distributed object technology. McKesson's InfoLink is a distributed sales information system using a mix of Web and CORBA technology. InfoLink illustrates the requirements of information systems in a networked economy and shows some problems technology leaders are facing today.

3.4.1 InfoLink Functionality

McKesson Corp. is a leading provider of health care products and services to retail pharmacies, hospitals and health care networks. Managing this vast distribution network effectively requires accurate tracking of thousands of products sold across dozens of territories. In order to make sales representatives more effective, McKesson built a sales-information network that gives its 500 remote sales representatives all over the United States "live" access to product, customer and commission data in a centralized information warehouse. The application called *InfoLink*, is deployed in a heterogeneous network environment of UNIX, S/390 and Windows NT servers and is using CORBA technology.

InfoLink provides comprehensive sales information for staff and customers. The users access the system two to three times a day and get customized information based on their user account. McKesson's sales staff can review pricing, inventory and monthly or annual totals from any location where they can get their laptops up on the Internet. Moreover, McKesson customers are able to review the current status of their business with McKesson, down to the invoice level. InfoLink delivers comprehensive historical data that includes much more current information than was previously provided. It also delivers analytical tools that enable both McKesson and its customers to analyze site or system purchasing patterns. Currently the system is merely used for information retrieval, however, in the future it should also be possible for sales representatives to input new data into the system via a forms-based interface on the Web. The fast access to customized data increased the productivity of sales personnel tremendously. They download all the needed data and can use it in spreadsheets and presentations for the customer.

3.4.2 Multi-tier Architecture

The objective in designing InfoLink was to make data universally available and up-to-date, while at the same time, to keep deployment and management of the application software central. It consists of multiple layers (see Fig. 2.). Its front-end applications and the Web server reside at the company's San Francisco headquarters. The system's back-end sits some 100 miles away, at McKesson's nationwide Drohan Data Center in Sacramento, where another server runs the database connectivity software that links the company's Web server to a very large data warehouse with about 2.5 terra byte of data. The information warehouse is updated on a regular basis and takes snapshots of various legacy systems.

Maintenance costs of the user clients and training of sales representatives were a major issue during the design phase, so the system architects decided to implement simple HTML front ends. This achievement enabled McKesson to deliver a very powerful system to the end-users with minimal training, no deployment costs, and no incremental or special hardware or software requirements. This significantly reduced the cost of ownership. However, as the application is accessed over the Internet, security was a big concern. So all communication with the InfoLink Web server is conducted over SSL and firewalls are protecting the application server as well as the back end servers.

The application layer is the heart of InfoLink and it compiles data from various sources like Lotus Notes databases and the Oracle Information Warehouse into a customized HTML page. During its development the InfoLink architects had to follow several design goals. McKesson is a rapidly expanding company, where mergers and acquisitions can occur at any time. This is the reason for a very heterogeneous and rapidly growing network infrastructure within the company. So *scalability* of the system as well as *platform independence* have been important goals. The system architects decided to implement the application layer in Java, and use a commercial CORBA ORB implementation as a distribution mechanism. The Java language ensures platform independence. CORBA provides interoperability between objects, built in (possibly) different languages, running on different machines. Moreover, CORBA ensures an order of scalability, which would not have been possible with CGI-based applications. In McKesson's object model, nearly 2000 Java objects serve roles ranging from HTML page formatting and Java code generation to transporting the data from server to server.

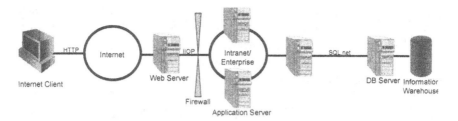

Fig. 2. InfoLink architecture

Seven developers have been involved in the InfoLink project, mostly having a general programming and systems development background. The project took five month of analysis and design and two month of actual implementation to set up the application layer of the system. During the development the team worked closely together with the sales force and made extensive use of HTML prototypes as a means of communication.

3.4.3 Evaluation

There are a couple of benefits, which make InfoLink very valuable to McKesson. First, McKesson's computing infrastructure is highly heterogeneous and includes legacy databases, groupware systems and components of enterprise software vendors. CORBA allows gluing this puzzle of systems together into a meaningful information source for the user. Second, the Web front end guarantees universal access and low maintenance costs on the client side. The major obstacle, during the development of the system was the lack of a CORBA component market. Nearly all application objects and even basic object services had to be custom developed. According to one of the system architects, development could have been much more effective, if the team could have bought components with generic functionality on the market. In general, however, InfoLinks is seen as a successful model and the architecture will also be used for future information systems of McKesson.

4 Towards Electronic Commerce Components

OMG's OMA and CORBA-based frameworks got a lot of attention during the last couple of years. IBM released the ComponentBroker, a full implementation of the CORBA Object Services. Netscape built an ORB implementation in its Web server and browser software. So applets don't need to download ORB functionality in order to access a CORBA server on the Internet. Many big software vendors licensed CORBA implementations and even the Java language (version 1.2) contains a lightweight ORB implementation, called JavaIDL. So it is likely, that CORBA will remain an important infrastructure for enterprise applications. On the other hand critics are claiming that important new technologies are missing in the OMG standards. Developers demand standards for mobile code or mobile state. Moreover, there is still no retail market in reusable CORBA components and often it is even hard to find implementations for basic Object Services.

4.1 Software Components

The difficulty with object frameworks is that they are abstract reusable "designs" which have to be dealt with by expert programmers to specialize and make them concrete (Thompson et al., 1998). Object frameworks that heavily rely on implementation inheritance are white-box frameworks that are published together with their source code. Component-based software like Microsofts ActiveX/COM or JavaSoft's JavaBeans has quickly become a popular programming paradigm of choice. This new notion of Componentware should enable rapid application assembly from off-the-shelf, pre-packaged software objects (Pfister, 1998). The developer begins with a set of unrelated components and must decide how to assemble them. This is reuse by composition, whereas object frameworks are mainly reuse by inheritance. Through scripting languages or visual builder tools like JavaSoft's BeansBox it should be much easier to glue together components into a working application.

The first noteworthy example of a black-box software component market was sparked by Microsoft's Visual Basic, a rapid-application-development tool based on a none-object-oriented programming language. Visual Basic comes with a large set of prebuilt components, so-called Visual Basic Controls (VBXs) and later OLE Custom Controls (OCXs). Packages with sets of Visual Basic controls can be bought from many third-party vendors.

4.1.1 Definitions

The software community does not yet agree on what a software component is exactly. For example, some authors (Hoque and Sharma, 1998) see a component as a group of objects, hidden behind a well defined interface. For this publication we define a *component* as a specific piece of functionality that can be accessed by other software through a contractually specified interface. They are self-contained, clearly identifiable artifacts that describe and/or perform specific functions (Sametinger, 1997). The component is a black box, where all interactions occur through the published interface. They can be deployed independently of each other and are subject to composition by third parties. This allows software building blocks from different origins that can be composed such that they work together in a meaningful way. Developers can focus on their core competence, whereas buyers can pick the best products among all vendors and integrate them in a plug-and-play manner. Component-oriented programming can be seen as the next level of abstraction after functions, modules and classes.

A *container* provides an application context for one or more components and provides management and control services for the components. Components come in various granularities like simple GUI widgets or complex services such as an account management function. Componentware promises several advantages over current approaches.

- Components enable a higher level of abstraction in programming. Application programmers can build applications without writing all the code from scratch.
- Component software combines the advantages of custom software and packaged software. It enables solutions that are better evolvable, i.e., which scale better, are more readily maintainable and can be extended incrementally over time. A component implementation can be replaced by a new version if its interface remains the same. This is an important advantage, as it allows the whole software system to evolve.
- Component-based software engineering shortens the time to market. Components can be developed in parallel if it is clearly defined in advance what each component should provide. Moreover, visual programming and scripting languages lead to increased productivity.
- A main advantage of component software is the creation of markets. A developer can buy the more generic features of an application, and concentrate on the more specific features. The consequence is a third party market of vendors specializing in certain application domains. Component software allows the buyer to pick and choose the best products among all vendors in the world, and integrate them in a plug-and-play manner.

In contrast to object frameworks, a *component framework* defines rules for independently developed and dynamically loadable components, rather than for classes that are linked together. Traditional object frameworks are linked statically, whereas component frameworks are linked dynamically upon loading. A component framework is a collection of component interfaces that embodies an abstract design for solutions to a family of related problems. In contrast to most object frameworks, component frameworks are black-box frameworks, i.e. frameworks that can be used without access to their source code.

4.1.2 Component Composition

The ideal scenario of component-based software engineering is to build applications by assembling high-level components. Component engineering is software development for reuse. If components are not available, they can be built out of lower-level components. This process is called software composition. One way to glue together components is through scripting languages. Ousterhout (Ousterhout, 1997) distinguishes scripting languages such as Perl, Python, Tcl or Visual Basic from system programming languages like C, C++ or Java. Scripting languages provide a higher level of programming and weaker typing than system programming languages. The development of applications is faster and the languages are easier to learn, because they have simpler syntax. This is a key issue for the adoption of component technology, especially as the programmer community has changed and there are many casual programmers. Products such as Microsoft's Visual Basic and Borland's Delphi have been used in application development for years and serve as good examples of component-assembly development models. This combination provides maximum flexibility and choice to the sophisticated developer actually building the components, but keeps development simpler for the application developer.

4.2 Component Models

A *component model* is a set of guidelines for creating components that will work together to form a larger application. It specifies the structure of its interfaces and the mechanisms by which it interacts with its container and with other components. For components to interoperate effectively, a component model should specify several characteristics (Bellur, 1998): *Properties* give an abstract view of the externally visible state of a component. *Introspection* is a means of reflecting on the component's capabilities and enables building tools to look at a component and analyze how it works. *Customization* of a component's property values enables developers to use application-building tools to change the component's events. There must be a way to store the newly customized features of a component *persistently*. An *event model* allows specifying the propagation of occurrences of activity. Finally, there should be instructions for *packaging* components for distribution and installing them. Currently the most wide-spread component models are ActiveX controls and JavaBeans. The next sections shall give a brief overview about these two component models.

4.2.1 ActiveX Controls

Microsoft's first version of Object Linking and Embedding (OLE) offered simple cut-and-paste capabilities. When OLE2 came out, Microsoft introduced its underlying communications layer as a separate entity called *Component Object Model* (COM). Developers could create language-independent components called OLE controls, or OCXs. The COM model differs from CORBA in that an object may provide not only one, but an arbitrary number of interfaces to each of which there can exist arbitrary numbers of external references. Once officially introduced, an interface may never be changed again. Every COM interface provides the method QueryInterface. It allows navigating between COM interfaces and is the way COM achieves polymorphism. If it is necessary to extend an interface, the new functionality must be provided as a new, additional interface. This simplifies a migration from old software to new software by allowing the support of old and new interfaces at the same time during the transition period. COM is a binary standard, meaning that the memory layout of an interface, the calling conventions, and the code file formats are completely determined by COM. OLE controls are useful only on a single machine, so they are not distributed objects.

In 1995 Microsoft announced a new generation of OLE/COM. COM was upgraded to DCOM that adds support for distributed objects, using a simplified implementation of DCE as its basis. DCOM treats client and server symmetrically in that a client doesn't know whether it calls a client-side stub or the real server, and a server doesn't know whether a server-side stub or a real client calls it. An ActiveX object is a DCOM object. The next generation of COM, called COM+ is a more abstract definition of how objects and classes are represented in memory. It should provide garbage collection and similar to CORBA many services, including security and transaction services.

4.2.2 JavaBeans

In contrast to ActiveX, JavaBeans is a platform-neutral component architecture for the programming language Java. With its inclusion in the JDK 1.1, JavaBeans promises to be a major contender in the component arena. A Bean is a visual component that adheres to the JavaBean interfaces for its interaction with other components. Beans are self-describing through the introspection and reflection classes. Reflection permits objects to examine each other at runtime to discover the capabilities of objects. The BeanInfo class is another way to find out information on a Bean at runtime. A Bean can be customized by editing its property sheet. In the Netscape environment, JavaBeans can be manipulated through JavaScript, a simple scripting language. JavaBeans can incorporate distributed object mechanisms like RMI or CORBA. The properties, methods and events of a JavaBean can easily be wrapped into a CORBA server by paralleling many of the key architectural designs of Java-Beans in CORBA. For example, the methods of a JavaBean can be exposed as a member method of a CORBA interface. The properties of a JavaBean can be exposed as a CORBA attribute. The events of a JavaBean can be exposed using the CORBA Event Service. Since JavaBeans can act as both CORBA servers and CORBA clients, this design provides a way to transform JavaBeans into a distributed component architecture. This opens the door to writing powerful distributed applications with easy deployment.

4.3 Server-side Business Components

Modern business applications are often composed in multi-tier architectures (see section 3.4.2.), where most of the applications logic is moved from the client to the server. A multi-tier approach increases an applications scalability, performance and reliability. Component models like JavaBeans or ActiveX have a historical origin in the assembly of user interfaces, where they are used to route user interface events such as mouse clicks and keyboard entries. The most common example of a component is a GUI widget, such as a button or a file selection box. However, in many approaches component technology is also applied on the server side. The most interesting future component markets will probably be for business components (often called *business objects*) on the server side, rather than on the client side where the margins are much lower and the requirements more generic. They are modeled after the real world to provide certain business functions like Customer, Order or Product.

Server components can be replicated and distributed across any number of servers to foster system availability. Server-side component models need to provide additional features like transactions, persistence, concurrency control and security. They are mostly non-visual and execute within a container that is provided by an application execution system such as a transaction processing monitor, a Web server or a database system. In December 1997 Sun released a draft specification for Enterprise JavaBeans, a component architecture for building server side components in Java. Enterprise JavaBeans add transactions, state management, and deployment time attributes to the JavaBeans model. Java clients should be able to communicate with Enterprise JavaBeans using RMI. Non-Java clients can invoke the application using CORBA IDL running over IIOP.

The primary obstacle for a business component infrastructure is the lack of interoperability between component models. To aggregate a collection of large-grained business components (possible from multiple vendors) into a useful application, the components must be able to communicate with each other. Those business component frameworks are just starting to emerge. Current component models are platform- or language dependent. Since there is no interoperability between vendor's component models, one cannot expect to write components that will run seamlessly in different vendor's environments. This confuses developers and lowers the adoption rate. Currently there is an OMG Component Model and a Scripting Language RFP. An OMG component model brings together ease-of-use and the interoperability of CORBA standards. This could increase the adoption rate of CORBA components. For the OMG a CORBA component model is an opportunity to gain critical masses. In their Component Model RFP, OMG identifies a clear appeal from the marketplace "for a distributed component model that is capable of inter-operating with other emerging component technologies, particularly the Java-Beans component model". This could lead to easy-to-use server components for order-entry, payment, or shipment.

Standards for component models are important, but by no means sufficient to fully exploit the potential of the component software market. For this to happen, more vertical, i.e. domain-specific standards are necessary as well. Components targeted at different domains cannot interoperate even if they use the same object model. It can be expected that over time, more and more specialized interface standards will be developed for domains such as financial services, database connectivity, electronic commerce and so on. Examples are Java Database Connectivity (JDBC) or OLE for Retail Point-of-Sales (OPOS). JDBC is a standard interface for Java components that need to access relational databases. OPOS drives peripheral devices such as bar code readers. Creating standard frameworks for business components is a very challenging technical, political, and financial undertaking. These domain-specific standards will probably be defined by user organizations rather than by vendors, since they require more domain knowledge than vendors typically have.

5 Applications of Electronic Commerce Components

The following sections provide some examples for the transition towards component frameworks. This illustrates the way many new electronic commerce applications are designed and implemented. We selected the Oracle Network Computing Architecture, the SAP Business Framework and Suns Java Electronic Commerce Framework as prominent examples.

5.1 Oracle Network Computing Architecture

The Oracle Network Computing Architecture (NCA) is a cross-platform environment for developing and deploying network-centric applications for both the Web and the corporate enterprise. NCA consists of three distinct tiers, the universal data server, the application server and a universal client.

NCA focuses on component-based development in a network-centric computing environment, tied together using industry standard protocols including CORBA, Java and HTTP. The plugable components in the architecture are called cartridges. Cartridges are business objects, which combine small-grained objects into useful components. They can be written in any number of languages including Java, PL/SQL, Perl and C and take advantage of the CORBA infrastructure. Developers create NCA solutions by either building cartridges from scratch or integrating them with purchased cartridges from third-party suppliers. There are three types of cartridges in the NCA. Client cartridges like Java applets or plug-ins contain visualization logic for extending or enhancing user presentation services on the client tier only (see Fig. 3.). Application server cartridges contain application/business logic. The application server acts as the container providing security, transaction management and load balancing. Data cartridges are restricted to the universal data server and contain data manipulation logic. The so-called Inter-Cartridge Exchange is the NCA protocol that will provide a COM/CORBA bridging mechanism which should enable ActiveX/COM clients to access NCA cartridges through IIOP.

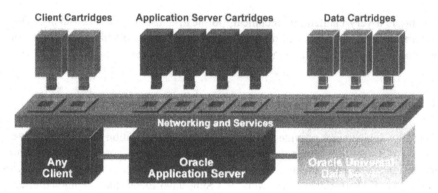

Fig. 3. Oracle network computing architecture

5.2 SAP Business Framework

SAP is a market leader in client/server enterprise application software. R/3 Releases 1.x and 2.x integrated applications through access to the same database. Now R/3 Release 4.0 provides a so-called Business Framework. Companies can use the Business Framework to combine individual components such as "Human Resources", "Consolidation", or "Availability-to-Promise", even if these components do not belong to the same R/3 release. A company about to upgrade one component will not be forced to upgrade the other components as well. A SAP Business Component supplies a dedicated, encapsulated business functionality via stable interfaces. A component of this type has its own development, implementation and maintenance cycles and can run on its own dedicated database. SAP Business Workflow and Application Link Enabling (ALE) are two techniques, used to integrate the whole system and map a business process across Business Components. Via the Business Information Warehouse it is possible to give managers a single view of the whole system across all installed components.

Access to Business Components is provided through Business Objects and their corresponding BAPIs (Business Application Programming Interface). BAPIs provide access to the SAP functionality for third party programmers and can also be accessed from DCOM, CORBA or Java clients. SAP Business Objects are representations of real-world entities such as "customer" or "invoice". Business Objects structure the interfaces to Business Components. So a Business Component represents the functionality of a set of semantically related SAP Business Objects which are supplied to a company in the form of a separate, executable software product. Release 3.1 included 28 different components for Internet applications, for example, for sales order creation via the Internet or for creating requirement requests. Newer releases will also make existing R/3 functionality available in the form of business components.

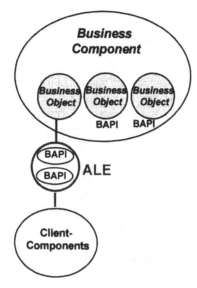

Fig. 4. SAP application link enabling

SAP is founding member of the *Open Applications Group (OAG)*. OAG was formed in 1995 as a non-profit organization and tries to establish independent standards for interoperability among enterprise software applications. The Open Applications Group is building specifications that define the business object interoperability between enterprise business applications. Most major enterprise software vendors like IBM, J. D. Edwards & Company, Oracle or PeopleSoft joined the company to achieve standards at the business component level. The Open Applications Group is undertaking three projects to standardize integration among the member vendors' software solutions. The names of these projects are Project A, Project B and Project C.

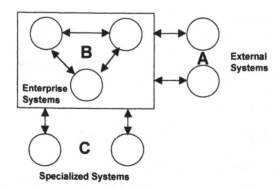

Fig. 5. OAG standardization projects

Project A will specify the integration of enterprise systems with the systems of other enterprises, for example, enterprise accounting systems to bank systems. Electronic Data Interchange (EDI) and Electronic Funds Transfer (EFT) are examples of the areas that Project A will focus on. *Project B* focuses on integration between enterprise business applications, for example, Vendor X's Accounting systems to Vendor Y's Manufacturing system, or Vendor Y's H/R to Vendor Z's Accounting systems. Project B is defining and implementing standards that create a common way to integrate enterprise logistic and manufacturing applications to the enterprise accounting business application. Some of the applications that Project B is integrating include Inventory, Customer Order Management, Purchasing, Manufacturing and Personnel. *Project C* focuses on the integration of specialized applications and the enterprise business applications. Specialized applications operate at the execution level of an enterprise and are mostly of complementary nature to the enterprise business applications. The OAG specifications are called OAGIS, which stands for Open Applications Group Integration Specifications. It can be expected that OAGIS will be an important standard in the area of business components.

5.3 Java Electronic Commerce Framework

The Java Electronic Commerce Framework (JECF) is an open platform for the development of electronic commerce applications in Java. It provides functionality that reduces the time and effort for developers to build electronic commerce applications. The Java Commerce APIs implement basic services within the Java Electronic Commerce Framework. They provide services that allow developers to easily create new electronic commerce applications, like on-line shopping malls, home banking or electronic brokerage. The Java Commerce APIs provide an encrypted database that can reside on the user's local hard drive and can securely maintain a customer's privileged information.

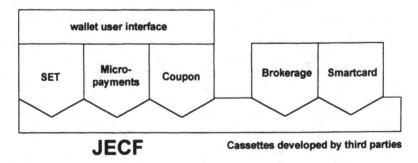

Fig. 6. Java Electronic Commerce Framework

A commerce bean is a reusable commerce component that meets specific interface requirements. It can implement an operation like purchasing or financial planning, a protocol like SET, a user interface component or the information of a credit card or voucher. For example the JECF could use a purchase operation bean in conjunction with a protocol bean to perform an online purchase. Commerce beans are currently undergoing a transition towards the JavaBean specifications. Commerce beans are contained within cassettes. A Cassette is a Java archive file (JAR) that is persistent on the client and is digitally signed with one or more roles, which provide specific capabilities to the contents of a cassette. So a cassette is a "package" for commerce beans and their resources.

The JECF Graphical User Interface, known as the "Java Wallet" is a single, pluggable user interface for cassettes. A consumer uses a Java-enabled browser to navigate an on-line merchant's virtual mall and select goods or services for purchase. He can also access the Java Wallet for home banking and portfolio management. Privacy of user's data is protected through the use of encryption and digital signatures. Developers can redesign the look and feel of the Java Wallet. The Java Wallet provides a secure means to make purchases using preferred payment types and protocols. The functionality can be extended, by installing new cassettes into the JECF. The Java Wallet allows developers to add new payment protocols, which can be downloaded as cassettes and plugged into the Java Wallet. Another JECF tool is the Java Shopping Cart, an applet that can store a customer's selected items before completing an on-line purchase. Applets can include interfaces to cassettes, which provide additional services like payment processing, security services or customer profile services.

6 Conclusions

The development of electronic commerce applications is a huge and fast moving field. Due to the mix of technologies and standards, electronic commerce has become one of the most complex areas in the information systems field. New software engineering concepts play an important role for the design and implementation of new electronic commerce applications. A general trend of all the different approaches is to enable a marketplace of third-party components. It is yet unclear, which component standard will dominate, but once a standard has reached a critical mass of support, the economy of scale cannot be beaten by a proprietary approach.

7 Appendix: Interoperability Standards for Electronic Commerce

Interoperability for components across the Internet is the critical enabler for electronic commerce. CORBA and DCOM provide very powerful protocols, however, for the thousands of CGI-based solutions on the Internet, these two options are not easily accessible. For example, it is not possible for a client to access the IDL interface of an electronic commerce server, unless the client is written in a language, for which there is a CORBA mapping like C++, C, Smalltalk and Java. Whereas CORBA and DCOM are very helpful to glue together components of different vendors within an application, there is a strong movement towards document-centric protocols for the interoperability between electronic commerce applications of different market participants. Document-centric messages can be handled by simple Web-server scripts as well as sophisticated applications based on distributed object technology. Thus, new document-centric electronic commerce standards will have a major influence on the implementation of electronic commerce applications on the Internet. In the next few sections we describe a selection of approaches.

7.1 From EDI to XML/EDI

Some of the first approaches in this direction come from an Internet Engineering Task Force (IETF) workgroup covering EDI (EDIINT), which has recommended standards for secure, interoperable electronic data interchange over the Internet. Member companies have demonstrated exchange of documents over SMTP using the Secure MIME (S/MIME) protocol. Two draft standards have been proposed: MIME-based secure EDI, and EDIINT functional specifications. Many companies have applied Internet-EDI in business-to-business commerce (Segev et al., 1997). The problem with EDI standards like ANSI X.12 or UN/EDIFACT is that start-up and support costs are very high, due to their inherent complexity. For small and medium-sized enterprises this has often been no solution. Moreover, EDI standards do not integrate very well with the omnipresent Web infrastructure. Thus, many new approaches use XML as an underlying basis.

Created and developed by the W3C XML Working Group, the eXtensible Markup Language (XML) version 1.0 is (as of February 10, 1998) derived from the widely used international text processing standard SGML (Standard Generalized Markup Language, ISO 8879:1986). Intended for use on the World Wide Web. XML still retains ISO 8879's basic features - vendor independence, user extensibility, complex structures, validation, and human readability - in a form that is much easier to implement and understand. XML is primarily intended to meet the requirements of large-scale Web content providers for industry-specific markup, vendor-neutral data exchange, media-independent publishing, workflow management in collaborative authoring environments, and the processing of Web documents by intelligent clients. The language combines the simplicity of HTML with the computability of EDI standards. XML suggests a way to make transaction sets easier to define and provides "self-describing" messages. Microsoft and Netscape promised support for XML with style sheets in their Web browsers. Advantages of XML-based standards are:

- Through Style Sheets (XSL, CSS) one can define different views on a document and make it displayable in a Web-browser. Thus XML documents are machine as well as human readable.

- XML has no extra infrastructure requirements. XML-documents can be handled both by simple server and by sophisticated applications based on distributed object technology. XML documents can be routed via standard Internet protocols like HTTP, FTP or SMTP. A wide range of freeware XML parsers is already on the market.
- XML has wide industry support (Microsoft, Netscape, Sun, etc.)and is emerging as the de-facto standard for many Web-based languages like RDF, PICS, CDF and OFX. Netscape and Microsoft will include XML parsers into the next release of their Web browser.

However, XML alone doesn't solve the interoperability problem. The tags need to be semantically consistent across merchant boundaries at least for the value chain of a given industry. In general, XML DTD's may be defined on a document by document, application by application, industry by industry or on a global basis. This allows flexibility and allows XML to emulate other existing proprietary or standard data formats, thus making the data more easily transferable between application formats. The following sections demonstrate some of the use of XML for Internet Commerce.

7.2 OTP - Open Trading Protocol

OTP is a protocol for interoperability of electronic purchases on the Internet that encapsulates payment protocols and offers/invoice/receipts for payment and delivery. OTP is focused on interchange between consumers, merchants and support services. The Open Trading Protocol (OTP) Consortium, a group of over 30 companies lead by Mondex, has released a draft standard (currently version 0.9) aimed at the retail trade on the Internet. OTP is a protocol for the development of software products that will permit product interoperability for the electronic purchase that is independent of the chosen payment mechanism - OTP encapsulates the payment with the offers/invoice/receipts for payment and delivery. It complements today's electronic payment protocols by addressing trading - the process of doing business.

OTP seeks to enable electronic commerce by supplying the equivalent of traditional, mostly paper based, methods of trading. The negotiation of who will be the parties to the trade, how it will be conducted, the presentment of an offer, the method of payment, the provision of a payment receipt, the delivery of goods and the receipt of goods. The OTP standards complement but don't replace protocols like SET by providing a set of rules that cover the following:

- offers for sale
- agreements to purchase
- payment (by using existing payment products)
- the transfer of goods and services
- delivery
- receipts for purchases

- multiple methods of payment
- support for problem resolution
- payment brand and protocol selection

The Open Trading Protocols identify four Trading Exchanges that involve the exchange of data between the Trading Roles. The Trading Exchanges are:

- Offer: The Offer Exchange results in the merchant providing the consumer with the reason why the trade is taking place. It is called an offer since the consumer must accept the offer if a trade is to continue.
- Payment. The Payment Exchange results in value of some kind being transferred between the consumer and the value acquirer. This may occur in either direction
- Delivery. The Delivery Exchange transmits either the on-line goods, or delivery information about physical goods from the deliverer to the consumer, and
- Authentication. The Authentication Exchange can be used by any trading role to authenticate another trading role to check that they are who they appear to be.

OTP Transactions are composed of various combinations of these Trading Exchanges. For example, an OTP Purchase transaction includes Offer, Payment, and Delivery Trading Exchanges. The protocol is freely available to developers and users, and builds on XML. It is one of the most comprehensive uses of XML to date. The specification provides detailed definitions of an entire series of transactions between consumers, merchants and associated service providers. The protocol is not "owned" by any one company, and its development will be managed by an independent organization. The OTP specification has been designed to support and complement other specifications like SET (Secure Electronic Transactions) and the EMV (Europay, MasterCard and Visa) chip card specification, to offer a consistent online interaction for consumers, merchants and banks using any number of payment options. OTP is designed to promote retail commerce on the Internet, however, it is still some distance away from full production.

7.3 OFX - Open Financial Exchange

OFX is a specification for the electronic exchange of financial data between financial institutions, business and consumers via the Internet, focused on the desktop PC. OFX was developed by CheckFree, Intuit and Microsoft. It supports a wide range of financial activities including consumer and small business banking; consumer and small business bill payment; bill presentment and investments, including stocks, bonds and mutual funds. Other financial services, including financial planning and insurance, will be added in the future and will be incorporated into the specification.

Open Financial Exchange is a broad-based framework for exchanging financial data and instructions between customers and their financial institutions. It is an open specification that anyone can implement: any financial institution, transaction processor, software developer, or other party. It uses widely accepted open standards for data formatting (such as SGML), connectivity (such as TCP/IP and HTTP), and security (such as SSL). Open Financial Exchange defines the request and response messages used by each financial service as well as the common framework and infrastructure to support the communication of those messages. OFX is based upon SGML and, like XML, it is an attempt to take the best features of SGML and remove much of the associated complexity. OFX is not technically an XML application. The syntax of OFX differs from XML applications in that OFX omits end-tags. Like XML, OFX is designed to be both easy to learn and extensible. In the FAQ document of May 1998, explicit reference is made to greater XML compliance as a goal: in the changes from version 1.02 to 1.5, "Open Financial Exchange has made a move towards XML compatibility . . ."

The Open Financial Exchange (OFX) and Integrion Financial Network (GOLD) standards do overlap considerably in the services that they describe. So, the Banking Industry Technology Secretariat (BITS), consisting of CheckFree, Integrion, IBM, Intuit and Microsoft, announced that a new open framework for the exchange of financial data and instructions will be published 1998. The unified specifications will merge the GOLD and OFX specifications.

7.4 OBI

In May 1997, the OBI (Open Buying on the Internet) consortium (more than 50 members) released the OBI standard v. 1.0. The OBI standard is an open, flexible framework for business-to-business Internet commerce solutions. It is intended for the high-volume, low-dollar transactions that account for 80 % of most organizations purchasing activities. The OBI standard is concerned with transactions between business-to-business trading partners that are characterized as frequent or repetitive purchases of high-volume, low-dollar transactions with a small number of Selling Organizations typically paid out of overhead. Such transactions are typically for commodity goods and services such as office supplies, scientific supplies, MRO (maintenance, repair & operations) supplies, PCs, temporary help, etc. These goods and services are often described as indirect or 'non-production" materials because they are not used in a production or manufacturing process. So the specification is applicable only to a narrow market segment of business-to-business commerce on the Internet. It defines requirements for how catalog and procurement software should handle a very limited set of purchasing transactions for a very narrow segment of electronic commerce. Within this narrow scope of Internet commerce, it does an admirable job of pulling together the many facets required to conduct a safe and secure purchasing transaction.

The OBI architecture is built on existing standards in order to maximize interoperability and decrease implementation costs. The following table from the OBI Standards document summarizes those existing industry standards that OBI compliant systems must adopt.

Table 1. Technical Standards relevant to OBI

Purpose	Standard
Content display	Evolving standards for Web browsers as specified by W3C
Order requests and OBI orders	ANSI ASC X.12 850
Order transmission	HTTP 1.0 using SSL
Secure internet communication	SSL v. 3.0
Cryptography	SSL v. 3.0 API
Public key certificates	X.509 v. 3 certificates
Payment protocols	SET

For ordering goods over the Internet, OBI proposes the transmission of an EDI ANSI X12.850 Purchase Order along with appropriate security and digital certificates. So OBI-compliant solutions must include the ability to map EDI data formats to and from existing catalog, inventory control and purchasing systems. Yet the OBI purchasing process assumes that buying organization's requisitioners begin their search by selecting a product category from the buying organization's purchasing homepage and are then linked to a single selling organization's catalog to locate products that meet their needs. The OBI standard makes no provision for buying organizations to be able to select and procure products and services provided by vendors competing with each other in an open marketplace. The OBI purchasing process assumes that buying organizations only have one or a few approved selling organizations for each category of commodity items.

7.5 Summary

XML-based interoperability standards promise to be a good candidate for future interoperability standards on the Internet. The requirements imposed by XML are minimal and it can easily be transformed into other representations. XML provides a high-level approach that does not require a particular distributed object technology, but holds the promise to allow mappings from XML documents onto CORBA objects as well as DCOM components. It is still an open question which of these standards will succeed and who should manage their evolution. Since few standards will have dominance, it is not unlikely that application vendors in this arena will achieve interoperability between systems through the agreement of meta-protocols.

References

Bellur, U., "The Role of Components & Standards in Software Reuse," *Position Paper for the OMG-DARPA-MCC Workshop on Compositional Software Architectures,* (08/1998), URL = http://www.objs.com/workshops/ws9801/.

Bichler, M.; C. Beam and A. Segev, "Services of a Broker in Electronic Commerce Transactions," *International Journal of Electronic Markets* 8, 1, (1998)

CommerceNet, "Catalog Interoperability Study: Issues, Practices & Recommendations," *CommerceNet Research Report*, February 27, 1998.

Hoque, R. and T. Sharma, *Programming WebComponents*, McGraw-Hill, New York et al. 1998, p. 28.

Keller, A. M.: "Smart Catalogs and Virtual Catalogs," in Proc. Of the *International Conference on Frontiers of Electronic Commerce*, (1995).

Lewandowski, S. M., "Frameworks for Component-Based Client/Server Computing," *ACM Computing Surveys*, 30, 1, (1998).

McConnell, S., "The OMG/CommerceNet Joint Electronic Commerce Whitepaper," (12/1997) URL = http://www.osm.net/about/library.html.

Moessenboeck, H., "Trends in Object-Oriented Programming," *ACM Computing Surveys*, 28A, (4), 1996.

Orfali, R. and D. Harkey, *Client/Server Programming with Java and CORBA*, John Wiley and Sons, New York, NY 1997.

Ousterhout, J. *"Scripting: Higher Level Programming for the 21st Century,"* (12/1997),
URL = http://www.sunlabs.com/~ouster/scripting.html.

Pfister, Cuno, *"Component Software: A Case Study using BlackBox Components,"* (01/1998),
URL = http:/www.oberon.ch/docu/case_study/index.html.

Thompson, C., Linden T. and B. Filman, *"Thoughts on OMA-NG: The Next Generation Object Management Architecture,"* (08/1997)
URL = http://www.objs.com/staging/OMG-OMA-NG.html.

Sametinger, J., *Software Engineering with Reusable Components*, Springer, New York 1997, p. 68.

Segev, A., W. Dadong and C. Beam, *"Designing Electronic Catalogs for Business Value: Results from the CommerceNet Pilot,"* Fisher Center for Management & Information Technology, U.C. Berkeley, CA, CMIT Working Paper 95-WP-1005, October 1995.

Segev, A., J. Porra and M. Roldan, "Internet-based EDI strategy," *Decision Support Systems*, 21, (1997), 157 – 170.

Sokol, P., *From EDI to electronic commerce: a business initiative*, McGraw-Hill, New York, NY, 1995.

CHAPTER 16
Electronic Commerce and Digital Libraries

Andrea L. Houston[1] and Hsinchun Chen[2]

[1]ISDS Department, Louisiana State University, Baton Rouge, LA 70803,
ahoust2@lsu.edu

[2]Management Information Systems Department, University of Arizona, Tucson, AZ 85721,
hchen@bpa.arizona.edu

In this chapter we discuss digital libraries from an electronic commerce perspective. The focus is on what the two have in common. The first section is an introduction which discuses some of the impacts that digital libraries and electronic commerce have had on our lives. The second section discusses common driving forces behind the two. The next section discusses common challenges, with an emphasis on the digital library perspective. The fourth section discusses several common issues, in particular, social, legal, quality, security and economic issues that both digital libraries and electronic commerce must address. The discussion in the fourth section primarily presents a digital library perspective, although the issues are important to both digital libraries and electronic commerce. Finally, the chapter closes with a conclusion.

Keywords: Digital Libraries; Electronic Information; Information Retrieval

1 Introduction

Advances in information technology and information management are dramatically changing our lives, especially the way we conduct business (e.g., electronic commerce) and locate and access information (e.g., digital libraries). Information, as discussed in this chapter, should be thought of in the broadest sense including at a minimum, text, numeric, image, video, and audio forms.

Exploiting information-related advances has become a strategy that few businesses can afford to ignore. For example, two years ago very little business was conducted over the Internet. Today an informative and engaging web presence is becoming a competitive advantage that organizations are aggressively pursuing. Consumers can locate information about a company or product using the World Wide Web (WWW). They can also order products and services through web-based catalogues and shop in web-based virtual shopping malls, browsing and purchasing products and services from more than one corporation. A variety of financial services (stocks, loans, banking, bill payment, etc.) are also available over the WWW.

Eventually, even highly personal and interactive services such as medical diagnosis and treatment recommendations for house-bound patients will be available online. It is not unlikely that the next generation will live in totally wired homes verbally interacting with intelligent virtual agents who will manage their homes and their lives. These agents will automatically perform such services as: ordering groceries and other products; scheduling services; providing reminders for appointments and errands; paying bills and handling other financial tasks; filtering mail; recommending articles and news items to read or (more likely) view; recommending and scheduling entertainment; performing background checks on child-care providers and other home-oriented service providers (gardeners, pool maintenance, repair and remodeling, cleaning, catering, etc.).

The location and provision of information traditionally performed by libraries and librarians has also dramatically changed. Clients no longer need to leave the home or office to locate and access information as it is usually available on-line via a digital gateway provided by a library (or other information provider, e.g., electronic publishers or individuals) (Wiederhold, 1995). Clients are no longer limited to information physically available in the nearest library. Today, through inter-library agreements, they have access to information from a wide variety of globally distributed information repositories (sources). Eventually, we will be able to take virtual tours of museums, historical sites and natural wonders as well as attend virtual concerts and theater performances, or watch an variety of types of movies, in addition to reading, viewing or listening to books, articles, lectures and music, all through our local library gateway.

What do electronic commerce and digital libraries have in common other than the fact that information technology advances have dramatically changed them? For one thing they both are involved with "the creation of information sources and the movement of [that] information across global networks" (Adam et al., 1996). This means that many of the technological changes and economic pressures driving the explosive growth and changes are the same. Similarly, both areas are concerned with the identification and delivery of *relevant* information to interested customers. This means that they face many similar issues, in particular similar economic, social, legal, quality and security issues. In this chapter we will explore some of these similarities, including the driving forces and the issues confronting both the providers and the users of electronic information.

2 Common Driving Forces

Electronic commerce and digital libraries involve organizations meeting the information needs of their clients via electronic information and global communication networks. To do so effectively requires a combination of technological advances and the ability of an organization to design, construct, manage and use global electronic networks (Mansell, 1996). Organizations must also be able to rapidly adapt to dynamic changes in technology and to cope with the size, scale and complexity of both the networks themselves and the information available through them (Atkins, 1997).

Flexibility, nimbleness and creativity are important abilities to differentiate an organization from its competitors.

Not only is the information exchange medium changing from physical objects to networks, but the information itself is changing which in turn has an impact on the medium. Traditional information exchange was textual or numeric, involving simple, standard data types. Electronic information exchange now includes audio, image and video data as well as a need for "graphical" information (i.e., the continuous output of an EKG machine). These data types require more bandwidth for transmission. Furthermore, there is no single internationally accepted transmission standard for any one of them often making information exchange challenging.

2.1 Common Goals

Both electronic commerce and digital libraries can be thought of in terms of a common generic model proposed by Adam et al. (Adam et al., 1996): "providers (information providers, merchants, retailers, wholesalers) make multimedia objects available to consumers (customers, information seekers, users) in exchange for payment." A generic system for either electronic commerce or a digital library could be characterized as "a collection of distributed autonomous sites (servers) that work to together to give the consumer the appearance of a single cohesive collection" (Adam et al., 1996). In practice, each site will most likely store a large number of information objects in a wide variety of formats on a wide variety of storage media (Lynch and Garcia-Molina, 1995). Consumers accessing the information will have a wide range of expertise in key access-related areas such as computer literacy, collection navigation abilities, and domain knowledge (Atkins, 1997).

Electronic commerce focuses on business-related interactions and transactions that serve the needs of consumers, sellers, intermediaries and producers of goods and services. Digital libraries focus on interactions between information producers (authors, publishing companies, government organizations), "librarians" (information locators, indexers, and filterers), and information seekers. Digital libraries use electronic commerce techniques when determining appropriate pricing and cost models for their services. Electronic commerce uses digital libraries as information repositories (Adam et al., 1996; Kalakota and Whinston, 1996; Lynch and Garcai-Molina, 1995).

One of the main goals of any organization involved in the information business is to add value to information that it provides or manages. The most common kind of added value is *access*. Access value either improves access time (retrieval speed and/or timeliness), availability (recall), content (relevance) or some combination of the three (Atkinson, 1996). Historically, organizations focused on generic improvements. The current trend is to customize or tailor improvements to information access at the *individual* client level.

2.2 Advantages of Electronic Information

The advantages of electronic information for digital libraries and electronic commerce are:

- *Access* - Electronic information is more readily available to customers (assuming that they have devices to generate, transmit and receive it) as there is no (or a dramatically reduced) purchase and delivery cycle. Customers don't need to travel to access information as it is always available on-line. There also is less effort for the information provider. Electronic information need only be created and stored *once* to be immediately available over a network simultaneously to multiple users as opposed to multiple copies being generated over time and provided to customers via traditional (manual) distribution channels (Kalakota and Whinston, 1996; Lesk, 1997; Reddy, 1996).
- *Flexibility* - The content of a single item of electronic information can change frequently using just one copy, something not possible in non-electronic media which requires modifications and updates to be republished as revisions or new editions. While this allows errors to be corrected and the most up-to-date information to be available, it can cause problems for archiving, and differentiation between multiple versions and authors. One way of addressing this issue and increasing flexibility is by creating links to modified and related information via hypermedia and hypertext functionality. Another approach, taken by Wilensky (Wilensky, 1996) (Berkeley), is the multivalent document approach in which "complex documents comprise multiple layers of distinct but intimately related content".
- *Economics* - Electronic information is cheaper to produce, store, distribute, and reproduce or copy. Furthermore, information providers can cooperate with each other by providing a gateway or links to information managed or provided by others. This allows providers to specialize on certain kinds of information thus conserving acquisition and production budgets while still providing access to a wide range of information (Lesk, 1997).
- *Preservation* - Electronic media does not disintegrate as readily as other types. Paper is a particularly vulnerable medium as it is susceptible to the problems of acid paper and binding disintegration as well as destruction through innocent physical handling and vandalism. Other kinds of media (including tape, images, negatives, vinyl records, etc.) are susceptible to disintegration due to pollution, catastrophic events (floods, and other natural disasters), humidity, light, insect and other kinds of pests, mold and mildew, vandalism and human handling.

Nonetheless, there are advantages to paper and other non-electronic forms of information. Some of these include (Kalakota and Whinston, 1996; Lesk, 1997):

- *Economics* - While electronic information may be cheaper to produce, store, modify and distribute, it is still much easier to determine a fair or market price and cost for a physical object or copy. To-date, there isn't a commonly accepted economic model that can accurately and fairly determine either costs or prices for electronic information.

- *Ownership Issues* - When information providers own a physical copy, decisions about acquisition and archiving are relatively straightforward. If information providers only own a link or gateway connection to the information certain kinds of problems arise (Feldman, 1997). For example, if an information provider decides to cancel its subscription to regularly published information (such as a journal) how will access be controlled? Obviously access to future issues should not be permitted but the right to access past issues has already been negotiated and paid for. Dynamically keeping this kind of information accurate increases the record-keeping and access control policies, procedures and processes for information providers. What should be done about an information provider that goes out of business or an information item that goes "out of print"? In both cases the information provider can no longer afford (or wish) to support physical storage. How can the rights of owners of links to that information be protected?

- *Copyright Protection* - With physical copies it is easier to track copyright infringements (at least there is physical evidence for prosecution purposes). Copyright violations are more difficult to track when anyone with on-line access can download information, plagiarize or modify it, and upload it making the "new" version available to others.

- *Quality Control* - The publication business (especially reputable publishers, editors and other kinds of information providers) lends credibility to information *content*. Consumers are less concerned about fraud, plagiarism, and unreliable or invalid information with non-electronic formats. Most non-electronic information (especially scholarly information) is subject to some kind of peer review, editing or similar validation process, further augmenting perceptions of quality.

- *Stability* - Physical copies also provide a kind of stability to information, as changes or modifications cannot be made except in revisions or new editions which are easily distinguishable from the original. Similarly, it is easier to distinguish multiple versions of information as well as the contributions of multiple authors and reviewers on physical copies.

- *Volume Control* - Traditionally, customers limited the volume of information they searched physically - only so much information was physically accessible. In cases of excessive volumes of available information, the advice of an expert was often sought. Now that anyone can become an information provider, the volume of information available has dramatically increased and will continue to do so. Even domain experts cannot keep up with this explosive growth in volume, making it more important for information consumers to filter out irrelevant information and information of questionable quality.

- *Quality of Experience* - Not everyone prefers to interact with a computer in order to get information. Many express strong preferences for "curling up with a good book", an emotion few express towards a computer. The quality of a computer sound system can rarely compete with the quality of a high-end home sound system or the acoustics of a finely engineered music hall or theater. The same is true of the image quality available on computer screens. Most people would agree that computers in general are at the low end of the scale for viewing images and movies.

2.3 Economic Pressures

Although the increase in electronic information is partially driven by economics, the economic pressures are slightly different for electronic commerce and digital libraries. There is an obvious economic advantage to both of them from a storage and preservation perspective. Electronic information is less expensive to store and easier to maintain. There is also an obvious economic benefit from the ability to provide a previously unattainable level of service, i.e., "individual words and sentence search and delivery of information to the user's desk-information that does not decay with time, whether it is words, sounds or images" (Lesk, 1997). In addition, previous information that was either unavailable or difficult to attain is now readily available electronically (i.e., large government collections).

In the case of electronic commerce, Malone (MIT) argues that there are three main economic effects enabled by technology (Mansell, 1996):

- *Communication effect* - increased amount of information exchanged at a reduced cost;
- *Brokerage effect* - more effective match between buyer and seller; and
- *Integration effect* - move effective stage coupling in the value-added chain.

While digital libraries are subject to the economic benefits of the communication effect, there are other economic pressures unique to them including:

- *Inflation* - an extremely rapid rise in library operating costs (especially in acquisition or collection expansion, particularly of scholarly journals). In the past 20 years, journal prices have soared by 400 percent while book and monograph prices have increased by 40 percent (Frye, 1997);
- *Volume* - an explosion in the amount, variety and complexity of available information;
- *Maintenance* - the preservation crisis in existing collections, especially with regard to acidic paper (nationally the replacement cost of disintegrating print materials extrapolates to approximately $35 to 45 billion (Frye, 1997));
- *Multimedia* - the increasing amount of information available in multimedia format which requires special viewing or listening facilities. The cataloging and storage requirements for multimedia information are also different from traditional print information;
- *Collaboration* - the advantages (both economic and improved level of service) from resource sharing among both libraries and other information providers;

- *Timeliness* - as electronic information is easy to produce, distribute and duplicate with few of the costly problems of multiple handling and redistribution, it encourages not only a dramatic increase in cost efficiency, but also a dramatic savings in time (Ginsparg, 1997); and
- *Scholarly Communication* - experts agree that the most significant economic factor driving digital libraries is the severe cost problem associated with scholarly communication (Drabenstott, 1993), in particular the excessive cost of providing access to an *appropriate* number of scholarly journals (Atkinson, 1996; Frye, 1997; Lesk, 1997) to maintain an *adequate* level of service for customers. For example, according to Andrew Odlyzko (Bell Labs), "a good mathematics library spends $100,000 per year on journal subscriptions, plus twice more on staff and equipment. [The] US spends as much money buying mathematics journals as NSF [the National Science Foundation] spends on mathematical research" (Odlyzko, 1996).

2.4 Technological Advances

There are many technological advances in information production, management and distribution that are responsible for *enabling* the increase in electronic information. They are too numerous to describe in detail but include such things as advances in: 1) storage media; 2) digitization or information capturing techniques (i.e., OCR technology); 3) automatically indexing and organizing large volumes of information (Schatz and Chen, 1996); 4) computing speed; 5) network technology (including data compression); 6) content-based search and retrieval (Schatz et al., 1996); 7) feature-based or texture-based search and retrieval (Smith, 1996); 8) data compression and full-text indexing (Witten et al., 1994); 9) resource or knowledge discovery; 10) multimedia and hypertext; 11) standards (i.e., Standardized General Mark-up Language (SGML), and Hypertext Mark-up Language (HTML)); 12) visualization techniques (Rao et al., 1995); 13) object-oriented techniques; and 14) improvements in user-interface design (Drabenstott, 1993; Kessler, 1996; Lynch and Garcia-Molina, 1995).

3 Common Challenges

Information providers have always been concerned about the quality (accuracy, completeness and timeliness) and the availability of information (ease of access, ease of use, timeliness and preservation) (Kessler, 1996). From a technical perspective, common challenges for electronic information fall into three general categories: 1) information acquisition and storage; 2) techniques to identify (locate), retrieve and filter relevant information from vast collections; and 3) providing universal access from a wide variety of information sources to a wide variety of information seekers.

3.1 Information Acquisition and Storage

The first major challenge for electronic information is that most information is not digitized. This is particularly true of existing information. In the future, policies can be established to digitally create new information, but the immediate challenge is to determine how to cost-effectively convert non-digitized information. Conversion challenges include both a technological component (e.g., improving OCR technology, advances in storage media) and an evaluation component (e.g., selection and prioritization of information to convert, choosing the appropriate level(s) of digitized quality - critical for images). Other related challenges are identifying methods to capture and index continuous media in real time and techniques for processing, storing and managing vast volumes of extremely complex electronic information (Adam et al., 1996; Christel et al., 1995; Wactlar, 1996).

The ultimate goal is not to keep a pristine, stagnant historical repository, but to encourage information use and reuse by interested consumers. This requires some kind of universal, and probably automatic (due to the volumes involved) indexing or feature identification mechanism for *all* data types that can be used to classify information for later extraction. At a minimum, electronic information metadata (information about the information features) needs to include feature relationships (for example, spatial, temporal and other domain-dependent logical relationships) and the ability to describe non-numeric and numeric features (Smith, 1996). Much of the research on feature extraction has been done in the area of image databases and video indexing.

Another major problem is the dynamic nature of electronic information (Huser, 1995). The content can change over time requiring either multiple copies or versions to be individually stored, or some mechanism that allows version differentiation for a single copy (Levy and Marshall, 1995). Electronic information facilitates multiple authorship and collaboration (integrated or leveled). Consumers need to be able to easily differentiate the contribution of each author.

Information collection managers need to develop mechanisms to determine what information and which version(s) to include in their collections. This can create information ownership and archiving issues. For example, if an information provider decides to only keep a pointer or link to a certain piece of information, then what happens when the owner(s) or manager(s) of the electronic copy decide it is no longer cost-effective to keep it? What are the responsibilities of the owner to notify pointer or link owners of changes or deletions (a classic problem on the WWW)?

3.2 Relevant Information Identification and Filtering

Assuming that information providers and managers can solve the acquisition and storage challenges, the next set of challenges involve finding ways to make the *right* information available to the *right* customers at the *right* time to improve decision making and maximize the utility of the information (Kalakota and Whinston, 1996; Lynch and Garcia-Molina, 1995). Not only must customers be able to identify or locate information potentially relevant to them, but they must have some way to either filter information so that only the most relevant information is returned and organize (via a ranking or categorization scheme) volumes of potentially relevant information into manageable units. Most users do not have the time to wade through vast amounts of information looking for the critical key informational gems. It is likely that intelligent artificial agents will be heavily involved in coping with the challenges of information location and filtering (Atkins et al., 1996; Knoblock et al., 1996).

There are at least two different kinds of information location processes. The first kind is useful in a broad-based search where the information need has not yet been narrowly defined. Recall is most important in this kind of search. Due to the volume of information returned, effective organizing and classifying techniques must be provided. Relevant information will probably be broadly dispersed among several distributed heterogeneous information sources. Therefore, the key challenge will be to present a seamless information integration or combination to the customer. Customers interested in this kind of search will probably want the information to be summarized for quick perusal (Schatz et al., 1996). Many of the problems and solutions associated with this kind of challenge have been well documented in the heterogeneous and federated database literature.

The second kind of information identification process involves a very narrow, well-defined and focused search. This kind of search requires very detailed information, most likely from a single information source. Precision will be most important and therefore effective filtering techniques will be required to return a small amount of the *most* relevant information. One challenge will be determining which information source best matches the customer's information needs.

In either case, the user interface will be critical. Even the most relevant information is worthless if the customer cannot understand the presentation (Saracevic and Kantor, 1997a). The best electronic information systems will have uniform but customizable, dynamic user interfaces that can smoothly integrate existing common data types (text, numeric, audio, video and image) from structured and unstructured sources with specialized types of data (maps, three-dimensional data, and continuous graphical data) and potentially new data types (Adam et al., 1996). These systems will incorporate algorithms and techniques that enable semantic interoperability, so that customers can search in unfamiliar domains of knowledge (each with its own specialized vocabulary and ontology) using familiar vocabularies and ontologies (Atkins, 1997; Lynch and Garcia-Molina, 1995). There is an extensive literature on the problems of semantic interoperability and content-based retrieval.

Techniques must also be developed to effectively chunk or package information into units that do not overwhelm either the cognitive abilities of human customers or the physical capacity of the networks and systems transporting and storing the requested information. The rich human-computer interaction literature covers many of these topics.

Another important aspect of information location, is finding key relationships, especially in distributed, heterogeneous information sources. Data mining, the extraction of patterns, associations and anomalies from large data sources, is necessary from both the provider and consumer perspective. Providers are interested in access and purchase patterns, exploiting this information to improve decision making and identify potential customers. Typically customers are loath to provide this kind of information about themselves. Fraud detection, local vs. regional differences in customers and changes in customer requirements over time are other relationships and trends that providers are interested in. Customers are interested in identifying underlying trends in information, especially information that improves cost minimization and purchasing decisions. Although data mining techniques currently exist, they are not sophisticated enough to handle either the volume or the complexity of existing information. The extensive data mining literature explores the challenges in this area.

3.2 Providing Universal Access

The ultimate goal of many of national level initiatives (i.e., the National Information Infrastructure - NII initiative) with respect to electronic information, is universal access. This is consistent with the traditional goals of information providers, from an economic perspective and a social perspective. For universal access to be accomplished information providers need to solve the problems of integrating distributed heterogeneous information and information sources, designing and implementing effective user interfaces and solving the "vocabulary problem" (via semantic interoperability) (Schatz and Chen, 1996).

One of the challenges to providing universal access is devising techniques that will assist a wide variety of information display devices in handling voluminous, diverse and complex electronic information. Not only is there a variety of operating systems in the computer domain, but there will be a wide variety of other non-computer information display devices (e.g., palm tops, televisions, fax machines, video monitors, modems, and other information "appliances") to cope with. Accommodating legacy information display devices and receivers is probably a more difficult problem than accommodating and integrating legacy information and information sources (Tennant, 1997).

Another challenge is that there is a limited amount of bandwidth available for the transmission of electronic information that must accommodate an increasing number of information providers and customers and increasingly complex (and large) data sets. For equitable universal access to be achieved, intelligent use of the bandwidth, including the ability to guarantee bandwidth for a given period of time (in particular for law enforcement and emergency situations) must be identified and policies to support such uses enacted.

These challenges when combined with the economic pressures faced by information providers (in particular libraries) have led to a vision held by many of information providers behaving as "gate-keepers" and the service (or set of services) that they provide as a "gateway" to information or knowledge (Dowler, 1997; Drabenstott, 1993; Olsen, 1997; Rockwell, 1997). Indeed, several university libraries currently describe themselves in this manner.

4 Common Issues

As the use of electronic information increases, its impact on our lives also increases. Often this results in humans interacting with information and each other in novel ways usually without the benefit of policies, procedures and guidelines to govern appropriate behavior. Both information providers and customers come from a diverse and complex global community, each with their own unique blend of cultural perspectives. Furthermore, the roles of information providers and customers are blurring (Wiederhold, 1995). There are several social-economic issues, unrelated to the more technically oriented challenges discussed above that arise from this blend of diversity, universal access, novel interactions, and blurring of roles and boundaries. Some of the major areas of concern are: social issues, legal issues, quality and security issues, and economic issues (Lynch and Garcia-Molina, 1995).

4.1 Social Issues

There are several kinds of social issues faced by both electronic commerce and digital libraries. The major ones include:

- *Literacy* - in order to be an electronic information provider or consumer, a certain basic level of education or training is required, i.e., a basic competence in the operation of a computer or other piece of equipment that either generates or receives digitized information. Although some basic language and communication skills are required to interact electronically, multimedia frees producers and consumers of electronic information from the literacy levels currently required by printed information.

  A related issue is who will be responsible for providing these basic computer skills and training. Should training be freely available through public education systems or should it be part of the paid-for services provided by organizations in the information business? Will access to training as well as access to the appropriate equipment (computer) and facilities (an account and storage space on a server) separate society into information "haves" and "have-nots"? If so, what are the implications of this division?

- *Cultural Biases* - Filtering and organizing electronic information to assist customers in coping with the problem of information overload is a service which can be viewed as having the best interests of the customer in mind. However, there is also the possibility that the result, deliberate or unintentional, is that the cultural biases and social values of the service provider are being imposed on the customer (Atkinson, 1996). The simplest example of this is language bias. Should customers be required to access information in the language it was generated in, or should part of an information service be the ability to translate information into the customer's language of preference?

Translation of words (written or spoken) is relatively straightforward, but what about translation of non-language information (i.e., images or music)? Furthermore, information considered publicly appropriate for one group of people may be offensive or even illegal for another (Kessler, 1996). One solution may be to develop highly sensitive and individually customizable user-interfaces that could accommodate a given individual or group's cultural and linguistic preferences (Ferguson and Bunge, 1997).

• *Ethical Considerations* - The traditional librarian perspective is that information providers have a responsibility to ensure public access to information as equitably as possible socially and economically. This perspective has recently been augmented by marketplace forces in electronic commerce which also encourage information providers to support universal (public) access at a reasonable fee (Atkinson, 1996). However, not all governments, organizations or social groups support universal access, and may indeed actively attempt to restrict access to certain kinds of information deemed inappropriate.

Universal access also encounters another set of ethical problems related to censorship and cultural bias. As pointed out earlier, not all information is appropriate for all groups. Different individuals and cultures have different opinions about the accessibility and even the definition of material that could be considered due to background (racial, religious, cultural), sex (including sexual preference), age and health including such information as: pornography, material generated by hate groups and other racial or religious persecutors, sexual predators (particularly child predators), drug dealers, terrorists and other criminals (Lesk, 1997). Should there be some kind of a limit on who can be an information provider (and if so, how could such a limitation be imposed and by whom)? Or should there be limits on what kinds of information an individual customer can receive (who has the authority to determine and impose such limitations, and how might it be accomplished)?

Now that almost anyone can be an electronic information provider, it is easier to perpetuate other questionable ethical acts, for example, it is harder to detect plagiarism. The shear volume of electronic information makes it very difficult to enforce copyright laws or to even detect illegal copies. False representation and false information can easily be provided electronically, leading to concerns about information quality. These ethical considerations are challenging enough within a given nation or culture, but electronic information is available globally, and different nations and cultures have very different perspectives, definitions, and social guidelines with respect to concepts such as plagiarism, copyright laws, and "truth in advertising". Do advances in information technology and electronic information provision and consumption foster or encourage unethical conduct or is ethical conduct indifferent to such advances (Rush, 1996)? How can internationally accepted ethical codes be developed and enforced in light of these issues?

Privacy and privacy-related questions are another group of ethical issues that arise with respect to electronic information. Providers want information about purchasing habits, credit history, debt ratio, tax and other financial information, investment preferences, employment history and other personal information that will help them better target customers and identify new customers as well as provide the ability to determine if price differentiation is possible between different customers. Often this involves information that individuals do not want organizations to have (and sell to each other). Related issues are concerns about who owns health and medical information and when can it be used to discriminate prices with respect to insurance policies and other health-related services or discriminate between individuals with respect to hiring, firing and promotion decisions. Similar concerns arise with respect to criminal record information.

- *Equality* - This set of issues involves questions such as, is there equal access to information and do individuals have an equally likely chance of providing electronic information. Experiences from some forms of electronic scholarly publication are very positive. A good example is the e-print archive for high-energy physics. In this case, access by status and country is more equal in the electronic version than the printed version as there is no need to be on any kind of distribution list (via social and professional connections) for electronic distribution (Ginsparg, 1997). The information is posted, and anyone can access it. There are other instances, in the vast biomedical collections for example, where the volume of information is so huge, that consumers tend to request information by a very small set of well-known and respected authors, journals, research centers, or some combination making it extremely difficult for newcomers to get recognized and accepted as information providers.

  This tendency also occurs in the marketplace. Consumers when faced with an overwhelming amount of information, tend to filter by "name-brand" companies or products, rewarding established organizations and making it extremely difficult for new enterprises to break into the market. Fears about the lack of quality control in electronic information drive this tendency even more dramatically. Information providers may have no difficulty making electronic information accessible, but how can consumers be encouraged to access the available information equitably?

  Another concern is that as the lines between the provision of information and information services become blurred between public entities and private entities, what incentives will there be to encourage private entities to provide their information and services freely and equitably to all? Won't it be in their economic interests to target certain information consumers and focus attention and accessibility on this group while ignoring others? What kinds of social mechanisms should be implemented to encourage equitable information availability?
- *Benefit* - Advances in information technology and information management clearly have dramatic societal implications (Bishop and Star, 1996). Education (Marchionini and Maurer, 1995), employment, the nature of work and the work-

place, and the general quality of life are all impacted. It is not yet clear who will benefit from these advances and if the benefits will be equitable or not. It is reasonable to suggest that it may be important to investigate what factors influence the rate and degree of acceptance and adoption of electronic information over non-electronic forms and what social and economic mechanisms are effective in facilitating and moderating such changes (Bishop and Star, 1996; Ginsparg, 1997; Lynch and Garcia-Molina, 1995).

4.2 Economic Issues

Information providers need to get paid for providing information. Otherwise there is no incentive (in the private arena, for example a video store) or no ability (in the public arena, for example a traditional public library) to provide it. If a provider invests in equipment and other resources necessary to produce electronic information, does that give it the right to profit from the consumption of that information? How much profit is appropriate? If others modify the information (some kind of value-added service or simple modification), are they entitled to profit as well and if so, what is the equitable distribution of that profit (Rush, 1996)? According to Saracevic and Kantor (Saracevic and Kantor, 1997a) "the value of information rests with improvements in decision-making." But the same information can be used in dramatically different ways with dramatically different results, so how can improvements in decision-making be evaluated, especially in the short term when payment is required?

In order to determine profit, an information provider needs to have some concept of the cost of providing the information or service. Unfortunately, the general consensus is that the current cost models and financial instruments used in traditional information production and consumption do not adequately address the needs of electronic information. Fixed cost models are insensitive to changes in content and costs. Electronic information comes in a variety of formats with different associated production and distribution costs. Cost models that are flexible and adaptable are required to handle the diversity and complexity inherent in electronic information (Adam et al., 1996; Choy et al., 1996).

A related value-based question is: As information services shift from labor-intensive to automatic and information technology-intensive processes, one of the questions becomes can a manual effort actually provide more value-added benefit (through greater precision for example) than an automated effort (Ginsparg, 1997)? Should there be a difference in pricing strategies for labor-intensive vs. automated information services? How will information providers determine the costs of providing previously unavailable information (Adam et al., 1996)? Historically, information provision and services are typically not broken down into individual transactions or monetorized (Rockwell, 1997). As a result, not only do the institutions themselves have little idea what an information transaction is worth, but information consumers have no idea what the costs, appropriate price or value of the information is (Lesk, 1997). Indeed, this is such a difficult challenge that Saracevic and Kantor

(Saracevic and Kantor, 1997b) developed a derived taxonomy to address the problem of determining or measuring the *value* of an information provider's (specifically a library) information and services. This problem is acerbated by electronic information which has almost a zero incremental reproduction and viewing cost, increasing the expectation that access should be free or extremely cheap.

Library services are typically subsidized, and the profession's ethic has traditionally been that services should be offered at no cost to the public. Therefore, librarians are typically more concerned about the possibility that economic inequities would lead to some consumers opting not to seek information thereby creating a class of informationally and economically poor than determining prices and costs for individual service transactions. As a result, cost containment has been the major method of trying to maintain an acceptable level of service in the face of increasing expenses. Technological advances such as client-server architecture and international standards for software and documentation (i.e., SGML), the use of Commercial-off-the shelf (COTS) products and re-using or sharing resources among institutions were the primary cost containment techniques (Drabenstott, 1993; Rockwell, 1997).

Nonetheless, economic information is not free. Some method of compensation is necessary. Currently, there are at least two basic electronic information compensation models: 1) allowing free access but charging for content (i.e., freely accessing the index and table of contents, but charging for anything more) and 2) charging for access but allowing free perusal and consumption of the content (Lesk, 1997). These two models are not mutually exclusive and conflicting, as both comfortably co-exist in cyberspace.

Many different electronic information funding models have been proposed, but the basic models are either time-based (payment for unlimited access for a given unit of time, e.g. a month), request-based (payment per request), or some combination of both (Adam et al., 1996; Drabenstott, 1993). Some possible models include (Lesk, 1997):

- Institutional (public and private) subsidies - the current model for most information providers;
- Free general services and charging by transaction for unusual services, especially those requiring any human intervention - an existing viable business model (i.e., warranties) that may make sense for all information providers in the future;
- Charging consumers for everything - assumes that producers can cost and transactionalize information services (for example this model works in video stores). Some common suggestions include charging by: connect time, CPU usage, fee-per-search, fee-per-hit or retrieval, and download fees. A problem with all of these suggestions is that in general consumers, do not understand how they work. This creates a situation where charges appear to be unpredictable, resulting in unreasonable or unpredictable consumer behavior which is distressing to information providers;

- Subsidizing services through providing advertising space (typical of magazines, television, and WWW);
- Other subsidizing mechanisms perhaps including pledge breaks (public appeals for donations similar to public television and radio);
- Taxes or other sources of public funds;
- Subscriptions (pay for a given length of time i.e., a year) or licenses (viable concept in the software market);
- Memberships similar to "buying clubs" where individual consumers pool their resources to allow access to information (pricing issues could be resolved via price discrimination, non-linear pricing and service bundling (Kluiters, 1997). This model and the subscription model could include "bounties" for signing up new members;
- Charge information providers a per-unit fee for the "privilege" of having their information and services accessible, then charge information consumers for the nominal incremental cost of accessing the information (similar to a per-page author charge under consideration by some journals);
- Opportunity cost - measures the opportunity cost of providing information or a service as opposed to measuring the cost of expended resources. "Opportunity cost is determined by the relationship between supply and demand for a given resource, so that the opportunity cost of an idle resource is close to zero but that of an overutilized resource is so high that it is basically unaffordable" (Adam et al., 1996); and
- Using a detailed byte-by-byte charging algorithm - an interesting idea from Ted Nelson (CNRI) and CMU's NetBill project (Lesk, 1997).

Electronic information economic models require a series of specialized costing and pricing algorithms that can dynamically determine the cost and price of an information or service and modify the model with a variety of environmental factors including supply and demand (Choy et al., 1996). From an information consumer's perspective, these algorithms need to provide cost minimization and multiple provider billing (Paepcke et al., 1996). From an information provider's perspective, the algorithms need to rapidly and dynamic respond to changes in supply and demand while exploiting new marketing opportunities (Lesk, 1997).

Some interesting electronic financial instruments have been developed extending the concept of electronic information to payment methods. They include:

- Digital or Electronic Cash - turns real currency from a banking institution into digital cash ("cyberbucks"). Security is handled via public key encryption. An example is DigiCash's Ecash (http://digicash.support.nl).
- Electronic Wallet - electronic transactions are charged to a credit card account. Security is handled via public key encryption. An example is CyberCash Wallet (http://www.cybercash.com/).

- Electronic Data Interchange - EDI - trading partners agree to exchange transaction information directly. Typically direct access is provided via dial-up connections or a proprietary network.

4.3 Legal Issues

There are several issues related to laws and governmental policies. Since electronic information exchange occurs on a global level, national governments will have to negotiate an international level policy framework that can accommodate the exchange of information across international boundaries and differences in cultural values and laws (especially with respect to copyright, intellectual property, privacy, information ownership, fraud and other business crimes, taxation and currency exchange) (Prentice, 1997). Just as an example, the current export regulations on encryption systems (presumably for reasons of national security) significantly inhibit the development and implementation of a secure, worldwide network infrastructure (Adam et al., 1996; Lesk, 1997).

Other more localized legal issues surrounding electronic information include (Lesk, 1997):

- *Unauthorized access* - electronic information appears to be more vulnerable to unauthorized access, theft and fraud than physical copies as it is harder to detect. A variety of techniques are being investigated to help insure the security of electronic information, including such topics as "firewalls", electronic signatures, encryption, special "rendering" or viewing software or hardware, and electronic watermarks.
- *Liability* - traditionally US law distinguishes between authors and publishers who were held responsible or liable for information that they produced and organizations like the post office, libraries and bookstores who merely distributed the information. Electronic information providers can distribute as well as produce information. Many system administrators are aware of the difficult legal questions regarding their responsibility and the responsibility of the organizations they work for (especially public ones such as universities, or private subscriber on-line service providers like AOL) for information published, displayed or distributed from their sites.

In situations where electronic information has multiple authors, and multiple versions how can expertise be determined and liability assigned? For example, according to current US law, the publisher or author of a book that contains bad advice on investments is not liable yet a stockbroker is liable for bad advice on investments. How will electronic information be handled? Who will determine who is liable, when, and for what?

- *Trademark Infringement* - in the US two organizations can have the same trademark or name as long as they are well-distinguishable and separable businesses.

Commonly used examples are: HP hot sauce and HP electronics (Hewlett-Packard) or Sun Oil (Sunoco) and Sun Microsystems. With the current Internet addressing systems, only one of them can have the .com address (for example, Sun Microsystems owns the www.sun.com address). Savvy Internet individuals realized this early in electronic commerce and registered for addresses that contained trademark names of large or popular organizations. Consumers guessing at the Internet address of an organization, product or service based on its trademarked name, may or may not connect to the appropriate site.

Another related problem is that individuals can copy or scan in trade-marked images (for example a state or university seal or commercial caricature), and use them as wall-paper or images on their own personal web pages. Similar to copyright protection, many organizations require notification and/or payment for permission to use their trademarks as it is often interpreted as an organizational endorsement.

- *Copyright and Intellectual Property Rights* - copyright issues, in particular copyright violation and the related intellectual property rights issues are probably the major legal concerns with respect to electronic information. It is generally agreed that without some form of intellectual property protection and reward system, many information providers will have no incentive to generate the information, at least not in an electronic form (Lesk, 1997). Pamela Samuelson (Samuelson, 1995) from Berkeley is a well-know authority on the topic from the perspective of electronic information.

Virtually anything that can be copyrighted, can also be digitized. Once digitized, anyone with a computer can copy it, modify it and distribute to anyone else that has access to a network. The regulations that exist today - which include: no downloading at all; no electronic storage (view only); no copies or distribution, even internally; no copies or distribution to third parties; and specific limitations on various types of use - are largely ignored by information consumers (Kalakota and Whinston, 1996). Information providers implicitly endorse this behavior by "looking the other way" in many instances.

Changes in US laws with respect to the definitions and legal treatment of electronic information, especially its transmission are being proposed. These changes are not necessarily in the best interests of consumers. For example, if digital transmission is no longer defined as "publication" but rather as "copying", then providers of the information are not required to file a copy with the Library of Congress, and are not subject to the current copying rights available under the "first sale" and "fair use" doctrines. Legal rights with regard to copies are more restrictive than publishing legal rights (Lesk, 1997).

Most experts are of the opinion that new copyright laws and practices, at least with respect to electronic information are going to have to be created as the speed of technological advancements have left the legal systems far behind (Kalakota and Whinston, 1996; Unsworth, 1997). Electronic information is easy to copy and redistribute, but it is difficult to detect a valid copy from an illegal one. New copyright laws and practices must be enforceable and therefore will probably rely on new technology to help protect copyrighted material from unauthorized access (Ching et al., 1996; Garrett and Lyons, 1993), reproduction, manipulation, distribution, and performance or display. New technology will probably also assist in the detection of copyright violations through new methods of authentication, management of copyright protected material (such as the clearinghouse model used predominantly by the music industry), and licensing techniques (Kalakota and Whinston, 1996).

Copyright laws and laws regarding intellectual property rights, key to the viability of certain types of electronic information generation, vary dramatically across international boundaries. Attitudes, biases, definitions and values with respect to these issues also tend to vary across cultures within national boundaries (Mansell, 1996).

There are several methods currently under investigation to protect intellectual property rights and copyright of electronic information. They include: (Lesk, 1997)

1. Fractional Access - this works only for very large information sources (e.g., LEXIS/NEXIS) as the value of the information source lies in the *volume* of information and the knowledge that can be gleaned from analyzing or "mining" the *entire* information source. There is no economic advantage to copying small portions of the data, and illegally copying the entire data source should be relatively easy to detect.

2. Interface Control - this solution requires a proprietary interface, implying that universal access is no longer possible as only information providers and consumers with access to the proprietary interface can produce and access the information.

3. Hardware Locks or "dongles" - this is the hardware equivalent of interface control (a software solution). Access to information is restricted to those individuals who have the proprietary access hardware (video games such as Sega or Nintendo are good examples). Furthermore, this solution has encountered consumer resistance as it is expensive and requires frequent upgrades typically not compatible with older software.

4. Information Repositories - in this solution legitimate copies are only available from one large repository or source. Any other copy is not legitimate. Some organizations exploring this approach include: InterTrust (previously EPR - Electronic Publishing Resources) and CNRI (Corporation for National Research Initiatives, currently working with the US Copyright Office) both from the US and Imprimatur (Intellectual Multimedia Property Rights Model and Terminology for Universal Reference) from Europe.

5. Steganography - this solution involves the embedding of hidden messages in the information. Each legal copy is labeled with a different identification number and illegal copies could thus be tracked back to the original purchaser (i.e., "digital water-marks"). The major problems are that the "hidden" codes or messages are easy to remove and hard to insert and while it appears to work with complex images it does not work with simple text and may not even apply to audio data.

6. Encryption - in this solution the information is encrypted (sometimes in cryp-tolopes or secret envelopes), and cannot be interpreted without the encryption key (software or hardware dependent).

7. Economic Approaches - these solutions attempt to identify ways to make it un-economical to pirate or illegally copy electronic information. Some examples of ideas include: provider page charges to reduce the per-copy price, site licenses to reduce on-site cheating, and advertiser supported publications.

8. Flickering or "Wobbling" - these solutions employ information technology that allows an information consumer to view but not capture information (Lesk, 1996).

4.4 Quality and Security Issues

There is a definite need to build credibility for on-line information. Many informa-tion consumers are of the opinion that "Information that you get for nothing over the Internet is worth nothing" (Lesk, 1997). This opinion is founded primarily on the well-know low quality of information on many netnews groups, and the lack of information quality control on personal home pages. Unfortunately none of the ex-isting searching engines have a way of evaluating electronic information quality (traditional information quality cues are typically missing) and therefore no way of sorting or filtering information by quality.

This lack of information about quality tends to encourage information consumers to limit searching to known experts (authors, WWW sites, organizations, publishers or journals, etc.) or information recommended by known experts. Some search en-gines do allow consumers to profile an expert or group of experts and request similar information (i.e., give me information identical to what Joe Einstein requests). In-formation integrity is still a problem however because electronic information is so easily modified. An information consumer is rarely guaranteed that the information of interest was truly generated or endorsed by the expert.

Currently, electronic scholarly publishing is a hotly debated topic. Much of the concern centers around the questions of the information and intellectual quality (Drabenstott, 1993; Peek and Newby, 1996). One of the quality-related concerns that can be addressed electronically is peer-review (a traditional form of quality control in academic publications). However, without peer review mechanisms, the quality, validity and viability of the electronic information in is at best, suspect.

Ginsparg's observations about the on-line e-print system (high particle physics) support the belief that high quality, valid, electronic scholarly communication and publishing is possible. "The electronic form, once posted to an archive is instantly publicized to thousands of people, so the embarrassment over incorrect results and consequent barriers to distribution, is if anything increased (not decreased). Such submissions cannot be removed but can be replaced by a note that the work has been withdrawn as incorrect, leaving a more permanent blemish than a hard copy of lim-ited distribution that is soon forgotten" (Ginsparg, 1997).

Issues of security and control are related to quality issues. Electronic information needs to address security in at least four areas (Adam et al., 1996; Kalakota and Whinston, 1996):

- *confidentiality* - protecting access to the contents of electronic information (especially sensitive electronic information, such as personal financial or health information, and strategic business or national information) from unauthorized access and distribution.
- *authenticity* - not only attributing electronic information to the correct information provider, but validating the information as original, accurate, and correctly attributed. This can be especially difficult in multi-authored and multi-versioned electronic information environment (Wiederhold, 1995). One area where authenticity is important, but it is equally important to preserve confidentiality is in electronic peer review (or a validation process of any kind where anonymity is important).
- *integrity* - protecting the contents of electronic information from unauthorized modification. This type of security involves a balance between easily enabling authorized updates and preventing unauthorized ones. The authenticity of modifications must be verifiable (also challenging in a multi-authorized and multi-versioned electronic information environment).
- *privacy* - protecting the access and usage patterns of information consumers from unauthorized access and resale. This form of security was discussed earlier.

An important challenge for the implementation of any security technique is to balance the need for security with the need for performance (access and timeliness). Authorized access and modification must not be so difficult that it is never attempted, or abandoned before completion. Information is not valuable if it is not accessible, timely or useful. Likewise the validation techniques while they must be as accurate as technically feasible, cannot be so time and resource intensive that the accessibility and timeliness of the information is compromised.

4.5 Standards

There is an especially important need for internationally accepted technical standards with respect to the representation, formatting, transmission, and protocols for electronic information. This is the only way to ensure compatibility and therefore interoperability between equipment, data, practices and procedures, all of which is necessary to achieve the goal of universal access (Kalakota and Whinston, 1996; Kessler, 1996; Paepcke et al., 1996; Tennant, 1997) and global electronic information exchange. Yet as pointed out earlier, there are many social, cultural and political barriers to overcome when developing usable and acceptable international standards, even when the benefit to all is clear.

There are several international organizations concerned with standards. The International Organization for Standardization (ISO) is involved in many different kinds of standards development, including standards that relate to electronic information (e.g., SGML). Another is the Internet Engineering Task Force (IETF) - see http://www.ietf.org - which is specifically interested in Internet architecture and smooth Internet interaction and operation (Kessler, 1996).

At a national level, while document standards such as SGML, HTML, TEI (Text Encoding Initiative), VRML (Virtual Reality Markup Language), and MARC (Machine-readable Cataloging) exist, in practice much of the electronic information interaction occurs via e-mail, anonymous ftp, Gopher, and WWW browser platforms with TeX, LaTeX, PostScript, PDF, ASCII text, Word and WordPerfect formatted documents. Most of these formats do not have existing mechanisms to distinguish the contributions of multiple authors and multiple versions, nor do they have the ability to include active links to other electronic information. Many of the formats used in practice are commercial, and therefore proprietary, which means that they are not platform independent and cannot be readily transmitted or accessed by all. Will common practice dictate what standards become accepted or will some governing body take responsibility for thoughtful and independent (unbiased) planning and design? If a set of standards is accepted and adopted, what kind of translation capability from these "legacy" formats will be provided?

5 Conclusions

There are many challenges and important issues associated with electronic information that have not yet been solved. Indeed they are in part responsible for "slowing down" the growth and expansion of electronic information in our everyday lives. But the advantages, especially the economic ones, appear to outweigh the disadvantages and most will agree that electronic information already has a major impact on our lives which will only increase as advances in information technology and information management continue.

While it is not known what the future will look like and what solutions will be brought to bear on many of the challenges and issues discussed here, one thing is known for sure. Whatever solutions are developed and implemented will never be final. Electronic information and the environment that it has created will continue to evolve. New challenges and new issues demanding new approaches will appear as new technologies become available. As electronic information changes and evolves the needs of information providers and consumers will change and evolve, perhaps in ways that we cannot yet imagine. The result is a self-perpetuating cycle in electronic information of new technology creating new challenges, situations and needs which in turn will drive the investigation, development and deployment of more new technology.

References

Adam, N. and Yesha et al., Y., "Strategic directions in electronic commerce and digital libraries: Towards a digital agora." *ACM Computing Surveys*, 28, 4, (1996), 818-835.

Atkins, D. E., "Report of the Santa Fe planning workshop on distributed knowledge work environments: Digital libraries." Supported by a Grant from the National Science Foundation (NSF-IRI-9712586) to the University of Michigan School of Information, March 9-11 1997.

Atkins, D. E., Birmingham, W. P., Durfee, E. H., Glover, E. J., Mullen, T., Rundensteiner, E. A., Soloway, E., Vidal, J. M., Wallace, R and Wellman, M.P., "Toward inquiry-based education through interacting software agents." *IEEE Computer*, 29, 5, (1996), 69-75.

Atkinson, Ross., "Library functions, scholarly communication, and the foundation of the digital library: Laying claim to the control zone." *Library Quarterly*, 66, 3, (1996).

Bishop, A. P. and Star, S. L. "Social informatics of digital library use and infrastructure." *Annual Review of Information Science and Technology*, 31, (1996), 301-401.

Ching, N., Jones, V. and Winslett, M. "Authorization in the digital library: Secure access to services across enterprise boundaries." in Proc. of the *Third Forum on Research and Technology Advances in Digital Libraries (IEEE) ADL '96 Forum*, (1996), 110-119.

Choy, D. M., Dwork, C., Lotspiech, J. B., Anderson, L. C., Boyer, S. K, Dievendorff, R., Griffin, T. D., Hoenig, B. A., Jackson, M. K., Kaka, W., McCrossin, J. M., Miller, A.M., Morris, R. J. T, and Pass, N. J. "A digital library system for periodicals distribution." in Proc. of the *Third Forum on Research and Technology Advances in Digital Libraries (IEEE) ADL '96 Forum*, (1996), 95-103.

Christel, M., Kanade, T., Mauldin, M., Reddy, R., Sirbu, M., Stevens, S. and Wactlar, H. "Informedia digital video library." *Communications of the ACM*, 38, 5, (1995).

Dowler, L., "Gateways to knowledge: A new direction for the Harvard College Library." In *Gateways to Knowledge: The role of academic libraries in teaching, learning and research*. Lawrence Dowler, editor, MIT Press, Cambridge, MA, 1997.

Drabenstott, K M., "Analytical review of the library of the future." Council on Library Resources, 1400 16th Street, N.W., Suite 510, Washington, DC 20036-2217, 1993. research assistance by Celeste M. Burman.

Feldman, S., "Advances in digital libraries '97." *Information Today*, 14, 7, (1997), 12-13.

Ferguson, C. D. and Bunge, C. A. "The shape of services to come: Values-based reference service for the largely digital library." *College and Research Libraries*, 58, 3, (1997), 252-265.

Frye, B. E. "Universities in transition: Implications for libraries." In *Gateways to Knowledge: The role of academic libraries in teaching, learning and research*. Lawrence Dowler, editor, MIT Press, Cambridge, MA, 1997.

Garrett, J. R. and Lyons, P. A. "Toward an electronic copyright management system." *Journal of the American Society for Information Science*, 44, 8, (1993), 468-473.

Ginsparg, P., "First steps toward electronic research communication." In *Gateways to Knowledge: The role of academic libraries in teaching, learning and research*. Lawrence Dowler, editor, MIT Press, Cambridge, MA, 1997.

Huser, C., Reichenberger, K., Rostek, L. and Streitz, N., "Knowledge-based editing and visualization for hypermedia encyclopedias." *Communications of the ACM*, 38, 5, (1995), 49-51.

Kalakota, R. and Whinston, A. B., *Frontiers of Electronic Commerce*. Addison-Wesley Publishing Company, Reading, MA, 1996.

Kessler, J., *Internet Digital Libraries: The International Dimension*. Artech House, Inc., Boston, MA, 1996.

Kluiters, C. C. P., "Delivering "building blocks" for digital libraries: First experiences with Elsevier electronic subscriptions and digital libraries in Europe." *Library Acquisitions: Practice and Theory*, 21, 3, (1997), 273-279.

Knoblock, C., Koller, D., Shoham, Y., Wellman, M. P., Durfee, E. H., Birmingham, W. P. and Carbonell, J., "The role of AI in digital libraries." *IEEE Expert*, 11, 3, (1996), 8-13.

Lesk, M., "Digital libraries meet electronic commerce: On-screen intellectual property." in Proc. of the *Third Forum on Research and Technology Advances in Digital Libraries (IEEE) ADL '96 Forum*, (1996), 58-64.

Lesk, M., *Practical Digital Libraries: Books, Bytes and Bucks*. Morgan Kaufmann Publishers, San Francisco, CA, 1997.

Levy, D. M. and Marshall, C. C. "Going digital: A look at assumptions underlying digital libraries." *Communications of the ACM*, 38, 5, (1995), 77-84.

Lynch, C. and Garcia-Molina, H., Interoperability, scaling and the digital libraries research agenda. A Report on the May 18-19, 1995 Information Infrastructure Technology and Applications (IITA) Digital Libraries Workshop, August 22 1995.

Mansell, R. "Designing electronic commerce." In *Communication by Design: The Politics of Information and Communication Technologies*. Robin Mansell and Roger Siverstone, editors, Oxford University Press, New York, NY, 1996.

Marchionini, G. and Maurer, H., "The roles of digital libraries in teaching and learning." *Communications of the ACM*, 38, 5, (1995), 67-75.

Odlyzko, A. M., "Tragic loss or good riddance? The impending demise of traditional scholarly journals." In *Scholarly Publishing: The Electronic Frontier*. Robin P. Peek and Gregory B. Newby, editors, The MIT Press, Cambridge, MA, 1996.

Olsen, J., "The gateway: Point of entry to the electronic library." In *Gateways to Knowledge: The role of academic libraries in teaching, learning and research*. Lawrence Dowler, editor, MIT Press, Cambridge, MA, 1997.

Paepcke, A., Cousins, S. B., Garcia-Molina, H., Hassan, S. W., Ketchpel, S. P., Roscheisen, M. and Winograd, T., "Using distributed objects for digital library interoperability." *IEEE Computer*, 29, 5, (1996), 61-68.

Peek, R. P. and Newby, G. B., *Scholarly Publishing: The Electronic Frontier*. The MIT Press, Cambridge, MA, 1996.

Prentice, A. E. "Copyright, WIPO and user interests: Achieving balance among the shareholders." *The Journal of Academic Librarianship*, 23, 4, (1997), 309-312.

Rao, R., Pedersen, J. O., Hearst, M. A., Mackinlay, J. D., Card, S. K., Masinter, L., Halvorsen, Per-Kristian and Robertson, G. G., "Richer interaction in the digital library." *Communications of the ACM*, 38, 5, (1995), 29-39.

Reddy, R. "The universal library: Intelligent agents and information on demand." In *Digital Libraries Research and Technology Advances*, Nabil R. Adam, Bharat K. Bhargava, Milton Halem, and Yelena Yesha, editors, Berlin, Germany, May 15-17, 1995 (1996). Advances in Digital Libraries Forum, Springer-Verlag. ADL '95 Forum at McLean, Virginia, USA, selected papers.

Rockwell, R. C. "The concept of the gateway library: A view from the periphery." In *Gateways to Knowledge: The role of academic libraries in teaching, learning and research*. Lawrence Dowler, editor, MIT Press, Cambridge, MA, 1997.

Rush, J. E., "Foreword." In *Scholarly Publishing: The Electronic Frontier*. Robin P. Peek and Gregory B. Newby, editors, The MIT Press, Cambridge, MA, 1996.

Samuelson, P., "Copyright and digital libraries." *Communications of the ACM*, 38, 5, (1995), 15-21 and 110.

Saracevic, T. and Kantor, P. B., "Studying the value of library and information services. Part I. Establishing a theoretical framework." *Journal of the American Society for Information Science*, 48, 6, (1997), 527-542.

Saracevic, T. and Kantor, P. B. "Studying the value of library and information services. Part II. Methodology and taxonomy." *Journal of the American Society for Information Science*, 48, 6, (1997), 543-563.

Schatz, B. and Chen, H., "Building large-scale digital libraries." *IEEE Computer*, 29, 5, (1996), 22-26.

Schatz, B., Mischo, W. H., Cole, T. W., Hardin, J. B., Bishop, A. P. and Chen, H., "Federating diverse collections of scientific literature." *IEEE Computer*, 29, 5, (1996), 28-36.

Smith, T. R., "A digital library for geographically referenced materials." *IEEE Computer*, 29, 5, (1996), 54-.

Tennant, R., "The grand challenges." *Library Journal*, 122, 20, (1997), 31-33.

Unsworth, J., "Some effects of advanced technology on research in the humanities." In *Gateways to Knowledge: The role of academic libraries in teaching, learning and research*. Lawrence Dowler, editor, MIT Press, Cambridge, MA, 1997.

Wactlar, H. D., Kanade, T., Smith, M. A. and Stevens, S. M. "Intelligent access to digital video: Informedia project." *IEEE Computer*, 29, 5, (1996), 46-52.

Wiederhold, G., "Digital libraries, value and productivity." *Communications of the ACM*, 38, 5, (1995), 85-96.

Wilensky, R., "Toward work-centered digital information services." *IEEE Computer*, 29, 5, (1996), 37-44.

Witten, I. H., Moffat, A. and Bell, T. C., "Compression and full-text indexing for digital libraries." In *Digital Libraries: Current Issues*. Bharat K. Bhargava Nabil R. Adam and Yelena Yesha, editors, Springer-Verlag, New York, NY, 1994. Digital Libraries Workshop DL 04, Newark, NJ, May 19-20, 1994, selected papers.

CHAPTER 17

Intelligent Software Agents for Electronic Commerce

Kristin M. Tolle and Hsinchun Chen

Management Information Systems Department, University of Arizona, Tucson, AZ 85721,
ktolle@bpa.arizona.edu; hchen@bpa.arizona.edu

This chapter is a survey of intelligent software agents in general and more specifically electronic commerce agents (ECAs). We begin with basic definitions and discuss the history and economic reasoning motivating the development of software agents. This is followed by a description of agent characteristics and a taxonomy showing where ECAs fit into the landscape of software agent research. How agents accomplish their goal seeking is described along with the learning and action mechanisms. Specific examples of electronic agents are given along with the economic and ethical impacts they are currently having on the marketplace and the potential impacts they may have in the future.

Keywords: Electronic Commerce Agents; Intelligent Software Agents; Economic Impacts of Agents; Internet Consumer Behavior

1 Introduction

Electronic commerce (EC) and software agents are two of the hottest fields of research in information science. As the Internet is rapidly becomes a popular marketplace for consumers and sellers of goods and services, combining these two research areas offers lucrative opportunities both for businesses wishing to conduct transactions over the World Wide Web (WWW) and for developers of tools to facilitate this trend.

The focus in this chapter will be on software agents specifically designed for electronic commerce activities. We will briefly describe the history of agent research in general, defining characteristics of agents, and will touch on the different types of agents. Following this introduction we will describe the learning and action mechanisms that make it possible for agents to perform tasks. Finally, we will describe the issues associated with the deployment of electronic commerce agents (ECAs).

Readers interested in more detailed coverage of the topics described in this chapter are invited to investigate the following web sites and the documents they reference: University of Maryland's AgentWeb site http://www.cs.um bc.edu/agents and MIT Media Lab's software Agent Group http://agents.www.media.mit.edu/gro ups/agents.

2 What Are Software Agents?

It can be argued that there are nearly as many definitions of what an agent is as there are researchers and developers in the field—perhaps more. Some definitions give broad characterizations, while others carefully detail what their authors perceive to be the "best" definition of an agent. The examples that follow define a specific type of agent with which this chapter is concerned—those typically referred to as "intelligent" or "autonomous" software agents.

An IBM white paper found at http://www.networking.ibm.com/iag/iag wp1.html defines a software agent as:

> *"An Intelligent agent is software that assists people and acts on their behalf. Intelligent agents work by allowing people to delegate work that they could have done, to the agent software. Agents can, just as assistants can, automate repetitive tasks, remember things you forgot, intelligently summarize complex data, learn from you, and even make recommendations to you."*

Hayes-Roth's description found in (Hayes-Roth, 1995) includes the temporal aspect in defining intelligent agents:

> *"Intelligent agents continuously perform three functions: perception of dynamic conditions in the environment; action to affect conditions in the environment; and reasoning to interpret perceptions, solve problems, draw inferences, and determine actions."*

From these descriptions it is apparent that agents are assistive computer applications designed to perform a set of tasks for their users. Agents operate in a variety of ways and are employed in a diverse set of domains. Some can learn how to accomplish tasks for the user by interfacing directly, either through direct programming manually, while others learn by employing artificial intelligence (AI) techniques to observe users' actions and attempt to replicate them. Some agents are stand-alone single applications designed for a specific purpose, while others are highly interactive with users and other agents in order to accomplish their goal-seeking activities. Key characteristics and learning methods are described in more detail later in this chapter.

2.1 Agent History

The beginnings of agent research can be traced back to 1977 during the early studies in distributed artificial intelligence (DAI). Carl Hewitt described his concurrent actor model (Hewitt, 1997) as a computation agent that has a mail address and a behavior. Actors communicate with each other via message passing, carrying out their actions concurrently. In 1986, Marvin Minsky gave a similar description in his book *The Society of Mind* where he described societies of goal seeking agents. Many of the questions he asked about how agents should interact, learn, and carry out tasks (Minsky, 1986) later became a model for researchers in the creation of intelligent agents.

The study of intelligent agents began around 1990 when people such as Alan Kay (Kay, 1990) and Nicholas Negroponte (Negroponte, 1990) proposed that human computer interfaces needed to be drastically changed to evolve into devices that could interact with users in a more human-like manner. Since that time a great deal of the research in this area has been fostered by the MIT Media Lab, Cambridge, Massachusetts. Researchers at MIT are making great contributions to a field of study known as "behavior-based" agents. Behavior-based is a term used to describe an agent which attains most or all of the key characteristics of an intelligent, autonomous agent.

2.2 Why Are Agents Important?

Agents are typically employed to perform tasks that are too difficult or mundane for their human counterparts (Hayes-Roth, 1995). Much of intelligent agent research is centered around the fact that more and more "untrained consumers" are using computers and interfacing with the World Wide Web (WWW) and thus require more efficient, easier, user-friendly ways to navigate and do business in this dynamic digital world (Foner, 1995). This is especially true due to the myriad problems being caused by the increasing amount of online information available on the WWW (Chen et al., 1998). Intelligent agents have the potential to hide the technical details while providing a high level of access to "newbies" or novice users. This potential capability is often a driving force behind the business strategies for the development of many of the electronic commerce shopping agents.

Software agents are big business. Many corporations are touting the inclusion of agent technology in their software applications. Large firms such as IBM, Microsoft, HP, Sun, Oracle, Apple, Lotus, and AT&T have either gone on record as researching agent usage or announced the inclusion of agents in their products. Most notably, Sun and IBM offer workbench tools that allow for easy incorporation of agents into Java applications. Academicians are also capitalizing on the popularity of software agents with such noted researchers as MIT Media Labs' Pattie Maes and University of Washington Computer Science professors Daniel Weld and Oren Etzioni have started venture-backed companies Agents, Inc. and NETbot respectively.

How big is the agent market? It has been predicted that in the next 5 to 10 years most new information technology development will be affected and many consumer products will contain embedded agent-based systems (Guilfoyle, 1995). The estimated market for agent software and products for the year 2000 is 3.9 billion, in contrast to the estimated 476 million for 1995. Specifically related to electronic commerce, in 1996 more than half of US Internet users purchased merchandise online, and sales totaled 500 million US dollars (Hamilton, 1997). The author of this article called these figures "much understated" because they failed to include users who consulted the Internet before purchasing offline.

2.3 Characteristics of an Intelligent Agent

Agent researchers often attribute very humanistic characteristics to intelligent agents. Key characteristics listed below are similar to those found in (Weld and Etzioni, 1995) as well as many other papers.

Autonomy: An intelligent agent must be able to act independently of the user. It should sense changes in its perceived environment and be able to take necessary actions to complete the goals that have been collaboratively contracted between the agent and the user. To classified as autonomous an agent must be:

- Goal-oriented: accept user requests and be responsible for deciding how and where to satisfy those requests.
- Collaborative: interact with users to request clarification; may modify or refuse to satisfy certain requests.
- Flexible: have the ability to choose which actions to invoke and in what sequence, depending on the state of its external environment.
- Self-starting: be active not only when it is invoked by the user, but also sense changes in the environment and determine when to take which action.

Personalizable/Adaptability: An intelligent agent must be able to work within an agreed upon framework to accomplish tasks specific to a particular user. It must have the ability to learn a user's preferences and then act accordingly on behalf of the user. This learning can be accomplished either by the agent being manually programmed by the user or by "watching over the user's shoulder." The latter method employs machine learning techniques in order to discover how the user performs some task. After the agent is "trained" it can then gradually take over accomplishing the task for the user (Foner, 1995).

Even if the same agent software is employed at two different locations, over time each agent should build and refer back to information it has gathered from its specific user. By doing so, agents which were identical at the onset will often react differently to a given situation once they are "trained" to perform tasks which match a particular user's preferences (Maes, 1995).

Communication Ability/Mobility/Discourse: Intelligent agents should have the ability to communicate easily with users and other agents across different system architectures and platforms. This ability is critical in order for the agent to develop a good understanding of its user and the environment in which it must operate. Being able to interact with other agents of a similar nature enhances the agent's knowledge acquisition capability by providing it with multiple sources of information for the development of its knowledge base. This assists in overcoming the "slow learning curve" typically associated with agents that are trained through repetitive user interaction.

Risk and Trust: The agent must perform with a level of ability that results in the user trusting it to act on his/her behalf. In order for the user to become comfortable with delegating duties to an agent, even for simple, non-critical tasks, there must be confidence that the agent will act as expected in most situations. Without trust the user is unlikely to use an agent.

Temporal Continuity: The agent must remain active over extended periods without user interaction. For some agents, time not spent carrying out user tasks is spent analyzing memory and determining correlations between features and actions taken (Maes, 1994). Some action triggering events often occur when the user is not directly interfacing with the agent. The agent can meet user needs more effectively, and with better perceived performance, by handling tasks as they are presented, rather than delaying action until is it invoked by the user.

Domain/Expectations: Interaction between users and agents are more successful if expectations are clearly defined. In dynamic and unpredictable environments, which is often the case in real-world applications, users should expect that the agent will, at least occasionally, pursue an incorrect course of action--even after an extensive training period. However, an agent should be expected to obtain a reasonably effective level of performance within a specific domain.

Cooperation: The user and the agent should be able to communicate to construct a contract specifying the tasks to be performed. This implies that on-going "conversations" will result in a collaborative agreement about tasks, goals, and actions the agent is to perform. Intelligent agents respond to user stimuli as peers, making suggestions and requesting additional information. This type of cooperation enables an agent to perform well in highly dynamic environments.

2.4 Types of Agents

It is impossible to list all the agents currently available, particularly because new agents are surfacing all the time. Figure 1 is an extension of a model found in (Franklin and Graesser, 1996) and attempts to show graphically show the major categories of agent development and domains. As the diagram depicts, the domains of agent deployment are diverse.

Artificial Life has been placed as a sub-family under Entertainment Agents as that is the classification it is given by its creators along with **knowbots** and **MUDs**. Artificial Life agents are "behavior-based" agents that attempt to synthesize biological life forms. They are often employed as interactive games as they are in the demos available from the Artificial Life homepage http://gracco.irmkant.rm.cnr.it/lui gi/lupa_algames.html. Knowbots are agents that occupy multi-user dimension (MUDs) game spaces. They offer assistance to game players in the MUD and often employ natural language processing techniques to interpret and respond to user dialogues.

Much recent agent research deals with a more lucrative category, Task Specific Agents. Task or Domain Specific Agents shown in Figure 1 have four sub-families: Personal Assistant or Shopping Agents, Information/Internet Retrieval, Education, and Optimization or System Administration Agents.

Personal Assistants and **Shopping Agents** generally operate in a small specific domain of a user's computing environment. Their purpose is to make users' computing time more efficient. Examples of this type of agents are e-mail assistants that sort, and in some cases, delete, e-mail messages or data categorization agents, which try to categorize large amounts of information into manageable chunks. We will discuss in more detail task-specific agents designed to be personal shoppers who assist consumers in purchasing products electronically over the WWW and electronic meeting facilitation agents which assist in the categorization of textual information.

Information Retrieval (IR) and **Internet Agents** are search engines which typically assist users in locating information on local Intranets, information databanks, and the WWW. Most of these agents have a single common entry point for all users and therefore cannot be customized. We will discuss an agent that is designed to locate information on Intranets and Internet more precisely than typical implementations of Internet agents.

Education Agents interact with users in a training capacity. Most of them are targeted to interact with children and teach specific topics, such as spelling, in a game-like atmosphere.

Optimization/Systems Administration Agents are designed to do the work of computer systems operators. For instance, they are able to determine where in a multi-host system applications will run most efficiently or what location of data files will result in the best data access times. Since computing environments are usually dynamic relative to some patterns of peak computing times, these agents are able to interact with the host systems more efficiently than humans to make decisions that optimize system performance (Chavez et al., 1997). A common implementation of an agent's decision-making strategy is based on a "bidding" or marketplace model.

The final sub-family under software agents, which will not be covered in this chapter, is viruses.

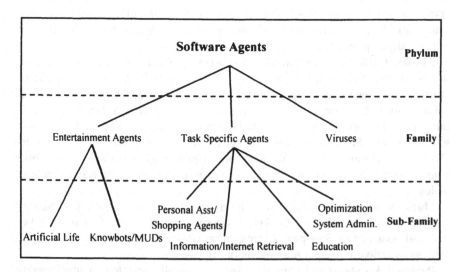

Fig. 1. A taxonomy of software agents

3 How Agents Perform Goal Seeking Behavior

The two major components of an individual agent are the way in which it learns and the way in which it carries out its tasks. Learning mechanisms define an agent's ability to gain and retain information about a particular user. Many agents contain no learning component--they simply act on a predefined set of programmed rules, which are updated as necessary by the developers. Agents of this type cannot be individualized to a particular user. However, agent research has been evolving and many agents contain some capacity for learning that makes them individualizable and deployable in dynamic environments such as the Internet.

Action mechanisms define how agents accomplish tasks. Sometimes an agent is a complete system. More frequently, the agent is made of many separate components, often referred to as specialized agents, which may have conflicting goals. We next discuss different types of learning and action mechanisms.

3.1 Learning Mechanisms

There are three methods of developing agents: user programmed, knowledge-based approaches, and machine learning approaches (Maes, 1994). Although the last of these is the generally accepted method for creating an autonomous agent, the others merit mentioning because they can be used in conjunction with machine learning approaches to improve the initial success of an intelligent agent.

End-User Programmed: This method requires the user to program the agent to perform required tasks. The user sets up the foundations by which the agents makes decisions and carries out tasks. This method can work well for static environments, but has not been as viable in more dynamic environments.

- Advantage: User will more readily trust the agent to act independently. The user can be certain of the action an agent will take, given a particular situation.
- Disadvantage: Creating and maintaining the agent is too difficult for most users. There is no method by which an agent learns or develops its perceptions about the environment, thus the user must continuously revise the agent's decision-making parameters in order for it to operate in dynamic environments.

Knowledge-Based: Another name for a knowledge-based agent is an expert system. A knowledge-based agent typically exists in a highly domain-specific field. A software engineer provides the agent with a large set of background knowledge about the user and the environment within which the agent will operate. This type of implementation is common for intelligent user interfaces such as web browsers.

- Advantage: Provides a homogeneous interface for all users.
- Disadvantages: Takes a lot of domain specific knowledge. It difficult for software engineers to implement and maintain. There is no custom interface which is spe-

cific to the user and the user's preferences are forgotten as soon as the application closes.

Machine Learning: Machine learning implies that the agent will adapt and learn through interaction with a user.

- Advantages: The user builds a relationship with the agent through training, thereby reducing some of the issues surrounding competence and trust. It is much easier for software engineers and end users to implement a machine learning approach. The agent continues to improve its performance over time without the need for additions to its knowledge base.
- Disadvantages: Extensive repetitive behavior is required to train the agent.

Combination Approaches: Intelligent agents must have some minimum background knowledge to perform initially. Machine learning can be combined with either knowledge-based or user developed approaches in order to achieve better performance at the onset. This essentially provides the advantages of the methods above, while reducing or removing many of the disadvantages.

3.2 Machine Learning Approaches

There are four methods by which an agent can learn and improve its behavior over time (Maes, 1995): Observing and imitating the user, receiving positive and negative feedback, receiving explicit instructions, and asking other agents for advice.

Observing and imitating the user: Observing the user means that the agent monitors the user's activities and then creates rules which are stored in a database and referenced by the agent. This database is also referred to as an agent's knowledge base. The information contained within the database is highly dynamic.

Receiving positive and negative feedback from the user: Receiving positive and negative feedback is an indirect method by which an agent learns. In this case, an agent may make some recommendation about what it thinks the user will do. If the user positively reinforces the agent by agreeing with the agent's chosen action, the agent gives the weight of the rule which resulted in reaching the proper conclusion a higher weighted value. If the user selects another alternative, the agent will then lower the weight of that rule. These weights are stored along with the rules in a database.

Receiving explicit instructions from the user: Explicit instructions are received when an agent and a user go through a training set which is set up for the purpose of teaching the agent about the user's preferences.

Asking other agents for advice: This learning method involves agent collaboration (Chen et al., 1996). The agent can interface with other agents that are similar in nature and ask their advice given a specific event. This usually occurs either when an inexperienced agent is unable to immediately determine what action should be taken or when an agent initiates exploratory communication with fellow agents for certain classes of events.

3.3 Action Mechanisms

Given a task, an agent will choose and act on the basis of:

- The perceived environment: before acting the agent makes an assessment of the current situation in the user's environment.
- The internal needs of the agent: The goal the agent is to act upon is reviewed.
- The agent's recent history: The situation is compared with the database of information the agent has amassed, and the knowledge is applied to the situation (Maes, 1994).

As previously mentioned, an agent relies on a knowledge base of information made up of weighted sentences which enable the agent to make judgments about possible actions. Each sentence is evaluated and given a point estimate or score. The sum of the differences for all weighted sentences is used to suggest a course of action. A confidence level is generated based on the proximity of neighbors, the closest neighbor's recommended course of action, and previously memorized examples of similar situations. Depending on the resulting confidence level, a percentage score from 0 to 1, the agent will act independently, suggest a course of action, or ask the user for advice.

In many behavior-based applications, user-controlled threshold levels are allowed to be set. If the confidence level falls within the "do it" threshold the agent will act on the users behalf autonomously. If the confidence level is below the "do it" threshold, but above the "tell me" threshold, the agent will suggest a course of action, but not take the action without the users approval. If the confidence level is below the "tell me" threshold, the agent is unsure how to proceed and requires the user to "show" it the correct course of action. As the user's confidence in the agent increases, the threshold can be changed to a level at which the agent rarely has to ask the user for advice on how to act, only in unusual or unique situations.

Communication with other agents is also important. Cooperation among agents fosters "societies" of agents (Minsky, 1986), which collaborate to meet user goals. Collaborative implementations focus on the interaction between agents with potentially conflicting goals, communication between agents, and decomposition and distribution of tasks. It is this interaction rather than an individual effort which enables the agent system as a whole to meet user needs. Agents can either exist in functional hierarchies to accomplish heterogeneous modular tasks or collaborate on tasks in a homogeneous way (Edmonds et al., 1994). More collaborative implementations allow for the sharing of information between agents, which further facilitates the learning process.

4 Electronic Commerce Agents

Electronic Commerce Agents (ECAs) often incorporate a financial or business component into the agent architecture. Either they are directly responsible for the exchange of funds over the Internet (for example an agent designed to pay remittances electronically) or they are implemented to generate or locate information which is necessary to the user or business which "employs" them. Information accessibility is becoming of particular importance in today's dynamic marketplace--providing support and success to firms which make investments in technology to support the gathering and assimilation of both internal and external information available to the firm.

Electronic commerce of the future is described as a "massive economy of online services linked together so that businesses routinely outsource functions such as fulfillment and shipping" (Hamilton, 1997). Distributors will "go virtual" by outsourcing physical warehousing and movement of goods. As we move from local to global economies, ECAs will become increasingly important to users and businesses.

4.1 ECA Characteristics and Examples

The most commonly available implementation of ECAs to the general public are shopping agents, also known as "metashoppers." We will discuss in more detail two shopping agents of varying degrees of complexity and capability which allow for purchasing products over the Internet: Jango and FireFly. An information gathering agent, the Itsy Bitsy Spider, is an example of an information generation agent-one which provides better precision in the locating of information than traditional search spiders.

Jango (http://jango.excite.com/index.dcg) from NETbot, Inc., is a shopping agent created by agent researchers Daniel Weld and Oren Etzioni. Jango is deployed under the Internet search engine Excite (http://www.excite.com/) as a shopping service. Similar to Internet and IR agent applications, Jango has a common user interface, rather than a customizable one. It has no built in capacity to store information about a user's searching preferences. Each time the user visits the site, it is as if it were the first time. Jango searches Internet web sites to find different sources for items the consumer may be interested in purchasing. Like a regular search engine, Jango searches based on the information entered by a user and returns all possible sources for requested items displaying all possible alternatives. Consumers must visit the Internet suppliers' sites in order to actually purchase products.

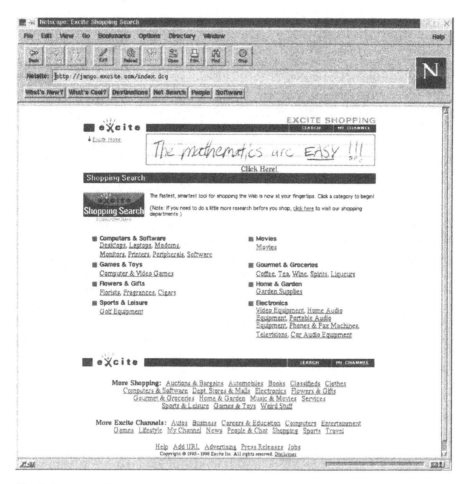

Fig. 2. Jango metashopper in excite

One of Jango's strengths is that it can search for a wide variety of products from more expensive items such as automobiles, furniture, and golf clubs to incidental items such as videos, spirits, and groceries. It has fast response time, but it may not perform an exhaustive search. Users are not given the opportunity to specifically select supplier sites. Another weakness is the common user interface. Jango retains no information about a consumer's preferences. However, this type of implementation matches the user search strategies of most Internet search engines such as Excite. Also, since it only reports the source and pricing for the goods and services the consumer is interested in, it relies on the supplier's source site to handle the purchasing aspect. This is a much easier strategy to implement as it avoids the necessity of dealing with electronic commerce issues such as security.

Fig. 3. Firefly from Agents, Inc.

Firefly from Agents, Inc. is a more sophisticated type of shopping agent. Interestingly, unlike the newly available Jango, it was one of the first shopping agents available on the WWW (commercially available circa 1996). Unlike Jango, Firefly has its own site instead of being embedded in a larger environment and users are required to provide a login name and password, since Firefly retains user information. Unlike other web sites which subsist on targeted advertising, Firefly doesn't require the user to fill out demographic questionnaires. Instead Firefly "learns" the preferences of the user through interaction and stores them for future visits. The more the user interacts with its agent, the better the system gets at predicting the user's preferences.

Firefly's main purpose is to match consumers with music they might be interested in purchasing (although for a short period, it also offered video cassettes). Users train the agent by ranking music they have previously listened to on a scale of 1 to 7.

The agent tracks the rankings along with genre preferences of a particular user. After a brief training period, the agent can predict and recommend other similar music to the user and can even predict his/her ranking of a music selection not previously encountered, by comparing the ratings and music tastes of the user to those of other users with similar musical tastes.

The greatest advantage of Firefly is that it remembers each individual user. Each time a user logs in and interacts with the agent, Firefly updates its information. Therefore, the agent can adjust when a user's purchasing preferences change. Update occurs automatically, unseen to the user. Agents, Inc. and its advertisers reach customers by using the psychographic profile of the user maintained by the agent. Specifically targeted advertisements can be sent to the user's screen--an advantage that common user interfaces do not possess.

A disadvantage is that the agent must be trained and thus requires periodic interaction in order to remain helpful. However, this disadvantage is outweighed by the marketing potential. A more serious disadvantage is the limited product range--music CDs and tapes. However, the links to other interesting shopping sites and the fact that many users log in simply to converse with other users and/or enjoy the novelty of the agent's musical suggestions overrides this disadvantage. Thousands of people visit Firefly's site daily and while they visit the site they are shown advertisements which are likely to be of interest to them.

The Itsy Bitsy Spider (http://ai.bpa.arizona.edu/) from the AI Lab at the University of Arizona is an Internet/Intranet information retrieval agent. The agent's main purpose is to combat the information overload problem occurring on the Internet. The need for such an agent becomes apparent when simple queries to Internet search engines result in thousands of hits, most of which are only marginally relevant.

Instead of focusing on standard keyword searching like most Internet agents and web crawlers, the Itsy Bitsy Spider (IBS) attempts to match entire pages. The user inputs the URL of a starting page(s) which represents the type of information the user is seeking. Through the user specified criteria, the agent searches for pages on the Internet or a local Intranet which are most similar to the starting page(s) and reports the results back to the user.

The page matching is a fairly simple concept which has dramatic results in the precision of retrieved pages. The agent converts the starting page(s) into a vector of search terms. Pages located on the Web which have a higher number of co-occurring terms with the starting page are selected as matches. Users can specify the number of pages to retrieve, the number of levels to search from the original page and/or the length of search time.

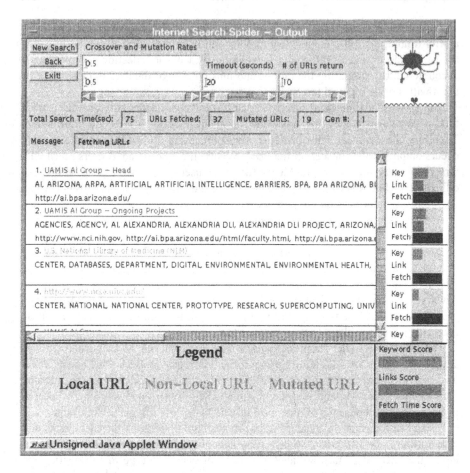

Fig. 4. The Itsy Bitsy Spider

The greatest advantage of IBS is the ability to retrieve a concise number of highly relevant URLs. The accuracy is driven by support for an entire textual vector of search terms (all terms that appear in the starting page). A disadvantage is that the tool is slower than other search engines. However, by using the agent's Java interface, users can see interim results instead of waiting for the entire search to complete before being able to look at retrieved items. Also, users have control over the waiting period by being able to specify search-time duration and the number of levels to search. As with Jango, IBS does not have the ability to conform to a particular user's requirements. All users rely on the same interface to enter query information.

These examples represent only a few of the ECAs available on the World Wide Web. Among the list of newly available metashoppers are Roboshopper (http://www.roboshopper.com) and Shopping Explorer (http://shoppingexplorer.com). Both provide features similar to Jango's. They query online stores for specific products in parallel and then return the results in a list that allows the user to choose which stores to shop. Other search engines, such as Yahoo, are also rumored to be investigating the implementation of metashoppers (Andrews, 1997).

4.2 Role of ECAs

Agents are designed to engage and help all types of end users (Minsky, 1986). They are not designed as replacements, but rather counterparts or helpmates to users in a complex and dynamic world.

An interesting paper by Chen et al. (Chen et al., 1996), describes one of the few comparisons of agents and their human counterparts. It was discovered that an agent was less precise in categorizing concepts generated during a GroupSystems® electronic meeting. However, the agent was five times faster than its human counterpart.

The rigorous study compared the performances of 12 professional meeting facilitators to those of a meeting categorization agent for four different electronic meeting sessions. The conclusion was that it was most effective to combine use of the agent and a human counterpart to create meeting categories more rapidly. Employing the agent as a first cut categorizer followed by refinement by a human facilitator reduced the categorization time and resulted in excellent precision.

Previous research has shown that systems designed to replace humans in a specific domain (usually in reference to expert systems) have experienced low adoption rates (Carroll, 1987), but users appear to be more receptive to agents because they are perceived to reduce workload by assisting them in accomplishment of tasks. Instead of purporting to be human replacements, as did the expert systems of the past, agents recently are gaining research support and usage as user enhancements.

5 Caveats

5.1 Ethics and Legal Issues

Who should have access to the data maintained and updated by an intelligent agent? Agents will often interface with similar agents to improve their overall performance. It is conceivable that an agent seeking to collect information about users could represent itself to the user's agent as a similar agent just looking for assistance (Maes, 1995).

Is there a difference between companies that maintain and sell databases of their customers' addresses and buying preferences and those that create and store user's e-mail addresses and psychographic profiles so advertisers can better target their customers? These types of applications and how the information they generate is used are described in more detail in (Flynn, 1996; Glave, 1996). No legal precedent has been set on this issue. However, companies like Agents Inc. have made it their policy to protect their users' privacy. In a recent article in IEEE expert, Vice President Yezdi Lashkari stated, "The user is the owner of private data. We're simply the custodian" (Hedberg, 1996).

Security issues regarding the Internet are a pervasive and well publicized problem. Hackers stealing credit card numbers and students breaking Internet security codes have filled the headlines ever since the introduction of the WWW. Convincing consumers that their credit information is secure is something that must occur before Internet commerce moves from the early-adopter stage to a main stream activity. With the standardization of communication languages between Internet agents comes the possibility of agents being created to gather information surreptitiously.

Larry Foner plainly states in (Foner, 1995) that "The sometimes conflicting goals of utility and privacy can be reconciled if the system is designed from the beginning to protect privacy while enabling distributed, shared computation." He suggests we motivate the development of a toolkit for agents which incorporates privacy. Many of the new Java toolkits claim to have this ability without compromising inter-agent communication (Krulwich, 1997; Lange, 1996). Prominence of this issue has been driven by companies conducting electronic commerce and electronic data interchange over the Internet.

5.2 Economic Issues

People often associate the ability of an ECA's ability to "shop around" with the possibility of paying a lower price. It is assumed that since users can look at a variety of sources before they buy and can ultimately choose the vendor with the lowest price that EC agents can create lower overall prices for goods purchased over the Internet. However, there have been documented cases in which Internet buyers may actually have paid more for an item than a non-Internet purchaser.

Since agents (and unassisted Internet shoppers) often rely on pricing available on the web, they are not aware that an unadvertised lower price for the same item may exist off the Internet. Lee (Lee, 1998) reported that car buyers in Japan actually paid more for cars they purchased over the Internet than the average Japanese car buyer. In this case, however, the cars had to pass an inspection to be considered for auction, making them of potentially higher quality than cars purchased via other methods. There are also issues associated with being unable to look at an item, or in the case of the Japanese car market, test drive an item to make sure it meets the user's needs and that it is not defective in some way.

Many companies are investigating the incorporation of billing into their web sites (Roberts, 1998). As these types of sites move from the planning stages into reality consumers will be able to have their agents take care of the mundane task of paying bills. Paying bills over the Internet offers advantages to consumers and and billers alike. Consumers will no longer have to mail in payments, saving postal costs. Billers will be able to "close the payment loop" between the consumer and the banking industry. However, consumers must be convinced of the security of payments made in this manner before they move from the early-adopter stage to routine consumer behavior. Lack of infrastructure, along with virtually nonexistent legal and regulatory frameworks, have forced businesses and users to be cautious in the capitalization of electronic commerce on the Internet (Hamilton, 1997).

5.3 Social Impacts

With the amount of development underway in the field of software agents and the increased focus on agents by academic institutions and industry, it is clear that agents will have a strong impact on the way that we use and will use software in the future (Tolle, 1997). By definition, an agent's purpose is to make computer use easier. Interfaces are becoming more intuitive, customizable, and user-friendly. Reducing the complexity of using computers is opening the door to a new class of computer users. The statement "Grandma is online" is no longer a funny story, but an example of the accessibility offered by the new agent interfaces to the WWW.

References

Andrews, W., "Shopping Agents: Promising Tool or Fad?." *WebWeek*, 3,33, (1997), 12-14.

Carroll, B., "Artificial Intelligence: Expert Systems for Clinical Diagnosis: Are They Worth the Effort?." *Behavior Science*, 32, (1987), 274-292.

Chavez, A, Moukas, A.G. and Maes, P., "Challenger: A Multi-Agent System for Distributed Resource Allocation," from *International Conference on Autonomous Agents*. Marina Del Ray, California, (1997).

Chen, H., Chung, Y., Ramsey, M. and Yang,C.C., "An Intelligent Personal Spider (Agent)for Dynamic Internet/Intranet Searching." *forthcoming in Decision Support Systems,* (1998).

Chen, H., Houston, A., Yen J. and Nunamaker, J., "Toward Intelligent Meeting Agents." *IEEE Computer*, 29,8,(1996), 62-70.

Edmonds, E., Candy, L., Jones, R. and Soufi, B., "Support for Collaborative Design: Agents and Emergence." *Communications of the ACM*, 37,7,(1994),41--47.

Flynn, L.J., "Agents Track the Once and Future Consumer." *The New York Times,* (1996).

Foner, L., "Clustering and Information Sharing in an Ecology of Cooperating Agents or How to Gossip without Spilling the Beans," from Proceedings of the *1995 Conference on Computers,Freedom, and Privacy* (1995).

Franklin, S and Graesser, A., "Is it an Agent, or just a Program?: A Taxonomy for Autonomous Agents." from Proceedings of the *Third International Workshop of Agent Theories, Architectures, and Languages*. Springer-Verlag,(1996).

Glave, J., "AI Technology Watches What You Read, Sells Accordingly." *Wired News,* (1996).

Guilfoyle, C., "Vendors of Agent Technology," from *UNICOM Seminar on Intelligent Agents and their Business Application*. London., (1995), 135-142.

Hamilton, S., "E-Commerce for the 21st Century." *IEEE Computer*, 30,5, (1997), 44-47.

Hayes-Roth, B., "An Architecture for Adaptive Intelligent Systems." *Artificial Intelligence: Special Issue on Agents and Interactivity*, (1995), 72.

Hedberg, S., "Agents for sale: first wave of intelligent agents go commercial." *IEEE Expert*, 11,6,(1996), 16-19.

Hewitt, C., "Viewing Control Structures as Patterns of Passing Messages." *Artificial Intelligence*, 8,3,(1997), 323-364.

Kay, A., *The Art of Human-Computer Interface Design*, Addison-Wesley. Chap. User Interface: A Personal View, (1990), 191-207.

Krulwich, B., "Automating the Internet: Agents as User Surrogates." *IEEE Computing*, 1,4,(1997), 34-38.

Lange, D. B., *Java Agent Transfer and Communication Interface "(J-ATCI)"*. Technical report. IBM Tokyo, (1996).

Lee, H. G., "Do Electronic Marketplaces Lower the Price of Goods?." *Communications of the ACM*, 41,1,(1998), 73-80.

Maes, P., "Agents that Reduce Work and Information Overload." *Communications of the ACM (CACM)*, 37,7,(1994), 31-40.

Maes, P., "Artificial Life Meets Entertainment: Lifelike Autonomous Agents." *Communications of the ACM, Special Issue on New Horizons of Commercial and Industrial AI*, 38,11,(1995).

Minsky, M., *The Society of Mind.* Simon and Schuster. New York, 1986.

Negroponte, N., *The Art of Human-Computer Interface Design*, Addison-Wesley. Chap. The Noticeable Difference, (1990), 245-246.

Roberts, W., "Billers Pave Way for Web Payments, but Consumers are Leery." *WebWeek*, 4,2,(1998), 16-17.

Tolle, K. M., "Intelligent Agents: Definitions, Designations, and Development," *Proceedings for the Sixth Intl. Conference on Information Systems Development*, ed. Plenum Press, New York. (1997), 275-290.

Weld, D and Etzioni, O., "Intelligent Agents on the Internet: Fact, Fiction and Forecast." *IEEE Expert*, 10,4,(1995), 44-49.

Part V
Business-To-Business Electronic Commerce

CHAPTER 18
Electronic Catalogs in the Web-Based Business-to-Business Procurement Process

John P. Baron[1], Michael J. Shaw[2], and Andrew D. Bailey, Jr.[3]

[1]Department of Business Administration, University of Illinois at Urbana-Champaign, Urbana, IL, USA, j-baron1@uiuc.edu

[2]Department of Business Administration, and Beckman Institute for Advanced Science & Technology, University of Illinois at Urbana-Champaign, Urbana, Illinois, USA, m-shaw2@uiuc.edu

[3]Department of Accounting, University of Illinois at Urbana-Champaign, IL, USA, jabaile@uiuc.edu

---

Electronic catalogs [e-Catalogs] are becoming the gateway to Electronic Commerce on the Internet. Most of the research and applications to date have centered on supplier based catalogs. There are at least as many business buyers as there are suppliers and yet little information is available to these buyers concerning the benefits, costs, and managerial considerations associated with the use of e-Catalogs. We examine e-Catalog issues from the business buyer's viewpoint. We concentrate particularly, on the use of web-based supplier catalogs in the management of procurement transactions. After reviewing the Web-based e-Catalog system design issues, we consider tangible and intangible aspects of cost/benefit relationships when adopting a Web-based procurement/purchasing system [WBPS]. There are some obvious tangible and intangible benefits. However, when adopting a WBPS, it is important for management to address the organizational issues very early on to assure organizational buy-in. We consider the various managerial issues that need to be addressed to assure a successful implementation.

Keywords: Electronic Catalogs; Business-to-Business; Procurement; MRO; Indirect Purchasing

---

1 Introduction

Electronic Commerce [EC] is expanding at a phenomenal rate. This is particularly true in the Business-to-business sector. Despite of this fact, little research is available about the costs and benefits associated with EC implementation. We examine the EC implementation issue from the business buyer's viewpoint, we are particulaly interested in web-based supplier catalogs and the management of the supply chain for Maintenance, Repair, and Operations [MRO] purchasing.

The first half of this paper examines electronic catalogs [e-Catalogs] and procurement systems from several different conceptual viewpoints. We define the e-Catalog concept and consider their importance to buyers and suppliers. The paper also looks at procurement systems and the utilization of e-Catalogs as electronic marketplaces. In the second half of the paper we turn to the application issues by reviewing of our research efforts with Caterpillar Inc. and their MRO procurement system.

1.1 e-Catalogs

An electronic catalog (e-Catalog) is generally used by individuals or organizations to present the items available for sale in a more timely and effective manner than possible using a physical catalog or agent. Alternative terms used for the e-Catalog concept are storefronts, web-stores, web-catalogs, and Internet-catalogs. Each of these terms refer to the same basic concepts described below. Suppliers and retailers recognize that electronic catalogs, whether in the form of stores or books, are a new means of accessing both old and new markets [Wyckoff 1997, May 1997] and are valuable only if they can be easily located and referenced by the customer. The Internet provides the means for ease of access and use in an e-Catalog environment. The Internet's easy and inexpensive access to global networks support rapid and extensive Electronic Commerce [EC], and particularly e-Catalog, development. Because EC and e-Catalogs topics are too extensive for a single paper, we limit our focus to the use of web-based e-Catalogs in MRO purchasing. MRO is an important component of Business-to-Business Electronic Commerce (BEC) applications and a good example for our purposes.

e-Catalogs are particularly important in MRO purchasing as the type of supplier involved usually deals with a large number of buyers and stocks a large number of items. For example, the latest physical catalog from W.W. Grainger, one of the largest industrial distributors, is six inches thick, has in excess of 3,900 pages, and weighs over five pounds. It also may be out of date before it is distributed. The cost of mailing this item to thousands of customers is a significant component of Grainger's sales expense. On the other hand Grainger's e-Catalog website is always up to date, is easily accessed by their customers and is much less expensive to maintain than its physical counterpart. The future of the paper catalog must be very limited indeed.

MRO purchases, also referred to as indirect purchases, have a much smaller transaction size and a greater frequency than do direct purchases related to production [Leenders 1997]. However, indirect and direct purchases are generally processed by the same systems and share the same expenses. Thus the ratio of processing costs to the value of the average indirect order is much higher than the similar ratio for the average direct order. Improvements in the cost to value ratio can have a very positive effect on the net income of both the buying and the selling organizations [Leenders 1997].

The Internet and the World Wide Web [Web] provide a cheap and reliable method for business buyers to access the electronic catalogs of suppliers and, by this means, significantly reduce the amount of costly human resources utilized by MRO systems. Because human error is the most frequent point of failure in MRO systems, less reliance on human effort reduces the number of problems incurred by the supplier which, in turn, reduces the critical cost to service the buyers [Lohr 1997, Paul 1997]. The benefits to the buyer are not as clearly identifiable. The buyer may now perform certain activities previously handled or supported by the supplier which would increase his expense. One objective of this paper is to clarify the benefits accruing to the buyer when using suppliers' electronic catalogs in their procurement process. In addition the paper addresses the technological, organizational, and structural considerations related to or required to achieve maximum benefits when implementing a Web-based procurement/purchasing system [**WBPS**].

2 e-Catalogs and EC

EC is a nebulous term in that it may have many different valid representations depending on the aspect of EC the researcher is examining [Sokol 1995, Adam 1996, Ahuja 1997, Kalakota and Whinston 1996, Clarke 1993]. Given the meaning of the words electronic and commerce, we define EC as the exchange of goods or services via a system based on electronic communication or storage. In this manner an electronic catalog can be defined as a listing of items and descriptions via a system based upon electronic storage. EC can include different mechanisms such as use of the telephone or CD catalogs, and may even include e-Catalog where software agents negotiate exchanges occurring entirely through electronic systems. The minimal purpose of e-Catalogs is to provide an information source. The minimal purpose of EC is to facilitate the exchange of goods or services which requires the exchange of information. Thus, we see that the e-Catalog is a component of EC. For e-Catalogs to be a significant contributor to commerce they must add value to EC, i.e. the e-Catalog must be more effective than competing processes or products.

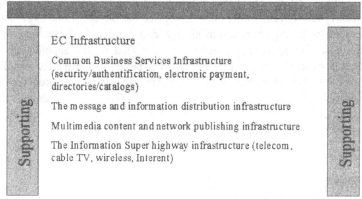

Electronic Commerce Applications

Supply chain management, Video on-demand, Remote banking,
Procurement and Purchasing, On-line marketing and advertising,
Home shopping

EC Infrastructure

Common Business Services Infrastructure
(security/authentification, electronic payment,
directories/catalogs)

The message and information distribution infrastructure

Multimedia content and network publishing infrastructure

The Information Super highway infrastructure (telecom,
cable TV, wireless, Interent)

Supporting

Supporting

Public policy
legal and privacy
issues

Technical Standards for
electronic documents, multimedia
and network protocols

Fig. 1. The electronic commerce framework

The value added nature of e-Catalogs. To understand the value added by electronic catalogs, we have to understand where they fit in the EC environment. Kalakota and Whinston (1996) provide us with a representation of the EC environment. In their framework [figure 1] technical standards and protocols are the backbone of the common infrastructure that supports the various commerce applications (page 4). In their representation e-Catalogs are one of the common infrastructure items used to accomplish EC applications. Shaw (1997) develops an EC model based on the Open Systems Interconnection (OSI) protocol. Shaw [figure 2] includes ten layers of functionality in the model; requirements, application, information, distribution, interface, messaging, authentication, data, security, transmission. In this model each lower layer services the needs of the layer above. In the Shaw framework electronic catalogs relate to both the application and the information layers. Both the Kalakota-Whinston and the Shaw models include electronic catalogs as one of several components in the EC environment. We rely on the Shaw model because we believe it provides a better structure for evaluating the value added nature of electronic catalogs in the EC environment.

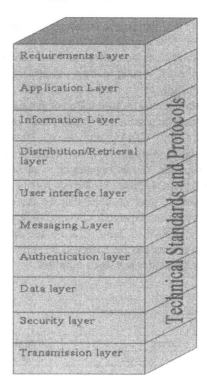

Fig. 2. The layered architecture for electronic commerce

In Shaw's OSI based model the electronic catalog connects the distribution services layer with the user requirements layer. The electronic catalog is the means by which the user views and interacts with the supplier's information. While other applications can provide similar services, electronic catalogs provide a range and effectiveness of service that exceeds any competing application. For example, physical catalogs are cumbersome to use, require large storage areas, become dated soon after being published, and make searching and comparison very difficult. CD catalogs are also apt to be out of date soon after publication. They also require physical storage and either replication for each user or some means of remote access and control. The interactive possibilities of web-based electronic catalogs greatly reduces physical storage and makes continuous updating effective and efficient. In addition a hierarchy of information can be made available where the user accesses only the amount of catalog information required to make a decision. The added value of Web-based electronic catalogs is in their ability to simplify search, maintain currency, and adapt, while making the location and evaluation of supplier's goods easier and more effective than other methods.

The Goals of e-Catalog use. The advantages gained in using Web-based e-Catalogs is dependent upon the extent to which the buyer utilizes the information made available by suppliers and the degree of integration that is achieved between the suppliers and the buyer. The degree of integration desired has organizational, strategic and functional implications for both buyers and sellers. The extent of utilization by buyers and suppliers is related to their perceptions about the value of e-Catalogs to the business strategies.

Buyers and suppliers are expected to have different perceptions as to the value of EC and e-Catalogs. For example, a supplier might want to capture a buyer by locking him into a proprietary set of e-Catalog applications. However, due to the availability of competing e-Catalogs this approach may limit the number of buyers who are willing to utilize the supplier. It is in negotiating to satisfy their joint goals that buyers and suppliers adjust their processes to new environments.

There are eight organizational goal variables that we associate with the use of e-Catalogs. Suppliers and buyers are expected to have different views about many of the variables. The views, presented in Table 1, are based on our understanding of general practices. These practices can be observed in normal commercial transactions and are not specific to particular buyers or suppliers.

Table 1. e-Catalogs and associated goal variables

Goal	Buyer	Supplier
Access to e-Catalog	Easy access	Easy access
Discovery of information in e-Catalog	Simple and quick based on generic terminology	Simple and quick based upon the supplier's terminology and search technique
Price specificity to the buyer	Specific to buyer	Specific to buyer
Content	Common format	Accentuating the points upon which the supplier chooses sell
Comparison	Easy to compare products internally and to other suppliers	Limited to internal comparisons
Substitution	Across all suppliers/manufacturers	Limited to the supplier's items
Specificity of the applications	Universal applications – buy and learn once use everywhere	Proprietary to the supplier – if you go elsewhere you must relearn
Trust	Provide a high level of trust	Provide a high level of trust

Easy access to the supplier's information is something both parties can agree is important to the mutual success. Buyers and Suppliers will also agree on the need and importance for simple methods for the quick discovery of information within a site. The focus of the buyer is generally on the use of generic interfaces and terminology when using a variety of supplier offerings. If they must use proprietary interfaces or special terminology, they prefer would be for their own. While the focus of the supplier is on the simple and quick, they prefer using proprietary interfaces and terminology as often already exists in their current applications and databases. In addition many suppliers utilize terminology as a means of product differentiation. Suppliers and buyers can agree that a final decision requires that the price the particular buyer will be charged is clearly displayed and accurate. The reason the buyer wants accurate information is obvious. The supplier might wish to obfusicate in hopes of segmenting the market. This is difficult to accomplish in traditional settings and even more difficult in an EC environment. Accurate price display can create trust in the supplier and limit suppliers losses when other organizations attempt unfair pricing practices. The buyer favors content information tailored to meet his particular needs, his own format, or at least information in a common format to allow for the ease of use and of cross supplier comparisons. The supplier favors information and format that stresses his particular product, price and quality advantages. The buyer wants to be able to compare a variety of suppliers side by side while the supplier prefers being able to explain his item in his own manner. The buyer wants to be able to determine what parts can be substituted for other parts across the full range of suppliers while the supplier wants to limit this capability to substitute items in other e-Catalogs. The supplier wants to use his proprietary system so that the cost of using alternative suppliers is high. The supplier hopes to atract buyers on quality, price and selection and to hold them, in part, due to the high cost of changing systems. The buyer, of course, prefers a universal system and low costs

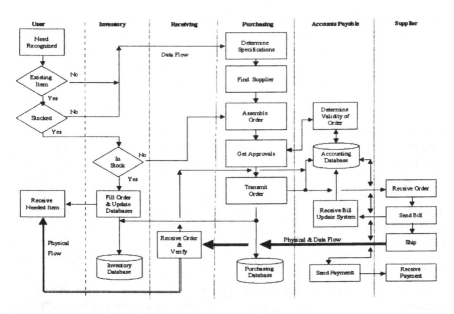

Fig. 3. A generic view of procurement

to move across supplier eCatalogs. Both the buyer and the supplier want a high degree of trust on both sides of the exchange. Trust issues are complex and include supplier/buyer reputation, payment terms, and many other aspects about each transaction. However, we are confident when we say that the greater the trust. the more likely that the transaction will occur.

e-Catalogs can only add value to commerce by satisfying the goals of the buyers and suppliers. This is not an easy task as the goals differ between buyer and supplier. We next address how these mechanisms work and how they integrate the procurement processes.

3 Procurement, e-Catalogs, and Electronic Markets

We have discussed what e-Catalogs are, why they are important, and user goals. In this section we look at the procurement process in electronic markets and at e-Catalogs as part of EC procurement process. We use the procurement process because it highlights the nature of the information exchange that takes place both internal to an organization and between the buyer and seller. Our examination of electronic markets illustrates how e-Catalogs enhance the ability of partners to communicate. We use practical examples to make our point.

3.1 Procurement

Procurement refers to the processes used by a buying party in locating, purchasing, and moving materials from suppliers to the buyer's point of need [Bowersox 1996]. Figure 3 illustrates the flow of information and materials in a generic procurement process. There are five entities in figure 3; users, inventory, receiving, purchasing, accounts payable, suppliers. This is not an exhaustive list but rather represents the main players in the procurement process. The process begins when a user recognizes a need for an item. The user may be a secretary who needs pens, a production supervisor who needs sheet metal, or a procurement specialist reacting to a production requirement report. The user can be almost anyone in the organization. In our work we concentrate on non-production procurement users. After recognizing the need the user determines if the item needed has been ordered before. It is at this point in MRO procurement processes that most of the errors and problems originate. This is because, perverse as it may seem, in most procurement systems the information needed for accurate processing is usually in the wrong place. The user finds that he does not have access to supplier catalogs and the other information necessary for a good decision. Further, Purchasing often does not have first-hand knowledge of the user requirements or becomes confused by the stated user requirement.

Those familiar with purchasing systems will recognize that a great deal of the procurement process has been automated, including communications with suppliers. However this automation breaks down due to several factors. Figure 4 illustrates the interaction of various areas of a buying organization with each other and with suppliers in a traditional procurement process. This is a high level representation of the paper and information flows never the less it gives you some idea as to the complexity of the interactions. The figure provides some insight into the number of times that information has to change hands and form. Each change contributes to the potential for inefficiency and error. EC and e-Catalogs may contribute to simplifying traditional procurement processes and thus contribute to increased efficiency and lower error potential.

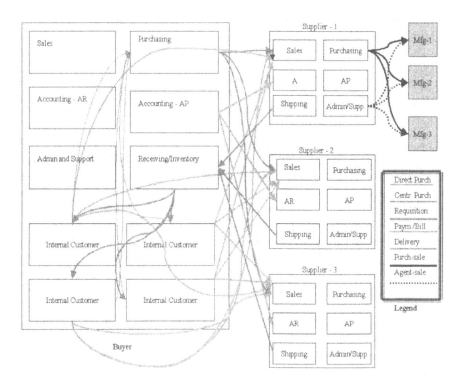

Fig. 4. Communications, both internal and external, deriving from procurement

3.2 Electronic Markets and Forms

Inter-organizational Information Systems [IOIS] like those supported by EC have been the subject of study for some time. These are systems that allow two or more organizations to exchange information in an automated and electronic form [Cash 1985, Choudhury 1997]. Malone, Yates, & Benjamin (1987) established two forms of IOIS's, the market and the hierarchy. Malone et al., relate coordination and production costs to organizational form. The coordination costs for a market are high in comparison to those of a hierarchical form of organization while production costs are higher in a hierarchical form of organization in comparison to those for the market based solution. EC can drastically reduce the cost of coordination, data gathering and analysis, thus making the market form of organization applicable in a broader range of circumstances. Choudhury (1997) adds a third form of IOIS and defines the three as [figure 5]:

1. Electronic Monopolies – IOISs that supports a sole source relationship for a product or set of products usually by the buyer's choice
2. Electronic Dyads – bilateral IOISs where EDI links are common examples
3. Multilateral IOISs – such as electronic markets

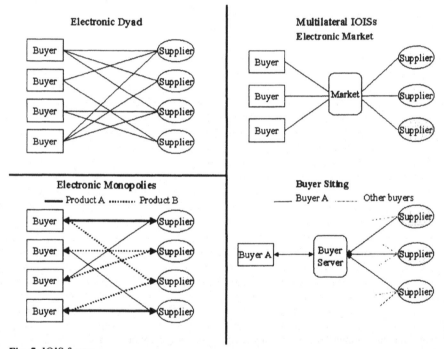

Fig. 5. IOIS forms

3.3 Examples of Electronic Market Forms and e-Catalogs

The electronic monopoly model offers the opportunity for the greatest degree of integration between the parties because the exclusivity of the buyer/seller relationship inherent in the monopoly form makes it less costly to integrate and increases the likelihood of cooperation. It also reduces search costs for the items covered by the agreement as the agreement artificially limits the search space. The benefits accrue at the cost of supplier selection by the buyer. The electronic purchasing system under development by the University of Illinois utilizes electronic monopolies for a selected number of items. This makes sense because the purchasing power of the university is concentrated allowing the university to achieve better terms than they would be able to obtain if purchases were fragmented by buyers among several suppliers. To guard against the deterioration of the seller's terms the University will perform periodic reviews of alternative sources.

The electronic dyad, where the buyers and suppliers establish non-exclusive links on a one to one basis, is the most common form of IOIS currently utilized. Suppliers make their information available to any buyer that can connect to their site. Many suppliers offer some limited form of integration if the buyer registers with them. This allows both parties to form a degree of trust. Due to the potential number of differing application platforms the level of integration is generally minimal. Connection Online [CCO] is an example and was started by Cisco Systems, inc. to facilitate the updating of its product catalog and to provide other customer service. CCO originally had two software agents and currently has ten to assist the users. Cisco supplies Internet hardware and applications, its products can require a high degree of specification. Prior to CCO it took an average of two days for the representative and customer to configure the Figure 5 equipment. Post CCO the average time is 15 minutes of the customer's time only. Cisco expects to transact over $1,000,000,000 of business via CCO in 1998 and fully 70% of its business is currently transacted via CCO with a minimum of human intervention.

This service provides Cisco with a tremendous advantage over its competitors as it can configure, deliver, and update its equipment faster and cheaper than those utilizing non-internet systems do. The business has proven so successful that they have formed a separate division to market it. From a buyer's viewpoint there are benefits from improved quality and reduced order time, but it also makes it difficult to go elsewhere as the costs are so attractive.

Multilateral IOIS have had only limited success. Quite a number of marketspaces using a multilateral IOIS form have started. A significant portion of these have failed. The successful marketspaces are distinguished by their ability to find a motivated and existing clientele to support them. Thus an industry member organization, such as plastic tubing users, has a better chance of surviving than does a general marketspace startup with no pre-existing client base. The notable exception to this observation is the success of General Electric's Transaction Processing Network [TPN]. TPN serves as a general marketspace for a large number of suppliers and buyers.

Steinfield, Kraut, and Plummer (1995) review Malone, et al's (1987) work and argue that the expanded use of networks did not produce the expected move to the marketspace form. A possible rationale for the failure to observe such a shift is that the cost of existing private networks inhibited the full benefits of networking from being realized. Empirical evidence does support the idea that Internet EC does produce significant savings in coordination for simple transactions. General Electric's Transaction Processing Network [TPN] has shown that as the capability to transfer of information over the Internet increases the complexity of the transactions that will occur also increases. Thus as the applications have evolved to transmit complex data, such as CADCAM drawings, over the Internet in a timely and secure manner the transactions involving these types of data have also increased. This demonstrates the robustness of Internet EC for the future.

TPN's success is explained by GE's procurement size. As the largest manufacturer in the world, GE conducts an enormous amount of procurement for its own purposes. Thus it is able to spread the cost of development and maintenance of the TPN system over a large transaction base. GE developed their own internal electronic procurement market that offered its divisions access to a large number of suppliers in a standardized, secure, affordable, informative manner. It was able to attract a large number of suppliers to participate as it opened a vast market to them that did not require costly private networks and their specialized applications. Once this was done GE recognized the potential to make the TPN cost center a profit center by selling the service to outsiders.

TPN was initially called GE Marketplace and began its commercial operations in the third quarter of 1994 over a private GE network. The name was changed in the second quarter of 1995 to TPNPost but otherwise remained the same until the third quarter of 1996 when GE made TPN available to other organizations. By that time GE had 10,000 suppliers networked. By the year 2000 GE expects to transact fifty percent of its business over TPN, more than one billion dollars worth of goods. [Smart 1996]

TPN provides a framework for suppliers and buyers to meet and do business. It supplies a variety of applications and systems for negotiating, bidding, payment, and display. In addition buyers and suppliers can form their own private networks based upon selective membership. Special applications are used to evaluate the buyers and suppliers according to the network's criteria for membership. This ensures the members of certain characteristics on the part of the buyers and suppliers.

GE currently claims several hundred members for TPN. The exact amount of business conducted via TPN is not published and it must be remembered that within that business is GE's own procurement. Most other third party marketspaces do not have any assured volume as TPN does with the GE purchasing. As a result several have failed due to their inability to attract enough buyers and sellers. Currently most third party marketspaces are based upon specific markets, often organized by industry coalitions.

An example of a mixed form of electronic marketspace is W.W. Grainger, a large MRO supplier operating throughout the USA. Grainger traditionally published catalogs and sent sales representatives to a large number of businesses to procure orders. As previously mentioned, their latest physical catalog is 3,964 pages. Their web site provides access to all of the items in the catalog with current prices including any special contracted prices that the user's organization has negotiated. In addition, the e-Catalog provides information on the availability of items and additional information about the items themselves. Grainger acts like most other supplier sites operating as electronic dyads. However, they are also willing to act as an organization's MRO purchasing broker in a form of electronic monopoly. The benefits to the buying organization are a reduction in the cost of MRO processing and in the size of inventory.

From the supplier's viewpoint the Monopoly model has the greatest value while the Buyer sited model has the least value. If the buyer-sited model were tied to some limitation on the number of suppliers then its value would be much closer to that of the Monopoly model for the supplier. The Electronic Dyad and Market models do not strongly support the supplier's view of the goals for e-Catalogs nor do they strongly support the buyer's view of the goals. The buyer's views are most strongly supported by the buyer-sited model while the Monopoly model is about equal with the electronic dyad and market models. The satisfaction of either the buyer's or the supplier's view of the goals for e-Catalogs is not the only factor in deciding on the model to use. Other considerations include competitive forces, pricing, and strategy, which are examined in the intangible section.

3.4 Internet-based e-Catalogs and the Procurement Process

The Internet provides a transparent means of communication between the suppliers and buyers. The user need only know the address of the other party. Even though the Internet is a complicated network of switches, communications lines, software, and equipment, it is of no concern to the users. The key to this simplicity is the separation of the various user organizations into islands with their own internal networks connected to the Internet by a common protocol [Andreoli 1997, Shaw 1997, Signalnet 1997].

A supplier-sited catalog uses the Internet as a means of communication. The supplier typically integrates his catalog and his support applications. In the same manner, a third party can integrate the various services that he provides. Note that in the latter case the market is the focus and therefore both the suppliers and buyers are external to the site and must utilize the Internet to access the site.

A buyer-oriented architecture is illustrated in figure 6. The figure includes an internal catalog and a "conceptual external catalog". The external catalog can remain conceptual or be given a reality by compiling the various suppliers' data in a format specified by the buyer. If the external catalog remains conceptual it is maintained as a set of URL links to the various supplier sites. For optimal effectiveness, converting the buyer catalog to a real local catalog requires the cooperation of the suppliers. The formatting issues are not trivial in themselves. In addition, when the buyer populates an internal catalog with information about the supplier's available items the internal catalog will soon be out of date unless it is updated on a regular basis. The supplier's cooperation in pushing updates to the buyer in the appropriate formats is much more effective and efficient than the buyer having to pull this information from the supplier's database. The implications and incentives for the development of Buyer/Seller partnerships are obvious.

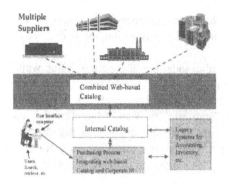

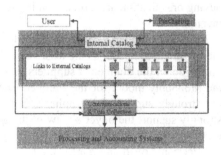

Fig. 6a. External catalog   **Fig. 6b.** Conceptual external catalog

Historically, price has been a prime factor in choosing a supplier. However, given competition and the ready availability of price information, this attribute is becoming less of a differentiating factor for suppliers. The trend is toward a reduction in the number of suppliers and a stronger relationship with those remaining suppliers to assure the best mix of price, quality, and delivery for the intended purposes. On the surface this would seem to run contrary to the capabilities provided by the Internet, i.e. ease in searching for the cheapest price. However, when price comparisons become easy and cheap, price ceases to be an effective marketing mechanism. Another important characteristic of the Internet is its support for inter-organization integration. Buyers and their suppliers can easily integrate production and BackOffice systems/processes across the firms in much the same way divisions of a single organization have done in the past. Thus it is important in choosing a supply partner to consider not only price but also a number of less tangible factors that contribute to inter-organizational integration. These factors include concerns for quality, trust [in an open web environment trust is a commodity that has to be earned and consequently has greater value], resources, and process savvy.

Figure 7 illustrates the situation from figure 4 after the introduction of internets and e-Catalogs. The same interactions are present but they have been integrated though internal and external networks and the use of e-Catalogs. The integration refers to the communication process and information exchange not to the methodology and use. The independence of the internal and external entities is maintained while the efficiency and effectiveness of common communications processing and information protocols are achieved. A number of larger firms have instituted this type of process earlier by utilizing proprietary applications and networks. Because of the cost of participation the benefits have never expanded beyond the immediate entities. The cost to participate is high and is directly proportional to the number of links that are established. The auto industry has pushed such technology for a decade and realized significant benefits. However, even General Motors, which can require suppliers to participate, utilizes such systems for only a small fraction of its procurement activities. Its suppliers have had little success in extending the links back in their own supply chain.

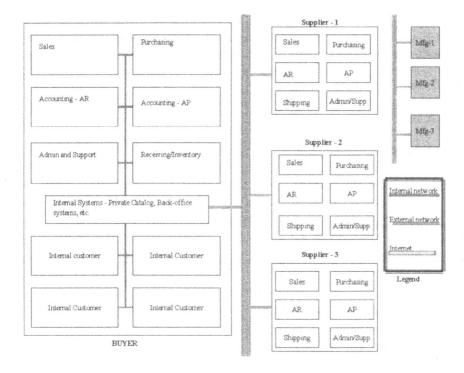

Fig. 7. Procurement with electronic communications

4 Caterpillar

Our research with Caterpillar investigated the application of electronic commerce to the management of purchasing and procurement processes. The purchasing and procurement processes include: product selection, source selection, price negotiation, order placement, order fulfillment, and payment. The purchasing and procurement process can utilize electronic catalogs and other electronic commerce components, such as Electronic Data Interchange (EDI), allowing transactions, even payment, to be handled electronically. The specific problem focus of this project was the management of indirect purchasing at Caterpillar. The project considered the incorporation of Web technology to shorten process time, eliminate paper work, and reduce (human) transaction errors. We also considered whether the utilization of Web features could create additional competitive advantages Caterpillar.

One of our first endeavors was to examine all of the current e-Catalog applications available. This is an impossible task as new applications are constantly being introduced and old ones, two or three months old, are being refined or scrapped. CommerceNet's site, http://www.commerce.net, lists a great number of EC suppliers and sorts them by product type. In Table 2 we list several of the major e-Catalog

solution suppliers and rate their products in nine categories. These ratings are judgmental and based upon published data. The number of applications available made it
infeasible for us to conduct tests of each application. Rather, we examined the literature available on each system and based our judgements on this information.
Those interested in more quantitative analysis can look at the popular press, any
number of technical magazines run evaluations of these types of applications on a
regular basis.

Table 2. Features of e-Catalog systems

Solutions / Functions	GEIS TPN	Elekom	Acquion GETS	Ariba ORMS	Connect Purchase-Stream	Actra Order Expert
Catalogue management: Ease of update; catalogue depth and flexibility	A	A	A	B	U	A
Security: Strengths and levels of security measures	A	U	B	U	B	A
Approval Process: Flexibility; customizability; degree of automation	B	A	U	A	A	A
User Interface: Customizability; consistency; intuitiveness	B	A	A	A	A	A
Search Engine: Strength of the engine; methods of search	A	U	B	U	B	A
Other merchandising application: Product display for customer convenience	B	A	U	U	B	A
Reporting: Are user data analyzed to track purchasing trends	U	A	U	A	A	U
Automated transaction: Payment method, tracking purchase	A	A	B	A	B	A
System integration: Degree of integration with Accounting system, purchasing and current Lognet	U	U	A	B	A	A

A – Excellent   C – adequate   E - not available
B – good   D - present but abilities doubtful   U - unknown

One important criterion not present on the table is the orientation of the application. By this we mean whom it is designed for, the supplier, buyer or some third party. We found that few products were designed for the buyer, apparently because the first drivers in e-Catalog development were suppliers. Also it turns out that buyer orientation is much more complicated to implement and maintain. In the following sections we review our research results as they pertained specifically to Caterpillar. We generalize and provide directions for others where possible.

5 Results

The analysis performed for Caterpillar demonstrated significant tangible value in utilizing e-Catalogs in the MRO procurement process. This result occurs even though the Caterpillar processes are already below the industry average in cost per transaction. Specifically it is estimated that the transaction cost could be reduced by 25% and the cycle time by 33% by introducing web-based e-catalog procurement. Both the cycle time and the transaction cost include all components from the initial recognition of need to its final satisfaction. Given the size of the organization and its existing networks and equipment the implementation cost is relatively small in comparison to the potential savings. The intangible value added was much more difficult to access but clearly of importance to Caterpillar.

5.1 Tangible Value

Caterpillar wanted to know if they could obtain a market advantage by adopting a WBPS. They were concerned with the technical, organizational, and market issues and desired a cost/benefit analysis to support any position. Organizational issues included the internal user's charge for the system, how to gain user acceptance, and how to implement given the variety of existing environments. The concerns are not simply about cost. They also relate to; the organization's technological structure and capabilities, the organization's culture and structure, and to the structure of the markets in which Caterpillar operates. We found it useful to group these concerns as tangible and intangible issues. The tangible items are those that are relatively easily measurable in quantitative terms, generally those of an economic or financial nature. An item that can be measured but where the cost of measurement is believed to outweigh the benefit or where historical or other information is simply not available is grouped with the tangible items. Items that are not easily measurable in quantitative terms are intangible. Clearly the boundary between tangible and intangible is both situation specific and judgmental. However, we believe you will find the distinction useful.

We have identified five tangible factors of potential benefit associated with e-Catalog procurement environments. These are Cycle Time, Transaction Cost, Error Rate, Inventory, and the Item Prices. We used the available data to assign values in each of these areas. Where the information available on the proposed environment was insufficient to make precise measurement possible estimates were made by the local experts. In addition we divided these items into a number of subsections to reduce unintentional biases. Where there were aggregate values available we were able to compare them to the sum of the subcategories of the estimated values as accuracy crosscheck.

Cycle time is the time from the identification of the need for an item to the fulfillment of that need. If all else remains the same then the faster the cycle time the lower the total cost to complete the transaction. There are several important components of cycle time. The four major components of cycle time considered were needs recognition, processing, supply, and receipt. Recognition includes the time from the identification of the need until that need has been transmitted to the purchasing system. Processing involves the order creation, approval, recording, and transmission to the supplier. Supply is the time from transmission to the time of delivery. Receipt is the time from delivery by the supplier to the time that the purchased goods become available for use. A WBPS can reduce the time to identify the needed item, the time and costs to process the order, and the recording of the order. If the buyer and supplier are well integrated then it can also reduce the time to transmit the order and reduce delivery time.

Transaction costs include staff, systems, and operational costs involved in processing an order starting from the recognition of the need until the need is satisfied. The major components of the transaction cost are search, process, transmission, verification, delivery, and error. Reduced cycle time results in the reduction of some of these costs. However, there may also be costs associated with the effort to reduce the cycle time. For example, if reducing cycle time results in higher error rates the change may ultimately produce higher transaction costs. Errors occur in input, processing, transmission, supplier, and delivery.

In the ideal system all items arrive just in time [JIT], thus eliminating the need for inventory. However, inventory also serves as a buffer against the possibility of production shut downs due to the lack of key input items. Maintaining inventory is a cost that must be weighed against the consequences of not having an item when needed. While this remains true in EC systems it can become a much smaller factor as the system responds much more quickly to need. The levels of inventory prior to a move to EC can be compared to the levels needed after the move to measure the potential inventory cost savings.

Purchase price can also be reduced due to the increased availability of and better negotiation potential. Inventory can be reduced as the knowledge about utilization increases and there is increased confidence in the ability to procure items, as they are needed. Thus even Caterpillar can obtain some inventory savings, despite a very efficient inventory process already in operation.

We analyzed the components of the cycle time for the improvements that might occur at Caterpillar. We considered the cost impact of a decreased number of difficult to process items when the new system is in place. We applied the resulting changes in cycle time to the staffing requirements and determined the net effect on purchasing transaction cost. We found that the improvement in cycle time alone produces an estimated 25% improvement in the staffing cost and that the estimated change in the number of difficult items provides an additional 6% savings.

In many firms the inventory size reduction, based upon the effect of the reduced cycle time, could be significant. In an organization where the inventory is currently maintained internally, a reduction of 25 to 30 percent is not an unreasonable expectation. However, due to the advanced nature of the current inventory system at Caterpillar, this factor was not considered significant in the overall analysis. Savings through price reductions did offer an opportunity for significant savings. Since price reduction translates directly to net income determination, any reduction in average prices paid for MRO items will show up in increased net income. As the percentage of the all purchases related to MRO is estimated to be from 40 to 60 percent of all indirect cost it is obvious that even a small change in the average price paid has a large potential impact on net income. The estimated change in the average price paid contained too many variables to arrive at a precise result. However our rough estimate ranges from a 1 to 10 percent improvement. The tangible costs of the new environment were, because of Caterpillar's advanced systems, minor in comparison to the benefits. The networks and equipment were already in use and the legacy systems are able to support the introduction of WBPS. The major new expense was expected to be in systems development and is expected to be limited to the cost of three analysts.

5.2 Intangible Values

In addition to the analysis of quantifiable savings, we created a list of intangibles where Caterpillar might obtain some benefit. We defined each issue and provided our best subjective assessment. We identified five categories of issues: Integration with existing business processes, Technology problems, Organizational culture Issues, Strategic issues, and Operational issues. Each of these areas was judgmentally evaluated to assess benefits versus costs, as a component of the intangible portion of the value formula.

Integration with existing business processes: Most organizations have a significant investment in their existing (Legacy) systems. Abandoning Legacy systems is often not economically desireable. Therefore, any new system must make use of the major existing systems at least until the Legacy systems hit the replacement point in their lifecycle. However, new systems should not be designed as simple extensions of the old. This approach will limit their future usefulness. A common approach to this integration problem is to design an interface between the new and old systems such that they can inter-operate without becoming interdependent. The standardization of this type of interface for a new technology is termed an envelope and it allows the firm to use the best and most extensible new technology while retaining the Legacy systems.

Technology problems: The integrity of an organization's data is very important, at least as important as safeguarding the cash. Thus any electronic system that allows either inside or outside users access to either data or other asset equivalents needs to be designed such that there is little chance of mis-use. EC by its nature allows for an increased possibility of security problems simply because it opens the systems to more users, both internal and external. Increased awareness of this factor is necessary and additional hardware/software is sure to be required. One common security device associated with the Internet is the firewall, a device that stands between the internal system and the external network. By tracking the information coming in, it protects the system by allowing access only to valid users for a valid request.

There are a large number of internal processes used to support the procurement process. It is important that any EC systems be able to interact well with these supporting systems to maximize the benefit from EC while maintaining security.

Organizational Issues: An EC technology implementation must support the organizational mission where ever the technology is used. If IT is used for one specified purpose it can be optimized to that task. If that system will be utilized for several different tasks it must be "optimized" based upon the overall or average usage. Therefore we need to know where the technology will be used and under what conditions must it work.

Who will use the technology and when it will be used should drive the type of technology adopted. A computer scientist sitting in an office can make effective use of much different technology than can a shop foreman with no computer experience trying to use the technology to obtain immediate answers in a time stress situation.

It is human nature to take the easiest course to accomplish a task. Given that new technology introduces new cost, both in dollars and learning, why would an individual on the line choose to use new technology over the old and familiar? The organization needs to develop incentives to make the use of new technology attractive and important. The organization must remove disincentives to the use of new technology to gain the full benefit of the change. Disincentives are usually unintended, as an organization does not generally spend money to improve something and then intentionally tell people not to use it. Unintentional or not, some perfectly good current policies may have a chilling effect on the utilization of new technology. Two of the primary disincentives to the use of new technology is increased cost and difficulty in use. Every firm recognizes that technology costs money, some firms seek to recapture their investment by charging the users an additional fee. When new systems are implemented, particularly in the critical inception stage, additional costs can be a strong disincentive to utilizing the new system, particularly if the old system appears to function adequately. In fact, it can be very beneficial to give the new technology an initial cost advantage, at least for some initiation period. In any case the introduction of a new technology requires a marketing strategy, including clear positive incentives, to assure a successful introduction.

Strategic Issues: Many suppliers are pushing the use of Web-based e-Catalogs as a means of improving their own processes. It is estimated that the majority of suppliers will be utilizing the Internet and e-Catalogs as their primary sales tool in the near future and that soon after that the majority will be using Web-based e-Catalogs as their only catalog tool. The organization that makes the move early may have a short-term strategic advantage. However, the protocols used by that organization must be able to adapt to whatever the norm becomes or else the initial advantage may becomes a disadvantage

Increased information means that the performance of both the purchasers and suppliers can be better monitored within and across the organizations. The strategic use of this information is an important value added aspect of the new technology. This is expected to have a positive result on purchasing economies, but the extent of the benefit is difficult to measure. The mirror of this is that the suppliers can better monitor buyer performance.

Operational Issues: The integration of the new systems with the legacy systems entails some cost. Depending on the nature of the existing systems this cost will vary with the degree to which the new environment must be adjusted to allow for integration. Ideally the new systems should seamlessly integrate with the legacy systems allowing the organization to replace only the minimum necessary components of the legacy systems. Generally the integration process is not so easy and can require changes to the e-Catalog system. Where the value of the existing system is high and the changes to both the Legacy systems and the new e-Catalog system have little effect, there is no problem. It must be remembered that the legacy systems should not determine the capabilities of the new system. If this is allowed to occur you will build a new system based on old standards. At Caterpillar the integration was reasonably straight foreward as their systems required little modification to work with the planned e-Catalog.

6 Critical Success Factors

We have categorized the factors critical to the success of the purchasing system implementation according to the views of the various interested parties in Table 3. The interested parties we consider are the suppliers, the internal users of the purchasing systems, and the members of the purchasing area. The table highlights those areas where a lack of agreement between user/purchasing/supplier goals might be detrimental to the success of the e-Catalog purchasing system implementation. We evaluate eight factors. Two factors numbers 4 and 5 involve party conflicts potentially detrimental to the success of the effort. Two other factors, numbers 2 and 6, represent possible significant conflicts. In each of these cases the accomplishment of the goal may be apparent to only one party. The benefits of achievement of the goal have to be made apparent to all players to assure the success of the new system.

Table 3 documents the critical success factors we identified. These are real issues that should be resolved before the project implementation begins. Obtaining the supplier cooperation for a buyer-sited e-Catalog seemed to be a difficult proposition. In discussions with suppliers it was found that they were willing to trade information to become a member of a restricted set of suppliers. Restricting the set of suppliers in a buyer-sited e-Catalog may be necessary as a matter of practicality and effectiveness. The effort to maintain e-Catalogs with many suppliers is an enormous task.

Table 3. CSF's as incentives for the stakeholders

	Factor	User	Purchasing	Supplier
1	Price Paid/Charged	Reduced	Effective	Increase in net return
2	*Cost to use/ operate/ participate*	*Apparently cheap*	Savings exceed the expenses	Increase in net return
3	Complexity	Significant reduction	Significant reduction	Decreased
4	Flexibility	Increased or at least maintained as is	Decreased or maintained as is	Decreased/Increased
5	Control	Decreased	Increased	Decreased/Increased
6	*Transaction Costs*	*Apparently decreased*	Decreased	Decreased
7	Cycle Time	Significant reduction	Effective	Decreased
8	Errors	Reduced without effort	Reduced	Improved relationship

It eventually became apparent to us that the most critical success factor was the internal players' perception of the project. The users would have to recognize its value to them. Thus the organization must make a concerted effort to demonstrate the value at the user level before they adopt the new system if they expect willing participation. Even in hierarchical organizations there is a difference in result produced by enthusiastic and unenthusiastic participation.

The issues above are not independent of each other or of the tangible factors discussed earlier. The analysis of the tangible items assumes that the majority of users adopt the new environment. However, as seen in the CSFs one of the problems is the possibility that users will not see the benefits to adopting the new system. It is important to address the transparency of incentives. It is also necessary to recognize that many of the individuals that utilize the new system will be unfamiliar with the technology. It is, therefore, important to make the technology easy to learn and use.

7 Lessons

The move to an e-Catalog environment can be quite beneficial. However there are a number of lessons to keep in mind. The context of the given situation must be considered first. This includes an analysis of both the internal and external environment. Savings are possible but not guaranteed and while there will be problems they are manageable. Such a move seems inevitable but it doesn't necessarily have to be today.

7.1 Context is the First Consideration

EDI, a form of EC, is extensively employed at Caterpillar and has proven to be quite beneficial to their business. However, the extent of benefit attainable with EDI is limited by use of proprietary networks, limited information exchange, and limited integration. Couple this with the cost of establishing EDI and it becomes apparent why EDI did not achieve the degree of use at Caterpillar that had been expected. The EDI limitations are the very reason why the use of the Internet makes such a difference in the potential benefits of EC. On the Internet many of the restrictions encountered with EDI are eliminated and overall performance is greatly enhanced. In addition the cost of providing the service is drastically reduced so that the cost/benefit ratio is improved from both sides.

The benefits that can be achieved in implementing an e-Catalog environment are contingent upon the degree of EC that is established [Choudhury 1997]. Table 4 illustrates a number of attributes that can be considered to obtain an estimate of the degree of EC in a given situation. There is no established formula to calculate this value. Implementing EC need not require acting on all attribute areas at once. However, it is worthwhile to remember that the benefits achieved are more than additive as the attributes are not independent and therefore limiting one may have an adverse effect on others.

Table 4. Design attributes of e-Catalog systems

Attribute	Description
Search	Ease of finding information – fundamental attribute
Data	The amount of information available for exchange and the quality of it
Speed	How fast the transmission of the information occurs
Integration	How the e-Catalog integrates internally, with legacy systems, and externally
Payment	The manner in which payment takes place
Delivery	How is the item delivered, tracked, and recognized upon delivery

7.2 Savings Possible but not a Given

Information technology has been examined this decade for demonstrable benefits and various research has reported the absence of quantifiable benefits in excess of the costs. Other research has sought to explain this anomaly to some degree of success. However to assume that e-Catalogs will provide savings is not assured and the effort that proceeds under that assumption may be doomed. The move may be dictated by strategic factors much as other IT has been. If you can only find it via e-Catalogs you have to use them.

7.3 Problems are Probable but Manageable

Since e-Catalogs are complicated and the process can be quite different from current practices it is often viewed as a quagmire. However, with careful analysis and planning the move to the e-Catalog environment can be relatively problem free. The key is in addressing the CSFs and the other intangible factors discussed.

7.4 Move is Inevitable but not Necessarily Immediate

Caterpillar has recognized the inevitability of the move to the Internet and e-Catalogs. Their suppliers are increasingly pushing for such a move. The tangible values are positive and the intangible issues with the proper treatment can also be positive. The organization has recognized that an early move on their part will allow them to have more control of the manner in which it is done and will be beneficial to the company. The organizational, structural and technological problems have been identified and can be addressed in an effective manner. However, without first examining the situation as was done, the organization could have assumed from the tangible value that the move was positive and then be surprised by a negative result. It is also possible that another organization might find the tangible values less attractive. By including the positive aspects of the intangible issues, it recognizes the need for a move and avoid any future problem.

8 Conclusion

Henry Ford didn't invent the automobile, but he did apply mass production techniques to its manufacture [Wyckoff 1997]. EC and e-Catalogs are not new and don't have to be invented. The application of the Internet to EC and e-Catalogs, however, is akin to Ford's use of mass production techniques – revolutionary. Given a broad definition of EC, it is difficult to find transactions that can not involve EC in some manner [May 1997]. Thus, the question to be asked is not what transaction involves e-Catalogs but what techniques should be applied at what time to maximize the benefit and minimize the risks of a WBPS.

We have shown several examples of e-Catalogs that have been successful and discussed the benefits that they provide. In addition we examined the complications involved in the implementation of an e-Catalog environment as observed at a large mid-western manufacturer. Most researchers agree that e-Catalog use is expected to continue to grow. Where e-Catalogs will end up is a point less agreed upon. In a similar case in the seventies, the airlines were faced with the dilemma of whether or not to open up their reservations systems. Those that extended their reservations systems, as an extranet, achieved a strategic advantage that only ended because of the courts. And those that didn't embrace the extension faced a strategic disadvantage that took quite some time to overcome.

The use of e-Catalogs is rapidly becoming a necessity. The sooner that buyers choose to use them the more influence they will have on how they are used. However the organization must first determine that their use is appropriate in their organization and market and that they have the structure and technology to make effective use of e-Catalogs. If there are negative from the mentioned review, then they should decide how to change them before trying to implement a system that will be of reduced value.

References

Adam, N.R. & Yesha, Y. (1996), Electronic Commerce an overview, in Electronic Commerce: Current Research Issues and Applications, edited by N. R. Adams & Y. Yesha. Published by Springer-Verlag, Berlin, Germany.

Ahuja, V. (1997), Secure Commerce on the Internet. Published by AP Professional, a division of Academic Press, Inc., N.Y.

Allen, Cliff & Kania, Deborah (1997), Web Catalog. Published by John Wiley & Sons, inc., New York.

Andreoli, Jean-Marc, Pacull, Francois, & Pareschi, Remo (1997), XPECT: a framework for electronic commerce. Published in IEEE Internet Computing, July-August, pp 40-48.

Boar, Bernard H. (1994), Practical steps for aligning information technology with business strategies: How to achieve a competitive advantage. Published by John Wiley & sons, inc., New York.

CBN (1997), Commerce by the Numbers.
URL = http://www.computerworld.com/emmerce/depts/ststs/bus.html.

Chronister, Kristian (1997), Study: Online sales to Top $1.5 Trillion. Electronic Buyers News, May 5th.

Danish, S. (1996), How to build a Successful Business-to-Business Online Catalog, published by SAQQARA Systems, Inc., 1230 Oakmead parkway, Sunnyvale, CA.

Drucker, Peter F., "Management", Harper and Row, New York, 1/74.

Gage, Deborah (1997), Cisco's Chambers: E-commerce to explode. PC Week, November 18th, URL: http://www.zdnet.com/pcweek/news/1117/18ecisc.html.

Holtzman, J. (1997), Can electronic commerce pass the ACID test?, in Electronics Now, V68, 3/97, pp 78-80.

Kalakota, R. & Whinston, A. B. (1996), Frontiers of Electronic Commerce. Published by Addison-Wesley Publishing Company, Inc., N.Y.

Kambil, A. (1997), Doing business in the wired world, in Computer, volume 30, number 8, may, pp 56-61.

Keller, Arthur M. (1997), Smart Catalogs and Virtual Catalogs, Readings in Electronic Commerce, R. Kalakota and A. Whinston (Eds.), Addison.Werley, New York, 1996.

Leenders, Michiel R. & Fearon, Harold E. (1997), Purchasing and Supply Management, 11th edition. Published by Richard D. Irwin, Chicago, IL, USA.

Lohr, S. (1997), Beyond Consumers, companies Pursue Business-to-business Net Commerce, in The New York Times - Cyber Times, April 28.

McComb, Gordon, (1997), Web Commerce. Published by John Wiley & sons, inc., New York.

McKendrick, Joseph (1997), Will Internet Rattle too Many Chains?. Cardinal Business Media, Electronic Commerce, April 25th,
    URL = http://www.midrangesystems.com/Archive/1997/apr25/el100601.htm.
Malone, Thomas W.; Yates, Joanne; & Benjamin, Robert I. (1987), Electronic Markets and Electronic Hierarchies. Communications of the ACM, June, Vol. 30, No. 6, pp 484-497.
May, Thornton A. (1997), Electronic Commerce: 3 Truths for IS. Computerworld, April 21st,
    URL = http://www.computerworld.com/leadership/970421leadership.html.
Morgan, David (1997), Lotus exec see huge business-to-business Internet market, Reuters June 4th.
Quarterman, John S. & Carl-Mitchell, Smoot (1994), The Internet Connection. Published by Addison-Wesley Publishing Company, New York.
Segev, A., Wan, D., & Beam, C. (1995), Designing Electronic Catalogs for Business value, CITM Working Paper CITM-WP-1005, The Fisher Center for Information Technology and management. Haas School of Business, University of California, Berkeley,
Seminerio, Maria M. (1997), Business-to-business E-commerce set to explode study says. ZDNN, July 28th, URL = http://www3.zdnet.com/zdnn/content/zdnn/0728oo06.html.
Shaw, N. G. (1997), Foundations of electronic commerce, in Crossroads the ACM student magazine, fall, pp 17-19.
Shaw, N. G. & Yadav, Urya B. (1997), Characteristics of systems requirements for Electronic Commerce. Published in AIS Americas Conference on Information Systems 1997.
Signalnet (1997), Electronic Commerce: a fundamental Architectural shift a technical primer. URL:http://www.signalnet.com/papers2.htm
Smart, T. (1996), Jack Welch's Cyber-Czar. Business Week, August 5th.
Sokol, P. K. (1995), From EDI to electronic commerce: a business initiative. Published by McGraw-Hill, N.Y.
Steinfield, Charles; Kraut, Robert; & Plummer, Alice (1995), The Impact of Interorganziational Networks on Buyer-Seller Relationships. Journal of Computer-Mediated Communication, Vol. 1, No. 3.
Vicente, Jose P. (1998), E-commerce Reshapes U.S. Retail Landscape. In Technology News, February 3rd., URL = http://my.exicte.com/news/r/980204/15/tech-retail.
Wong, William T. & Keller, Arthur M. (1994), Developing an Internet Presence with On-line Electronic Catalogs, Stanford Center for Information Technology, October 9th.
Wyckoff, Andrew (1997), Imagining the impact of electronic commerce. OECD Observer Oct-Nov, n208, pp 5-9.

CHAPTER 19
The New Economy Electronic Commerce, and the Rise of Mass Customization

Bill Fulkerson[1] and Michael Shank[2]

[1]CIS-Technology Integration Deere & Company, Moline IL, USA, wf28155@deere.com

[2]Principal, IBM Consulting Group, New York, NY, USA, Shankm@us.ibm.com

We assert that the New Economy, together with the advent of electronic commerce, has moved mass customization beyond the realm of myth and mystery for many firms and squarely into the realm of mandatory consideration. The shift away from mass marketing and toward mass customization parallels a similar shift away from mass communication (broadcasting) toward targeted communication (direct addressing). We observe that this phenomenon has enabled a new wave of customer intimacy. Firms are responding by fundamentally changing their manufacturing, distribution, and delivery of products to enable economical mass production of customized goods. The full implications of this apparent paradigm shift remain unpredictable. We posit that this shift offers the global society the potential of profound benefits as well as the risk of substantial cost.

Keywords: Electronic Markets; Transaction Cost Economics; Information Economics; Organizational Structure; Consumer Behavior; Business Strategy; Mass Customization; Mass Production

1 Introduction

If there is one common visceral sense shared by executives today, it is that their business has changed or is about to change. Across all industry, reliable and proven ways of conducting business are changing as new forms emerge to challenge conventional business practice. The observable symptoms of change are everywhere, as demonstrated by these examples:

- Television, catalogs, and the Internet have made successful inroads into traditional retail distribution channels–enabling competitors and brokers to enhance customer value by providing more goods and services for less cost.
- Product differentiation has become commonplace as manufacturers have adopted innovative ways of packaging product with service and/or information components.
- Marketing, manufacturing, and distribution alliances make possible integrated offerings.

- Products customized for individual tastes are available by the availability of made-to-order using materials and services procured from across the globe.

Customer expectations in this era of mass customization are remarkably similar to those held by customers in the pre-industrial age. Whether dealing with an artisan/craftsman or a corporation, customers want a high quality, economically priced, readily available product.

The shift in organizational infrastructure to meet customer expectations is indicated in the Figure 1 (Gray, 1998). The size of each rectangle indicates the relative importance of the organizational element it represents. For example, the role of the distributor dominates the left organizational structure but plays a lesser role in the middle organization and then disappears in the right organization.

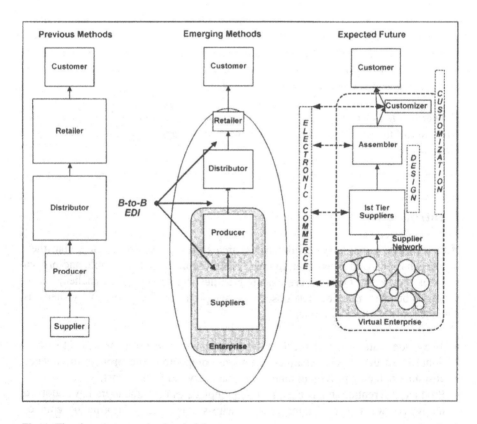

Fig. 1. The changing organizational structure

Initially, the organizational elements were loosely linked in pairs and absent of any true coordination. The producer pushed inventory through the distribution network to the retailer. Since supplier and producer schedules were determined by forecasts, uncontrolled inventory often accumulated when demand levels declined below forecasts.

With satisfaction of pent-up demand, the need to control cost while producing for declining markets motivated producers and suppliers to limit their independence for the to benefit from collaboration at the level of an enterprise. The rise of Electronic Data Interchange (EDI) in the grocery industry has generally permeated commerce to facilitate business-to-business exchange of orders, operating information, and logistics status. The adoption of pull systems prompted the declining role of distributor and retailer as flow manufacturing enabled a build-to-order order fulfillment process.

We anticipate the next phase in organizational change to be the rise of the virtual enterprise. This type of organization will consist of a select group of first-tier suppliers coupled with a loose knit network of secondary and tertiary suppliers directly supporting a producer engaged in design and assembly. It will be tightly linked to the customer in a production demand flow system enhanced by the ability to support mass customization. The Internet will enable this linkage along with proprietary Extranet networks to provide global electronic commerce (EC) capability. The shrinkage of time and distance by EC will reinforce the adoption of the principles of the new economy that make mass customization economically feasible.

Our argument, presented in the following sections, is organized as follows. In Section 2.0, we introduce an experiential description and indicate the new rules of the tacit knowledge of the New Economy. The effect of supply outstripping demand explains the rise of the customer, the role of the service economy with unbundled products and services, and the virtual enterprise as a solution to the need for agile response of the producer. The role of Electronic Commerce is explained in Section 3.0. The elements of mass customization, namely modular design and rapid response, are presented in Section 4.0. The chapter ends with a near-term forecast and a cautionary warning in section 5.0.

2 The New Economy

In the New Economy, people work with their brains more than their hands and, enabled by communications technology, pursue global competition. Because the rate of change increases rapidly, innovation becomes more important than mass production and venture capital pursues new concepts rather than new machines (Wired, 1998). The New Economy's "focus upon the moment of exchange, and not on the system as a whole, has been profoundly absorbed into the worldview of the modern citizen." (Mulgan, 1998) To accommodate for this myopic focus upon a transaction based economy, firms must reconsider their basic strategic assumptions. "[M]any of the prevailing mainstays of strategic analysis—including economies of scale, experience curves, industry analysis, and market share—need to be reconsidered in light of the new competitive structures and organizational forms made possible by the dominance of services and their technologies." (Quinn, 1992)

Some strategists predict that existing value chains will fragment into multiple businesses, each of which will develop their own sources of competitive advantage (Evans and Wurster, 1997). When individual business functions having different economies of scale or scope are bundled together for the convenience of the customer, firms sacrifice potential competitive advantage of the separate functions for the good of the enterprise. Unbundling these functions to form separate businesses can achieve a competitive advantage. However, this alternative to devolve the enterprise or its value chain is an unlikely scenario in a conventional strategic analysis. Firms must adopt a dynamic approach to developing strategy that can accommodate the dramatic changes destined to occur in markets.

2.1 New Rules

The changes in the economy and organizations that have accompanied the transition from mass production to mass customization require new economic rules. These new rules do not negate the old rules of a resource-based economy; they only explain the new outcomes that occur in an information-based economy.

In a resource-constrained economy, products can be viewed as "congealed resources with a little additional knowledge." Limitations such as supply constraints, rising costs, and diminishing profits associated with a static state of equilibrium can ultimately stifle returns on investment. In an information-based economy, products can be viewed as "congealed knowledge with little additional resources." The previous resource based constraints need not limit returns. The new rules can be explained as follows (Arthur, 1996):

- Development costs are high relative to production costs. Thus, unit production cost falls as sales volume increases (e.g., a pharmaceutical).
- Networks of users produce sales volumes that make a product the *de facto* industry standard (e.g., the Windows operating system).
- Extensive training is required for productive use. Once customers have invested resources in training to use a product, they prefer to update their skills incrementally rather than reinvest resources to learn a new product (e.g., single source provider of an airline fleet).

In an economy of increasing returns, a firm with an advantage over its competition often continues to maintain and extend its advantage. Also, a firm may operate in the twin economic worlds of increasing and diminishing returns. Manufacturing and other mass production operations face diminishing returns while the logistics, branding, marketing, and distribution operations are subject to increasing returns. At the end of their life cycle, some original knowledge-based products may become virtual commodities (e.g., the IBM PC).

Service firms, particularly information-based businesses, benefit from the networked structure of their business, the intimate relationship required in delivering their services, and the ability to rapidly tailor their offering to fulfill customer expectations and needs. Success in the realm of decreasing returns requires planning, control, and optimization in a static economic environment while success in an economy of increasing returns requires more dynamic and adaptive responses such as:

- Building an "installed customer base"—often achieved by initial discounting to buy market share.
- Recognizing the existence of ecology of products with members actively managing the product interdependencies and market feedback loops. (e.g., Wintel)
- Watching carefully for the "next big thing" and moving quickly to capitalize on the opportunity. (e.g. the Internet supplanting on-line services)

2.2 Customer as Queen

Supply has outstripped demand in the New Economy and the customer has become Queen. In their book, *The Profit Zone* Slywotzky and Morrison motivate a customer-centric perspective with this opening statement:

Thirty years ago, the customer didn't matter. That sounds heretical, but it is true. In the postwar business landscape of the 1950s and 60s, customer demand outstripped capacity. It was a supplier's world and large monolithic companies ruled. These sellers were in the economy's driver's seat. Today, in contrast, the number of customers is dwarfed only by the amount of information available about each option. There has been a secular shift from the supplier to the customer. Highly competitive markets and abundant information have placed the customer at the center of the business universe.
(Slywotzky and Morrison, 1997)

The customer-centric perspective reveals gaps in performance impossible to perceive from the producer-centric perspective. "The gap between the ideal product and service benefits desired by customers and what they are actually able to purchase" is the customer sacrifice (Hart, 1996). The concept of customer sacrifice can be used to explore missed opportunities of best-of-breed firms that may have highly satisfied customers but still miss the opportunity to delight the customer by meeting their individual needs. One strategy suggests that firms that discover this customer sacrifice gap should fill it, but initially only for their best customers (Pepper and Rogers, 1997a and 1997b). They recommend that firms consider the lifetime value of customers and pursue a share of customer strategy rather than a share of market strategy. With an investment in interactive technology and increased computing power, firms can capture and analyze every interaction they have with a valuable customer.

Over time they can form a "learning relationship" with the customer and give the customer exactly what he or she wants (Pine et al., 1995).

Peppers and Rogers justify their advice that firms move from mass marketing to 1:1 (one-to-one) marketing to the individual on these grounds:

- Customer preferences differ across granular segmentation rather than across broad demographic categories.
- Customer expectations are set by contact with anyone or any firm.
- Economical computation (analysis and storage) and numerous interactive opportunities to learn about customers abound (Burke, 1996).

These changes, referred to as marketing's electronic revolution or the move from traditional marketing to information-driven marketing (Deighton and Blatberg, 1995), include a shift away from market segmentation, whereby all customers with the same profile are treated identically. Instead, advertising, promotions, and ultimately pricing are narrowed to appeal to a specific individual rather than broadened to appeal to "typical" members of a group. In the New Economy, distribution channels link directly to consumers or attempt to co-manage consumers when distribution intermediaries are used. R&D priorities are driven by consumer needs and not just by the firm's core competencies. Some products and services are outsourced to better serve special customers. The emphasis of tracking and monitoring transactions changes the firm's performance metrics from periodic market share and sales volume toward continuous customer retention, cost of customer acquisition, and customer lifetime value (Deighton, 1996).

The information required to enable these marketing shifts may not be obtained cheaply as customers stop providing personal information for little or nothing in return (Hagel and Rayport, 1997). Customers have amassed a very rich and valuable store of information from multiple sources: cookie technology on Internet browsers; financial information captured in Quicken; on-line banking and credit card access; frequent flyer programs; and the ability to tie one's household data into other data sources such as Nielsen television data. Firms that act to leverage this type of data may find themselves earning the role of infomediary (i.e., information intermediary) when the power of information shifts to the customer (Komenar, 1997). Francis Swain, the technology manager of Dorr Farms, understands the value of data when he says, "My dream is not to farm but to own the information company that farmers hook up to for information on logistics, crop data, whatever." (Ferder, 1998)

2.3 Unbundling Products and Services

The adoption of a customer-centric orientation has lead firms to disassemble traditional packages of products, services, and information and reassemble them into new bundles at substantially the same cost. This approach to customers enables firms to maintain or increase the price of goods and services by addressing customer value. In the New Economy, flexible service offerings are one way to tailor products. This approach requires firms to understand their operations and customers well enough to successfully customize. Readily available sources of interactive marketing data have fueled the move toward tailored products and services.

Historically, firms have adopted flexible offerings more often in the product area than in the service area. However, in the New Economy, this approach may be a mistake since services accounted for seventy-seven percent of all employment and seventy-five percent of GNP in the United States in 1990. In addition, service related activities contributed most of the value-add in most manufacturing organizations and sixty-five to seventy-five percent of costs (Quinn, 1992). Many firms have ignored their service offerings to the extent that they do not know what service offerings the customer values. Thus, they neither know the cost to deliver service nor have they determined the price the customer is willing to pay (Anderson and Narus, 1997). Companies that create flexible service offerings from their standard services and enhance them with new or optional services have the opportunity to increase customer value and to reduce operating costs.

The following examples illustrate a common principle: all the companies have adopted the one-to-one marketing principle to achieve increasing returns via innovative application of the Internet's interactive capabilities. Through development of a purposeful learning relationship with their customers, they serve them better individually and simultaneously establish a higher customer switching cost. The more business these firms conduct with a customer, the better they understand and can benefit that customer. The larger the customer base, the better their customer preference databases reflects all customers. Eventually, a standard database of preferences could be shared across multiple businesses with customer approval and authorization to exploit the benefits of mass customization and EC.

E-trade: This Charles Schwab on-line discount brokerage service offers a new price point for securities trading. Schwab has 860,000 on-line account holders out of its 4.4 million total account holders. Of these customers, 182,000 primarily trade through the Internet. Schwab's on-line commerce accounts for approximately one-half of Forrester Research's estimated $111 billion annual on-line securities trading. Schwab's stock trades at a price multiple of four times annual sales and 32 times 1997 profits. Schwab offers its customers "anytime, anywhere, any way" access to an increasingly diverse and tailored set of products and services.

Amazon.com: This on-line catalog of 2.5 million book offers titles to prospective buyers that is many times what can be stocked at an average retail bookstore. With interactive searching capabilities, it has reduced the purchaser's searching transaction cost by an estimated 50 times and can provide instant inventory information. In addition, Amazon.com provides information typically offered by specialty bookstores, such as reviews from other readers and recommendations for similar books. Among these services are the ability to tailor a selection of books for a customer's preferences. In addition, personalized communications inform customers of reviews, releases, and other information tailored to their wants and needs.

Firefly: This "recommender" technology, purchased by Microsoft in 1998, is featured at its BigNote music site, http://www.bignote.com. Firefly asks consumers to rate music they know in order to match them with consumers with similar preferences. Data mining is used to make recommendations to the consumer on other music that he or she might enjoy given the preferences of others with similar tastes. The same recommendation system technology (and similar systems such as GroupLens, LikeMinds, and WiseWire) is being applied to preferences for many different items such as books, World Wide Web sites, and search results. Firefly's main site currently links consumers to the movie site FilmFinder, as well as to sites by Yahoo to recommend World Wide Web sites and by Barnes and Noble to recommend books. Firefly also maintains user-created chat rooms and bulletin boards to help like-minded individuals find one another and develop communities of interest around their shared preferences—thus customizing an individual's social experiences on the World Wide Web (Dragan, 1997).

Lee Printware: This T-shirt and sweatshirt subsidiary of VF Corp, had EDI links to its largest customers for years. Each time it wanted to add another customer, it had to deliver a turnkey system to the customer, thereby adding to Lee's training, support, and maintenance costs. The system was proprietary, difficult to use, and expensive to maintain. Lee has now implemented an Internet solution, "TieNet," which allowed it to put twelve of its largest distributors (ninety percent of its wholesale business) on the system in four months at a total cost of $125,000. Customers use World Wide Web browsers to place orders, check availability, and review order status. John Davis, vice president of information services for Lee, points out that with EDI each distributor had to invest $20,000 in hardware and software. Once the TieNet system was "built for one customer and sitting on our server, then it's just a matter of adding users and passwords. If they have a browser, that's all it takes." (Info Week, 1997) TieNet provides tailored inventory order management for each of Lee Printware's distributors.

2.4 Rise of the Virtual Enterprise

As implied by our title, the New Economy and Electronic Commerce have given rise to the era of Mass Customization. Dramatic changes in the structure of society and its commercial organization structure follow as a direct consequence. The New Economy's "focus upon the moment of exchange, and not on the system as a whole, has been profoundly absorbed into the worldview of the modern citizen." (Mulgan, 1998) No where is the effect of organization change more profound than in the discrete manufacturing sector where producers match their production rate closely with customer demand to provide a rapid, economical response to changing order patterns. The rise of customer expectation for a unique product requires manufacturers to embrace homogenous production of a wide variety of products. Producers' operating in a build-to-order mode control inventory levels with process triggers (both physical and electronic) that pull inventory through the supply chain as needed.

Push vs. Pull: The concepts of the supply chain and pull manufacturing systems have gained prominence with the general acceptance of the just in time (JIT) production philosophy (Bermudez, 1996). Push systems, typically associated with mass production methods, incorporate master schedule forecasts to initiate production in anticipation of demand. The finished product is pushed into the distribution network for later retail sale. Traditional manufacturing organizations, practices, and computer systems developed for these build-to-inventory markets have proven unworkable in the era of build-to-order markets.

Orders, rather than forecasts, drive pull systems. This direct linkage of actual demand to production planning and execution enables manufacturers to react rapidly to consumer orders and provides an opportunity to achieve price realization. For example, producers can implement yield management strategies that reward long range purchase guarantees with lower prices and exact premium price for short-term delivery appear on the horizon. As a result of these strategies, firms can reserve capacity for premium priced short-term orders while rejecting long-term orders. For perhaps the first time, orders will have unequal value to a firm.

Extended Enterprise: Excellent supply chain management calls for sales and operations planning that transcend company boundaries. It must involve every link of the supply chain (from the supplier's supplier to the customer's customer) to develop forecasts collaboratively and then maintain the required capacity to meet these forecasts across the enterprise. Channel-wide sales and operations planning can detect early warning signals of demand lurking in customer promotions, ordering patterns, and restocking algorithms and takes into account vendor and carrier capabilities, capacity, and constraints. Coordination of manufacturing scheduling and inventory deployment decisions can pay off handsomely, improving fill rates, asset turns, and cost metrics for all concerned.

The cost of distribution, marketing, and sales constitutes as little as ten percent to as much as eighty percent of the product cost. An erroneous prediction of high demand lead to excess inventory, the cost of which was hidden by the accounting practices of the distribution network. But with the advent of electronic commerce, the old cost model does not pertain. As the manufacturer synchronizes production with demand and delivers directly to the customer, finished goods inventory can be reduced at the distribution end of the supply chain, leading to lower costs and higher profits. To achieve real economy, the manufacturer must couple real-time demand information from the supply chain, the capability to produce goods under a flow manufacturing philosophy, and creative use of outbound logistics to reduce the volume in the inventory "pipeline."

Fisher argues that firms must choose the right type of supply chain for their business. He proposes two types of supply chains depending upon the type of product supported. Efficient chains support products (functional) where predictable delivery volumes and continual improvement are key to cost control. Responsive chains support products (fashion or technology) where guaranteed availability and rapid response to changes in demand levels are key to obtaining price realization (Fisher, 1997).

In a simulation study of the impact of information sharing on order fulfillment in divergent assembly supply chains (like Fisher's responsive type), Shaw found that efficient information sharing enables inventory cost reduction while maintaining acceptable order fulfillment cycle performance. One may conjecture that information, which provides the basis for enhanced coordination and reduced uncertainty, can substitute for inventory. This work may lead to development information-based rules of inventory management that will complement the current rules that balance lead-time and holding costs (Strader et al., 1998).

"[T]he manufacturing/distribution supply chain can act to amplify market variability rather than to dampen it." In one analysis that incorporated a multiechelon model (wholesale, retail, market) in an environment of nonstationary demand, the results suggest the benefits of reducing demand variation by filtering retail orders through distribution centers rather than filling them directly. These results were highly dependent upon the industry as typified by wholesaler lead-time, inventory control policies used at each echelon, and retail order patterns (Aganha and Cohen, 1998). Filtering through distribution centers counters the effects of forecast errors, grouping orders into batches to obtain administrative efficiencies, use of promotional sales programs to meet marketing goals, artificial customer orders placed to hedge availability in periods of decreasing supply.

Flow Manufacturing: Demand Flow Technology® (DFT) a shop floor control strategy developed by J_c-I-T Institute of Technology, Inc. incorporates modern manufacturing principles to pull raw materials and products through the production process. The pull begins at the point consumption controlled by production triggers (kanban) that match the rate of production with rate of customer demand. A factory organized according to DFT principles exhibits flexibility in the face of changing demand levels and the capability to incorporate technological innovations as they occur. Although a firm may incorporate several elements of DFT, its full adoption requires major changes in corporate culture, organizational structures, management attitudes, worker relationships, as well as process-line designs from a traditional plant (Emmanuel and Miller, 1998).

DFT enables production of a high quality product in the shortest production time and at the lowest possible cost by reducing the amount of non-value-added work. In the abstract, the flow process reduces to a sequence of tasks to assemble the product dictated by a flat bill of material and paced by actual demand. The typical flow line consists of a single assembly line supported by linked synchronous feeder lines, adjacent asynchronous machine cells, and JIT delivery of purchased materials delivered at point-of-use (Constanza, 1994). Thus, DFT controls inventory levels but more importantly, retains the inventory in its most flexible (and economical) state, as raw material.

DFT requires careful assembly line design to ensure economical operation and nearly perfect quality levels for smooth operation. As material flows from one workstation to the next, built-in quality procedures instruct the worker to check the work performed at the prior operation. This direct linkage reduces the number of defects that can build up in the system and provides instant feedback to the problem operation. Accordingly, DFT management requires metrics that balance manpower, material, and capacity constraints to accommodate anticipated fluctuations in product mix and production volume. Since the control of production rate requires changing work assignments, a flexible, cross-trained work force becomes an imperative (Bermudez, 1996).

3 Electronic Commerce

The answers to three questions provide the visibility needed to enable organizational change and the transition to mass customization: (1) WHO has my goods? (2) WHERE are my goods? (3) WHEN will my goods arrive? They inform the system about the state of goods throughout the enterprise network across procurement, production, distribution pipeline, warehouse, or retail display.

In commerce, oral statements, written contracts, and digital messages have all, at one time or another, be adopted to execute a business transition. Oral messages and paper transactions often spawn secondary and tertiary transactions into the system that can disrupt the process flow by shear volume if not beuracracy. Digital messages can have the same effect. However, properly designed process flows implemented with electronic commerce (EC) in mind allow information open accessed to the transaction by all parties.

EC encompasses all business-to-business and business-to-customer transactions that involve the buying and selling of goods and services, and the transfer of funds, through digital communication. It includes all inter-company and intra-company functions (such as marketing, finance, manufacturing, selling, and negotiation) that enable commerce and, electronic data interchange, file transfer, fax, and interaction with a remote computer. Recently, the scope of EC expanded to include the business-to-customer relationship including buying and selling over the Internet, and all other ways of doing business over digital networks.

EC originated during the 1970's in the grocery and transportation industries as electronic data interchange (EDI) to facilitate the electronic exchange of routine business documents. It expanded across other industries as cost reduction pressures prompted systems professionals to develop data transmission conventions to enable the computer-to-computer exchange of machine-readable data through the use of standard formats and content. Although the existing information technology limited EDI applications to replacement of paper documents with electronic versions of those same documents, significant savings were realized by limiting the number of people required to handle purchase orders and to maintain reliable communication with suppliers. Progressive companies have recently begun to adopt EDI to manage orders.

The long-term benefits promised by EDI require its full integration throughout business systems of producers and the multi-tiered supply chain. Although many secondary and tertiary members of the supply chain initially complied with the producer's EDI standards, they have never fully integrated EDI into their business culture and practices. As producers and members of the first tier suppliers continued to expand their reliance upon EDI by implementing multiple related transaction sets many of the secondary and tertiary suppliers did not follow their lead and are unable to reciprocate with appropriate transactions.

Table 1. Phases of collaboration in EC

Partnership relationship	Description	Supply chain integration support	Types of information
Transactional	Computer-to-computer transmission of fixed structure transactional information.	• No support of synchronized planning. • Support of synchronized execution.	• Purchase orders • Invoices • Order acknowledgement • Load tendering • Load acknowledgement • Freight invoicing • Freight payment
Information sharing	Trading partners share and exchange information.	• Supports synchronized, but not independent planning. • Maximum support of integrated solution.	• Order status • Shipment tracking and tracing • Sales forecasts • Production schedules • Inventory levels • Product designs and specs • Product descriptions and prices • Sales promotional calendars.
Collaborative	Trading partners jointly develop plans	• Supports joint synchronized planning. • Minimum support of integrated execution.	• New product plans • Product design and technical specs • Product packaging • Pricing promotion plans • Demand plans • Replenishment plans • Store layout and shelf utilization.

Source: AMR Research, 1998

In spite of these disappointments, companies have begun to act to obtain the benefits of real-time information sharing and transactions to support synchronized, optimized supply chain planning and execution. They plan to move goods from end-to-end of the supply chain in a just-in-time (JIT) fashion to reduce the inventory in the pipeline and avoid delays induced by funds transfer or for credit-checks.

Generally, trading partnerships evolve over time, often starting with transactional exchanges and moving toward information sharing. Electronic collaboration is usually the final form of relationship established between trading partners. This is achieved by building upon previously established transactional and information-sharing infrastructures (Lapide, 1998). The three phases of collaboration in EC shown in Table 1 provide a useful picture of the past, present, and future of business-to-business EC.

4 Mass Customization

Mass customization aims to satisfy the customer with product variety and customization economically and quickly. The willingness of customers to pay more to satisfy their special needs justifies its adoption in low- to medium-volume markets. Indeed, intense competition in today's business environment mandates that firms attend to both efficiency and perceived customer value.

Quinn points out that that a number of firms (primarily service-oriented firms) have managed to capture "both lowest-cost outputs and maximum personalization and customization for customers," and in so doing they have achieved mass customization (Quinn, 1992). Given the advances in manufacturing technologies, the importance of service, and new levels of marketing sophistication and interactive technology, the new commerce holds great potential for mass customization. Three factors that contribute to mass customization and market fragmentation (Anderson et al., 1997):

- Direct customer addressing coupled with profitable production of variety;
- Delivery channel diversity to exploit direct customer addressing and variety; and
- Customer expectation for customized products, expanded services, and immediate availability through a preferred delivery channel.

The impact of mass customization, broadly implemented, would substantially change the competitive landscape in the global economy. According to John Landry, the chief technology officer for IBM/Lotus: *I'm not talking about incremental change here. I'm talking about a set of technologies that will be as significant in impact as assembly-line technology was to mass production, and as mass-media technology was to mass-marketing. But this internetworking technology will replace many of the advantages of mass production and mass marketing by allowing for mass customization...creating, in some industries, custom goods better, faster, and cheaper than mass-produced goods and providing the framework for addressing individuals with custom marketing and messages and individualized service* (Tapscott, 1995).

A recent study of mass customization in the manufacturing sector of the United Kingdom found that of the firms that implemented mass customization, twenty-one percent increased their market share, twenty-four percent decreased the time to respond to customer orders, fourteen percent increased their profitability, and five percent cut manufacturing costs. Barriers to mass customization included inflexible factories, customization expense, rigid information systems, change management, difficulties understanding what customers really want, and suppliers who could not match mass customization requirements (IBM, 1997). These three components leverage the interactive nature of new commerce technology, allowing firms to respond flexibly from a stable and cost-effective operations base (Shank, 1997):

1. A customer interface that allows customers to easily state their preferences and that adds value by assisting customers in determining preferences;
2. A configuration system, software, or manual that takes the customer's order and manages the capability modules that must be brought together to respond to the request; and
3. A capabilities management system that identifies required capability modules, adjusts them, and manages extended enterprise interfaces for capabilities obtained outside (or across) the firm.

4.1 Design

Mass customization strategies vary across industry, product, and customer but all depend upon appropriate designs. They obtain economy of scope through adoption of modular designs that fulfill customer preferences for a few changeable features (non-enduring) in conjunction with many features that do not change (enduring). This modular concept maps enduring customer needs to a static product platform and non-enduring preferences to interchangeable functional modules that can be mated with the platform via a standard interface (Sahiwal, 1997).

Modularity is a strategy for organizing complex products and processes efficiently (Baldwin and Clarck, 1997). A modular system is composed of units (or modules) that are designed independently but still function as an integrated whole. Designers achieve modularity by partitioning information into *visible design rules* and *hidden design parameters*. Modularity is beneficial only if the partition is precise, unambiguous, and complete.

The visible design rules pertain to decisions that affect subsequent design decisions. Ideally, visible design rules are established early in the design process and communicated broadly to those involved. Visible design rules fall into three categories:

- An *architecture* that specifies what modules will comprise the system and their function.
- *Interfaces* that describe detailed module interactions including fit connectivity, and communication.
- *Standards* that specify test procedures for conformity to design rules and to measure module compatibility and interactions.

The hidden design parameters pertain to decisions that do not affect the global design but relate to a single local module. These parameters can be chosen late, changed often, and communicated only with the local module design team.

Modular systems are difficult to design because the visible design rules, that must be specified in advance, require an intimate knowledge of the end-customer's application and of the inner workings of the product. The time saved in parallel development of independent modules may be lost during the final system integration. In particular, engineering details that once were of little concern to marketing executives may now play a prominent role in their early strategic decisions.

Modular design alone does not guarantee successful mass customization strategy. Successful mass customization incorporates derivative product families to smooth progression to the next product generation, modular design to enable economical upgrades, and exploitation of the pricing advantages obtained from product differentiation in areas where the customer perceives value. The value of any product or service is derived from its ability to meet a customer's priorities. Customer priorities are, in simple terms, the things that are so important to them that they will pay a premium for them or, when they don't get them, they will switch suppliers (Slywotzky and Morrison, 1997).

Since the early 1900s, advocates of mass production have argued that its full potential could not be realized unless product design, sales, and delivery were standardized as well. The 1950s relaxed this extreme position to accommodate customization within market segments. A five-step continuum from pure standardization (or mass production) to pure customization (or craft production) in the design, fabrication, assembly, and distribution of an item has been proposed (Lampel and Mintzburg, 1996). Products can range from being commodities to being one of a kind items. In fact, most firms that embrace mass customization today operate in the middle of this continuum in the "customized standardization" mode that incorporates standardized design and fabrication with customized assembly and distribution.

The implicit modularity in these strategies enables designers to develop product that meet customer needs, can be fabricated and assembled to meet those objectives, and are readily distributed. Without an extended customer view, the full potential for product diversification can not be realized. For example, a component supplier must understand the economic motivation of the manufacturer procuring the components, the distributor of the finished goods, as well as the end-use customer to design a component for a modular product.

Parametric computer-aided design tools and flexible manufacturing technologies enable the transition from the pure strategies (located at either end of the continuum) toward the hybrid strategy (located in the middle). The product focus deals with the enduring features of the product while the customer focus deals with the non-enduring aspects of the product. These two elements merge during the fabrication and assembly processes. Product differentiation that resides in the distribution channels remains distinct from production itself. However, the essential link to the customer occurs at both the enterprise (production) and distribution levels.

4.2 Production

The shift from mass production to mass customization involves a shift from deriving profits from volume to deriving profits from variety. However, just as with modularity, product variety alone is not sufficient for firms to be successful in mass customization. In order to benefit from a mass customization strategy, manufacturers must seek out "good variety" but avoid "bad variety." The value judgements of good and bad relate directly to the economics of production. Good variety encompasses changes or additions that increase customer value in excess of the cost incurred in the product, its production, or in requisite organizational complexity. Bad variety increases these costs without an offsetting increase in customer value.

The attempt to overcome the cost and constraints of time and space with information technology follows directly after an era in which product proliferation was seen as the solution to meeting customer expectations. Firms have used new product introductions and line extensions as competitive weapons, as ways to attract and retain customers in an increasingly competitive and overcrowded marketplace. Many of these products have missed the mark or simply maintained competitive parity. In an attempt to more efficiently differentiate their products and services and give customers more of what they want rather than more variety, some firms have adopted mass customization to more efficiently customize or bundle products and services to meet the needs of each individual consumer or business customer.

The automobile manufacturers, operating in an assemble-to-order mode, have perfected mass customization in recent years. Open any World Wide Web page or new car shopper catalog and you will find vehicles specified by model along with a series of options for tailoring your order to meet a variety of appearance, performance, and economic preferences. Lower volume heavy equipment manufacturers mode of operation more closely resembles configure-to-order. They also offer a choice of models but the add-on components are more highly configured than the option packages offered by the automobile industry. This second group of manufacturers runs the risk of introducing "bad variety" in a counterproductive attempt to delight the customer. The following examples describe two industry leaders that have met the challenge of operating profitably near the highly risky end of the continuum between assemble-to-order and configure-to-order.

John Deere: In 1992, John Deere introduced a new line of row crop planter products together with new production methods. Previously, the planters were mass-produced for inventory in a batch build process. Picking the required components and options from inventory and shipping them unassembled to a dealer for final assembly completed the order fulfillment process. However, the design complexity of the new line of planters required a more controlled assembly process than could be provided at a dealership.

John Deere responded to this opportunity by refurbishing its production facility to support elements of flow manufacturing and embracing a team oriented assembly process and pay system. To support and sustain its commitment to meet customer expectations for product variety, availability, and quality, they adopted a genetic algorithm-based sequencing system in 1994. The sequencing system produces an assembly line lineup that minimizes the number of production constraints encountered to fill committed orders in a profitable manner.

Thus, John Deere addressed the issue of "good versus bad" product variety by directly confronting the issue of production complexity. Although technically not intended for mass customization, Deere's modular approach to product design enables it. The improvements in factory volume, finished product inventory cost, and order cycle time have justified the cost of changing the production method (Fulkerson, 1997).

Textile Clothing Technology Corporation: Operation of $(TC)^2$, the Textile Clothing Technology Corporation in Cary, North Carolina, demonstrates the potential for combining the technology of the New Economy, EC, and ability to meet individual customer preferences for competitive advantage. Organized originally a textile research consortium, $(TC)^2$ has organized from being a network of textile and clothing manufacturers to become a virtual corporation. They produce custom orders from data obtained by digital body scan from custom design terminals located in stores. The virtual organization fills orders broadcasts over the network through a reverse auction to determine which firms will provide the individual components of the order such as fabric, buttons, or cut and sew operations. These individual components are fabricated, manufactured, or pulled from stock and assembled for next-day delivery by exploiting existing inbound and outbound material logistics systems (Upton and McAfee, 1996).

5 Conclusions

We have explored the implications of the New Economy and Electronic Commerce upon the rise of mass customization and organizational change in the service industries and discrete manufacturing. Although much of the discussion has focused upon technology, the issue is not technology as an end in itself but technology as the means to the broader societal changes that it produces.

The shift away from mass marketing toward mass customization parallels a shift away from mass communication (broadcasting) toward targeted communication (direct addressing) along with complementary moves in the area of distribution logistics. The areas of communication and logistics appear to be co-evolving as advancements in one-area precipitate advancements in the other. "Throughout the twentieth century physical mobility and communications grew in tandem rather than as substitutes. The spread of the telephone accompanied that of commuter railways and trams, the radio accompanied the spread of cars and airplanes, the television that of motorways and jets, and everywhere the graphs of traffic movement move in parallel with the graphs of communication usage. [...] [Connectivity] tends to be cumulative. Each new medium of communication does not replace its predecessor so much as complement them." (Mulgan, 1998)

Communications has progressed from early stages (one-to-few and one-to many) to advanced stages (few-to-many and many to many) within the last century. One effect of this communications revolution may be a "new economics of information" that will transform the very structure of society. When the trade-off between richness (bandwidth, customization, and interactivity) and reach (size of audience) is eliminated, specialized communication channels will no longer be necessary and everyone can communicate richly with everyone else on the basis of shared standards. This highly connected model of communications might be called a hyperarchy after the hyperlinks of the World Wide Web. "When the principles of hyperarchy are thoroughly understood, they will provide a way to understand not only positioning strategies within business and industries but also more fundamental questions of corporate organization and identity." (Evans and Wurster, 1997) This hyperarchy effect can be already observed as firms are fundamentally changing their manufacturing, distribution, and delivery practices to enable mass customization. The emergence of hyperarchy is depicted in the changing structure of manufacturing organizations depicted in Figure 1.

The full implications of this apparent paradigm shift remain unpredictable. This cautionary note reflects the attitude of a growing group of "technorealists" who challenge society to think critically about the role that tools and interfaces play in human evolution and everyday life. They remind us that "the current tide of technological transformation, while important and powerful, is actually a continuation of waves of change that have taken place throughout history. Looking, for example, at the history of the automobile, television, or the telephone—not just the devices but the institutions they became—we see profound benefits as well as substantial costs. Similarly, we anticipate mixed blessings from today's emerging technologies..." (Technorealism, 1998)

References

"Making it for you--personally." *The Foundation for Manufacturing and Industry, Department of Trade and Industry*, IBM Consulting Group, February 1997.

"Strictly Business." *Information Week.* March 17, 1997: 38-44.

Aganha, M., and M. Cohen, "The Stabilizing Effect of Inventory in Supply Chains", *Operations Research*, Volume 46, Supplement Number 3, (1998): pages s72-s83

Anderson, E., G. S. Day, and V. K. Rangan. "Strategic Channel Design." *Sloan Management Review.* Summer 1997: 59-69.

Anderson, J. and J. A. Narus. "Capturing the Value of Supplementary Services." *Harvard Business Review.* January-February 1995: 75.

Aurthur, B., "Increasing Returns and the New World of Business." *Harvard Business Review.* July-August 1996: 100-109

Baldwin, C. Y.; K. B. Clark, "Managing in an Age of Modularity", *Harvard Business Review*, September-October 1997: 84-93

Bermudez, J. *Synchronized and Flow: Manufacturing Techniques to Support Supply Chain Management.* Advanced Manufacturing Research, Report on Manufacturing, March 1996.

Burke, R. "Virtual Shopping: Breaking in Marketing Research." *Harvard Business Review.* March-April 1996: 120-131.

Carayannis, E. and J. Alexander, "Electronic Commerce and Knowledge Economics, Trust and Coopetition in a Global Business Environment, *Journal of Internet Banking and Commerce,* http://www.arraydev.com/commerce/jibc/9703-05.htm, accessed 7/6/98

Costanza, J., *The Quantum Leap in Speed-to-Market: Demand Flow Technology & Business Strategy,* J_c-I-T Institute of Technology, Inc., Englewood, CO, 1994

Deighton, J. and R. Blatberg. "Marketing's electronic revolution." *Advertising Age.* October 25, 1995.

Deighton, J., "The Future of Interactive Marketing." *Harvard Business Review.* November-December 1996: 151-162.

Dragan, R. V. "Advice from the Web." *PC Magazine.* September 9, 1997: 133-144.

Emmanuel A. K. and R. A. Miller, Demand Flow Technology® for Transnational Companies, http://www.gsia.cmu.edu/afs/andrew/gsia/bosch/work/kam pou ris.html, accessed 6/26/98

Encyclopedia of the New Economy, http://www.hotwired.com/special/ene/.

Evans, P. B. and T. S. Wurster, "Strategy and the New Economics of Information", *Harvard Business Review,* September-October 1997: 71-82.

Ferder, B. J., "Agriculture's Future: The Digitally Enhanced Megafarm." *The New York Times.* May 4, 1998.

Fisher, M. "What Is the Right Supply Chain for Your Product?" *Harvard Business Review.* March-April 1997: 105.

Fulkerson, B. "A Response to Dynamic Changes in the Market Place." *Decision Support Systems.* Vol. 21, No. 3, November 1997: 199-214.

Gray, M. Unpublished internal communication, Deere & Company, 1998.

Hagel, J. and J. F. Rayport. "The Coming Battle for Customer Information." *Harvard Business Review.* January-February 1997: 53.

Hart, C., "Made to order." *Marketing Management.* V 5(2), Summer 1996: 11-23.

Komenar, M., *Electronic Marketing: Comprehensive Marketing Techniques to Help You Reach a Broader Market.* New York: John Wiley & Sons, 1997.

Lampel, J. and H. Mintzberg. "Customizing customization." *Sloan Management Review.* Fall 1996: 21-30.

Lapide, L., "Are We Moving from Buyers and Sellers to Collaborators", *The Report on Supply Management,* AMR Research, Boston, MA, July 1998

Mulgan, G., *Connexity: How to Live in a Connected World,* Harvard Business School Press, Boston, MA, 1998

Peppers, D. and M. Rogers. *Enterprise One To One.* New York: Doubleday, 1997

Peppers, D. and M. Rogers. *The One To One Future: Building Relationships One Customer at a Time.* New York: Doubleday, 1997.

Pine, B. J., D. Peppers, and M. Rogers. "Do You Want To Keep Your Customers Forever?" *Harvard Business Review.* March-April 1995: 103.

Quinn, J. B., *The Intelligent Enterprise.* New York: The Free Press, 1992.

Sahiwal, R. "New Product Development Process for Mass Customization", Unpublished manuscript, 1997.

Shank, M. "Mass Customization: Implementing the Adaptable Organization." Unpublished IBM Consulting Group white paper, 1997.

Slywotzky, A. and D. J. Morrison, *The Profit Zone: How Strategic Design Will Lead You to Tomorrow's Profits,* Times Business-Random House, 1997

Strader, T. J., F. Lin, and M. J. Shaw, "Simulation of Order Fulfillment in Divergent Assembly Supply Chains", *Journal of Artificial Societies and Social Simulation* vol. 1, no. 2, 1998 [web page] <http://www.soc.surrey.ac.uk/JASSS/1/2/5.html>

Tapscott, D. *The Digital Economy: Promise and Peril in the Age of Networked Intelligence.* NewYork: McGraw-Hill, 1995

Technorealism, [web page] http://www.technorealism.org/ [Accessed 12 may 1998].

Upton, D. M. and A. McAfee. "The Real Virtual Factory." *Harvard Business Review.* July-August 1996: 123

CHAPTER 20
Supply Chain Processes and Relationships for Electronic Commerce

Daniel E. O'Leary
Marshall School of Business, University of Southern California, CA, USA
oleary@usc.edu

In this chapter, I survey recent developments in supply chain relationships that have been designed to exploit technology. Firms are now in a position to more tightly link themselves with other firms through their use of supply chains in order to attain greater efficiencies.

Keywords: Supply Chain Management; Electronic Commerce

1 Introduction

Supply chain processes and relationships increasingly are designed to exploit changes in technology. The purpose of this paper is to summarize some of the changes that have taken place in those processes and relationships. Changing supply chain processes have evolved from classic paper-based systems and documents, towards reengineered processes that involve electronic capture and transmission of less document information. Supply chain relationships have evolved from loosely coupled relationships into virtual organizations, coupled with integrated enterprise resource planning systems.

In particular, this paper elicits a number of specific changes in supply chain processes that have been designed to speed transactions and improve the quality of information, including,

- Electronic data interchange to facilitate speed and quality of information interchange,
- Gathering information directly from the source, rather than have one accountant talk to another,
- Suppliers determining order quantities and order times for buyers,
- Elimination of invoices saving administrative work,
- Using barcoded labels to help eliminate invoices and facilitate improved quality of information,
- Automating the matching of goods ordered and received,
- Developing different payment triggers, such as paying for inventory when received or used.

Further, supply chain relationships have changed to accommodate changes in technology and changes in reengineered processes:

- Firms interfacing enterprise resource planning systems to facilitate inter-organization interchange and access to information, and
- Firms developing virtual organizations through integration of their supply chains.

2 Supply Chains

At the simplest level the supply chain consists of a single link between a supplier and a buyer, for example, where a supplier provides goods to a retailer. In more complex settings there can be multiple interlinking chains, with both extended supply chains into suppliers and out of the buyers, where buyer and seller roles become intermediary roles. In addition, there can be multiple inputs to any buyer or multiple outputs from any seller.

2.1 Sources of Costs in the Supply Chain

There are three primary sets of costs in any supply chain: inventory; adminstrative and information flows; and production and transportation costs. Supply chains are beginning to address issues such as minimization of these costs across the supply chain.

Inventory: Supply chains are linked by common, often conflicting, interests of getting products to customers in order to meet demand and yet a desire to limit inventory, ultimately system-wide.

> *Guessing consumer demand is a little like forecasting the weather. So manufacturers and retailers usually build up inventories to make up for the imperfections in their predictions. But inventory costs money. Stockpiles take up space, and companies have to pay people to do something as routine as moving them to one side of the warehouse from another. What's more they tie up cash that companies could be using for things like splashy marketing and dreaming up new products.* (Brownlee, p. R12 1996)

Administrative Costs and Information Flows: In order to control inventory and respond to customer demand, supply chains are linked together through flows of information regarding the purchase and sale of goods. That information is communicated either on paper or electronically on a number of documents. Administrative systems have been built up to process these information flows. In many cases, administrative activities can be shifted from buyer to seller or seller to buyer in the supply chain. However, with a shift of activities there is generally also a shift of administrative costs from one party to the other. In some cases, these shifts in administrative costs results in changes in other costs, such as production or transportation costs.

Production and Transportation Costs: The third category of costs in the supply chain are production and transportation costs. In supply chains, we will see a supplier take on additional administrative costs from the buyer, in order to smooth and/or decrease its production and transportation costs, while decreasing its cycle time.

3 Communication Processes

Classic communication between supplier and buyer was done using paper-based systems. Increasingly, those paper-based processes are being replaced using electronic data interchange (EDI).

3.1 Classic Paper Based Systems

Classic supply chain system documents are paper-based, with a number of inherent limitations. Documents are used to create other documents. As a result, the probability of an error increases as information is transcribed from one document to another. Further, some of the developers of documents and some environments, e.g., loading docks, are seen as having limited reliability. Although, paper documents can be inputted to a computer-based environment, development and data entry of document information requires multiple transcriptions of the data. As a result, such processes can result in the introduction of additional errors into the system. Paper-based systems also are dependent on ensuring that all appropriate departments get copies of the documents necessary to do their job. If even a small percentage of those documents get lost or misplaced there can be gaps in the systems and orders can go unfilled.

3.2 Electronic Data Interchange

Electronic data interchange is the electronic transmission of data in standard format. Typically it takes the form of particular documents such as purchase orders or invoices. When compared to paper, EDI can have a substantial impact on the costs.

> *RJR Nabisco estimates that the cost of processing a paper-based purchase order is $70, whereas the same transaction performed through EDI costs less than $1.* (Millman, 1998, p. 83)

Differences in costs arise for a number of reasons. EDI documents only need be entered one time, thus cutting down on administrative costs and costs due to errors. EDI transactions typically originate from reliable sources and locations. Accordingly, in general, EDI transactions have greater source reliability than many paper processes. Since EDI is in electronic format, EDI transactions can be made accessible to a range of users simultaneously through use of an integrated database system. With access to an integrated database system there is no need to ensure that a paper copy is available at all appropriate locations.

Historically, EDI-based systems can require substantial expense. In part, the expenses of operating an EDI system derive from use of costly value added networks (VANs). However, with the advent of the Internet, the underlying cost structure may be changing. For example, for EDI over the Internet, in some settings, according to Cone (1998, p. 107) small suppliers can get into EDI for well under $1000.

4 Purchase Order Processes

There have been two trends facilitating reengineering of purchase order processes: changing how the information is gathered and changing who originates the order.

4.1 Purchase Order Processes

Typically, purchase orders originate when an ordering department indicates that there is a need for some goods to be purchased, e.g., to be used in a production process. Generally, the ordering department is responsible for choosing the amount of goods to be ordered, when they are needed, etc., based on their assessment of their particular needs. The internal order is copied onto a purchase order form which establishes the legal contract between the supplier and the buyer. A copy of the purchase order is kept in purchasing, one is sent to the ordering department, one is sent to accounts payable, one is sent to the receiving dock and two are sent to the buyer. Of those two sent to the buyer, one is signed and returned to the supplier indicating acceptance of the contract.

4.2 Reengineering How Purchase Order Information Is Captured

For computer-based systems, order information can be captured in paper form and then placed into the computer (as in a classic paper-based process), or it can be directly input into the computer by the purchasing department, gathering the information directly from the source. Unfortunately, the more times that any data is handled the higher the probability of an error. As a result, information generally has a higher quality if information is directly gathered from the source. Accordingly, origination of purchase orders can be reengineered by directly inputting information into electronic form rather than cascading through paper and then into electronic format.

4.3 Which Company "Writes" the Purchase Order and "Determines" Quantity?

In classic systems the ordering company determines order information, writes the order and then sends the order to the supplier. Unfortunately, ordering departments vary in their quality of being able to assess the need and timing of goods. However, determining order quantity is a decision that affects both the ordering and supplying company. If goods are not on the shelf then consumers cannot buy them hurting **both** supplier and retailer. Further, unfortunately, different potential ordering departments may have limited understanding of purchasing, including what to purchase and how much to purchase. Accordingly, in some situations the supplier may better understand consumer needs and thus be in a better position to write the purchase order and choose what and how much should be ordered. In other settings, buyers wish to shift administrative costs out to sellers. As a result, there has been a shift of the generation of some purchase orders from particular buyers to suppliers.

In order for suppliers to make such decisions they need information on sales. At least two arrangements have found use in order to provide suppliers with that information. First, information on shipments from warehouses was sent to suppliers to facilitate their determination of orders. However, there is a lag between actual customer demand at the retail level and new shipments from stores to warehouses. Further, those delays are not under the control of the supplier, since they are a function of the buyer's systems. Second, information on actual customer purchases from the retail stores also have been used to facilitate determination of orders. Generally, suppliers prefer this data since it is not delayed or messaged by buyer systems. Accordingly, it allows direct development of "better" order.

In addition, suppliers like to be in a position of determining orders since that information can be used to smooth supplier production and transportation needs. As a result, the supplier trades off potentially increased administrative requirements for the ability to reduce its costs in other areas.

5 Receiving Documents

Information about receiving goods from buyers is captured in the receiving memorandum. Technology provides a tool to facilitate reengineering of receiving memorandums using scanning.

5.1 Receiving Memorandums

When the goods are received they are examined at the receiving dock and the quantity received is recorded. Receiving information is entered on a receiving memorandum. If there is a purchase order system, then when the goods are received the personnel on the loading dock check to ensure that goods received have been ordered by consulting their copy of the particular purchase order. A copy of the receiving memorandum is kept in receiving and a copy is sent to the accounts payable department, indicating that goods can be paid for because they have been received.

Unfortunately, loading docks are not seen as the most reliable source of information. Weather conditions, employee capabilities, employee interests and other factors can have a negative influence on the quality of the information about arriving goods. As a result, accounting processes typically require invoices, in part to confirm what was shipped from supply chain partners.

5.2 Reengineering Receiving Memorandums

However, as an alternative to having the loading dock prepare a receiving memorandum, shipments can be accompanied by bar code tags, originating from the vendor, that contain information as to who shipped the goods, what goods are contained in the shipment, how much was shipped, etc. Those tags can then be scanned by dock workers with the result that the bar coded information is then directly captured in electronic format. Adopting use of the bar codes and scanning technology releases some of the concern for reliability of dock workers processing information. In addition, bar codes can effectively replace invoice information, offering a more timely multiuse source of information. Bar coded tags that accompany shipments offer an approach to communicating information about the shipment that is fast and provides quality less costly information flows.

6 Invoice Processes

One of the parameters in the design of supply chain management is the invoice process. An important way of redesigning is to actually remove invoices from supply chain systems.

6.1 Invoices

Invoices typically are sent after the goods are sent. Generally, one invoice is generated for each purchase order. In some cases one invoice is generated for each shipment. At the receiving company, after receipt of the invoice, the invoice is matched with the purchase order and receiving memorandum to make sure that the company is being billed for the goods that it ordered and received.

Invoices differ from the purchase order and receiving memorandum (both generated internally), because they provide external evidence of the purchase. As a result, one of the primary forces for keeping invoices are those concerned with classic internal controls, such as the internal or external auditor. In some countries the concern for control afforded by invoices is embedded in the law, e.g., Belgium, by requiring that invoices be issued for purchases.

6.2 Reengineering Invoice Processes

Since the generation of any document can result in errors, the more documents that are generated the higher the number of errors. As a result, in general, the more invoices, the more errors on the invoices and the more errors in matching. Further, if there are many invoices then those invoices are likely to be distributed over time, with some arriving sooner, rather than later. Thus, the number of invoices can interfere with timely and quality processing. In addition, generating and processing invoices has a large administrative cost, typically measured on a per invoice basis. As a result, one approach to potentially decreasing administrative costs is to decrease the number of invoices generated or received. Accordingly, reengineering of invoice processes have focused on reducing the number of invoices.

Single Invoice: Processing a lot of invoices is expensive. As a result, some companies, such as K-Mart have begun to have their suppliers provide them with a single invoice covering all the purchases made from all branches of the supplier. This approach results in a shift of administrative costs from the buyer to the supplier. By requiring the supplier to put all purchases on a single invoice the buyer cuts down on buyer's matching processes, and as a result on its own administrative costs. However, requiring a supplier to put all information on a single invoice makes a substantial requirement of the supplier's information systems. In particular, the supplier's systems now need to provide summarized information rather than individual purchase order transactions. Summarization processes can generate errors. As a result, supplier systems have to be constructed so that they facilitate the ability to generate a single invoice.

No Invoices: Invoices are not really needed if all other systems work the way they are supposed to. If the supplier sends what is on the purchase order and if transportation works as it is supposed to then the purchase order and receiving order quantities will be the same. As a result, the invoice should only contain redundant information. In addition, if the goods are accompanied by a bar coded summary of the goods, then that information can substitute as the invoice. Accordingly, for either or both reasons, some companies such as Ford have eliminated the use of invoices (Hammer 1990).

7 How Can "Matching" be Reengineered?

Prior to payment, the appropriate documents are matched, in order to ensure that payment is for what was ordered and received. Matching provides a control over supply chain transactions.

7.1 Matching Purchase Order, Receiving Memorandum and Invoice

Administratively, the accounts payable department typically is responsible for matching each invoice with its corresponding purchase order and the receiving memorandum generated with the receipt of the goods. If the information is the same on all three documents then the documents are matched and the invoice is paid. If the information is not the same then any anomalies must be corrected or accounted for before the bill is paid.

7.2 Reengineering the Matching Process

Costs associated with the matching process are dependent on the number of documents being matched, with some predictable tendencies:

- the more paper the higher the probability of an error.
- the more documents the higher costs of matching
- the more waiting the higher the probability of a lost document or error in information

As a result, reengineering the matching process has taken three directions. First, the matching process is designed to use electronic-based information. Accordingly this requires the reengineering of the purchasing process: directly entering information from purchasing; scanning receiving information; using EDI to communicate invoice information. Second, the number of items being matched has been reduced at firms such as Ford (Hammer 1990). Rather than matching the purchase order, the receiving memorandum and the invoice, only the first two are matched. The invoice is not included since the information on the invoice should be redundant. Third, since there are a reduced number of documents to match, it is easier to build a system to automate the process. The role of humans becomes one of resolving anomalies.

8 Payment

Payment is triggered by document flows in classic supply chain processes. Alternative triggers derive from the flow of materials, and can be the basis of reengineering the payment process.

8.1 Classic Payment Trigger

Invoices are sent from the supplier's accounting department to the buyer's accounts payable department to trigger payment of the supplier. Based on the terms of the invoice, such as net 30 days, the buyer is required to pay the supplier.

There are at least three limitations of this approach. First, in this arrangement, payment occurs when one firm's accounting department contacts the other firm's accounting department. As a result, there is a layer of overhead with accountants talking to accountants. Second, payment is limited to receipt of all the appropriate documentation. Any lost or missing documents will slow the payment process. Third, using the invoice as a trigger ultimately limits the type of payment arrangements, and as a result, the extent of the supply chain integration.

8.2 Payment Triggers

Although historically payment for goods has been triggered by the invoicing process, there are other potential triggers for generating payment for goods. Additional event triggers include when goods are received and when goods are used.

When Received: According to Hammer (1990), Ford pays for the order when it arrives. In this setting there is no need to wait for or process an invoice. When goods arrive there is a matching process that takes place between the purchase order and the receiving information (scanned bar codes). Matching is facilitated since fewer documents make it easier to match and fewer documents suggest that there will be fewer document-specific errors.

The matching process is automated. If there is a direct match then there is no problem and the goods are paid for. If there is no direct match, then the goods are treated as an anomaly, given additional attention.

In addition, information is captured regarding different supplier's record of shipping what they were supposed to ship: Does goods purchased equal goods received? That information is used to determine whether or not the buying firm continues to use the supplier. Too many anomalies and the firm is replaced by another supplier.

When Used: Another approach is where actual "use" triggers a payment for goods. As reported in Brownlee (1996), Colgate has agreements with a number of suppliers where suppliers are responsible for making sure that the goods are available on the premises of Colgate's production facilities. Whenever Colgate uses the goods that triggers a payment. In this setting, a purchase order and receiving information could substantially precede the use of the goods. In this setting there is no apparent need for an invoice, since the buyer is the first to know how much of the supplier's goods have been used. As noted by Brownlee (1996, p. R12)

...in exchange for giving some suppliers quicker notice on shifts in its own demand, Colgate doesn't have to pay for the product ingredients it orders until those powders and liquids have actually been used. That's not a big hardship for the suppliers, though: The new system takes less time to crunch numbers so they get paid more often.

9 Company Electronic Interfaces

In order to integrate across firms there needs to be an ability to have firm's systems "talk" to each other. Communication of data using EDI is being replaced with inter-firm communication across integrated enterprise resource planning systems.

9.1 Loosely Coupled Using EDI

EDI allows loosely coupled firms to communicate across the supply chain. EDI communication from firm to firm can be accomplish for some standard documents using universal translators. These translators accommodate a wide range of inputs and outputs. As a result, firms in the supply chain need only limited commitment to computer-based supply chain management systems.

9.2 Reengineering Using Integrated Enterprise Resource Planning Systems

Enterprise resource planning (ERP) systems provide an individual firm with substantial capabilities to plan and control its own resources. Some of the better known ERP systems include SAP's R/3, Oracle, PeopleSoft, Baan and J.D. Edwards. Some see ERP systems as the one of the primary tools to facilitate reengineering documents and processes (e.g., Gendron 1996). As a result, in order to implement reengineered processes, such as those listed in this paper, an ERP system can be a useful tool.

In addition, if different firms use the same ERP systems then inter firm communication of supply chain information can be facilitated and supply chain partners can integrate with each other and others in the supply chain. For example, Colgate (Brownlee 1996) is using SAP to integrate back to its suppliers. According to Brownlee (1996, R. 12) Colgate is "... supplying a handful of its most critical suppliers with computers loaded with R/3 and plugged directly into the Colgate system."

This integration results in what is known as a virtual organization, which Goldman et al. (1995, p. 7) define as one "...where complementary resources existing in a number of cooperating companies are left in place, but are integrated to support a particular product effort for as long as it is viable to do so. ... Resources are selectively allocated to the virtual company if they are underutilized or if they can be profitably utilized there more than in the 'home' company." In addition, Goldman et al. (1995) note that virtual organizations are designed to facilitate three types of competition, each of which is supply chain related:

- create or assemble productive resources quickly
- create or assemble productive resources frequently and concurrently
- create or assemble a broad range of productive resources (e.g., research, manufacturing, design, etc.).

The use of information technology in virtual organizations is an effort to improve the productivity, increase response speed, and facilitate concurrent productive activities. Information technology is used aggressively, replacing or supporting human actions, rather than relying on traditional administrative systems.

10 The Relationship Between the Buyer and the Supplier

Classic supply chain relationships place firms in primary or secondary supply relationships. However, in some supply chain settings the technology is pushing some of those relationships to more integrated relationships, ultimately resulting in a smaller number of suppliers.

10.1 Primary or Secondary Supplier

In classic supply chain settings, supplier relationships are less than exclusive, and lack integration. For example, United Stationers is the primary supplier for some buyers, but in some cases they are a busy phone line away from not even being a supplier. According to the CIO of United Stationers,

> Ninety-three percent of our orders come in, computer to computer, over proprietary EDI...-like lines. If our computer system doesn't respond, our customers have their ordering systems configured to automatically dial our competition. (Zerega 1998, p. S8)

10.2 Integrated Supplier

However, in some supply chain settings, more integrated supplier - buyer relationships are being developed. Rather than choosing a different supplier if the phone is busy, firms are developing more integrated relationships that allow development of more information on which to choose suppliers for particular shipments. For example, as part of being a supplier to Colgate, as noted above, Brownlee (1996) reported that suppliers were required to implement particular software, SAP's R/3.

Colgate's use of these ERP systems eliminates some classic asymmetries of information. Historically, if Colgate made an order they had only historical information regarding that firm's past ability to provide supplies that would meet its production needs. However, with their current network of integrated ERP systems, they have real time information available about their supplier's inventory. Using the ERP system (Brownlee 1996, R. 12), "Colgate's plan is to use its network to get a peek at customer's stockpiles, while allowing its suppliers to look at Colgate's inventory as well."

10.3 Smaller Numbers of Suppliers

Further, as noted in Brownlee (1996), Colgate's new system tends to favor a supply chain with fewer suppliers. In order to be fully integrated with Colgate's supply chain requires that each supplier have SAP's R/3. As a result, this limits the potential suite of suppliers.

In addition, since Colgate and their suppliers have access to critical information about each other, they have other reasons to limit the number of suppliers. First, Colgate uses resources monitoring its suppliers through those systems. As a result, since resources are finite, its efforts must be limited. Second, if too many firms have access to Colgate's information then it may find that its information could be used against itself. As a result, there is a tendency to work with fewer trusted suppliers.

11 Which Firm Decides Which Approach Is Used?

What factors lead one firm or a group of firms to dictate which portfolio of technology solutions is used? There appear to be a number of factors, including market power, technological leadership, recognition of the business problem and existence of deep pockets.

11.1 Market Power

Introduction of an approach such as a single invoice or no invoice, or use of an ERP system across a supply chain probably requires substantial market power. For example, Colgate apparently has that market power in order to get the necessary cooperation from their suppliers. Since Colgate supplied the software, implementation is apparently in concert with Colgate's needs, e.g., a common set of product numbers could be used to facilitate ordering processes. However, the supplier's costs for maintenance and use of the software can be substantial, beyond Colgate's initial purchase of the software. For example, suppliers will need workers to massage the software to meet some of their own requirements. Accordingly, Colgate's influence must be substantial.

11.2 Technological Leader

It is likely that any firm dictating any technology solution is a technology leader or first mover on the use of technology. As an example, Colgate was apparently one of the first adopters of SAP's R/3 enterprise resource planning system. As noted by Brownlee (1996), "When it comes to taking an all-out plunge into SAP's hot selling application, Colgate is clearly ahead of the pack ...."

11.3 Business Problem Solution

In addition, it is also likely that the implementing firm recognizes the importance of technology as a means to solve business problems, not just a technology for technology sake. For example, as noted by Brownlee (1996, R12),

As soon as a customer walks into a Wal-Mart, Target or Kmart store and buys a tube of toothpaste Colgate wants to know. With the help of R/3, Colgate is able to look at some of its customers' inventories and spread the data instantly to virtually every nook in its supply chain. ... Before Colgate set up its new system ... it had a business problem.

11.4 Deep Pockets -- Substantial Financial Resources

As an example of the importance of "deep pockets," Colgate's widespread use of SAP and Colgate's purchasing the system for some suppliers required substantial financial investment. A 1996 survey by Gemini Consulting found that an average implementation of SAP averaged $7.5 million. As noted by Brownlee (1996), "Colgate won't say how much it has spend on the system, but it is weaving R/3 into every corner of its core operations."

12 Summary

This paper has investigated how supply chain documents and processes can be reengineered in order to ultimately facilitate electronic commerce.

- Classic paper processes were reengineered as EDI,
- Purchase orders have been reengineered to accommodate supplier writing buyer orders,
- Receiving memorandums were reengineered so that now the receiving dock does not originate any new documents, but instead scans an existing one,
- Invoices were eliminated because they carry redundant information,
- Because invoices have been eliminated, the matching process that supports payment has been reengineered, and
- Since the matching process is reengineered, different payment triggers could be used to reengineer the payment process.

Further, reengineering these processes has facilitated changes in supply chain relationships

- ERP systems were used to reengineer the way that firms interact electronically, ultimately forming virtual organizations designed to improve a firm's competitive response,
- Ultimately, resulting in new more integrated relationships with fewer suppliers.

Technology advances and development of interlinking software has facilitated integration of suppliers and buyers through the supply chain as part of the development of electronic commerce. Different supply chain arrangements reflect different levels of integration. In particular, inter organization integration is occurring from two different directions.

First, adoption of technology is forcing integration across firms. In order to be able to supply a company like Colgate, supply firms need to employ a particular ERP system. In addition, the use of that system facilitates loss of asymmetries of information that historically could provide suppliers with potential advantages, such as, lower costs through keeping lower inventory. Now that Colgate and its suppliers both have access to additional information about each other, many of the potential advantages of asymmetric information have been lost.

Second, technology changes are facilitating integration between firms never before achievable. At the extreme, multiple organizations can become an integrated network referred to as a virtual organization. Colgate's adoption of SAP's R/3 allows it to see if its suppliers have enough inventory and allow its suppliers to closely track Colgate's demand. Until recently, Colgate was unable to perform these activities internally, let alone with respect to their suppliers.

Acknowledgement. The author would like to thank the referees for their comments on an earlier version of this paper.

References

Brownlee, L., "Overhaul," *Wall Street Journal*, Wednesday, November 18, 1996, p. R12 and R. 17.

Gendron, M., "Learning to Live with the Electronic Embodiment of Reengineering," *Harvard Management Update*, November 1996, p. 3-4.

Goldman, S., R. Nagel, K. Preiss, *Agile Competitors and Virtual Organizations*, Van Nostrand Reinhold, New York, 1995.

Hammer, M., "Reengineering Work: Don't Automate, Obliterate," *Harvard Business Review*, July/August 1990, pp. 104-112

Millman, H., "A Brief History of EDI," *Infoworld*, April 6, 1998, p. 83.

Zerega, B., "United Stationers: Pushing for Success," *Infoworld*, April 20, 1998, p. S8

CHAPTER 21
Supply Chain Management: Developing Visible Design Rules across Organizations

B. Rachel Yang

Department of Business Administration, University of Illinois at Urbana-Champaign, Champaign, IL, USA, ryang@uiuc.edu

This chapter proposes an integrating view of Supply Chain Management as a set of Visible Design Rules that govern interactions across independent organizations, each with its own hidden operational and organizational information. Applying the principle of modularity from computer architecture to supply chain studies, we specify the basic three elements of visible rules: architecture, interfaces, and standards in the context of supply chains. Subsequently we discuss a set of measurable operations performance metrics, interfaces among supply chain partners in the form of processes that cut through multiple layers of the chain, and partnership and network structure as the architecture of supply chains. We suggest that supply chain management studies and practices should focus more on the overall visibility of standards, interfaces, and structure instead of probing into each organization's detailed planning and operations, to allow for the maximum flexibility for them to change and innovate. The ultimate goal is to achieve an agile supply chain with quick and accurate response in a fast changing business environment.

Keywords: Supply Chain Management; Design Modularity; Visible Design Rules; Performance Metrics; Process Interfaces; Architecture

1 Introduction

Ever since the concept of *Supply Chain* was first used in the late 1980's to describe the whole sequence of activities spanning from sourcing raw materials to getting finished products into the hands of end customers, there has been an increasingly large number of articles written on this subject. Business journals run series of reports on new supply chain practices and success stories. Consulting companies set up specialized departments and conduct supply chain projects using it as a powerful value-enhancing methodology. Academic researchers develop models and data analyses to further our understanding and knowledge in this intricate yet important matter.

The advance in this area has achieved several benefits. It has heightened the industry awareness of a potential new breakthrough in logistics and inter-organizational coordination in order to cut costs and gain profitability, after decades of efforts in improving manufacturing efficiency and continuous improvements within organizations. Companies as diverse as Federal Express, Proctor & Gamble, and Hewlett-Packard have recognized *Supply Chain Management* (SCM) as their cutting-edge business strategy in the 1990's. The cross-functional and inter-organizational nature of supply chain also changed the landscape of management studies towards more interdisciplinary approaches across functional areas such as manufacturing, logistics, engineering, marketing, information system, strategy, and economics. Old models are revamped, and new opportunities are opened up, all of these reflected in conference sessions, workshops, and special issues of journals dedicated to the topic.

Despite the elevated awareness and enthusiasm, there seem to exist a lot of different approaches and sometimes conflicting issues, which leaves us with a field without a set of common definitions and an integrating framework. For example, in resource planning, some studies adopt a hierarchical structure to examine interactions among various levels, while others still focus on traditional aggregate planning models within organizational boundary. Some inventory studies are expanded to multi-echelon models but more are not. In vendor management, JIT II delivery calls for vendor proximity, close synchronization, and hence stable partnership, while virtual organization and strategic alliances advocate fast partnership turnover. All these issues are relevant, but what is missing is an integrating framework to link them. This is clearly an acute problem facing researchers and practitioners in this area, as the proliferation of SCM studies heightens the need for such a framework, and a continuing lack of it will undoubtedly hinder further advancement.

One consensus in SCM is that all studies agree supply chain is a complex, interactive, and dynamic system, linking a group of partners of suppliers, manufacturers, distributors, and retailers, each with a set of functions of design, engineering, production, purchasing, logistics, marketing, customer service, information system, and so on. How can we construct a framework that would preserve the excellence within each player and each function that we have achieved so far, and meanwhile create a new synergy from an integrated supply chain?

2 Principle of Modularity

Modularity has been known as an effective strategy for organizing complex products and processes efficiently. According to Baldwin and Clark (1997), design modularity is defined as building a complex product or process from smaller subsystems that can be designed independently yet function together as a whole. It is achieved by partitioning information into *visible design rules* (or *visible information*) and *hidden design parameters* (or *hidden information*). Visible design rules fall into the following three categories:

- An *architecture*, which specifies what modules will be part of the system and what their functions will be.

- *Interfaces* that describe in detail how the modules will interact, including how they will fit together, connect, and communicate.
- *Standards* for testing a module's conformity to the design rules and for measuring one module's performance relative to another.

Modularity has proven to be a powerful tool to ensure innovativeness of each member module and flexibility of the whole system. It gives independent design teams, within the same organization or scattered around the world working for different suppliers or manufacturers, freedom to experiment on their smaller modules by working on the hidden information within the modules, as long as they still comply with the overall visible design rules. The large number of independent and parallel experiments gives the overall structure ability to change, innovate, adapt, and grow, all of which characteristics of a flexible system. On the other hand, modular systems are much more difficult to design, as designers must have profound knowledge of the modules and the overall product or process.

These benefits and challenges were revealed in the world's first modular computer, the IBM System/360 in 1964. Before that, each mainframe computer had its own operations system, processor, peripherals, and application software. System/360, for the first time, consisted of a family of computers of different sizes for different applications that used the same instruction set and shared peripherals. To develop it, IBM set up a central processor control office to establish and enforce visible overall design rules, and dozens of design teams that had full control over the hidden design elements in their modules. This approach took far more resources to develop than expected, but the increased costs were more than compensated by the huge commercial and financial success. IBM changed the competition landscape in the computer industry, but newcomers with their compatible and better modules, such as printers, terminals, memory, software, and even central processing units, ultimately drove this dynamic and innovative industry to evolve from mainframe, minicomputer, personal computer, to the new world of networked computing.

A whole set of terminology of design modularity, such as visible and hidden information, architecture, interface, and standards, was then developed in computer architecture (Hennessy and Patterson, 1990), and later companies like Sun Microsystems, used the principle to their advantage to defeat its rival Apollo Computer in the workstation market. In a separate but not unrelated endeavor, modularity is not an unfamiliar name for people in production and operations management as they have used it in organizing complex manufacturing processes into modules or cells. It was argued that Henry Ford's largest contribution at the beginning of this century was not the idea of moving assembly line, but rather the thinking of dividing task into small manageable pieces, or modules (Womack et al, 1990). It unleashed the amazing productivity out of newly industrialized workers transformed from a huge reservoir of farmers and immigrants with little training, and hence lent the possibility to a mass production boom. In the last two decades, advanced technology brought about large sophisticated systems like Flexible Manufacturing Systems that facilitate the implementation of Group Technology and Cellular Manufacturing. A century's continuous advancement has improved efficiency and flexibility to the extent that new breakthrough is hard to achieve within an organization, therefore attentions were turned towards the slacks and wastes across organizations.

Into the picture enters Supply Chain Management, which answers this question by advocating more coordination and integration among all activities involved in putting a final product into an end customer's hands. Studies have revealed that improving one channel member's performance will not necessarily improve that of another member or the whole channel, as in the case of frequent discount and promotion causing undesirable forward buying. This is in the line of our understanding that local optima do not always lead to global optima. We have also observed the facts that a not-well-thought-out partnership seriously blocks the potential of local improvement, for example, for a supplier to innovate the product or a distributor to adapt to a changing market. Therefore, in order to leave enough room to encourage each player to change and innovate, while keeping the coordination seamless and the system flexible to re-configure, it is necessary and important to separate the visible information from the hidden information and focus on the former. How much have we achieved on understanding the visible design rules of supply chain management? In the subsequent sections we examine the standards, interfaces, and architecture as the three basic elements of visible supply chain design rules. Table 1 highlights the hidden and visible information in supply chains.

Table 1. Separating the hidden and visible information in supply chains

Hidden information (within each function or organization)		• Layout design • Quality management • Aggregate planning • MRP
Visible information (across functions and organizations)	Standards	• Inventory turnover • Response and cycle time • Service level and order fill rate
	Interfaces	• Order fulfillment process • Product development process • Customer service process • Logistics process
	Architecture	• Modular product • Flexible process • Quick and accurate response

3 Supply Chain Standards

Supply chain management aims at ultimately improving customer satisfaction level while reducing overall costs and speeding up turnaround times (Davis, 1993). Customer satisfaction is assured by having the right product at the right place at the right time. Overall costs along supply chain include sourcing, producing, transporting, distributing, and servicing costs. Relevant turnaround times include the response time from order placing to order fulfillment, and product development time from conception to market introduction.

Traditional approaches often achieve a subset of these objectives at a significant sacrifice of others. For example, customized production or make-to-order approach gives customers maximum satisfaction in terms of the right product, but usually takes a high cost and a long lead-time. Mass production or make-to-stock approach, to the contrary, is able to maintain low cost and consistent quality, but it only yields standardized products that may not match customers' specific needs. Furthermore, because it relies on a homogeneous market with stable demand, product life cycles and product development cycles are often very long.

As more companies strive to pursue excellence in cost, quality, time, and customer satisfaction, combing the strengths of make-to-order and make-to-stock seems to be the solution. As a result, a new approach of "make-parts-to-stock-and-assemble-end-products-to-order" is established. As end products are assembled to orders, customer satisfaction will be high and the order placement to fulfillment lead-time will be short. As parts are made to stock, production, storing, transportation costs will be low. This is basically the modularity concept, but stretched out across organizational boundaries along supply chains. Supply chain becomes a physical identity that coordinates goods and information flows to carry out this strategy. This *mass customization* approach inevitably imposes new challenges to product design and supply chain design, raising questions such as where to differentiate the product, and where to store inventories along the supply chain.

To reduce the supply chain objectives on customer satisfaction, cost, and responsiveness into measurable parameters for purposes of testing new initiatives and evaluating new partners, it is important to develop a set of *supply chain performance metrics*. In observable and measurable operations terms, we suggest the following parameters:

- Inventory Turnover
  It defines how many times annual are sales compared with inventory level. Sales and inventories can be measured at various points of the channel or the total channel level.
- Response Time
  It defines a good or information "travel" time from one point of supply chain to the other, for example, from placing an order to initiating production runs to shipping to customers, or from conceiving a product concept to introducing to markets. It can be also called lead-time or throughput time.

- Cycle Time
  It defines how often we get goods or information out of the supply chain pipeline. A long product development time does not prevent frequent product introduction as long as the channel is well synchronized.
- Service Level
  It defines the percentage of time that the supply chain point is not out of stock.
- Line/Order Fill Rate
  It defines the proportion of demand that a line item (or orders of several line items) is filled by on-hand stock or within mutually agreeable time frames.

The purposes of developing these metrics for supply chains are:

1. Benchmarking within and across industries (such as auto, computer, packaged goods, apparel, etc) to establish a set of standards;
2. Testing new supply chain initiatives, such as vendor-managed inventory, continuous replenishment, every-day-low-price, etc;
3. Evaluating suppliers and channel partners, such as third-party logistics, virtual integration, etc.
4. Sharing among supply chain members, together with orders and sales information.

As we have observed the propagated and amplified impact of variability and dependency from downstream members to upstream members in the classical "Beer Game" and "Bullwhip Effect" (Lee et al, 1997), we can further measure and incorporate variances of the above parameters into the supply chain testing and evaluating standards.

4 Supply Chain Interfaces

The protocol of interaction among supply chain members can be represented as a *process that cut through multiple layers*. A process is a group of activities with sequential or parallel relationships that span over a period of time. Now we discuss some processes that are specific to supply chains. These are a few generally identified processes, and we hope more studies will uncover more. It is exactly the integrating nature of these processes across functional and organizational barriers that suits the need of supply chain design and improvement so well that from the very beginning, supply chain studies are generally believed to be process-based.

4.1 Order Fulfillment Process

A process from the moment a customer places an order to the time the order is delivered to the customer, which involves order taking, inventory control, sourcing and procurement, production scheduling, manufacturing and packaging, warehousing and transportation, and possibly other after-sales service and disposition activities.

The biggest problems with many companys' order fulfillment processes are erratic orders, orders that do not reflect real consumer demands, and long order transmission and goods transportation times with large variations. The result is a typical phenomenon of simultaneously having high level of costly inventories and low level of order fill rates (Lee and Billington, 1992).

Some supply chain strategies have proved to be effective in this regard, as listed below, with their underlying philosophies and examples of companies that have successfully implemented the initiatives. The success of these programs rests on a channel-wide member participation and coordination.

- POS: point-of-sales data see-through recognizes a common mistake that manufacturers mis-interpret orders as real market demand and consequently over-make or under-make products, which causes overstock or shortage in the channel. Passing the end sales data up the supply chain will alleviate the problem, and has been used by large retailers like Wal-Mart that are electronically linked with their major suppliers.
- JIT II: just-in-time-II, successfully implemented at Bose, extends the waste-free "right item, right amount, at right place, when just needed" JIT concept from manufacturing to transportation, and requires vendors to have presence and involvement at the manufacturer's factory floor to secure a seamless transportation-production scheduling coordination.
- CRP: continuous replenishment program emphasizes cutting down transportation batch size to make more frequent and flexible deliveries. Campbell Soup is a good example of inducing its customers that are supermarket chain stores into this program.
- ECR: efficient consumer response was pioneered by Proctor & Gamble to actively go down the supply chain into its customers, all the way through to the store level, to stabilize planning and ordering to improve the manufacturer's efficiency and enhance values for customers.
- EDLP: everyday low price, used by retailers like Hill's Department Stores, in contrast to frequent discounts and promotions generally used in the 1980's and still used at some retailers, is effective to prevent "forward-buying" and stabilize order patterns.

4.2 Product Development Process

A traditional product development process, whether it is a phase-review process or an engineering development process, starts from a design concept and ends with a manufactured product. This process is expanded in a supply chain system with cross-functional and cross-organizational cooperation:

- "Con-current Engineering" involves team members from engineering, production, marketing, purchasing, quality control, and service support functions, with each member representing their own functional objective but working together towards the common goal of fast and successful product development.
- The product development process includes more activities and affects more supply chain partners. New product conceptualization in "Quality Function Deployment" starts with collecting information about and feedback from customers, and "Design for Manufacturability" is extended to "Design for Parts Supply" and "Design for Distribution." Companies like IKEA have broadened their product development process, which does not end until the new product is successfully introduced in diverse markets.

4.3 Customer Service Process

A process that is triggered by a service call from customer, which subsequently may involve field service, technical support, parts supply, feedback to product design, and other necessary activities to make customers satisfied.

Current studies on customer service focus on the front end of the process, i.e. the point of customer contact, and fail to recognize it is the whole process of organizing parts and diagnosis information flows that determines the quality of service. Resources usually deployed in a service process include personnel with diagnosis and repair capability, needed spare parts, and supporting databases and tools. Be it a phone/on-line consultation or a field visit, a service process has several unique aspects such as: (1) response time is critical as customers are frustrated; (2) demand for parts and services is difficult to predict; (3) service area is geographically dispersed. These all lead to maintaining large detailed databases and building costly high inventories of parts, personnel, and equipment at various points of the supply chain to prevent stockouts, or risking customer satisfaction. Therefore it is important to carefully consider trade-offs between cost and response time when making decisions about how many service bases to install and where to store service parts, and to standardize service procedures in the process.

4.4 Logistics Process

Any logistics activity involves at least two members in a supply chain, and these activities range from outbound/inbound transportation to warehousing, and involve decisions such as carrier selection and management, transportation mode, inventory control, and freight bill auditing/payments.

Logistics practices have experienced a rapid change from mostly independent efforts in the past towards more emphasis on partnership and coordination. Freight consolidation and logistics outsourcing are two important trends reflecting this change. Two new practices are examples showing the direction of this change:

Cross-docking: Goods arriving at a warehouse will be assorted and re-bundled at receiving without entering the warehouse, ready for shipping out according to a delivery schedule. It is used as a part of the overall supply chain "Fast Flow" program in companies like Sara Lee Knit Products.

Third-party logistics: A company recognizing its core competence not in logistics may turn to a third-party for part or all of its outbound and inbound transportation and warehousing needs. Companies such as Federal Express have been able to use their "best-in-class" expertise and develop innovative technologies like automatic delivery tracking system, to help their customers focus on their own core competence.

We have described four common processes in supply chain: order fulfillment, product development, customer service, and logistics. Once the process that describes the interface in a specific supply chain setting is identified, we can use general process analysis tools, such as process flowcharting and bottleneck analysis, to map out the entire process flow with goods and information, uncover redundancy and gap, and identify output-limiting bottleneck. More techniques such as business process re-engineering can also be applied in these supply chain processes.

5 Supply Chain Architecture

A supply chain architecture stipulates a group of *partners and structure* of their relationships. It answers such questions as: Should company X be part of the system? If yes, what functions should it perform? What is the general structure of the network?

Supply Networks: Constructing a supplier base includes make/buy decision, vendor selection, and vendor management. Traditionally manufacturers have leaned towards vertically integrated, but now even large companies outsourced some production and service. There is a spectrum of supplier-buyer relationship ranging from adversarial and open-market view of suppliers to single or dual source of supply over an extended period of time. How well the vendor can work together, for example, in Just-In-Time delivery and joint product development, is very important to the manufacturer's success as now the whole supply chain competes together as one identity.

Distribution Channels: Building distribution channels requires decisions such as own sales-force versus independent agents, how many layers of the channel, how many dealers in each territory. The new trends in this area include the shift of channel power towards buyers, and emergence of new media such as Electronic Commerce, all leading towards possibilities of bypassing some traditional middlemen such as wholesalers and some retailers.

Strategic Alliances: Sometimes competitors form temporary alliances to fend off new and powerful entrants. This forges some horizontal links in supply chains as they share suppliers or distributors. Sometimes buyers and suppliers form more lasting alliances to develop new products or markets, but unlike the traditional vertical integration, these alliances do not involve capital ownership or even contractual agreement. This practice is a new solution in today's business world with fast changing technology and market. Consequently "virtual organizations" are formed, disassembled, and reconfigured frequently, achieving the high flexibility and rate of innovation in the opening discussions.

Information Architecture: One driving force behind the advancement of supply chain practices is the ability to acquire, store, and transmit data through new information technologies. Companies like Baxter have intentionally designed and updated their information system links to reach and retain more customers (Venkatraman and Short, 1992). The information architecture of a supply chain is the inter-organizational-information-system (IOIS). In terms of the visible design rule we discussed earlier, the more traditional architecture in this area was *Electronic Data Interchange* (EDI), which requires special cable connection and rigid data format, but insures high security level. More companies seem to move toward the new *web-based architecture*, where it is easier to transform data in any form and connect or disconnect to any partners. But security over the Internet is still a issue of concern.

In addition to the physical architecture of the number of nodes and arcs in the supply chain network, incentive problems remain to be important in any effort and profit sharing relationships. Hidden information and moral hazard concerns are present in supply chain contract designs, and game theory is relevant in understanding the way that channel members jointly maximize and subsequently divide the pie of channel profit.

6 The Goal: Agile Supply Chain

Fisher (1997) has identified the product characteristics that stipulate the right type of supply chain to be either efficient or accurate. The benefit of developing supply chain linkages as visible design rules is to make *a dynamically agile supply chain*. This can be achieved by applying the modularity principle systematically throughout *product-process-channel design*.

Modular Product: According to Sanchez and Mahoney (1996), modular product architecture creates information structures for modular product development process and modular organization design. Therefore product modularity is fundamental for process flexibility and supply chain agility. Companies like Benetton and Hewlett-Packard have developed product design strategies such as "Postponement" to delay product differentiation on those features with high demand uncertainty to the last possible point of their supply chains (Lee and Feitzinger, 1997).

Flexible Process: A flexible process is able to handle a wide range of components, products, and information, and is fast in adapting to any changes (Suarez et al, 1995). Manufacturing flexibility includes mix flexibility, volume flexibility, and new product flexibility, and relies on modular product development as well as close relationships with materials suppliers and parts subcontractors.

Quick and Accurate Response in a Transparent Supply Chain: There have been studies on using "Quick Response" and "Accurate Response" programs in order to improve supply chain speed and flexibility, by carefully assessing demand forecasts and costs of stockouts and markdowns (Fisher et al, 1994). Other studies examined the possibility of applying "Lean Production" to cut down inventory and delay in international supply chains (Levy, 1997). Together they demonstrate the need for a transparent set of design rules for global supply chains that are characterized by long lead-times, expensive freight, and large economical, political, and cultural diversity.

7 Conclusion

We have proposed that supply chain is the paradigm for *organizing complex goods and information flows* efficiently, therefore more focus should be put on developing a set of visible design rules across functions and across organizations in terms of standards, interfaces, and architecture. There are still some remaining questions, such as how to codify the visible design rules, is it possible to capture them into computer programs, and how the visible design rules can evolve over time. Just as the computer industry's visible rules evolved from the initial mainframe to the current networked computing, we saw some evolutions in the sections of supplier networks, distribution channels, strategic alliances, and finally the inter-organizational information systems. These are positive changes that are helping companies and their supply chains better positioned in the new landscape of Electronic Commerce.

References

Baldwin, C. and K. Clark, "Managing in an Age of Modularity," *Harvard Business Review*, September-October, 1997.

Davis, T, "Effective Supply Chain Management," *Sloan Management Review*, Summer, 1993.

Fisher, M., "What is the Right Supply Chain for Your Product?" *Harvard Business Review*, March-April, 1997.

Fisher, M., J. Hammond, W. Obermeyer, and A. Raman, "Making Supply Meet Demand in an Uncertain World," *Harvard Business Review*, May-June, 1994.

Hennessy, J. and D. Patterson, *Computer Architecture: A Quantitative Approach*, Morgan Kaufman Publishers, 1990.

Lee, H. and C. Billington, "Managing Supply Chain Inventory: Pitfalls and Opportunities," *Sloan Management Review*, Spring, 1992.

Lee, H. and E. Feitzinger, "Mass Customization at Hewlett-Packard: The Power of Postponement," *Harvard Business Review*, January-February, 1997.

Lee, H., V. Padmanabhan, and S. Whang, "The Bullwhip Effect in Supply Chains," *Sloan Management Review*, Spring, 1997.

Levy, D., "Lean Production in an International Supply Chain," *Sloan Management Review*, Winter, 1997

Sanchez, R. and J. T. Mahoney, "Modularity, Flexibility, and Knowledge Management in Product and Organization Design," *Strategic Management Journal*, Vol. 17, 1996.

Suarez, F., M. Cusumano, and C. Fine, "An Empirical Study of Flexibility in Manufacturing," *Sloan Management Review*, Fall, 1995.

Venkatraman, N. and J. Short, "Beyond Business Process Redesign: Redefining Baxter's Business Network," *Sloan Management Review*, Fall, 1992.

Womack, J., D. Jones, and D. Roos, *The Machine That Changed The World*, Rawson Associates. 1990.

CHAPTER 22

Web-based Global Supply Chain Management

Gek Woo Tan[1], Michael J. Shaw[1], and William Fulkerson[2]

[1]Department of Business Administration, and Beckman Institute for Advanced Sciences and Technology, University of Illinois at Urbana-Champaign, Urbana, IL, USA, g-tan@uiuc.edu; m-shaw2@uiuc.edu

[2]CIS-Technology Integration, Deere & Company, Moline IL, USA, wf28155@deere.com

A key constituent of supply chain management strategies is information sharing. Software component technology facilitates information sharing by providing a means for integrating heterogeneous information systems into virtual information systems. Extranet technology facilitates information sharing between an enterprise and its business partners as well as its customers through the Internet. These two technologies enable new strategies that integrate information systems and improve supply chain networks. We discuss the application of these strategies to supply chain processes.

Keywords: Global Supply Chain Management; Information Sharing; Component Technology; Extranet; Information Systems Integration

1 Introduction

A supply chain is a network of business units and facilities that procure raw materials, transform them into intermediate goods and then final products, and deliver the products to customers through a distribution system. Supply chain management (SCM) is concerned with the management of these activities such that the product passes through the chain in the shortest time with the lowest cost (Lee et al 1995). As supply chain networks (SCNs) become increasingly global, coordination between processes are more crucial. The focus of SCM has shifted from engineering efficient manufacturing processes to the coordination of activities in the SCN through knowledge management.

Information sharing is a key ingredient in coordination of SCNs. Programs like Just-in-time (JIT) in production as well as continuous replenishment program (CRP) and quick response programs (Hammond, 1993; Fisher et al., 1994) in retail rely on the dissemination of scheduling, shipment or manufacturing information to the parties involved. Information sharing improves coordination between the supply chain processes to enable the material flow, and reduces inventory costs (Strader et al. 1998a).

A major barrier towards information sharing is the incompatibility of different computer systems. Frequently, each strategic partner develops its own proprietary systems which make information systems (IS) integration across enterprise boundaries difficult. Channel partners have to invest in electronic data interchange (EDI) technology in order to implement CRP or JIT strategies. The drawbacks of EDI are (1) a heavy investment for each participant, (2) the reach of EDI systems is limited because each EDI system is different due to a lack of standardization. Web technology overcomes the system incompatibility problem by encapsulating enterprise systems as object components, made accessible by standardized interfaces, and defining a protocol for transmitting documents between these components. Using Web technology, we can form virtual information systems (VIS) from different enterprises' heterogeneous IS. This improves SCN management by (1) reducing production costs through lower procurement and distribution costs, (2) better utilization of resources through enterprise specialization, and (3) greater integration of SCN activities through the virtual integration of IS.

This paper is organized as follows: we first discuss the characteristics of products and supply chain networks and describe the Web-based SCN in Section 2. We describe component technology in Section 3 and Extranet technology in Section 4. In section 5, we show how these two technologies improve the various supply chain processes. We use an SCN example from John Deere & Company to illustrate our work in Section 6. We discuss some issues of the Web technology in Section 7 and conclude in Section 8.

2 Web-based Supply Chain Network

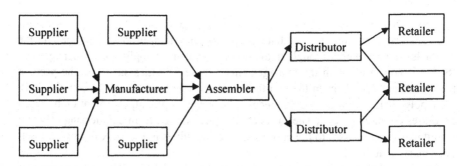

Fig. 1. A generic supply chain network

A supply chain network (SCN) is a series of value-added processes (also called tier, state or phase) owned by one or more enterprises, as shown in see Figure 1. The chain starts with the raw-material supplier and ends with the consumer. Each intermediate tier is a supplier to its adjacent downstream tier and a customer to its upstream tier. SCNs are becoming complex for two reasons. First, increased labor costs forces enterprises to source from countries with cheaper labor in order to keep production costs down and stay competitive. Second, consumers are becoming more sophisticate, demanding customized products that better meet their needs. The increase in product variation makes demand forecasting more difficult as an enterprise now has to deal with several demand patterns (one for each product type) instead of a single demand pattern. Furthermore, increased product types results in a greater number of suppliers to manage and higher coordination costs. In addition to optimizing its processes within itself, the enterprises within a supply chain must now coordinate with each other. Supply chain management (SCM) has two goals: (1) coordinate the activities of each tier, as well as the transition between tiers to facilitate the smooth and efficient flow of products down the value-added chain at the least cost, (2) match the supply with the market demand.

These two goals are translated into two SCN paradigms: the *make-and-sell* and *sense-and-respond* (Bradley and Nolan, 1998). The fundamental disposition of a "make-and-sell" company is to pre-package and shrink-wrap as much as possible to take advantage of economies of scale, and then to offer persuasively what has been made. Service is a way of enhancing the attractiveness of the product. Frequently, the product process and manufacturing capacity drive the production process. In contrast, a sense-and-respond company concentrates quickly responding to specific market needs. The product itself can only be one component of the complete service response. Production is driven by consumer demand and market conditions.

The nature of the product determines which SCN paradigm is more appropriate (Fisher 1997). Functional products are typically staple necessities and have long life cycles, stable demand patterns and low product differentiation. Given this fairly stable environment, the focus of the SCN is efficient production by exploiting economies of scale. Innovative and customizable product demands, on the other hand, are more difficult to predict. Examples of innovative products are fashion apparel that changes every season and high-tech products that become obsolete very quickly. These products have short life cycles and generally a longer lead time. Lead-time reduction strategies like JIT are not applicable because the product manufactured, and hence the raw materials required and possibly the suppliers change from season to season. Since the long-lead time coupled with short product life limits the number of production cycles producers must accurately read consumer preference in order to avoid stock-out or excess inventory problems. The challenge is thus to match the supply with market demand. The appropriate SCN strategy favors postponement of product differentiation and the ability to quickly change the composition of the SCN as it responds to the dynamic environment. Customizable products form a third category that have a very high degree of product differentiation, which makes it infeasible to stock all product variations. While the overall demand quantity may be relatively stable, the difficulty lies in anticipating the product mix. Such products generally require a modular design with substitutable components that can be assembled together based on customer orders. Table 1 summarizes the characteristics of the product types and their corresponding SCN.

Table 1. Characteristics of product types and the corresponding SCN

	Physically efficient process	**Market-responsive process**	
Product characteristics	*Functional product* • Stable demand pattern • Long life cycle • Low product differentiation	*Customizable product* • Semi-predictable demand pattern • Medium life cycle • High product differentiation	*Innovative product* • Unpredictable demand pattern • Short life cycle • High/low product differentiation
SCN goal	Supply at the lowest cost	Customize product to individual demand	Match supply with market demand
Key action	Coordinate activities of channel partners	Assemble product to customer demand	Sense market signals and respond
SCN objective	*Efficient*	*Customizable*	*Responsive*
Nature of OFP	Supply driven	Demand driven	Demand driven
Demand mgt policy	Make-to-stock	Assembly-to-order	Make-to-order
Strategies	Efficient replenishment	Mass customization, postponement	Postponement, sense and respond
Information sharing	• Inventory movement • Production schedule • Production capacity	• Customer orders	• Customer sales • Customer feedback
Examples	Grocery, gasoline	Cellular phones	Fashion apparel

Lack of information sharing is a common root cause for supply-chain related problems. One example is the so-called bullwhip effect, where a slight variation in demand at the consumer end results in wild swings at the supplier end. The bullwhip effect is attributed to four causes: demand signal processing, batch ordering, price fluctuation and shortage gaming (Lee et al., 1997b). In demand signal processing, for example, because consumer sales quantity is not passed to the upstream levels, each tier is forced to predict the demand based its adjacent downstream order. This results in multiple forecasts, with predicted errors escalating as the distorted demand information travels upstream. Meanwhile, supplier's production information (e.g. capacity and lead-time) is not shared downstream. In the case of large consumer sales coupled with long lead-times, downstream customers only get their orders partially fulfilled. This leads into a vicious cycle of shortage gaming and large demand swings. Countermeasures include consumer direct ordering, computer-aided ordering, sharing point-of-sale capacity and inventory data, vendor-managed inventory, and continuous replenishment program (Lee et al., 1997b, Lee et al., 1997a). These solutions boil down to the need for information sharing and an information infrastructure to support it.

Different types of SCNs may require different information sharing strategies. Lin and Shaw, for instance, developed a simulation model that tests and evaluates SCN designs and strategies (Lin and Shaw, 1998; Lin et. al., 1998). One of the experiments was to test the effects of information sharing up and down the supply chain. The results of information sharing are summarized as follows: (1) reduced cycle times at downstream tiers, (2) significantly reduced inventory cost at all tiers, especially at tiers where product assembly takes place, (3) reduced tardiness at downstream tiers where assembly takes place, and (4) reduced tardiness on meeting customer lead times at all tiers. In general, querying supplier capacity helps estimate material arrival times and generate more achievable build plans. This is especially significant in convergent SCNs with a large number of suppliers. Querying demand from customers lowers inventory costs and better meets customer demand by carrying or producing the desired products only when they are needed. Demand information is critical for OFP improvement in a constantly changing market. Information sharing enables the demand management policy to shift towards assembly-to-order and a greater degree of customization. These findings support the Lee's conclusion that information sharing increases SCN visibility and reduces the bullwhip effect.

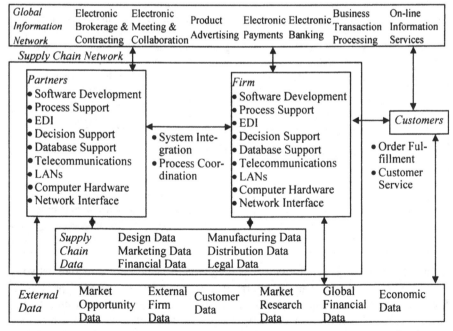

Fig. 2. An information infrastructure framework for supporting Web-based supply chain network (*Source*: Strader et al., 1998b)

Table 2. SCN process problems and how the Web can be used to alleviate these problems

SCN processes	SCN problems	Web application in SCN processes	Web impacts on SCN processes
Product development	• Need for richer communication across product development cycle • Long development time	• Implement the concurrent design framework • Foster collaboration	• Reduction in product development time • Knowledge sharing • Increased design collaboration
Order fulfillment process	• Bull-whip effect • Long product development time • Inaccurate demand forecast • Multiple demand forecasts • Inventory buildup	• Enables rapid assembly of IS into virtual business IS • Enables JIT and CRP strategies between enterprises without heavy EDI investments • Sharing demand and supply information	• More accurate demand forecast • Elimination of intermediaries • Formation of virtual IS • Direct-to-consumer sale • Increased enterprise specialization • Reduced inventory
Procurement	• Long lead time • Inflexible relationships due to high switching costs • Incompatible processes & systems	• Enables online bidding and auction processes • Electronic catalogs • Integrates search and ordering	• Greater flexibility in choosing partners • Shorter sourcing cycle • More responsive SCN • Reduce search costs and errors
Customer service	• Personalized service is costly • Response time can be long if not coordinated	• Enables enterprise to provide personalized service at low cost.	• Personalized service at low cost • Increased consumer control • Increased coordination to improve service level

In order to implement information sharing, an information infrastructure network is needed to support the various information requirements of the SCN processes. Figure 2 shows such a framework for supporting virtual organizations from (Strader et al., 1998b). The SCN can be viewed as an instance of a virtual organization, which is defined to be a temporary network of companies that come together quickly to exploit fast-changing opportunities (Byrne et al., 1993). The enterprise IS supports supply chain processes and process coordination within enterprises and between enterprises. In addition, the framework also includes (1) a global information network for supporting various electronic services like brokerage and contracting, payment and banking, transaction processing, (2) electronic access to external environment data, and (3) electronic connections to customers that support activities such as order fulfillment and customer service.

The Web infrastructure serves as an implementation of this framework with the Intranet supporting intra-organizational business processes, the Extranet interconnecting an enterprise to its partners and the Internet linking the enterprises to their customers, other institutions and agencies. Component-based development specifies an approach for building modular business applications that can be assembled to form business systems. As virtual organizations are formed from independently-owned corporations, their corresponding IS are assembled together to form virtual information systems.

Web facilitates information sharing and process integrating by providing the infrastructure as shown in Figure 2. Table 2 shows how Web technology addresses the problems of the various SCN processes and how they can be improved. We will next discuss two enabling technologies for Web-based SCNs—component technology and Extranet.

3 Component Technology

The concept of component technology was first developed to achieve more productive software development. Component-based development (CBD) enables prefabricated, pre-tested and reusable pieces of software to be assembled together, thereby enabling very flexible applications to be built rapidly.

We expand the definition of the component environment to include software components (also called component objects), interfaces, component framework, object broker, repository and communication network. Szyperski and Pfister define a software component to be a unit of composition with contractually specified interfaces and explicit context dependencies (Szyperski and Pfister, 1997). It can be independently deployed and is subject to composition by third parties. Software application programs, system management facilities and other services are examples of component objects. A component's interface defines access points that allow its clients to access the services it provides. It is a set of methods that does not change throughout its lifetime and is globally uniquely identifiable. The interface may be hard-wired into the component (like COM objects) or separately implemented as interface adapters (like CORBA objects). A component framework is a software entity that supports components conforming to certain standards and allows instances of these components to be "plugged" into the framework (Szyperski, 1998, p. 280). It establishes environmental conditions for the component instances and regulates how they interact with each other. The component broker and repository are necessary for the successful implementation of a component-based software system. Given a request, the broker identifies a component instance that fulfills the request, locates it and plugs it into the framework. Its function is to select and assemble component instances belonging to different IS into a VIS, analogous to the formation virtual enterprises from separate enterprises. In current component technology software like CORBA and COM, the broker's function is limited to locating and forwarding required documents; it does not possess the sophistication to perform selection and evaluation yet. The communication network is the network that physically links IS together.

Component technology provides seamless communications between applications residing in different IS. When a client object invokes a call, the request is passed to its interface adapter stub which invokes the call to the broker. The broker searches from the repository for the location of the object that implements the request, passes to it the parameters, invokes its method and returns the results to the client's interface adapter. The process is transparent to the client who views the call as a local call (Orfali et al. 1996, p. 68).

Modularity is the key property of component technology. Customizable products can address individual needs better than standardized products, but they are more complex and more costly to produce. Modularity manages complexity by enabling a complex product to be assembled from smaller subsystems that can be designed and built independently yet function together as a whole (Baldwin and Clark, 1997). Complexity comes from the number of ways to assemble the pieces, not in the pieces themselves (Simon, 1981). The key to rapid customization is customization through the selection and assembly of modular pieces, not in the individual crafting of the system. The system may be a product with different parts, an information system with different applications owned by different departments, or a virtual organization with different functional departments owned by different corporations.

In an environment with unpredictable changes, the success of an organization lies in its ability to respond and adapt itself to these changes. Different types of partnerships require different levels of information sharing (Seidmann and Sundararajan, 1998). Component-based development allows each business applications to be independently developed and assembled according to the needs of the SCN. In addition, it enables strategies for information sharing and integration as follows:

1. *Modularization and encapsulation*—Each component in an IS can be separately developed or purchased, and then assembled to form the final system. The CBD process is (i) simpler because the inter-dependencies between components are reduced, (ii) faster because components can be bought or developed by a third party, and (iii) more flexible as components are acquired when needed.
2. *Plug-and-play component development*—CBD aims to develop component objects that can be easily plugged into frameworks with minimal user effort in integration. For example, a supplier who won a bid to supply to a manufacturer in an online bidding process can plug its procurement software to the manufacturer's IS to access its production schedule and requirements and automatically forward the orders to the supplier's IS.
3. *Enterprise specialization*—Because IS *components* can be combined, each enterprise can specialize in developing modules for its core processes and collaborate

with enterprises specializing in complementary processes. For example, a retailer can turn over its procurement process to its supplier (as in CRP) or engage an independent 3rd party vendor to perform the procurement process, and focus its resources to better understand and meet consumer needs.

4. *Dynamic SCN configuration*—Specialization and collaboration go hand-in-hand. An enterprise which specialize in certain processes needs other enterprises to perform the other processes. Component *technology* enables enterprise partners to collaborate and assemble VIS according to their needs, resulting in dynamic SCN configuration.

5. *Integration of business processes of cross-industry partners*—One of the emergent behaviors in electronic commerce is in the *convergence* of services in different industries, especially in consumer services. For example, Web travel sites bundle together services from the airline, hotel and vehicle rental sectors as well as other tourism information.

4 Extranet Technology

Just as component technology facilitates information sharing at the enterprise level, Extranet facilitates information sharing between strategic partners as well as the customers. It connects multiple and diverse organizations online behind virtual firewalls, where those who share in trusted circles can network in order to achieve commercial-oriented objectives. It extends the business enterprise to include strategic partners, suppliers, distributors, contracts and others that operate the physical walls of the organization but are nonetheless critical to the success of business operations.

Security and access privileges are two of the most important issues in Intranet/ Extranet. Companies want to link up the computer systems within their organization boundaries as well as outside the boundary but at the same time prevent illegal access. The most common practice is to set a firewall around the company's information system, and sometimes between departments. The firewall proxy server or router programs scrutinize messages from outside the firewall to determine whether they are allowed inside the firewall (Sheldon, 1996). Partners of the company are given accounts and passwords to access the company's systems via Extranet.

There are three justifications for developing an Extranet. The first is to leverage existing investments in information technology. Many companies already have their documents on line and also have Internet access. Some of them have also adopted EDI to coordinate with the channel partners. By choosing to deploy an Internet-based application that is already supported by the technology already in use by the partner, companies will avoid a lot of hassles associated with custom clients. Second, because the Internet is governed by standards, any Extranet applications developed to these standards will virtually be guaranteed to work with the browsers, reducing the application developing time. Third, it is possible to customize Extranet applications to match the business model of individual partners. This approach reduces the cost to staff human service representatives. Furthermore, these applications are available and accessible on a 24-hour basis, improving customer satisfaction.

The components of an Extranet generally include network access, servers, business applications and interface software. Since an Extranet spans multiple remote organizations, Internet connectivity is required among the participants. Connections may be via dedicated Internet lines or dial-up via modem. Extranet servers house the tools required for a successful Web presence which include the functionalities like security, access control, transaction management, site operations, multiple-platform compatibility, deployment versatility and an extensible and scaleable architecture. Business applications provide the functionality for Extranets to serve as valuable tools for electronic commerce or other collaborative business objectives. Extranet solutions must be extensible enough to include the addition or modification of applications as business goals and objectives evolves. Interface layers are bridges between system software and graphical user presentation that exist within any software product. Effective Extranet interfaces address four interaction scenarios: individual, one-to-many, two-way, many-to-many interactions.

Three types of Extranet models have arisen in general practices: secured intranet access model, specialized application model and electronic commerce model (Bort and Felix, 1997). The *secured intranet access model* allows partners directly into the corporate intranet, either through the Internet or via a direct, dial-up connection. This type of Extranet is suitable for strategic partners that are crucial to the enterprise. With the *specialized application model*, the Extranet is an application developed specifically for partners that may also be part of the intranet. This type of Extranet is suitable for important partners that are important, though not key to the survival of the enterprise. The *electronic commerce model* uses electronic commerce techniques to service a partners segment, including similar security architecture and transaction processing. This type of Extranet is suitable when the partners segment contains hundreds of companies. In general Extranet applications should be simple and work reliably. Security is imperative as trust may be compromised. A ramification of a breach in security could be far greater than whatever data was lost.

The Extranet makes information sharing and customization strategies possible. One of the original reasons for building an Extranet is to link an enterprise to its business partners. By sharing process information such as manufacturing schedule and production capacity and external information such as consumer demand, an enterprise is able to better coordinate its activities with those of its upstream and downstream partners. The bullwhip effect demonstrates how lack of accurate consumer demand information causes inventory problems that compound as orders travel up the supply chain.

Extranet also allows low-cost customization for both consumers and producers by facilitating information exchange. Consumers are able to initiate customization by selecting information that they are interested in receiving. From the consumer selections, producers are able to construct consumer profiles which allow producers to better design products/services to meet consumer preferences.

5 Web-based Supply Chain Processes

In this section, we show how the strategies enabled by component technology and Extranet are used to improve supply chain network (SCN) processes. An SCN is made of enterprises which are held together for the purpose of fulfilling the demand of the consumers, and delivering the intermediate product from one enterprise to another as it travels through the process chain. On a physical level, the SCN can be viewed as a container with the enterprises as the components. On a conceptual level, the SCN is the framework that holds the product development process, procurement process, order processing and forecasting, order fulfillment process, distribution process and customer service support together. Insufficient information and communication cause problems that can be overcome by component technology and Extranet by facilitating cross-boundary information sharing. In the remainder of this section, we illustrate how the procurement process and order fulfillment process are improved by the new technologies. In particular, we show how Extranet-enabled online bidding process increases the flexibility of the SCNs, and how component technology enables tighter coordination between the processes by integrating the various enterprises' IS into a VIS.

5.1 Procurement Process

Procurement is part of the order fulfillment process (OFP) that deals with the acquisition of input materials from upstream enterprises. The procurement process has three parts: (i) searching and selecting the supplier, (ii) negotiating terms and establishing a contract, and (iii) executing out the contract. The search process leads to the selection of the supplier that is best able to provide the input requirements in terms of cost and quality of product and service (e.g. timeliness. The relationship between the supplier and the immediate downstream enterprises may be long term as in a partnership, medium term as in a project contract or short-term as in a one-time purchase, depending on the product type (see Section 2).

Extranet facilitates the selection and negotiation activities in the procurement process. Figure 3 shows an online bidding process. A 3rd party acts as a broker to provide the space in which the bidding commences including maintaining a database of bidding information and negotiation tools like group ware systems. A manufacturer submits its product specifications to the pool of suppliers, who evaluate them and submit their bids. The manufacturer then selects a supplier and the two parties negotiate the contract on-line via the Extranet. The supplier fulfills the terms of the contract and sends the required product to the manufacturer who pays for it. Web technology reduces the time taken to transmit bids between suppliers and customers, and also gives accesses to greater pool of suppliers and customers respectively.

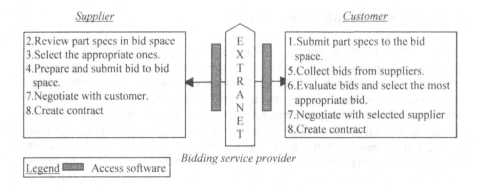

Fig. 3. Online bidding process

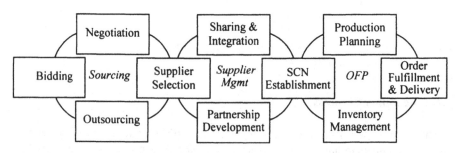

Fig. 4. The bidding, supplier management and order fulfillment cycles in SCN

The relationship between sourcing, supplier management and order fulfillment cycles is generalized in Figure 4. The objective of the sourcing cycle is to identify a suitable supplier for procuring an outsourced product through the bidding and negotiation cycle. In supplier management cycle, the focus is to develop a relationship between strategic partners through information sharing and systems integration. In the OFP cycle, the relationship with the supplier is already established. The goal of the OFP is thus to ensure an efficient order-fulfillment-deliver cycle by managing inventory and production planning.

Figure 4 captures both long-term and short-term procurement relationships. Functional products that have predictable consumer demand patterns favor a long-term procurement relationship for efficiency purposes. The sourcing cycle is performed once, and the next step is the building and cementing of relationship between the selected supplier and the manufacturer through the integration of the two corporations' IS. Once the connection is established, the manufacturer just runs through the OFP cycle without needing to go through the previous two stages. EDI technology is one popular solution to cross-enterprise IS integration. However, the heavy capital investment and the proprietary nature bar the participation of smaller companies in such partnerships and force enterprises to stay with the same partners. Adoption of component technology could reduce the barrier to systems incompatibility and enable the supplier's IS to be compatible with that of the manufacturer. This property is particularly appealing to medium-term partnerships where enterprises do not want to commit themselves to a particular supplier or are unable to lay out the capital for EDI development.

For innovative products, the sourcing cycle may be invoked each time the enterprise runs through the OFP cycle. Because of the short product life, manufacturers are producing different products each cycle which requires different inputs and hence different suppliers. Furthermore, the needs of an enterprise can change dynamically. A responsive SCN is both responsive and flexible enough to choose the most appropriate supplier at a given time. The online bidding capability made possible by Extranet technology improves the procurement process in two ways: first, it reduces the time taken to bid and negotiate. Second, it provides the manufacturer a large pool of suppliers from which to choose, and vice versa. This pool increases the probability for a good match between the manufacturer and supplier in every procurement process.

5.2 Order Fulfillment Process

The order fulfillment process (OFP) includes the SCN processes like procurement, order processing, production and distribution. The objective of SCM is to optimize the OFP by coordinating the supply chain activities and streamlining the transition of intermediate products from enterprise to enterprise via efficient logistics management. It starts with the consolidation of demand forecasting and incoming orders. Based on the production quantity, the production schedule is generated and input materials procured. The enterprise then manufactures and assembles the products before shipping them to the downstream customer.

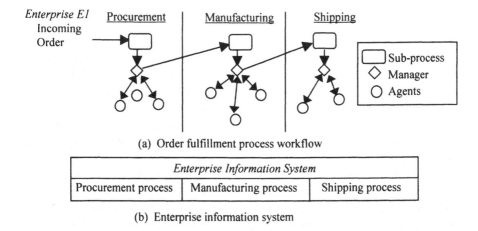

(a) Order fulfillment process workflow

Enterprise Information System		
Procurement process	Manufacturing process	Shipping process

(b) Enterprise information system

Fig. 5. Traditional order fulfillment process

In a typical enterprise, all processes are owned and performed by the same enterprise *E1*, as shown in Figure 5a. The agents perform the various activities in each process, controlled by the manager. The white icons indicate that all agents belong to *E1*. The IS is often a system that handles all processes (see Figure 5b).

Figure 6 shows the OFP in a component environment where not all the activities are performed within an enterprise. Different activities in the OFP are performed by different enterprises, as shown in Figure 6a. In the manufacturing process, for example, some parts are manufactured in-house (white icon) while other parts are outsourced or purchased from other enterprise (patterned icons). The manufacturing manager manages the manufacturing activities as well as the bidding and negotiation processes for outsourcing. Some processes are completely managed by an external

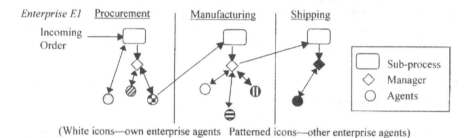

(White icons—own enterprise agents   Patterned icons—other enterprise agents)

(a) Order fulfillment process workflow

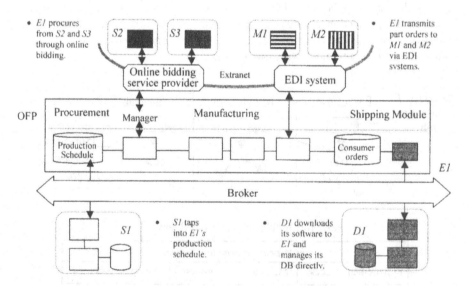

(b) Component-based information system

Fig. 6. The multi-enterprise OFP in a component environment

enterprise. For example, shipping process is managed by distributor $D1$ which takes care of delivering the finished products to the downstream customer. Other processes may not require an explicit manager to coordinate. For example, staple input materials suppliers like $S1$ can run $E1$'s scheduling software via the object request broker (ORB) to find out its production schedule and deliver the input materials accordingly. The procurement manager just needs to handle one-time transactions and other unexpected procurements (i.e. $S2$ and $S3$)

The corresponding IS is component-based where each process's applications have been divided into modules. Other enterprises can access $E1$'s scheduling software or directly plug into its module. $D1$ directly plugs its distribution software into $E1$'s shipping module since it is managing $E1$'s shipping process. Supplier $S1$ has direct access to the $E1$'s scheduling software in the procurement module since it has a long-term relationship with $E1$. The procurement manager negotiates short-term purchasing contracts with $S2$ and $S3$ via the online bidding service. The manufacturing manager places orders for the outsourced parts with manufacturers $M1$ and $M2$ through the EDI systems. The IS in Figure 6b is in effect a virtual IS, formed by integrating the ISs of the various enterprises.

Each sub-process in the OFP is driven by information—how much to produce, when to produce, how much to procure, who to procure from, produce in-house or outsource parts, who to ship to etc. Each piece of information affects the downstream process. In enterprise with proprietary information systems, information sharing occurs only within the enterprise, making it difficult for other enterprises to participate in the process. Transactions outside the enterprise must be explicitly made. Hence, the enterprise handles the entire OFP as shown in Figure 5.

The OFP in Figure 6 is a multi-enterprise system with different tasks performed by different enterprise. Component technology facilitates information sharing among enterprises. For example, instead of developing an explicit module to handle shipping, the enterprise plugs a distributor's shipping module into its information system. Through Extranet, suppliers access the enterprise's scheduling software to obtain up-to-date production information and coordinate their output with the enterprise's production schedule. Hence OFP becomes a collaborative effort instead of a single-enterprise effort. The participants of the OFP can also change dynamically. For example, in single transactions, the procurement manager may select different suppliers thereby optimizing each transaction. Using online bidding and auctioning systems, the enterprise may also bid to supply to downstream customers.

6 Example: A Flexible Web-based SCN Supporting Mass Customization at John Deere

Efficient SCM must balance conflicting constraints. For example, the fluctuating demand pattern of highly customized products is difficult to forecast. The production unit requires an accurate demand forecast to optimize the production and procurement processes. The marketing unit, on the other hand, prefers to retain the flexibility to adjust the demand forecast to accommodate unpredictable demand. Web technology helps to resolve these conflicts by supporting the needs of both production and marketing. We use a John Deere planter example to illustrate how Web technology enables its SCN to support mass customization.

6.1 Background

John Deere began manufacturing agricultural equipment in 1837 with the self-scouring moldboard plow. Among its many current products is the row crop planter (see Figure 7). Although John Deere offers its customers more than 75 models of planters, with the choice of options a planter can be configured in over 1.6 million ways.

A typical planter consists of a rectangular frame, two marker arms and multiple row units along with corresponding seed, fertilizer, herbicide, and insecticide containers. The frame varies in length, to accommodate the varying number and type of row units ordered. Several design options facilitate transportation of the planter between the fields. Customers can also choose among several types of mechanical marker arms that assist the operator to plant straight rows. Also, the planter can be configured to plant many types of row crops, and a variety of soil and field conditions.

Fig. 7. An example of John Deere's planter (*Source*: John Deere)

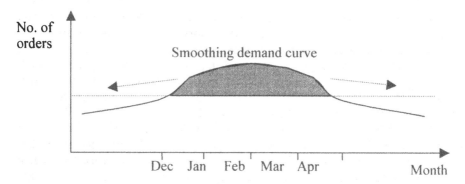

Fig. 8. Demand of planters on a yearly basis

The demand for planters is seasonal, with the highest orders in the period between December and April (see Figure 8). To smooth out the demand curve, the factory brings forward some production ahead of the forecasted peak. Dealers receive financial incentives to place orders early. Although demand levels may be predictable, anticipation of the correct model and option mix is quite difficult. The traditional method to hedge against fluctuating demand by carrying large inventory violates the build-to-order strategy. Instead, by buying-to-plan and building-to-order, John Deere aligns its SCM and production strategy to meet anticipated demand while accommodating variation in the level of demand.

John Deere planters are assembled under a built-to-order strategy that incorporates Just-in-Time production of components in manufacturing cells adjacent to the assembly line and point-of-use delivery of purchased components. This mixture of purchased raw material to support cellular production adjacent to the line and JIT delivery of purchased components at point of use complicates John Deere's SCM strategies but enables efficient production.

Correct sequencing of orders for production can mean the difference between meeting or missing an order delivery date (Davis and Meyer, 1998). An efficient assembly sequence balances production performance (worker productivity, operational efficiency, product quality and order cycle time) while controlling cost (among contributing production modules and suppliers). It must accommodate two forms of constraints: strong (illegal and prohibited from occurring) and weak (legal but penalized in proportion to cost). Non-manufacturing constraints such as customer service policies, market-planning goals, order fill priorities, and product distribution strategies must also be included. SCN strategies are an integral part of achieving efficient production schedules.

6.2 Web-based Supply Chain Network Architecture

John Deere's environment is not unique. Companies like John Deere have three common goals in managing their SCN. First, facilitate information sharing so that the factories would be able to better manage the peak demand as shown in Figure 8.

Second, rapidly reconfigurable SCNs that respond to variability in the model mix and option mix. Third, a retail distribution network that accommodates one-to-one marketing. The Web-based SCN architecture enables them to meet all three goals.

In general, most SCNs adopt a hybrid of the make-and-sell and the sense-and-respond approaches because each class of product components exhibits different characteristics and has different requirements. For example, the John Deere planter incorporates highly customized parts such as plastic components as well as commonly used parts like hydraulic hoses, pumps and gauges. The Web architecture and Extranet technology enables an SCN to support these different types of requirements. Prior to the rise of electronic commerce, two strategies were used to procure these highly customized components: opt for a short lead time by holding a large inventory of the full range of parts and incur a high inventory cost, or place individual orders and experience a long lead time. The new technologies shorten the lead-time by propagating the customer orders to the suppliers as they are needed. This approach can be achieved with the *secured intranet access model* by incorporating these suppliers into manufacturer's corporate intranet and allowing them access into its master production schedule. For the commodity parts sourcing, the *electronic commerce model* allows the manufacturer to effectively manage these non-strategic suppliers.

These two categories of requirements mirror the long-term and short-term relationships that exists among strategic business partners. Highly customized parts typically require special manufacturing capability that lead to increased switching costs and to long-term relationships. A manufacturer may also choose to pursue long-term relationships with suppliers supplying low-variation products for efficiency purposes. For example standard components produced from raw materials in production cells adjacent to the assembly line, like John Deere's marker arms can adopt Web EDI to reap the benefits of JIT strategies. The universal access property of the Web allows the manufacturer to coordinate with strategic partners across the world and build a truly global SCN. Manufacturers generally have a short-term relationship with suppliers of commodity priced materials because they prefer to retain the flexibility to select the supplier that best suit their needs. The availability of online bidding systems enhances this flexibility by widening the pool of suppliers that the manufacturer can choose from.

Extranet facilitates the propagation of demand information from retailers to manufacturers. In the past, manufacturers utilized automatic inventory replenishment strategies to distribute products to retailers based on the percentage of products sold in the previous years. However, fluctuating annual demand patterns made this formula inaccurate. Increasing the stock-level to cover the error in the formula lead to high carrying costs due to the wide range of models and options offered.

A Web-SCN enables producers to transit from an automatic inventory replenishment system to an available-to-promise. An Extranet links the dealers into a network with the manufacturer through the *specialized application model*. Once manufacturers have adopted available-to-promise capability for build-to-order strategies, advanced strategies such as profitable-to-promise are possible. Systems that allow customers to select the production slots much like airline agents reserve seats on a particular flight create the opportunity for dynamic pricing based on production schedule and capacity.

The Web-SCN enables retail distributors to embrace one-on-one marketing since product information can be readily customized to inform customers and guide their selections. Dealers can track individual sales and construct personalized maintenance schedules for each product sold. Dealer networks can be created to share resources as well. For example, retailers can share inventories of wholegoods and service parts to improve service levels and control inventory costs.

Table 3 lists the specific issues of a traditional SCN and the enhancements made possible by Web technology.

Table 3. Summary of the enhancements to traditional SCN using Web technology

SCN processes	Traditional SCN issues	Web technology enhancements
Demand	• Cyclical demand pattern • Complex product mix	• Facilitates demand information sharing • More accurate demand forecast
Product design	• Highly customizable product • Product has both customizable and commodity parts	• Facilitates mass customization through postponement strategy • Facilitates design collaboration
Order fulfillment and distribution	• Global organization • Global sourcing • Large dealer network	• Facilitates coordination and resource sharing • Facilitates communication between suppliers, dealers and customers
Enterprise resource planning	• Hybrid SCN for commodities as well as specialized components • Build-to-order production strategy • Supplier management for both long-term and short-term supplier relationships	• Better inventory management through JIT and CRP strategies • Online bidding enables flexible short transactions • Supports both cost-efficient and market responsive SCNs
Customer service	• Improved product info dissemination to dealers • Available-to-promise guarantee for customer orders	• One-on-one customer service • Guidance for product selection • Customer-scheduled ordering

7 Discussion

Web technology facilitates cross-enterprise information sharing through inter-connectivity and integration. Extranet interconnects enterprises to their strategic partners as well as to their customers. However, current Web-based applications are relatively simple and are currently limited to information sharing type applications like content providing and online-catalog transaction applications. Software component technology, on the other hand, enables a deeper level of business process integration by allowing one enterprises' software to be plugged into another's framework. The drawback is that its reach is much more limited, requiring participants to use component software. This excludes the average consumer from the network.

Web-based technology brings about changes in the structure and behavior of enterprises changes the configuration of SCNs. First, the barriers erected by proprietary systems would be down, allowing companies that do not have EDI linkages to enjoy the advantages brought about by EDI systems as well. Trust and relationships between channel partners in an SCN would probably play a more important role as the switching cost due to system compatibility is reduced. Companies would probably compete on other terms such as the quality of product, customer service, the timeliness of product delivery etc. Second, as companies specialize in their key processes, there would be an emergence of a new breed of companies specializing in performing subsidiary tasks. Third, there would probably be an increase in the number of virtual enterprises as specialized firms band together to provide the entire repertoire of SCN functions.

One issue of concern in Web-based technology is security. Proprietary systems, though expensive to develop and difficult to cooperate with in joint ventures also makes it safer since it is less accessible. This issue is currently addressed in Web technology to make computer systems less vulnerable and for safer information transmission over Internet.

8 Conclusion

The focus of this chapter is to show how Web technology improves supply chain network management through information sharing and information systems integration. Different types of products require different types of supply chain network. The trend towards customizable products makes supply chain management more complex. Large product variety requires more product types which in turn requires more suppliers. Demand forecasting is made more difficult as the enterprise now has to forecast for each product type instead of a single generic type. Information sharing between enterprises and consumers helps to alleviate some of the supply chain problems.

The World Wide Web provides the information infrastructure for information sharing. One enabling technology, component technology, facilitates the integration of heterogeneous information systems from different corporations. Another technology, Extranet interconnects enterprises and their strategic partners. These two technologies makes possible strategies that support flexible procurement, mass customization and personalized customer service and increases the responsiveness of the supply chain network. As an example, we show how a Web-based supply chain network supports the mass customization of John Deere's planters.

Reference

Baldwin, C. Y., and K. B. Clark, "Managing in an age of Modularity," *Harvard Business Review*, Sept-Oct (1997), 84-93.

Bort, J., and F. Bradley, *Building an Extranet*, John Wiley & Sons, Inc., New York, NY,1997.

Bradley, S., and R. Nolan, *Sense and Respond: Capturing Value in the Network Era,* Harvard Business School Press, Boston, MA, 1998.

Byrne, J.A., R. Brandt, and O. Port, "The Virtual Corporation," *Business Week,* February 8, (1993).

Davis, S., and C. Meyer, *Blur:The Speed of Change in the Connected Economy*, Addison-Wesley, Reading, MA, 1998.

Fisher, M. L., "What is the right supply chain for your product?" *Harvard Business Review*, Mar-Apr (1997), 105-116.

Fisher, M. L., J. H. Hammond, W.R. Obermeyer and A. Raman, "Making supply meet demand in an uncertain world," *Harvard Business Review*, May-June, (1994), 83-93.

Hammond, J. H., "Quick Response in Retail/Manufacturing Channels", in *Globalization, Technology and Competition*, S.P. Bradley, J.A. Hausman and R.L. Nolan (Eds.), Harvard Business School Press, 1993.

Lee, H. L., and C. Billington, "The Evolution of Supply-Chain-Management Models and Practice at Hewlett-Packard," *Interface*, 25, 5, Sept-Oct (1995), 42-63.

Lee, H. L., V. Padmanabhan, and S. Whang, "Information Distortion in a Supply Chain: The Bullwhip Effect," *Management Science*, 43, 4, April (1997a), 546-558.

Lee, H. L., V. Padmanabhan, and S. Whang, "The Bullwhip Effect in Supply Chains," *Sloan Management Review*, 38,3, Spring, (1997b), 93-102.

Lin, F., and M. J. Shaw, "Supply Chain Strategies for Order Fulfillment", *International Journal in Flexible Manufacturing Systems,* (1998), forthcoming.

Lin, F., G. W. Tan, and M. J. Shaw, "Multi-Agent Enterprise Modeling," *Journal of Organizational Computing & Electronic Commerce*, (1998), forthcoming.

Orfali, R., D. Harkey, and J. Edwards, *The Essential Distributed Objects Survival Guide*, John Wiley & Sons Inc., New York, NY,1996.

The Sante Fe Institute, Swarm Web pages, URL = http://www.santafe.edu/projects/swarm/

Seidmann, A., and A. Sundararajan, "Sharing Logistics Information across Organizations: Technology, Competition and Contracting," in *Information Technology and Industrial Competitiveness: How IT shapes Competition"*, Kemerer C.F. (Ed.), Kluwer Academic Publishers, Boston, MA, 1998, 107-136.

Sheldon, T., *Windows NT® Security Handbook*, Obsborne McGraw-Hill, Berkeley, CA, 1996.

Simon, H. A., *Sciences of the Artificial*, MIT Press, Cambridge, MA, 1981.

Strader, T. J., F. Lin, and M. J. Shaw, "Simulation of Order Fulfillment in Divergent Assembly Supply Chains," *Journal of Artificial Societies and Social Simulation*, 1, 2, (1998a), URL=http://www.soc.surrey.ac.uk/JASSS/1/2/5.html.

Strader, T. J., F. Lin, and M. J. Shaw, "Information Infrastructure for Electronic Virtual Organization Management," *Decision Support Systems*, 23, (1998b), 75-94.

Szyperski, C., *Component Software: Beyond Object-oriented Programming*, ACM Press, New York, 1998.

Szyperski, C., and C. Pfister, "Workship on Component-Oriented Programming," in *Special Issues in Objected-Oriented Programming - ECOOP96 Worship Reader*, Mühlhäuser M. (Ed.), dpunkt Verlag, Heidelberg, 1997.

**Part VI
Enterprise Management**

CHAPTER 23

Virtual Organizations and E-Commerce

Paul Gray and Magid Igbaria
Department of Information Science, Claremont Graduate University, Claremont, CA, USA,
Paul.Gray@cgu.edu; Magid.Igbaria@cgu.edu

In a virtual organization, goods and services are accessible without face-to-face contact with other people. In such organizations, computers and telecommunications substitute for physical location. Virtual organizations are particularly suited for E-commerce because the contact between the customer and the vendor is a home page on the Internet. This chapter discusses the forces, dilemmas, issues, and implications of ongoing virtual organizations and their relation to E-commerce. It describes the four main driving forces (global economics, policies and politics, the enlightened population, and technologies) and the issues and complexities that these forces impose. Distributed organizations based on telecommuting and temporary alliance of multiple organizations are described as specific instances of virtual organizations.

Keywords: Virtual Organizations; Virtual Corporations and E-commerce; Telecommuting; New Ways of Working

1 Introduction

In E-commerce, a business organization can be located anywhere in the world since it is linked to its customers not by physical presence (as in a retail outlet) but by communications and computer networks. Most organizations involved in E-commerce are conventional in that they have one or more physical places of business. However, there are organizations that are "virtual" in the sense that they are not located in a single place but are distributed or are temporary combinations of consultants and small firms joined together for a specific purpose.

2 Thinking About Virtual

What do we mean by virtual? Here are quotations of four definitions:

- Being such in essence or effect though not formally recognized or admitted (Webster Dictionary, 1990)
- Existing or resulting in essence or effect though not in actual fact, form, or name. (Microsoft Bookshelf, 1995)

- Pertaining to a functional unit that appears to be real, but whose functions are accomplished by other means (IBM Dictionary of Computing, 1996).
- Significant enhanced effects or actions, physical behavior of non-physical entities, and the supporting use of telecommunications and computing technologies. (Grenier and Metes 1995).

These definitions imply a mode of organization once based exclusively on physical contact being transformed to one where goods and services are accessible without face-to-face contact with other people. From one point of view, then, all E-commerce is virtual. In this chapter, however, we will take a much narrower view and consider only organizations which are virtual and which are engaged in E-commerce.

The virtual world involves a change from the physically oriented structures of the 19th century to the non-physically oriented communications structures (i.e., structures without constraints of place and time) of the 21st century. Figure 1 shows a framework for thinking about the virtual world.

DRIVING FORCES	VIRTUAL ARRANGEMENTS
• Global economics • Politics and policies • Enlightened population • Technology	• Telework • Computer-supported cooperative work • Virtual corporation • Virtual community

Fig. 1. Framework for the virtual world

In this chapter, we discuss the first three arrangements shown in Figure 1: telework, cooperative work, and the virtual corporation.

3 Driving Forces

3.1 Global Economies

Economies are now global. Firms routinely move an important piece of work, such as a proposal, across time zones and countries so they can work on them literally around the clock. A project may involve many people who never see one another yet work closely together through electronic mail, video, and other technological aids.

Borders are becoming transparent for trade as regional trading blocs such as NAFTA and the European Union move forward and as global money nears a reality. For trade, English is starting to be a universal language. Whether these changes are good or bad is still a matter of dispute. Nonetheless the global economy is here.

3.2 Policies and Politics

The world's trading partners have differing views of governments' role in IT implementation. Governments, businesses, and users, have concerns about ownership, access, and distribution of information. Some European countries already view the free flow of information as a way to improve their economies and are instituting policies which clearly demonstrate their commitments toward creating a global marketplace. For example, the Danish government is aggressively pushing the country toward a virtual workplace. It has developed a technical blueprint for achieving this goal including a plan to have 75% of the households equipped with personal computers and modems by the year 2000.

3.3 Enlightened Population

Use of the virtual technologies requires individual computer literacy. Countries in which people are schooled in basic computing have a temporary edge in working virtually. However, this edge will disappear as older workers leave the workforce. Work processes are being redefined and people are adapting to the accompanying social and physiological changes. An example of this change is the disappearance of the employment security once offered by large corporations.

3.4 Technology

Technology by itself does not ensure the coming of the virtual workplace. Rather, it is an enabler. We are seeing a cornucopia of supporting technologies, including the Inter/Intranet, World Wide Web (WWW), electronic mail, groupware, videoconferencing, workflow, data management, data warehousing, and improved networking capabilities.

4 Forms of Virtual Organizations

Virtual organizations actually come in two forms.

1. Continuing firms without offices.
2. Temporary organizations formed to accomplish specific projects.

4.1 Firm Without Office

This statement is not quite correct. To comply with Securities and Exchange Commission rules, all companies must have an address. Even VeriFone, now a division of Hewlett Packard, the quintessential company without an office, does have a base in Redwood City where some of its computers are located. When it was founded, it consisted of individuals scattered from New York to Hawaii who worked where they lived and met occasionally (typically at an airport hotel) as needed.

This company is the world's largest supplier of electronic credit-card verification equipment (that is the swipers that tell the merchant to accept or reject your card). Its main means of communication among its 1800 employees is electronic mail using Digital Equipment Corporation VAX's and leased lines. Its offices are where the employees are at any given moment. No one has a secretary but everyone has a laptop. There are no paper memos. People who won't use a keyboard need not apply for work.

The idea behind a dispersed, mobile company such as VeriFone is to create a firm that is close to its customers. It also provides the capability of making time zones work for the company rather than against it. VeriFone managers can (and do) pass projects (particularly proposals for new business) from one continent to another to keep them on track and on time.

With everyone on-line it is possible to accumulate expertise quickly. One story told by VeriFone concerns a salesperson trying to close a deal in Greece. The negotiations hit an impasse when the salesperson did not have specific information the bank wanted. He asked for and received a grace period of 24 hours to find the answer. He posted an urgent request via e-mail from his hotel room, asking if any of his colleagues had faced a similar scenario. He received 24 responses overnight and was able to close the deal the next morning.

What makes this example even more interesting is the fact that VeriFone uses relatively modest technology: ASCII character-based E-mail as opposed to high bandwidth applications such as videoconferencing or multimedia for coordination.

4.2 Temporary Organizations

The project organizations that make Hollywood films are an example of the temporary organization form. A team of free-lance workers and small companies is assembled for each new film project. After a film is completed, the team created for this project dissolves. However, since film making, like most types of businesses, involves relatively small groups of creative people, many people find themselves working together over and over. More generally, groups from different organizations, often staying in their own location and having different cultures, work together toward a particular output.

Virtual corporations are an organizational innovation. They are temporary networks of independent companies--suppliers, customers, even erstwhile rivals--linked by information technology to share skills, costs, and access to each others Instead of expanding the business or buying out another company, an organization may elect to create an alliance or partnership with another company. This organizational arrangement is particularly prevalent in midsize US manufacturing companies. Virtual alliances where the structure is predicated on competency needs is very different from traditional alliances, where partnerships are based on convenience (cost, location, etc.).

The arrangement may involve equal partners, a prime systems contractor and major component subcontractors (e.g., airframes, wing assemblies, tail assemblies), or the equivalent of the Japanese keiretsu, an ongoing coalition of contractors working on a particular product over time. From the viewpoint of the individual professional, their primary time is allocated to the joint work product. Thus, they spend their time working in their own location but being connected to other members of the team electronically through electronic mail, electronic data interchange, and other means of communications.

Virtual business relationships turn out to be more complex than the traditional model. They are created and dissolved quickly. Two companies in partnership on one project may be bitter rivals in another. Differences in corporate culture must be worked out. Ways have to be found to protect company secrets such as special formulas or marketing strategies.

5 Technology That Makes Virtual Organizations Possible

Virtual organizations are possible because the convergence of computers and telecommunications make coordination possible even when the participants are geographically separate. Collaborative applications include computer-based conferencing (including e-mail), shared applications and data bases, workflow software, project management software, and video conferencing to name just a few. It is the ability to cooperate through technology that makes the virtual organization possible.

6 The Virtual Worker

Not only can companies be virtual, but individual workers as well. Figure 2 shows the set of possible arrangements.

In conventional work, people come to the same place and typically work fixed hours. This has been the arrangement in offices and factories going back into the 18th century. The first type of virtual arrangement is *telecommuting* (e.g., Nilles et. al., 1975; Gray et. al., 1996) In telecommuting, workers are connected digitally to their firm, working either at home or in a workplace close to their home called a *telecommuting center*. For such workers, telecommuting may be daily or on some days during the week. The workers interact with their organizations through voice and computer and, in some cases, via video.

		Organization		
		Same place	Multiple locations	Virtual(No office)
Employees	Same place	Conventional	Consulting firms	------------
	Different place	Telecommuters	Hoteling	Completely virtual firm

Fig. 2 Examples of possible arrangements of employees and organizations

6.1 Multiple Locations

Some employees work in multiple offices. For example, auditors and consultants in large accounting firms spend a portion of their time in their assigned company offices or cubicles and the rest at client locations or traveling. For such firms, a large fraction of the office space stands empty much of the time. Becker and Steele(1996), for example, found that over 60% of the office space in major corporations was empty at any given time. The response to this approach has been "hoteling". That is, just as hotel rooms are identical and are assigned to travelers when they arrive, workers are assigned office space when they come to the work place. Their papers and personal items are moved into their temporary quarters. Hoteling is discussed further in Appendix I of this chapter.

6.2 No Office

In a completely virtual firm that does not have offices, the members of the firm work at or near their homes, which may be anywhere, and meet periodically as needed. In this arrangement, all communication is electronic. That is, the organization itself is run as E-commerce.

6.3 Computer Supported Cooperative Work

In a virtual organization, just as in a conventional one, teamwork is critical. Computer-supported cooperative work (CSCW) is about using teams to support the flexibility of virtual work, which allows work to take place anywhere, anytime. Figure 3 is a 2x2 matrix that shows the four combinations of time and place involved.

	SAME PLACE	DIFFERENT PLACE
SAME TIME	Group decision support systems	Videoconferencing
DIFFERENT TIME	Project scheduling tools	Electronic mail, computer conferencing

Fig. 3. Examples of time and place combinations

In a virtual organization using different time/different place communication, people have the opportunity to decide when they want to communicate, the form of communication, and how the communication will proceed.

The use of CSCW to improve communication in virtual organizations is not without its problems. Success rates of CSCW technologies are contingent on the people who use them. It is not the technology that is the problem, but the social aspects of using the technology. In E-commerce, where the payoff comes from the exchange of accurate information as well as payment, the social aspect is as important the as the technical.

6.4 Management Control

Virtual organizations do need coordination. That is, the usual control functions that management performs need to be done whether workers are in the same location, or in groups at different locations, or working alone. The classic control tasks become more difficult when managers who are used to working in line-of-sight supervision attempt to supervise workers who are dispersed. Research by Westfall (1996) indicates that there is a natural tension between managers and workers that can be explained by agency theory (Eisenhardt 1989) and by institutional theory (Powell 1991). In brief, agency theory indicates that managers assume that workers (agents) shirk and, conversely, workers worry about not being recognized by managers for the good work that they do. Institutional theory indicates that in many institutional cultures, workers located remotely are assumed to be "on the beach" rather than working. These and other findings on telecommuting are discussed further in Appendix II of this chapter.

7 Virtual Organizations and E-commerce

Virtual corporations are an organizational form particularly suited for E-commerce. In E-commerce, where the contact between customer and vendor is entirely digital, the customer does not know whether company is co-located or virtual. Furthermore, the customer should not care since, like *Land's End*, a company that is a voice at the end of a telephone line, an E-commerce organization is a home page on the Internet.

Requirements for a virtual firm engaged in retail E-commerce are no different than those for a conventional firm. The company requires a company identity on the Internet (home page, etc), an electronically accessible catalog, a warehouse or the ability to act as a broker and order just-in-time, good telecommunications and computer capabilities. Both the telecommunications and the computer can be either insourced or outsourced. That is, the company can create and maintain its own technology (insource) or hire another firm to provide technology services (outsource). In the latter case, the company and its oursourcer form a virtual corporation. Advertising on the web or in conventional media is used to reach customers so that they look at the firm's home pages.

8 Advantages and Disadvantages

In deciding whether to form a series of alliances and create a virtual organization for E-commerce, the advantages and disadvantages of virtual organizations need to be considered.

The strategic reasons for forming a virtual organization are summarized by Goldman, Nagel, and Preiss (1995) and verified by Palmer (1998):

1. Sharing infrastructure, R&D risk, and costs
2. Linking complementary core competency
3. Reducing the time from concept to cash through sharing
4. Increasing the facilities available and the apparent size of the organization
5. Gaining market access and sharing customer loyalty.

Grimshaw and Kwock (1998) considered the advantages and disadvantages for combinations of small to medium sized companies who are able to respond quickly to change, with the results shown in Table 1.

9 Examples

This section describes several additional virtual organizations engaged in E-commerce. They cover a range of fields (a magazine, a software retailer, a bookseller, a vineyard, and a travel agency). The products are both intellectual and physical. Their main distinguishing characteristic is that they are not conventional store-based or catalog based retailers. For each organization, its internet address follows its name. The first two (Datamation and Egghead) are examples of companies that started out as conventional firms and, when faced with economic difficulties, converted to being virtual. The other three were founded as virtual companies.

Table 1. Advantages and disadvantages of alliances

ADVANTAGES	
• Increasedcompetitive capability and flexibility	Partners can pool core competencies and add new ones as needed. They can respond more quickly to changes in the marketplace.
• Improved Customer Service	Virtual organizations have greater customer focus and market response. Linking with clients in design and other processes reduces errors and improves service.
• Lower costs	For example, reduced rent, cycle time for design, development, and production
• Better communication and internal control	By working in teams rather than a hierarchy, intra-organizational communication improves
DISADVANTAGES	
• High investment and operational costs	Lower costs (above) are counterbalanced by increased investment in infrastructure, coordination costs, training, and maintenance
• Legal problems	Ownership rights for copyrights, designs, products
• Trust and respect	Unless there is trust and respect among partners, projects break up
• Culture clash	Partners coming from different business and national cultures must work together

Datamation: (http://www.datamation.com). Datamation is a well-respected periodical in the field of information systems. Established in 1957, its history spans the mainframe, PC, and client-server eras. It was distributed free of charge to senior people in the field who qualified and made most of its revenue by selling advertising to computer and software manufacturers. In January 1998 it announced that it would no longer produce printed copies and publish entirely on the Internet. The conversion to a virtual product was based on economics. Datamation, despite a circulation of 199,000 and a staff of only 20 or so, was losing money. It had developed an excellent web site and is continuing with the web site version.

Egghead: (http://www.egghead.com). Egghead, a pioneer in selling PC software at retail, converted to being a virtual company in February 1998. Although Egghead, founded in the mid-1980's, reached a peak of over 200 retail outlets, in recent years had been unable to meet the competition of the megastores that sold both hardware and software. Egghead launched its on-line store in September 1997 and then bought Surplus Direct, a computer discount reseller which runs an auction service on the net (www.surplusauction.com). In February, it closed all its remaining 80 stores, reduced its workforce from 1000 to 200, and became a virtual company, now known as Egghead.com Inc.

The basic marketing strategy of Egghead.com Inc. is that it is an established national brand name competing in an E-commerce market for computer goods at retail (estimated to be over $3 billion by 2001). Because it is well-known, Egghead.com believes that it will be more likely to attract customers in E-commerce than companies without brand identification. . To spread that brand name, it signed marketing agreements with Yahoo and others to advertise.

Amazon.com: (http://www.amazon.com). Amazon.com, a virtual bookstore, opened in July 1995 to "offer products that educate, inform, and inspire." The concept was to build an online store that was user-friendly: easy to navigate with a wide range of selection. By using information technology, Amazon.com provides features to simplify book purchases. Its search engine allows customers to search by title, author, subject, keyword, ISBN, publisher, or date of publication. Other features include 1-ClickSM (a secure ordering system) and a file of customers' recommendations on specific books. Amazon.com offers 3 millions books, CDs, audiobooks, DVDs, and computer games to 2.5 million people in more than 160 countries.

Virtual Vineyards: (http://www.virtualvin.com). Virtual Vineyards, a direct marketer of fine foods and wines on the Internet, was opened in January1995. Their approach has been to try to differentiate the company as an on-line specialty retailer. Using information technology to sell wine, the company tries to "give potential customers in-depth information about the wines being offered and the people who made them" with buying comfort and an easy-to-follow user interface.

Internet Travel Network: (ITN) (http://www.itn.net). Internet Travel Network (ITN), is an Internet-based travel agent founded in January 1995 to "develop and market high-quality, easy to use travel reservations services for the leisure and business travel industry." ITN provides customers with real-time data and allows reservations to be made in all airline CRS systems, linking more than 2 million registered users and 4,000 member travel agents. With 20 million hits per month, the Internet reservation system allows individuals and travel agencies to arrange and purchase air tickets (including seating and meal selections, frequent flyer account numbers, preferred gateways and routings), reserve car rentals, and book hotel stays.

10 Policy Issues

The driving forces and the nature of E-commerce lead to policy issues that need to be resolved. These issues include global policy and economics, social and human behavior, organizational structures, and family structure. In the following paragraphs we present the conventional wisdom on these issues. However, in many cases, the underlying research to prove or disprove the arguments has not yet been done.

10.1 Global Policy

Global policy and economics establish the legal framework and the set of rules by which virtual organizations will conduct E-commerce. Since its inception, the Internet has been an open culture in which information is exchanged freely. However, increased commercialization and globalization makes this openness inefficient and policies to balance openness and marketplace efficiency difficult to formulate (Press, 1994). For virtual organizations, the following issues common to all E-commerce are of particular importance.

- access rights
- information security and privacy
- secure monetary exchange
- taxation

Failure to appropriately address these issues can lead to a loss of confidence in the underlying technologies and thereby create significant barriers to virtual organizations.

Access Rights: The virtual organization depends on its ability to communicate without censorship and to have the protection of intellectual property rights protection afforded by copyright[1]. Virtual organizations in E-commerce operate globally and thus need access rights on a global basis. Unfortunately, not all countries provide the same protections, in part because of cultural and political differences.

In the United States, copyright laws are twenty years old, and thus do not interpret issues such as fair use that arise in an electronic world (Miller, 1996). Judicious global solutions to the access rights issues are not imminent. Individual countries may resolve problems within their borders, but resolutions need to cross global boundaries. There is progress. For example, Singapore is working to merge censorship laws without negatively impacting technological breakthroughs.

Security and Privacy: A robust security scheme is a fundamental requirement for virtual organizations if they are to engage in widespread commerce on the Internet. An adequate security solution includes requirements to (1) maintain confidentiality to the parties involved in the transaction, (2) authenticate the parties involved in the communication, (3) provide data integrity, (4) provide for future non-repudiation by the parties involved in the transaction, and (5)provide the ability to hide parts of a transaction from viewing by other parties. Confidentiality is typically provided through encryption. Authentication, data integrity, and non-repudiation are enabled through digital signatures and public-key certificates. With the growth of virtual organizations, the next generation of standards is needed to resolve scaling problems of the Internet and handle security, auto-configuration, and real-time services (Hinden, 1996).

Internet security and privacy remain elusive. People won't use the technology to deal with virtual organizations unless they are confident their transactions are secure and private. Further complicating this issue is the fact that such standards are not the responsibility of one specific body. There are competing standards organizations each with members protecting vested interests.

---

[1] We use the term "copyright protection" generically to refer to all forms of protection of intellectual property

Monetary exchange methods: The virtual organization requires secure, universal monetary exchange on a global basis to function effectively. That is, in the long term, it would be difficult for them to operate in a mixed mode where most transactions involve using media over than the Internet for exchange. The virtual organization does not care whether the standard form of exchange on the Internet turns out to be electronic checking, a digital cash standard, or a specific digital money. Forms of monetary exchange on the Internet are discussed in Chapter 13.

Taxation: Virtual organizations are particularly sensitive to taxation issues since they are located in many places simultaneously. From the point of view of these organizations, they seek taxation rules which should be simple, transparent, accommodate different tax systems, and should not distort nor hinder their competitiveness in electronic commerce.

Uniform Commercial Code: To overcome the possibilities of different jurisdictions having different commercial policies, virtual organizations are particularly interested in having the Universal Commercial Code extended so that it covers their activities in a uniform manner. Three groups have been working on developing model laws (The National Conference of Commissioners of Uniform State Law (NCCUSL), the United Nations Commission on International Trade Law (UNCITRAL) and the International Chamber of Commerce). Of these, UNCITRAL was furthest ahead in mid-1998, having completed a model law.

10.2 Social and Psychological Issues

"People issues," that is, the social and psychological impacts of virtual organizations on both the worker and the E-commerce customer, are created by the virtual organization. In this section we discuss how the virtual organization changes the way people relate to one another.

Interaction and homogeneity: The prevalence of virtual organizations, in which people telecommute and use the Internet for their commercial transactions, could lead towards greater isolation and less of a sense of community with physical people. Simply put, there is a significant reduction in the amount of time spent physically interacting with other people. The impacts of such behavior on adults and children raised on a somewhat steady diet of metaphysical activities are not known.

The degree of homogeneity exhibited by participants in a virtual society is a critical issue. Virtual interaction may allow people to more easily seek out others who espouse their own beliefs than could be done in a physical world. Consider the Usenet groups and electronic Bulletin Boards available today in which people can share ideas and knowledge on a particular subject. It is unclear whether these activities create homogeneity among people or whether such interactions more often viewed as a convenience for a particular time. Another deliberation is the degree to which physical contact needs to supplant the electronic element. Gergin (1991) uses the theory of social saturation to support his premise that we are becoming more and more alike. Since modern communication exposes people to more opinions, values, and lifestyles, other people are assumed to be the same as oneself, thereby leading to homogeneity.

Another effect on people is the result of being expected to be available for work 24 hours a day. This infringement on personal lives can be daunting. A few years ago it was a status symbol to carry a pager for it signified that one had critical knowledge or skills or was wired in to important people. Today, some workers view a pager as a leash that allows their superiors to call on them anytime and anyplace. The 7x24 uptime is a particular problem for virtual organizations, visible only on the Internet, and serving multiple time zones.

Time compression and expansion: While virtual communication provides faster transmission of information, it also allows people to do things on their own schedule and in their own time. That is, there a simultaneous compression and expansion of time. CSCW, for example, supports this flexibility in people's schedules (Shneiderman, 1993). The use of CSCW to improve communications is not without its problems for success rates of CSCW technologies are contingent on the people who use them. For example, Zigurs, et al. (1988) studied the impact of Group Decision Support Systems (GDSS) on influence and performance and found minimal improvement over groups of people who did not use technology. We believe it is not the technology that is the problem but the social aspects of using the technology.

10. 3 Process

This section explores issues related to the way work and activities are accomplished. Process ramifications of virtual organizations influence the way people are taught and learn, the way people work, and the way in which goods and services are delivered.

Education: Schein (1993, pp. 85) stated that "Only a few years ago we were saying that the 'management of change' is the biggest challenge organizational leaders face. Today we hear that the problem is no longer the management of change, but the management of 'surprise'...". The challenge in living through a time of surprise is that one can't anticipate what skills or knowledge will be beneficial at any point in time. If the unexpected is to become part of the expected environment, then people must find methods to cope if they are to survive in that environment. An oft-proposed method is through greater emphasis on personal responsibility, individual empowerment and innovation (Herriot and Pemberton, 1995; Hammer and Champy, 1993; Drucker, 1988). An essential aspect of this method is the ability of individuals to learn and apply knowledge to new situations.

Redesigned Work Processes: Virtual organizations involve redesign of work processes. Unfortunately, reengineering projects have not been very successful in transforming organizations. (Cranier, 1996). For the virtual organizations to evolve, work processes will need to exploit technologies to reduce cycle time, remove the barrier of distance from interactions, and improve the quality of information created (Pyle, 1996). There have been some successes of process reengineering using electronic commerce including one at Bell Atlantic Corporation in which an end-to-end corporate procurement process was implemented using electronic commerce technology (Sivori, 1996). But methods guaranteed to succeed are not yet available.

Simplified Distribution: Virtual organizations operate in electronic markets, that is information systems supporting or coordinating one or more phases of the business life cycle. The importance of electronic markets is that they are available 24 hours a day, have the potential to move markets closer to a perfect economic state (supply side equals demand side) thereby reducing transaction costs (Schmid, 1994).

Electronic markets in the virtual world are *marketspaces* as opposed to *marketplaces* in the physical world (Rayport and Sviokla 1995). In the physical model, value is added to the organization through a set of linear activities whereas in the virtual model, the events are nonlinear. The matrixed activities of the virtual model provide the capability to access and distribute products through varied channels.

Electronic markets have the potential to eliminate much of the agency work currently performed in the physical world; e.g., travel and real estate agents. For example, ITN is a travel agency that adapted the virtual organization form. Computer Reservation and Global Distribution Systems in the tourism industry such as the SABRE system developed by American Airlines are EM's that have significantly reduced costs in the tourism industry by opening up direct access to travel agents and consumers. A natural extension of disintermediation is the potential change in governance. In representative government, people elect others in the hope that they will, on balance, serve as their agent. In a virtual government, these agents may no longer be necessary because people could perform governmental functions virtually (e.g., virtual voting on issues, teledemocracy, the virtual town hall).

10.4 Organizational Forms and Norms

The hierarchical structure, with well-defined lines of command, control, and communication, is not optimal for virtual organizations. Rather, virtual organizations work best as empowered, networked structure built through alliances and partnerships.

Networked Organization Structures: A transformation from the traditional, centralized hierarchical organization to a networked, decentralized structure is underway. Globalized organizations must be agile, flexible, and boundaryless (Eichinger and Ulrich, 1995) which is possible under a network organizational model. Tapscott and Caston (1993, p. 33) describe this new structure as being flexible and "based on cooperative, multi-disciplinary teams and businesses networked together across the enterprise".

The importance of structure in any organization is to establish a set of rules for decision making. Since virtual organizations are networked, they work best if they use a "fuzzy" model rather than the traditional crisp or mechanistic structure. (Buchanan and Boddy, 1992). Unfortunately, because of its newness, few organizations have as yet successfully adopted the network structure. Thus, companies going "virtual" have significant challenges to overcome in order to flatten their organization structures from hierarchical to networked and to push decision making to lower levels (Fonda and Rowland, 1995).

Empowerment: One of the critical management issues for virtual organizations is the empowerment of workers enabled through technology to create value for the organization (Clement, 1994). In a virtual organization, the individual worker or team must take responsibility since there is little hierarchy to which to refer. Results of a study conducted by Clement showed that while computing technology contributed to the organizational reformation process, the initiative of the workers to take control over their lives was just as critical. However, an empirical study of workplace empowerment (Thorlakson and Murray, 1996) indicated little support for positive effects related to empowerment.

Alliances and Partnerships: Virtual organizations involving alliances and partnerships are complex. They are created and dissolved more quickly than the traditional model. These new relationships impact corporate culture. A major concern for companies entering into such business arrangements is how to protect trade secrets, marketing strategies, and other proprietary information.

Family Arrangements: Working adults are finding it increasingly challenging to strike a balance between work and family. The number of American families with stay-at-home mothers is below 10% (Schepp, 1990), and one in four workers has assumed responsibility for eldercare (Lefkovich, 1992). The flexible work arrangements offered through teleworking or telecommuting provide employees with a mechanism to handle these problems.

Teleworking is not a panacea. One study indicated that people who telecommute experience marital and family tensions that emanate from merging home and office (Snizek, 1995). This includes the perception by other family members that one is not really working when at home. A lack of recognition as being both a housewife or house-husband and a valuable employee can be discouraging. A movement to a family structure combining work and home has implications which force a worker to assume concurrent or dual roles. Telecommuters who aren't able to assume the model of the traditional workplace (physical and mental separation of work and personal responsibilities) find it difficult to be effective and productive in either role.

11 Conclusions

This chapter presents the forces, dilemmas, issues, and implications of ongoing virtual organizations and their relation to electronic commerce. It identifies and discussed the four main driving forces (global economics, policies and politics, the enlightened population, and technologies) and the issues and complexities they impose. It describes the boundaries of the virtual organization in its relation to electronic commerce. The distributed organization based on telecommuting and the temporary alliance of multiple organizations are described as specific occurrences and manifestations of virtual organizations. We hope this chapter contributes to the understanding of the major issues and complexities involved in the evolution to virtual organizations as a dominant force in electronic commerce and will stimulate research of these organizations in field settings.

Appendix 1 Hoteling and Other New Ways of Working

The way people work in offices is changing. Data indicate that even if workers come to a central location full time, the typical office for people in field sales, project management, audit, and consulting is unoccupied over 50% of the time. Managers look at this occupancy level and conclude that large sums are being spent unnecessarily on office space (rent, phone, furniture, computers). This situation is further exacerbated when workers telecommute.

One of the approaches being used by large firms such as Ernst and Young (accounting and consulting), IBM, and Chiat/Day (advertising) to reduce office costs and to (hopefully) improve productivity is to use non-territorial offices, a concept called hoteling. The name of the concept comes from the way hotels are organized. A person going to a modern hotel is assigned a room that is identical to every other room. If the same person comes again for another stay, they are assigned to a different room that is identical to the one they occupied previously. The guest doesn't care which room they have since they are all the same. Carried over to an office setting, when a person arrives, they are assigned an office space depending on availability. Their use of the space may range from a few hours to a few days. However, at the end of this time the office is reassigned.

The operation at Chiat/Day is typical. Each employee has a locker that contains their personal material but no particular workspace. The person calls in ahead of time to notify their concierge that they will need an office. Their personal belongings are moved into the office assigned. They are handed a mobile telephone which has their personal number and which they take with them as they move around the building. Thus, they can always be reached. Some of the space saved from having fewer offices is used to create additional areas (called "activity zones") for different purposes (e.g., where people can mingle, where teams can meet, where individuals can do quiet work). Group members use their assigned office or whichever activity zone makes the most sense for their current activity.

Typical non-territorial offices accommodate from 3 to 10 employees per workspace. As a result, real estate costs are reduced. Increasingly sophisticated, easy to use telecommunication tools (e-mail, voice mail, fax, cellular phones, and high speed modems) allow employees to work remotely. When not in the non-territorial office, they can maintain communications from home, from client's facilities, and from their cars. They can work virtually anywhere, anytime.

Appendix 2 Telecommuting

In telecommuting, professionals work in their homes, in a telework center, or at a client's office rather than in their own organization's office. Experience has shown that telecommuting increases worker concentration and productivity by providing quiet space and by taking workers out of the interrupt mode that is so prevalent in most offices. Furthermore, experience has shown that telecommuters work best if they are in this mode only part of the time, such as three days a week.

Additional telecommuting benefits include:

- Reducing the number of trips required, particularly during rush hours. This reduction reduces the requirements for increasing urban highway and public transport capabilities.
- Reducing expensive downtown real estate needed.
- Reducing the wages that have to be paid individuals since employers, in effect, pay the employee's commuting costs as part of their wages.
- Reducing employee stress.

Telecommuting is a radical notion in the workplace because it separates the two classic functions of supervision: seeing that the worker is busy and checking the technical content of what the worker is doing. Supervisors have great difficulty making this separation. This problem is mitigated somewhat in a telework center, where a local supervisor can check on the intensity of the work.

Telecommuting tends to be a privilege given to workers who have been with a company for some time and who are trusted. Even then, not all workers are suited for telecommuting. Some people working at home cannot resist the temptations of the refrigerator, alcohol, television, or requests for taking care of family matters. Others feel isolated because they crave the social contact that the office provides. An advantage of telework centers over telecommuting from home is that these centers allow people to get away from home and provide the social contact they need.

Although the supply aspects of telecommuting appear to be a solved problem, the demand side is not. Supervisors tend to worry: "are they working"? Telecommuters wonder if they are being overlooked for promotions and assignments. Some feel that being out of sight, they are out of mind for appropriate evaluation of their contribution and appropriate rewards. Recent work at Claremont Graduate University shows that these phenomena can be explained by agency theory that tells us that work can be viewed as an implied contract relationship between employer and employee. Under such a contract, workers can be evaluated based either on their behavior or the outcome of their activities. For example, for professional work, it is difficult to write contracts that stipulate deliverables exactly. Thus, for telecommuting, the relationship must be evaluated in terms of behavior.

Research results dating back to the 1960's show that telecommuting cannot be full time. Studies done in London and Stockholm showed that it was possible to move entire groups out of the crowded central cities. However, it was also found that for people to work together there needs to be an initial contact for each side to size up the other and establish a relationship. Thereafter, it is possible to work for extended periods (3 to 6 months) before face-to-face contact is needed again to strengthen the social bonds.

References

Becker, F. and F. Steele, *Workplace by Design: Mapping the High Performance Workscape*, Jossey-Bass Publishers, San Francisco, CA, 1995.

Buchanan, D. and D. Boddy, *The Expertise of the Change Agent, Public Performance and Backstage Activity,* Prentice Hall, Englewood Cliffs, NJ, 1992.

Clement, A. "Computing At Work: Empowering Action by Low-level Users," *Communications of the ACM,* 37,1, (1994), 53-63.

Cranier, S., "The Rise of Guru Skepticism," *Management Today*, March, (1996), 48-52.

Drucker, P. F., "The Coming of the New Organization," *Harvard Business Review*, 68, 1, (1988), 3-15.

Eichinger, R. and D. Ulrich, "Are You Future Agile?" *Human Resource Planning,* 18,4, (1995), 30-41.

Eisenhardt, K.M., "Agency Theory: An Assessment and Review", *Academy of Management Review,* 14,1, (1989), 57-74.

Fonda, N. and Rowland, H., "Take Me to Your (Personnel) Leader," *Personnel Management* 1, 25, (1995), 18-20.

Gray, Paul et. al., "The Demand for Telecommuting" *Information Systems Management,* 14, 1, (1997), 1-15.

Gergin, K. J., *The Saturated Self: Dilemmas of Identity in Contemporary Life*, Basic Books, New York, 1991.

Goldman, S., R. Nagel, and K. Price *Agile Competitors and Virtual Organizations: Strategies for Enriching the Customer*, Van Nostrand Reinhold, New York 1995.

Grenier, R. and Metes, G., *Going Virtual, Moving Your Organization into the 21st Century*, Prentice Hall, Englewood Cliffs, NJ, 1995.

D. J. Grimshaw and F.T.S. Kwock, "The Business Benefits of Virtual Organizations" in Igbaria, M. and Tan, M. (eds.) *The Virtual Workplace*, Idea Group Publishing, Hershey, PA, 1998.

Hammer, M. and J. Champy, *Reengineering the Corporation, A Manifesto for Business Revolution*, HarperCollins, New York, NY, 1993.

Herriot, P. and C. Pemberton, *Competitive Advantage through Diversity: Organizational Learning from Difference*, Sage Publications, London, UK, 1995

Hinden, R. M. "IP Next Generation Overview," *Communications of the ACM,* 39,6, (1996), 61-71.

IBM Dictionary of Computing on Disk, McGraw-Hill, New York, NY, 1996.

Lefkovich, J. "Business Responds to Eldercare Needs," *HRMagazine*, June, (1992).

Microsoft Bookshelf, Microsoft Corporation, Redmond, WA, 1995.

Miller, L., " Protecting Cybersurfers, Creators is a Balancing Act," *USA Today,* June 29, (1996).

Nilles, J.M., et. al., *Telecommunications Transportation Tradeoffs: Options for Tomorrow*, John Wiley & Sons, New York, NY, 1975.

Palmer, J. W., "The Use of Information Technology in Virtual Organizations" in Igbaria, M. and Tan, M. (eds.) *The Virtual Workplace*. Idea Group Publishing, Hershey, PA, 1998.

Powell, W.W., "Expanding the Scope of Institutional Analysis" in W.W. Powell and P.J. DiMaggio (eds.) *The New Institutionalism in Organizational Analysis* The University of Chicago Press, Chicago, IL, 1991, 183-203.

Press, L.. "Commercialization of the Internet," *Communications of the ACM*, 37, 11, (1994), 17-21.

Pyle, R., "Commerce and the Internet," *Communications of the ACM*, 39,6, (1996),23.

Rayport, J. F. and J.J. Sviokla, "Exploiting the Virtual Value Chain," *Harvard Business Review*, 75, 6, (1995), 75-85.

Schein, E. H., "How Can Organizations Learn Faster? The Challenge of Entering the Green Room," *Sloan Management Review*, 34, 2, (1993), 85.

Schepp, B., *The Telecommuter's Handbook: How to Work for a Salary Without Ever Leaving the House*, Pharo Books, New York, NY, 1990.

Schmid, B. "Electronic Markets in Tourism," in Proc. of *ENTER 94*, Innsbruck, Austria, 1994.

Shneiderman, B., *Designing the User Interface, Strategies for Effective Human-Computer Interaction*, Addison-Wesley, Reading, MA, 1993.

Sivori, J. R., "Evaluated Receipts and Settlement at Bell Atlantic," *Communications of the ACM*, 39, 6, (1996), 24-28.

Snizek, W. E. , "Virtual Offices: Some Neglected Considerations," *Communications of the ACM*, 38, 9, (1995), 15-17.

Tapscott, D. and A. Caston, *Paradigm Shift, The New Promise of Information Technology*, McGraw-Hill, New York, NY, 1993.

Thorlakson, A. J. H. and R.P. Murray, R. P. "An Empirical Study of Empowerment in the Workplace," *Group and Organizational Management*, 21, 1, (1996) 67-83.

Webster's Ninth New Collegiate Dictionary, Merriam Webster, Springfield, MA, 1990.

Westfall, R., "The Microeconomics of Remote Work" in Igbaria, M. and Tan, M. (eds.) *The Virtual Workplace*, Idea Group Publishing, Hershey, PA, 1998.

Zigurs, I., M.S. Poole, and G.L. DeSanctis, "A Study of Influence in Computer-Mediated Group Decision Making," *MIS Quarterly*, December (1988) 625-644.

CHAPTER 24
Web-enabled Data Warehouse

Ye-Sho Chen[1], Bob Justis[2], and Edward Watson[1]

[1]Department of Information Systems and Decision Sciences, E. J. Ourso College of Business Administration, Louisiana State University, qmchen@unix1.sncc.1su.edu; ewatson@1su.edu

[2]Department of Management, E. J. Ourso College of Business Administration, Louisiana State University, mgjust@unix1.sncc.1su.edu

In this paper we review the basic architecture of a Web-enabled data warehouse. Industrial practices and valuable Web sites developed by leading vendors on the topic are provided. The usage of information usually follows the 80/20 rule, e.g., 80% of usage involves only 20% of resources and 80% of queries are requested by 20% of users. This phenomenon is also reported frequently in Web-enabled data warehouse. To enrich the literature, we propose an 80/20-based methodology to build such a Web-enabled data warehouse.

Keywords: Data Warehouse; Web Technology; Web-enabled Data Warehouse; 80/20 Rule

1 Introduction

In his well-known book on *Building the Data Warehousing*, Inmon (1996) defines a data warehouse as a "subject oriented, integrated, nonvolatile, and time variant collection of data in support of management's decision." The subject-oriented data is one structured around the major interests in the enterprise, e.g., cycle time, cost structure, and quality, and largely independent of the operational applications. Typical sources of data for integration include operational databases, legacy databases, and external sources of data such as demographic databases. Nonvolatility of data means that data warehouse data is loaded and accessed, but update of data rarely occurs. The time variant characteristics of data include long time horizon, sophisticated snapshots of data, and time as a key element in the data structure.

Initially, a data warehouse was built for decision support (Poe et al., 1998). The users tend to be internally trained decision-makers who need the data warehouse to conduct various ad hoc and routine analyses for solving problems. Now due to reasons such as pressures of competition and cost reduction, results justification, and improvements in enabling technologies (SUN, 1997), the user group is expanded to include those closely related to the problems, e.g., less trained internal users and external users such as customers, suppliers, and partners. A Web-enabled data warehouse (WDW) enables the diverse group of users to access and query the data warehouse through a Web browser. For examples, internal users may use company's Intranet to conduct trend analysis and forecasting; customers may use Internet to determine what mix of products to buy to minimize the costs; and suppliers may use Extranet to forecast new supplies needed for the next period of time.

The WDW topic is gaining in popularity recently due to the tremendous advantages a company can benefit from it (SUN, 1997; Miley, 1997), including expanded role of the data warehouse in the organization, e.g., high availability and performance; extended use of the data warehouse cost-effectively, e.g., lower cost of application deployment and management, lower training costs, and unified data support; and extended use of the data warehouse with less complexity, e.g., self-service access. In order to achieve a successful implementation, other issues other than the benefits have to be considered (Craig, 1997), including security, business value, impact assessment, setup and management, and tools and support for global requirements.

A WDW is typically built evolutionarily and is a never-ending journey. In order to do it right at the beginning, a good architecture serving as the vision for building the WDW is needed. In Section 2, we discuss the basic architecture of a WDW. Valuable Web sites on the topic developed by leading vendors are provided. The architecture helps us define various important components in building a WDW. Practices of the WDW in various industries are discussed in Section 3. One particular area which we like to address in this paper is the important roles the 80/20 rule plays in building a WDW. The empirical phenomenon is frequently reported in analyzing the usage patterns of a WDW (Kelly, 1996; Kelly, 1997), e.g., 80% of the queries are requested by 20% of the users. To take advantage of those usage patterns, a WDW design methodology based on the 80/20 rule is introduced in Section 4. The methodology integrates three important frameworks: Barlow's (1995) Frequency Marketing, Ives and Learnmonth's (1984) Customer Service Life Cycle (CSLC), and Alter's (1996) Work-centered Analysis (WCA). The methodology may provide a solution to the problem encountered by most of WDW developers (Stedman, 1998), i.e., "more than half of data warehousing projects either fall behind schedule or get put on hold." Finally, issues for future research on the WDW are discussed in Section 5.

2 The Architecture of Web-enabled Data Warehouse

In this section, we review the architecture of data warehouse and how to put the architecture on the Web. Valuable Web sites on the WDW architectures developed by leading vendors are also provided.

2.1 The Architecture of Data Warehouse

According to Inmon (1996), there are four generic levels in the architected environment of data warehouse (Figure 1): the operational level, holding data serving, for example, online transaction processing activities; the data warehouse level, holding mostly primitive and not updated data; the departmental (or data mart) level, containing almost exclusively derived data; and the individual level, performing mostly online analytical and heuristic analyses. To move from the operational level to the data warehouse level, data integration is needed. It is a very time consuming process that involves the activities such as data cleansing, extraction, and merging. To move from the data warehouse level to the data mart level, data transformation is needed which involves the activities such as data aggregation and propagation. Data mining is used to analyze patterns of the data residing in the data marts, which will enable the users to make better decisions. As we can see, building a data warehouse using the architected (or top-down) approach is quite time consuming. Another alternative (the bottom-up approach) shortens significantly the time of construction by moving from the operational level to the data mart level (Kimball, 1996; Hackney, 1997).

Based on the four architected levels of environment, different vendors have their own detailed strategies of implementation. For example, consider SAP's Business Information Warehouse (BIW) concept (Figure 2a) and the SAP R/3 BIW architecture (Figure 2b) developed based on the concept. SAP was founded in 1972 and has grown to become the world's fourth largest software company in the world (ASAP Consultancy, 1996). SAP offers a unique system that supports nearly all areas of business on a global scale. The business information warehouse is a concept that is able to be realized in practice because all the integrated SAP system components can be called upon to supply data that is structured in accord with the enterprise data model that has been established for a particular company. The BIW collects data from both SAP applications and external systems and tailors it to meet the specific requirements of production and controlling staff and of company management. This results in new opportunities for decentralized "self-control" at the department level. SAP has implemented this logical enhancement to core controlling functions in its Logistics Information System (LIS) for sales, purchasing, production, plant maintenance, and quality management; in the Financial Information System (FIS) for customers and vendors; and in the Human Resources Information System (HIS).

The BIW shown in Figure 2b is a data warehouse solution tailored to work with R/3. The top layer of the figure depicts the Business Explorer, comprising BIW's client components for the end-user. The middle layer represents the BIW Server and the bottom layer represents the OLTP systems from which source data is extracted. The BIW performs three primary functions: data warehouse management and administration, data storage and representation, and analysis and reporting. Within any data warehouse, data must first be extracted from diverse sources and then mapped to the specific data structures required for analysis and reporting. Most data warehouse solutions are designed to extract and map data at the level of individual database fields without recognizing the business relevance of that data. Data and its business relevance therefore have to be modeled and coded individually for each user organization as do extractionand mapping. If changes are made to the underlying business processes, this can have an impact on the entire flow of data and may result in significant maintenance overhead. The Production Data Extractor is a set of programs that extracts data from R/3 OLTP applications. The staging engine is employed to implement data mapping and transformation as a metadata-driven process that is automated throughout. An administrator's workbench tool set with a user-friendly GUI is available that allows the BIW administrator to perform all data warehouse construction and maintenance tasks within a single, unified environment.

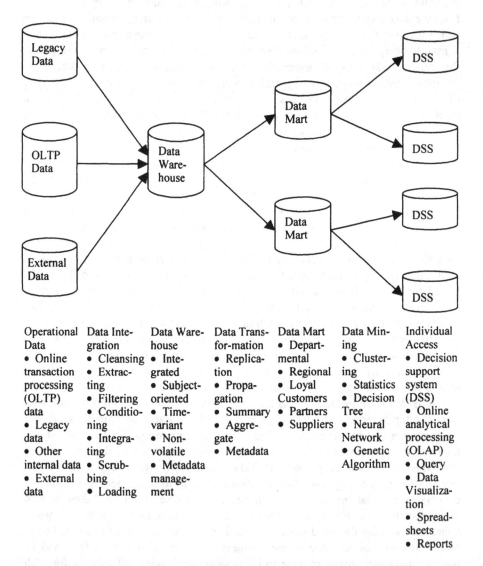

Operational Data	Data Integration	Data Warehouse	Data Transformation	Data Mart	Data Mining	Individual Access
• Online transaction processing (OLTP) data • Legacy data • Other internal data • External data	• Cleansing • Extracting • Filtering • Conditioning • Integrating • Scrubbing • Loading	• Integrated • Subject-oriented • Time-variant • Non-volatile • Metadata management	• Replication • Propagation • Summary • Aggregate • Metadata	• Departmental • Regional • Loyal Customers • Partners • Suppliers	• Clustering • Statistics • Decision Tree • Neural Network • Genetic Algorithm	• Decision support system (DSS) • Online analytical processing (OLAP) • Query • Data Visualization • Spreadsheets • Reports

Fig. 1. The four levels of architected environment of data warehousing (Inmon 1996)

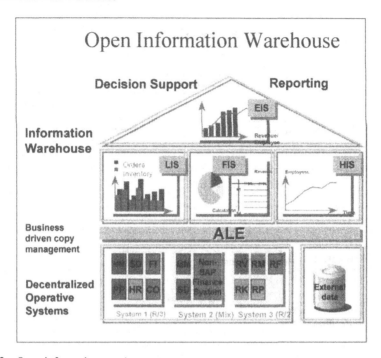

Fig. 2a. Open information warehouse concept

BIW allows the end user to look at data from many different perspectives, to transparently combine data from various sources, and to drill-down from one level of detail to another. To make this possible, BIW stores data in multidimensional form. InfoCubes are the central containers of data used in reports and analysis. Hierarchical relationships for characteristics play an important role in analytical and reporting activities. For example, cost centers are usually hierarchically structured; products are generally grouped into product family hierarchies. BIW allows a hierarchy to be modeled over the value domain of one or more characteristics. These hierarchies are independent of InfoCubes and may be used as the basis for aggregation and drill-down criteria within reports. Metadata (information about information) is central to the data warehouse concept. It is used to describe the source, history, and many other aspects of the data. Metadata allow information stored in BIW to be used effectively for reporting and analysis, and ensure that all users have one version of the truth. The user access information held in InfoCubes through reports. For each report, there are numerous different views that display information according to slice and dice operations performed by the user. In other words, a report is not a static snapshot but a gateway through which the user can explore the underlying data.

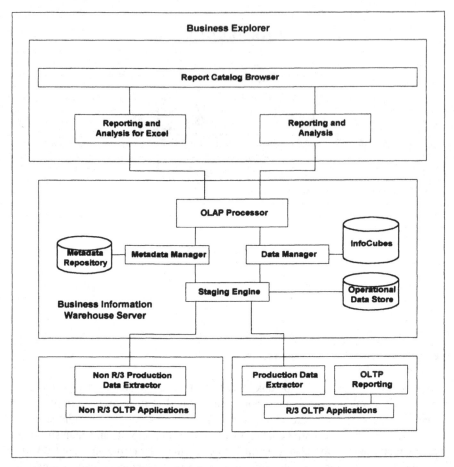

Fig. 2b. Components of the SAP R/3 business information warehouse

2.2 Putting the Data Warehouse on the Web

In order to put the data warehouse on the Web, several new layers of Web technology, such as Web browser, Web server, and Web gateway (SUN, 1997), have to be added in between the users and the original data warehouse architecture. For example, Figure 3 shows Oracle's WDW architecture with five tiers (Burleson, 1997): presentation tier, comprising a thin-client Web browser; publication tier, comprising the standard HTTP listener for HTML documents; application tier, comprising Web server and the applications it enables; data tier, comprising the data warehouse or data marts which may be derived from the data warehouse or from the data sources directly; and source tier, comprising any number of data sources with the data extracted, transformed, and transported to the data warehouse or data marts.

Figure 3 also shows two paths to access the WDW. The user of path A sends a request to the Web server through a Web browser. The Web server kicks off the Web
application server, which passes the request to the express server via the express
Web agent. The express server executes the procedure that was named in the URL.
If the data needed is already cached on the express server, it gets the data from there;
if not, it gets it from the data warehouse residing in the universal server. Express
server then processes the request and generates an HTML document, which is then
sent back in the reverse route to the end user. Path B is identical to A until the activation of the Web application server, at which point the user's request is translated
by the NCA cartridge into PL/SQL statements. If the data is already in the data mart,
the procedure obtains it from there; otherwise, the procedure executes against the
data warehouse and caches the result in the data mart. The data is then sent back in
the reverse route to the end user.

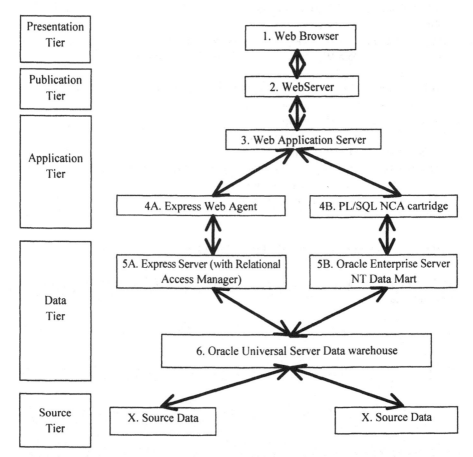

Fig. 3. Oracle's five-tiered architecture of Web-based data warehousing (Miley 1997)

2. 3 Valuable Web Sites

Shown below are some valuable Web sites for further reading on the WDW architecture:

- HP's Web-enabled OpenWarehouse,
  http://www.hp.com/computing/framed/enterprise
- IBM's Visual Warehouse, http://www.software.ibm.com/data/vw
- Informatica's PowerMart, http://www.informatica.com
- Information Builders' Incremental Warehouse,
  http://www.ibi.com/products/webfocus/overview.html
- Informix's Universal Warehouse,
  http://www.informix.com/infmx-cgi/Webdriver
- Microsoft's Active Data Warehousing,
  http://www.microsoft.com/data/oledb/olap
- MicroStrategy's DSS Web,
  http://www.strategy.com/Products/Web/index.htm
- NCR's Scalable Data Warehousing, http://www3.ncr.com/sdw
- Platinum's DecisionBase,
  http://www.platinum.com/products/dataw/dbase_po.htm
- Red Brick's Warehouse, http://www.redbrick.com
- SAS' Web-enabled SAS System,
  http://www.sas.com/software/web_enablement
- Sun's Java-enabled architecture,
  http://www.sun.com/products-n-solutions/ solutions/nba/warehouse
- Sybase's Adaptive Component Architecture,
  http://www.sybase.com/ datawarehousing

3 Practices of Web-enabled Data Warehouse

The following table summaries success stories of the WDW implementation in various industries.

Table 1. Success stories of the WDW implementation

Industry	Case/Reference	Brief Description
Banking	Republic Security Bank (Simpson, 1998)	Extracting up-to-date, detailed data analyses from the banking industry's multiple database sources
Entertainment	Pacific Bell Videl Services (Crawford, 1998)	Improving customer acquisition and retension
Healthcare	National Institutes of Health (Mahaffey, 1998)	Providing a better way for users to access and analyze enterprise information
Insurance	State of Washington (Coleman, 1997)	Enabling users to have more control over their data and how it gets used
Manufacturing	Alarming Profits at Harris Semiconductor (Barquin and Edelstein, 1997)	Providing manufacturing information along with an alarm system that quickly identifies desirable and undesirable changes in the factory that may impact profits
Military	Data Warehousing at the Naval Surface Center, Dahlgren Division (NSWCDD) (Barquin and Edelstein, 1997)	Empowering the end user so they can satisfy their own dynamic information requirements
Personal Expressions	Hallmark Cards (Marshall, 1997)	Leveraging the overwhelming preference for the Hallmark name through mass merchandise outlets
Retailers	Kimball (1996)	Tracking value propositions in the demand/supply chain management
Telecommunications	Mattison (1997)	Showing how dozens of companies using advanced data warehousing and data mining tools to solve the most immediate telecommunications problems
Transportation	Brussels Airport Terminal Company (Dejalle, 1998)	Integrating terminal operations to meet increased demand
Utilities	CLECO (Clark, 1997)	Helping marketing determine what services the utility customers really wanted, while enabling management to better control costs and expenditures

4 Building the Web-enabled Data Warehouse: The Frequency-based Approach

In this section, we show the important roles the 80/20 rule plays in building a WDW. Five principles are derived from the 80/20 rule. In order to take the advantage of the principles, we propose a frequency-based methodology for building the architecture of the WDW. Three predecessors of the methodology are reviewed, including Frequency Marketing, CSLC, and WCA. The procedures for using the methodology are then discussed. The relationship between the methodology procedures and the five principles derived from the 80/20 rule is also discussed.

4.1 The Important Roles of the 80/20 Rule

Consider Figure 3 again. Path A uses OLAP for multidimensional ad hoc querying. The path works for executives who need a sophisticated tool to do multidimensional analysis on an ad hoc basis. Path B, on the other hand, is set up to work against a data mart to increase performance of standardized queries and reports to be used by several user groups. The creation of the two paths suggests two types of classification: users and requests. Path A is designed for a group of significant users, e.g., busy executives, who tend to conduct ad hoc queries, a kind of requests, which is hard to predict and standardize. Path B, on the other hand, is designed for different groups of users whose requests tend to be predictable and can be standardized for reducing the cycle time of requests. In terms of the two-path usage framework, the 80/20 rule says: 20% of the users (queries), make up of 80% of the resources for responding user's requests. These two types of classification coupling with the 80/20 rule are very important for building a successful WDW since their requirements drive the needs of appropriate data sources, the design of the data warehouse, data marts, and ultimately, the decision support applications.

Using the 80/20 rule as the keywords to search on the literature and the Web, we summarize the important roles of the 80/20 rule in building a WDW in the following table. The first design factor considers the very important question confronted by most of teams interested in building a WDW, e.g., where to start? Principle 1, implied from the 80/20 rule, says that one shall start with a simple project with high business impacts. Enhance the first iteration WDW continuously when there is a proven success. Once a well-crafted project has been chosen, the next step is to gather the corresponding data, cleanse them to maintain the high data quality. Even though insuring high data quality is a very important practice in designing a WDW (Brackett, 1996; Tayi and Ballou, 1998), Principle 2 says that there is no way to gather and cleanse the required data in a short time frame. Instead, one shall focus first on the small set of vital data, do it well and move on to the rest of required data. Once the data warehouse is built, the next step is to do data aggregation for the data marts. The 80/20 rule says that 20% of the aggregates will be used and reused continuously, resulting in 80% of performance improving. Thus, Principle 3 says that one needs to use a good hybrid OLAP tool which can maximize the utility of the 80/20 rule. Once the departmental level is dealt with, one needs to consider the specific user needs. Principle 4, based on the 80/20 rule, suggests that a simple tool kit be used to deliver the majority of user needs. Dedicated and expensive tools can be induced later for the rest of high power and sophisticated users. Finally, for maintaining the built WDW, Principle 5 stresses the importance of self-sufficiency by well-defined procedures and good user training. By doing so, it will reduce the headache of managing the WDW.

Table 2. Important roles of the 80/20 rule in building a WDW

Design Factor	The 80/20 Rule	Reference	Implication
Where to start the WDW project?	80% of the system value is produced in 20% of the total time.	Daly (1998); Gilman (1998); Kelly (1996, 1997); Poe, Klauer, and Brobst (1998)	Principle 1: Start with a *small* project that has the most significant impacts on the business and continue building on the *success* evolutionarily.
Data c*leansing*, when moving from the operational level to the data warehouse level.	20% of the data may meet 80% of needs.	Atre (1998)	**Principle 2:** Start with the *small* set of vital data with high quality and continue cleansing and incorporating the rest of data evolutionarily.
Data *aggregation*, when moving from the data warehouse level to the departmental level.	80% of the performance improvement will be achieved by only 20% of the candidate aggregates.	Stamen (1998); Sahin (1998); Kelly (1998)	Principle 3: Use a *hybrid* OLAP technology which utilizes Relational OLAP tools 80% of time and Multidimensional OLAP tools 20% of time to make queries and reports.
Complexity of *user needs*, when moving from the departmental level to the individual level.	80% of users require only simple reports that take only 20% of resources to create.	Eckerson (1998); Flohr (1997)	Principle 4: Start with *simple* tools that can satisfy most of the user's needs and continue using dedicated tools for the rest, only when there are proven *success*.
Maintaining user needs, after the WDW project is finished.	80% of users' report needs can be accommodated by 20% of the current reports.	Glassey (1998)	Principle 5: Start with lots of *simple* steps for users to produce their needs. Train them with those steps and encourage *self-sufficiency*.

4.2 Predecessors of the Frequency-based Methodology

Frequency marketing, deriving from the frequent-flyer programs beginning in 1981, is an idea of rewarding a business' most frequent (and profitable) customers based on the 80/20 rule. Applying the concept to WDW, we may classify customers (users) and services (requests) into "frequency" classes, respectively. The frequency is defined in a general sense. It could be the number of occurrences or the required attention level. For examples, the frequency classes for the customers may be frequent (or loyal), infrequent, and potential; and for the services may be basic, intermediate, and advanced. The combination of the two classifications generates nine versions of business processes for WDW.

Inside each business process, the CSLC may be used to model the services to the corresponding class of customers. In the content of the WDW design, the framework recognizes four stages through which a customer will pass for the service:

- Before requesting any service, the customer will have *requirements* specific to the service, which is available, but the customer is unaware of it or doesn't know where to find it.
- Having decided to use the service, another set of questions related to *acquisition* arises. In this stage, the questions of the customer will be more focused relating to how easy it is to use the server and the time needed to use it.
- Now that the customer has signed up with the service, questions related to the *ownership* arise as to the use, support, and maintenance.
- The end of the cycle, or *retirement*, brings about additional opportunities for the use of the WDW. Customers will again be looking for new services, thus they may become customers again. Thus, the life cycle may loop back to the requirement stage when there is a need for upgrading the service or replacing it with a new one.

To build the WDW supporting the CSLC in each business process, Alter's WCA framework may be used which consists of six interrelated elements: business process, "a related group of steps or activities that use people and information to create value for internal or external customers"; products or services, the "output of the business process"; customers, "those who use the outputs of the business process"; participants, the "people who enter, process, or use the information within the system"; information, such as "data input, related data, and output"; and technology, the "tools that either perform, work directly, or are used to perform work."

4.3 The Frequency-based Methodology

Figure 4 shows the blueprint of the frequency-based methodology which integrates three important frameworks: Barlow's Frequency Marketing, Ives and Learnmonth's CSLC, and Alter's WCA. The procedures for using the methodology are discussed below.

4.3.1 Customized Products/Services

The first step of the methodology follows the suggestion by Billington (1997) on how to customize for the real world: identify the loyal customers, figure out what they need by way of customization, and align service processes with those needs. Our procedure starts with classifying the *customers* into the "frequency" classes, e.g., frequent, infrequent, and potential, and then the *products/services* into the "frequency" classes based on, e.g., the number of occurrences or the complexity level. An example of the products/services classes may be simple, moderate, and complicated. The complicated cases tend to occupy 80% of time for the services, although they are only 20% of the requests from the customers. After the two classifications, a 3x3 frequency matrix, such as the one shown in the upper-left corner of Figure 4, is defined.

Now, *prioritize* the nine different versions of business processes in the frequency matrix. Each of the nine processes has its own WCA with its business process being described by the four stages of the CSLC. For example, the WCA of business process 1 is provided to serve frequent customers on simple cases. This business process will include the stages of requirements, acquisition, ownership, and retirement in the CSLC. The process numbers 1 to 9 may serve as a prioritized way for building the WDW. Consider, for example, the process of serving frequent customers on simple cases. By definition, the process has the most many customers to serve and the most many cases to deal with, it is obvious that this process shall be the first for introducing the WDW. On the other hand, the demand for complicated cases requested by potential customers is quite uncertain, thus the corresponding business process shall be the last to be incorporated into the WDW implementation. Building the WDW project based on the prioritized processes follows Principle 1shown above, i.e., starting with a *small* project that has the most significant impacts on the business and continue building on the *success* evolutionarily.

4.3.2 Intensifying the Focus in Each Business Process

The next step is to identify the focus of the four stages of the CSLC in each business process and *intensify* the services related to the focus. Although each of the nine business processes has the four stages cycle to care about, the intensity of care needed for the four stages is quite different among the nine processes. For example, for the process serving frequent customers on simple cases, the focus of customer service shall be more on the later parts of the life cycle, i.e., ownership and retirement. This is because those customers know who you are (frequent customers) and what they want (simple cases). The company shall devote more resources on the after service activities so that the customers may keep on coming back. On the other hand, for the potential customers requiring complicated services, the focus shall be on the early parts of the life cycle, i.e., requirements and acquisition. Both are designed to show who you are and what specific services you can provide to the potential customers. Building the WDW project supporting the intensified focus follows Principle 2 discussed above. This is because data needed for the focussed activities are relatively small comparing with data needed for the whole business process. Thus, extra effort may be spent on this small portion of data to maintain high data quality.

	FREQUENT CUSTOMERS	INFREQUENT CUSTOMERS	POTENTIAL CUSTOMERS
SIMPLE CASES	WCA 1	WCA 4	WCA 7
MODERATE CASES	WCA 2	WCA 5	WCA 8
COMPLICATED CASES	WCA 3	WCA 6	WCA 9

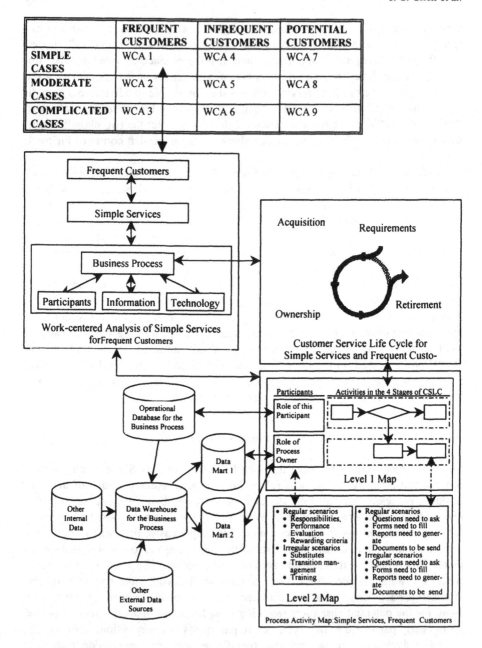

Fig. 4. The frequency-based work-centered analysis framework

4.3.3 Identifying Participants and the Information They Need

The third step is to describe, for each WCA, *participants* who will be involved in the work center, what roles they play, and the *information* they need to do the work. To that end, a detailed process mapping has to be carried out and documented. As is shown in Figure 4, the process activity map consists of two levels. The first level documents the role each of the participants needs to play, the activities need to be done, and the points where the coordination between the participants are needed. A very important thing needed to be documented in the second level of the map is the scenario management, which includes what shall be done in the regular and irregular scenarios. The regular scenarios for each role may include responsibilities, performance evaluation, and rewarding criteria. The irregular scenarios may include substitutes available, transition management, and training. For each activity and coordination performed by the participants, the second level documents in every scenario the detailed things such as questions asked, forms needed to fill, reports need to generate, and documents need to send. Once the process activity map is documented, an operational database for the business process can be built to support the participants the online transaction processing activities on the daily basis. An example is shown in the left lower corner of Figure 4.

To track, analyze, and improve the performance of the business process, a WDW is needed for participants to access for various process related decision-makings. For example, the process owner, in addition to the daily operations, also needs to track periodically the performance of the business process, such as quality, service, cost, and cycle time. That is, decision support applications, such as ad hoc queries and standard monthly comparative reports, are needed for the process owner. To satisfy the demands of the process owner, several data marts may be derived from the data warehouse to increase the performance of the queries. Based on the 80/20 rule associated with Principle 3 above, i.e., 80% of the performance improvement will be achieved by only 20% of the candidate aggregates, data marts may be built for those frequently asked queries. In addition, the 80/20 rule for Principle 4 indicates that 80% of users require only simple reports that take only 20% of resources to create. Thus, those simple reports need to be identified and implemented first to reduce the time of building the WDW.

The process activity map is a very useful tool for modeling the information needs of the participants. Based on the online transaction-based queries, forms, and reports documented in the process activity map, the entity-relationship diagram for the operational database may be constructed (Kroenke, 1998) and the database can be built accordingly. Furthermore, based on the entity-relationship diagram, the decision support requirements documented in the process activity map, e.g., online analytical queries and reports, and other internal or external data sources, one may construct the blueprint of the WDW (Silverston et al., 1997) which includes aggregation levels, facts, dimensions, attributes and their hierarchies, the star schema, and the corresponding relational tables.

4.3.4 Selecting the Tools and Building the System

The fourth step of the methodology is to configure the information technology tools needed to support the work. There are many *technical* factors to consider when choosing the right tools (White, 1998), e.g., data integration and transformation, metadata management, speed and reliability. When using the frequency-based methodology, the tools shall enable the prompt classification of a customer request in terms of customer type and product/service type and trigger the appropriate business process to respond to the request. Principles 3 and 4 above also provide additional guidelines for evaluating the products. Since building the WDW project is a very expensive investment, the project team will be confronted with *economical* questions raised from many non-technical people, e.g., how to relate this investment to the business bottom line?

Figure 5 shows a pictorial approach to evaluating various IT investment alternatives (Chen et al., 1997). The approach is based on Oracle's CB-90 methodology for quantifying the IT investment (LaPlante, 1994; Semich, 1994). Associated each alternative are three numbers: *value* (0 to 5), *cost* (the radius of the circle), and *risk* (0 to 5). The value, cost, and risk, are the aggregation of various tangible and intangible value, cost, and risk propositions, respectively. For example, one of the value propositions is the impact of the alternative on the company's top ten agenda and one of the risk propositions is the possibility of losing or not being to hire good people. By looking at the picture, one can immediately come to the conclusion that Alternative 1 is the best choice, since it has the highest value, the lowest risk, and the lowest cost. Besides being able to compare alternatives of IT investment easily, the approach may be enhanced (Chen and Chong, 1998) to address the economics questions after the implementation of the chosen alternative, e.g., where is the circle now? and where will be the circle next year?

4.3.5 Managing the System

The data warehouse shall be built evolutionarily based on the priority of the business processes. For example, Figure 4 shows that the data warehouse is built for the WCA 1 whose business process has the highest priority. Figure 6 shows how to build the data warehouse evolutionarily for the business processes with priorities 1 and 2. Managing the WDW after it is built is not an easy task (Inmon et al., 1997). Three major things shall be considered, i.e., how to make the system and the business process it is supporting more efficient, effective, and innovative. An example of *efficiency* is to Principle 5 above to make the users more self-sufficient by giving simple-steps just-in-time training. An example of *effectiveness* is to use data mining techniques (Cabena et al., 1998, Adriaans et al., 1996) to build models of the typical buying patterns of loyal and potential customers. Appropriate marketing campaigns will follow when the models are well understood. The WDW technology provides tremendous amount of opportunities for innovative business process reengineering (BPR) (Kelly, 1996; Kelly, 1997). On the one hand, the customer service tracking in the WDW may suggest BPR is needed. On the other hand, the BPR effort may lead to better operational databases which again leads to better data warehouse and data marts for better customer service tracking.

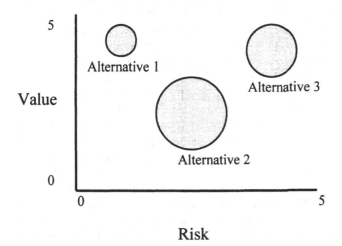

Fig. 5. A pictorial approach to evaluating IT investment (Chen et al. 1997).

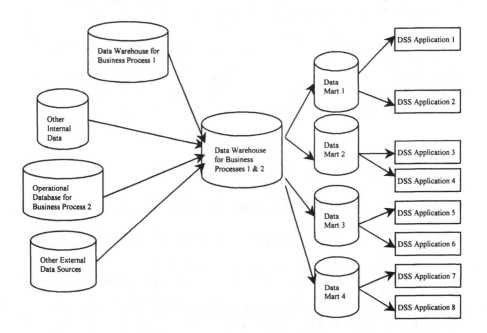

Fig. 6. How to build a data warehouse evolutionarily

5 Conclusion

In this paper we firstly reviewed Inmon's (1996) four levels of architected environment of data warehouse. As an example of implementation of the architected environment, SAP's Business Information Warehouse (BIW) solution is discussed. The BIW is a state-of-the art, end-to-end data warehouse solution that gives knowledge workers rapid access to data from SAP systems, from other enterprise applications, and from external sources (e.g., content provides such as Nielsen). BIW is SAP's new generation of data warehouse technology, raising the capabilities first shown in the Open Information Warehouse to a completely new level. In order to enable users access the data warehouse easily and reduce the cost of managing the system, putting the data warehouse on the Web has been popular. BIW is the ultimate web-based information warehouse that seamlessly integrates data warehouse, and executive information systems with business operations and a common business framework and data structure.

Oracle's 5-tiered architecture for building a WDW was used to explain in more details the connection between the Web technology and data warehouse. Strategies of WDW implementation by leading vendors were also included. Real life practices of the WDW in several industries were also briefly described. In addition to helping us understand the Web connection, Oracle's 5-tiered architecture also enable us to see the importance of the 80/20 rule in building a WDW. An 80/20-based methodology was therefore proposed for building a WDW. In addition, a pictorial approach to evaluating the WDW investment was also discussed.

Besides the Web connection, data warehouse is moving into its second generation (Kelly, 1997). The new generation promises more powerful tools (Inmon, 1998) for sophisticated business intelligence applications (White, 1998), such as market management, risk management, and fraud management (Cabena, et al., 1998). Data mining and its related tools play a very significant role in delivering a successful second-generation data warehouse (Inmon 1998).

References

Adriaans, P. and Zantinge, D., *Data Mining*, Addison-Wesley, England, 1996.

Alter, S. *Information Systems: A Management Perspective*, Benjamin/Cummings, Menlo Park, CA, 1996.

ASAP Consultancy and Jonathan Blain, *Using SAP R/3: Special Edition*, Que Corporation, 1996.

Atre, S., "Rules for Data Cleansing," *ComputerWorld*, March 9, (1998), 72-73.

Barlow, R.G., "Frequency Marketing", *Marketing Encyclopedia*, J. Heilbrunn, Editor, American Marketing Association, 1995.

Barquin, R. and Edelstein, H., *Planning and Designing the Data Warehouse*, The Data Warehousing Institute Series from Prentice Hall, 1997.

Billington, J., "How to Customize for the Real World," *Harvard Management Update*, (1997), URL = http://www.hbsp.harvard.edu/frames/groups/newsletters/feature.html.

Brackett, M.H., *The Data Warehouse Challenge: Taming Data Chaos*, John Wiley & Sons, New York, 1996.

Burleson, D., *Oracle Data Warehousing*, The Coriolis Group, Inc., Scottsdale, Arizona, 1997.

Cabena, P. Hadjinian, P. Stadler, R., Verhees, J., and Zanasi, A., *Discovering Data Mining: From Concept to Implementation*, IBM International Technical Support Organization, Prentice Hall, New Jersey, 1998.

Chen, Y.S., Chong, P.P., and Walsh, K., "A Self-Adaptive Paretoan Approach to Information Technology Investment," *Informs San Diego*, Spring, May 4-7, 1997.

Chen, Y.S. and P. Chong, "Information Productivity Modeling: The Simon-Yule Approach", *Encyclopedia of Library and Information Science*, 61, 24, (1998), 170-200.

Clark, R. "CLECO and Brio Technology," *DM Review*, 7, 7, (1998), 110-111.

Coleman, M. "State of Washington and Red brick," *DM Review*, 7, 7, (1997), 122-123.

Craig, R., "Data Warehousing and the Web," *Oracle Magazine*, XI, 5 (1997), 11-12.

Crawford, G. "Pacific Bell Video Services & Information Advantage," *DM Review*, 8, 8, (1998), 58-59.

Daly, D., "Evolution Not Revolution: A Client/Server Migration Strategy," *Data Warehouse Resources*, Data-Warehouse.Com, March (1998),
URL = http://www.data-warehouse.com/resource/articles/daly4.htm.

Dejalle, A., "Brussels Airport Terminal Company and Brio Technology," *DM Review*, 8, 8, (1998), 64-65.

Eckerson, W.W., "One-stop Shopping for Business Information," Patricia Seybold Group, August (1997), URL = http://www.reportmart.com/WHITEPAP/patricia.htm.

Flohr, U., "OLAP by Web," *Byte*, September (1997),
URL = http://www.byte.com/art/9709/sec6/art6.htm.

Gilman, M, "A Consultant's Methodology," *Data Warehouse Resources*, Data-Warehouse.Com, March (1998),
URL = http://www.data-warehouse.com/resource/articles/gilma8.htm.

Glassey, K.L., "Implementing a User-centric Data Warehouse," Brio Technology, March (1998), URL = http://www.brio.com/library/imp.html.

Hackney, D., *Understanding and Implementing Successful Data Marts*, Addison Wesley Developers Press, MA, 1997.

Inmon, W.H., *Building the Data Warehouse*, 2e, John Wiley & Sons, New York, 1996.

Inmon, W.H., Welch, J.D.., and Glassey, K.L., *Managing the Data Warehouse*, John Wiley & Sons, New York, 1997.

Inmon, W.H., *Second Generation Data Warehousing/Practical Data Mining*, Kiva Productions, Inc. (1998), URL = http://www.kivaproductions.com/topics.html.

Ives, B. and G.P. Learnmonth, "The Information System as a Competitive Weapon," *Communications of the ACM*, 27, 12 (1984), 1193-1201.

Kelly, S., *Data Warehousing: The Route to Mass Customization*, John Wiley & Sons, New York, 1996.

Kelly, S., *Data Warehousing in Action*, John Wiley & Sons, New York, 1997.

Kelly, T.J., "Dimensional data Modeling," *Sybase Consulting*, March (1998), URL = http://www.sybase.com/services/dwpractice/dimensional.html.

Kimball, R., *The Data Warehouse Toolkit*, John Wiley & Sons, New York, 1996.

Kroenke, D.M., *Database Processing*, 6e, Prentice Hall, New Jersey, 1998.

LaPlante, J., "No Doubt About IT: The CB-90 Methodology," *ComputerWorld*, August 15, 1994, 86.

Mahaffey, J.A., "NIH and Prism Solutions, Inc." *DM Review*, 8, 5, (1998), 74-75.

Marshall, T., "hallmark Cards and MicroStrategy," *DM Review*, 7, 7, (1997), 114-115.

Mattison, R., *Data Warehousing and Data Mining for Telecommunications*, Artech House, Inc., Norwood, MA, 1997.

Miley, M., "Building a Web Warehouse," *Oracle Magazine*, XI, 5 (1997), 51-75.

Poe, V., Klauer, P., and Brobst, S., *Building a Data Warehouse for Decision Support*, 2e, Prentice Hall, New Jersey, 1998.

Sahin, K., "Multidimensional Database Technology and Data Warehousing," *Acumate ES*, March (1998), URL = http://www.kenan.com/acumate/byln_mdw.htm.

Semich, J.W., "Here's How to Quantify IT Investment Benefits," *Datamation*, January 1994, 45-48.

Silverston, L, Inmon, W.H., and Graziano, K., *The Data Model Resource Book*, John Wiley & Sons, New York, 1997.

Simpson, L. "Republic Security Bank and M&I data Services," *DM Review*, 8, 8, (1998), 62-63.

Stamen, J., "OLAP, MOLAP, Overlap," *Byte*, August (1996),
URL = http://www.byte.com/art/intervu/oracle.htm.

Stedman, C., "Warehousing Projects Hard to Finish," *ComputerWorld*, March 23 (1998), 29.

SUN, "Web-Enabled Data Warehousing with Sun and Java," SUN White Paper, August (1997), URL = http://www.sun.com/products-n-solutions/solutions/nba/warehouse/ documents/WebWP.html.

Tayi, G.K. and Ballou, D.P., "Examining Data Quality," *Communications of the ACM*, 41, 2 (1998), 54-57.

White, C., "How to Choose the Right Data Warehousing Tools," Database Associates International White Paper, *ComputerWorld*, March 2, 1998.

White, C., "The IBM Business Intelligence Software Solution," Prepared for IBM Corporation, *Database Associates International*, January (1998),
URL = http://www.software.ibm.com/data/pubs/papers/bisolution/index.html.

CHAPTER 25
Intranets: An Internet Inside the Organization

Dave King

Comshare Inc., Ann Arbor, MI 48108, USA, dking@comshare.com

Since their inception in the mid 1990's, adoption of intranets by large and medium sized organizations has increased at much the same rate as the Web at large. Just as public Web sites have evolved over time, so have intranets. No longer are they simply used as a publishing medium; now they encompass a variety of applications designed to support decision making, complex business processes, and communication and collaboration among teams. This chapter examines some of the technical underpinnings of intranets, considers the differences among intranets, extranets and the Internet, and explores those situations and applications where intranets are preferred to traditional client/server offerings.

Keywords: Collaborative Application; Extranet; Dynamic Database Access; Firewall; Intranet; Internet; TCP/IP; Return on Investment; Virtual Private Network (VAN); Workflow

1 Introduction

In January of 1995 Tom Davenport, a university professor and columnist for InformationWeek, proposed the idea of utilizing Web technologies to support internal business processes. As he put it,

> *Though the current version of the Web is interesting enough, the prospect of Web-based architectures within companies is perhaps even more exciting. The Web offers a model for how businesses will soon display and access internal information. A company could have, as it were, its own internal Web-only some of which would be accessible to outsiders. Just as we now navigate through Web servers worldwide, we could then navigate through a range of information available in large organizations.*
(Davenport, 1995)

A short time later, in the April, 1995 issue of *Digital News and Review*, Stephen Lawton used the term "intranet" to describe the use of Web and other Internet technologies for internal organizational purposes (Hinricks, 1997).

Today, there is ample evidence that a substantial percentage of large organizations and enterprises, especially in the U.S., have implemented or are in the process of implementing intranets (Intranet Journal, 1997). A survey by Hambrecht and Quest indicated that 85% of the Fortune 200 firms had developed or were developing intranets. Forrester Research put the figure at 67% for firms in the Fortune 1000. IDC's survey of U.S. and European firms found that 77% of U.S. and 75% of European organizations were already using or expected to be using intranets within the year. More recently, a survey conducted by Information Week (Violino, 1998) revealed that 90% of their InformationWeek 500 (firms with the largest information technology expenditures) had already implemented intranets. Regardless of the exact figures, it is obvious that intranets have experienced the same type of exponential growth as the larger Internet and Web and show no signs of letting up.

In this chapter we explore the intranet phenomenon. In particular we will address the following questions:

1. What is an intranet?
2. What sorts of applications are best delivered over an intranet?
3. What are some examples of companies who are realizing the benefits from intranet applications?
4. Once started, how does an intranet evolve over time?
5. What does it take to turn an intranet into an extranet?

2 What Is an Intranet?

2.1 Intranets Defined

While the term "intranet" has been defined in a variety of ways, we take it to mean "the networks, clients, servers, and applications that support an organization's internal operations and communications when those systems are built on Internet standards and protocols in an open systems environment" (Ware et. al., 1998).

The public Internet offers a variety of client/server applications including the Web, file transfer, e-mail, newsgroups, and chat. Each of these involves a particular type of client, a particular type of server, and a particular protocol that defines how clients make requests and how servers respond to those requests. Below is a list of the specific communication protocols on which these applications are based:

Application	Communication Protocol
Web	HTTP – Hypertext Transport Protocol
File transfer	FTP – File Transfer Protocol
E-Mail	SMTP – Simple Mail Transport Protocol
Newsgroups	NNTP – Network News Transport Protocol
Chat	IRC – Internet Relay Chat

While each of the above client/server applications entails a specific protocol, they all rest on TCP/IP – the transmission control protocol (TCP) and internet protocol (IP) that ties together clients and servers on the Internet. Basically, IP defines the dotted addressing scheme (e.g. 130.211.5.14) that enables a client machine to locate a server machine on the network and vice-versa, while TCP defines exactly how the communications (requests and responses) between machines are to be structured as data packets. Adoption of TCP/IP as a universal communication standard has enabled a diverse range of hardware to be inter-networked together into the global configuration called the Internet.

In the recent past, many organizations have invested time and money in establishing proprietary networks and creating or purchasing various client/server applications to run on those networks. Many of the networks utilized Novell's Network Operating System (NOS) or Novell's Netware with the IPX protocol. The use of proprietary networking systems and protocols makes it difficult to tie together disparate hardware and to create scalable applications. These are some of the reasons that organizations have adopted TCP/IP as the standard for their internal local area networks (LANs) and wide area networks (WANs) and have turned to various Internet protocols in order to deliver information and applications

While there are some exceptions, the vast majority of intranets rest primarily on Web standards and protocols. This means that intranets are usually implemented by creating a "Web" inside the organization. Assuming that an organization already has a TCP/IP network in place, an intranet usually starts when one or more departments decides to make various documents or departmental information available over an internal Web. This usually entails:

- Turning a departmental workstation or PC into a dedicated server machine.
- Assigning the machine a Web address (in Web vernacular a Web address is called a Uniform Resource Locator or URL), e.g. www.mydepartment.com.
- Installing Web server software on the machine, e.g. like Microsoft's Internet Information Server (IIS).
- Converting the documents or information to static HTML Web pages and storing the pages in the appropriate subdirectories on the dedicated server.
- Establishing a security policy for the pages (e.g. are the pages to be password protected or not).
- Advertising the availability of the site and opening it for business.

Figure 1 below provides an overview of the components, standards and protocols for a departmental Web site.

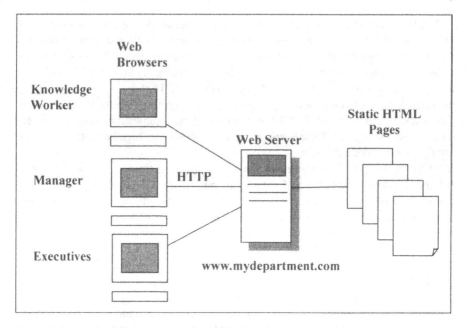

Fig. 1. Departmental intranet

2.2 Differences Between Intranets and the Internet

Most organizations that have implemented intranets allow end users to access the larger Internet. From an end user's perspective, the two networks appear cotermi-nous. For example, an organization might create an internal Web site for tracking competitors. Here, the pages at the site could link to other pages at this site or other sites within the organization, as well as to pages at sites outside the organization. The seamless interface between the sites both within and outside the organization are made possible because intranets and the Internet both rely on the same standards and protocols.

How is an intranet distinguished from the Internet? The bottom line is that intra-nets and the Internet are not distinguished by their underlying architectures. Their architectures are basically the same. What distinguishes the publicly accessible Internet from an intranet is the difference in focus and content. The following table summarizes some of the distinguishing characteristics (Hinrichs, 1997):

Table 1. Differences between intranets and the Internet

Intranets	Internet
Proprietary information	Public information
Aimed at employees	Aimed at outsiders
Collaborative communications	Financial transactions
Process oriented	Sales and marketing oriented
Transforms organizations	Transforms customer/sales cycle
Emphasis on work groups, teams and intradepartmental flow	Emphasis on single point of contact with the organization and user profiling
Creates a learning organization	Creates brand awareness
Needs to be highly decentralized	Needs to be highly centralized.

So, where does the intranet end and the Internet begin? Usually, the clients and servers on an intranet sit behind a "firewall."

A firewall is a computer-based device that prevents unauthorized access to an organization's internal network. At the same time it provides external Internet access to users. With a firewall a company can control what type of access is permitted...If you go hunting around the network administrator's shop for a machine with a big sign on it saying 'Firewall,' you won't find it. A firewall usually isn't a single machine, in fact, it might not be a machine at all, but rather a program (Pfaffenberger, 1997).

2.3 Extranets Defined

Along with other security measures and devices, firewalls not only permit outgoing traffic but also control incoming traffic. For instance, a salesperson who is on the road might dial into an online service like AOL, connect to the Internet through AOL's Web browser, and (with the right user id and password) directly access his or her organization's intranet via this connection. In the same vein, an organization can permit similar types of access to individuals outside the organization, like suppliers, distributors, or other partners. The virtual networks that provide external access to internal intranets have been given the name "extranets." The relationships among the Internet, intranets and extranets are depicted in Figure 2. Later, we will describe how extranets work and provide real-life examples of their use.

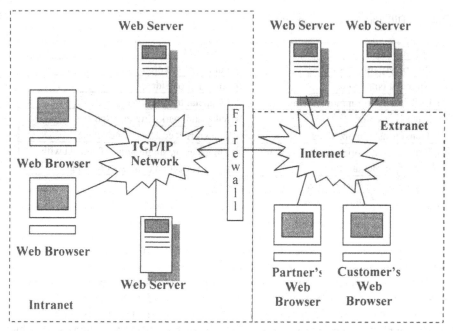

Fig. 2. Virtual network blending the Internet, intranets and extranets

2.4 A Sample Intranet

Comshare's InfoWeb is illustrative of many of the intranets developed by commercial companies, especially those who utilize Web protocols and standards. Comshare is a software vendor of packaged and custom applications for management planning and control (e.g. software applications for creating budgeting systems). Comshare has approximately 450 employees worldwide and revenues of $60-$70 million dollars. The homepage for Comshare's InfoWeb is displayed below in Figure 3.

A cursory review of the homepage reveals that it provides links to: pages about company news, human resource information, product and project status, a calendar of events, customer support services, computer system support, other internal Web sites, and a mechanism for searching the contents of the intranet. Clicking on a link takes the user to the associated page. For example, clicking on the "Benefits (US)" link under the Employee heading takes the user to the page shown in Figure 4.

Fig. 3. Comshare's infoWeb homepage

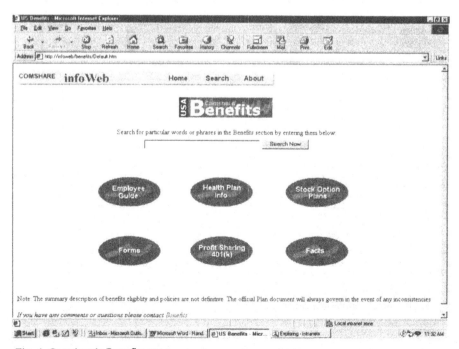

Fig. 4. Comshare's Benefits page

For the most part, the pages on the InfoWeb site are static Web pages that reside on a single Web server (in this case Microsoft's Internet Information Server). The site also provides access to other Web servers both internal and external to the company and allows distributors and customers extranet access to the customer support system. For some of these sites the Web pages are generated in a dynamic fashion based on the results of queries to relational databases. The overall architecture of InfoWeb is shown in Figure 5.

Like other intranets, InfoWeb has gone through a series of incarnations. Originally, the information on InfoWeb resided on separate Web servers that were under the control of the individual departments providing the information – in essence separate Web sites. Each site had a different "look and feel" with different navigational schemes. A few of these sites seemed to undergo continuous change. After 9-12 months of operation, the IS department decided that the users would be better served by coalescing most of these individual sites into a single site. The information is still provided by the individual departments but IS assumed editorial and administrative responsibilities for the site and its contents. Those sites that remained autonomous – like Product Development and Helpline-- were encouraged to adopt a similar look and feel. Although differences still persist among the individual sites on the InfoWeb, the differences are not as radical or apparent as earlier versions.

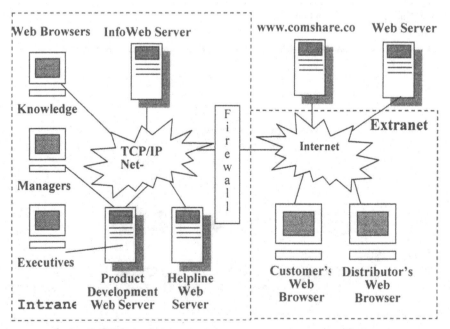

Fig. 5. Comshare's infoWeb architecture

The shift towards centralized control of Comshare's InfoWeb corresponds quite closely to the advice offered by a number of sources. As DeWire (1998) puts it:

Many corporations are realizing that their intranets have grown into massive, uncontrollable beasts that require new data management strategies. When an organization gets ready to build an enterprisewide intranet, it first needs to find all the existing "autonomous" internal Web sites. These folks then need to be convinced that they should be brought into a single standard and that the Web group should have centralized responsibility for them. The Web group – steering committee, a council, etc. – is the governing office for intranets.

Establishing a single standard can be accomplished in a variety of ways

3 Why Intranets?

In addition to the fact that they are based on pervasive Internet standards and protocols and can leverage an organizations existing infrastructure and applications investments, the rapid adoption of intranets and intranet applications can be attributed to a variety of other factors. Relative to other more traditional client/server applications, including groupware like Lotus Notes and message-based applications, intranets offer the following advantages:

- Centralized maintenance and administration with applications deployed directly from servers without the need for software releases, updates or patches on client desktops.
- Lower "total cost of ownership" (TCO) because of the availability of free Web servers (e.g. Apache or Microsofts IIS) and free Web browsers (i.e. the Netscape Navigator and Microsoft's Internet Explorer).
- Platform portability where applications are written once and then installed on a platform of choice without the need for software re-writes or re-complication.
- Ease of use achieved through a universal client interface – the Web browser – that provides end users with a simple, straightforward frontend to varied applications.
- Easy access to up-to-date information which are made available "anytime and anyplace."
- Fast and easy application implementation attained through the use of simple standards (e.g.HTML the hypertext markup language) that makes it possible for "authors" to create and distribute content with minimal skills.

4 Intranet Applications

The InformationWeek (Violini, 1998) survey of executives cited above lends some credence to the fact that early intranet implementations were focused on human resources, while recent applications have recognized that intranets provide an effective way to support organizational decision making and to automate business processes. When asked, "Which business applications are accessible over a browser on your corporate intranet?" 60% of the executives at the InformationWeek 500 firms indicated that their intranets provided access to human resources, 55% to decision support, and 37% to workflow processes. A recent series of articles appearing in the online Intranet Journal offers a detailed look at a variety of applications supported by the current generation of intranets. The list below summarizes the possibilities by major functional area.

Human Resources

Employee handbook	Telephone directory
Benefits information	401K center
Employee surveys	Internal recruitment
External recruitment	Candidate screening
Organizational charts	Newsletters
Company calendar	Employee classifieds

Sales and Marketing

Product demos and scripts	Product information
Sales forecasts and reports	Sales contact management
Sales lead management	Market research
Prospecting	Press releases
Sales team collaboration	Online sales training

Calendars for trade shows, seminars, advertising and PR campaigns
Solicit input from field personnel

Financial and Accounting Applications

Financial reports	Policies and procedures
Budgeting	Asset management
Expense reports	Unit reporting and forecasting
Payables/Receivables	Payroll

Customer Service and Support

Order entry and tracking	Problem entry and tracking
Bug fixes	Warranty claims and processing
Problem escalation	Training for service and support staff

Customer accounts consolidated from multiple sources
Frequently asked questions (FAQs)
Customer information entry and update

Engineering

Project conferences	Project documentation
Engineering change orders	Workflow management
Standards and methodologies	Engineering libraries
Technical papers	Prototype applications
QA feedback	Project management

Shared development of products and documentation

Regardless of the industry in which they operate, most organization's intranets encompass a combination of the above applications. Netscape's public Web site provides a collection of case studies describing the intranets at a number of commercial firms and the applications they service (Netscape, 1998). Below is a summary of the applications detailed in these case studies:

Company	Application
Bay Networks	On line access to sales-order status, product availability, sales leads, and sales appointments.
	General corporate news and data with full text search capabilities.
	Forms entry for all corporate administrative activities including travel requests, facilities requests, accounting forms, and HR benefits forms.
	Online discussion groups for engineering, sales, and marketing on competitive issues, software applications, and product introductions.
BC Tel	Virtual HR providing access to all human resource programs InfoSource offering 1600 customer service reps access to product, service, customer and competitive information.
Booz-Allen	Knowledge-Online, a repository of the firm's knowledge and expertise
	Database driven expert skills directory for matching staff skills with client needs..
	Online newsgroups for discussing company and non-company related topics.
Ciba-Geigy	Access to company information about organization functions, services, corporate news,
	Worldwide employee directory
	Ordering of services and products.
Grupo Financiero BITAL	A collection of online HR applications including an: employee health plan guide; telephone directory; and employee magazine

Daily postings of company reports and bank news.
Bulletin board discussion groups of bank related issues and activities.

ICA
Fluor Daniel

Coordination, collaboration and communication about industry projects including access to published, categorized ISO 9001 procedures with search capabilities
Online access to CAD and other project information for worldwide collaboration on design projects.

Italtel

14web, a central source of information providing online access to a company directory, product documentation, product demonstrations, software downloads, training courses, etc.
Online monitoring of the company's plants and networks.
Electronic Press Review, a daily internal publication with archived issues and full text search capabilities.

Johnson
Controls

A large scale, global directory infrastructure with daily updates from Control Data X.500 directory and Oracles databases.

Knight-Ridder
New Media

Financial personnel from distributed locations can access central Oracle Financials database.
Access to customer service records.

Litton
Industries

Online capital forecast planning with ability to request, analyze and approve out-of-plan capital acquisition requests.

Centralized database of approved vendors for government related projects.
Intranet forms for querying the Computervision CAD files in a legacy database. Files can be viewed with a browser plugin.

Nomura Research Institute

The Digital Office providing access to company notices, business reports, policies and rules, employee information, and training course, help desk reports, and sales and operation support data.

Scotia Capital
Markets

Online research reports, help, worldwide employee telephone book, closing prices, etc. with full text search capabilities.

An institutional investors Fixed Income Trading System for placing orders for bonds and other fixed income instruments.
An extranet offering retail clients the ability to trade online.

Thailand National Science and Technology Development Agency	Online access to a company newsletter, press releases, announcements, calendar of events.
	Newsgroup discussion centers and departmental news forums for project and assignment collaboration.
US West	The Global Village offering access to the Rumor Mill, online discussions; the life situations database, and corporate newspaper. Online support for customer service representatives enabling them to determine availability of telephone facilities and services
Xilinx	Crossroads intranet providing access to competitive information, sales materials, legal documents, product specific information, and project information. An extranet providing manufacturing partners online access to manufacturing specifications and sales partners access to customer information.

None of these applications appears automatically when a Web server is installed. Instead, they all require programming and often involve linking the server to existing data sources. The difference between programming for intranet (or Web) applications and traditional client/server applications is that the programming is simpler. The Web server vendors, like Microsoft and Netscape, provide tools that enable the "average" programmer to create an application, even if the application requires real-time access to relational database sources.

5 Identifying Intranet Opportunities

While intranet applications offer many advantages relative to more traditional applications, there are several instances where the traditional solutions are preferred. How do you determine whether a new application should be implemented as an intranet or an existing application should be converted to an intranet? There are no hard and fast rules for making this determination. The Intranet Journal (1998) offers five characteristics to look for in identifying business processes that can be handled or improved by intranets:

- Traditional Paper Publication – processes that involve production, distribution and update of dynamic information that is usually published on paper. A number of HR documents fall into this category, as well as marketing (product lists) and sales literature (e.g. price lists).

- Multiple Data Sources – processes that involve consolidation and integration of information from multiple data sources. Most organizations, for example, have multiple customer databases including orders, account information, customer service reports, and the like. Instead of creating an integrated data warehouse, an intranet can be used to create a virtual data warehouse by using an intranet application to access and integrate the data in a consolidated report.
- Distributed Collaboration – processes that require daily communication and collaboration between individuals and teams at multiple locations. Engineering teams and sales teams, for example, are often geographically dispersed. These teams require frequent communication and collaboration, not only among themselves but also with other teams. Standard Web technologies provide a simple means for posting project, company, and customer information in support of these teams. In house newsgroups and chat facilities support online discussion and collaboration among team members at different locations.
- Locating Online Content – processes that require people to find or requisition information. A number of proprietary systems have been developed for searching large scale document databases (e.g. reference manuals). Lotus Notes is one example that has been employed by a number of companies. Verity's Agent-based systems are another. For the most part these proprietary systems are best suited for LAN environments and required specialized software to be installed on the end user's desktop. In contrast, the online search facilities provided with most Web server software provide a simpler and cheaper alternative to the proprietary systems. These intranet search facilities operate in much the same way that the search engines (e.g. Yahoo, Infoseek, and Excite) operate on the World Wide Web.
- Modernizing Legacy Applications – processes that run in mainframe environments that require improved "ease of use" or integration with newer systems. A number of companies are in need of updating existing systems, especially legacy systems. Many of these existing systems rest on relational databases. As noted, Web server software provides the means to access relational database information in a straightforward fashion and to make this information available to geographically dispersed audiences in a secure and flexible manner.

6 Intranet Evolution

6.1 Evolutionary Stages

Some experts contend that, once established, intranets undergo a natural evolution, progressing from organized chaos through various stages or models to the pinnacle of a virtual organization. Ware et. al. (1998) describe the progression in this manner:

While there is nothing absolute or deterministic about the pattern, we have seen this progression (with minor variations) often enough to believe it reflects a natural experiential learning process for organizations.

The progression to which they refer includes the following stages: playground; communication enabler; knowledge enabler; workflow enabler; collaboration enabler; and virtual organization.

In a similar fashion, Gonzales (1998) sees the Web and intranets "evolving from a publications platform to a high value applications environment." She has identified four models of Intranet design where "the levels of interactivity and the variety of features increase in each subsequent model." The key differentiator among the models is the type of interaction, communication and collaboration they support. The models include the: Publication Model ("I publish, you read"); Asymmetric Interaction Model ("I ask, you respond"); Symmetric Interaction Model ("We all have a chance to talk and listen, ask and respond"); and Synchronous Virtual Environment ("This is the way we work").

While there are simple differences between the numbers and names used by the two typologies, both typologies highlight similar facts about the evolution.

Intranets usually begin life as playgrounds or underground movements championed by one or more intranet evangelists. As the number of departmental Web sites increases, there is pressure to control the growth, content, and "look and feel" of these sites. The pressure towards centralized control often comes from MIS or IT – the department charged with overall responsibility for the network on which these sites live. Actual control of the intranet often resides with a central Intranet committee whose members consist of the departmental "webmasters" charged with maintaining the content of the intranet. Control usually takes the form of standards and rules pertaining to issues like "look and feel," security, site maintenance, and the like. For example, early in the development of the "Global Village" intranet at U.S. West, the webmasters in various departments formed the US West Web Developer's Coalition to serve as a coordinating body for sharing expertise, experience, and for addressing the above issues (Gonzales, 1998). Today, many organizations bypass the chaos associated with the playground or underground stage and use an Intranet Committee to design their intranets from the start.

During the initial stages of an intranet, most of the content comes in the form of static Web pages that are electronic versions of printed materials like company newsletters, HR policy manuals, product literature, and the like. From a technical standpoint, this type of information is easy to convert to Web format and to administer. Compared to the printed version, the intranet version saves on printing costs, widens the audience of readers, provides up-to-date information, and is searchable.

Overtime, as an intranet grows, the content becomes more dynamic and sometimes more collaborative. From our standpoint, there is no predetermined pattern to why, when and how these changes occur. Instead, whether the content becomes more dynamic or collaborative really depends on the business processes the organization is trying to support. However, it is the case that creating, maintaining and administering dynamic or collaborative content on an intranet requires considerably more technical expertise than simply publishing static Web pages.

6.2 Dynamic Data Access

Many of the sample intranet applications summarized earlier require access to data housed in a relational database. Customer accounts, sales leads, and project schedules are some examples. While it is possible to automatically create static pages based on the records in a database, it makes little sense. Usually there is too much data, the data are too dynamic, and the needs of the end users so varied, that it is almost impossible and too time consuming to anticipate what sorts of static pages would have to be created to satisfy the users' needs. Obviously, it makes more sense to provide users with access to the database, letting them (in a controlled fashion) formulate their own queries.

The process of providing end users with real-time access to a database via an intranet is fairly involved. The process is outlined in Figure 6 below.

Basically the process works like this:

1. The user accesses a Web page containing a Web-based entry form that enables the user to indirectly formulate a database query. A Web-based entry form contains a set of input boxes, selection lists, and buttons where the user enters data that correspond to the values of one or more fields in the underlying database. For instance, there might be textbox for entering a customer's name or a drop down list that lets the user select the name.
2. The user completes the form by clicking on a "submit" button. This sends the data entries to a specified Web server on the intranet. Although the user can't see it, the Web page containing the entry form also provides the name of the Web server where the data are to be sent, as well as the name of a program or special Web page that will process the data received by the server.
3. Upon receiving the data, the Web server invokes the designated program or special Web page and makes the data available to that program or page. In the past most of these programs were "common gateway interface" (CGI) programs. That is, programs written in C, C++, Visual Basic, Perl, or some other language that included CGI subroutines that allowed the program to received data from a Web server and to return results (in the form of dynamically created HTML pages) to a Web server. Today, many of these programs are actually written in JavaScript or VB Script that is embedded directly in a Web page and executed on the server (known as server-side scripting as opposed to scripts that are executed by the Web browser). So, instead of invoking a program, the Web server accesses the special Web page and executes the script commands contained in the page. The availability of server-side scripting has greatly simplified that task of creating applications that provide real-time access to a database.
4. When the CGI program or special Web page begins execution, it takes the data that has been entered and formulates an SQL query that it submits to the database.

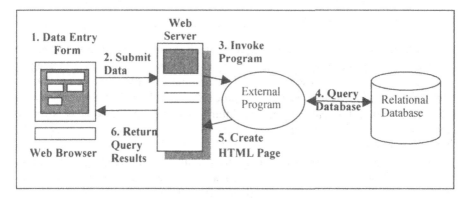

Fig. 6. Intranet access to a relational database

5. Once the query has been completed, the same program or special page takes the query results and dynamically constructs a Web page that is passed back to the server.
6. Finally, the Web server returns the resulting Web page to the end user.

6.3 Collaborative Applications

In a collaborative intranet application, end users "write as well as read." BITAL's online bulletin boards for discussing bank related issues, Booz-Allen's online newsgroups for discussing company related issues, and Thailand NSTDA's online forums for collaborating on research projects are illustrative of this type of application. The prototypical collaborative application is the UseNet newsgroups found on the larger Internet. Online forums like UseNet are organized by topics and subtopics. Within a topic or subtopic, users can post messages or respond to messages posted by others. The initial message and the associated responses form a message "thread."

While it is possible to create a collaborative application from scratch, most organizations rely on packaged software designed specifically for this purpose. One alternative is to implement a newsgroup or NNTP server inside the firewall. In essence the organization creates its own UseNet newsgroups. Newsgroup servers are packaged with both Microsoft's Internet Information Server (IIS) and Netscape's SuiteSpot Server. This technology was used by the three organizations listed above. Another alternative is to use specialized Web software designed specifically for collaborative applications. O'Reilly's WebBoard is a conferencing system that supports multiple, threaded, subject-based discussions. Another product that can be used for this purpose is Allaire Forums. Finally, Lotus Domino is a special server that "Webifies" Lotus Notes, a collaborative application that is widely used in many larger organizations.

6.4 Workflow Applications

Like collaborative applications, workflow applications are a type of groupware. The term workflow refers to the automatic routing of documents through a messaging system in support of business processes. Unlike online discussion groups or forums that are information-centric, workflow is process-centric. Workflow applications can be used to control processes such as billing, purchase authorizations, expense authorizations, or any other business process where the sequence and timing of the stages is important.

Prior to intranets, workflow systems were built with proprietary client/server software packages and relied on e-mail protocols and backbones to move the documents from one stage of the process to another or from one person involved in the process to another. In contrast intranet and extranet workflow relies on Internet protocols and specialized applications to accomplish the same tasks. Again, it is possible to create a workflow applications from scratch. In *Understanding Intranets*, Greer (1998) details an application built by Emery Worldwide to handle United States Post Service (USPD) second-day airmail. The application provided inventory management that tracked the pickup, delivery and on-hand inventory of second-day priority mail containers across twenty geographically dispersed Emery sites. The system was built using Java as the development language, Remote Method Invocation (RMI) to manage software objects on the distributed network and involved communications among a variety of servers on the network. Because most organizations don't have the skills required to build a workflow system from scratch, most organizations rely on packaged software to accomplish the feat. Jetform's Formflow, Lotus Domino, and Ultimis Workflow are examples of commercial products that support intranet workflow (Hills, 1996b).

7 From Intranets to Extranets

An extranet opens an organizations intranet to the outside world. It supplies a communication link between an organization and its partners – dealers, distributors, contractors, suppliers, subsidiaries, and even a company's own sales representatives. The focus of an extranet is on the organization's "supply-chain" community. Prior to the advent of extranets, most organizations relied on the face-to-face contacts, phone, fax, e-mail, newsletters, and proprietary electronic data interchange (EDI) to communicate and collaborate with its partners.

Extranets can provide:

- Key customers with product updates, order status, account balances, and online support.
- Sales representatives, dealers, distributors and subsidiaries with access to customer records, competitive data, pricing information, and inventory.

- Repair and support personnel with product release notes, parts catalogs, and on-line technical manuals.
- Joint venture partners with project status updates, financial report, and research reports.
- Vertical industry partners an online forum and news from trade associations.

Previously, online communications between partners often relied on expensive, proprietary software applications that operated over value added networks (VANs). This is why EDI, which utilized this technology, never enjoyed widespread popularity, especially among medium-sized and smaller firms. In contrast, implementing an extranet is relatively simple and cost effective. The only requirements are that a partner has a Web browser and access to the larger Internet and that an organization opens it's intranet to a selected part of the outside world.

There are a variety of options which allow partners to connect to an organization's intranet – a dial-up connection, private (leased lines), a Web server outside the firewall, and a secure tunnel on the Internet (Pfaffenberger, 1998):

- Dial-up – An organization can install a remote access server (RAS) which enables a partner (or other employees) to utilize a modem to dial into the organizations intranet. The partner is required to have a user id and a password to gain access. Although relatively slow, a dial up connection is very secure.
- Private Lines – An organization can install, or lease from one of the telcos, a private high-speed line that connects its network to the partner's network. This virtual private network is both high speed and secure. However, it can be expensive, especially if there are multiple partners involved.
- A Server outside the Firewall – When an organization creates a Web site open to the public at large, the server sits outside the organization's secured network. An intranet server can also be placed on the other side of the firewall and secured with user ids and passwords. In this way only authorized users have access to the data. Because a server of this sort is susceptible to "hacker" attacks, this approach is only recommended when the data are not particular sensitive.
- Secure Tunnel – In this option the partner "tunnels" into the intranet over the public Internet. Encryption is used at both ends of the tunnel to secure the communication. Tunneling of this sort is supported by a network technology called the Virtual Private Network (VPN). Figure 7 provides an overview of a VPN. In the past the firewalls at both ends of the VPN needed to be the same brand. The new VPN standards have relaxed this requirement. Again, many companies rely on the telcos or other Internet Service Providers (ISPs) to manage their VPNs.

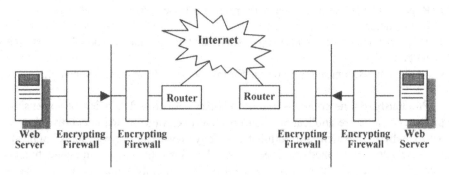

Fig. 7. Architecture of a virtual private network (*Source*: Dewire, 1998)

8 Conclusions

A Meta Group study found that intranets achieved a 38% return on investment (ROI) with applications based on static pages yielding a 22% ROI, collaborative applications producing a 40% return, and dynamic applications generating a 68% return (Greer, 1998). The return was independent of the size of the application with departmental intranets having as much impact as enterprise wide applications. The real key was the alignment between the application and the business strategy it was designed to support.

In the future, organizations will no longer be able to consider intranets in isolation. Their Internet, intranet and extranet strategies will have to converge. The term "I-net" has been used to cover all three types of applications (Dewire, 1998). A high return on "I-net" investments will require an organization to not only understand its own internal operations but also the requirements and business needs of its customers and trading partners.

References

Davenport, Thomas, "Use The Power Of The Web -- The Internet's World Wide Web offers a model for businesses to display internal information," *InformationWeek*, 9/16 (1995), URL=http://www.techweb.com/se/directlink.cgi?IWK19950116S0065

Dewire, Dawna, *Thin Clients: Delivering Information Over the Web*, McGraw-Hill, New York, 1998.

Gonzales, Patricia Stone, *21ˢᵗ Century Intranet*, Prentice-Hall, New York, 1998

Greer, Trevor, *Understanding Intranets*, Microsoft Press, Redmond, Washington, 1998.

Hills, Mellanie, *Intranet Business Strategies*, Wiley, 1996a.

Hills, Mellanie, *Intranets as Groupware*, Wiley, 1996b.

Hinrichs, Randy J., *Intranets: What's the Bottom Line*, Prentice Hall, 1998.

Intranet Journal, "Fifty Ways to Put an Intranet to Work," Intranet Journal, (1998), URL=http://www.intranetjournal.com/features/fifty.

Loshin, Peter, *Extranet Design and Implementation*, Sybex Network Press, San Francisco, 1997.

Netscape,"Customer Profiles," Netscape, (1998), URL=http://Home.netscape.com/comprod/at_work/customer_profiles

Pfaffenberger, Bryan, *Building a Strategic Extranet*, IDG Books, Foster City, CA, 1998.

Violino, Bob, "Defining IT Innovation," *Information Week*, 9/14 (1998), URL= http://www.informationweek.com/700/innovate.htm.

Ware, J., Gebauer, J, Hartman, A and M. Roldan, *Search for Digital Excellence*, McGraw-Hill, New York, 1998.

CHAPTER 26

Decision Support Applications in Electronic Commerce

Clyde W. Holsapple[1], Kshiti D. Joshi[2], and Meenu Singh[3]

[1]School of Management, Carol M. Gatton College of Business and Economics, University of Kentucky, Lexington, Kentucky, cwhols@pop.uky.edu

[2]School of Accounting, Information Systems, and Business Law, Washington State University, Pullman, Washington, joshi@cbe.wsu.edu

[3]Computer and Technical Sciences Department, Kentucky State University, Frankfort, Kentucky, msingh@gwmail.kysu.edu

Electronic Commerce (EC) signifies a fundamental shift in how organizations operate, interact, and compete. Decision making is a common thread underlying all EC transactions, shaping all activities in a value chain/supply chain, and feeding off of EC information exchanges. Supporting this decision-making is an important aspect of EC. The overwhelming success of the Internet has opened uncharted opportunities for all organizations to use this technology as a basis for Web-oriented decision support systems(WODSSs). Here, we explore decision support applications that are emerging all along the EC frontier, focusing on those that are delivered across the WWW. This includes the positioning of decision support within the EC realm, a survey of decision support initiatives on the WWW, and the introduction of three taxonomies for guiding study and research: a Subject-Oriented Taxonomy for studying WODSSs used in EC in terms of the subjects about which they can provide knowledge; a Technique-Oriented Taxonomy by which a WODSS is viewed in terms of the knowledge-management technique employed to implement it; and a Coordination-Oriented Taxonomy which deals with the coordination of distributed components of a WODSS. In conclusion, we present some observations about avenues for future research and development of decision support applications in EC.

Keywords: coordination; electronic brokerage; electronic commerce; knowledge-management technique; web-oriented decision support system

1 Introduction

At the cutting edge of business today, electronic commerce (EC) signifies a fundamental shift in how organizations operate, interact, and compete. It is emerging as a key enabler in changing the way companies do business and represents one of the most intriguing challenges facing the business world today (Yadav et al. 1997). Electronic commerce represents a new universe of value creation for consumers and organizations (Applegate et al., 1996). The driving force behind this redefinition of business is the perception that information, its dissemination, and ease of access are crucial to the effective functioning of any organization (Kalakota and Whinston, 1996). Through a host of technological advances, highlighted by global interconnectivity via the World Wide Web(WWW), a wealth of real-time information is available online. WWW founder Tim Berners-Lee (1996) sees the Web as a vast, rapidly changing information resource. One of the major uses of timely information is the support of decision making.

Here, we explore decision support applications that are emerging all along the electronic commerce frontier, with a special emphasis on those that are delivered across the WWW. The exploration includes the positioning of decision support within the EC realm, a survey of decision support initiatives on the WWW, and the introduction of three taxonomies for guiding study and research. The coverage is organized as follows: Section 2 establishes a contextual perspective for examining decision support applications in electronic commerce. In Section 3, we summarize research and practice along the DSS dimension of EC. Section 4 introduces a subject-oriented taxonomy for studying DSSs used in EC and illustrates it with examples from the Web. Section 5 shows how Web-oriented DSSs can be classified based on the knowledge management techniques they employ; illustrative examples are provided. In Section 6, we introduce a coordination-oriented taxonomy that involves two dimensions for studying Web-oriented DSS possibilities. We close with some observations about avenues for future research and development of decision support applications in electronic commerce.

2 Context

Internet-facilitated electronic commerce represents one of the most exciting and potentially significant emerging market opportunities available today (Auger and Gallagher, 1997). Yet, to many, electronic commerce is a confusing subject involving an incredible amount of jargon, numerous claims, and rapid change. Often, it is poorly understood or narrowly understood, meaning different things to different people and reflecting varying backgrounds, job functions, professional orientations, and so forth. Electronic commerce has become such an enormous field that there is to be found a rich variety of descriptions and definitions of it, each having its own views and merits (Holsapple and Singh, 1998).

Many of the views and definitions of EC stress the use of technology for handling buying-selling transactions. Others emphasize that it involves the use of technology for exchanging information. Yet other views concentrate on identifying EC activities or EC effects. For our exploration of decision support applications in EC, we adopt the following unifying definition of electronic commerce:

Electronic commerce is a knowledge-centered approach to achieving business goals in which technology enables or facilitates activities in and across the value chain, as well as decisions that underlie those activities
(Holsapple and Singh, 1998).

Decision making is a common thread underlying all EC transactions, shaping all activities in a value chain or supply chain, and feeding off of EC information exchanges. Supporting this decision making is an important aspect of electronic commerce. Indeed, Kalakota and Whinston (1996) speculate that the next wave of corporate electronic commerce innovations will be aimed specifically at decision support.

In the knowledge-based view of decision support systems (Holsapple and Whinston, 1988, 1996), a decision is a piece of knowledge indicating the nature of an action commitment; it is produced by manipulating other knowledge of various types (including information), and the production effort can be aided by a computer-based system that is able to store and process knowledge representations. Such a system is a decision support system (DSS). A DSS's knowledge repository can be physically distributed, as can its knowledge processing capabilities (Holsapple and Whinston, 1986). DSSs developed and used for electronic commerce over the Internet tend to be distributed mechanisms for knowledge management.

The immense and growing body of knowledge that exists on the Web can be processed in various ways to support decision making. General browsing activity can be undertaken to obtain knowledge or simulate ideas in the course of decision making. It may even help in recognizing the need for a decision. Interactions with a Web site can result in problem solving that provides some specific piece of knowledge required in decision making. Of course, the ultimate value of the Web's knowledge for supporting a particular decision maker depends on what knowledge happens to exist there and how easy it is to access. But we can say with certainty that both consumers and managerial decision makers will increasingly plug into external technological structures to draw on knowledge resources that enhance decision making performance, resources that they themselves are unable or unwilling to manage (Holsapple and Whinston, 1996).

The Web has been discussed extensively in the popular press as an entertainment and information resource and it is fast becoming a major new setting for DSS access, deployment, development, product information, and research (Power, 1997). Bhargava et al. (1997) state, "All emergent markets for decision technologies that we are aware of are hosted on the Internet - in particular, on the Web ." The goal for the WWW makes it an ideal distribution system for the DSSs of the future (Gregg and Goul, forthcoming).

The advent of new programming language environments (e.g., Sun's Java, script languages based on Web URL conventions), combined with the introduction of client-server architecture in organizational computing platforms, has opened new opportunities for DSS researchers and builders to develop distributed, network-based DSSs (Bui 1997).

The trend is clear. The overwhelming success of the Internet has opened uncharted opportunities for all organizations, large and small, to use this technology as a basis for Web-oriented decision support systems (WODSSs). Albeit in its infancy, decision support on the Web is already happening. Numerous decision support facilities are readily available via the Web. Researchers and practitioners have started to publish and share ideas, insights, and observations on the convergence of the DSS field with the EC frontier. Examples include finding DSS resources on the Web, deploying DSSs on the Web, and designing protocols, architectures, and tools that facilitate decision-making processes in the context of electronic commerce.

3 DSS Initiatives in Electronic Commerce

We are rapidly entering an era that will be dominated by knowledge-based organizations in a knowledge-based society (Toffler, 1990; Drucker, 1993). The very nature of organizations is changing from an emphasis on working with materials to an emphasis on working with knowledge (Holsapple and Whinston, 1987). Each such organization is populated by a community of knowledge workers who are interconnected by a computer-based infrastructure. The computer-supported knowledge-intensive business tasks they perform comprise the fabric of electronic commerce. The dominant technological features of a knowledge-based organization (be it a single firm or a virtual, network organization) are local workstations, support centers, communication paths, and distributed knowledge storehouses (Holsapple and Whinston 1987).

Each workstation is a computer local to a knowledge worker. It has a local repository of knowledge and software for manipulating knowledge in support of the worker's performance of business tasks such as decision making. Support centers (e.g., servers) are shared, possibly remote, computers also able to do knowledge manipulation and draw on contents of distributed knowledge storehouses. The communication paths define a network (e.g., internet, intranet) that connects workstations, support centers, distributed knowledge storehouses, and external technological structures. Thus, each workstation is a knowledge worker's portal into a world of electronic commerce.

Continuing developments in the interrelated fields of artificial intelligence, decision support systems, and organizational computing will play a crucial role in the design, construction, and ongoing management of knowledge-based organizations (Applegate, Cash, and Miles, 1988; Holsapple and Whinston, 1996). From a DSS vantage point, a key challenge is how to exploit advancing technology to implement DSSs that improve the global decision making performance of an organization's knowledge workers. Broadly speaking, the purpose of a DSS is to improve the decision-making ability of knowledge workers by allowing more or better decisions within the constraints of cognitive, temporal, and economic limits; a DSS increases a user's productivity in handling the knowledge involved in decision making (Holsapple and Whinston, 1996). "In the future, we can predict confidently that every knowledge worker will have to do some form of DSS" (Ba, Kalakota, and Whinston, 1997). This prediction is in line with the trend in organizations today where more and more decision making is being driven down to lower echelons. This new form of organizational architecture requires radical changes in the treatment of DSSs (Ba, Kalakota, and Whinston, 1995).

The field of decision support is expanding rapidly into the world of electronic commerce. From being primarily personal support mechanisms, DSSs are moving to be *shared commodities* across the organization (Turban and Aronson, 1997). Organizations can use intranets and the Internet to deliver high value applications to decision makers around the world. Corporations are developing distributed DSSs (intranets and extranets) that enable easy access to knowledge stored in multiple locations, permit collaboration among decision-making participants, and foster knowledge sharing worldwide. Artificial intelligence methods are improving the quality of decision support, becoming embedded in various processors such as search engines and intelligent agents. The paramount challenge is development and delivery of decision support technologies that are architecture neutral, portable, dynamically adaptable to ever changing decision situations, and efficient in consuming system resources (Bui, 1997). Here, we summarize research initiatives that contribute to meeting these challenges, plus progress to date in delivering distributed decision support.

3.1 DecisionNet

DecisionNet is a research initiative that aims to advance the distribution of DSSs using the Web (Bhargava et al., 1997). Various computer-based decision technologies are now available in the academic, research, and commercial environments. However, use of these decision technologies is below potential because of a reliance on traditional software distribution strategies that are not particularly suited to small and specialized niches of the decision technology marketplace. Traditional mechanisms for distributing decision support software (e.g., value-added retailers of shrink wrapped software) require each component of the solution package to be acquired, installed, and executed on a user's computational platform. This raises various problems for both consumers and providers such as awareness, accessibility, compatibility, applicability, advertisement, and version management (Bhargava et al., 1997; Kalakota, Stallaert, and Whinston, 1996).

The awareness problem results when potential users are not always aware of relevant decision support technologies. If they are aware, they may not have access to, or own a copy of, technologies that might benefit them. Such technologies can require specific hardware and software configurations not possessed by potential users. Due to the complexity of developing decision technologies, many of them exist only as broadly-applicable general solutions, needing further customization before users can apply them. As new technologies are developed, their providers need proactive ways of advertising and informing potential customers. Moreover, providers must offer and maintain product versions that are consistent with the shifts in user platforms.

The DecisonNet objective is to use enabling features of the Web to address these problems. It provides solvers and allow for their remote execution. It is a brokered system that facilitates transactions between providers and consumers of decision technologies. Developers of solvers provide their solvers to be included in the DecisionNet and all users must register in order to use solvers from the system. Registered DecisionNet subscribers can access all DecisionNet services via a Web browser. They do not have to download, install, and execute the solvers on their own computational platforms. Instead, they access solvers remotely and run them on the provider's platform. This allows use of a solver on an as-needed basis (e.g., fee for use rather than purchase), even if a user does not have the necessary platform to run it.

3.2 Protocol Suite to Automate DSS Deployment on the World Wide Web

Modern organizations are undergoing significant transformations leading to major restructuring initiatives, eliminating management layers and empowering line personnel with greater decision making duties. However, today's line personnel typically have neither the budget nor the training to develop specialized, customized DSSs. Information system departments are also undergoing significant change. Some are being distributed into functional areas and many face increased outsourcing of application development, including DSSs. At the same time there are technological advances in end-user-interfaces, database management, model management systems, and AI.

Given these trends, Goul et al. (1997) call for a paradigm shift in DSS deployment involving the design, development, and validation of a protocol suite for deploying and sharing specific DSSs by commercial and academic entities, whereby those DSSs are accessible to end-users through the WWW. Already, users of WWW browsers can find and use Web sites that address their individual decision support needs, and/or the needs of their organization. However, current browsers do not have the ability to conduct intelligent searches for specific decision support resources independent of a decision maker who is busy with other matters. This inability exists because there is no common framework for intelligent DSS search.

With an agreed-upon suite of Open-DSS protocols, there is opportunity to develop the type of browsers end-users need in order to be led to specific decision support resources (Goul et al., 1997). In addition, the proposal of a suite of Open-DSS protocols can help to bring about standards. Such standards would be important for guaranteeing the integrity of specific decision support resources and would also help to yield a high level of service.

In the proposed open-system, decision support resources are to be distributed on individual Web pages, consistent with the way other knowledge is currently being offered. The Open-DSS protocol suite requires a DSS builder to also supply information about the specific decision support resource. This includes its purpose, computing environment, data inputs, and data outputs. It would be specified by the builders at the time of resource creation and could then be used to aid the discovery of desired decision support. Specialized WWW search agents (e.g., softbots, spiders, wanderers) would be used to identify addresses and build an index of protocol-compliant decision support applications. This index could then be searched by decision makers or their agents to identify resources that satisfy user-stipulated search parameters.

The open protocol contributes to the disintermediation of the WWW. It allows individual users or automated intelligent search agents to find any protocol-compliant resource, not just those posted with an individual broker. However, the open system has no mechanism to control what is put on the Web and portrayed as a DSS. As a comparison, note that in the DecisionNet approach, a DSS broker in the guise of DecisionNet is used to provide access to high quality, tested DSSs; specialized search agents or specialized browsers are unnecessary as search is required only within the index of registered DSSs. An extended version of the Open-DSS protocol proposed by Gregg and Goul (forthcoming) is designed to support deployment capabilities of both the open-system DSS and DecisionNet.

3.3 Electronic Brokerages for Decision Support

Kalakota, Stallaert, and Whinston (1996) point out that DSSs can be devised to take advantage of the wealth of real-time information (e.g., exchange rates, commodity prices) available through global interconnectivity. Such DSSs will be very different from traditional ones in the sense that they should be able to access and process knowledge from various sources worldwide, as well as accept user-specific (local) data requirements or constraints. They point out that these DSSs can be made publicly available over the same interconnected medium (e.g., the Internet) eliminating the need for a decision maker to acquire an individual copy of the software. Because support offered by such a DSS could be charged on a fee-per-run basis, the DSS plays the role of an electronic brokerage, where value is added through information collection, processing, and/or synthesis. This approach has been detailed for the class of DSSs that use domain-specific operations research (OR) solvers as decision aids to derive proposed solutions to user-stated problems (Kalakota, Stallaert, and Whinston, 1996).

As the number of domain-specific OR solvers publicly available increases, finding the correct OR solver (or server) in cyberspace may take considerable time. To ease this limitation Kalakota, Stallaert, and Whinston (1996) advocate intermediaries on the Web, called *electronic brokerages*, that maintain directories of information about available data sources, solvers, and other services on the Web. They identify four major benefits that enhance problem-solving efficiency in the Internet environment: minimizing knowledge search costs for the consumer in a distributed environment; creating a Yellow Pages directory that - in addition to directing users - provides an evaluation scheme for various pertinent resources; coordinating activities on the user's behalf during the OR transaction; and providing efficient post-processing facilities, such as result and report generation which conform to a user's graphical user interface.

Such brokerages can be staffed by *soft OR agents*. These are programs that know about a user's tastes, budget, and schedule and take care of personal jobs centered around managing knowledge. They execute rudimentary search and derivation of knowledge. A brokerage contains soft OR agents that maintain knowledge about users, OR servers, and data available in their various directories. These agents are triggered by incoming requests from a user via his or her Web browser and HTML documents. The request-reply sequence is accomplished using mail-enabled computing. One of a broker's soft OR agents is responsible for data collection from data servers on the Internet, checking data format and conversion, data transfer to the OR tool servers on the Internet, invoking an OR solver, and finally transferring outputs to the end-user as an HTML document. To a user, this soft OR agent is the DSS.

3.4 Intranet Decision Support

Organizations have become increasingly distributed, resulting in dispersed knowledge repositories. The idea of a centralized storehouse that holds all of an organization's knowledge is often simply not practical. For organizational decision support, a main objective is to achieve knowledge integration, so that a decision maker can easily select what is needed from distributed sources, share knowledge across applications, and have a stable repository for long term knowledge archiving. One approach to this objective is an intranet decision support framework comprised of a client-broker-server architecture to provide decision makers with accurate, comprehensive, consistent information (Ba, Kalakota, and Whinston, 1997).

The intranet decision support framework advocates creation of three kinds of intermediation agents to perform brokerage services between knowledge sources and decision makers, using structured documents such as Standard Generalized Markup Language (SGML). Interface agents reside on each client and perform knowledge base query processing and presentation. Retrieval agents reside on the broker server and interact with various directory services to find the knowledge needed by a user. Gateway agents ensure that knowledge sources on different servers are directly TCP/IP accessible or fit the Web environment.

The intranet DSS has four kinds of directories. The broker directory keeps track of company-wide knowledge that enables a broker to provide users with enterprise perspectives in their decision making. The other three directories (called data, model, and tool) could be located on either the broker server or individual departmental servers. Data directories maintain information about data (meta data). Model directories contain information on previously built decision models that can be used as building blocks for new model formulations. Tool directories maintain a list of solvers with their attributes.

3.5 Multiparticipant Decision Support on the Web

A multiparticipant decision support system (MDSS) is a computer-based system that supports the decision-making efforts of a decision maker comprised of multiple participants (Holsapple and Whinston, 1996). A major class of technology used in building MDSSs is groupware. This technology is designed to help enhance group performance (e.g., group decision making). Some is for use in special purpose decision rooms. However, it is increasingly developing in the direction of supporting groups whose participants work in different places at different times.

The Internet and the Web hold many possibilities for groupware (Fellers, Clifton, and Handley, 1995). Dennis (1998) lists four compelling technical reasons that make the Web and groupware a natural combination: the standardization of protocols and architecture enable true platform independence at the client side; the Web provides universal access without making any distinction where one is in relation to the server; no additional software is needed on the client once it has web access; the idea of a Web server. It follows that Web-based groupware is an important technology for creating multiparticipant WODSSs.

Today there are more than 75 Web-based groupware systems, with new ones being added every week (Dennis, Pootheri, and Natarajan, 1996). For instance, TCBWorks (http://tcbworks.cba.uga.edu/tcbworks/), developed at University of Georgia, is first-generation Web groupware that enables people working in different places and times to interact, discuss issues, and make group decisions. It is designed to support structured discussions and multicriteria decision making on a series of topics. It enables groups to build and edit pools of knowledge that aid in decision making. Other web groupware systems are web conferencing systems that power discussion forums on the Web. For example, with CU-SeeMe by Cornell University (http://cu-seeme.cornell.edu), a user can videoconference with another site located anywhere in the world. Multiple parties at different locations can participate via their own desktop computer in a CU-SeeMe conference wherein they strive to reach a joint decision. Web-based negotiation support systems are yet another kind of multiparticipant decision support facility. Examples include the INSPIRE and INSS systems developed at Carleton University (http://www.budsiness.carleton.ca /interneg).

3.6 Consumer-Oriented Decision Support Systems on the Web

On the Web today, numerous decision support resources are readily available on a vast array of sites to support both every day and major decisions that consumers make. Often, these facilities may not be thought of or labeled as DSSs. Nevertheless, they provide decision support in one way or another. Some of these sites provide support in a passive way - a user visits the site, finds some relevant knowledge, and factors it into his or her decision making. Other sites are interactive. They allow users to pose a problem and receive a solution (i.e., some relevant knowledge) that can be factored into making a decision about the problem.

Specific examples of passive and interactive decision support resources abound on the Web today. For example, **MyYahoo** (http://my.yahoo.com/) is a customizable version of Yahoo that allows users to build content modules such as a portfolio module that offers personalized knowledge for supporting investment decisions. In this module, the securities (including stocks and mutual funds), purchase price, and number of shares can be entered. A user can then track relevant information such as delayed quotes, trends, earnings per share, P/E ratios, news and profiles of companies invested and so forth. **The National Association of Realtors** site (http://www.realtor.com/) supports decisions about home buying. In their own chosen locales nationwide, potential home buyers can enter required search criteria such as type of home, approximate price, minimum number of bedrooms, baths, and square footage. To enhance the search a user may also enter optional search criteria including general features of homes, interior and exterior requirements, lot size. Homes that come closest to user's desires are listed in the order of closest match. For support of travel decisions, one may visit sites such as Microsoft's **Expedia** (http://expedia.msn.com). Expedia provides a world guide, hotel directory, travel magazine, expert opinions, and travel tips all rolled into one. It can also serve as a personal travel assistant remembering information such as past and future travel plans, airplane seat and meal preferences, frequent flyer numbers, and so forth. Such sites as these provide decision support to masses of consumers on a daily basis.

3.7 WODSS Taxonomies

The foregoing research and practitioner efforts to enhance decision support on the Web reflects a considerable range of WODSS perspectives and issues. For the most part, these efforts have focused on certain WODSS aspects, without considering the emerging WODSS phenomenon as a whole. There are diverse kinds of decision support systems available on the Web today and all are, obviously, not the same. Consequently, some framework is needed to help users, developers, educators, and researchers bring some structure and organization to the young WODSS field. To achieve this purpose and highlight future WODSS possibilities in electronic commerce, we introduce three taxonomies in the sections that follow.

One obvious taxonomy is to categorize WODSSs according to the subject areas about which they have knowledge. This is particularly beneficial for users and educators. Another useful way to look at WODSSs is in terms of the knowledge-management techniques they employ. This taxonomy, discussed in Section 5, classifies WODSSs based on the particular technique or techniques used for representing and processing knowledge. It is of principal interest to WODSS developers who select techniques and tools to build WODSSs. While it may also be of interest to developers, a third taxonomy is advanced to provoke WODSS researchers. Described in Section 6, it identifies different possibilities for coordinating the distributed components of a WODSS. Each of these possibilities suggests various research topics that deserve further investigation.

4 Subject-Oriented Taxonomies

One way to organize an understanding of WODSSs is in terms of the subjects about which they can provide knowledge. Such a taxonomy is of principal value to prospective users. The potential user of WODSSs has in mind a subject about which he or she needs further knowledge to factor into a decision making process. Within or across decision processes, knowledge may be needed about multiple subject areas. That is, a user typically has a need for knowledge in multiple subject areas. It follows that a taxonomy of WODSSs organized according to such subjects would be useful. In each category, the user would identify decision support resources pertaining to a particular subject of interest. The result is a user-specific, subject-oriented directory of decision support resources on the Web.

Of course, decision makers differ on what subjects are of interest, reflecting variations in the decision domains with which they deal, in their approaches to decision making, and in their individual knowledge preferences. Subject categories can be defined broadly or as relatively narrow niches. They may be organized in a hierarchical fashion, with narrow subject categories being clustered into broader multi-subject categories. It can also happen that subjects overlap. Thus, determining universally acceptable categories for a WODSSs subject-oriented taxonomy may not be feasible. Nevertheless, we can propose a collection of subject categories as a starting point for modification and extension by users to suit their own needs.

Table 1 presents subject-oriented taxonomy of decision support resources relevant to consumer decision making. For each category, it shows examples of sites that provide knowledge in the indicated subject area. This may be knowledge selected from a repository at the site or knowledge derived at the site. The specific categories in Table 1 are drawn primarily from a substantial compilation of DSS instructional materials existing at http://www.uky.edu/BusinessEconomics/dssakba/ and used in DSS coursework assignments. It appears that the taxonomy can be of some benefit to DSS educators and students in structuring study of WODSSs, as well as benefiting DSS users. Higher level categories could be imposed on those shown in Table 1. For instance, the vehicle, travel, and real estate subjects could be clustered into a category dealing with knowledge for purchasing decisions.

A companion subject-oriented WODSS taxonomy can be devised for managerial decision making. Following from the EC definition introduced earlier, its subject categories would mirror the major activities in a value chain. These are the 1) primary activities of inbound logistics, production, outbound logistics, sales and marketing, and customer service, and 2) support activities of infrastructure, human resources management, technology development, and purchasing (Porter, 1985). Each of these is a subject area of knowledge that could be addressed by decision support resources on the Internet or an intranet. For instance, Aspect Development Publishers has constructed a Web site (http://www.aspectdv.com) that provides knowledge to support procurement decisions.

A browser's bookmark facility can be used to keep track of favorite decision support resources in each subject area, with a folder being created for each category.

Alternatively, meta sites can be constructed such that their links to decision support resources are organized according to subject. Consumer World (http://www.con sumerworld.org) is an example of such a meta site for consumer decision making.

Table 1. A subject-oriented WODSS taxonomy with examples

Problem domain	Specific examples	URL
Career decisions	CareerSite virtual resources, online job search facilities	http://www.cereersite.com/
	COMPUTERWORLD Online Career Agent	http://careeragent.computer world.com/
	JobSmart career guides, salary surveys	http://jobsmart.org/jobsmart. htm
Financial decisions	Deloitte & Touche's PeerScape, company analysis, research	http://www.peerscape.com/
	Financenter calculators for invest-ment, advisory reports	http://financenter.com/invest .htm
	Prudential Securities advice, strate-gies, calculators	http://www.prusec.com/
Health decisions	Lifelines, knowledge about preven-tive care	http://www.lifelines.com
	Medscape, knowledge about medical specialties, medical calculators	http://www.medscape.com
	Pharmaceutical Information Net-work, knowledge about drugs, their uses, side effects	http://pharminfo.com
Insurance decisions	Financenter calculators for key in-surance decisions	http://www.financenter.com/ insure.htm
	Quicken InsureMarket, online insur-ance resource, comparisons, tips, risk evaluator	http://www.insuremarket.co m/
	SmartCalc modifiable calculators	http://www.smartcalc.com/S martCalc/do-cs/calclist.htm
Investment decisions	BigCharts, online charting, quotes, research	http://www.bigcharts.com/do cs/about.htm
	Fidelty online investment solvers, news, data	http://personal12.fidelity.co m:80/
	MyYAHOO! customizable personal quotes, related news	http://my.yahoo.com/
Relocation decisions	Financenter calculators, advice for finding realtors, mortgages, renting vs. owning	http://www.financenter.com/ homes.htm

Table 1. continued

Problem domain	Specific examples	URL
	Homebuyer's fair relocation calculators to compute cost of living, moving cost, relocation wizard plan moving with a custom timeline	http://www.homefair.com/home/
	Virtual relocation, calculate the financial impact of relocation, cost-of-living summaries and analysis	http://www.homefair.com/home/
Retirement decisions	ATR social security estimator, news about social security reform, taxes	http://atr.org/
	Financenter calculators for retirement decisions, advice for retirement plans, IRA's, credit reports and monitoring	http://www.financenter.com/retire.htm
	T. Rowe price calculators, profiles, FAQs	http://rps.troweprice.com/main.html
Vehicle decisions	Autoweb, car search, buying guide, auto talk	http://www.autoweb.com/
	Carpoint, car searches, pricing, descriptions	http://carpoint.msn.com/Home/Highlights
	OnlineAuto, car searches	http://www.onlineauto.com

5 A Technique-Oriented Taxonomy

Regardless of various subject domains, WODSSs can be viewed in terms of the knowledge-management technique employed to implement them. This is of particular interest to developers who must choose and use these techniques. The technique-oriented WODSS taxonomy stems from an application of the generic DSS architecture, which involves four interrelated components: a language system comprised of all messages a DSS can accept, a presentation system comprised of all messages a DSS can emit, a knowledge system (KS) comprised of all knowledge a DSS has stored and retained, and a problem processing system (PPS) which is the DSS's software engine (Holsapple and Whinston, 1996). The first three are systems of knowledge representation. The fourth element is what works to recognize and solve problems. In doing so, a PPS exercises one or another technique for processing knowledge representations in the KS. This gives rise to many special cases of the generic DSS architecture, each specializing in a particular technique(s) for representing and processing knowledge (Holsapple and Whinston, 1996). Table 2 presents a WODSS taxonomy based on common knowledge management techniques. Although other techniques exist (e.g., neural network) and new techniques may be devised, these categories seem to be the most prominent. The categories are illustrated with WODSS examples.

A text-oriented WODSS supports a decision maker by providing knowledge represented as electronic documents. Its PPS accepts requests to access desired chunks of text from those held and possibly hyperlinked in its KS. The access can involve exploratory browsing in search of stimulative ideas that have a bearing on a decision to be made. It may be a focused search for some particular piece of knowledge needed to make a decision. Or it may be knowledge delivered via push technology or intelligent agents. The KS contents can be electronic versions of alerts, research reports, news, tutorials, guidelines, advice, procedures, descriptions, narratives, and so forth. Extending in the direction of multimedia, the textual representation may be accompanied by pictorial images, graphics, and audio such that the hypertext WODSS becomes a hypermedia WODSS.

In a database-oriented WODSS, the KS contents are organized in a highly structured fashion according to some data model (e.g., in relational tables or multidimensional cubes). The knowledge tends to be primarily descriptive and can be extremely voluminous. Examples include descriptions of historical price patterns of stocks, real estate for sale, job openings, vendors, and product specifications. Some of the database content may be represented as pictures, text, video, or audio in addition to customary numeric and string values. The PPS includes a database control system, plus an interactive query processor and/or various custom-built processors. Its main function from a user's viewpoint is to conduct selective searches of KS databases and present the resultant knowledge to be factored into decision making.

The user of a spreadsheet-oriented WODSS inputs data values describing some problem of interest (e.g., a what-if problem). The PPS uses formulas held in the KS to calculate a solution to that problem. The values are typically input by filling in slots on an electronic form, although there may be some variations such as responding to a menu that lists possible values. The slots can be arranged in a conventional spreadsheet grid patterns, but often appear in a more free form pattern without display of the formulas. These free-form renditions of spreadsheets are often called worksheets, calculators, or electronic forms (Holsapple and Whinston, 1988); each is comprised of knowledge about the data entry form, the formulas that are to be applied to entered data, and the presentation of calculation results. The PPS that uses these KS contents is able to process indicated forms, execute stored formulas, and produce indicated presentations of results to be factored into a user's decision making.

A *solver* is an executable algorithm that can solve any member of a particular class of problems. The calculator defined by spreadsheet formulas or that underlies a worksheet form could be regarded as a simple kind of solver. But much more complex algorithms, involving more than expression evaluation or sequences of assignment statements, are the focus of solver-oriented WODSSs. Their solvers address such problem classes as simulation, regression, portfolio analysis, or linear optimization. A solver-oriented WODSS can be fixed (i.e., part of the PPS) or flexible (i.e., part of the KS) (Holsapple and Whinston, 1996). It accepts a user's statement of a problem, and may even assist in formulating the problem statement. Where there are multiple solver candidates, the problem statement identifies which is to be used. A problem statement will also either include or indicate where to access any data that pertain to characterizing the problem. The PPS executes the selected solvers to derive knowledge (i.e., a solution) that is presented for the user to factor into a decision-making episode.

Table 2. A technique-oriented taxonomy with examples

Orientation	Specific examples of URL	Knowledge provided to users
Text	Jobsmart http://jobsmart.org/	Career, resume, guidance; job tips
	Expedia http://www.expedia.com/	Travel alerts, news, tips, guidelines
Database	National Association of Realtors http://38.248.210.43/home.htm/	Search database of over one million homes using user-specified screens
	OnlineAuto http://www.onlineauto.com	Search database of pre-owned and new autos using user-specified screens
Spreadsheet	SmartCalc http://www.smartcalc.com/SmartCalc/docs/calclist.htm	Numerous calculators for consumers
	Diversified Investment Retirement Solutions http;//www.divinvest.com/023DIA.html	Worksheet for savings rate calculation
Solver	Diet Problem http://www.mcs.anl.goy/Home/otc/Guide/CaseStudies/diet/index.html	Results from online linear optimization solver that finds cheapest combination of foods to satisfy daily nutritional needs
	Cutting-Stock Problem http://www.mcs.anl.goy/Home/otc/Guide/CaseStudies/cutting/index.html	Results from integer programming solver that minimizes waste in cutting small orders from large stock
Rule	Spacecraft Environmental Anomalies Expert System http://envnet.gsfc.nasa.gov/Expert_System/Expert_System.html	Provides advice about causes of anomalies in the space environment
	Confined Spaces Advisor http://www.osha.gov/wren/csa.html	Provides expert advice on protecting workers from confined space hazards
Compound	MoneyNet http://www.moneynet.com/home/MONEYNET/homepage/homepage.asp	Provides news, quotes, profiles; generates graphics from historical price database; portfolio worksheet
	Homebuyer's Fair http://homefair.com/home/	Provides tips, guidelines; selects from databases with school, crime, city snapshot information; various relocation calculators

A rule-oriented WODSS represents and processes reasoning knowledge in the guise of rules. Each rule specifies what conclusions can be drawn under certain circumstances. The KS contains one or more sets of rules representing expertise that can be used to derive advice about situations in some domain of interest. The PPS accepts (and may guide) a user's characterization of a situation and does logical inference with a KS rule set to produce advice (i.e., knowledge) that a user can factor into decision making.

A compound WODSS is one that makes substantial use of two or more knowledge management techniques. For instance, a WODSS that supports investment decisions could use text management (e.g., to provide knowledge about recent news, company profiles, analysts' reports, and investing principles), database management (e.g., to furnish knowledge about company fundamentals, analysts' ratings, price and volume histories), and spreadsheet management (i.e., to furnish knowledge about impacts on portfolios). A compound WODSS could be built with a single PPS that tightly integrates multiple knowledge management techniques (e.g., using the synergistic approach to software integration) (Holsapple and Whinston, 1996).

In each of the above WODSS categories, the knowledge management technique(s) a developer chooses determine(s) how the KS contents are structured and what kinds of problem processing can be done by the PPS. Although WODSSs have been built in each category, there appears to be considerable room for improving development tools to facilitate a developer's efforts in using one or another knowledge management techniques on the Web (Kalakota and Whinston, 1997). One approach for progress along this line is for tool vendors that specialize in a particular technique to consider how to extend their current tools in order to ease the development of WODSSs.

6 A Coordination-oriented Taxonomy

The final taxonomy introduced here stems from the recognition that the PPS and KS of a WODSS are distributed. Each has local and remote components with the distributed PPS components working together to process knowledge existing in the distributed KS components: that is, the distributed components of a WODSS need to be coordinated in some fashion. Variations in how this can be done gives rise to a coordination-oriented taxonomy of WODSSs that is of interest primarily to researchers and developers.

One way to organize an understanding of coordination in WODSSs is in terms of two underlying dimensions: *distribution* and *assistance*. The first of these refers to the pattern of distribution among local and remote components of a WODSS. Is it a simple pattern with few components or a complex pattern with many components? Is the pattern known and fixed in advance of decision support, or does it unfold in the course of a decision support session? Whereas the distribution dimension characterizes the structure subject to coordination, the assistance dimension characterizes the dynamics of coordination. Are the interactions among distributed components direct and unassisted, or is there an intermediary that assists with coordinating the interactions? The taxonomy identifies three cases of distribution and two cases of assistance, giving rise to the six types of WODSSs shown in Table 3.

All three cases of distribution involve a local processor. They differ in terms of remote components: a single remote domain processor, a fixed set of multiple remote domain processors, and a variable set of remote domain processors. A domain processor is typically accompanied by a knowledge-store on which it operates to recognize and/or solve problems in a particular domain. It employs one or more knowledge management techniques to address problems in some subject area. The two cases on the assistance dimension are non-brokered and brokered. In the former, the local processor and domain processors interact directly with each other, coordinating their own respective activities (possibly under a user's guidance). In the brokered case, one or more brokers intervene to guide such coordination efforts as managing supplier-consumer relationships, simultaneity constraints, task-subtask relationships, and resource allocation. Thus, the six types of WODSSs differ in terms of the configuration of domain processors and brokers that, along with a local processor, constitute their respective PPSs. They also differ in terms of the accompanying KS contents.

The problem processing system of a Type I WODSS is comprised of a local processor on a client computer and a domain processor on a server. The local processor is commonly a browser which enables the user to invoke the domain processor, view its responses, and execute applets it provides. The domain processor is server software that manipulates (e.g., stores, selects, derives, presents) representations of domain knowledge residing on the server. This includes CGI scripts which are gateways allowing the acquisition of knowledge from other application systems (i.e., other support centers). The knowledge storehouse(s) manipulated by a domain processor is the remote portion of a WODSS's knowledge system. It may be represented as HTML hypertext, databases, worksheet forms, solvers (e.g., applets), rules, and so forth.The local portion of the KS is modest, consisting of the domain processor's URL and browser settings reflecting a user's preferences.

Separately, neither the local processor nor domain processor can function as the PPS of a WODSS. Together, they function as a distributed PPS that is able to accept a user's problem solving (or problem recognizing) requests within the subject domain covered by the domain processor, and provide corresponding responses (i.e., knowledge) that can be factored into the user's decision making. Coordination mechanics are largely embedded within the pps elements based on standard protocol assumptions. A Type I WODSS is appropriate when a single Web site is sufficient for meeting a decision maker's knowledge needs. Creating such a WODSS is accomplished by identifying the URL of such a Web site for bookmarking. This identification may be a lengthy process involving considerable Web exploration (via a search engine and/or surfing). Or, it may involve simply the acceptance of the URL from a trusted source such as a publication or advisor.

Table 3. A coordination-oriented taxonomy

ASSISTANCE / DISTRIBUTION	Non-Brokered		Brokered	
Single	**TYPE I**		**TYPE II**	
	PPS	**KS**	**PPS**	**KS**
	Browser + DP	Browser Settings URL of Remote Site Domain Knowledge	Browser + Broker + DP	Browser Settings URL of Remote Site Broker Knowledge Domain Knowledge
Multiple/ Fixed	**TYPE III**		**TYPE IV**	
	PPS	**KS**	**PPS**	**KS**
	Browser + [DP$_1$: DP$_n$]	Browser Settings URLs of Remote Sites Domain Knowledge	Browser + Broker + [DP$_1$: DP$_n$]	Browser Settings URLs of Remote Sites Broker Knowledge Domain Knowledge
Multiple/ Variable	**TYPE V**		**TYPE VI**	
	PPS	**KS**	**PPS**	**KS**
	Browser + [DP$_1$: DP$_i$]	Browser Settings URLs of Remote Sites Domain Knowledge	Browser + Broker + [DP$_1$: DP$_i$]	Browser Settings URLs of Remote Sites Broker Knowledge Domain Knowledge

DP : Domain Processor
DP$_i$: a variable number of sites
DP$_n$: a fixed number of 'n' known sites

PPS : Problem processing System
KS : Knowledge System

A Type II WODSS has Type I features plus the inclusion of a value-adding broker(s) as a third constituent of the PPS. A broker can be thought of being a facilitator. Because the distribution pattern is relatively simple, the roles that a broker could play are somewhat limited. One way that a broker could add value is to customize the user's interactions with the local and/or domain processors. The broker would assume responsibilities for knowledge presentation and rendering at the client site (Ba, Kalakota, and Whinston, 1995). Based on its knowledge of the client environment and the user's presentation preferences, the broker would examine a response from the domain processor to determine what program to invoke to produce an appropriate customized presentation of the response (i.e., as a substitute for a standard browser presentation). Just as such a broker functions as a part of the WODSS's problem processing system, the knowledge that it uses (including its library of presentation programs) functions as a part of the WODSS's knowledge system.

Another example of a broker in a Type II WODSS is one that coordinates user requests rather than responses to the user. It may be convenient for a user to issue some requests or parts of requests in ways that are not readily accommodated by a browser. For instance, a request could be very large, involving entire files of data needed to fully characterize a problem. A user would prefer not to interactively enter this data in browser-presented forms. The files of data on the client may not be arranged in formats that are directly useable to a domain processor. A broker could add value by coordinating the transferal from client files to the domain processor. Based on an indication of what portions of client files are relevant for a request, the broker would use its knowledge of those files' structures and of the input format requirements of the domain processor to perform the desired mapping. Such a broker would thus function as a part of the PPS and the knowledge it draws on (including a library of mapping modules) functions as part of the KS.

Brokers like those outlined above are instrumental in extending a WODSS's language system and presentation system beyond what is available in a Type I WODSS. Using a suite of Open-DSS protocols for domain processors (along the lines of those noted in Section 3.2) would be helpful in implementing such brokers. It is conceivable that the broker and its knowledge could reside on the client side or server side, at the same or a different support center than that where the domain processor resides.

A variety of research issues exist for the first two WODSS types, including the following: Would it be beneficial to devise a "thin" browser, simplified to have only those features that are useful for Type I and Type II WODSSs? If so, exactly what features should be included? Are there additional features, beyond those available in common browsers, that would be beneficial to include in the WODSS's local root processor? For instance, can the browser's message managing capabilities be effectively integrated on the client with other knowledge management techniques (e.g., using a synergistic approach to software integration (Holsapple and Whinston, 1996)), giving a local as well as remote domain processing capability? Where should a Type II broker reside and what tools would be helpful in developing these brokers? Would it be feasible and useful to incorporate broker capabilities into the local processor, rather than treating them as separate entity within the PPS? What can the developer of a domain processor do to increase the likelihood of its inclusion in large numbers of WODSSs?

It may happen that a decision maker is unable to construct a suitable Type I or Type II WODSS because of an inability to identify a domain processor with capabilities sufficient to meet his or her decision support needs. However, those needs may be met by a set of domain processors in a Type III WODSS. For instance, in making investment decisions, it may be desirable to use all three domain processors shown for the investment subject area in Table 1. The local processor in the Type III case behaves as it does in the Type I case, with the exception that it has bookmarked multiple domain processors. Sequencing the use of these PPS components within a decision-making episode is at the discretion of the user.

There may be multiple levels of domain processors within the set that participates in the PPS. Domain processors whose URLs are held in the local portion of the knowledge system form the first level. The second level (if any) is comprised of useful domain processors not in the first level, but which are linked to by KS contents for first-level domain processors. Third and subsequent levels are similarly identified. Creating a Type III WODSS is accomplished by identifying first-level URLs for bookmarking (e.g., in a folder reserved for the WODSS). With this type of WODSS, a user uses the local processor to contact a desired domain processor, submit requests to it, present responses from it, and perhaps execute applets that it provides. As demanded or inspired by the flow of problem recognition/solving transactions within a decision making episode, the user contacts other domain processors in the set. This may involve remembering responses from one processor and then entering parts of these responses in requests to another domain processor (an inconvenience that does not exist with Type I WODSSs). Over time, it can happen that a routine pattern for processor contacts emerges, becoming a user's habitual or standard for using the WODSS.

A Type IV WODSS has the Type III features, plus the inclusion of a value-adding broker(s) in the PPS. Such a broker could perform facilitation activities like Type II brokers. But because of the existence of multiple domain processors, additional coordination issues arise that may be facilitated by Type IV brokers. For instance, it may be that the identification of the set of n domain processors is done by a broker (i.e., the broker's URL may replace URLs of the first level of domain processors in the local KS). It is the broker that ensures the quality (i.e., utility and validity) of domain processors that it identifies. The broker may document the qualities of identified processors for user viewing. DecisionNet (Section 3.1) is an example of such a broker.

Beyond identification and quality assurances, brokers in a Type IV WODSS may facilitate supplier-consumer relationships among domain processors. Rather than the Type III approach of having a user pass results from one processor to another, a broker may take care of this (performing any requisite reformatting transformations along the way). In the case of large volume transferals, such a capability is a big time saver. In effect, this kind of brokerage facilitates the management of a knowledge supply chain within the WODSS. A Type IV broker may also determine or recommend patterns of domain processor contacts. This could be based on its recognition of a user's habits, an analysis of domain processor's capabilities with respect to user needs, an ability to do task-subtask coordination, or the conduct of an auction among the n domain processors for the right (perhaps compensated) to perform some needed processing.

A variety of research issues exist for Type III and Type IV WODSSs including the following: What are the relative advantages and disadvantages of these types of WODSSs versus Types I and II? From a user's perspective? From a domain processor developer's perspective? What features could be added to a Type I local processor to better cope with multiple domain processors (e.g., an ability to annotate bookmarks, rate the domain processors on various dimensions, recall/highlight second and lower level processors that are most valuable, automate the pattern of contacts)? Should brokerage functions be partitioned among specialized brokers or combined in a super broker? Where should a Type IV broker reside? To what extent can or should brokerage function be incorporated into local or domain processors? What can the developers of brokers or domain processors do to increase the possibility of widespread inclusion in WODSSs?

It may happen that a decision maker is unable to identify a fixed set of domain processors appropriate to his or her needs. In situations where the decisions to be made are very unstructured, this becomes more likely. Rather than working with familiar domain processors, the decision maker is in more of an exploratory mode regarding the constitution of a WODSS. There are few (if any) preconceptions about what domain processors to use. Instead, the WODSS is constructed on the fly, in the course of making a decision. The local processor is present and one or a few domain processors have been identified as with Types I and III. But, additional (as yet undetermined) domain processors are needed.

By ad hoc identification and evaluation of candidate processors, those to be used in the Type V WODSS are determined. Identification of candidates may occur via hyperlinks from domain processors already included or via recommendations from personal or published sources. A priori, the variable number of domain processors to be used in the WODSS is unknown. As each new one is included, the local processor may keep track of its URL. After the decision making episode with a Type V WODSS concludes, the WODSS may be either thrown away (i.e., a record of the domain processors used is discarded) or reviewed and reworked (e.g., possibly discarding domain processors that proved to be of marginal value) to evolve into a Type III WODSS.

Like a Type V WODSS, a Type VI WODSS has a variable number of domain processors identified in the course of working on a decision. But its PPS also includes a broker(s). A broker for a Type VI WODSS could perform any of the functions carried out by Type II or IV brokers. However, it may also be equipped to cope with the variable number of just-in-time domain processors. Search engines, directories, and metasites are straightforward examples of such brokers. A more extensive example, which can be personalized to an individual user, is the softORagent described in Section 3.3. Each of these kinds of brokers becomes the local processor's main entry point into the Web for identification, evaluation, and use of domain processors that can provide knowledge to be factored into the concurrent decision process. With a Type VI WODSS, the Web itself serves as a vast distributed processor and knowledge storehouse through which a broker helps light a path for the decision maker.

Research issues for Type V and VI WODSSs include the following: Can a Type V WODSS have any ongoing existence beyond the decision episode during which it is created and used (e.g., retaining portions of its KS as a basis for the next Type V WODSS that is created)? What local processor facilities would be helpful in using a Type V WODSS to establish or evolve into a Type III WODSS? What are the best sources other than brokers, for obtaining the "seed" URLs for a Type V WODSS? Under what circumstances is one kind of Type VI broker preferred to others? What technologies and methodologies are needed to customize Type VI brokers for individual user's tasks and needs in discovering and evaluating domain processors? Under what conditions are Type VI WODSSs preferred to Type IV WODSSs, and vice versa? When should creation of a Type V or VI WODSS be terminated by abandoning further efforts to identify and evaluate domain processors?

7 Conclusion

Hundreds of companies have built technologies that aim to enable electronic commerce in a variety of ways. These technologies have been used to develop a multitude of EC applications. Some of these applications are for processing transactions. Other EC application systems (or parts of them) are for providing decision support. In the world of electronic commerce "...home-run opportunities belong to companies with people who deeply understand how the Internet as a channel can serve that industry. These companies will build Websites that aggregate buyers and sellers to help facilitate both the decision making process and the subsequent delivery of products or services" (Gurley, 1997).

Advances in technology will ease the development of decision support application systems in electronic commerce and enhance the potential effectiveness of such systems. Researchers will lay the groundwork for these advances by addressing issues in such topic areas as local processors, domain processors, brokers, their interplay, and their deployment. The research initiatives summarized in Section 3 are important first steps in the direction of improved DSS applications in electronic commerce. The taxonomies provide ways of organizing research efforts.

For instance, investigation of local processors would provide a better understanding of issues such as those that follow: Using bookmarks to do site-hopping is primitive; maybe the PPS's local processor should have multiple slots, one for each site (a multitasking browser). Domain processors are often independent; could a local processor provide a common interface for coordinating transfers of knowledge among them (e.g., perhaps using a clipboard feature to move knowledge among domain processors, using some form of mapping so that an output schema of one domain processor would be accepted by an input schema of another)? The local KS has potential to be more than a bookmark; perhaps it should be able to store a user profile to customization of decision support behaviors, or the local KS may hold frequently needed knowledge for requests so that it can be used again without re-typing given a user profile; a browser may be more intelligent in contacting and using relevant sites; it can evaluate results obtained from sites. Macro capabilities may be useful in a local processor. A local processor should give users a chance to edit and annotate bookmarks and folders; this could allow it to keep a user's ratings of sites and automatically display them during navigation. We contend that efforts to address research issues in any of the topic areas can benefit from a knowledge management view of decision support (Holsapple and Whinston, 1996), of organizations (Holsapple and Whinston, 1988), and of electronic commerce (Holsapple and Singh, 1998). This view serves as a unified perspective for appreciating the growing convergence of these three areas.

References

Applegate, L. M., C. W. Holsapple, R. Kalakota, F. J. Radermacher, and A. B. Whinston, "Electronic Commerce: Building Blocks of New Business Opportunity," *Journal of Organizational Computing and Electronic Commerce*, 6, 1 (1996), 1-10.

Applegate, L. M., J. I. Cash, Jr., and D. Q. Miles, "Information Technology and Tomorrow's Manager," H*arvard Business Review*, November, 1988.

Auger, P. and J. M. Gallaugher, "Factors Affecting the Adoption of an Internet-Based Sales Presence for Small Businesses," *The Information Society*, 13, 1 (January-March 1997), 55-74.

Ba, S., R. Kalakota, and A. B. Whinston, "Executable Documents as the Basis for DSS," *ISDSS Conference Proceedings Volume 2*, Hong Kong, 1995, 373-379.

Ba, S., R. Kalakota, and A. B. Whinston, "Using Client-Broker-Server Architecture for Intranet Decision Support," *Decision Support Systems,* 19, 3 (March 1997), 171-192.

Berners-Lee, T. (interview), "Web Inventer Berners-Lee Reflects on the Web's Origins and Future," *PC Magazine On-Line*, May 30, 1996,
http://www.zdnet.com/news/trends/t960530b.htm.

Bhargava, H. K., R. Krishnan, and R. Muller, "Decision Support on Demand: Emerging Electronic Markets for Decision Technologies," *Decision Support Systems*, 19, 3 (1997), 193-214.

Bui, T. X., "Decision Support in the Future Tense," *Decision Support Systems*, 19, 3 (1997), 149-150.

Dennis, A. R., S. K. Pootheri, and V. Natarajan, "TCBWorks: A First Generation Web-Groupware System," http://tcbworks.cba.uga.edu/, 1998.

Drucker, P. F., "The Age of Social Transformation," *Atlantic Monthly*, 274, 5 (1994).

Fellers, J. W., A. Clifton, and H. Handley, "Using the Internet to Provide Support for Distributed Interactions," *Proceedings of the Twenty-Eight Annual Hawaiian International Conference of System Sciences*, 1995, 52-60.

Goul, M., A. Philippakis, M. Y. Kiang, D. Fernandes, and R. Otondo, "Requirements for the Design of a Protocol Suite to Automate DSS Deployment on the World Wide Web: A Client/Server Approach," *Decision Support Systems*, 19, 3 (1997), 151-170.

Gregg, D. G. and M. Goul, "A Proposal for an Open DSS Protocol," *Communications of the ACM*, forthcoming.

Gurley, J. W., "Creating a Great E-Commerce Business," *Fortune*, March 16, 1997, 146-148.

Holsapple, C. W. and A. B. Whinston, *Manager's Guide to Expert Systems*, Irwin,Homewood, IL, 1986.

Holsapple, C. W. and A. B. Whinston, "Knowledge-Based Organizations," *The Information Society*, 5, 2 (1987).

Holsapple, C. W. and A. B. Whinston, *The Information Jungle*, Dow Jones-Trwin, Homewood, IL, 1988.

Holsapple, C. W. and A. B. Whinston , *Decision Support Systems: A Knowledge-Based Approach*, West, St. Paul, MN, 1996.

Holsapple, C. W. and M. Singh, "Knowledge-Oriented Approach to Electronic Commerce," *Kentucky Initiative for Knowledge Management*, Research Paper No. 116, 1998, College of Business and Economics, University of Kentucky.

Kalakota, R. and A. B. Whinston, *Frontiers of Electronic Commerce*, Addison-Wesley, Reading MA, 1996.

Kalakota, R., J. Stallaert, and A. B. Whinston, "Worldwide Real-Time Decision Support Systems for Electronic Commerce Applications," *Journal of Organizational Computing and Electronic Commerce*, 11, 32 (1996), 11-32.

Porter, M., *Competitive Advantage*, Free Press, NY, 1985.

Power, D. J., "Finding Decision Support Systems Resources on the World-Wide Web," http://dss.cba.uni.edu/papers/dssresources.html.

Turban, E. and J. E. Aronson, *Decision Support Systems and Intelligent Systems*, Prentice Hall, NJ, 1998.

Yadav, S. B. and N. Shaw, "A Comprehensive Framework for Understanding Electronic Commerce," *Proceedings of the 1997 Information Resources Management Conferences*, Vancouver, 446-450.

Part VII
Information Services and Digital Products

CHAPTER 27
The Internet Information Market:
The Emerging Role of Intermediaries

P. K. Kannan[1], Ai-Mei Chang[2], and Andrew B. Whinston[3]

[1]Department of Marketing, The Robert H. Smith School of Business, University of Maryland, College Park, MD 20742, USA, pkannan@rhsmith.umd.edu

[2]Information Resources Management College, National Defense University, Washington, DC 20319, USA, chang@ndu.edu

[3]Department of Management Sciences and Information Systems, University of Texas, Austin, TX 78712, USA, abw@uts.cc.utexas.edu

This chapter surveys the market for information and information products on the I-Way with a specific focus on marketing information that is generated, collected, and processed and/or marketed /distributed on the Internet. We describe the nature of such information and information products with illustrative examples and highlight the unique features of the Internet information market. We discuss, from economic and social perspectives, the evolution of specific organizational and social structures that are necessary for a thriving information market on the Internet and provide evidence of such trends on the I-Way.

Keywords: Marketing Information; Marketing Research; Information Economics; Consumer Privacy; E-Communities; Intermediaries

1 Introduction

It is undeniable that the Internet is fast changing the ways in which commerce is conducted currently – from marketing products and services to businesses and consumers to understanding consumer behavior and interacting with businesses and consumers regarding their preferences and needs. While some view the Internet as another channel to reach markets, others are of the opinion that the Internet transcends the traditional channel functions and is a paradigm change from traditional channels. Whatever be the perspective one adopts, it is a fact that the new "channel" is ushering in changes at many levels in the market – at the organizational as well as at consumers' level (Business Week, 1997a). The purpose of this chapter is to explore these changes and trends in the context of the marketing information and information products market.

The central theme of our chapter can be clearly understood in the context of Figure 1. In traditional commerce, organizations and consumers interact with each other – through information exchanges and transactions – in a medium which is, for most part, non-electronic and which consists of conventional channels. The features of these channels largely determine the organizational forms, industry structures, and societal forms that characterize traditional commerce. When the non-electronic medium is replaced/augmented by the Internet, the interactions between organizations and consumers are subjected to the unique features of the Internet medium. Some of these features include instantaneous global reach (geographical independence), an order of magnitude increase in the scale and dimensionality of information, asynchronous two-way interactions, decreased transaction costs, control over participant identities and anonymity, rapid spread of information, complete and accurate capture of all transactional information, and so on. The questions of interest to both academics and practitioners are: how will the medium affect the organizational forms and market structure and how will society and consumers react to the medium and its impact on organizations and markets? These questions, as we will see, have special relevance to markets that are digital in nature – information products and information services, whether generated and produced on the Internet or otherwise – as the unique features of the Internet impact these products and services more significantly than any other. An understanding of this impact will be useful in designing organizational structures, setting up institutional guidelines and commercial policies, and designing consumer co-operatives that facilitate the best use of the Internet as a commercial medium.

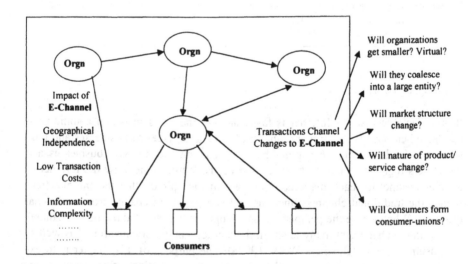

Fig. 1. Market interactions and medium of interactions

This chapter is organized as follows. In Section 2 we present some illustrations and features of the Internet information market and some examples of how marketing information is generated on the Internet. These examples cover both business-to-business situations as well as consumer-oriented cases. Section 3 focuses on the business-to-business information market and argues how reputation and quality effects play a part in shaping the organizational and industry structures. In Section 4 we focus on the consumer-information market and examine the issues that impact both organizations and consumers that are unique to the Internet medium. In Section 5 we discuss the emergence of electronic communities among consumers and businesses as a reaction to the Internet medium and how they play a key intermediary role in the information market. We present our conclusions in Section 6.

2 The Marketing Information Market

Our definition of the Internet based marketing information market is as follows. The market encompasses (1) organizations that generate, collect, process, and/or market and distribute, on the Internet, information about organizations, transactions, and customers in distinct markets, both virtual and real, (2) buyers of the information (organizations or individuals), and (3) consumers who provide information about their demographics, interests, lifestyle, and transactions. The common medium that links all players in the market is the Internet, which is used for information generation and/or marketing, transacting and distributing information and information products.

From a process-oriented viewpoint, providers of market information products can be classified as primary research providers and secondary data providers. Primary research providers supply custom research products that are designed and collected specifically for a client. Many marketing information services have started using Internet as the medium to collect primary data to capitalize on its channel-specific advantages. The transmission speeds, storage capacities and global reach of the Internet allow real-time interactions with consumers, transmission of rich multimedia content, and lower transaction costs in obtaining responses. These advantages have given rise to new and innovative primary research techniques such as online focus groups, web panels, pop-up surveys and e-mail surveys. Many organizations (NFO Research, SurveySite) have set up interactive survey panels to evaluate product positioning, to collect consumers' attitudes and beliefs regarding brands, and to understand their purchasing habits (Wylie 1997). Some organizations use virtual reality techniques to conduct primary research using simulated products, services, and shopping environments (Dellacave 1996). Such real-time feedback has helped many information producers to rely more on the Internet environment for information generation. In addition, there are many other firms that use Internet purely as an advertising and transaction medium for primary research products (e.g. ROI). Providers of secondary data, which is data gathered previously for other projects but has relevance to the current project, have been using the online delivery channel even before the advent of the Internet. However, many of these organizations have started using the Internet as an alternative delivery channel (e.g., Dialog, Lexis-Nexis, EDGAR). Such secondary data cover published data, online databases, geographical information systems, and market research reports, some of which cover commerce on the Internet itself.

From a content generation viewpoint, marketing information on the Internet can be classified as information generated outside the Internet and as information generated within the Internet. Most online databases provide information collected outside the Internet domain. In addition, many organizations, realizing the earning potential of data they have stored of their customers, transactions, credit histories, and competitors in their data warehouses, are beginning to sell the information over the Internet (McCullough 1998). Some Internet based organizations have already started collecting information on their online markets – details of transactions, customer web-visits, click-streams, demographics, and such – using sophisticated measurement technologies (Hamlin 1997). There are market research firms on the Internet which measure consumers' reactions to different web-sites and sell the aggregated information product to web-based clients (e.g., Customer Insites).

An interesting development in web-generated marketing information market is the evolution of organizations that "compensate" consumers for providing information on their demographics, interests, and lifestyle. Most such organizations provide "freebies" in the form of free e-mail, coupons, and monetary compensation to consumers in return for their information (CyberGold, Juno.com, HotMail). These organizations, in turn, use the information to attract revenue from advertisers who wish to reach out to their target segments. Another novel way marketing information is collected is through electronic communities (e-communities). These are virtual communities of online users who share similar interests and interact with each other. As community members interact with each other and community facilitators/sponsors exchanging comments, reviews, attitudes and beliefs about the subjects of their interest, they generate valuable information that marketers would be willing to pay for. Members also provide information on their demographics when they enroll in the community. This information can be used by e-communities to attract advertisement revenue and community exchanges could be sold as information products. As the Internet grows, many e-communities are evolving rapidly (Business Week, 1997b) and thus the potential for marketing information generated on the Internet may be limitless in the short run.

It is clear from the preceding discussion that, as commerce on the Internet grows, there will be an exponential growth in marketing information that is generated on the Internet. As the network effects start manifesting, the number of organizations that will enter the market to provide information products, generated either on the Internet or otherwise, is also likely to increase significantly. What will be the impact of this growth on the marketing information market? What are the facilitators and barriers to the growth of the information market? How would consumers (both organizations and individuals) react to the increasing need for consumer information and the increasing number of suppliers that can generate them? In order to answer these questions, it is useful to categorize market transactions in the information market as business-to-business transactions and consumer-oriented transactions. Business-to-business transactions are characterized, on the supply side, by market research firms and online data servers and, on the demand side, by corporate/organizational clients. Market research firms enter into business contracts corporate clients generally on a turnkey basis, but also focus on building long-term relationships with clients through account cultivation and management. Online servers may supply data to clients on the basis of connect-hour prices or yearly subscriptions. In consumer-oriented information transactions, the supplier is the individual consumer or an e-community and the buyer is an organization. Thus, marketers and advertisers pay for the access to consumer information either from individual consumers or from e-communities. Other organizations may pay the individual consumers using "freebies" instead of monetary compensation. In the following sections, we address the basic questions from the perspective of business-to-business (B2B) information market and from the perspective of consumer-to-business (C2B) information market.

3 The B2B Market

It is necessary to understand the nature of the product and transactions in the B2B information market to appreciate the issues involved in the Internet-based market. The quality and reliability of marketing information products are generally difficult to define or assess especially those products that are predictive in nature such as market forecasts, economic forecasts and market potential studies. A supplier may expend "significant" effort, use appropriate technologies and produce a "good" quality forecast, but environmental uncertainties may render the forecasts to be wrong. Therefore, the customer using the information to make their decisions may consider the information to be of "poor" quality. Since quality of the product cannot be inspected as in the case of physical products, information products present difficulties in assessing whether the supplier has expended significant effort in producing the product or not. Such problems in measuring the quality of the information products make it difficult to tie the price of the information products to an outcome-based measure. These difficulties force both suppliers and buyers of such products to closely evaluate the risks in transacting business with each other.

There are different kinds of risks that buyers and suppliers face. From the buyer's viewpoint, there is risk involved in contracting for the supply of information without being able to observe its quality, instead relying on the supplier's overall reputation. Suppliers, on the other hand, expend "significant" effort in producing quality information, yet the product could be perceived as being unreliable, because of factors beyond their control. This could damage their reputation and prevent them from forging a long-term relationship with the buyer. If buyers recognize the risk suppliers face and want the suppliers, nevertheless, to expend "significant" effort and not cut any corners in producing the information, the buyer will have to offer a price that is *incentive compatible*. That is, pay a price high enough to induce the supplier to be honest and not cheat in information production. At the same time, the price offered should be greater than or equal to what the supplier could get from other buyers for the same information, that is, a price that guarantees supplier's *reservation utility*. Our research has shown that the minimum price the buyer can offer that satisfies the above conditions is higher when there is greater uncertainty (or noise) in assessing the quality/reliability of the information product (Kannan et al 1997). In other words, if the supplier's efforts have little impact on determining the *observed* reliability of the information they supply, the buyers will have to pay a higher price to ensure significant effort from the supplier in producing the information. From the supplier's viewpoint, the situation is as follows: when the supplier faces higher uncertainty in how the information's quality is perceived, greater are the chances that it will be marked as a poor supplier even when it expends significant effort. This may lead to loss of reputation and lower chances of a long-term relationship with the buyer. To compensate for this potential loss, the supplier will have to charge higher prices to maximize its expected revenues in the long run.

On the Internet-based information market, many of the above problems worsen. The Internet provides significant opportunities for information suppliers to set up servers and supply information products because of the relatively small overhead and low barriers to entry. As a result, there is no control over the number of information suppliers or the quality of information products that are available on the Internet. In addition, the customization afforded by the channel makes it difficult to compare the quality of the information products. There may be many sources for the same information with widely different prices. Thus consumers may face difficulties in identifying reliable suppliers. They may obtain information regarding the quality of information products from different vendors, but for information products, which must be consumed to know the quality, no amount of information will suffice. Under such a situation, when buyers do not have adequate information about product quality, their willingness to pay for the information may depend on their *expected* level of quality available in the market. Thus, they may evaluate all products to be of the same average quality and be willing to pay just the average price. If the high quality information suppliers are not able to convince the consumers regarding their products' worth, there is no incentive for them to produce such products. Thus, they may stop producing high quality information products. This limits the market availability to just low-quality products or "lemons" (Choi, Stahl and Whinston 1997). This may, over time, lead to further lowering of expected valuation of the information products and further decline in the quality of available products. This slide to a market of lemons is a real danger for the Internet-based information market.

The inherent nature of the information products also plays a crucial role in setting buyers' expectations about the Internet market. It is a fact of life that many marketing information products show high variations in content from one supplier to another. Given the high variation in the content – for example, market forecasts -, many buyers perceive value in obtaining highly targeted information products from a number of suppliers rather than obtaining omnibus information from a few sources. Given the value of multiple perspectives on a fast-changing market such as the IT market, the information products provided by these suppliers are viewed more as being complements rather than substitutes (Sarvary and Parker 1997). Combined with our argument that such information products are also likely to cost more because of their inherent uncertainty, we have a situation where high priced, high variance products are being purchased by buyers from multiple suppliers. As Internet expands, more sources become available, many with low or no reputation. Buyers cannot use price as a quality indicator in differentiating among the suppliers, there are difficulties in identifying reliable information sources, all of which present ideal conditions for a breakdown of the market mechanism. However, we argue in the following subsection, that emergence of powerful intermediaries will prevent such a breakdown, instead make the Internet-based information market stronger.

3.1 Impact of Intermediaries

The emergence of intermediaries can significantly alter the scenario for the Internet-based marketing information market. They can contribute to an efficient market by adding value in market transactions in five distinct ways (Figure 2): (1) researching buyer information needs, (2) acquiring relevant information products from suppliers, (3) managing intellectual properties and copyright, (4) authenticating information suppliers, and (5) complementing, processing, and adding value to information products. Intermediaries' role in researching customers' needs can contribute to lower search costs as they have expertise in identifying information suppliers and knowledge of the suitability of the diverse and complementary information from different sources for buyer needs. Searches by inexperienced users over the Internet can result in high costs due to information overload. Intermediaries can provide a valuable service in this context because of their expertise in searching and their extensive knowledge of the suppliers, their contents, and value. This cost advantage will get even better as intermediaries acquire specialized knowledge and expertise over time.

Intermediaries can also play a crucial role as intellectual property managers in ensuring that the value of information products remains high. By entering into contracts with information suppliers for information products that are routinely demanded by buyers, intermediaries can help in building a strong market and ensure property rights. Contracts could cover the product form (information streams, levels of aggregation), price and schedule (how often) of electronic transfers. Since intermediaries ex-ante would not know the exact information that buyers would demand but only its broad nature, they might enter into yearly contracts for information with suppliers. Such contractual agreements can lead to a stable information market. In addition, because the scale of purchase from the intermediary is larger, the acquisition costs would be much lower than for direct sale to buyers.

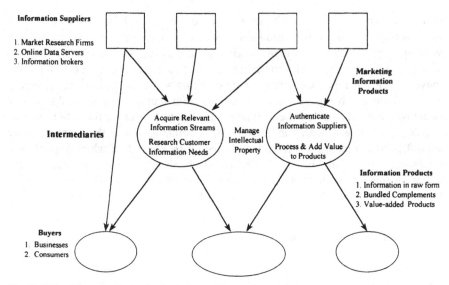

Fig. 2. Role of intermediaries in the information market

Intermediaries can also provide the critical service of monitoring and authenticating the information suppliers through inspection of supplier processes. While this may add to the costs, intermediaries can exploit their scale of operation and decrease the per-transaction cost of acquiring information products. Intermediaries can also help develop new suppliers, which may be impossible for buyers to develop on their own because of the costs involved. Thus, access to certain key information can be obtained only through intermediaries. On a related note, approved suppliers of information to well-known intermediaries can use the authentication as a "stamp of quality" in selling their information to other intermediaries and customer groups. Thus, the authentication role of intermediaries may prevent the market for information from sliding into a "market for lemons". Intermediaries can also play a key role in complementing information from different sources, bundling them as information products, and adding value through further analyses so that the customer needs are met. Such *customization* ensures that the information market does not turn into a commodity market.

Finally, even disregarding the transaction cost advantages that we have alluded to in the previous paragraph, intermediaries can *reduce* costs in the Internet-based information market. This cost advantage arises from controlling the risks associated with buying information products on the Internet. When multiple suppliers supply information products through intermediaries and the intermediary merely bundles these products (without adding any value), it still reduces the chances of the bundle being perceived as unreliable. This reduction in uncertainty leads to lower *incentive compatible* prices that the buyer has to offer for significant effort from the suppliers, than when the supply is made directly from the suppliers. Intermediaries may incur significant additional costs in monitoring and ensuring that the suppliers put in significant effort. Even with the additional costs, research has shown that the resultant decrease in price per information product is substantial (Kannan et al 1998). The intuition is as follows. When suppliers supply one information product they have a greater risk to their reputation in supplying directly to buyers. The intermediaries supply multiple, complementary products from multiple suppliers that evens out the uncertainties. This lowers the risk to the intermediary's reputation and leads to lower prices. Also, when the intermediaries are in the market for the long term, they can also punish the low-quality suppliers and drive them out of the market. This reduces the risk of low-quality supplies in the market.

3.2 Open Issues

We have argued so far that intermediaries can prevent the Internet-based information market from becoming a chaotic market for lemons. We have also shown the importance of intermediaries' actions in monitoring suppliers and safeguarding against fly-by-night operators supplying low quality products. However, we have assumed that buyers will flock to buy from intermediaries instead of directly buying from suppliers. This needs some explanation and clarification. Reputation of organizations plays a significant role in business-to-business transactions. This implies that buyers use reputation as a proxy measure for evaluating the quality/reliability of the information products. Buyers' risk in transacting business with organizations with no reputation remains the same whether the other party is an information supplier or an intermediary. This leads to two inferences. First, marketing information suppliers with established reputation in other markets could enter the Internet market much more successfully than new suppliers who start out on the Internet. By supplying to multiple buyers, established suppliers with reputation can realize similar risk reductions and associated cost reductions as the intermediaries discussed in the previous sub-section. Second, intermediaries starting out on the Internet will have to build their reputation just as anyone else starting out on the Internet. Building reputation will take some time. This has important implications for which organizations can play the role of powerful intermediaries on the Internet information market.

Since reputation effects are strong in the B2B market, it is clear that organizations with established reputation in other markets can use Internet as an important channel to further their market shares. Thus, firms with strong brand presence such as A.C. Nielsen, IRI, and other large market research firms are in an ideal position to emerge as intermediaries by integrating down vertically. Some of these firms are already taking on the role of intermediaries in other markets. Other possible candidates are electronic communities, which are still evolving on the Internet. Business communities such as TPN-GEIS develop network of reliable suppliers that buyers in the community can leverage. Similar models for the information market can provide all the benefits of an intermediary. (We discuss the intermediary role of e-communities later in this chapter).

The other issues that need to be resolved for the continued growth of the market are institutional in nature. The first is the development of standards and passage of copyright laws for electronic transfer and re-transfer of information. Since the marginal cost of producing an information product is almost zero, information sold by suppliers could be re-sold in the same or altered form. To protect suppliers' interests this gray area needs to be appropriately resolved. The second issue is the evolution of contractual agreements similar in spirit to the ones governing EDI transactions that could render transactions over the Internet to be more formal. This will aid rapid exchange and processing of information products on the Internet.

4 The C2B Market

One of the most exciting developments in the realm of Internet commerce is the ability to mass customize products and services. The Internet provides interactivity, means to obtain quick feedback from consumers on many information dimensions such as consumer behavior, attitudes, interests, lifestyle, and demographics. Advances in information processing and storage technologies have made it very inexpensive to collect such information, process the information, and customize offerings to consumers. These form the foundation for such concepts as "one-on-one" marketing, mass customization, relationship marketing, micro-marketing, etc. In the marketers' ideal world, consumers would freely provide such information to marketers, who would use them to customize products, price discriminate consumers, and use the information in any way to their advantage. Marketers value such consumer information and in traditional markets employ various market research techniques to collect such information. Sometimes they buy the information from databases. With the advent of the Internet, consumers are realizing the importance of their personal information and the value it has for marketers. In addition, there is heightened sensitivity among consumers regarding how the information is used, how it is resold, and how it contributes to many unsolicited mailings and "spam" messages and to total loss of privacy. Given the above situation and the need for personal information for targeted marketing, marketers have started compensating consumers for their personal information (Hagel and Rayport 1997). From the marketers' viewpoint, this is a compensation that is well spent as it obviates the need for costly mass advertising instead using the budget for micro-marketing. This has led to the evolution of a different kind of information market on the Internet – marketers buying personal information from consumers, and hence our term consumers-to-business (C2B) market.

4.1 Issues

In order to understand the basic issues confronting the C2B market, it is necessary to review the tension that exists between consumers' need for privacy and the marketers' need for their personal information. From the consumers' viewpoint, there are inherent risks in giving away their personal information. First, there is the "nuisance" effect. That is, the personal information could be bundled and sold to other marketers who may use the data to target consumers to sell their own products/services. Consumers are targeted with unsolicited information or "junk" mail, which is a cost to the consumers. Second, there is a more serious effect when marketers use the information to price discriminate consumers, which then may reduce consumer surplus. This is something consumers may want to guard against. Third, there is a risk of invasion of privacy, which is a cost to the consumers in various ways. The net impact of these effects is consumers become risk averse to sharing their personal information with marketers. On a positive note, the personal information when used correctly can reduce the search costs for consumers, as they would receive information on products/services they are interested in directly from the marketers. Also, if there is some monetary compensation for sharing the personal information consumers can benefit. From the marketers' viewpoint, there are some risks too. These relate to the quality of information they receive from consumers. In order to use the information profitably for targeting consumers, marketers need reliable information. However, many surveys of consumers on the Web indicate that around 40-50% of the consumers misrepresent at least some personal facts (GVU Survey 1997a). This could be mainly due to their inherent risk-averse orientation or their desire to protect privacy. It could also be due a basic mistrust of marketers' intentions regarding the use of information. For example, they could believe that there are no benefits of any kind to consumers in providing personal information. If the information that marketers get from consumers contain significant misrepresentations, then the usefulness of such information for targeting purposes is quite limited. If marketers are risk averse in their information transactions with consumers, then the outlook for the C2B information will be bleak. The risks involved for both parties in transacting business could stifle market growth.

Unlike in a traditional market, where sellers take the initiative and risks to develop the market, the C2B market needs to be developed by the information buyers, in this case, the marketers. (In a strict sense, the developmental effort is still performed by the seller who needs the information to sell his products/services more efficiently and effectively, but if the focus is only on consumer information as the product our above statement is justified). The consumers who can sell their information to the buyers are risk-averse in this market. This risk arises from the fact that they are uncertain about the outcome of the transaction: (1) could it lead to privacy problems, price discrimination or nuisance effects? (2) Would there be benefits such as reduced search costs? In the context of such uncertainties, the marketers would have to make higher payments to consumers in order to get them to participate in a market relationship. Once this relationship is established and consumers experience the benefits and none of the anticipated ill effects, there would be significant reduction in uncertainties. Logically, this could lead to lower payments in exchange for information, as consumers would be more willing to share their information. Once the relationship is established, it could also reduce the chances of consumers misrepresenting their personal information.

What are some ways to overcome the uncertainties associated with the outcome of information transactions? One obvious strategy is to make an attractive "signing" bonus to consumers when they enter into an agreement to exchange information for a nominal compensation. As consumers become aware of the benefits of sharing their information, additional information can be obtained more easily. There are two problems with this strategy. First, marketers take on a high risk by committing money up-front. Consumers could sign-on and terminate the relationship at any point after getting the bonus. Also, from the consumers' viewpoint, a significant signing bonus may only add to their uncertainties as how the information will be used if the marketer could afford to pay such a bonus. Other strategies work at reducing the uncertainties associated with the outcome.

The first strategy is to provide clear indications to consumers that the marketer has a well-defined policy on safeguarding consumer privacy, and provide the contents of the policy. Many consumers are willing to share their information with marketers if they knew how the information was going to be used (GVU survey 1997b). Also, uncertainties would be greatly reduced is they knew that the information was not going to be re-sold to other marketers (GVU survey 1997b). The recent FTC investigations against GeoCities for misleading consumers on what they did with the personal information (InternetNews, 1998) goes a long way in assuring consumers that marketers would take honest measures to adhere to their privacy policies. The second strategy is to get certification from organizations such as TrustE on adherence to standard consumer privacy policies. Such authentication is becoming very popular and the certifying organizations conduct audits of the companies they certify. This would help in building consumers' trust and reducing uncertainties.

In addition to the above strategies that marketers could adopt, there are organizations emerging on the Internet which help in organizing the market for consumer information and render the market more efficient. One of the features of these organizations that may be attractive to consumers is that they act as intermediaries between the consumers and marketers. This gives them to opportunity to aggregate personal information and sell it to marketers while at the same time safeguard individual privacy. In the following subsection we discuss the different business models these intermediaries follow and their relative impact on the growth of the information market.

4.2 The C2B Intermediaries

The C2B intermediaries aim to match marketers that sell products/services with the appropriate target consumers who might be interested in those products and services. The intermediaries trade marketing information. They collect personal information from consumers and using this information they provide product and service information through interactive advertisements to the consumers that marketers would like to target. The intermediaries charge marketers for the opportunities to direct advertisements to the consumers (thereby generating revenue) and they compensate consumers for the information and for viewing/interacting with the advertisements. The compensation takes many forms: it could be free e-mail service, free Internet access, cash, promotional rebates and coupons or point-reward that can be exchanged for a variety of goods and services. Currently, there are more than a hundred such intermediaries on the Internet vying for consumers' information on the Internet. Each intermediary employs a different business model to attract Internet users to enter into agreements with their organization, ensure user involvement with the advertisements, and charge marketing organizations for the advertisements. In general, they can be classified into two main categories based on the business model they adopt: the *community* model and the *pay-for-performance* model, although there are many variations within each category (Chang et al 1999a).

The intermediaries following the community model provide free services such as e-mail access, chat groups, news, weather and magazines, etc. in much the same way as a no-frills Internet Service Provider. Some intermediaries provide (1) free service software that users can install on their computers and (2) free access to these services (through local lines) that users can tap into at no extra cost other than subscribing to a local telephone line. Others use their web-sites to provide such service. In return, the users signing up with these intermediaries provide detailed demographic, lifestyle and/or product/service preference information. Intermediaries sell advertising opportunities to client organizations and tailor advertisements to user groups based on the information they provide. When users sign on and use the free services such as e-mail, chat rooms, news, etc., these tailored advertisements are directed at them as banners/background, at strategic locations on the interface screens. Some examples of intermediaries that follow the community model include Juno, which provides free e-mail service with 6-7 million subscribers; Hotmail, an Internet-based e-mail service provider claiming a 14 million subscriber base, YahooMail, NetAddress, RocketMail, etc. (users need to have access to the Internet to use these e-mail services and get a password to link to the e-mail services; these e-mail services tend to be very versatile in transmitting various data formats and files). Some also provide chat rooms, discussion forums, and opportunities to play games with other members (e.g., YahooMail). Since such services foster a sense of community among the members, we use the term "community" model. The degree of community atmosphere, of course, varies.

The intermediaries following the pay-for-performance model operate in a much different manner as compared to the community model. When users sign up with these intermediaries, they provide demographic and product/service preference information as they would do with the community model organizations, but they do not get any free service. Instead they get paid cash or bonus points for viewing and interacting with the advertisements that are tailored to their preferences and sent to them via e-mail or flashed at them at certain web-sites. If the users fail to interact or remain passive to the advertisements, they do not get paid; they accrue the payments or bonus points only when they interact and hence the term "pay-for-performance". The accrued cash can be used in many ways – deposited in a bank account, used for buying products at web-sites, obtain rebates, etc., while the accrued bonus points can be redeemed for products/services in a manner similar to the redemption of frequent-flyer miles or loyalty points. The advertisers who advertise through these intermediaries get charged on the basis of verified responses from users who interact with the advertisements (on the basis of "click-throughs"). Examples include Cybergold.com, launched in 1996, that offers incentives ranging from 50 cents to several dollars for such activities as viewing and interacting with advertisements, visiting web-sites, taking surveys, filling out application and registration forms, making purchases, etc. (with a limit of one reward per person per action), and BonusMail.

Both types of intermediaries are helping the C2B information market to grow as they target different segments of consumers and operate in different markets. Some intermediaries that follow the community model by providing free e-mail service, chat room, news, etc., target users who do not have access to the Internet from their home (Juno.com). Many community models are offered on the Internet, which means users need to have access to the Internet first before using the free service. The competition in this market is fierce as many web-sites offer free e-mail in the hopes of becoming users' "portal" site. For a user to participate in a pay-for-performance model, he/she also needs to have access to an Internet or e-mail service first. This implies that the pay-for-performance models are targeted at current Internet users. While CyberGold targets the sophisticated "surfers", and BonusMail assumes that the user has an e-mail address already. Juno.com targets the naïve first-time users who would like to have access to e-mail, chat room service, etc, which is potentially a larger market than the market of Internet users. Hotmail, which follows the community model, assumes that the user has access to the Internet and thus may compete with CyberGold for users' attention. It may be conjectured that the community models act as a training ground for users to become more comfortable with e-mail and other services before they spend their own money to get these services.

4.3 Consumers' Valuation of Benefits

The success of intermediaries' efforts in expanding the market for consumer information using an ad-revenue model may ultimately depend on consumers' valuation of the benefits they derive in exchanging their information. From the consumers' viewpoint, the valuation of the services and incentives offered by intermediaries has two components. One is the valuation of the compensation for information, offered in various forms, and the other is the valuation of the advertisements that the consumers view and interact with. The value of advertisements arises from the fact that they reduce the search costs of consumers in acquiring goods and services. As much as the advertisements focus on goods and services that the consumers are interested in, this is not an issue. The consumers' valuation of the compensation provided by intermediaries has to be viewed in the context of the hidden costs that consumers incur in obtaining the compensation. For example, in the community model, the free services of the intermediary provide the means for the consumers to interact with others. While they are viewing the advertisements that appear on the screen they are also performing some useful tasks – composing an e-mail, or chatting with a community member or watching news, etc. The advertisements are passive. When consumers interact with the intermediaries they are motivated by their needs to interact with other users, get news, or something other than the need to view advertisements per se. This is not the case with the pay-for-performance model, where consumers expressly log on with the intermediary to interact with/process the advertisements, visit web sites, etc. However, the incentives they get are cash or bonus points that can be exchanged for many things, not just free e-mail or chat room service.

The valuation of compensation in its different forms may vary across population and, thus, intermediaries following different models may attract different kinds of consumers. It may be conjectured that, on the basis of the valuations, the community model may foster more loyalty among its users than in the pay-for-performance model where its users may be more likely to switch from one incentive to the other. By the same token, the community model may provide more opportunities for the intermediary to target advertisements to its user base, as their interaction with the intermediary may be motivated by greater needs than just to view the advertisements per se. In the pay-for-performance model the user may interact with the intermediary to purely view and process the advertisement. This has its advantages in that it guarantees the processing/interacting with the advertisement, while in the community model there is no such guarantee that the user processed the advertisement. Thus, in one model we have higher participation, no guarantees on advertisement interaction, but a higher cognitive processing if interaction does occur and in the other model we have guaranteed interaction with the advertisements but possibly with lower cognitive processing and a lower overall participation rate.

Given the variation in consumer valuation of the compensation, one of the challenges that intermediaries face is how to develop strategies to attract consumers with higher thresholds of participation at the same time minimizing the costs of obtaining information. Specifically, the issue is how to attract consumer information of higher valuation by selectively providing higher incentives to those consumers who are cognitively involved with the advertisements (similar to the price discrimination problem). This is a more pressing challenge for a pay-for-performance intermediary as there could be a segment of users who, motivated purely by financial incentives, could be clicking on all advertisements while providing unreliable information about themselves and thus taking undue advantage of the intermediary.

5 Electronic Communities

In our discussions of both the B2B and the C2B markets, electronic communities or community-type models played a prominent role as intermediaries. Many such e-communities are rapidly evolving on the Internet, some organized by community members themselves, some organized by marketers, and some by third parties who act as intermediaries in Internet transactions. In many cases, marketing information is generated within communities themselves that may be valuable to marketers. Given its growing importance in the Internet-based information market, it is necessary to devote some discussion to e-communities and their role in the market.

E-communities can be defined as *social* aggregations of a *critical mass* of people on the Internet who engage in public discussions, *interactions* in chat rooms, and information exchanges with sufficient *human feeling* on matters of common interest to form webs of *personal relationship*s (Chang et al 1999). The common needs, which drive this aggregation, could be social as well as commercial. This bonding is further strengthened by personal relationships that ensure some degree of loyalty of the members to the community. It is not uncommon to find communities for business organizations – communities of buyers and sellers, such as GE Information Services' Trading Process Network (GEIS-TPN), a community of GE suppliers and other buyers, CommerceNet, etc. These business communities consist of a critical mass of members whose needs are mainly *commercial* and who use the communities mainly for *networking* and building *business relationships*. These business-to-business communities may lack the human element and the social interactions, they nevertheless can be considered as communities.

5.1 Information Generation in E-Communities

Figure 3 provides an overview of the information generation process within communities. Members' input to the community consists of information content in the form of comments, feedback, elaborating their attitudes and beliefs, and informational needs. Members may provide such content unsolicited or in response to queries by other members or the organizer of the community. Thus, members provide useful information that is retrieved and used by other members of the community. The community organizers may also put in their own content which members may find very valuable. For example, the organizers of BioMedNet , a medical community, provide content in the form of information on latest medical research and techniques, which the physician members would find very useful. In such communities, the members would also be willing to pay *subscription fees* to become members of the community as they may highly value the information they receive from the community. For becoming members of communities such as America Online or CompuServe members need to pay subscription fees. Such subscription fees may be viewed as a charge that members need to bear to be part of an exclusive community or for accessing the content in the communities that they value.

A community brings together consumers of specific demographics and interest. This presents opportunities for transacting business and communicating messages about products and services, of interest to consumers and which marketers and advertisers value and are willing to pay for. Thus, e-communities can attract ad-revenues from advertisers eager to communicate their messages to community members. (This is currently a significant source of revenue for e-communities). There are also other opportunities for value creation. These arise from the marketing information that is generated within communities, which the environment (marketers and advertisers among others) would find valuable. Such information include demographics and psychographics of members, their attitudes and beliefs about products, services, and issues, their behavior data with regard to business transactions within communities, and information on their interactions and interaction dynamics. Such information could be sold to marketers and advertisers if the members do not object.

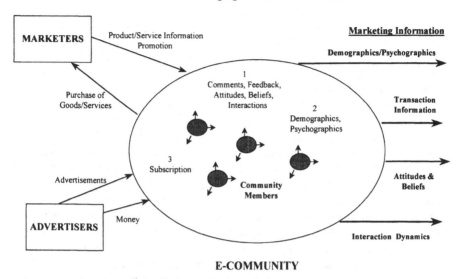

Fig. 3. Information generation in electronic communities

Transaction of information products in communities also depends on who organizes the community and who owns it. Transaction-oriented communities are generally organized, controlled and run by marketers. The marketing information generated in these communities may reside with the marketers who may or may not sell such information. In many cases, marketers who own e-communities can use such information to derive synergies for other related business functions, such as better customer service, mass customization in service and delivery, marketing research feedback, etc. If the community is controlled and owned by members themselves, the main focus of such communities is to derive sole benefits for the members and value is created in content exchange and/or through subscription fees. If the community organizers and those who run it are not marketers, advertisers or members but unrelated third parties, such communities are in a better position to leverage the full range of possibilities of information exchange. We focus on the intermediary role of e-communities in the next sub-section.

5.2 Intermediary Role of E-Communities

E-communities are increasingly called upon to play the role of intermediaries in Internet-based transactions. Communities such as Parentsplace.com and TPN-GEIS are good examples of communities that were started out by marketers and buyers to aid their businesses, but ended up being intermediaries (Chang et al 1999b). Members enroll in communities to forge ties with other members, extract or download content of good quality from the community, and provide content of their own to others. Marketers on the other hand look for access to targeted consumers, transact business with community members and buy information that is generated within the communities. E-communities as intermediaries have to ensure: (1) that the content input by community members, advertisers, and marketers are of good quality, and (2) that members' privacy is protected even as appropriate relationships are forged between community members and marketers. There are several issues involved in ensuring the above conditions.

Content Quality: If content is generated by community organizers (as in Bio-MedNet) then their editorial staff is responsible for maintaining its quality. However, if content is member generated then maintaining quality may not be an easy task. Such member input could vary from opinions to experiences and reviews where it may be difficult to judge its quality. There is nothing stopping a community member from inputting deliberate lies, misrepresentations about their experiences about products/services, and misleading other community members. In most cases, e-communities can put up a disclaimer regarding the member-generated content -- they cannot fully vouch for the quality of the content, they are the opinions of individuals and so on. But unless there is some intervention to assure quality, the community can easily disintegrate, as serious community members will start looking elsewhere. The intervention can be in the form of moderators in chat rooms or editors who will continuously monitor the nature and quality of input and interactions and take action against members who continuously disrupt the community. Ensuring the quality of information from advertisers and marketers may also be difficult, but in most cases the e-community can rely on their corporate image and reputation as proxies for their information quality. E-communities can thus ensure that their community members are not subject to the manipulations of fly-by-night operators and their schemes.

Preventing Free-Riders: For a community which relies on members' input for information generation, members who "free-ride" can be a problem. For example, consider an e-community devoted to vacation travelling. Members can access useful information from travel agents and other marketers of vacation packages, but other members' reviews of and experiences with different packages can be much more useful. If community members participate in a community only as "lurkers" and do not contribute any useful information (by trying out a package/service themselves), then the community can suffer (Choi, Stahl, and Whinston 1997). Over time such free-riding can lead to paucity of useful content in the community and reduce the value of the information generated. Thus, as an intermediary e-communities have to ensure active participation of members possibly through economic incentives.

Maintaining Member Privacy: Members who join e-communities usually provide personal information to the community organizers. This information is usually needed to better meet member needs of social interaction and commercial interactions. The community organizers also need the information to maintain the relative homogeneity of the community in terms of interests and/or demographics. In addition, e-community can also generate significant information regarding members' interests through chat rooms and discussion groups where they interact with other members. E-communities can also track members' transaction information. While all such information has value for marketers and advertisers, most members expect e-communities to respect their privacy and safeguard their personal information and not let advertisers and marketers use the information indiscriminately to "spam" members. Members also expect similar privacy in dealing with other members. Thus, e-communities may choose to use *aggregated* personal information to provide to marketers and not divulge individual-level information.

Meeting Marketers' Needs: Advertisers and marketers expect value for the revenue that they provide e-communities by way of ad-fees and commissions. They derive such value through communicating their messages to the right target segment, forging long-term relationships with members, and getting information on how best to meet their needs. This implies that corporate clients expect to get from e-communities "good" quality demographic and interest information. In addition, they would like to focus on individual consumers and their specific needs to take advantage of the one-on-one marketing opportunities that the Internet facilitates. This implies that corporate clients may demand individual level data from e-communities even as e-communities are concerned about protecting members' privacy.

Maintaining Critical Mass: For any community to thrive it needs to have a critical mass. If the chat rooms and discussion rooms are empty or do not have new content, membership dwindles quickly. Business-to-business communities are also similar in this respect. For example, Industry.Net was never able to attain the critical mass in time for the community to thrive. Since many businesses adopted the "wait-and-see" approach, the community never took off. Critical mass is necessary for membership growth and for healthy revenues from corporate clients. As intermediaries e-communities have a special role to play in maintaining a critical mass.

5.3 E-Communities in the Value Chain

E-Communities' impact in the value chain of the Internet-based information market can be inferred by comparing a market without e-communities and a market with them acting as intermediaries. In general, marketers will incur a significant cost in obtaining personal information directly from consumers on the Internet. This cost is higher (1) for marketers with lower reputation, (2) as there is more uncertainty regarding the outcome of the sharing, and (3) as the percentage of consumers in the target population who already share information with other marketers is lower. When a marketer's reputation is low, consumers' perception of overall success of the marketer's project will be low and there will be higher uncertainty regarding how the information will be used. That is, consumers will perceive that the marketer cannot gather information from a significant number of consumers. If the return for information is in an abstract form – better service and better quality that cannot be easily perceived – then, given the risk averse nature of consumers, they may seek higher returns. By the same token, if consumers already share their information with other marketers already, the marginal return they may seek from sharing the same information may be much lower than otherwise (that is, their marginal costs of sharing their private information are much lower now).

Let us now consider the market with e-communities acting as intermediaries. When consumers provide their private information to the e-community, the e-community could have a conflict of interest with the members. That is, the intermediary could do whatever they wanted with the information. How can consumers avoid having to monitor the community? This can be done through the intermediary entering into contracts with the consumers, providing an attractive return in exchange for their information. If the intermediary fails to do so, the intermediary will face the disintegration of the community. This threat of disintegration is enough incentive for the e-community to honor the contracts, since not doing so will threaten its well being. How does the intermediary recoup this expense? The first way is through the diversification it provides. That is, consumer information is provided to multiple marketers and, therefore, the probability of an eventual success increases significantly. This can be viewed as a reduction of uncertainty on the consumers' part through the law of large numbers. The second way is through protection of privacy. Intermediaries are in a good position as third parties with no connection to marketers to provide mechanisms and assurance for consumer information protection. By crafting clever mechanisms for consumer privacy and securing members' trust can lower the expected return that consumers expect for their private information. Third, given the different relationships that the intermediary can forge with multiple marketers, they would be in a much better position than individual marketers to provide value to members in terms of product/service information content and varied choice. This reduces consumers' search costs. This also enables them to secure members' trust in less time than would be possible for an individual marketer, as they would not be hindered by an agenda of pushing a specific product/service at members. By the same reason, intermediaries can better fulfill the social needs of members through chat rooms, discussion rooms, and content as compared to marketers. As intermediaries can effectively provide a variety of services to members of an e-community, they are also in a better position to maintain the critical mass of members and help grow the community. The net effect is that those consumers, who prefer to remain on the sidelines when a marketer approaches them for private information, are more likely to join an e-community because of the increased probability of success with their information. The protection of privacy also increases their likelihood of joining the e-community.

While maintaining the privacy of consumers can lower the costs of procuring consumer information, it is also necessary for e-communities to meet the needs of marketers to keep the revenue flowing into the communities. Such a trade-off can be accomplished by clever mechanisms such as FireFly's Passport. FireFly collects demographic and psychographic information from those consumers who apply for the passport and offers them full control over their personal information as to what could be shared and what not, who to share with and who not to, and so on. When members enter the web sites of marketers who are clients of FireFly, they provide their passports, which depending on their previous consent, provide the appropriate personal information to the marketer. The marketer uses this information to personalize his service and product offering to the members, develop a relationship with the customer, direct the customers to their own communities with like-minded members and so on. Such schemes provide the balance between consumers' need for privacy and marketers' need for personalization.

6 Conclusions

We started out this chapter asking a very fundamental question: how will the Internet as a channel affect the organizational forms and market structure and how will society and consumers react to the medium and its impact on organizations and markets? We have presented scenarios in the B2B market and the C2B market that clearly indicate the emergence of intermediaries as a likely change in the market structure. We have presented arguments to highlight their role in rendering the markets efficient and their crucial role in the generating growth in the markets. We also discussed the likely candidates for intermediaries in these markets. The arguments clearly indicate the importance of electronic communities in the Internet-based marketing information market. E-communities can offer a win-win situation for both consumers and marketers and can reduce the tension between marketers' need for marketing information and consumers' need for privacy. E-communities can have a similar impact in the business-to-business market by reducing uncertainties in transactions between information sellers and buyers and by preventing a slide to a market of "lemons".

It is clear from our discussion that the Internet medium presents special opportunities and challenges in marketing information products. In fact, emergence of intermediaries whether they are e-communities or others can be viewed as a reaction of the market players to deal efficiently with the challenges and take advantage of the unique opportunities that Internet channel presents. It is also clear that the power balance between marketers and consumers, which hitherto had been heavily tilted in marketers' favor, is slowly shifting towards the consumers. This is a trend that is going to continue as Internet commerce grows and is likely to transcend the Internet to other channels too. There are many interesting issues to explore in this realm and we hope that the thoughts expressed in this chapter will contribute in some way to this exploration.

References

Business Week (1997a), "Service with a Click", March 24, p. 19.

Business Week (1997b), "Internet Communities", May 5, p. 64-80.

Chang, A., P. K. Kannan, and A. B. Whinston (1999a), "The Economics of Freebies in Exchange for Consumer Information on the Internet: An Exploratory Study," (forthcoming), International Journal of Electronic Commerce.

Chang, A., P. K. Kannan, and A. B. Whinston (1999b), "Electronic Communities as Intermediaries," *Proceedings of the 32nd Hawaii International Conference on System Sciences*, January, (forthcoming)

Choi, S., Stahl, D.O., and Whinston, A. B., (1997), *The Economics of Electronic Commerce*, Macmillan Technical Publishing, Indianapolis, IN.

Dellacave, T. (1996), "Curing Market Research Headaches: Virtual Reality Technology is Putting Companies in Their Customers' Shoes", *Sales and Marketing Management*, Vol. 148, July, p. 84-85.

GVU's 7th WWW User Survey (1997a),
    http://www.gvu.gatech.edu/user_surveys/survey-1997- 04.

GVU's 8th WWW User Survey (1997b),
    http://www.gvu.gatech.edu/user_surveys/survey-1997-10.

Hagel, J. and J. Rayport (1997), "The Coming Battle for Customer Information", *Harvard Business Review*, January-February, p. 53-65.

Hamlin, Charlie (1997), "Market research and the wired consumer", *Marketing News*, June 9, Vol. 31, No. 12, p.6.

InternetNews (1998). "GeoCities Settles with FTC over Privacy Violations," August 13, (www.internetnews.com)

Kannan, P. K., A. Chang, R. Kali, and A. B. Whinston (1997), "Online Marketing Information Intermediaries: An Economic Model and Analysis", Working Paper, University of Maryland, Marketing Department, November.

Kannan, P. K., A. Chang, and A. B. Whinston (1998) "Marketing Information on the I-Way," *Communications of the ACM*, Vol. 41, No. 3 (March), p. 35-43.

McCullough, Dick (1998), "Web-based Market Research Ushers in New Age," *Marketing News*, Sept. 14, p. 27-28.

Sarvary, M and P. Parker (1997), "Marketing Information: A Competitive Analysis", *Marketing Science*, Vol.16, No.1, p. 24-38.

Wylie, K. (1997), " NFO Exec Sees Most Research Going to Internet", *Advertising Age*, Vol. 68, Issue 20, May 19, p. 50.

CHAPTER 28
A Strategic Perspective of Internet Information Providers

Alexandre Barsi Lopes and Dennis Galletta
University of Pittsburgh, Katz Graduate School of Business,
alopes@pitt.edu; galletta@vms.cis.pitt.edu

Forecasters predict that the new century will usher in more extensive commercial impacts of the Internet that will dwarf those achieved in the late 1990s. Strategic models need to be applied to understand electronic commerce from two perspectives: one that emphasizes the structure of the entire industry, and one that emphasizes the contribution of the particular resources of an individual firm. This chapter provides structural and resource-based analysis of Internet information providers (IIPs) along with consideration of issues important in the generation, processing, storage, and transmission of information. Structural issues address risk, barriers to entry, bargaining power, and substitute goods available in an industry, while resource-based issues focus on a particular firm's balance of property versus knowledge, as well as its information capacity, exclusivity, and overall reputation. In general, resource-based analysis implies that generation and processing of information are knowledge-based resources, while storage and transmission are property-based resources. Structural analysis implies that there is a large and ever-increasing amount of competitiveness in the industry, bringing into doubt the effectiveness of adopting a price/cost strategy. Combined analysis leads us to conclude that knowledge-based resources will be more effective in achieving competitive advantage than property-based resources because the former will provide more capability for all-important product differentiation.

Keywords: Resource-based theory; structural perspective; strategy; strategic analysis; Internet; electronic commerce; competitive advantage

1 Introduction

From the Agricultural and Industrial ages arose a new kind of economic engine of our society: the generation, storage, transmission, and processing of information. It is believed that approximately 50% of all workers in the USA and Canada work in information-related activities (Poirier 1990). The primary showcase of the information age is the Internet, the global computer network that is becoming more and more indispensable to our activities and way of living every day.

The explosive expansion of the Internet provides an excellent example of network externality: The more an information network expands, the more people become attracted to it. The Internet has indeed been attracting a growing number of users, including those with no previous experience with computers. As the number of regular users speeds past the 50 million milestone at the rate of 71,000 new users per day (Editor & Publisher 1997), the Internet becomes a tempting medium for commerce (Notess 1996). Several new ventures have emerged that focus specifically on selling information through this medium (Blake 1995).

At this writing, there is no single model of how to conduct business on the Internet (Tedesco 1997). Several facts contribute to this situation. Rapid changes in technology enable new, unanticipated applications at every turn. The user base has been changing as well, from a population of highly experienced computer professionals to those who can be considered computer-naïve: the late adopters (Mossberg 1997). Also, firms who are leaders in providing tools and leading-edge examples to the rest of us have different origins and stakes, different visions of the Internet's future, and different notions of the ways to achieve these visions. Finally, there is social controversy surrounding the Internet, especially those related with property rights, law enforcement, security, and users' accessibility rights.

Because of these difficulties, it is important for the field to generate models for understanding the phenomena surrounding the Internet. While these models will not solve the problems, they can form the basis for a strategic analysis of the commercialization of information on the Internet.

In this analysis, we define *Internet Information Providers* (IIP) as those firms (or business units within larger corporations) that, using the Internet as the transmission medium, distribute information to customers and other end users. The transaction of interest may involve a subscription (with or without charge), a charge per unit of time consumed, or a charge per unit of information consumed.

The main objective of this paper is to formulate a series of general propositions that can be used to develop a business model for commercialization of information on the Internet. These propositions will be based on two distinct, major, and complementary perspectives of strategy: the structural perspective and the resource-based perspective.

We begin by characterizing information activities and the information value chain. The following sections introduce a series of propositions regarding the commercialization of information on the Internet based, in turn, on the structural perspective and the resource-based perspective. The last section presents conclusions about what we learned applying these models to Internet Information Providers.

2 Information Industry Activities

Information can be manipulated in four fundamental ways (Davis and Davidson 1991): *Generation* gathers and codifies environmental events, *processing* modifies information into a more useful form, *storage* attempts to safely preserve the information for later use, and *transmission* distributes the information to the users. A firm can perform any or all of these services, which can be viewed either as discrete independent activities or as a chain of interdependent activities.

Generation: News agencies such as Reuters (www.reuters.com) and financial agencies such as Bloomberg (www.bloomberg.com) would be considered as primary examples of companies dedicated to the generation of information and knowledge. Reuters creates news stories that clarify world events, while Bloomberg offers results of financial analysis for investors.

Processing: Information processing can exist by itself as in the case of companies that provide software generating graphical analyses of raw data. However, all other activities (generation, storage, and transmission) also involve some kind of information processing. Bloomberg processes data to create summaries of industries or their subsets.

Storage: There are several companies, most notably Hoovers (www.hoovers.com) that specialize in maintaining large databases. Huge repositories are available throughout the Internet, ranging from nearly complete collections of informal newsgroups kept by Deja News (www.dejanews.com) to official federal tax forms made accessible by 1040.com (www.l040.com).

Transmission: Some companies provide physical access to the Internet. Most visible are telephone carriers such as MCI (www.mci.com) and Sprint (www.sprint.com).

As mentioned above, a company can decide to focus only on one of these activities or integrate them in a chain (see Figure 1). Bloomberg Financial Services is an example of a company that executes all activities in a chain (Nee 1996). The firm captures and generates information through an internal news agency and by performing financial analyses, and processes and stores this information for future distribution either through a proprietary network or through the Internet.

Even if a company specializes in only one type of information activity (for example, only information storage or information generation), it has to execute all the other information activities to manipulate information. This is true even if these other activities are not significant in terms of the final product. For example, a company that specializes in creating and maintaining large databases must develop processes for obtaining the information, processing it, and organizing its structure for insertion into a database. It must also deliver the information contained in the database to its clients. In this case, these activities (generation, processing and transmission) are performed to support the main activity developed by the company: information storage.

Furthermore, a company may perform two or more information activities but each of the activities can generate autonomous information products. For example, Reuters generates information that feeds both real time and Internet services but it also sells this information (or a variation of it) to different newspapers around the world (Hayes 1996; Ojala 1996).

In the following sections we will examine Internet information providers from both structural and resource-based views of strategy. The resource based-view of the firm provides a useful complement to Porter's (Porter 1980) well-known structural perspective of strategy, by focusing on individual firms' specific assets, instead of industry-based factors (Miller and Shamsie 1996). A resource-based analysis of competition differs from that derived from an economic perspective both in its explanation of behavior within an industry and in its normative implications (Collis 1991). This difference arises not out of the analysis of product market position for which the resource-based of the firm offers no new insights, but from its analysis of the assets that a firm accumulates over time. The two approaches are therefore complementary, with one explaining the value of competitive outcomes in the product market, and the other explaining the dynamic aspects of firm behavior with regard to the accumulation and disposition of the firm's resources (Collis 1991).

The structural perspective of strategy focuses on the whole industry in which an IIP operates, identifying and analyzing the competitive forces that work in this industry and the competitive strategies that interact with these forces and result in a firm's competitive position. The resource-based view stresses the peculiarities and strengths of each firm that belong to an industry, identifying how these idiosyncratic characteristics can generate competitive advantage. While the structural perspective is a macro, industry-level approach, the resource-based view is a micro, firm-level view. The use of both will allow a complementary and comprehensive analysis of different firms competing in an industry.

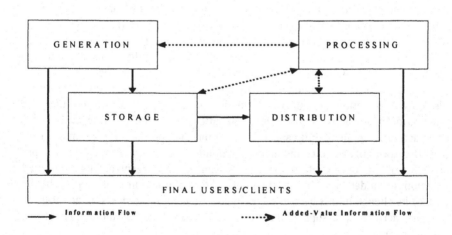

Fig. 1. Information value chain

3 Structural Perspective of Strategy

The structural perspective of strategy posits that the structural characteristics of an industry determine the levels of performance that a firm can achieve (Porter 1980; Barney 1986; Roquebert, Phillips et al. 1996). This perspective strongly illuminates economic and technological forces within an industry (Lenz and Engledow 1986), and emphasizes the role of management in searching for attractive industries that provide high profitability (Grant 1991).

According to this perspective, the main attributes that have impact on firm's returns are the existence and degree of product differentiation in the industry, the overall elasticity of demand for the industry, the existence and value of barriers to entry, and the number and relative size of the firms (Barney 1986; McWilliams and Smart 1993). The structural perspective has as its environment a set of competitive forces that establish both opportunities and threats (Lenz and Engledow 1986), where the attractiveness of the industry and the firm's relative position within the industry are fundamental to its success (Porter 1991; Carrol 1993). Therefore, the structural perspective can (Amit and Schoemaker 1993): (1) assess the profit potential of various industry participants by focusing on the external competitive forces and barriers that prevail in different product/market segments; and (2) identify the industry-level factors that keep a firm competing in an industry.

Competitive advantage in this perspective results from a firm's ability to perform the required activities at a collective lower cost than rivals, or perform some activities in unique ways that create buyer value and hence allow the firm to command a premium price (Porter 1991). Several drivers of competitiveness can lead to above-normal performance (Porter 1991): scale, cumulative learning in the activity, linkages between the activity and others, the ability to share the activity with other business units, the pattern of capacity utilization in the activity over the relevant cycle, the activity's location, the timing of investment choices in the activity, the extent of vertical integration in performing the activity, institutional factors affecting how the activity is performed such as government regulation, and the firm's policy choices about how to configure the activity independent of other drivers.

Relatively recent developments and extensions of the primordial conceptual references in the structural perspective, such as the modification of the unit of analysis from the entire industry to strategic groups, have increased its role in business planning (Porter 1981). These strategic groups are composed of firms that are attempting to modify or exploit similar structural characteristics of a given industry (Barney 1986). Therefore, members of a certain strategic group act in a similar way and possess relatively equal strategies. This extension of the structural perspective relaxes the assumption of firm homogeneity within an entire industry and allows more explanation of variation in performance.

Indeed, several industry factors may be used to explain unusually high profitability achieved by firms competing in this given industry. Meta-analysis indicated that several industry-level factors (such as industry concentration, industry growth, capital investment, size and advertising) have a significant impact on firms' performance (Capon, Farley et al. 1990). However, other studies have shown that firm-level factors can be used to explain a larger amount of diversity among firms' profit-ability (Jacobson 1990; Roquebert, Phillips et al. 1996).

Two points should be made before proceeding with a detailed analysis of an ge-neric IIP industry. It is important to notice that an almost infinite number of potential markets could be served by Internet information providers. We do believe that com-panies that distribute information on the Internet share a certain number of charac-teristics, either because of the characteristics of information as a product or because of the transmission medium (or because of the interaction of both). Nevertheless, we may classify IIP industries and companies on a continuum of possible types of in-formation being provided. At one extreme of this continuum are decision-making/economic transaction-related sites, which provide information for financial investment, information about business and industry trends, information about prod-ucts, etc. One example would be the Nasdaq site about financial investment (www.nasdaq.com). At the other extreme we have leisure-related sites (sports, en-tertainment, etc.). The example here could be Microsoft's Cinemania, with reviews and news about movies (cinemania.msn.com). In the middle of the continuum we could have, for example, online newspapers or magazines with a more general fo-cus, services that could be used for both economic transaction-related activities and leisure. The example could be the New York Times' site (www.nytimes.com).

It is also important to observe that some IIPs can obtain profits from different sources other than users' subscriptions and other direct charges. For example, many sites today have their profits based solely on advertising (Blake 1995). Other sites may acquire profits from transactions related to the information they provide. Travelocity (www.travelocity.com), an Internet based travel agency, offers free in-formation about flights, car rentals, and tourist destinations. However, this firm benefits from the transactions that are conducted through the site, like a traditional travel agency.

The structural perspective of strategy provides a useful framework for strategic analysis. Porter's (1980) model (in the structural perspective) defined five competi-tive forces that affect the degree of competition in a specific industry: suppliers, customers, current competitors, potential industry entrants, and substitute products. Each force and its application to IIPs will now be described.

3.1 Suppliers

The bargaining power of information suppliers is, on a large scale, related to the scarcity of information they provide and to the threat of vertical integration they present (Porter 1980). A firm that is the sole supplier of information will have strong bargaining power. Information uniqueness may come from many sources, including exclusive access to information or from a provider's reputation, for example. At the other extreme, when the information is widely and inexpensively available, the bar-gaining power of suppliers of that information would be very low.

The stronger position for information suppliers can also derive from the low investment needed to create and maintain an Internet site (Kambil 1997). Because the Internet provides a very inexpensive medium to those that sell information to reach final customers, information suppliers (companies that generate information) normally can bypass any kind of information intermediaries. For example, while it is possible to find information about the NBA in both ESPN (espn.sportszone.com) and CNNSI (www.cnnsi.com), much of the same information can also be found at NBA's official site itself (www.nba.com). Likewise, income tax forms, available from 1040.com (www.1040.com) are also available at the IRS site itself (www.irs.ustreas.gov). It seems that, if a user has some expertise with Internet search mechanisms, he/she will be able to find alternative sources for that information. Therefore, if the existence of an IIP is dependent on information provided by third parties, it is in a precarious position because of the presence of numerous other inexpensive sources of the same information.

There are some ways, however, in which an IIP can leverage relationships with suppliers. The IIP can, for example, act as a channel between multiple suppliers and multiple customers, operating essentially as an interface. When faced with a situation of uncertainty or lack of familiarity, customers tend to persist with a simpler representation of the world (Sheth and Parvatiyar 1995). If an IIP can centralize information coming from different sources and present this information in an organized way to the customer, the customer may stick with this IIP instead of trying to search for alternative sources on the Internet. This arrangement would also be beneficial to the providers, because this channel could be an alternative source of profits to them. America Online (www.aol.com), for example, is a company that has been very successful in establishing its channeling interface.

The number of suppliers and the structure in which they are organized is fundamental to the success of the IIP acting as a channel. For example, it is possible to find information about companies and corporations in several sites in the Internet, including the companies' own sites. However, the difficulties and costs involved in this time-consuming effort are large. Therefore, it makes sense that companies specialized in maintaining and distributing huge databases (such as Hoovers) can be profitable with the Internet.

3.2 Clients

Two factors give bargaining power to clients when they seek information products on the Internet. First, there are few switching costs involved in the substitution of an Internet information service. Therefore, clients are only tied to an IIP when there is the belief that the relationship provides some benefit to them. If contracts are created, they are often more like subscriptions than long-term associations; clients find they are not tied into long-term arrangements that prevent them from seeking alternative services from other IIPs. In cases where there are no fees received from clients, and revenue is derived only from advertising, switching costs are limited to the time it would take to find an alternative source and learn how to use it. As in commercial broadcasting, the clients' power is in their numbers, making the site attractive to advertisers.

The second and most significant advantage for the client side comes from the number of alternative services that are available. A search engine will often yield several sites contained the desired information, many of which are free. This tilts the power balance even more steeply toward clients.

Only when two conditions occur simultaneously might the IIP have advantage over clients. The first condition is that the information sold by the IIP is unique or exclusive. A basic way to generate exclusive information comes from value-added activities such as processing the information in some unique way. Even when the raw information is freely available on the Internet, the additional analysis, graphics and processing may be quite valuable to the clients. In the case of ESPN and CNNSI, for example, even considering that we can find the results and other basic information about sports in many other sites, the analysis presented in the site is normally the exclusive property of these sites.

However, there needs to be careful selection of information to provide, or the exclusivity will be wasted and the market will be too small to be justified. We can hardly imagine enough people paying enough to justify a site containing exclusive information about a third-division soccer team in Ceara, Brazil. To have an edge over the clients, the IIP has to provide information whose expected utility to the client is high, or at very least, higher than its cost. For example, clients would pay a substantial amount for information that would help them save a great deal of money. Therefore, an IIP only has bargaining power over clients if it offers information that is both exclusive and with high expected utility.

3.3 Potential Industry Entrants

For several reasons, barriers to entry for providing information on the Internet are almost nonexistent. First, information is intangible, does not obey laws of physics, and is infinitely replicable (Poirier 1990). Therefore, there are potentially no economies of scale in the production of new information. Second, because information can be manipulated, combined, and processed in many different ways, depending essentially on the creativity of those involved in information manipulation, there are potentially infinite opportunities for differentiation. Third, capital requirements to create an Internet business are relatively small, due to continuous decreases in the costs of information technology (Hawkings 1994; Kambil 1997). Fourth, as we discussed above, clients' switching costs are relatively small, making the adoption of new entrants relatively easy. Finally, the Internet itself provides the distribution channel that is used by IIPs to reach its clients, eliminating problems of competition over distribution channels.

Therefore, together with the threat of vertical integration from information suppliers, it is expected that the lack of barriers to entry will keep the provision of information on the Internet highly competitive.

3.4 Current Participants

One factor that can affect the direct competition between IIPs is the Internet's exponential and highly-publicized growth in the last few years. The high rate of increase in the number of users (potential customers) is accompanied by less need to gain market share by stealing existing customers of other IIPs. For now, it almost seems that all IIPs can grow substantially, with a perhaps temporary absence of a "zero-sum game."

Other factors, however, may increase the competition among IIPs, especially when these firms are aiming for small markets. First, a large number of firms provide information on the Internet, and for almost any kind of information we can find several different providers. Second, there is once again the effect of low switching costs. Third, the firms that are selling information on the Internet have very diverse origins. Some of them are affiliated with larger, disparate corporations in a variety of industries (Notess 1996), while others were created specifically for doing business on the Internet (Blake 1995). This situation generates an abundance of business models and visions among the participants, which leads to an abundance of opportunity for competition. Finally, there could be high strategic stakes involved, because of the commonly-held prediction of continued future growth of Internet business and incursion of its impact into the daily lives of more and more people with less and less computer experience.

Thus, we believe that, with so many participants, so many different visions, and so much belief in rising stakes, the competition among IIPs will eventually become very large, especially in those contexts where there is a high degree of adoption of potential customers.

3.5 Substitute Products

Three characteristics give information services on the Internet an advantage over substitute products. There is great potential for nearly continuous updating, multimedia capabilities, wide and instantaneous distribution, and interactivity.

IIPs provide services that can be updated several times a day, which is especially useful when the information is volatile as, for example, stock quotes. Also, IIPs can carry multimedia files containing elements such as video and sound, giving them a clear competitive edge over newspapers and magazines unless CD-ROMs are bundled with them. Manufactured products such as magazines and CD-ROMs are produced in a fixed quantity and circulated to a pre-established distribution channel, while Internet information can reach thousands or millions of browsers with equal ease.

While television and radio also offer multimedia and can reach large numbers of people quickly, these media do not provide interactivity. The exchange of information between the user and the IIP cannot be reproduced easily with radio and television. Interactivity allows the user to narrow the focus of interest in the content that is provided by the IIP. Also, the Internet itself provides a media for exchange of opinion, because both parties can communicate using e-mail or discussion groups.

Obviously, we are still far from a problem-free Internet. Language differences can constrain market size, and bandwidth limitations prevent the use of highly sophisticated multimedia content. However, current work on language translation and use of satellite and cable TV infrastructure might reduce these difficulties.

3.6 Differentiation x Price/Cost Strategy

An analysis of the five competitive forces involved in industries encompassing IIPs lead us to the conclusion that the most appropriate strategy in these industries is differentiation. First, there is a large number of competitors and, due to the lack of barriers to entry, the expectation of more and more competitors over time. Second, there is a lack of perfect substitutes; on the contrary, people seem to be turning away from some conventional media such as television and long-distance calling toward the Internet (Find/SVP 1997). Third, there is a proliferation of different visions for the future of the Internet, involving hardware, software, concepts, etc., leading not only to a competition for prices but a competition for the implementation of visions. Fourth and finally, due to the number of information sources on the Internet, especially free sources, clients have a strong position, leading IIPs to work even harder to achieve a large customer base. All of these factors, especially the existence of free sources of information, lead IIPs to try to differentiate their services in order to grow.

At the same time, the existence of alternative free services works against using a price/cost strategy. It is difficult to compete in price or cost when there are a number of free alternatives. Furthermore, many information products have similar problems because information has two interesting characteristics that make it an unusual resource: intangibility and infinite replicability. It is difficult to imagine a price/cost strategy applied to a product that has these characteristics, because the product itself can be reproduced with almost zero cost. Also, it is difficult to appraise information. How can we appraise, for example, the application of an analytical procedure to data recovered from stock markets? How can we appraise the convenience of having an electronic newspaper instead of a printed copy? How can we appraise search mechanisms or portal sites? Finally, there is some controversy involving competitive price moves in online industries. We can take the recent example of America Online, which some time ago reduced its monthly subscription fee and quickly gained so many new customers in a short period of time that they overloaded their servers (Gurley and Martin 1997). Even while industry observers complained against price decreases (Fong 1997; Gurley and Martin 1997), the price move was followed by other online providers, diminishing America Online's advantage.

We are not saying here that a price/cost strategy is completely infeasible. However, because of characteristics of information as a product they are difficult to implement and may be rapidly assimilated and imitated by competitors, which can lead to price wars in detriment of all participants in the industry. Thus, a differentiation strategy looks more appropriate for IIPs, especially in an environment that is likely to become more competitive in the future as the rate of adoption begins to peak.

3.7 Propositions from the Strategic Perspective of Strategy

From the analysis of IIP using the strategic perspective of strategy, the following propositions can be derived:

- P1. Dependence of an IIP on information provided by third parties will increase its risk. This risk, however, may be minimized in the cases where the IIP can serve as a channel for several other IIPs.
- P2. The bargaining power of clients will exceed that of IIPs because of the number of alternative information sources. An exception to that rule occurs when an IIP provides information that is both exclusive and high in expected utility for the client.
- P3. The few barriers to entry, large number of participants and, consequently, different visions about the future will make the competitiveness among IIPs increase, especially in markets where there are a large number of potential adopters, a large expected profitability, and high strategic stakes.
- P4. IIPs will have an advantage over non-Internet substitute products in the cases where multimedia, fast update and interactivity are important.
- P5. Differentiation-related strategies will be more effective that price/cost-related strategies when an IIP seeks competitive advantage.

4 Resource-Based View

The resource-based view emphasizes the resources that individual firms have developed to compete in their environment (Miller and Shamsie 1996), with the assumption that these resources are heterogeneously distributed across industries (Barney 1991) and these resources were acquired through limited competition before they became valuable (Peteraf 1993). The resource-based view explains long-lived differences in firm profitability that cannot be attributed to differences in industry conditions (Peteraf 1993). Firms obtain competitive advantage by using strategies in which they exploit their resources, and therefore respond to environmental opportunities while neutralizing external threats and avoiding internal weaknesses (Barney 1991). The resource view has been used to formulate a new and more dynamic (in comparison to neoclassical theory) model for competition, where competition and lack of equilibrium are conditions leading to firms' innovative behavior (Hunt and Morgan 1995; Hunt and Morgan 1996).

Resources include all of a firm's assets, capabilities, organizational processes, special attributes, information, knowledge, etc., that it controls for conceiving and implementing strategies that improve its competitive advantage (Barney 1991). Here we use Grant's definition of competitive advantage (Grant 1995), that states that when two firms compete, one firm possesses a competitive advantage over the other when it earns a higher rate of profit or has the potential to earn a higher rate of profit. Resources confer competitive advantage to a firm to the extent that they are rare or hard to imitate, have no direct substitutes, and enable companies to pursue opportunities while avoiding threats (Miller and Shamsie 1996). In other words, the ability of a firm to achieve an advantageous, firm-specific resource improves the way in which the firm can compete in its specific industry (Aharoni 1993).

To confer sustainable competitive advantage, a firm's resource should possess four different attributes (Barney 1991):

(a) it must be valuable;
(b) it must be rare among firm's current and potential competitors;
(c) it must be imperfectly imitable; and
(d) there cannot be strategic equivalent substitutes for this resource that are valuable but neither rare or imperfectly imitable.

The lack of imitability of a resource can be caused by three factors (Barney 1991): unique historical conditions, elusive linkages between causes and consequences, and the presence of a socially complex environment.

The resource can be derived from unique historical conditions and a competitor organization should follow the same path to acquire the resource. An example is given by the Japanese automakers and their network of suppliers (Dyer 1996). These networks have permitted that Japanese automakers to obtain sustained competitive advantage in comparison to their American counterparts (at least in some segments). These networks, however, were very difficult to imitate because they were developed through mutual trust relationships over a long period of time. Unless their competitors develop the same trajectory, they probably will not be able to develop equivalent networks. In the specific case of online information, this may be the case of Reuters, the largest online financial information company in the world with earnings topping $ 586 million in 1995 (Hayes 1996). This company has a history of 145 years generating and distributing financial information, ranging from using doves in the early years to their current real time electronic networks to perform this task.

Because there may not be a clear link between the resources and the outcomes, it is often difficult to identify the causes of the sustained competitive advantage. Again, Japanese companies during the 80's can provide a useful example. Despite many studies trying to identify the factors that made Japanese companies superior in some industries, no clear causal relationship was found between a certain bundle of firm-level characteristics and superior performance (Chow, Shields et al. 1991). In the case of online information products we can cite as an example America Online. Despite problems with connectivity that America Online clients have found (InfoWorld 1997), this company is still a market leader by a large margin in the provision of online information for broad markets (Monash and Barlow 1997). However, there is no clear understanding of the source of this success. Possible reasons cited include technological infrastructure, reputation, and establishment of brand. (Kawasaki 1997; Monash and Barlow 1997).

The resource may be originated by complex social phenomena occurring in a complex social environment, making it difficult for a firm to manage the process. For example, in the case of clan-form companies (Ouchi 1980) that possess competitive advantage, is difficult to identify exactly which characteristics of the firm provide this advantage. One specific example in the arena of online information products is Bloomberg, a company that provides financial information, considered by some the "biggest financial information success story of the past decade" (Willoughby 1995). Part of this success is attributed by the company's founder to their corporate culture, "where the employees act as if they were the owners" (Dumaine 195).

Six major categories of resources have been suggested (Grant 1991): financial, physical, human, technological, organizational and reputation. However, this classification does not give a precise idea about how resources can evolve through time and how these resources are fitted to the environment surrounding a company. Another categorization scheme is proposed by Miller and Shamsie (1996) classifying resources into two categories: property-based and knowledge-based. Property-based resources are those legally controlled by a specific firm, whose competitors are not permitted to acquire those resources; they are tied to specific and well-defined assets. Thereby, the firm can obtain superior performance until the market changes and devalues that resource. Knowledge-based resources are protected from imitation because they are subtle or hard to understand, involving talents that are elusive and whose connection with performance is hard to understand. Knowledge-based resources typically are better designed to respond and adapt to the challenges facing the organization.

Furthermore, Miller and Shamsie (1996) consider that each kind of resource is more appropriate for a certain type of environment: property-based resources fit better with a predictable environment and knowledge-based resources with an uncertain environment. Because property-based resources are designed primarily to provide an organization with a high-degree of control, they are likely to be of most value in a stable and predictable environment, where the firm can maintain their relevance. When the environment is unpredictable, property-based resources may be rapidly depreciated by the changes in the context in which the organization is embedded. On the other hand, unpredictable and unstable environments form the ideal settings for knowledge-based resources, where these resources can be used to anticipate and respond to changes posed by the environment. It does not mean that these resources are irrelevant in stable environments but in the latter context the use and development of knowledge-based resources could represent a waste of firm efforts and financial resources.

In the resource-based perspective, the origin of a company and its capability to implement synergy among activities are very important, because they enable the exploitation of resources that a firm owns. According to Ansoff (1987), synergy is the capacity of utilizing and combining several resources of a company in order to produce an outcome that is greater than simply the sum of activities. Synergy gives the company more flexibility in the market (Ansoff 1987), decreases the amount of capital necessary to enter an industry (Porter 1980), and represents an opportunity that should not be overlooked (Hax and Majluf 1996).

In this section we described the Resource-Based view of the firm, identified the main characteristics of resources and introduced a classification scheme where we can categorize resources according to their relationship with property and knowledge and their fit with the environment. In the following section we will use the concepts of resources as they relate to the information industry to develop a series of propositions regarding the possibilities that IIPs have to achieve competitive advantage.

4.1 The Resource-Based View and IIPs

Because of technological uncertainty, the lack of business models, potential competitiveness, strategic interests and different dimensions of competition, we believe that knowledge-based resources will be more effective than property-based resources in achieving competitive advantage in the commercialization of information on the Internet.

First, there is technological uncertainty. The relatively recent explosive growth of the Internet brought a new wave of technological development in the transmission of online information, especially those regarding the transmission of multimedia features (Cohen 1997; Wagner 1997). New standards have been developed for data compression and new forms of presentation and advancements in programming languages used in the Internet have contributed to new improvements in the technology. The decision about the type of technology to be adopted now is also much more difficult because there is a great uncertainty about which of these new technologies will become the "de facto" standard in online transmission.

Second, as we mentioned before, online information acquired a strategic dimension with the development of the Internet, with several companies beginning to use the Internet to disseminate their information. Information companies with good reputations have been trying to build on those reputations, launching new Internet counterparts to their successful newspapers and databases (Information Today 1996; Jenkins 1996; Notess 1996). The perspective that online information will constitute a great source of profitability in the future has been attracting firms from all segments and therefore increasing the competition among those that commercialize information. However, there is still no clear model of how to conduct business in the Internet, and this lack of a consistent model leads to high uncertainty regarding the expectations about those ventures (Tedesco 1997).

Finally, the competition among IIPs involves separate dimensions. For example, there is competition between services that can be accessed directly and those that are aggregated within a larger product (for example, information provided by America Online and CompuServe) (Kobielus 1996). There is also competition between paid and free IIPs, provided that the person searching for the information has some degree of expertise with search engines (Kawasaki 1997).

These conditions comprise a very uncertain and dynamic environment, where knowledge-based resources have a more effective contribution to competitive advantage than property-based resources.

Each of the four information activities has different potential for generating competitive advantage for an IIP. This potential depends essentially on the amount of reliance an information activity has on technological aspects of competition. Resource-based theory scholars believe that is very unlikely that computers and information technology by themselves can be a source of sustained competitive advantage, essentially because the machines are generally commodities and nearly-identical units can be bought nearly anywhere (Barney 1991; Miller and Shamsie 1996). Therefore, we believe that if an information activity is essentially dependent on information technology it will be associated with property-based resources and it will constitute a competitive advantage only in exceptional cases.

Information generation can provide competitive advantage when the firm creates information that is unique and whose expected utility is high. The expected utility of information relies on its scarcity and may vary according to its purpose, especially when related to decision making activities and efficiency maximization in the performance of certain activities (Melody 1987). A strong capability of information generation means that this kind of company would have significant capacity to build a product repository from which it could extract the information necessary to supply specific demands. An information repository with comprehensive content and adequate structure could facilitate the strategic development of products to different markets. This ability should be considered a knowledge-based resource because it requires subtle capabilities that cannot be controlled and legally owned.

Unique knowledge about specific ways to process information can also result in competitive advantage to an IIP. There are risks associated with the commoditization of information, especially when this information can be obtained from several sources (Gandy 1992). IIPs may alleviate this risk by creating value through the aggregation of more and more services, especially in the analysis of the information (Ojala 1990). Acting in this way, IIPs abandon the role of information brokers and assume the role of information consultants (Broughton, Blackburn et al. 1991). These companies would not simply facilitate the access to information, but by its aggregation they would be creating unique new information that could be valuable for users.

Processing activity also creates information but in a way that differs from information generation activities. Mainly the difference stems from the possible use of third party information, instead of direct acquisition. The advantage is gained by unique and valuable ways of analyzing and processing the information. If a financial company developed a useful way to analyze financial data, for instance, and can use this technology on data provided by stock markets, this company could be more successful penetrating a market or expanding its market share. Processing activities should be considered knowledge-based resources because of the same reasons we use to classify generation activities in this category: subtle abilities that cannot be either physically acquired or legally controlled.

The other two information activities, storage and transmission, are heavily related to information technology and, consequently, the likelihood that these activities may generate competitive advantage is small. In the case of transmission, the Internet itself imposes a restriction to the IIPs that desire to use information transmission as a way to acquire competitive advantage. IIPs have only a limited set of options to control information transmission. They can, for example, increase the capacity of their servers, allowing better access and more speed in information retrieval. They can also manipulate the protocol in order to equalize transmission speed to their users. However, two important factors that affect information transmission are out of the control of IIPs. The first one is the speed of the user's connection, which determines the velocity of information transmission. The second is the network structure, where the transmission nodes are not controlled directly by anyone, being subject to external factors such as variability in physical lines and capacity of the intermediary servers. This structure works well to increase reliability and speed of a particular transmission, making use of alternative routes when desirable. However, it prevents the sending and receiving parties from controlling the flow of information, making competitive advantage due to transmission activities unlikely.

Storage activity is also essentially based on information technology, involving devices that have dropped in price most dramatically in the last few years (Hawkings 1994). Additionally, knowledge of how to create and maintain a database is publicly available and transmitted in journals and universities worldwide. Furthermore, new database tools, especially those equipped with interactive Fourth Generation Languages, facilitate the creation and maintenance of databases (Fichman and Kemerer 1993).

Obviously, a certain amount of talent is still necessary in the creation of the structure of a database. However, there are new tools provided in data warehousing and mining packages that provide new methods based on statistical procedures and artificial intelligence that can integrate apparently unrelated databases and create a single structure from which is possible to retrieve valuable information (Inmon 1996; Newing 1996a; Newing 1996b). Yet, in this case the value would be added by processing activities (unique ways of interpreting data) and not by storage activities. Thus, it is difficult to imagine that information storage activity can provide competitive advantage, essentially because it is associated with publicly available knowledge and information technology.

There are some circumstances, however, in which property-based resources such as information storage and transmission may result in competitive advantage. The first case happens when a firm has a reputation of reliability. Actually, reputation can be considered not only a valuable resource (Porter 1980), but also a resource that is very difficult to imitate because it relies on historical events (Barney 1991), giving us reason to classify reputation as a knowledge-based resource. In this case, firms based on property-based resources can leverage their activities and achieve competitive advantage. It should be noted that reputation would also improve the capacity of generating competitive advantage that knowledge-based resources have.

Size, amount of information sources provided, and access to exclusive sources can also be important to generate competitive advantage in the case of storage activity. If an IIP possess exclusive access to valuable information sources it can almost incorporate the advantage produced by information generation activities, since in the eyes of the client, the online information firm that is acting as a broker is generating new information. Size of the database and amount of information sources provided can also generate competitive advantage in a similar way. To the client, the amount of information that is accessible in a single location increases the attractiveness of the IIP.

An important observation is that these information activities may also represent cases of complementarity of resources, where joint use of resources can potentially yield a higher total return than the sum of returns that can be earned if each set of resources is used independently of the other. These types of synergy can be achieved in several different ways, from acquisition of a firm to the purchase of its services or goods (Chi 1994). Referring again to Figure 1, if a company that performs an information activity is close to the beginning of the chain, it will have more opportunity to reach clients and final users, either with "raw" information or with information processed in such a form as to contain added value. If a company is near the end of the chain, it will have fewer opportunities to add value to information and fewer channels by which it can increase its base of clients and users. Therefore, the combination of different information activities may be used to enhance the prospects of achieving competitive advantage.

4.2 Propositions from the Resource-Based View

From the analysis of IIP using the resource-based view of strategy, the following propositions can be derived:

- P6. Because technological uncertainty, the lack of business models, potential competitiveness, strategic interests and different dimensions of competition make the environment for IIPs unpredictable and dynamic, knowledge-based resources will be more effective than property-based resources in achieving competitive advantage in the commercialization of information on the Internet.
- P7. Information generation and information processing behave more like knowledge-based resources and information storage and distribution behave more like property-based resources.
- P8. A good reputation achieved by the IIP may "boost" the other information activities, making both knowledge-based and property-based resources more effective.
- P9. In the case of information storage, database size and amount of information provided may enhance the IIP's capacity to achieve competitive advantage.

- P10. In the case of both information storage and information distribution, exclusive access to information sources may increase the possibility of an IIP to achieve competitive advantage. Additionally, from the client's perspective, this may be considered a special case of information generation.
- P.11. The combination of different information activities may be used to enhance the prospects of achieving competitive advantage.

5 Conclusion

Structural and resource-based strategic theoretical bases provide a perspective that is simultaneously macro and micro in nature. The macro perspective addresses the general characteristics of the information industries comprised in the Internet, and the micro perspective describes potential competitive resources for IIPs.

From the structural perspective, it appears that the competitive forces in Internet information industries contain a high degree of competitiveness, especially when the Internet adoption process achieves it peak. The analysis of these forces lead us to conclude that price/cost strategies will probably be ineffective in this environment and, to survive, a company should pursue differentiation as its main strategy.

The resource-based view implies that each information activity is related to one of two basic types of resources: each is based either on knowledge or property. Due to the subtle requirements for performing these information activities, both generation and processing activities are knowledge-based resources. At the same type, storage and transmission activities are associated with information technology, which are property-based resources.

Form the combined analysis of the industry and the examination of information activities which yield rich, competitive resources, we propose that information activities related to knowledge-based resources, namely generation and processing, will be more effective in achieving competitive advantage than property-based resources, namely storage and transmission. Furthermore, information generation and processing can provide a company with the ability to create information that is unique and has high expected utility, giving this company the capacity to pursue a differentiation strategy.

Further research is still necessary to advance our knowledge in the area of commercialization of information on the Internet. The purpose of this paper was the development of a theoretical basis for future empirical research. From the discussion above, we would like to emphasize and recommend the use of complementary perspectives of strategy as a way to provide a strong and complete theoretical framework upon which this empirical research can be conducted.

Acknowledgement. Alexandre Barsi Lopes is a fellow of CAPES, Brasilia – Brazil.

References

Aharoni, Y. (1993). "In Search for the Unique: Can Firm-Specific Advantages Be Evaluated?" *Journal of Management Studies* 30(1): 31-49.

Amit, R. and P. J. H. Schoemaker (1993). "Strategic Assets and Organizational Rent." *Strategic Management Journal* 14: 33-46.

Ansoff, H. I. (1987). *New Corporate Strategy.* New York, Wiley and Sons.

Barney, J. B. (1986). "Types of Competition and the Theory of Strategy: Toward an Integrative Framework." *Academy of Management Review* 11(4): 791-800.

Barney, J. B. (1991). "Firm Resources and Sustained Competitive Advantage." *Journal of Management* 11(4): 99-120.

Blake, P. (1995). "Infopreneurs on the World Wide Web." *Information Today* 12(6): 12-13.

Broughton, D., L. Blackburn, et al. (1991). "Information Brokers and Information Consultants." *Library Management* 12(6): 4-16.

Capon, N., J. U. Farley, et al. (1990). "Determinants of Financial Performance: A Meta-Analysis." *Management Science* 36(10): 1143-1159.

Carrol, G. R. (1993). "A Sociological View on Why Firms Differ." *Strategic Management Journal* 14: 237-249.

Chi, T. (1994). "Trading in Strategic Resources: Necessary Conditions, Transaction Cost Problems, and Choice of Exchange Structure." *Strategic Management Journal* 15: 271-190.

Chow, C. W., M. D. Shields, et al. (1991). "The Effects of Management Controls and National Culture on Manufacturing Performance: An Experimental Investigation." *Accounting, Organizations, and Society* 16(3): 209-226.

Cohen, S. (1997). "A Guide to Multimedia in the Next Millenium." *Training & Development* 51(8): 31-39.

Collis, D. J. (1991). "A Resource-Based Analysis of Global Competition: The Case of the Bearings Industry." *Strategic Management Journal* 12: 49-68.

Davis, S. and B. Davidson (1991). *2020 Vision.* New York, Simon & Schuster.

Dumaine, B. (195). Volume Down at Bloomberg. *Fortune.* 131: 33-34.

Dyer, J. H. (1996). "Specialized Supplier Networks as a Source of Competitive Advantage: Evidence from the Auto Industry." *Strategic Management Journal* 17: 271-291.

Editor & Publisher (1997). 71,000 New Net users Every Day: New International Study. *Editor & Publisher.* 130: 41.

Fichman, R. G. and C. F. Kemerer (1993). "Adoption of Software Engineering Process Innovations: The Case of Object Orientation." *Sloan Management Review* 34(2): 7-22.

Fong, K. (1997). Let's face it: Flat-rate online pricing is insupportable. *Network World.* 14: 24.

Gandy, T. (1992). "The Dash for Data." *The Banker*(December): 59-60.

Grant, R. M. (1991). "The Resource-Based Theory of Competitive Advantage: Implications for Strategy Formulation." *California Management Review*(Spring): 114-135.

Grant, R. M. (1995). *Contemporary Stratgy Analysis: Concepts, Techniques, Applications.* Cambridge, MA, Blackwell Publishers Inc.

Gurley, J. W. and M. H. Martin (1997). The Price Isn't Right on the Internet. *Fortune.* 135: 152-154.

Hawkings, D. T. (1994). "Growth Trends in the Electronic Information Services Market: Part III." *Online*(January): 117-119.

Hax, A. and N. S. Majluf (1996). *The Strategy Concept and Process: A Pragmatical Approach.* Upper Saddle River, NJ, Prentice Hall.

Hayes, J. R. (1996). Acquisition Is Fine, But Organic Growth Is Better. *Forbes.* **158:** 52-56.

Hunt, S. D. and R. M. Morgan (1995). "The Comparative Advantage Theory of Competition." *Journal of Marketing* **59:** 1-15.

Hunt, S. D. and R. M. Morgan (1996). "The Resource-Advantage Theory of Competition: Dynamics, Path Dependencies, and Evolutionary Dimensions." *Journal of Marketing* **60:** 107-114.

Information Today (1996). "Database Race to the Web." *Information Today* **13**(7): 1,55.

InfoWorld (1997). "AOL: A Case in (Painful) Point." *InfoWorld* **19**(18): 74.

Inmon, W. H. (1996). "The Data Warehouse and Data Mining." *Communications of the ACM* **39**(11): 49-50.

Jacobson, R. (1990). "Unobservable Effects and Business Performance." *Marketing Science* **9**(1): 74-85.

Jenkins, M. (1996). The Washington Post Recover from a False Digital Start. *Branweek.* **37:** N14-N16.

Kambil, A. (1997). "Doing Business in the Wired World." *Computer* **30**(5): 56-61.

Kawasaki, G. (1997). Get off Steve's Case. *Forbes.* **159:** 110.

Kobielus, J. (1996). On-line Services Will Mutate to Survive in the Age of the World-Wide Web. *Network World.* **13:** 44.

Lenz, R. T. and J. L. Engledow (1986). "Environmental Analysis: The Applicability of Current Theory." *Strategic Management Journal* **7:** 329-346.

McWilliams, A. and D. L. Smart (1993). "Efficiency v. Structure-Conduct-Performance: Implications for Strategy Research and Practice." *Journal of Management* **19**(1): 63-78.

Melody, W. H. (1987). "Information: An Emerging Dimension of Institutional Analysis." *Journal of Economic Issues* **XXI**(1): 1313-1339.

Miller, D. and J. Shamsie (1996). "The Resource-Based View of the Firm in Two Environments: The Hollywood Film Studios From 1936 to 1965." *Academy of Management Journal* **39**(3): 519-543.

Monash, C. and L. Barlow (1997). "AOL Doesn't Suck!" *Upside* **9**(5): 76-88.

Mossberg, W. (1997). Computers Are Still Too Complicated, But Changes Are Coming. *Wall Street Journal.* New York: B1.

Nee, E. (1996). "Michael Bloomberg." *Upside* **8**(5): 36-53.

Newing, R. (1996a). "Data Mining." *Management Accounting - London* **74**(9): 34-36.

Newing, R. (1996b). "Data Warehousing." *Management Accounting - London* **74**(3): 21-22.

Notess, G. R. (1996). "News Resources in the World Wide Web." *Database* **19**(1): 12-20.

Ojala, M. (1990). "Institutional Investors Go Online." *Link-Up*(July/August): 28-29.

Ojala, M. (1996). "Reuters Profile: An Online House of Mirrors." *Database* **19**(4): 12-19.

Ouchi, W. G. (1980). "Markets, Bureaucracies, and Clans." *Administrative Science Quarterly* **25**(March): 129-142.

Peteraf, M. A. (1993). "The Cornerstones of Competive Advantage: A Resource-Based View." *Strategic Management Journal* **14:** 179-191.

Poirier, R. (1990). "The Information Economy Approach: Characteristics, Limitations, and Future Prospects." *The Information Society* **7:** 245-285.

Porter, M. E. (1980). *Competitive Strategy - Techniques for Analyzing Industries and Competitors.* New York, MacMillan/Free Press.

Porter, M. E. (1981). "The Contributions of Industrial Organization to Strategic Management." *Academy of Management Review* **6**(4): 609-620.

Porter, M. E. (1991). "Towards a Dynamic Theory of Strategy." *Strategic Management Journal* **12**: 95-117.

Roquebert, J. A., R. L. Phillips, et al. (1996). "Markets Vs. Management: What 'Drives' Profitability?" *Strategic Management Journal* **17**: 653-664.

Sheth, J. N. and A. Parvatiyar (1995). "Relationship Marketing in Consumer Markets: Antecedents and Consequences." *Journal of the Academy of Marketing Science* **23**(4): 255-271.

Tedesco, R. (1997). Roads Taken, Not Taken Toward Internet Profits. *Broadcasting & Cable*. **127**: 72.

Wagner, M. (1997). Microsoft, MCI Champion 'Net Video Technology. *ComputerWorld*. **31**: 43-44.

Willoughby, J. (1995). "Assembling an Information Giant." *Investment Dealers Digest* **61**(40): 14-19.

CHAPTER 29

A Strategic Framework for Electronic Commerce:
The Digital Production Cycle

Jaana Porra

Department of Decision and Information Sciences, University of Houston, Houston, TX, USA, jaana@uh.edu

In this chapter we introduce an all-digital production cycle. We explain how traditional industry value chains are being transformed in cyberspace. Our main argument is that an all-digital production cycle is emerging for electronic commerce firms with all-digital products. These all-digital products are created, manufactured, marketed, sold and delivered over the network in ten phases: (1) Strategy; (2) Concept; (3) Content Creation Plan; (4) Digital Acquisition; (5) Manufacturing; (6) Product or Service Version; (7) Electronic Commerce Policy; (8) Repository; (9) Electronic Distribution; and (10) Electronic Markets. We conclude that an electronic commerce enterprise manufacturing all-digital products may rely on a qualitatively different production cycle than a traditional business manufacturing physical products.

Keywords: Digital Production Cycle; Digital Product; Electronic Commerce Industry; Business Strategy; Business Model; Content Creation; Digital Manufacturing; Electronic Commerce Application

1 Introduction

Electronic commerce is the most significant strategic shift in applying computers to business since Porter's competitive advantage paradigm (cf., Porter, 1985). Porter's model moved the focus of information technology (IT) in organizations from an administrative role (supporting the core business functions) to direct business support (becoming a part of the core function). This changed the role of IT from a consumer of administrative overhead to a provider of competitive advantage. More specifically, competitive advantage using IT is developed by automating the value chain processes that involve: inbound logistics; operations; outbound logistics; marketing and customer service (Figure 1). With the integration of IT, products and services can: be delivered faster; produced at lower cost; and more clearly differentiated from competitors. With this paradigm shift, IT's role in the organization has also been enhanced by a shift in the opinion of IT's importance to business' strategic plans. It is now common to speak about competitively-advantaged information systems that directly affect the corporate value chain and thus the bottom line.

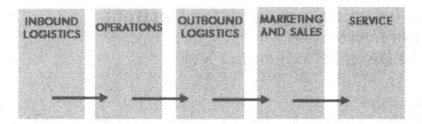

Fig. 1. Porter's value chain

Although merely a decade old, Porter's competitive advantage model is already being rethought in light of new technology forces (Tapscott, 1996). The most pervasive of these forces has been the introduction of the Internet for commercial use in 1991. This watershed marked the end of the not-for-profit Internet sponsored by non-profit organizations such as NSF and other large research institutions. That year the first fully commercial Internet connections became available from companies such as General Atomics, Performance Systems International and UUNET Technologies (Cronin, 1995). These firms were soon joined by others who agreed not to restrict commercial traffic on the Internet. This new commercial Internet created the first real opportunity for electronic markets. It offered a truly global publicly available computer network infrastructure with easy and inexpensive access. After nearly three decades of not-for-profit operation, the network was transformed into a worldwide digital marketplace practically overnight. This shift from a physical marketplace to a digital one does not simply reduce costs, speed up communications, and provide users with more timely information for the benefit of the value chain. Rather when information exchange becomes electronic, both subtle and dramatic changes in the nature of human and organizational communication occur. The new technology enables new kinds of relationships between organizations and people. According to Tapscott (1996), in the process, Porter's *value chain* is transformed into a *value network* as new relationships become possible. Instead of Porter's *value-added* technology application opportunities, the technology in the virtual world offers *value-generative* possibilities. Thus, the digital economy complements the traditional economy of products and services. However, it also supports a new all-digital environment where physical laws have been replaced with electronic ones. This paper proposes an alternative strategic model called the digital production cycle. This model assumes a network that provides a uniform electronic medium for the exchange of products and services and thus creates a richer context for commerce. By casting the strategic components of company in terms of a purely electronic environment, new relationships can be highlighted that more correctly capture the nature of electronic commerce.

2 Defining Electronic Commerce

Today there are several notions of electronic commerce. In Porter's context, it refers to improving the value network of suppliers, manufacturers, partners, distributors and customers. In this meaning, electronic commerce often stands for improved inter-organizational information systems that apply open standards such as EDI over the Internet and the World Wide Web (WWW also Web) (cf., Segev, et al., 1996, 1997). Additionally, electronic business opportunities require that traditional components be re-evaluated, reengineered or eliminated[1]. This type of electronic commerce is often also called *business-to-business* electronic commerce. Currently the IT application areas include supply chain management, just-in-time and continuous replenishment distribution and mass customization through data warehousing and data mining.

Another approach to electronic commerce called *business-to-customer* electronic commerce includes Internet and WWW-based retail operations. Both large corporations and small entrepreneurs can introduce new business models and concepts for a global consumer marketplace. Many only see the Internet as a new marketing tool or a new distribution outlet for old products. Others, however, see an opportunity to create novel all-digital products and services. These new products and services can be created, implemented, marketed, ordered, sold, distributed and paid for electronically over the Internet. The latter group qualitatively differs from the traditional electronic commerce participants in that their product or service can only exist in the context of this new virtual world. Such all-digital concepts include *electronic communities*, *search engines*, *interactive content, archives* and *chat rooms*. Examples such as these are predicated on either digitizing existing product or providing a digital alternative to traditional distribution. At the extreme of such purely electronic notions, is the idea of charging for virtual products that satisfy purely virtual needs. For example, "renting out a virtual shield in order to survive a virtual dragon attack while visiting a virtual dungeon" (Rocket Science Games) does not have a counterpart in the traditional commercial world. From this last perspective electronic commerce has already changed what constitutes "a viable business idea." In the Internet environment, the traditional high technology startup business models do not apply. Such models emphasize the hardware or software products meant for traditional not electronic commerce markets. In the world of the Internet, the concept of creating a tangible product out of the background context of the digital infrastructure is new and fraught with new problems and opportunities. As such, the digital production cycle model proposed here can be used as an alternative to the manufacturing-based strategy model of Porter.

Today's electronic commerce can support the traditional production cycle (manufacturing material goods in the real world) with the Internet and the WWW. But a second type of electronic commerce that includes products that are traditional but

---

[1] Among the first business transactions to be eliminated as unnecessary is the invoice (Verity, 1996).

whose production cycle can completely or partially be transferred into the virtual world as its business infrastructure evolves. These products include any intellectual property that can be digitized. Products that are candidates for digitization are software, books, motion pictures, music videos, music recordings, presentations, games, photographs, magazines, animations, and television broadcasts. This last type of electronic commerce encompasses those all-digital products that are produced in an all-digital production cycle and that would not exist outside the global public computer network. The division between business-to-business electronic commerce and business-to-customer electronic commerce illustrates two potentially distinct areas of electronic commerce with differing objectives and methods. We propose that an equally important distinction may be found between the traditional production cycle and an all-digital production cycle electronic commerce (Figure 2).

The traditional production cycle is well described by Porter (1985). The remainder of this text describes the all-digital production cycle. As Figure 2 indicates, most WEB-enabled firms currently operate somewhere between these two extremes. Most firms currently utilize a "partially digital production cycle" that combines phases from the two extremes. Such combinations are likely to be found in the transitional products of transitional industries that have been significantly impacted by the overnight appearance of electronic commerce on the Internet.

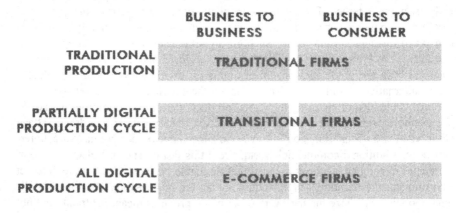

Fig. 2. Organizing electronic commerce

3 The Digital Production Cycle

The all-digital production cycle refers to a value network of businesses which together create a value generative digital production cycle. This cycle has ten phases which may all be digital: (1) Strategy; (2) Concept; (3) Content Creation Plan; (4) Digital Acquisition; (5) Manufacturing; (6) Product or Service Version; (7) Electronic Commerce Policy; (8) Repository; (9) Electronic Distribution; and (10) Electronic Markets. Thus, the digital production cycle refers to creating, marketing, selling and distributing all-digital concepts in an all-digital business environment. This environment, we propose, is different from the traditional business environment in several aspects (Figure 3).

First, in the all-digital environments *concepts (phase 2)* often are a combination of a business model and a digital product. Another way of defining a business model is to specify "the way revenues are created." In cyberspace the most common business models include: testing-free-of-charge; renting; renting-to-own; owning and subscribing-for-service (Porra, 1997). *Testing-free-of-charge* refers to a concept of providing the software for free for a specific period of time after which the product is automatically disabled (the product "expires"). Testing-free-of-charge may also translate into charging some customers while letting others "test" the product without expiration. For example, businesses may be charged while individual customers can use the software for free. *Renting* refers to a onetime fee for a digital service (e.g., the dragon shield rental fee). *Renting to own* refers to the possibility of owning the product after renting it for a predefined time period. *Owning* refers to conducting a payment transaction prior to the delivery of the digital product. *Subscribing for service* refers to the continuous renewal of a sales agreement.

The significance of the digital concept including a viable business model becomes clear in the context of the Internet. The network was originally designed for an easy, global distribution of ideas, products and services for free. With the addition of the commerce mechanisms, the ability to apply business models to the Internet's existing infrastructure became a reality. This allowed not only simple transitions to take place from physical to electronic markets, but provided new opportunities that are part of the infrastructure itself. For example, First Virtual, an Internet based company whose *business strategy* is to provide "secure credit card transactions over the Internet" draws its business from the public's concern for the security of the transport medium (Borenstein, 1996).

DIGITAL PRODUCTION CYCLE

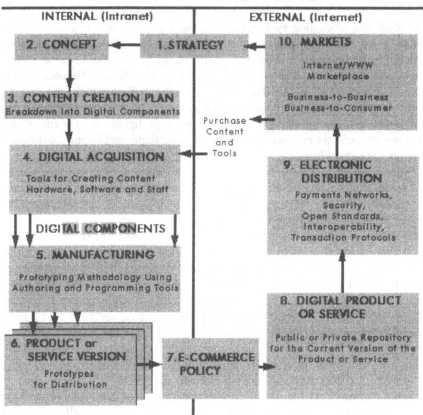

Fig. 3. An all-digital electronic commerce framework

Once the digital concept is defined, the creation of the *content* of the planned product or service is considered. In the *content creation plan (phase 3)*, the digital components of the concept are identified. Technically these components consist of combinations of video, audio, animation, graphics, programs and text necessary to deliver the product or service. But conceptually, they consist of the digital product *and* its infrastructure. For example, a content creation plan for a virtual music store must not only include the product itself (e.g., digital records) but might also include: WEB music clips for perusing, images of artist, text descriptions, lyrics, cover art, reviews, WEB site art and navigation. In the highly interactive WEB, the digital environment of the product and the infrastructure which delivers it is at least as critical as the digital product itself. Because digital commerce business models are included in the digital concept for the service or product, it is necessary to include plans for marketing, ordering, payment and distribution processes at this stage of planning. When business is conducted on the WEB, all of these external processes may have consequences when developing the digital components. Behind the digital content, a potentially elaborate set of software applications exists to process the business transaction. These may include applications for browsing, security, catalogs and storefronts, researching products, ordering, payments, on-line customer support, licensing, royalty accounting, royalty distribution, and on-line distribution (Porra, 1997). Moreover, the digital infrastructure may require interaction with the traditional corporate back-end systems to complete the transaction (Figure 4).

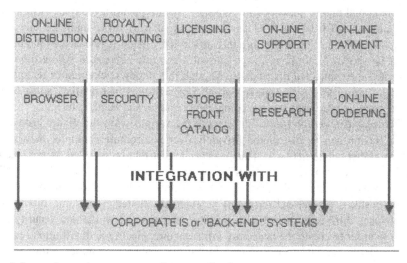

Fig. 4. Some electronic commerce software applications

After the content creation plan and plans for the supporting applications are in place, the *digital acquisition (phase 4)* of components can begin. This phase simply refers to choosing whether to make the digital components or to buy them. In this phase it is also necessary to determine whether to make, buy or rent the supporting software applications or whether partnering with a service provider (ISP) in areas such as on-line payments or security makes more sense. From a technical standpoint, making digital components refers to using tools such as cameras, musical instruments, keyboards, scanners and software in order to create input for the digital manufacturing process. This component development process has been enhanced through the explosion of WEB-based development tools, reusable digital objects and digital acquisition techniques that directly target the creation process.

The all-digital *manufacturing (phase 5)* process refers to rapid development of prototypes using the previously created digital components and supportive services and applications. Though representative of the kinds of prototyping methodologies used for traditional software development, manufacturing in this context assumes continuous revision. The purpose of manufacturing is not to perfect the product or service on the first iteration, but rather to create a digital product or service version that can be used to test the concept in the global digital market place. Thus, in all-digital production cycle, a *version (phase 6)* of the product or service is developed and given to testers or customers for feedback. The feedback in turn is used to enhance the next version of the product or service. Although the feedback from the digital market place is most likely to cause incremental changes in the product concept, changes in the manufacturing cycle and distribution are considered normal (Porra, 1996)[2].

The digital product or service versions are placed into a public or private *repository (phase 8)* that is accessible from the private corporate network (Intranet) or from the global public network (the Internet). Such repositories may be firm-owned WEB sites or WEB-based third party services such as cyber-malls or electronic communities. Before the digital product or service version is released to the public, it must be shown to conform to the current *electronic commerce policy (phase 7)* established for controlled distribution. Though this policy is external in its application, there are clearly e-commerce policy considerations that mediate some of the internal creative processes such as component creation and manufacturing.

Electronic distribution (phase 9) refers to the various ways the digital product or service version can be distributed privately over a corporate computer network or over the global public network. Thus, electronic distribution is based on approaches such as point-to-point delivery, distribution lists or public broadcast (Porra, 1997). This delivery may be on-demand (based on a retail order), periodical (based on a user or business partner subscription) or even unsolicited. Electronic distribution also includes third party distribution services, payment networks and security providers. In order to create the necessary infrastructure, electronic distribution requires open standards that ensure interoperability of the electronic commerce transactions across a variety of platforms.

The digital *marketplace (phase 10)* is perhaps the most problematic component of the production cycle to consider. Though the Internet was originally touted as the penultimate economic frontier, the economic reality has been less than expected. Though it is easy to see how electronic commerce works in theory, the practices of establishing Internet markets for products and services has been more elusive. As expected, successes have been found mostly in those industries that heavily rely on information distribution such as financial services, advertising, e-zines and communication. However, industries with strong intellectual property emphasis such as film or publishing may have more reservations about entering the digital market place until the infrastructure matures.

Regardless of the effectiveness of the electronic marketplace, the market feedback will continue to drive the e-commerce *strategy (phase 1)*. When the Internet was not-for-profit, it was significantly more difficult to estimate the worth of the

---

[2] Changes in the concept are relatively common in current Internet based businesses. For example, Lycos has changed its business model from renting advertising space on its Web site to selling access to electronic communities (that sell advertising space). The next change in the business model could be profiting from transactions initiated in electronic communities between the advertisers and the paying visitors of the electronic communities.

endeavor. But as is usual with large economic investments, Internet-dependent companies that fail to produce economic returns will have very short lives. Following this embryonic stage of the Internet where the possibilities seem unbounded, only a few strategies will survive and mature. The pace of change and the speed with which these forces interact will force firms to constantly revise their strategies. This assumption that the firms engaging in electronic commerce undergo perpetual revision is not far from the truth. Porter's sequential relationships in the value chain make each phase relatively independent. But, the cycle model proposed above demonstrates that the interplay between phases requires continuous reinvention and reconstruction. In the physical world of manufacturing, it may be possible to completely restructure one phase without modifying others. But in a fully digital world, simple changes in one area propagate quickly throughout the entire product cycle. This tight coupling between electronic content, its creation, and its distribution exists because of the commonality of form among the phases. As we move to all-digital commerce, we can expect that the best performers will be those firms that can quickly execute these versioning cycles.

The all-digital production cycle is meant to provide a simple framework to show the temporal dependencies that make up a product or service cycle. As with the most "life cycle" models, it is easy to see the steps that make up the "life" but more difficult to imagine the "cycle" of life. We submit that the importance of the processes outlined above are not their sequence but their recurrence. Failure to acknowledge the recursive cycling through the processes will result in products and services that become brittle with age and stagnate quickly. In the new digital world, the ability to revise and enhance may be even more important than correctly identifying the product/market combination initially. As has been shown repeatedly in the digital marketplace, the best technical product does not always win the market. It is the firm that can best position, revise and integrate that most often captures market share. This cyclic nature of this production model emphasizes this point. Change and flexibility should become the watchwords of electronic commerce in these early days.

4 Infrastructure

One fundamental characteristic of technology infrastructure is that it is only noticed when it does not work (King, 1997). So intertwined are solutions such as telephone networks with the ways of doing business that it is nearly impossible to say where technology ends and business practice begins. The electronic commerce infrastructure, however, has not advanced to this qualitative stage. Although nearly two million people in the United States have purchased something over the Internet (Hoffman, 1996), the electronic commerce infrastructure continues to evolve. However, before the digital production cycle can become reality, at least three levels of the infrastructure must to be in place (Figure 5.)

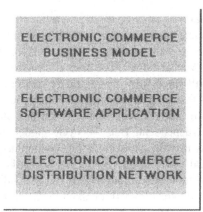

Fig. 5. Levels of electronic commerce infrastructure

First, electronic commerce business models have yet to mature. While traditional business models are clear about how and when a commitment to pay is initiated, the electronic environment does not have such clear practices. Due to the non-profit history of the Internet, it is common to deliver a product without expecting a commitment for payment in return. Though this practice is considered unusual in traditional commerce, it is so common on the Internet that it is often included in viable virtual world business models. However, until it is clear how a business transaction is initiated and conducted over the Internet, many potential customers will stay away.

The second limitation of the digital production cycle involves the existence of robust commercial software support. This means that all of the components (electronic marketing, advertising, manufacturing, product versioning, product browsing, electronic cataloging and storefronts, research tools for customers, ordering, sending and receiving payments, royalty accounting, distribution and security) must be supported by software applications. These applications must interoperate through standardized interfaces for a seamless shopping experience and to complete the business transaction. At this stage of electronic commerce's development such off-the-shelf components are not readily available. Though numerous products and proposals exist there is little standardization or a market leader that can demonstrate significant acceptance. The electronic marketplace will develop such standards and market leaders will emerge. But as of this writing, we may only assume that this infrastructure component will improve.

The third level of an electronic commerce infrastructure is the public global computer network. Today, the Internet provides this level of infrastructure. The growth of this network has been tremendous over the past few years. As the demand for Internet access expands, we can expect the network to expand to accommodate the demand. This expansion will be capital intensive and may lag behind the demands placed upon it by the marketplace. Even now we see network infrastructure problems (e.g., limited IP addresses and limited bandwidth). But proposed solutions (e.g., Internet II) abound. Though it is easy to criticize the current quality of the Internet infrastructure, its very existence is a tribute to the quality of the original ideas.

We propose that this early developmental stage of the electronic commerce infrastructure can be illustrated by this three level viewpoint in Figure 5. While the Internet is often touted as the electronic commerce infrastructure, in reality, it only provides the lowest level of the necessary functionality. The importance of a global public access network cannot be underestimated as the necessary prerequisite for electronic commerce. However, it only offers a starting point for a comprehensive solution for digital commerce whose true utility awaits the development of effective commercial software and business models that employ it.

5 Transformation of Industries

The transition from the traditional production cycle to an all-digital production cycle will first take place in industries such as publishing, broadcasting, and advertising. In the process, industries of content creation, content processing and content communication will collide and coalesce (Tapscott, 1996). Industries dealing with potentially digital products will have to restructure and reorganize their value networks. Three examples of potential value network reorganizations are: the software industry; the motion picture industry; and the publishing industry.

The traditional software industry value chain involves a software developer, publisher, distributor, retailer and the consumer (Porra, 1997). This value chain is held together with agreements between participants. Such rules dictate, for example, that new customers are for dealers; existing customers are for publishers; and that dealers only sell new products not upgrades (Figure 6).

While these agreements are binding in the real world, the virtual world does not recognize them. Instead, cyberspace is open for many permutations to occur. A developer may partner with a publisher, distributor, retailer or sell directly to the user. Similarly, a publisher may partner with a distributor or a retailer or sell directly to the user. Eventually, the digital marketplace, not the extant mutual agreements, will determine which permutation will prosper. Moreover, in cyberspace, old intermediaries are terminated (disintermediation) and new ones created (reintermediation). Figure 7 demonstrates this kind of restructuring which replaces the traditional value chain with a network of new relationships. Here again we see that the uniformity of the digital media creates opportunities which heretofore did not exist.

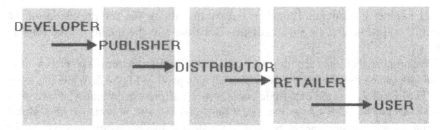

Fig. 6. The traditional organization of the software industry

Another well-known example of a potentially all-digital industry is the film industry. Today, "the industry" is divided into two tiers of film production and film distribution. Film producers do not distribute their own products and distributors do not produce films. In cyberspace such a division need not apply. As soon as the motion picture production cycle becomes all-digital, there is no reason why a digital motion picture product could not be created, developed, marketed and distributed to the customer directly over a computer network by the production company. To overcome the momentum of the film industry's established two-tiered model will require bandwidth of sufficient capacity to allow Hollywood movie quality to be transmitted over the Internet. Though this technology may still be decades away, the notion of transporting entertainment over the Internet has already at least captured the imagination of some creative content producers.

Another candidate industry for similar transformation is the publishing industry. Although daily and weekly news are readily available over the WWW, book publishers have been reluctant to digitize their product for Internet commerce because of the inability to collect revenues and fears of mass reproduction once the content reaches the Internet. Additionally, no easy way exists to consistently register, calculate and distribute the intellectual property earnings over the Internet. This lack of royalty accounting and distribution is only one of the missing links in an all-digital production cycle.

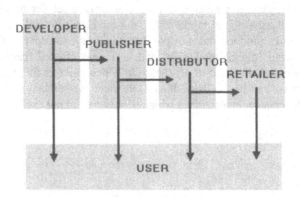

Fig. 7. In the digital production cycle all permutations are possible

To assimilate all of the industries that produce content that may be digitized into the fold of the Internet is not a realistic expectation. During this transition phase, many firms will opt to avoid the Internet as a fundamental commerce mechanism. Though many early adopters will fail for lack of infrastructure, lack of commercial tools or lack of appropriate business models, they will determine for the majority of late adopters how to operate successfully. It is the lessons gleaned from experiences with the new commerce marketplace that will guide the future.

6 Conclusions

Electronic commerce may include several potentially qualitatively differing types of commerce. While it has become common to distinguish between business-to-business electronic commerce and business-to-customer electronic commerce, it may be necessary to identify additional dimensions as well. In this text we have proposed that it may be necessary to consider the traditional value chain as being separate from an all-digital production cycle. While Porter's value chain model may help to adapt a traditional production cycle to the electronic era commerce in a transitional way, we propose that all-digital commerce may require reconstructing the production cycle itself. The premise behind this suggestion is that digital products do not need to follow the sequence of inbound logistics, operations, outbound logistics, sales, marketing and service like manufactured goods. Instead, digital commerce can benefit from the methods familiar from the content producing and software industries. Additionally, unlike traditional commerce, electronic commerce is bound by the conventions and technology of the Internet. Instead of attempting to force this network infrastructure to support traditional business models and practices, an alternative approach is to include the fundamental characteristics of the public network in business models and products themselves. The end result may be a qualitatively different commercial environment from that portrayed in Porter's competitive advantage model. Moreover, in all-digital businesses, what constitutes competitive advantage may be redefined in the process.

Electronic commerce is a new and rapidly evolving area. Any effort to include all of the diverse viewpoints into a framework is a challenging task. So much of the necessary research and real world experimentation of what works and what doesn't work has yet to be done that such framework can only be called tentative. Our attempt is clearly not comprehensive. There are many indications for the need to use many frameworks. Other authors have also indicated such needs in the form of both general electronic commerce networks (Kalakota & Whinston, 1996) and electronic commerce frameworks aimed at a specific industry (cf., Hamalainen, et al., 1996, for an electronic commerce framework for the education industry). Rather we have attempted to illustrate a particular viewpoint of electronic commerce that expresses the cyclic nature of the production environment. This structure outlines but does not of provide comprehensive steps at each stage. It serves to emphasize the continuous cyclical revision that is required to operate successfully in such a dynamic market-place as the Internet.

References

Borenstein, N., et al., "Perils and Pitfalls of Practical Cybercommerce," *Communications of the ACM,* 39,6(June), 1996, 36-44.

Cronin, M. J., *Doing more Business on the Internet -- How the Electronic Highway Is Transforming American Companies,* Van Nostrand Reinhold, New York, NY, 1995.

Hoffman, D. L., W. D. Kalsbeek, and T. P. Novak, "Internet and Web Use in the U.S.," *Communications of the ACM,* 39, 12, 1996, 36-46.

Hamalainen, M., A. B. Whinston, and S. Vishik, "Electronic Markets for Learning: Education Brokearages on the Internet," *Communications of the ACM,* 39, 6(June), 1996, 51-58.

Kalakota, R., and A. B. Whinston, *Frontiers of Electronic Commerce,* Addison Wesley Publishing, New York, NY, 1996.

King, J., *Retail Electronic Commerce,* A presentation, Center for Research on Information Technology and Organizations (CRITO), University of California, Irvine, 1997.

Porra, J., *Colonial Systems, Information Colonies and Punctuated Prototyping,* University of Jyvaskyla Studies in Computer Science, Economics and Statistics, 33, University of Jyvaskyla Press, Jyvaskyla, Finland, 1996.

Porra, J., *Electronic Software Commerce,* A Briefing Paper, The Fisher Center for Information Technology and Management, Walter A. Haas School of Business, University of California, Berkeley, 1997.

Porter, M. E., *Competitive Advantage -- Creating and Sustaining Superior Performance,* The Free Press, New York, NY, 1985.

Segev, A., J. Porra, and M. Roldan, *Internet-based financial EDI: the case of Bank of America and Lawrence Livermore National Laboratory Pilot,* The Fisher Center for Management and Information Technology, Walter A. Haas School of Business, University of California, Working Paper CITM-95-WP-1018, 1996.

Segev, A., J. Porra, and M. Roldan, "Internet-Based EDI Strategy," *Decision Support Systems,* 617, 21, 3 (1997), 157-170.

Tapscott, D., *The Digital Economy -- Promise and Peril in the Age of Networked Intelligence,* McGraw-Hill, New York, NY, 1996.

Verity, J. W., "Invoice? What's an Invoice?", *Business Week,* June 10, 1996, 110-112.

CHAPTER 30

The Emergence of Auctions on the World Wide Web

Stefan Klein

Department of Information Systems, University of Muenster, Muenster, Germany,
klein@wi.uni-muenster.de

Auctions are formalized trading procedures in which the trading partners' interaction is governed by specific rules for competitive bidding and trade execution. Auction markets provide procedures for the exposure of purchase and sale orders to the market participants in order to determine the price of trade objects. Empirically we find a multiplicity of auction types with different trade objects, access rules for participants, and trading rules. During the 1980s electronic auctions have been developed and implemented which distributed not only information about the trade objects electronically but also executed the trading process itself as computer-mediated process. The extensive proliferation of electronic commerce on the Web has accelerated the diffusion of electronic auctions. In this chapter we will present a framework of constituting elements of auctions and discuss the impact of the Web on the proliferation of auctions. The move-to-the-market debate is used as background to scrutinize success factors and limitations of electronic auctions.

Keywords: Electronic Auctions; Electronic Markets; Electronic Commerce; Transaction Cost Economics; Governance Structures

1 Auctions on the Web

"Auction markets provide centralized procedures for the exposure of purchase and sale orders to all market participants simultaneously."
(Lee 1996, 398)

Auctions are formalized trading procedures in which the trading partners' interaction is governed by specific rules for competitive bidding and trade execution. Auction markets provide procedures for the exposure of purchase and sale orders to the market participants in order to determine the price of trade objects. In many cases an auctioneer is functioning as an intermediary. Empirically we find a multiplicity of auction types with different trade objects, access rules for participants, and trading rules. Auctions are used for diverse and heterogeneous trade objects such as

- commodities like financial products, metals or agricultural products,
- perishable items like airline tickets or
- scarce or unique items such as advertising space or pieces of art.

Securities markets, the Dutch flower market and used care markets are among the most prominent examples of electronic auctions in which products are represented electronically and bidding is facilitated through some kind of electronic media. Electronic auctions are a special case of automated negotiations (cf. Beam; Segev 1997). Since the diffusion of the Web has gained momentum and the number of Web users is rising steeply, a proliferation of electronic markets, in particular electronic auctions, can be observed.

1.1 Types of Auctions and Motives of Participants

Auctions are typically classified according to (a) trading goods (e.g. rare goods, consumer goods or commodities, Beckmann et al. 1997), (b) whether they are procurement or sales auctions (Heck and Vervest, 1998) and (c) different mechanisms of price determination. English or Dutch indicates the direction of the clock (ascending, descending); some auctions are performed in real time while in others bids (or offers) can be submitted over an extended period of time and will be matched at a given date. We do, however, not emphasize the different mechanisms of price determination, but focus rather on the motives of the participants. While the analysis of Web-based auctions will focus on retail sales auctions which are targeted primarily at consumers, the first two types are mentioned in order to indicate the wide (and widening) spectrum of possible applications of auction mechanisms.

Auctions as coordination mechanisms: Auctions are increasingly used as an efficient coordination mechanism for establishing an equilibrium price. Examples are an automated auction among software agents to control air conditioning at Xerox (Markoff 1996), power auctions (Singh et al. 1997), or (in the future) auctions for the allocation of telecommunication bandwidth. In these auctions there is little or no human intervention during the trading since they conclude only when a price has stabilized.

Auctions as procurement mechanisms: What has been practice in public procurement and the construction industry for years, is currently spreading into many other industries: companies are publishing calls for tender and inviting submissions from a wide array of potential suppliers. At the end of the submission period, the tenders are ranked and the supplier is chosen. Many companies have found out that doing this via the Web is not only efficient but increases the likelihood of submissions because of the increased visibility of the call for tender (van Heck and Vervest 1998).

Auctions as social mechanisms for price determination: For objects that are not traded on traditional markets, which may be unique, or for rare items that are offered randomly or at long intervals, an auction creates a market place that attracts potential buyers. By offering numerous items at one time and by attracting a good amount of attention, these auctions provide the requisite exposure of purchase and sale orders and hence liquidity of the market in which a price can be determined. Typical examples of this pattern are auctions of art as well as auctions of communication frequencies (Lewyn, 1994; Cramton, 1995) and Web banner advertising space.

Auctions as efficient allocation mechanisms: For the allocation of limited resources, auctions are used to (dynamically) establish a price which reflects the scarcity of the resource and the preferences of the bidders. Klausz et al. (1998) have shown in an experimental setting of a university modem pool that auctions lead to a more efficient capacity utilization of congested IT resources. The impact of an electronic auction on price level is discussed by Lee (1998).

Numerous consumer items are difficult to market via established distribution channels. This typically occurs because they are (a) products with a limited shelf life or last minute products like seats in a scheduled flight, (b) overstocked products that need to be separated from the new product series, or (c) discontinued or reconditioned items.

In this case the auction is a separate distribution channel, targeted at a wide audience which might be prepared to accept the product restrictions in return for a significant discount. The auction gives customers the opportunity to indicate their price preferences and the suppliers the opportunity to study customer behavior. The auctioneer attempts to provide sufficient breadth and depth of the market, in order to continually attract interested buyers that have a high likelihood to find something and sellers that have a high likelihood of clearing there stocks if only they set the price low enough. A typical example of this type of auction is Onsale [http//www.onsale.com/] (Economist, 1997).

Auctions as highly visible distribution mechanisms: A fourth type of auction is similar to the third, as items are auctioned off as a kind of special offer. However, the set-up of the auction is different: typically one supplier auctions off a limited contingent of items and uses the auction primarily as a mechanism to gain attention and to attract those customers that are bargain hunters or are intrigued by the dynamics of the real time auction process. The airline seat auctions by Cathay Pacific, American Airline and Lufthansa fall into this category. Lufthansa has found out that a considerable number of participants in their monthly ticket auctions are already regular Lufthansa customers looking for a cheap ticket, e.g. for an additional weekend vacation or as a gift. Special cases are auctions in which the trading objects are donated and the auction return is dedicated for charitable purposes.

The motives and possible gains for the respective players vary with the different auction types. Table 1 gives a summary of the main motives.

1.2 A Case: Lufthansa Ticket Auctions

Since August 1997, Lufthansa is regularly auctioning off selected flight tickets via their Web site Info Flyaway [http://www.lufthansa.com]. Once a months, auctions run for a full day from 10 a.m. till 10 p.m. 50 separate auctions take place during an auction day. During one auction which typically lasts for ten minutes one set of tickets is auctioned off. There are on average 60 participants in the virtual auction room, about 20 of them are active bidders. An auctioneer is trying to induce participants to continue the competitive bidding process. The Lufthansa auction is an English auction with ascending prices, the ticket list price, however, is taken as an upper limit. Successful bidders are called after the auction in order to confirm the price and verify the credit card information. Typical bidders are participants in Lufthansa's frequent flyer program Miles & More and use Lufthansa's Web site regularly. The offered tickets are for carefully selected seats on less frequented flights on attractive routes. Auction tickets, which often are sold with a significant discount, are frequently used for an additional weekend trip or as presents. Lufthansa does no longer auction other trade objects which are outside its immediate business scope, because that would require an auctioneer's license.

The auction is runs by an independent agency, infoMedia, which offers a full auction service package [http://www.infomedia.de]. infoMedia compiles the auction catalog, registers the participants and run the auction system with a maximum load of 2000 concurrent participants or observers. The fee for one auction day including call center operation for 48 hours is about USD 10.000. Table 2 summarizes the components of the Lufthansa auction based on the transaction phase model.

Table 1. Motives of the participants in different retail auction types

Auction type / Role	Price discovery	Allocation mechanism	Distribution mechanism
Buyer	Experts/ professional collectors trying to acquire rare items at a reasonable price.	Bargain hunting. Gambling.	Bargain hunting, spontaneous purchases, e.g. of gifts. Gambling. Possible side motive: charity.
Supplier	Exposing items for sale to a sufficient breadth of demand. Hope for a high price.	Clearance of inventory. Gaining information about customers' price preferences.	Public and media attention, marketing and public relations. Direct sales channel. Possible side motive: charity.
Intermediary	Achieve high breadth and depth of auctions. High trading volume resulting in higher returns. Successfully conducted auctions will improve the auctioneer's reputation.	Achieve high breadth and depth of auctions. High trading volume resulting in higher returns. Successfully conducted auctions will improve the auctioneer's reputation.	Limited role because of a 1:n supplier:buyer ratio. Service provider for the supplier side.

For Lufthansa, ticket auctions are in the first place marketing events and experiments in the area of electronic commerce. The auction rules have been gradually adapted and modified based on the growing experience and response from participants. Despite limited advertising, the auctions have gained a lot of publicity, particularly in traditional media. One goal of the auctions has been to attract (potential) customers to the Lufthansa Web site, which is also a direct sales channel. Lufthansa has moved cautiously - without major advertising activities - in an attempt not to alienate travel agencies.

Despite the fact that marginal cost for additional passengers on seats that might otherwise not been sold are very low, the revenue generated from the ticket sales hardly justifies the Web auction in its current format. The benefits for Lufthansa are primarily in the area of marketing and market research. The auctions have generated plenty of publicity in traditional media, customer feedback and additional traffic on the Web site.

Table 2. Components of the Lufthansa auction

Transaction phase	Components
Information	Auction catalog (available tickets, rules and regulations) and timetable
Negotiation	Web-based auction system with a virtual auction room, English auction. Animation during the bidding process.
Settlement	Call center operation: successful bidders are contacted after the auction, the ticket price etc. is confirmed and credit card information is verified. Tickets are delivered per mail or stored for pick-up at the airport.

2 A Framework for Auctions

The impact of the World Wide Web on the diffusion of auctions is not yet fully understood nor do we have a sufficient conceptual basis to link auction design and effects. The following framework (Fig. 1) attempts to capture the complexity of auctions. It depicts the constituting elements of auctions and shall help to distinguish different dimensions of the Web's impact on their design and effects.

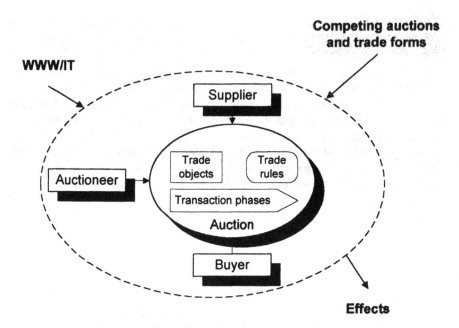

Fig. 1. The constituting elements of auctions

2.1 Auctioneer

By bringing together potential buyers and sellers, auctioneers create a marketplace and make current levels of supply and demand more transparent. The auctioneer provides the institutional setting for the different transaction phases of the trading process: information exchange, price determination, the trade execution and settlement. Electronic auctions depend even more than traditional auctions on a good reputation and quality guarantees, e.g. whether the trading goods are available and of the promised quality or whether trades are executed without frictions. While some of the traditional auctioneers like Sotheby's [http://www.sothebys.com] are slowly entering the field of electronic auctioning, we see a majority of new entrants. Some of them are affiliated with the suppliers of the trading goods, some emphasize their role as intermediaries who provide a whole range of services for electronic auctions. In particular, they offer auction engines and trading platforms for a variety of products and vendors.

2.2 Buyers and Suppliers

The number of buyers and suppliers respectively distinguishes different types of auctions. In the classical case, multiple buyers face multiple suppliers. In some of the sales auctions, like the Lufthansa auction, just one supplier faces multiple buyers. The inverse situation characterizes many procurement auctions, where one buyer faces multiple suppliers. (Heck and Vervest, 1998).

Among the main institutional design parameters are the access rules for buyers and suppliers. While wholesale auctions are targeted at an expert audience, retail auctions on the Web are often open to the general public. Individual auctions vary in respect of control mechanisms, required advance payments or other credible commitments of the participants. If the marketing purpose dominates, entry barriers are kept very low and payment authorization is often checked only after successful bidding.

2.3 Trade Objects

The variety of potential objects traded on auctions can be distinguished into three broad categories:

- For commodities, auctions improve the market transparency and facilitate ad-hoc price determination.
- For perishable products in a wider sense, such as airline seats or overstocked products, auctions attract potential buyers and they are distinct channels that allow vendors to maintain a different price level in the traditional sales channels.
- For scarce or rare products such as pieces of fine art, collectors items or communication frequencies, auctions are institutionalized procedures for price determination.

Electronic markets initially have been developed for commodities and products with simple and standardized product descriptions. As the Web lowers the cost of creating a marketplace it enables to extend the geographical range of auctions and to extend the auction mechanism to trade objects that have not been auctioned off before. The progress of technology allows to considerably extend this range and include objects that require complex descriptions. In addition, samples can be provided or experts can be involved to evaluate products and probably communicate with potential buyers electronically. The analysis of AUCNET, an electronic wholesale auction for used cars, has shown that in comparison to traditional auctions newer cars and cars in a better condition are auctioned off electronically (Lee, 1997). A possible explanation is that the complexity of the description rises exponentially with the age of cars.

2.4 Trade Rules

Numerous rules have been developed that govern the trading process, in particular the number and exposure of bids and offers and the trade execution. Reck (1994) has developed a taxonomy of auctions based on

- the number of bids and offers on each market side
- the form of bids (private - public)
- the number of items bought and sold per transaction
- the existence of sequencing rules
- the occurrence of transactions (periodic – continuous) and the ordering mechanism.

He has specified a set of generic rules and has indicated how these may be used to design new types of auctions. (1997).

Retail auctions on the Web are predominantly organized as English auctions. A competitive real-time bidding process in which the buyers can observe each other is compatible with the motives of buyers and suppliers likewise. This design reflects also technical restrictions with respect to synchronizing bids and providing reliable timestamps.

2.5 The Transaction Phases

The negotiation phase, in which prices are determined and contracts are closed, is the core of auctions. However, the preceding information phase is crucial for the number of participants and their level of interest. Clear and distinct information about trade objects and trade rules avoids frictions during and after the auction, especially in retail auctions with multiple non-expert participants.

A broad set of rules governs the settlement phase, the exchange and logistics of goods and payments. Entry fees and deposits are imposed to secure the seriousness of buyers. The separation of the price determination process and the physical logistics of the trade objects has improved the efficiency of auctions. Trade objects are only moved after they have been sold. These rules are complementing the actual rules for the price determination process (cf. Heck et al. 1997). The enforcement of these rules is meant to guarantee the correct execution of trades and is of utmost importance in an electronic environment.

2.6 The Impact of the Web

While most of the motives for auctions are independent of the underlying technology, we have scrutinized how the Web influences the constituting elements of auctions. The Web as a "global hyper-media computer-mediated environment" (Hoffmann, Novak 1995) represents the result of IT achievements in numerous areas: advanced client-server architectures, low-cost, widely diffused hyper-media clients, low-cost communication-infrastructure, platform independent software, etc. These features have an impact on the diffusion of auctions:

- The communication infrastructure with millions of potential trading partners facilitates the global visibility of offerings. Even highly specialized items for selective customer groups can thus be marketed efficiently.
- Standardized mechanisms for hyper-media representation of trade objects have increased the manageable and economically feasible complexity of electronic product descriptions.
- Generic auction engines and auction platforms which have been developed by specialized service providers reduce the set-up cost of auctions for suppliers and give them the option of running the auction themselves or use the services of intermediaries.
- The development and diffusion of standardized search mechanisms and event-driven notification of bidders as well as
- mechanisms for secure payments encourage customers to opt for Web auctions with electronic trade execution.

Table 3. Impact areas

Parameter	Impact of the Web
Auctioneer	Lower entry barriers, auction infrastructure can be used for multiple auctions of different trade objects. Risk of supplier auctions and disintermediation of auctioneers.
Suppliers and buyers	Customizable access rules, theoretically millions of potential customers can be reached. Auctions become a feasible option for many suppliers.
Trade objects	Focused product segments can be auctioned off, the technology extends the complexity of the product description.
Trading rules	The trading rules reflect the lack of a guaranteed service, rules can be changed quickly.
Settlement	For digital products the entire trading cycle can be handled on the Web, for physical products the trading process and the physical logistics of the trade objects can be separated, leading to a reduction of costs.

Heck and Ribbers (1996, see also Heck; Damme; Kleijnen; Ribbers 1997) have shown that the institutional arrangements of auctions, in particular the rules for trade object representation and examination, and the interests of stakeholders have a strong impact on the success of electronic auctions. Especially, if electronic auctions are competing with established auctions or efficient trading mechanisms.

2.7 Competing Auctions and Alternative Trade Forms

As the number of auctions, especially on the Web, is mushrooming, the amount of competition among auctions for comparable trade objects is rising. While this is beneficial in terms of general attention, it might limit the liquidity of less popular auctions. Further research is needed in order to determine what the critical success factors for individual auctions are. Likely candidates for success factors are as diverse as the reputation of an auction, trading rules, risk for the supplier and search cost for the buyer, the level of commissions and fees or the expected liquidity of the market.

Fig. 2 depicts the competitive environment of Lufthansa's ticket auction. Immediate competition from other ticket auctions can be neglected as there are no other ticket auctions for flights from Germany. However the auction has to be positioned in relation to traditional distribution channels, primarily travel agents, and emerging distribution channels like tourism Web sites, especially in the last-minute segment. Right now the positioning criteria for the ticket auction are a careful selection of tickets to be auctioned off and the emphasis on marketing benefits for Lufthansa. An alternative positioning of the auction would be to use it to sell small contingents of tickets on flights that are known to be fully booked. In this case, the auction would be a mechanism to allocate a scarce resource, to learn about customers' price preferences and to generate profits. However, the auction would have to be marketed totally different.

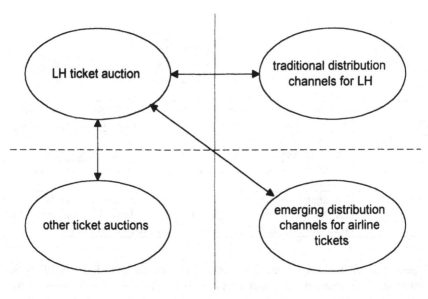

Fig. 2. Competitive environment of Lufthansa's ticket auction

2.8 Effects of Auctions

The motives of the participants which we have described are clearly pointing towards intended effects from the various players' perspectives. However, it is not only difficult to identify causal relationships between, e.g., trading rules and effects, but there are also numerous potential side effects. A major concern of the suppliers is that it will be difficult to isolate auctions from other sales and distribution channels because customers will adapt their buying behavior to flexible pricing. As a result, an increasing price pressure is feared which might not only affect the auctioned products but also - as a side effect - those products that have not been singled out for auctions.

In general, dynamic price determination leads to an extended price differentiation. Consumers might be confronted with an extended opportunity but also necessity to negotiate prices (Cortese and Stepanek, 1998). Auctions do not necessarily lead to lower prices (Lee, 1998). As auctions enable buyers to articulate their price preferences, suppliers might be prompted to design products that fall into the preferred price range. Given the dynamics of the underlying product markets and the individual market places where the respective products are traded, it is difficult to assess in general what the effects of auctions will be. In order to get a better sense of the potential benefits of auctions, we have distinguished determinants of buyer and supplier utility and indicated areas of auction design impact.

Supplier utility of an auction is a trade off between revenues from sold trade objects and intended side effects on the one side and auction costs and risks on the other. Table 4 gives a summary of suppliers' costs and benefits reflecting auction design parameters using the example of the ticket auctions. Costs and benefits have to be compared to alternative sales channels.

Table 4. Supplier utility of a ticket auction

Costs/benefits	Explanation	Impact of auction design
Revenues from sold tickets	Revenues have to be compared to alternative sales channels for a comparable selection of tickets, e.g. last-minute.	Selection and combination of bidding rules.
Intended side effects	Examples: customer relations, publicity, traffic on the Web site, market research, information about customer preferences	Organizational environment, marketing activities, analysis of results.
Auction cost	Cost components: fee for auctioneer, set-up cost for electronic auction, settlement cost (call center etc.). Costs have to be compared with alternative channels and their likelihood of selling selected tickets..	Auction set-up (make-or-buy, frequency, settlement arrangements).
Auction risk	Ticket not sold. Risk is low as unsold tickets can be returned into the pool of available tickets after the auction.	Selection of tickets, marketing of auction, timing of auction.

Customer utility is a trade off between the price of the trade object and the costs for obtaining the respective object. Table 5 explains customers' costs and benefits in the case of the ticket auction. In particular search and negotiation costs are subject to decisions about the auction design. In the future, agent technology can be used to reduce theses costs and make auctions even more attractive. Search agents might lower the search costs and bidding agents might lower the negotiation costs.

Table 5. Customer utility of a ticket auction

Costs/benefits	Explanation	Impact of auction design
Auction ticket price	Ticket price in relation to price on any other distribution channel.	Price limit.
Side effects	E.g. fun of bidding process.	Animated auction process.
Search cost	Invested time (opportunity cost) to find site(s) that sell wanted tickets at less than list price. Search costs turn into sunk costs, if wanted ticket not available.	Advertising, auction directories, agents.
Negotiation cost	In particular invested time (opportunity cost). Entry cost if there is an entry fee. Winners curse, if tickets are bought at a higher than necessary price.	Organizational set-up, access rules and bidding rules.
Auction risk	Wanted ticket sold to other bidder or final price too high.	

3 The Move-to-the-market Hypothesis Reconsidered

We have argued that empirical evidence suggests an extension of market mechanisms and we have tried to show how features of the Web are related to the accelerated diffusion of electronic auctions. We would now like to link these findings with the academic discourse about the impact of IT on governance structures and relate our findings about Web auctions to the respective arguments.

3.1 From Electronic Hierarchies to Electronic Markets

As early as 1987 Malone et al. have hypothesized about the influence of emerging information and communication technologies on the execution and coordination of economic transactions. Their claim is that IT will increasingly be used to coordinate economic activities and will consequently increase the share of market coordination over hierarchical coordination. Their argument is based on the transaction cost theory which compares coordination costs of different governance structures, e.g. markets and hierarchies: As IT reduces coordination (and information) costs, market transactions gain a comparative advantage. In greater detail, they focus on asset specificity and complexity of product description as transaction features, which determine the choice of coordination mechanisms. If both are high, hierarchical coordination is most efficient; if both are low, market coordination is preferable.

A number of the effects that Malone et al. (1987) have predicted, can be substantiated in relation to Web auctions.

Communication effect: Communication costs have been significantly reduced and the communication intensity has mushroomed. Information about the availability of trade objects on auctions can be retrieved globally and people can participate in Web-based auctions all over the world from their homes or offices.

Brokerage effect: "The introduction of the electronic auction can shift brokered or dealer markets into auction markets. ... The electronic auction substantially reduces coordination costs by allowing transactions to take place without middlemen." (Lee, 1996) Not only have traditional markets been complemented by electronic markets, but numerous new markets have emerged. As technology has lowered the set-up costs for auctions, suppliers and buyers can bypass many-to-many markets with auctioneers and establish one-to-many sales or procurement auctions respectively.

Decreasing asset specificity and time specificity: While Malone et al. argue that IT is reducing the asset specificity of production technology, the proliferation of the Internet and Internet-related standards and protocols (TCP/IP, Internet services, HTTP, VRML, Java etc.) have considerably lowered the asset specificity of IT investments and engendered the rise of new IT market segments. This trend however might be reversed in the future as the variety and complexity of Internet-related technology is rising quickly. Malone et al. (1987) have added time specificity as a further type of asset specificity. Contrary to their prediction that high time specificity leads to hierarchical coordination, electronic auctions are examples of coordination mechanisms targeted at time specific products such as last minute flights.

Rising complexity of the product description: Most significant progress has been made in extending the complexity of product descriptions while lowering their cost at the same time.

In sum, a number of Malone et al.'s predictions have been confirmed and the empirical evidence underscores the general line of their argument. However, the described development gives as well fresh evidence for the concerns of those researcher that have voiced rebuttals against Malone et al.'s claim.

3.2 Move-to-the-middle Hypothesis

The move-to-the-market hypothesis has been challenged by Clemons and Reddi (1993, 1994), who - again based on transaction cost theorizing and a limited amount of empirical evidence - propose the move-to-the-middle hypothesis. The move-to-the-middle is a double move: away from the hierarchical vertically integrated organization to a higher degree of outsourcing and at the same time away from faceless market relations towards a situation where the firm relies on a few co-operative partners. The first part of the move towards outsourcing is based on a reasoning similar to Malone et al. (1987): IT lowers transaction costs, the costs of coordination and monitoring and the relationship specificity of IT investments, and hence makes outsourcing an advantageous option. The role of IT in this process is to at least partly offset exogenous factors that usually increase transaction costs, such as relationship-specific investments, small numbers bargaining, demand uncertainty etc. The second part of the argument, however, gives reasons why companies increasingly choose long-term co-operative relationships instead of market relationships:

long-term relationships provide higher incentives to invest in IT and in the requisite organizational adaptations and learning processes (Seidmann, Wang 1992). At the same time long-term relationships provide some protection against the risks of opportunistic behavior and especially the loss of critical resources (Clemons, Row 1992).

An increasing number of suppliers can be taken as an indicator of the move-to-the-market. However, empirical findings show, on the contrary, that firms in many industries are reducing the number of their suppliers. Bakos' and Brynjolfsson's (1992) explanation is, that although overall Coordination costs are decreasing, this effect is often offset by an increasing demand for quality. As quality and non-contractible actions of suppliers become more important, the buyer has to provide incentives for the supplier to invest in underlying relationship specific assets. A limited number of suppliers is such an incentive as it increases the bargaining power of the supplier and reduces the risk of buyer defection. Their argument is that the importance of non-contractible issues in a supplier-buyer relationship determines the optimal number of suppliers. The buyer relinquishes part of his power in order to create an incentive for the supplier to invest in the relationship. It is a balancing act of control over gains from investments and quality improvements. Non-contractible properties of the relation are dealt with through contracts concerning the exclusiveness of the relation and a barter of power concerning the division of revenues. What we see is a growing reliance on (specific) institutional arrangements to provide the right balance of interests in the area of non-contractible and intangible aspects of inter-firm relationships.

The analysis of reasons for closer relationships among business partners contributes to the understanding of the design and success of Web auctions. So we are shifting the perspective from the question "what is the most efficient governance structure?" to the question "what can we learn from the governance structure debate about success factors of auctions?".

Re-intermediation: While some of the middlemen have been replaced, new cybermediaries have emerged. The versatility of Web technology enables auctioneers to use economies of scale and scope: an existing auction platform can be used for multiple auctions at the same time and can be extended to all types of trade objects.

Quality and trust: Non-contractible issues, such as quality and trust are crucial issues for Web auctions, however they can be facilitated by a strict institutional regime and auctioneers' trust building measures. When quality is a concern, a third party, the auctioneer, has to provide safeguards and control mechanisms to ensure the quality of the trade objects and reduce the hazards of the trade execution (cf. Bakos; Brynjolfsson 1992). The requirements of trust are applied to the selection of the auctioneer and the governance structure of the auction. I.e., we are distinguishing two types of relationships: the primary trade relationship between buyer and seller, and the service provision relationship between the auctioneer and the respective trading partners. The loose relationship among the trading partners is complemented with a trustworthy relationship between trading partners and auctioneer. However, a good reputation of the auction and (system) trust in the effectiveness of the institutional rules and the trade system may be functional substitutes for personal trust that results from a relationship. In a centralized market, the trading partners outsource the provision of safeguards for a flawless trade execution to the auctioneer and they build a fairly stable relationship with the auctioneer for that purpose.

Small number of suppliers: Applying Bakos and Brynjolfsson's (1992) argument to the development of auctions would suggest that trading partners will trade, despite a rising number of auctions, only with a small number of auctioneers. The risks of an increasing fragmentation of the auction market with increased competition among auction sites and diminishing liquidity for individual auctions clearly warrant a (virtual) consolidation of auction sites.

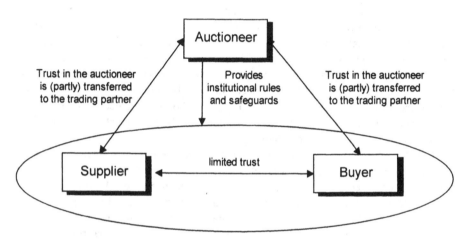

Fig. 3. Triangular trust relationship

3.3 Mixed-mode Hypothesis: Strategic Positioning of Web Auctions

In contrast to a dominating economic rationale, Holland and Lockett (1994) emphasize the strategic dimension of governance decisions. They propose what may be described as the 'anything goes' hypothesis, stating that whatever governance form a firm chooses, IT can be used to accentuate the effects of the chosen governance structure and to improve its efficiency. In hierarchical relationships information systems are designed to foster the organizational integration, in market relationships information systems reduce information and transaction costs and facilitate the ease of switching among several suppliers. In response to the primarily transaction cost oriented approaches, Holland and Lockett (1994) have developed an extended theoretical framework and have included business marketing, manufacturing strategy and organizational behavior literature. Based on these literatures and in contrast to the prevailing contextual determinism, they develop a research framework for coordination strategy and propose the 'mixed mode hypothesis': firms develop different forms of market and hierarchical relationships that are maintained simultaneously. The interrelations and interdependencies of governance structure, asset specificity, market complexity and Coordination strategy are analyzed in order to explain inter-organizational arrangements. Holland and Lockett (1994) have used five cases to illustrate different examples of vertical relationships on a continuum from a high level of organizational integration and hierarchy to fragmented business relationships and a market system. All but the market system example show a sequential combination of hierarchical and market arrangements. These mixed-mode arrangements combine the benefits of markets, such as high incentives to lower costs and improve quality, with the benefits of hierarchies, namely the efficient integration of operations.

The move-to-the-market debate is characterized by two major developments: The theoretical scope has been extended beyond transaction cost theorizing: organization theory and political economy (Bensaou 1993), resource dependence theory and network theory (Reekers, Smithson 1994) as well as business marketing, manufacturing strategy and organizational behaviour (Holland; Lockett 1994) have been taken into consideration and led to conceptually richer arguments. Throughout the debate, the initial question "what is the impact of IT on governance structures?" has been rephrased into "what is the strategic rationale for the selection and possibly combination of Coordination mechanisms?".

Holland and Lockett (1994) have emphasized the strategic rationale of governance decisions and have given a number of illustrative examples and cases of sequentially combined governance structures. The evidence of the Web auctions enables us to extend their argument in favor of concurrently combined governance structures: like oil wholesalers in the past have combined procurement from spot markets and from suppliers with whom they have a stable contractual relationships, companies are using Web auctions for the sale of returns and overstocks while they use at the same time traditional sales and distribution channels.

Strategic Positioning: The different types of auctions that we have distinguished, suggest a careful positioning of the auction mechanism by the suppliers, often complementing market or customer segments or other sales and distribution channels. Some examples are

- last minute offerings in tourism,
- relatively good used cars, as the complexity of the product description rises exponentially with the age or deterioration of cars (Lee 1997),
- special offers or stock-offers in the apparel business,
- offers that are restricted on traditional markets such as East African flowers (Heck; Ribbers 1996).

The examples are suggesting that companies are choosing not only sequential combinations of governance forms, like an auctions once a year which is pursued by a stable supplier-buyer relationship, but also concurrent combinations of different governance forms.

Mixed-mode Combination of Coordination Mechanisms: The New York Stock Exchange opens the trading day with a call market auction before switching to continuous market trading during the day (Bakos, 1998). Similar combinations of different auction types and coordination mechanisms can be used in other environments as well in order to respond to changing market conditions. Lufthansa, e.g., could use the English auction for the real-time auction and accept closed bids for any flight they are operating would be automatically matched according to predefined rules of availability and price-time priorities.

Image building: The high attention that Web auctions have drawn in the past, enabled suppliers to use them to carefully (re-)cast their image. While, e.g. the airlines have not fundamentally changed their pricing strategies, they have at least suggested a more flexible approach to pricing and have auctioned off limited contingents of tickets or offered tickets at lower prices for direct sale on the Web.

4 Conclusions

Web auctions and electronic markets in general have recently emerged at a high rate. Technological progress and the proliferation of global hyper-media communication infrastructures have enabled numerous players to expand the use of the advantages of auction mechanisms in an computer-mediated environment:

The Web has provided low-cost access to a global market space and at the same time highly focused customer groups. The wide availability of standardized software clients for the access to auctions, in most cases just Web browsers, has extended the group of potential participants. Cost-efficient communication infrastructures and low-cost market-engines have enabled auctioneers to set up auctions quickly and with limited investments. Expert examination and hyper-media representation of trade objects facilitate the separation of trade process and physical logistics of the trade items, thus lowering the transaction costs even further.

A simple conceptual analysis of this development against the background of the move-to-the-market debate has highlighted some of the success factors for electronic auctions as well as arguments for their strategic positioning:

H 1: The World Wide Web has reduced suppliers' and buyers' auction-related costs. For suppliers it has become less expensive to set-up auctions, to communicate the availability of specific trade objects and to describe electronically even complex trade objects. The Web enables suppliers and auctioneers to approach a global audience with very specific interests and needs, thus generating the requisite liquidity even for specialized market segments. For buyers, the cost to search for specific objects and to participate in an auction has been reduced. Consequently, new types of auctions are emerging and the trade object range has been extended into new domains.

H 2: Even more than traditional auctions, electronic auctions are exposed to the risk of fraudulent behavior such as misrepresentation of trade objects, missing rights, failure to settle deals or inability to pay. Design parameters for the auction, such as access rules and controls, and in particular the reputation of the auctioneer are safeguards for the participants. That means, that the low-trust market relationship among buyers and sellers is complemented by trust into the auctioneer.

H 3: Rather than becoming the only and ultimate governance form, auctions have gained a prominent place among and next to other forms of distribution or procurement. They are applied for specific customer or product segments, for direct sales or as marketing events.

The proliferation of Web-based auctions has also demonstrated that auctions are a very delicate instrument that can easily fail if one or several of the design parameters have been set in a wrong way. This article has attempted to raise the awareness about the impact of the Web and the complexity of design decisions. It has speculated about future directions of the development of electronic auctions, in particular

- the emergence of new auction rules,
- the extension of auctions into new domains,
- the development of new technologies in order to reduce buyers' search and negotiation cost even further.

Acknowledgement. I would like to thank Bob O'Keefe, Brunel University, and an anonymous reviewer for helpful comments and suggestions on earlier versions of this chapter.

References

Bakos, J. Y., "The Emerging Role of Electronic Marketplaces on the Internet," *Communications of the ACM*, 41, 8, (1998), 35-42.

Bakos, J. Y. and Brynjolfsson, E., "Why Information Technology Hasn't Increased the Optimal Number of Suppliers," *Sloan School of Management WP 3472-92*, October 1992.

Beam, C. and Segev, A., "Automated Negotiations: A Survey of the State of the Art," *Wirtschaftsinformatik* 39, 3, (1997), 263-268.

Beckmann, M.; Kräkel, M. and Schauenberg, B., "Der deutsche Auktionsmarkt: Ergebnisse einer empirischen Studie," *ZfB*, 67 ,1, (1997), 41-65.

Bensaou, B. M., "Interorganizational Cooperation - The Role of Information Technology an Empirical Comparison of US and Japanese Supplier Relations," in Proc. of the *International Conference on Information Systems (ICIS)*, (1993), 117-127.

Clemons, E. K. and Reddi, S. P., "Some Propositions Regarding the Role of Information Technology in the Organization of Economic Activity," in Proc. of the *Hawaii International Conference on System Science (HICSS)*, (1993), 809-818.

Clemons, E. K. and Reddi, S. P., "The Impact of I.T. on the Degree of Outsourcing, the Number of Suppliers, and the Duration of Contracts," in Proc. of the *Hawaii International Conference on System Science (HICSS)*, (1994), 855-864.

Clemons, E. K. and Row, M. C., "Information Technology and Industrial Cooperation," in Proc. of the *Hawaii International Conference on System Science (HICSS)*, (1992), 644-653.

Cramton, P.C., "Money Out of Thin Air: The Nationwide Narrowband PCS Auction," *Journal of Economics & Management Strategy,* 4 ,2, 1995, 267-343.

Cortese, A.; Stepanek, M., "Special Report on E-commerce: Goodbye to Fixed Pricing," *Business Week*, May 4, 1998.

Economist, *"On-line Auctions"*, Economist, May 31 - June 6, 1997.

Heck, E. van; Damme, E. van; Klejinen, J. and Ribbers, P. "New Entrants and the Role of Information Technology - Case Study: the Tele Flower Auction in the Netherlands," in Proc. of the *Hawaii International Conference on System Science (HICSS)*, (1997).

Heck, E. van and Ribbers, P. M. A., "Effects of Electronic Markets: An Analysis of Four Cases in the Dutch Flower and Transport Industries," in Proc. of the *Hawaii International Conference on System Science (HICSS)*, (1996), 407-416.

Heck, E. van ; Vervest, P., "Web-based Auctions: How should the Chief Information Officer deal with them?," Communications of the ACM, 41, 6, 1998, 99-100.

Hoffmann, D. L. and Novak, T. P. "Marketing in Hypermedia Computer-Mediated Environments: Conceptual Foundation," *Working Paper No. 1, Research Program on Marketing in CME*, Vanderbilt, January 1, 1995.

Holland, C. P. and Lockett, G., "Strategic Choice and Inter-organisational Information Systems," in Proc. of the *Hawaii International Conference on System Science (HICSS)*, (1994), 405-413.

Klausz, F. J.; Croson, D. C. and Croson, R. T. A. "An Experimental Auction to Allocate Congested IT Resources," in Proc. of the *Hawaii International Conference on System Science (HICSS)*, (1998), VI 363-373.

Lee, H. G. (1998): "Do Electronic marketplaces lower the price of goods?," in: Communications of the ACM 41(1), 1998, 73-80.

Lee, H. G., "Electronic Market Intermediary: Transforming Technical Feasibility into Institutional Reality," in Proc. of the *Hawaii International Conference on System Science (HICSS)*, (1997).

Lee, H. G., "Electronic Brokerage and Electronic Auction: The Impact of IT on Market Structures," in Proc. of the *Hawaii International Conference on System Science (HICSS)*, (1996), 397-406.

Lewyn, M., "What Price Air?," *Business Week*, March 14, 1994, 54-55.

Malone, T. W.; Yates, J. and Benjamin, R. I., "Electronic Markets and Electronic Hierarchies," *Communications of the ACM*, 30, 6, (1987), 484-497.

Markoff, J., "Can Xerox Auction off Hot Air?," *The New York Times*, June 24, 1996, D5.

Reck, M., "Formally Specifying an Automated Trade Execution System," *Journal for Systems Software*, 21, (1993), 245-252.

Reck, M., "Types of Electronic Auctions", in Schertler, W.; Schmid, B.; Tjoa, A M. and Werthner, H. (eds.) *Information and Communications Technologies in Tourism*. Springer-Verlag, Wien; New York, 1994, 236-243.

Reck, M., "Trading-Process Characteristics of Electronic Auctions," *International Journal of Electronic Markets*, 7 ,4, (1997), 17-23.

Reekers, N. and Smithson, S., " EDI and Interorganizational Coordination in the European Automotive Industry," in Proc. of the SISnet Conference (1994).

Seidmann, A. and Wang, E., "Electronic Data Interchange - Competitive Externalities and Strategic Implementation Policies," *Computer and Information Systems Working Paper CIS 92-03*, William E. Simon Graduate School of Business Administration, University of Rochester, May 9, 1992.

Singh, H.; Hao, S. and Papalexopoulos, A., "Power Auctions and Network Constraints," in Proc. of the *Hawaii International Conference on System Science (HICSS)*, (1997).

**Part VIII
Security, Privacy, and Legal Issues**

CHAPTER 31
Electronic Commerce: Privacy, Security, and Control

Daniel G. Conway and Gary J. Koehler

Decision and Information Sciences, Warrington College of Business, University of Florida, Gainesville, FL, USA, conwaydg@ufl.edu; koehler@ufl.edu

This chapter examines technical and non-technical issues related to privacy, security and control in Electronic Commerce. These issues are of great concern to consumers and businesses and continue to evolve at an impressive rate. This chapter presents many of the more common problems and fears that accompany electronic transactions as well as many of the behavioral and technical responses.

Keywords: Electronic Commerce; Security; Privacy; Encryption; Control; Authorization; Firewall; Public-key; Digital Signatures; Digital Certificates; Passwords

1 Introduction

This chapter examines issues of privacy, security and control in Electronic Commerce. Businesses and governments worry about the security of their systems. Consumers worry about their privacy and inappropriate use of their credit card numbers, pin numbers, passwords, etc. In any case, organizations and individuals want assurance and protection.

1.1 Privacy

Do you want to know Bill Gates' Social Security Number? The government tells you this at http://www.sec.gov/Archives/edgar/data/789019/0000891020-96-000072.txt. (It's 539-60-5125). The Privacy Act of 1974 significantly restricts Government agencies' use of Social Security Numbers and the disclosure of these numbers. Clearly there is a problem. And it isn't just with Social Security Numbers.

Individuals worry about inappropriate use of their credit cards, their bank or brokerage accounts and even their very identities. They worry about inappropriate access of their credit records, their medical records, their purchasing history, their criminal record (if any), and other personal information. Yet much of this is available online or during online transactions.

As you visit Web sites, your browser activities are often recorded both by your server and by the visited site's server. The sites you visit are also recorded on your computer for possible scrutiny by your boss. (The Electronic Communications Privacy Act gives the employer the right to monitor your e-mail and Web use.) To see the log of sites you have visited, type about:global on the Netscape Location field or open the Go menu for the Open History option under Internet Explorer. Browser cookies on your machine contain text about you that can be read by websites.

If electronic commerce is to become a standard marketing channel, the onus of privacy will be on the organizations that present their services or products on the Web. Organizations already worry about the same issues that individuals worry about especially as they relate to the integrity and security of their systems.

1.2 Security

In early 1998, news sources touted the arrest of "Analyzer" – an 18 year old Israeli hacker who had successfully penetrated Pentagon systems as well as a number of other U.S. government, commercial and educational systems (Martinez, 1998a; Smith, 1998). Although the Pentagon penetrations did not yield classified information nor did they lead to any tampering of information, the acts themselves are disturbing. Some hacker actions are clearly comical. An Air Force Web page on aviation statistics was replaced with a pornographic picture (CNNInteractive, 1996). Better yet, the CIA home page was altered to say "Central Stupidity Agency" (Drash and Morris, 1996). The General Accounting Office admits to over 250,000 hacker attempts to penetrate military sites per year with about half being successful.

Not all security threats are harmless. In 1994 Vladimir Levin electronically absconded with more than $10 million from Citibank (Burke, 1998). Fortunately, he was arrested in 1995 and all but about $400,000 was recovered. A recent congressional hearing mentioned a hacker breaking into a San Francisco power grid and shutting-down power for part of the city (http://www-nasirc.nasa.gov/nasa/index.html). Sometimes the damage is greater than the stolen resources. In 1988, Robert Morris unleashed an Internet worm that reputedly cost Internet sites over $98 million to rectify (see http://antivirus.min ingco.com/library/weekly/ aa101797.htm for details).

Cyberpunk: Outlaws and Hackers on the Computer Frontier by Hafner and Markoff (1991) discusses the Robert Morris worm escapade. Many other hacker exploits have been chronicled (see http://www.dowco.com/gor_books/net/cult ure/hackers.html for a nice list of books on hackers). Clifford Stoll's book *Cuckoo's Egg* (1989) tells how a 75 cent discrepancy in a computer accounting system led him to discover and eventually track-down an international hacker group responsible for stealing defense information. Perhaps the most celebrated hacker is Kevin Mitnick (see http://kevinmitnick.com/), known as Condor, who has been held in jail without bond since his arrest in 1995. His exploits have been reported in books like *Take-down: The Pursuit and Capture of Kevin Mitnick, America's Most Wanted Computer Outlaw-By the Man Who Did It* by Shimomura and Markoff (1996) and *The Fugitive*

Game : Online With Kevin Mitnick by Littman (1997). Another case discusses a truly scary episode about a mentally and physically disabled teenager (called Phantomd for Phantom Dialer) who wreaked havoc across the Internet and is chronicled in *At Large: The Strange Case of the World's Biggest Internet Invasion* by Freedman and Mann (1997).

The term "hacker" had been in use for many years, and originally meant an untrained individual who would try various actions to accomplish a task on a computer. It didn't enter mainstream usage until Robert Morris almost crashed the Internet in 1988 with his Internet worm. A hacker is now described as a person who breaks into computers for various purposes. More recently, the term "cracker" has been introduced to refer to unscrupulous juveniles who use the Internet to terrorize the public.

Are these highly publicized cases about hackers and crackers the exception? Apparently not. The Computer Emergency Response Team (http://www.cert.org/) received 39,626 e-mails and 1,058 hotline calls in 1997 affecting over 140,000 sites. Hacker and cracker computer crimes are estimated to cost businesses $10 billion annually (http://www.research.ibm.com/topics/popups/smart/security/html/gsal.html). These breaches are not limited to attacks from the outside. In a 1997 survey of 563 sites conducted by the Computer Security Institute (see http://www.goc si.com/csi/homepage.htm) with questions from the FBI, 75% reported financial losses from computer security breaches. Twenty-six of these respondents were able to quantify their losses:

- unauthorized access by insiders: over $3,000,000
- unauthorized access by outsiders: over $2,000,000
- telecommunications fraud: over $22,000,000
- proprietary information theft: over $21,000,000
- financial fraud: over $24,000,000
- sabatoge: over $4,000,000
- financial fraud: over $24,000,000

Another FBI study of 400 companies found almost half had experienced a breach in the prior year with one-third occurring even with firewall protection. (http://www.research. ibm.com/topics/popups/smart/security/html/gsal.html)

Organizations experience attacks from outsiders (hackers and crackers), from insiders in the form of fraud or espionage, from sabotage of services or files and from computer viruses, worms and the like. In Section II we discuss many security problems in detail.

1.3 Control

Many security and privacy threats exist on the Internet. In large part, these result from the basic design of the Internet. Section II discusses these factors. Fortunately, there are ways to lessen these threats. In Section III we discuss many types of control. Control methods extend from authenticating users with simple passwords through controlled access through firewalls. (Conceptually, a firewall is a computer or router placed between the Internet and the internal corporate network that runs software to screen network traffic.) Most security systems and systems designed to ensure privacy employ encryption methods. Encryption is discussed in detail in Section IV. This leads to a discussion of secure transactions in Section V.

1.4 Policies

Governments and Corporate policies play an important role in security and privacy. In Section VI we look at U.S. policies and initiatives. In Section VII we present a catalog of measures companies could take to better secure their systems. We conclude this chapter with a short summary.

2 Types of Security Problems

2.1 Introduction

Security problems can occur on any networked computer. Many of the problems are related to the exploitation of the original design of the TCP/IP suite of internet-working protocols, but most are due to configuration or operator carelessness. In this section, we first review how the TCP and IP protocols function as it relates to how they can be exploited. The hacking methods that take advantage of TCP and IP are not necessarily unique to that protocol and can be extended to other transport and addressing protocols. We next present security problems associated with viruses or downloadable executable code. Finally, operating system holes will be examined and additional information is presented.

It is worthwhile to review TCP and IP to better understand what makes them vulnerable to attack. Most Internet traffic is encapsulated in IP packets, including most information transferred from browsers and e-mail clients. The purpose of the IP protocol is solely to route packets from source to destination. It is unreliable in the sense that it does not perform packet recovery and does not guarantee a packet ever arrives at its destination. The data type encapsulated in an IP packet can be of any form, including text, sound, or graphic. An IP packet contains several information fields, including the source address, a 4-byte number under the current IP version, and the destination address, also a 4-byte number. These addresses, especially the source address, can be overwritten using specialized software in order to mislead a destination computer as to the origin of the packet.

TCP is a connection-oriented reliable transport layer protocol. Connection-oriented implies that the two machines first establish a session before any data is exchanged. Reliable implies that TCP is responsible for guaranteeing the delivery of data and is capable of recovering from lost, duplicated, and out-of-sequence datagrams. We will provide more detail of the protocols and their relevant header fields as we discuss the security problems that they present. For a more complete discussion of the TCP/IP family of protocols, see Comer and Droms (1995) and Stevens and Wright (1996).

2.2 Passive Sniffing

Passive sniffing attacks are often the first step that a hacker performs in order to gain information about a network. In this attack, a hacker captures packets traveling across a network. These packets contain information about both the source machine and the destination machine, including their IP address. The device used to capture networking packets is called a sniffer or a network monitor. They are readily available in the form of downloadable software on the Internet or can be rented using designated machines from network security companies. Monitoring software also comes with network operating systems, such as Windows NT. One can also write a sniffer using Tcpdump (Unix) or by extending the example code that accompanies the Windows Device Driver Kit (DDK).

Passive sniffing attacks can also capture usernames and passwords if such information is transmitted in plaintext or cleartext. Some of the more widely used TCP/IP application level protocols transmit login information in cleartext format, including FTP (File Transfer Protocol), Telnet (Terminal Emulation), and SMTP (Simple Mail Transfer Protocol). Thus, any device listening between the source and destination of the transmission can intercept the username and password in cleartext.

A sniffer captures all header fields of TCP, IP, and the MAC header (e.g., Ethernet) as well as the data field. The header fields contain addressing, transport, and checksum information while the data field contains application level protocol information. In an insecure connection, this could be the information involving usernames and passwords or the body of an e-mail message.

Also, HTTP is a cleartext protocol which uses TCP/IP as its transport and routing protocols, though it is not a member of the TCP/IP suite. A webpage form written in HTML which uses a GET or POST operation will also submit a request in cleartext. Consider the login page of the New York Times shown below:

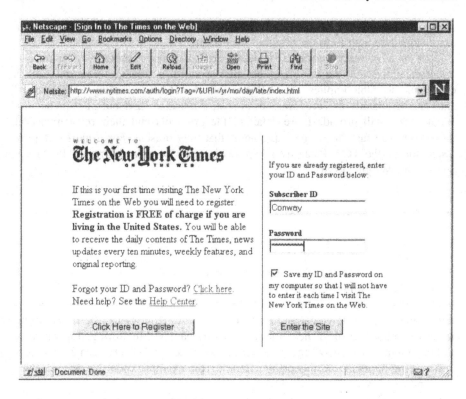

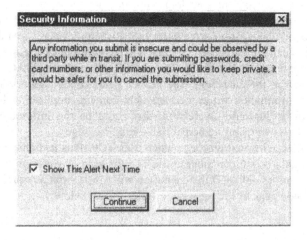

On this form, the user enters their subscriber ID (Conway) and password (My-Password). The password is of type 'password', so it does not appear on the screen. When browsers send cleartext information with GET or POST operations, a warning similar to the following appears:

The ensuing POST operation creates the following segment of the corresponding Ethernet frame captured by a sniffer:

55 73 65 72 3D 43 6F 6E 77 61 79 26 50 61 73 73 77 6F 72 64 3D 4D 79 50 61 73 73 77 6F 72 64	User=Conway&Pass word=MyPassword

Thus, the username and password have been compromised as they are transmitted across the network in cleartext. In general, it is recommended that users choose a different password for services that transmit passwords in cleartext.

To discourage such attacks on distributed networks, system administrators can employ user identification schemes such as Kerberos ticketing or a one-time password system. The Kerberos system has been built into Windows NT 5.0 and will be discussed in detail later. A one-time ticketing system assigns the user a new password each time the user logs out of a system. Both solutions can be attacked through other more sophisticated methods and both introduce new technical and behavioral issues. In either case, passive sniffing can still yield some information to the hacker if the data streams are not encrypted or digitally signed.

2.3 Active Sniffing or TCP Hijacking

Each computer on a network has a unique 4-byte IP address. Passive sniffing allows the hacker to learn a server's IP address and perhaps some addresses that a server trusts. Even if only the server's address is captured, a hacker might be able to guess trusted hosts by using nearby addresses. For example, if a server had an IP of 200.201.202.15, a hacker would likely attempt to spoof the IP 200.201.202.14 in an attempt to gain access to the server. Armed with such information, a hacker can attempt to assume the identity of a machine in the server's local network. This spoofing of a trusted client or server IP is common to many attacks. See http://main.succeed.net/~coder/spoofit/IP-spoof.1 for a detailed description of IP spoofing and accompanying code.

Each byte of data transferred between a client and a server is numbered in the TCP header to allow the receiver to reconstruct the original message. If a packet arrives with a sequence number that doesn't match the number the server is expecting, the packet is discarded. An R (reset) bit can also be used to break the connection if one of the communicating parties determines a connection should no longer exist. Of course, an intruder can thus send such flags to close other connections if that connection obstructs his objectives.

A TCP/IP connection is a three-step process, frequently called a three-way hand-shake. Each step of the process and the completed connection are all candidates for attacks. In the first step, the client sends a packet requesting a connection. In the packet heading, the SYN bit (Synchronizing segment) is set to indicate this initial request and an initial sequence number is sent. SYN packets are faster to send than they are to process, allowing a hacker to cripple a server by continuously transmitting such packets. If a server's incoming queue fills with such requests, subsequent packets are discarded. Normally, a hacker would spoof an unreachable IP so that the server would use up all its available connections attempting to complete the hand-shake with the non-existent host. This attack is called SYN flooding and it is frequently used to disable a communicating party so that a hacker can impersonate the host.

In step two, the server responds with a packet setting the SYN and ACK (Acknowledgement) flag set and its own initial sequence number. Finally, the client responds by acknowledging (ACK flag set) with an ACK packet and the connection is established. From this point on, only the ACK flag is set. There are other flags useful in other attacks that are not covered here.

A hacker that is between a client and a server and is able to spoof IP and sequence numbers can attack either machine in several ways. The hacker can disable one of the machines and take the identity of the other, or the hacker can mimic either machine and carry on conversations impersonating the other. A hacker could also attach additional information to a client request and strip the corresponding additional response from the packet before forwarding the remaining response to the client's original request. If a hacker desynchronizes the connection to impersonate a host, a flood of TCP ACK packets would likely be generated as the two original parties attempted to communicate with what they believed were correct sequence numbers. A host responds to each improper packet with an ACK packet, which in turn produces another automatically detected by software. See http://rootshell.con nectnet.com/docs/tc p_attack.ps.gz for a more detailed description of this type of attack.

2.4 Trust-Relationship Exploitation

A hacker could attack a remote server without being in a position to directly receive responses. In order to accomplish this, the hacker would need the server's IP, a trusted IP, and a guess at the server's initial sequence number. A trust-relationship exploitation attack works as follows. The hacker first disables the client using SYN flooding or attacks at a time they believe the client to be turned off. The hacker attempts to connect to the server using a spoofed packet with the disabled client's IP. If successful, the server responds to the client with an SYN/ACK packet, which the hacker never sees. The hacker guesses the server's initial sequence number and sends an ACK packet to complete the connection. Thus, the server believes the connection has been made with the trusted client when actually the client is unaware of the connection. The hacker then sends packets to the server in hopes of creating a back door, such as remotely setting up a user account on the server. This attack is blind as the server's response packets never reach the disabled client or the hacker. If the hacker has guessed the sequence numbers and a firewall has not discarded the packets as they entered the server's site, then the hacker has established the back door. Kevin Mitnick allegedly used this attack in his infamous attack on Tsutomu Shimomura's computers in San Diego, which ultimately led to the hacker's arrest. The attack is described at http://www.rootshell. com/docs/se quence_attacks.txt.

Having a firewall intercept packets as they entered a local network could prevent the above attack. Firewalls should be configured to reject packets from outside with IP addresses corresponding to hosts on the inside. Servers that are intended for public use, such as Web servers, should be physically separated from a local network by a firewall as well. Firewalls will be discussed in more detail in a following section.

Many more TCP/IP based attacks and routing attacks are available to hackers today and tested code is widely available. The curious reader should start at http://www.rootshell.com/ as a starting point for related documentation and code. Klander (1997) provides a description of many more such attacks as does Bellovin (1989).

2.5 Viruses

A computer virus is a computer program that executes on a host without the expressed consent of the operator. As a program, a virus can cause as much or as little damage as any other program. They can transmit sensitive information or reformat a hard drive. They can lock out the user by taking over the keyboard or mouse, or they can operate in a manner such that the user never knows they are there. Although virus detection software can detect and eradicate many common viruses, there is always a gap between when new viruses are written and when they are first detected and their footprints identified for inclusion in virus protection software.

A trojan horse virus is a computer virus that a user believes to be safe. The user executes the program and the virus takes control. Such a program could have been downloaded or received as an e-mail attachment. Downloading an infected executable program using FTP or accepting an e-mail attachment that contains a virus will not affect the host until the user executes the program. Many firewalls are configured to not allow attachments of any kind to penetrate as viruses can be so damaging. A hacker could easily replace a harmless executable with a malicious one as the file transferred by. We discuss this topic further in the section on firewalls.

A virus might also be placed on a computer by a hacker who has set up a secret account. Once the hacker logs into the system, they could replace any executable on the machine with their own code, which could then be executed by an unaware user or remotely by the hacker. Many times, viruses are spread accidentally, by exchanging infected diskettes for example. Virus checking software is designed to look for common traits in virus attacks, such as an increase in hidden files, boot sector inconsistencies, or executables that attempt to overwrite important system files. Executables that have mysteriously grown in size due to inserted code are also suspicious.

Memory resident virus checkers will also monitor the effects of executing programs to determine if they are attempting to take over vital system resources or modify system code. Although virus checkers have become significantly more sophisticated, will always be playing catch up. As more and more people attach their machines to networks, one can expect the proliferation and damage caused by viruses to continue to be significant.

2.6 Downloadables : Java and ActiveX Applets

Downloadable applets are programs that execute automatically upon download. These applets download automatically when host Web pages are accessed. After they are downloaded, they are immediately executed by the Web browser if the browser is configured to do so. Applets bring animation and interactivity to the Internet, but they also pose an obvious and significant security threat. The two most common types of applets, Java applets and ActiveX applets, approach the security issue from fundamentally different philosophies (see Venners, 1997a-1997c for a nice introduction to Java security architectures). Java applets are designed to operate inside a virtual machine embedded in the browser and have no access to the system itself. This is called the sandbox in which the Java program runs. As a result, Java applets cannot read or write from a computer's hard drive, initiate new processes, or perform network connections to computers except the one where it originated. This level of security is comforting to the user, but it also limits the usefulness of the application. ActiveX applets are programs that are executed and given full access to the operating system and system resources. As a result, they are a tremendous security risk, but are not limited in functional scope. This section discusses the Java security model in further detail. See Hughes et al (1997) or Yerxa (1997) for additional detail.

Java applets were designed to run independently of a computer's operating system. There are several layers to the security model. First of all, the Java language itself does not contain statements supporting indirect addressing. Thus, an applet cannot access memory outside of the applet's own memory block. The Java compiler enforces security as well by enforcing strong typing and class based objects. The compiler creates an intermediate form of program called byte code. This byte code is then downloaded.

Java Virtual Machines (JVM) are embedded in Web browsers and provide another level of security. The JVM written for various browsers are different, each allowing different levels of access corresponding to different levels of trust. The purpose of the JVM is to interpret the byte code and make sure the applet executes in the proper address space. The JVM prevents the applet from playing in other sandboxes and prevents programming errors, such as an indexing out-of-bounds array. The JVM itself consists of three parts: the Class Loader, the Byte-Code Verifier, and the Security Manager. The Class Loader loads all the necessary classes into memory at the request of the applet, as opposed to letting the applet manage the memory. It is possible to create byte-code without using a Java compiler and thus bypass the built-in language security features. The Byte-Code Verifier ensures that the applet was indeed created by a Java compiler by scanning the code for violations such as name space violations and object accesses in violation of the security model.

Finally, the Security Manager (SM) passes final judgement on whether or not a statement can execute. SM is itself a Java class, and users can write their own security managers giving applets different levels of access to system resources. SM monitors file access, system and network I/O, and process and thread creation among other things, and determines whether or not the action is permissible. Generally, JVMs embedded in browsers are very restrictive whereas JVMs built into operating systems are very lenient. Applets downloaded over the internet that are executed outside of the browser could therefore pose a security risk as the security manager used by the operating system would likely give the applet file access.

The goal of creating a perfectly secure language and virtual machine environment is ambitious. There are significant technical and marketing challenges to overcome in order to achieve such a goal and there are fortunes and futures in the balance. Java as a programming language will likely continue to grow in popularity as a networking and middleware language, apart from the JVM and the Internet downloadable debate.

Presently, Java and ActiveX applets approach security from opposite viewpoints, but that continues the change. Java applets and ActiveX applets can each be digitally signed to confirm their origins. Browsers can be configured to allow each type of applet different levels of access to system resources. JVMs are being loaded with more and more traditional operating system functions as operating systems are being loaded with more and more networking and security functionality. The marketing battles, legal maneuverings, and technical developments associated with applets will be interesting prominent in the media for years to come.

2.7 Operating System Holes

No widely used operating system today was developed with secure electronic commerce as the primary focus. As a result, additional operating system features supporting secure transactions are constantly being created to enhance current systems. Network administrators need to be constantly monitoring such developments and implementing the patches and enhancements as they become available.

The primary competing operating systems today are Windows NT, various versions of Unix, Novell's Netware, and perhaps the JVM. Windows NT is the fastest growing system but trails Unix versions substantially in revenue. Both Windows NT and Unix are heavily dependent on the TCP/IP suite of protocols and Novell is moving decisively in that direction. Novell is also establishing Java as the core of its future networking strategy. None of the systems is exempt from attack.

Unix is the oldest and most widely used networking operating system in use today. Unix has the advantage of having been tested and patched by hackers for decades. As a result, many of the security flaws are well known and fixes are widely available. Many of the attacks on Unix machines are TCP/IP based attacks where the hacker attempt to access root level processes, so called R-functions (rlogin, ...). These functions allow hackers to log in remotely, acquire directory and user listings, and create new accounts. It is recommended that administrators disable these functions on servers configured for public use. Administrators should see http://www.rootshell.com/ for descriptions of known attacks against various versions of Unix.

Windows NT, currently the 32-bit version, was developed more recently by experts who were well aware of the Unix security shortcomings. It is clear that Microsoft takes security very seriously judging by the vast amount of literature available at their Web site (see http://www.microsoft.com/security/). NT has not had the years of testing that Unix has had, but they are remarkably responsive in fixing holes as they are discovered. Administrators are strongly encouraged to consider NT service packs as they are developed and to monitor the Microsoft Web site regularly for developments. Netware has seen its market share negatively affected by the competition from NT, but remains strong with a large installed base and loyal customers. One advantage Netware had over Unix was in its use of IPX/SPX as its transport and networking layer protocols. Thus, traditional TCP/IP attacks would not work against a Novell network. In order to infiltrate such a network, one would first have to attack a host connected to a WAN by TCP/IP, take over that host, and launch an attack from there. Although possible and likely done successfully, it is a much more complicated process than TCP/IP attacks alone. As Novell migrates to TCP/IP, this advantage will be lost.

The JVM behaves enough like an operating system to warrant mention here. Due to the cryptographic and networking libraries shipped with the Java foundation classes, the JVM might be the closest thing to a networked operating system developed with secure electronic transactions in mind. Currently, Sun and IBM are developing a formal Java operating system. That system will have built in digital certificate verification, public and private key encryption methods, and secure protocol extensions to TCP/IP like Secure Sockets Layers. It is unclear how it will perform in other traditional operating system roles as it is still in early development. One would expect Windows NT 5.0 and future versions of Solaris to have similar functionality built-in as well.

2.8 How to Hack Information

As one might expect, the World Wide Web contains a vast amount of literature on network security in general and computer hacking in particular. A search on the words 'Network Security' currently returns over 7000 pages using a popular Web search engine. This figure, assumed to underestimate the actual number of sites, will likely grow significantly as electronic commerce continues its explosive growth.

One good starting location for documentation on security problems and hacking is http://www.rootshell.com. That site contains many of the more widely sited white papers on common hacker attacks as well as network sniffers and other tools. It is to the advantage of any network administrator to be aware of common protocol attacks as well as the location of the software to patch them.

3 Control

3.1 Focus Areas

Control is enforced at many points in a networked computing environment. Password systems are the most frequently encountered control systems for users. However, there are many points in a communication network where authentication of a packet takes place. These locations are entry points to a company network, a local network, or a personal machine. This section begins by surveying authentication systems, discussing the behavioral and some technical aspects of password and biometrics systems. It then examines firewall issues, including configuration and bypass. Some of the more technical aspects of authentication systems are presented in later sections covering encryption and privacy.

3.2 Access Control

Before authentication systems can be implemented, a policy stating who has access to what resource needs to be determined and formalized. Such local issues include access to personnel files, financial records, and other company proprietary information, as well as access to network applications that communicate beyond the firewall. Policies need to be clarified with regards to what types of documents, files, or applets should be allowed through the firewall. To most users, these policies will likely be unpopular and convincing education should accompany this effort. No user ever asked for less access to resources.

Access control also involves physical aspects of network security. Computers need to be physically secured and physical access to workstations, servers, and backup devices should be carefully regulated. A record should be kept mapping users with accessible devices. That record should be regularly updated and time stamped in the unfortunate event that evidence might have to be preserved.

3.3 User Authorization

Most personal computers and network operating systems require authorization from users in order to receive services. These systems can be based on passwords, physical characteristics like fingerprints, or complicated mathematical keys and algorithms. They are intended to keep unauthorized users out as well as document the entry and exit times of authorized users. Most user authorization systems classify the user into one of several categories, each with an appropriate level of read, write, query, or execute access. A network administrator manages these accounts and the username-password pairs are generally encrypted and stored locally. Hackers frequently target these password files as they attempt to capture account information or establish themselves as an authorized user.

3.4 Password Protection

In order for password systems to function as designed, the user and the computer need to keep a copy of the username and password in a secure location. Computers are generally better at this than humans are. Computers store such information in encrypted files. Humans store such information in cleartext on post-it notes and stick them to their monitors or under their keyboards. Neither place is considered very secure. Users need to be convinced that even if their particular data seems unworthy of protection, the networked machine still poses a security threat. Klein (1991) presents an excellent paper regarding password security.

One attractive solution to many password problems is the use of smart card technology. Smart cards store password or key information so the user is not tempted to write passwords or store them on their machines. This also allows for passwords to be more complex as they are not limited to characters available on keyboards. Users are not required to remember their passwords, though they are required to remember to carry their cards. Storing the card with the workstation or desk naturally reduces such advantages. Smart cards have the disadvantage that they require additional hardware on all cooperating hosts.

Authorization systems can also be designed so that more than one person must authenticate in cooperation for a user to be allowed access to a resource. For example, a bank vault may be designed so that no single person knows the entire combination, thus preventing any one person from having physical access alone. Mathematical algorithms have been devised that work similarly in concept. Such algorithms are called k-out-of-n authorization systems. The idea is as follows. Of the n persons who have key pieces, any subset of k persons can combine their keys to get access to a resource. The advantage of this system would be that a person's password, or key, could be accessed by an authority, but only with permission from at least k of the n trusted agencies. No one agency could act alone. Any stolen information containing a piece of the key would be without value. The US government is currently devising such a system. See Shamir (1979) or Stinson (1995) for a more detailed description of k-out-of-n authorization systems.

3.5 Biometrics

Passwords have many disadvantages. They are often forgotten, they are managed carelessly, and they are generally chosen poorly. One alternative to using text-based passwords is biometrics. Biometric systems create unique codes based on unique physical features of the human body, such as fingerprints, hand structure, and voice or retina characteristics. They share many of the positive features of smart cards but are much more difficult to lose or forget. Like smart cards, they require additional hardware to operate on all cooperating hosts. Due to the cost of the additional hardware and the required processing power for pattern recognition systems, they are not widely used today for general electronic commerce. However, there is much excitement in the field and potential exists for convenient authentication systems based on biometrics. Recent developments can be found at The Biometric Digest at http://webusers.anet-stl.com/~wrogers/biometrics/.

3.6 Content Security

Networked computers and firewalls can be configured to deny certain categories of executables from executing locally. The most common content security software are virus checkers. Virus checkers are programs that execute (usually automatically) whenever a user attempts to execute a program. The virus checker scans the executable code for suspicious behavior or addressing and alerts the user if something is found. Virus checkers can be configured to automatically scan files as they are stored locally. They also have a built-in timer that alerts the user when it should be updated. Updates are generally available via a network and upgrades can be performed automatically.

Content security more recently has expanded to include applets. Browsers and firewalls can be configured to deny applets internal access to a network. Management usually sets such policies. Browsers and firewalls can also be configured to refuse URLs based on some rating system. This can assist management (and parents) from allowing particular Web site information from propagating.

3.7 Firewalls and Network Security

Firewalls are software programs that provide a filter through which incoming and outgoing packets must pass. In their simplest form, they can admit a packet based on the value of a field in the packet header, such as an IP. In the figure below, the WWW server is configured to deny access to all requests accept those with network Ids 128.227.0.0.

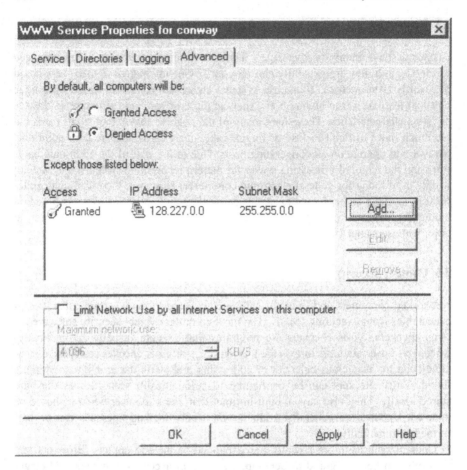

More sophisticated firewalls range in ability from application gateways and proxies to firewalls capable of stateful inspection. Such firewalls will be examined later.

A corporate network design would require a firewall be installed at each entry point into a network. If such a network were designed to include public servers such as a Web server, the design would likely include a firewall between the public server and the corporate firewall. This is accomplished by operating public services physically on a separate host. Public servers are common targets for hackers and attacks against such services are well documented and easily performed.

Firewalls can be configured to accept or reject packets based on IP addresses, port or application numbers, or any field in a TCP or IP packet. This type of firewall is called a packet filter. It examines the source IP address of a packet and makes an accept/reject decision based on either the network ID portion of the address or the entire address itself. Such a filter can prevent outsiders from entering, assuming they are using their true IPs, or prevent insiders from accessing particular Web sites containing unproductive or politically undesirable content. For example, some communist countries made access to the Wall Street Journal and other business publications unavailable to their citizens by not allowing any packets with IP Source Address = 206.157.193.* through their country's firewalls. Of course, it is easy for a site to change addresses or to mirror itself to another IP. It would be equally simple for a person to copy all the information contained in a public Web site to their own site and make it available from there. Such IP filters are generally not very effective.

Every TCP/IP service is identified by a number called a port number and placed in a TCP header. When the TCP/IP stack or firewall parses the TCP header, it finds this number and sends the data to the corresponding application. For example, port 80 is generally used for HTTP, port 25 for e-mail (SMTP), and port 23 for Telnet connections. A firewall can be configured to allow public access to ports 80 and 25, but not 23, for example. Similarly, it can be configured to allow only particular IPs to use Telnet services, and make public HTTP and SMTP to everyone. It is generally a good policy to restrict public access to as few services as possible.

When a client attempts to connect to a server, it initializes contact by sending a packet with a SYN flag in the TCP header set to one. If the connection is accepted, the server and client continue their communication using packets with an ACK bit set to one. Thus, if a firewall keeps records of all current connections, it can deny packets that are not the result of a previous request. This will prevent an outside attack from attempting to make a connection with an inside host. The firewall allows requests to pass out (SYN = 1, ACK = 0) but only responses (SYN = 0, ACK =1) are allowed to filter in. This type of filter can prevent many common types of attacks.

The File Transfer Protocol (FTP) is one of the more common internetworking protocols and occupies ports 20 and 21. This protocol differs in that it requires a port for managing the transfer and a port for the data transfer itself. When a client makes a request, it sends a packet (SYN = 1) to the server. If the server accepts the connection, it then sends a request to the client (SYN = 1) to establish the data transfer. If the ACK filter described above is in place, the data transfer connection will be denied, as the connection request will have originated from outside the firewall. Many firewalls support passive mode file transfers, which allow the client to make the data transfer request as well. Most Web browsers use passive mode by default.

TCP is designed to be a reliable transport protocol. Its sister protocol, UDP (User Datagram Protocol) is designed to be unreliable. Unreliable in this case implies a connection is not maintained or established at all. The UDP header in fact does not contain a SYN or ACK field. Such services that use UDP over IP include routing maintenance protocols and broadcasts. Unfortunately, they also include DNS, NFS, NetBIOS-over-TCP/IP, and NetWare/IP. These services can be easily corrupted or used as a launching point for other attacks.

The DNS protocol is used to map domain names such as www.java world.com to IP addresses such as 209.1.23.51. This is a common application level protocol used in electronic commerce. A client makes a request to a domain name server for the corresponding IP address of the given name. The server responds in a UDP packet with the IP. If all UDP services are disabled, all internal Web clients would be required to access external sites directly by using IP addresses. These are generally more difficult to remember and extremely difficult to guess. One solution is to limit such requests and responses to 'trusted sites'. However, a response could contain a spoofed IP response, giving a hacker limited access to a DNS port. Recently, router firewalls have expanded UDP packet management in order to keep track of requests and allow the corresponding responses. This does not prevent IP-spoofing, but it will deny a hacker from attacking without packaging the attack as a response to a request.

Another possible solution is to operate a DNS inside the firewall and configure it with only the sites you wish to allow your internal users to access. This solution will naturally require additional hardware and software as well as IS resources, but it would allow a firewall to deny all UDP packets. Keeping a DNS internal also would not prevent inside hackers from attacking hosts using UDP attacks. The external IP addresses stored at the internal DNS would somehow need to be maintained and verified as well. In other words, how do you know the IPs haven't been spoofed originally or tampered with internally? The solution does prevent the UDP attacks, but the IP packet filter issues remain.

A more sophisticated solution involves using proxy servers and application gateways. These servers accept the client request and perform the connections on behalf of the client. When the proxy is convinced the communication has completed successfully, it returns the results to the host. If the proxy is hacked and crippled, no internal host is affected by the shutdown and internal hosts can use a second proxy while the first is being reoriented. The use of a proxy prevents direct contact between a client and server and thus prevents all the problems associated with such connections. It also centralizes management of information access and allows one site use of an advanced TCP/IP stack while the internal hosts continue to use their previously configured stacks.

Proxy servers are also available that inspect each packet for suitability. Such products can also perform stateful inspection, a service that downloads an applet or distributed executable in its entirety and runs it prior to allowing it to reach its final destination. Upon downloading an executable attachment, a proxy would send the file to a screening computer. That computer would load and run the program to determine if it contains potentially damaging code, such as a virus. If the screening computer is not corrupted and other characteristics of the executable code are satisfactory, the code is considered safe and sent on to the destination computer. This type of service also centralizes virus control management and can assist in preventing inattentive users from compromising the internal network.

As users get more comfortable with and dependent on networking, they tend to resent the type of controls firewalls impose. As a result, more sophisticated users frequently install modems into their computers to allow them to work around firewalls. Modems used to bypass firewalls pose a very serious security threat as they are rarely configured to perform firewall responsibilities. Because many internal phone numbers are closely related, a hacker can easily attempt to call thousands of potential modems using specialized computer programs. Once a connection is made, the host computer is a significantly easier hacking target than a company firewall.

Dialup modems present a management problem as well. Such devices are very inexpensive and simple to configure. They are not always easy to detect due to clever physical placement. Users can easily make connections using readily available remote access software and tunneling protocols. (Tunneling protocols are used for end-to-end connections such as remote login to a server across the Internet.) As telecommuting and virtual office environments become more common, dialup modems and the corresponding security threats will likely continue to proliferate. Company network security experts should periodically use dialup hacking tools on potential phone connections to determine the existence of such devices. If it is determined that such a device is necessary, the administrator needs to assist the user in configuration or firewall implementation as well as manage related upgrades. The logging features should be enabled and periodic inspection of those files should be performed.

Much literature exists on the topic of Firewalls. Any Unix security text will cover the topic in great detail. Other sources include Ranum (1992), Hall (1997), and Willis (1997).

3.8 Network Address Translation

Many of the more common hacking attacks on a network are based on spoofing the network address of an incoming packet. Packet filters can be spoofed and persuaded into believing a packet originated from the inside when in reality it originated from the outside. Such attacks begin by the hacker capturing an internal IP via session hijacking, DNS request, or by accessing an internal Web server. Once the IP is known, the hacker can impersonate that IP in an attempt to pass through the firewall. A firewall can also play this game by capturing all IP addresses as they pass through and translating the network ID portion of the address to a different address. This is named network address translation for obvious reasons. Network address translation prevents outsiders from directly contacting internal hosts. If such an attempt is made, the firewall discards the package. This forces all communication to pass through the proxy and allows the proxy to determine the suitability of the packet.

Network address translation prevents end-to-end protocols by forcing all packets to pass through the translator. One such protocol, IPSec, encrypts the IP inside the packet and wraps that information in a second IP packet. Thus, each packet contains an IP and an encrypted IP. The network translation server would change the outer IP as it passed through the firewall, but the inside encrypted address would refer to the other IP. As a result, packets using protocols that secure and encrypt the IP address such as IPSec are received with an IP address different than their encrypted or hashed IP address. Such packets, designed to prevent such IP spoofing, and thus discarded by the end host.

IPSec would still be effective if the address translation firewall were configured to verify the packet was not spoofed by decrypting the encrypted address and comparing it to the advertised address. The firewall would then be required to repackage the packet using IPSec and using the true internal network address. This would establish an end-to-end communication with the external host and the firewall and an end-to-end communication with the firewall and the firewall and the internal host. Such services will likely become widely available as the IPSec protocol is formalized and implemented. See Cheng (1998) or Moskowitz (1997a) for a description of IPSec.

3.9 Some Commercial Tools

Many commercial tools are available for firewalls from various vendors. Those desiring to build their own firewall should consult Chapman and Zwicky (1995). The firewall newsgroup can be found at comp.security.firewalls and comp.security. misc. Other valuable resources include Telstra (http://www.tel stra.com.au/info/sec urity.html), COAST (http://www.cs.pur due.edu/coast/co ast.html) and CERT (mailto:cert-advisory-requests@cert.org). An Eggleston Web site offers over 10 links to firewall vendors (http://www.access.digex.net/~nua nce/security.html).

4 Privacy: Encryption and Virtual Private Networks (VPN)

4.1 Introduction

Privacy consists of disguising information. Information sent not as cleartext is called ciphertext. The first known effort to disguise information is thought to be that of Julius Caesar, who would conceal information by shifting letters to the right by three places. When the generals received his messages, they would know to shift the letters back three places. For example, the cleartext message "monday" would be concealed as the ciphertext "prqgdb". Anyone intercepting the message would thus need to know the encrypting key (shift letters by 3) in order to decrypt the message. Due to a lack of literacy and available analytical tools, this was a fairly successful cipher. This simple form of shifting is still done today to hide answers to riddles or other inappropriately placed statements on newsgroups. It is trivial for a computer to decipher as the encryption method is linear and thus subject to frequency analysis.

During the World Wars of the twentieth century, radio signals had to be encrypted to keep information out of enemy hands. Many complicated machines were developed to mechanically encrypt text, including the infamous Enigma machine of Nazi Germany. These machines were capable of encrypting messages in a far more complex mathematical manner than had been used before and hastened the development of the digital computer. The Japanese naval codes JN22, JN25, and Purple are also examples of sophisticated mechanized algorithms that were difficult to impossible to break by hand. Much of the groundwork for the field of cryptography was developed during this period and has only recently been declassified.

Due to the sensitive issues related to hiding information, it is believed that published literature is years behind secret research in cryptography. There has been much recent advancement of strong encryption methods, however, and those developments have set the stage for an inevitable showdown between government concerns and electronic commerce concerns. Banking and other international businesses that need to secure information want strong encryption to protect that information whereas the government wants the ability to access that information under certain conditions. Each camp has very strong reasoning to support their viewpoints. It is a difficult issue, one that will likely continue to create conflict for many years to come. See Section VI on "Government Policies and Related Issues" for references on current cyber laws.

This section on privacy will explain some of the more common encryption methods and developments in cryptography as they relate to electronic commerce, including public key and private key encryption.

4.2 Virtual Private Networks (VPN)

The Internet is a vast collection of interconnected computers. Passing information over any public communication network makes eavesdropping a concern for those sending sensitive information. If information is encrypted such that only a subset of the users can decrypt it, those users have established a VPN. It is virtual because the subnetwork does not exist independent of the internetwork, and it is private because only those computers with corresponding decryption keys can read the information. VPNs rely on encryption to block eavesdroppers. See Moskowitz (1997b) for a discussion of the term VPN.

The following notation will be used in this section for all algorithms.

P	Plaintext (or Cleartext)
C	Ciphertext
K	Encryption key
$e_k()$	Encryption function using key k
$d_k()$	Decryption function using key k

Using this notation, we deduce $e_k(P) = C$, $d_k(C) = P$, and $d_k(e_k(P)) = P$. There are various names for attacks against encrypted data based on the amount of information an attacker knows prior to the attack. The interested reader should consult Schneier (1996) for details.

The length of the key, measured in bits, is directly related to the strength of the algorithm. For example, the US government currently limits the key size of exported cryptographic algorithms to 40 bits under most conditions. Recently, Hewlett-Packard was allowed to export a stronger 128 bit encryption technology under certain restrictions. Currently, 128 bits is considered almost unbreakable. Most ATM cash machines use 56-bit encryption. The US Navy uses an extremely secure 4096 bit encryption algorithm. Many algorithms exist which can use variable length keys as well.

4.3 Secret Key Encryption

The oldest and most common form of encryption fits in the category of secret-key encryption, also called symmetric key or private key. When using this type of encryption, each user has the key that is used to encrypt and decrypt information. The Caesar cipher is an example of secret-key encryption. Most symmetric key algorithms have a computational speed advantage over public key algorithms. They however suffer from one drawback, which is how to securely get the key to both parties. When a user receives a private key, how does he know it came from a trusted source? Could the intended key have been replaced with a third party key? As we know, the IP address of the source could have been spoofed. Secret key algorithms are most effective when keys do not need to be distributed over a public network. ATM machines use secret-key encryption since the key can be determined at installation and the installation is carried out by trusted (we hope) parties.

DES, or Data Encryption Standard, is the most widely used secret-key algorithm. Developed in the early 1970s by IBM for the National Bureau of Standards (NBS), DES (1997b) became the US federal standard for use on all unclassified government communications. The US National Security Agency tested the algorithm and modified certain aspects of it, including reducing its key length from 128 bits to 56 bits and changing some of the non-linear inner workings. It was an unprecedented time in encryption as NSA only recently had admitted their very existence. The standard was published by NBS in January of 1977, likely due to a misunderstanding between NSA and NBS. It will likely be the last such NSA standard published. Cryptographers have been able to study the algorithm and its inner workings, but have had limited success using the information to improve attacks. Some of the more recent attempts, using differential cryptanalysis, have led researchers to believe that NSA has known about such potential attacks 20 years before the area was publicly researched. Many others believe NSA has a secret trap door or glass window into the algorithm, which allows them to quickly decipher DES encrypted information. No proof of such a system exists, but little is known about NSA.

The DES algorithm is a symmetric key algorithm and is available in hardware or software. It is a block cipher, in that it works on blocks of data at a time. The 56-bit DES encrypts 8 bytes or characters of data at a time. It begins by permuting the bits of both the data and the key. The key is then divided into 28 bit halves, and each half is shifted left based on which of the 16 rounds you are performing. The key is then reassembled and compressed in accordance with a known table to a length of 48 bits. The data is also halved and the right 32 bits are expanded according to another table resulting in 48 bits. An exclusive-OR is performed on the new 48-bit key and 48-bit right bits to create a 48-bit result. Though the above steps seem complicated, they are linear and trivial to decrypt.

The interesting and non-linear step of the DES algorithm involves Substitution-boxes, or S-boxes, as do many encryption algorithms. Consider the first S-box given below:

S-Box 1.

14	4	13	1	2	15	11	8	3	1	6	12	5	9	0	7
0	15	7	4	14	2	13	1	1	6	12	11	9	5	3	8
4	1	14	8	13	6	2	11	15	12	9	7	3	10	5	0
15	12	8	2	4	9	1	7	5	11	3	14	10	0	6	13

This step of the algorithm compresses the 48-bit result down to 32-bits by dividing the 48 bits into 8 groups of 6 bits. Each group has its own S-box and compression works as follows. Assume the first 6 bits of the current 48-bit result are 101011. Bits 1 and 6 are taken to create the row number and bits 2,3,4 and 5 are taken to create the column number. Rows and columns are numbered beginning with 0. Thus, the 6-bit result above would be substituted with the table entry from row (binary 11) 3 and column (binary 0101) 5. That table entry is 9. The number 9 in binary is 1001. Thus, the first 6 bits of the current 48-bit result 101011 is replaced with 1001.

This step is essential and not well understood. It is non-linear and appears optimized to withstand the newest forms of differential cryptanalysis. There are 8 such S-boxes, and each has been studied extensively. The 8 S-boxes compress the 48-bits back to 32-bits, which are permutated once again. Finally, an exclusive-OR is performed with the original left 32 bits of the data and the two halves are swapped. This entire algorithm is then performed 15 more times!

Remarkably, the same key is used to decrypt the information, except the key is shifted to the right during each iteration instead of shifting to the left. People new to the field of cryptography can't help but feel that the algorithm is overkill. However, with the increase of computing power combined with the decreasing cost, brute force attacks have been becoming more and more successful. In the software version, a 56-bit key generally corresponds to an 8-character password. This is particularly weak, as the keyboard does not contain keys which produce all the possible binary combinations. Humans are also notoriously poor at choosing passwords, which further restricts the possible keys to try in a software implementation. Mathematically, researchers have identified weak keys and ways to exploit the algebraic structure and many such poor choices have been published.

A natural extension of DES would be to encrypt with one 56-bit key k_1, and then encrypt with a second 56-bit key k_2. Would this not create a 112-bit key version of DES? This actually increases security by only 1 bit due to a type of attack called 'meet in the middle attacks'. However, performing three DES operations with three different keys, $E_{k3}(D_{k2} (E_{k1} (P)))$, does indeed double the key strength. This is called Triple-DES. HP's VerSecure uses Triple-DES. There are many less common forms of DES, including variations that employ other S-boxes, and the interested reader is again referred to Schneier (1996) for variations and related commentary.

4.4 Public Key Encryption

In 1976, Diffie and Hellman (1976) and Merkle (1978) first presented the concept of public key encryption. The idea was that the encryption and decryption keys were not the same, though with some additional information, one could be used to generate the other. This was a stunning finding which forever changed cryptography and its use in current internet protocols has made secure electronic commerce possible. In general, public key algorithms are significantly slower than secret key algorithms, and frequently a hybrid system is employed to improve efficiency.

With public key encryption, every sender and receiver has a public key and a private key. The public key is given out freely and the private key is never compromised. Thus, knowing a person's public key would allow anyone to encrypt a message, but only the owner of the private key could decrypt the message. This means that even the person encrypting the message could no longer decrypt the message. The main advantage of public key encryption is that the communicating parties need not meet prior to the secure exchange of information, provided that they trust that the public key did indeed come from the other party. This is a recurring problem in all forms of encryption. It will be discussed further in the section on digital signatures.

The first public key algorithm was based on an integer programming problem known as the knapsack problem. There are two forms of the knapsack problem, one that is trivial to solve, and a second that is NP-complete and therefore much more difficult to solve for large problems. If a person knows the key that maps the hard problem to the easy problem, he can publish the hard problem and keep the key private. Binary information can then be encoded as a difficult knapsack problem, which eavesdroppers could not solve in reasonable time. The owner of the private key could therefore convert the problem to an easy type and solve it by inspection. The knapsack algorithm is no longer considered a secure algorithm, though it is frequently used for demonstration, as it is easy to understand and does not depend on complex prime number theory.

Soon after, Rivest, Shamir, and Adleman (1978) created what is now the most common public key algorithm: RSA. It is also one of the easier to understand. The idea behind the algorithm is that it is difficult to factor large numbers. A large number in this case may contain over 200 digits. Factoring a large number has never been proven analytically to be impossible (or equivalently as difficult as a known hard problem), but centuries of mathematicians and recent digital attacks have been unable to advance the science of factoring. RSA essentially makes a very large number public and challenges hackers to factor it. Due to its popularity and importance in many protocols, we present a sketch of the algorithm below. Readers yearning for more details can find many electronic sources available on the Web, including www.rsa.com.

The algorithm first generates two (large) prime numbers p and q. The value n is computed as n = p*q. The encryption key e is chosen (randomly) such that e is relatively prime to (p-1)(q-1), implying they have no common factors. The values e and n are made public. The decryption key d can be calculated using the Euclidean algorithm such that

$$e*d = 1 \bmod (p-1)(q-1) \text{, or } d = e^{-1} \bmod (p-1)(q-1).$$

The value d makes up the private key. The original values p and q are secretly discarded.

To encrypt a message, one would use the equation $C = P^e \bmod n$. Thus, anyone with the public key (e,n) can encrypt a message. To decrypt the message, one would use $P = C^d \bmod n$. Thus, to decrypt the user would need to know the value of d. How can this value be computed? Recall, to get d, one needed e, p and q. The value e has been made public, so an attacker would need the values p and q. Given the public value n, p and q could be found only if n could be factored into its prime elements. As we noted, factoring large numbers is difficult.

As an example, let p = 13, q = 11, n = 143. I choose e = 23 to be relatively prime to (p-1)(q-1) = 120. Then d = 47 as (23*47) mod 120 = 1081 mod 120 = 1. Suppose I wish to conceal my message, which is represented numerically as 8. To encrypt, I use the formula C = 8^23 mod 143. With some calculation, this results in ciphertext C = 83. The message 83 is then sent across the network. The owner of the private key, 47, then uses the formula P = 83 ^ 47 mod 143. Again after calculation, P = 8. These small values of p and q result in an easily factored 143, thus such numbers would never be chosen. The mod formulas, including 83^47 mod 143, can be solved with relative ease on a spreadsheet.

What remains is to find large prime numbers. There are also good and bad choices for p and q and some poor choices for e (and thus d). Attacks on RSA have been primarily focused on which values of p, q, e, and d are considered weak. Attempts to factor faster, even using massively parallel machines and coordinated Internet attacks have not proven to be particularly promising.

The RSA algorithm is significantly slower than the DES encryption method implemented in hardware or software. When both are implemented in hardware, the RSA method is 1000 times slower than DES. In software, RSA is 100 times slower. Thus, hybrid methods have been created which combine both public key encryption and secret key encryption. The strength of a public key system is to allow parties to exchange information without having met previously to exchange a secret key. Thus, public key encryption is used to securely exchange the secret key, and the secret key is used for faster encryption. Secure sockets layers and Pretty Good Privacy are examples of protocols that use hybrid methods. See the section on secure transactions for details.

Hundreds of other tested encryption algorithms exist and have been used in commercial products. Some of the more common block ciphers include Lucifer (Smith, 1971), RC2 (proprietary system by RSA Data Security), IDEA (Lai and Massey, 1991), and Skipjack (proprietary code by NSA for the infamous Clipper

Chip). Lucifer was an early block cipher created by IBM labs. It has some similar features to DES including S-boxes and permutations, but the substitution structure is weaker than that of DES. It remains as a historical teaching tool, but it is vulnerable to differential encryption attacks. RC2 was designed as a replacement for DES by one of the world's most respected cryptologists Ron Rivest, currently at MIT. It is a 64-bit cipher with variable key size. The algorithm is proprietary, though some details have been presented. IDEA, or International Data Encryption Algorithm, is currently being used by PGP. The algorithm uses a 128-bit key and encrypts 64-bit blocks using efficient computer operations. IDEA has been patented and published, which gives it an advantage over RC2 in the battle for open standards. It has been optimized against differential cryptanalysis as well as Markov analysis, which the authors Xuejia Lai and James Massey created. IDEA is a strong contender to replace DES as the future standard. Skipjack was developed by the NSA for the Clipper chip series and was completed in 1990. It uses an 80-bit key to encrypt 64-bit blocks using 32 rounds of processing. It is most likely an extremely secure algorithm as NSA plans to use it in its Defense Messaging System. Currently, it is only being implemented in tamper-proof hardware to prevent reverse engineering. The algorithm was recently released by NSA.

4.5 Key Escrow

One possible compromise being pushed by world governments is the concept of key-escrow. The concept allows users to use stronger encryption methods but forces them to turn over their private key to an escrow agency, which can then be asked to turn it over to authorities under court order. There are many variations for implementation. Under one scenario, a user's private key would be partitioned into small units and turned over to separate escrow agencies. This would reduce the risk of the key being stolen from a particular agency as any piece on its own would be of significantly less value than having the entire key. Lotus and HP have released products that adhere to the escrow idea, however, it appears that they do so simply to acquire a market share. There are obvious marketing issues involved in selling software overseas that can be read at any time by the US Government.

Many issues remain legally and politically unresolved and undefined in regards to key escrow. Should a researcher be allowed to publish an encryption method for testing by others? Would any governments use this to monitor civil rights movements? Have any governments ever had a willingness to view personal information from rival parties? Would they use this technique to do so? What type of evidence gathered from using key-recovery would be admissible in court? There are many more questions yet to be resolved and many strong options have been expressed with regard to civil liberties, but the marketplace has begun to use this approach at least temporarily.

4.6 Advanced Topics in Encryption

Encryption is an exciting and mysterious science. It has an intriguing historical background and considerable unknown history. Today, it receives much interest from the popular press and much interest in the form of grants from various governmental agencies. Though the mathematics of encryption are somewhat complex, number theory and abstract algebra, and the algorithms seem bizarre and patternless, it is a topic which networking specialists need to be aware of in order to choose systems that adequately protect their information.

New technologies and designs are emerging which could significantly impact the science. One such technology is quantum computing. The idea is that a quantum computer could hold in its register the values 0 and 1 simultaneously. If a 32-bit register could hold all values, it could simultaneously hold over 4 billion values. Though many problems have yet to be worked out, it is estimated that a quantum factorization engine could factor 129-bit RSA in seconds (see Hughes et al., 1997). In 1994, Leonard Adleman brought the field of molecular computing into the mainstream when he solved a directed Hamiltonian Graph problem through methods using chemical reactions and separations. Other respected researchers in the area, most prominently the late Seymour Cray, have long portrayed this topic as being the future of computing. The process uses DNA-enzyme to perform pattern matching. Again, many problems have yet to be worked out, but preliminary work is encouraging.

Quantum cryptography has recently been revived as well and is currently being used by British Telecom for distances of up to 50 km connected by fiber optic cable. In this method, the sender transmits a series of photons down the fiber, randomly polarizing each photon in 45-degree increments. The receiver can measure the polarization only if the detector used is aligned properly. By chance, the receiver can measure 50% of the signals. The receiver than sends the sender the sequence of alignments he used. With some additional information and understanding, they now have a shared key. This system also has some drawbacks, but essentially it is working now.

Hardware implementations of algorithms, including the Clipper chip and smartcards, can be attacked by several approaches that fall in the category of fault cryptanalysis. This attack attempts to induce information by operating the hardware at the limits of voltage, temperature, or other hardware boundaries without corrupting the device. Methods that use parity bit information have also been proposed and tried. Finally, attacks that accurately measure the length of time a device uses to encrypt or decrypt can also yield information about the keys used. These methods, along with attacks involving electromagnetic radiation and electrical pulses should keep smartcard designers occupied.

Much exciting research is currently being done on encryption for use in secure commercial networks. Although it is widely thought that the NSA is years ahead of any published academic research, the algorithms available today are ample to safely protect user passwords and credit information for years to come. The use of encryption methods in secure protocols should become the emphasis for electronic commerce researchers. We continue by presenting some of the protocols used to secure electronic transactions and examine the area of digital certificates.

5 Secure Transactions

5.1 Introduction

Secure end-to-end transactions lie at the heart of electronic commerce. The fundamental issue is trust. In all secure transaction protocols and algorithms, some trust needs to exist. Many forms of trust are currently being marketed, but a few have emerged as competing standards. We examine how transactions can be digitally signed to verify the source and how digital certification assists with such verification.

Public key encryption was presented as a secure encryption method in that any message encrypted with a user's public key could only be decrypted with that user's private key. An equally useful consequence is the opposite: if Bob receives a message that can be decrypted with Alice's public key, then it must have been encrypted with Alice's private key. That implies that the message was in fact from Alice, as only she has the private key. Clearly, anyone possessing Alice's public key could decrypt such a message, so further measures must be taken to secure the message. Such methods are discussed below.

5.2 Hashing Functions and Digital Signatures

One of the disadvantages of public-key encryption is the speed of the implementation. Many documents may not need to be encrypted, but verification of the source may be essential. In this case, a hash or digital fingerprint of a document can be created, encrypted, and appended to the document. We examine this process and mention some of the more common hashing functions now.

A hashing function is a one-way function that takes a document and creates a significantly shorter digital summary, generally on the magnitude of 160 bits. Hash functions are one-way functions in that the resulting 160 bits can not be reverse engineered to produce the original document. They are designed so that it is extremely unlikely for two documents to produce the same hash. Because of this uniqueness, they are frequently referred to as digital fingerprints. Hashing functions need this uniqueness as they are used to determine whether or not the document has been changed, even if the change were just by one character or decimal place.

Several hashing functions have received governmental or commercial endorsement. The United States National Institute of Standards and Technology (NIST) has adapted the Digital Signature Standard (National Institute of Standards, 1994), or DSS for its standard. It was developed by NSA and uses the Secure Hash Algorithm, considered to be one of the most secure algorithms today. The algorithm is similar to one created by Ron Rivest in 1990 called the MD-4 (Rivest, 1991) (message digest #4) algorithm. It is likely DSS will become a standard in the same way that DES became a standard.

In a digital signature, a document's hash is encrypted by the sender's private key and the encrypted hash is attached to the document. This is significantly faster than encrypting the entire document and adds very little data to the transmission. When the message is received, it is hashed using the same hashing algorithm employed by the sender. The attached hash is then decrypted with the sender's public key and the two hashs are compared. If they are not identical, then the message must have been altered during transit, either from an error being introduced or by a hacker replacing or modifying the message or hash directly. In this case, the message is discarded.

Digital signatures can be used in many electronic transaction models. For example, programs downloaded over the Internet pose a tremendous security threat. Digital signatures can be used to verify that the program received was indeed sent by the assumed party. If you trust the party, you would then trust the software. Remote database updates work similarly. If you can verify the update came from the advertised source, you can update the database accordingly.

5.3 Trusted Third Parties and Digital Certificates

For any type of blind communication to exist, there has to be some degree of trust. At the very least, a user needs to trust the source of other public key. Is trust transitive? In other words, if you trust Bob, can you trust everyone Bob trusts? How far can such transitive trust be extended? If Alice and Bob each trust Trent, then Trent is called a trusted-third party. The market for trust is interesting from an economic point of view. Generally, economic analysis focuses on complementary and substitution effects. It is not yet clear how trust as a commodity can be analyzed and quantified. For a discussion of the economics of trust, see Whinston (Whinston et al., 1997).

Digital certificates are based on a common transitive trust. A digital certificate can have different forms. Consider an example X.509 (International Telecommunication Union format) certificate below, taken from a Netscape website example:
Certificate:

Data:
   Version: 0 (0x0)
   Serial Number: 1 (0x1)
   Signature Algorithm: MD5 digest with RSA Encryption
   Issuer: C=US, OU=Test CA, O=Netscape Communications Corp.
   Validity:
      Not Before: Wed Nov 23 14:30:35 1994
      Not After: Fri Nov 22 14:30:35 1996

Subject: C=US, OU=Test CA, O=Netscape Communications Corp.
Subject Public Key Info:
   Public Key Algorithm: RSA Encryption
   Public Key:
     Modulus:
       00:b4:6c:8a:ec:ba:18:7b:72:a1:3c:cb:e9:81:15:
       2d:df:9b:b2:82:5b:13:50:02:2a:fe:7c:51:07:e6:
       14:c3:60:ad:15:56:de:f0:a7:32:c1:a0:34:95:a3:
       6a:4e:bf:21:48:4a:4a:21:7d:6b:37:12:59:8a:b8:
       c9:65:ff:a7:45:a0:16:b7:e1:b8:cb:52:0e:16:bd:
       e0:16:dd:dd:a7:36:67:3e:09:b9:db:33:bd:74:fc:
       de:58:94:cf:28:b3:96:d5:8e:33:61:1f:cb:40:3f:
       2a:29:2d:0b:68:87:15:68:fd:09:00:e0:77:4e:d2:
       40:1a:3e:5f:9c:d3:cc:16:63
     Exponent: 3 (0x3)
Signature Algorithm: MD5 digest with RSA Encryption
Signature:
   55:79:c0:97:88:44:77:48:8a:48:7e:16:6a:d7:e5:3e:e2:f7:
   17:d0:d4:80:d8:92:95:e8:7c:12:9f:be:78:4b:a6:cb:e5:25:
   c9:db:d4:e0:d3:e7:c2:7b:56:03:f9:2a:7a:d5:09:53:48:86:
   37:b1:be:0b:21:1a:f5:0c:6c:96:2b:bf:70:8a:6e:c4:fd:ea:
   0f:90:35:7f:66:05:eb:f2:05:c2:20:3d:72:fa:52:ab:88:41:
   7b:3e:d8:10:23:59:e5:82:f9:71:86:66:12:ca:c5:f7:46:47:
   84:ad:56:66:a4:50:1c:ff:ac:12:a4:69:65:4a:d4:11:b7:a4:
   b1:4e

The certificate contains a version number, dates during which the certificate is valid, and some hexadecimal encryption information. Most importantly, the certificate contains a digital signature from the CA that states in essence that the public key can be trusted. A browser that trusts the CA can then verify that the public key does indeed belong to the server. It does this by first decrypting the hash with the CA's public key and then rehashing the certificate with the given signature algorithm and comparing the two values. If they match, then the certificate was created by the CA and should be trusted. The draft of the Internet X.509 Public Key Infrastructure (PKI) can be found at http://www.veri sign.com/ repository/ietf/draft-ietf-pkix-cmmf-00.txt.

The Secure Electronic Transaction (SET) certificate technology, developed originally by Visa and MasterCard, extends the X.509 certificate structure shown above in a manner such that the merchant never sees the credit card number. Used in conjunction with SSL, the consumer's credit card numbers never travel in cleartext and are never available to the merchant. This technology has the support of IBM, Microsoft, Netscape, GTE, RSA, and VeriSign, and is thus likely to become a standard for increasing the security of creditcard transactions. See http://www.visa.com/cgi-bin/vee/nt/ecomm/set/main.ht ml?2+0 for more details on this evolving technology.

Operating systems and browsers currently have some limited certificate handling built in. Microsoft NT 5.0 and Novell's NDS can store X.509 certificates and some extensions. It remains to be seen how well the big players work together. Meanwhile, other companies are introducing products that keep the user's private key off easily physically compromised machines. Such devices would store the user's private key on a smartcard or have the retrieval be based on biometrics such as a fingerprint. Current certificate authorities include VeriSign, GTE, VISA, and the US Post Office. Expect to see increased activity in this area.

5.4 HTTP and Secure-HTTP

HTTP is the protocol used to transmit requests and WWW pages between clients and servers. It is a cleartext protocol and the original designers had no reason to believe it would become the protocol backbone for Internet commerce. As a result, it has neither built-in encryption techniques nor any inherent way to exploit a public key infrastructure. The HTTP message format consists of a series of headers, a blank line, and a body. The headers list the request or response code and which MIME (Multi-purpose Internet Mail Extensions) formats are being used among other things. A browser request might look like the following:

```
POST /public/index.html
Accept: text/plain
Accept: text/html
Accept: image/gif
Accept: image/jpg
Accept: image/jpeg
Referrer: http://www.ufl.edu/business/faculty/dis.html
User-Agent: Mozilla/3.0
From: conwaydg@ufl.edu
** blank line **
username=koehler
&password=hoosier
```

It is the responsibility of the server to format the response in a manner that the client can interpret. As presented earlier, any device sniffing this network can obtain all the information from this message as it passes. Secure HTTP, or S-HTTP, was designed to address this problem.

S-HTTP extends HTTP to add security. It wraps any version of an HTTP message inside an S-HTTP message body. When a session is established, the client and server negotiate the cryptographic preferences each will be using and the client sends it's public key. The server then creates a session key and encrypts it with the client's public key. Upon receiving the session key, the client decrypts the message to obtain the key and the client and server exchange subsequent requests and responses encrypted with the session key. S-HTTP also supports digital signatures and can optionally support server side digital certificates as an additional security feature. Unlike HTTP, sessions are kept alive until the browser requests that they be terminated. This reduces the overhead from session negotiation.

5.5 Secure Sockets Layers

The most widely supported secure transmission protocol used today is Secure Sockets Layers (SSL) originally developed at Netscape . The protocol resides between an application and the TCP/IP protocol stack and thus can be used in any networked application. It has been submitted to the W3 Consortium working group on security as a standard protocol for Web browsers and servers. It has considerable support from industry and a very large installed base. SSL works as follows (http://home.net scape.com/assist/security/ssl/ howitworks.html).

When a browser is installed onto a client, it generates a public key and private key combination. The client requests a connection with a SSL server by sending a 'hello.client' message along with its public key, similarly to S-HTTP. The server responds with its public key in a message encrypted with the client's public key. The client then requests the session key in a message encrypted using the server's public key. The session key is created with each new session and is exchanged using the appropriate public keys. Server-side digital certificates are supported and SSL 3.0 supports client-side certification as well. Source code in C to create SSL compliant applications can be freely downloaded from Netscape's Web site.

Netscape Object Signing (NOS) works with SSL to allow downloaded objects to request access to a user's system resources. When such an object is downloaded, Navigator displays information regarding who signed the object and what resources were requested. The user then can choose whether or not to let the object pursue the resources. NOS allows servers to sign any object format. Microsoft has a similar technology called Authenticode which is available through Microsoft Internet Client SDK. It functions similarly, though the signature is embedded within the object itself.

5.6 S/MIME and OpenPGP

Secure MIME and OpenPGP (Pretty-Good Privacy - Garfinkel, 1995) are rival secure e-mail protocols that are currently incompatible. OpenPGP has a large installed base but momentum in the form of high-profile support (Microsoft, Netscape, IBM-Lotus Notes) seems to favor S/MIME. Each supports a different form of digital certificate with S/MIME supporting the more popular X.509 standard. PGP uses local certificate authorization to create a web of trust. Anyone in the web of trust can act as a trusted party for anyone else in the web. S/MIME uses the more common CA to issue and manage its certificates. There are advantages to each approach. Using an external CA like VeriSign can be more complicated than a small or middle-sized company requires whereas the web of trust created from PGP may be too large in a big company to be of any value. See Higgins (1997) for a comparison of the approaches.

5.7 Kerberos Key Exchange

The Kerberos authentication service was developed at MIT and is currently being implemented into Windows NT 5.0. It has the advantage of a single log-in for all services. The service works as follows. When a user logs into a network, the user is given a ticket-granting ticket (TGT) to take to the Kerberos server, which is the only host it trusts. The TGT is actually a block of information about the user and a time stamp encrypted in the Kerberos server's own key. This TGT is used to obtain service tickets from the central Kerberos server for use on other services.

When a user requests a service, S, it first must acquire a ticket from the Kerberos server, K. The server K verifies the TGT from the client and creates a packet for the desired service. The packet contains a ticket for the requested service and a randomly generated session key all encrypted in the client's public key. K also encrypts the session key and ticket using S's public key and sends it to S. S then waits for the client to connect. The client decrypts the packet to learn the session key. It encrypts the session key with the ticket using S's public key and sends it to S. S decrypts the message and checks if the session key matches the key sent from K. The client may also authenticate the server at this point as well. The session key is then used from this point to encrypt the session.

Kerberos is not intended to be a complete network security solution, but it does have some advantages. The single log-in feature is attractive as it simplifies the number of passwords a user must remember. The centralized key server simplifies management of the system. It is the foundation of OSF's DCE Security Service and will likely see strong market acceptance with the release of NT 5.0. It has the disadvantage that applications need to be re-written or Kerberosed in order to take advantage of the system's abilities. As of now, not enough such applications exist, though that again is likely to change quickly. See Neuman (1994) or Backman (1997) for a more detailed description.

5.8 Consumer Education

It often baffles computer security professionals when consumers freely give credit card information to strangers over a telephone or via mail or to potentially disgruntled employees at a gas station but are unwilling to transmit such information in encrypted form over the Internet. Many of the fears consumers have are based on media hype rather than on any truly measurable level of security. Massive marketing campaigns are currently underway to persuade consumers to feel as comfortable with electronic transactions as they do with other forms of transactions.

Consumers should remain cautious and seek education with regards to electronic transactions. For example, one company recently guaranteed the security of credit card numbers transmitted securely to their server. Such a guarantee is worthless, as there is currently no means for proving that someone stole the numbers online.

6 Government Policies and Related Issues

6.1 Key-Recovery Systems

The U.S. Government has struggled for a policy that balances the security needs of business and government and the privacy needs of individuals with the need to enforce laws, regulate public activities and provide national security. Electronic commerce needs secure transactions. Encryption methods provide one of the best answers.

But encryption can also secure illegal records and transactions. Terrorists and criminals can hide their affairs with strong encryption safe in the belief that their secrets are impenetrable.

Until the beginning of 1997 encryption software using keys larger than 40 bits could not be exported without government approval. This was relaxed to 56 bits by President Clinton but with a questionable provision: the software was required to have a key-recovery system that law-enforcement officials could use (with court permission) to obtain the key and decrypt information encrypted with that software. Most companies oppose this concept. It is almost comical to think that citizens of Italy or Russia could find comfort in the knowledge that the CIA could unlock their private information. Indeed, the Economic Strategy Institute has argued that U.S. companies stand to lose $35 billion over the next five years with this restriction (Borland, 1998a). In September of 1998, President Clinton approved the exporting of 56-bit key encryption without restrictions.

And 56-bit encryption is hardly a secure haven. Indeed, 56-bit keys have been cracked in as few as 39 days (Martinez, 1998b). 128-bit encryption is becoming a standard. Recently Hewlett-Packard received permission to export VerSecure, which provides 128-bit encryption. It does have a key access system but that can be disabled by the user.

U.S. officials have also argued for a domestic key-recovery system. France has a key escrow policy and other countries are considering such laws. American companies have lobbied against such laws (Borland, 1998b). A domestic key-recovery might cost U.S. companies $140 billion (Borland, 1998b). In a recent concession (Clausing, 1998), the Clinton administration allowed export of strong encryption software without a key access system but only for financial applications exported to nations with acceptable money-laundering laws.

An alternative solution is a proposed FBI cryptography laboratory, like the National Security Agency's (Borland, 1998b). Presumably, this lab could develop technical means to combat improper use of encryption.

All of this concern may become obsolete. Recently Rivest (1998) showed how confidentiality can be achieved without encryption through a process he calls chaffing and winnowing.

Whether this or other ideas eventually take-shape will prove interesting. Until then, great controversy will continue on this issue.

6.2 Cyber-Crime

There are several government initiatives that address security issues. Many efforts are concerned with protection of government systems. For a period, many Internet security issues were studied by the Federal Networking Council (FNC) (http://www.ccic.gov/cicrd/pca-wg/lsn.html) which was chartered to act as a forum for networking activities between federal agencies. A report on Federal Internet Security can be found at http://www.fnc.gov/fisp_sec_con tents.html. On October 1st, 1997, the FNC was de-chartered and many of their activities moved to the Large Scale Networking group of the Computing, Information and Communications R&D Subcommittee (http://www.ccic.gov/cic rd/pca-wg/lsn.html).

Recently U.S. Attorney Janet Reno announced the formation of the National Infrastructure Protection Center (Dornin, 1998). This cyber-crime center will link to other federal departments, to local and state police and to centers at universities. It will also coordinate with other nations. This center will combat hacker threats to national security.

A number of teams are available to handle security incidents resulting from cyber-attacks, including:

- Carnegie Mellon's Computer Emergency Response Team (CERT) Center (http://www.cert.org/)
- The Automated Systems Security Incident Support Team (ASSIST) for INFOSEC security (http://www.assist.mil/)
- The Forum of Incident Response and Security Teams (FIRST) representing over 60 teams from government, commercial, and academic groups (http://www.first.org/).
- NASA's Automated Systems Incident Response Capability - (NASIRC) (http://www-nasirc.nasa.gov/nasa/index.html)
- The U.S. Department of Energy (http://ciac.llnl.gov/)

CERT alone received 39,626 e-mails and 1,058 hotline calls in 1997 affecting over 140,000 sites.

There are many sources of information available on security. The National Institute of Standards and Technology has a Computer Security Resource Clearinghouse (http://csrc.ncsl.nist.gov/) which provides information on authentication, emerging technologies, encryption, security objects, virus information and a host of additional security issues.

The National Institute of Health maintains a site on computer security information at http://www.alw.nih.gov/Security/security.html. Likewise, a similar site by the Library of Congress can be found at http://lcweb.loc.gov/global/internet/securi ty.html .

6.3 Laws

Laws protecting privacy are plentiful. Some protect individuals while others spell-out the rights of government and businesses. Below is a brief summary:

- Privacy Act of 1974 – gives individuals the right to know about, to access and to correct personal information in federal databases and to limit the collection and disclosure of such information without consent;
- Right to Financial Privacy Act of 1978 - controls government access to personal financial records;
- Privacy Protection Act of 1980 - Makes it unlawful for government officials to search or seize materials possessed by "a person reasonably believed to have a purpose to disseminate...forms of public communication";
- Debt Collection Act of 1982 - Amendment to Privacy Act of 1974 and Federal Claims Protection Act of 1966 giving the federal government greater access to data and private sector sources for help in debt collection;
- Electronic Communications Privacy Act of 1986 - provides protection for all forms of electronic communication and their systems but does not cover individual LAN communications (http://www.eff.org/pub/Legislation/ec pa.law);
- Computer Security Act of 1987 - gave the National Bureau of Standards (now called the National Institute of Standards and Technology) responsibility for developing standards and guidelines for security and privacy of information in government systems (http://csrc.ncsl.nist.gov/secplcy/csa_87.txt);
- Video Privacy Protection Act of 1988 - prohibits selling of videotape rental data without consent or court order;
- Foreign Communications Free Trade Act of 1989 - regulates foreign electronic commerce;
- Computer Fraud and Abuse Act – prohibits unauthorized access to government systems (http://www-nasirc.nasa.gov/law/titl-18.html);
- Communications Assistance for Law Enforcement Act – details the responsibilities of telecommunications carrier's to cooperate in the interception of communications for legal purposes (http://cpsr.org/cpsr/privacy/epic/wiretap/1994_tele phony_law.txt); and
- Freedom of Information Act 1996 – all government agencies must disclose information kept on individuals except to the extent this violates an individual's privacy (and certain other exemptions).

Current laws and pending legislation dealing with security issues can be found at http://www-nasirc.nasa.gov/laws_bills.html.

7 Corporate Policies on Security, Privacy and Control

7.1 Introduction

Information security is much more a management issue than a technological issue. For a corporate policy to be effective, everyone must be involved. Security involves both behavioral and technical issues and therefore must have well defined goals and priorities. Involvement and education needs to be continuous. The potential damage from one disgruntled employee or one poor choice of password can easily exceed the cost of implementation and management of a sound policy. According to the 1997 CSI/FBI Security Survey (563 responses), 75% of respondents reported financial losses related to security violations. Losses averaged from $76,000 per virus attack to $957,000 for compromised proprietary information or financial fraud. Most respondents admitted they still had neither an emergency response team nor any policy for preserving evidence.

7.2 Develop Goals and Priorities

The goal of information security is to create a safe computing environment where the cost of violating security exceeds the value of the information lost or obtained by others. The first step in the process is to develop goals and priorities. A policy team should be established consisting of representatives from IT and non-IT functional areas. Representatives who have the most to lose from compromised or lost information generally make good members.

A policy should thus first identify what information is valuable and who should be allowed access to it. This risk assessment should attempt to quantify the impact of losing the data, both accidentally or underhandedly to potential enemies. This loss should be in monetary terms and downtime. Threats need to be prioritized based on the likelihood of occurrence. After careful assessment, the team should develop a plan to improve the current strategy. A disaster recovery plan should be formalized at this juncture. Officers on the team need to be identified and roles need to be defined.

Many tools exist that can be used to assist in identifying security problems in software, with SATAN (Security Administrator Tool for Analyzing Networks) being the most common tool. SATAN and anti-SATAN tools should be used to identify common configuration problems and security shortcomings. Security specialists may be useful at this point in the process as well. Users need to be informed of the security holes that cannot be closed by technical solutions, such as internal modem firewall bypass threats. SATAN code can be found at www.rootshell.com. Additional sources can be found at International Network Services homepage http://www.ins.com, and Network Computing's "How to Secure Your Network" at http://techweb.cmp.com/nc/netde sign/security1.html.

7.3 Detail Security Requirements

Security threats can come from inside or from outside the organization. Having identified valuable information and the users who should have access to it, the team should be able to define security requirements. Such requirements should be behavioral and technical and address both inside and outside threats.

Computer users are notoriously poor at choosing passwords. One necessary requirement for a company is to force users to choose non-trivial passwords. Having the system not accept passwords from a given list of poor choices can help enforce this policy. In fact, when a hacker attempts to guess passwords, he or she generally uses such a list. Even a list as long as a dictionary or lists from a baby-name book can be iterated through quickly in an attack. Hackers frequently attempt to capture personnel files in hopes of guessing user passwords. Such programs generally attempt combinations as well, such as first name and street address. For example, a poor choice of password might be a combination of a spouse's first name and street address, such as martha8431. Such a password might pass the password checklist, but it could be easily guessed based on personnel file information. Passwords should not be changed frequently as that leads users to paste them on their monitors or under their keyboards. Users should not be asked to remember more than one password for internal systems, or likely the same result will occur. Passwords of temporary users or users soon to leave the company need to be well managed. See http://rootshell.connectnet.com/docs/passwords_klein.ps.gz for a survey of password security.

External security generally involves hardware and software, rather than behavioral policies. Policies for firewalls and remote access need to be well defined. If the organization has information it wishes to make available to the public through ftp or http, it should designate servers solely for this duty and keep those servers outside of the company firewall. If the corporate policy is not to allow ActiveX to be used, it should be enforced at the firewall. All routers today already have built-in firewall capability, so most perimeter policies can be implemented without additional cost.

Security should be simple and if possible transparent to users. The policy should emphasize using the built-in security technology already in place. Services that are no longer used should be identified and disabled. PCs should automatically check for viruses upon boot and each time a diskette is inserted into a workstation. Requiring the user to do this manually will certainly doom the policy. Accounts should not be shared between users and users moving between departments should be assigned new accounts. E-mail client packages should be uniform throughout the company and encryption should be consistent. Users need to be educated as to when they are transmitting information in cleartext format.

7.4 Implement and Manage a Program

Network security can be technically complex, and implementation success depends on being able to communicate the plan clearly and easily to users. It is likely that some changes will be looked upon as inconvenient to the users, such as requiring passwords where none were required previously or by restricting the transfer of files or applets through a firewall. Users need to be educated as to why the new policy has been chosen and support from upper management might help justify the reasoning. New employees need to have this training as part of their general orientation.

As a company expands or contracts, their information requirements change. Management of a security policy consists of managing user accounts and passwords as well as making sure new equipment is properly configured. As unforeseen issues arise, they need to be treated promptly and results need to be shared with those affected by the issue. Users should be periodically and politely reminded of the importance of compliance both at a personal and company level. Users who have previously lost information to viruses or hardware failures can provide motivation to their more fortunate cohorts.

7.5 Audit for Compliance and Continuously Improve

As with any policy, there needs to be some penalty for non-compliance to help encourage compliance. If this penalty is well-defined and meaningful, the policy will more likely be observed with allegiance. Such penalties should reflect the policy's seriousness about the issue.

Periodically, users should be reminded through seminar or direct audit that compliance with the policy is still essential. Communication should remain bi-directional to help improve the overall system. Through periodic interaction, safe networking will become habit.

8 Summary

This Chapter focused on security issues, control and privacy. These issues are essential to widespread Electronic Commerce on the Internet. Business (and government) need to protect their systems. Individuals want assurance that their private information and resources, such as credit cards, are secure in Electronic Commerce transactions.

Before developing control procedures for security threats to business systems and methods to protect privacy, it is necessary to understand the types of threats that are possible. Many of the threats possible across the Internet are due to the original design of the TCP/IP. In Section II we first review how the TCP and IP protocols function to see how they can be exploited. Many of these same ideas can be used for other protocols. We next present security problems associated with viruses or downloadable executable code such as Java Applets or ActiveX routines. Finally, operating system holes were examined and additional information presented.

In Section III we turned our attention to control methods. This section began by surveying authentication systems, discussing the behavioral and some technical aspects of password and biometrics systems. It then examined firewall issues, including configuration and bypass. Some of the more technical aspects of authentication systems were presented in Section IV.

Section IV explained some of the more common encryption methods and developments in cryptography as they relate to electronic commerce, including public key and private key encryption. Passing information over any public communication network makes eavesdropping a concern for those sending sensitive information. When information is encrypted such that only a subset of the users can decrypt it, those users have established a Virtual Private Network. Virtual Private Networks form the backbone of secure transactions.

Section V detailed issues of secure transactions. . The fundamental issue is trust. In all secure transaction protocols and algorithms, some trust needs to exist. Many forms of trust are currently being marketed, but a few have emerged as competing standards. We examine how transactions can be digitally signed to verify the source and how digital certification assists with such verification.

Government laws, regulatory bodies, and law enforcement agencies shape the environment for Electronic Commerce. In Section VI we looked at the current state of key-recovery systems that government agencies seem dedicated to require by law. Such requirements already cost U.S. businesses in international trade. Whether it will also be imposed domestically remains to be seen. We also looked at many government initiatives that address security issues and reviewed laws that pertain to privacy and security.

Finally, in Section VII we focused on activities companies could undertake. Information security is much more a management issue than a technological issue. For a corporate policy to be effective, everyone must be involved. Security involves both behavioral and technical issues and therefore must have well defined goals and priorities. Involvement and education needs to be continuous.

References

Backman, D., "Kerberos: A Piece of the Net Security Puzzle", *Network Computing Online*, July, (1997).

Bellovin, S., "Security Problems in the TCP/IP Protocol Suite", *Computer Communication Review*, Vol. 19, No. 2, April, (1989), 32-48.

Borland, J., "Encryption Lawsuit back on 'Fast Track'," *CMPnet*, March 30, (1998).

Borland, J., "Will FBI Lab End Crypto Wars?" *CMPnet*, April 8, (1998).

Burke, B., "The Hacker Hall of Fame: A Rogues Gallery of High-tech Pirates," *BusinessToday.com*, February 25, (1998).

Chapman, D., & E. Zwicky, *Building Internet Firewalls*. O'Reilly & Associates, Inc., Cambridge, MA, 1995.

Cheng, P., J. Garay, A. Herzberg, & H. Krawczyk, "A security architecture for the Internet Protocol", *IBM Systems Journal*, (1998).

Clausing, J., "Administration to Allow Limited Data-Scrambling Exports," *New York Times*, July 8, 1998.

CNNInteractive, "Computer Hacker Plants Porno on Air Force Web Page," *CNNInteractive*, Dec. 30, (1996).

Comer, D., *Internetworking with TCP/IP, Volume I*, Prentice Hall, Englewood Cliffs, New Jersey, 1995.

Diffie, W., & M. Hellman, "New Directions in Cryptography", *IEEE Transactions on Infrormation Theory*, V. IT-22, n. 6, Nov (1976), 109-112.

Dornin, R., "Reno Announces New Center to Combat Cyber-crime," *CNNInteractive*, February 28, (1998).

Drash, W. & J. Morris, "Hackers Vandalize CIA Home Page," *CNNInteractive*, Sept. 19, (1996).

Freedman, D. & C. Mann, *At Large: The Strange Case of the World's Biggest Internet Invasion*, Simon and Schuster, New York, 1997.

Garfinkel, S., *PGP – Pretty Good Privacy*, O'Reilly & Associates, Inc., Cambridge, MA, 1995.

George, D., Study: "U.S. Vulnerable to Cyberterrorism," *CNNInteractive*, October 21, (1997).

Hafner, K. & J. Markoff, *Cyberpunk: Outlaws and Hackers on the Computer Frontier*, Simon and Schuster, New York, 1991.

Hall, E., "Internet Firewall Essentials", *Network Computing Online*, Nov, (1997).

Higgins, K., "S/MIME And OpenPGP Vie For Security Title", *Network Computing Online*, Sept, (1997).

Hughes, M., C. Hughes, M. Shoffner & M. Winslow, *Java Network Programming*, Manning Publications Co., Greenwich, CT 1997.

Klander, L., *Hacker Proof: The Ultimate Guide to Network Security*, Jamsa Press, Las Vegas, 1997.

Klein, D., "Foiling the Cracker: A Survey of, and Improvements to, Password Security", Software Engineering Institute, Carnegie Mellon University, (1991). Document reproduced at URL = http://rootshell.connectnet.com/docs/passwords_klein.ps.gz.

Lai, X., & J. Massey, "A Proposal for a New Block Encryption Standard", *Advances in Cryptology – EUROCRYPT '90 Proceedings*, Springer-Verlag, (1991), 389-404.

Littman, J., *The Fugitive Game : Online With Kevin Mitnick*, Little Brown & Co., Boston, 1997.

Martinez, M., "Pentagon Hacker Nabbed," *ABCNEWS.com*, March 19, (1998).

Martinez, M., "U.S. Wants Encryption Keys," *ABCNEWS.com*, March 2, (1998).

Merkle, R., "Secure Communication Over Insecure Channels," *Communications of the ACM*, v. 21, n. 4, (1978), 294-299.

Moskowitz, R., "IPSec For Communities Of Interest", *Network Computing Online*, Sep, (1997).

Moskowitz, R., "What is a Virtual Private Network", *Network Computing Online*, Sep, (1997).

National Bureau of Standards and Technology, NGS FIPS PUB 46, "Data Encryption Standard", National Bureau of Standards, US Department of Commerce, Jan (1977).

National Institute of Standards and Technology, NIST FIPS PUB 186, "Digital Signature Standard," U.S. Department of Commerce, May (1994).

Neuman, B., & T. Ts'o, "Kerberos: An Authentication Service for Computer Networks", IEEE Communications Magazine, Vol 32, Number 9, pp. 33-38, Sep (1994).

Ranum, M., "An Internet Firewall", *Proceedings of World Conference on Systems Management and Security*, (1992).

Rivest, R., "Chaffing and Winnowing: Confidentiality without Encryption," March 18, 1998, URL = http://theory.lcs.mit.edu/~rivest/chaffing.txt.

Rivest, R., "The MD4 Message Digest Algorithm," *Advances in Cryptology – CRYPTO '90 Proceedings*, Springer-Verlag, (1991), 303-311.

Rivest, R., A. Shamir, & L. Adleman, "A Method for Obtaining Digital Signatures and Public-Key Cryptosystems," *Communications of the ACM*, v. 21, n. 2, Feb (1978), 120-126.

Schneier, B., *Applied Cryptography : Protocols, Algorithms, and Source Code in C, Second Edition*, John Wiley & Sons, New York, 1996.

Shamir, A., "How to Share a Secret.", *Communications of the ACM* 22 (1979), 612-613.

Shimomura, T. & J. Markoff, *Takedown: The Pursuit and Capture of Kevin Mitnick, America's Most Wanted Computer Outlaw-By the Man Who Did It*, Hyperion, New York, 1996.

Smith, G., "Hacking Away at the Pentagon," *ABCNEWS.com*, March 3, (1998).

Smith, J., "The Design of Lucifer, A Cryptographic Device for Data Communications," *IBM Research Report RC3326*, (1971).

Stevens, W. & G. Wright, *Tcp/Ip Illustrated : Tcp for Transactions, Http, Nntp, and the Unix Domain Protocols (Vol 3)*, Addison-Wesley, Reading, MA, 1996.

Stinson, D., *Cryptography Theory and Practice*. CRC Press Inc., 1995.

Stoll, C., *The Cuckoo's Egg*, Doubleday, New York, 1989.

Venners, B., "Java's Security Architecture," *JavaWorld*, August, (1997).

Venners, B., "Security and the Class Loader Architecture," *JavaWorld*, September, (1997).

Venners, B., "Security and the Class Verifier," *JavaWorld*, October, (1997).

Whinston, A., D. Stahl, & S. Choi, *The Economics of Electronic Commerce*, Macmillan Technical Publishing, 1997.

Willis, D., "Villians in the Vault", *Network Computing Online*, Oct, (1997).

Yerxa, G., "Thwarting Malicious Java Attacks", *Network Computing Online*, Sept 4, (1997).

CHAPTER 32
The Emerging Law of Electronic Commerce

Jane Kaufman Winn
Southern Methodist University School of Law, Dallas TX, USA,
jwinn@mail.smu.edu

In this chapter, I define the scope of electronic commerce law and discuss how law can evolve in response to rapid change in social and business practices. I summarize how commercial law has adapted to electronic sales of goods using EDI and Internet distribution systems, discuss the strengths and weaknesses from a legal perspective of a new technology-based model for electronic commerce - digital signatures and public key infrastructure - and compare that model with others for managing the legal risks of electronic sales of goods. I also summarize how changes in payment system technologies and bank practices have produced new laws governing electronic payment systems; and how financial markets have moved to electronic systems for transferring investment securities.

Keywords: Electronic Contracting; Electronic Data Interchange, Public Key Infrastructure; Digital Signature; Certificate Authority; Trusted Third Party, Risk Management; Authentication; Security Procedure

1 Introduction

Doing business over the Internet may seem to raise breathtakingly novel issues in business law, but the law of electronic commerce is actually as old as the telegraph. It was not long after the telegraph entered into widespread use that the first case was litigated in which a party tried to avoid liability by claiming that an agreement reached by an exchange of telegrams could not constitute a valid and binding contract (Wright and Winn, 1998). Most courts in the US have risen to the challenge to look beyond form and evaluate the substance of the transaction, whether the new form of agreement was telegram, telex, fax or email. In some instances, however, there are laws that require a specific form be used by the parties in order to give their agreement legal effect, and in other instances, courts have been distracted or confused by new technologies, and refused to validate the parties' agreement. The question how commercial law will adapt to the new business realities of Internet electronic commerce can best be answered by looking at how the law adapted to earlier iterations of electronic commerce - in particular, electronic data interchange electronic contracting conducted over closed, proprietary networks, electronic funds transfer systems used by banks, and electronic settlement and clearing systems used in Wall Street.

This chapter will deal with the law of commercial transactions conducted electronically, whether done over open or closed networks. A commercial transaction in this context refers to a business transaction of a type normally conducted on standardized terms and in high volume. For example, a sale of goods, including the payment for those goods, is a classic example of a commercial transaction. In the US, a large part of commercial law is contained within the Uniform Commercial Code, a model statute which has been adopted as law in all fifty states with minor local variations, which has been supplemented by various state and federal laws and regulations. The analysis of commercial law issues in this chapter will take the provisions of the UCC as the starting point, and add reference to other sources and bodies of law as necessary.

This chapter will not give a comprehensive overview of all the issues raised by doing business over the Internet. For example, an audit of all the legal issues raised by doing business from an Internet site might include not just a review of commercial law issues but also patent, trademark and copyright law issues; advertising and consumer protection regulations including privacy law issues; antitrust and deceptive trade practices law issues; record retention and email policies; the design of security procedures and access controls; and tax law issues. Nor does this chapter provide any legal advice; specific questions of electronic commerce law should be pursued with qualified legal personnel.

While many of the issues raised by Internet electronic commerce closely resemble issues raised by earlier generations of technology such as telexes and faxes, what may be unprecedented is the degree to which electronic commerce is changing some of the basic principles upon which business administration has been based for decades. The volume and magnitude of changes in business practice that are occurring now as a result of adopting electronic commerce systems are putting tremendous pressure on traditional commercial law doctrines to adapt and evolve. Legal institutions can respond to these pressures in a variety of ways, and this chapter will consider the costs and benefits associated with different techniques for adapting law to new business practices.

This chapter will begin with a brief sketch of the methods for adapting commercial law to changing business realities in Section 2. Section 3 first analyzes the legal issues raised by selling goods using electronic contracting systems such as electronic data interchange, which have been extensively debated for over a decade. Legal issues raised by selling goods over open networks such as the Internet are considered next in Section 3, with a discussion of how new electronic commerce systems such as digital signatures and public key infrastructures may help reduce legal risks. Section 4 looks at electronic payment systems, including credit cards and wire transfers, and the laws governing them. This section analyses the significance consumer protection law in contributing to the current dominance of credit cards as the payment system for Internet retail commerce. Section 5 looks at the process by which financial institutions replaced stock certificates and bonds with electronic settlement and clearing systems, and how commercial law adapted to those changes. The law governing transactions in financial assets was first reformed during the 1970s when computers were first introduced into the process. When those reforms proved unsuccessful, lawyers revised the law again during the 1990s, but only after undertaking a careful study of actual Wall Street business practices. Section 6 presents conclusions that can be drawn from the analysis of these examples of how commercial law has adapted to electronic commerce technologies.

2 Adapting Commercial Law to New Business Realities

The most elementary way for business parties to adapt commercial law to new circumstances is through the use of contracts. Parties can depart from the terms of current standard form contracts to write new contracts describing new transactions and allocating new risks between the contracting parties. Failed transactions that result in litigation produce reported legal opinions that become case law which in turn helps parties predict how effective in fact their new contract terms are at regulating innovative business practices. The process of building new law through precedent can be slow and problematic, however, as the outcome of litigation is always somewhat uncertain. As contracts become more innovative, their enforceability becomes less predictable as a result.

When the parties are no longer confident that their contracts will produce predictable legal outcomes, they can lobby state legislatures or Congress to enact statutes to resolve the uncertain issues. While statutes may be more comprehensive and coherent than case law, the process of lobbying is also problematic as different interest groups may resist enacting legislation or may counter by offering undesirable alternative legislation. Furthermore, once a law is passed, even if it is found to be inadequate at resolving the matters it was designed to address, getting a statute repealed can be even more difficult than getting one enacted in the first place. The uniform law drafting process, coordinated by the National Conference of Commissioners on Uniform State Laws (Uniform Law Commission or ULC) is a collaborative process involving all fifty states that produces model statutes, and is an alternative route to getting legislation enacted. The ULC is supposed to reduce some of the uncertainty associated with law reform by providing a forum within which issues can be thoroughly and thoughtfully debated and consensus achieved prior to legislation actually being introduced in the states. But the uniform law drafting process may be even slower than other legislative routes and there is no guarantee any consensus or workable model will be produced. Because there are no easy solutions to the problem of adapting commercial law to meet the needs of innovative businesses, early adopters of new technologies have no choice but to tolerate a degree of legal uncertainty.

Under ideal circumstances, commercial law statutes should be reformed in response to significant changes in established business practices to reduce uncertainties that arise under existing law. Innovators start the process by using contracts to assign rights and responsibilities among themselves. Having lawyers individually negotiate and draw up contracts can be an expensive proposition, especially if the business party has to educate the lawyer about the basic business model the parties have developed as part of the drafting process, but it may be the only practical way for the parties to reduce some of the legal uncertainties arising out of innovative business practices. As experience grows and business practices that were once considered innovations become routine, parties to commercial transactions can standardize the terms of their contracts, minimizing or eliminating the role of lawyers in individual transactions. When contract terms and business practices become very standard and routine, commercial statutes can be revised to incorporate what can be thought of as default terms based on these standard contract terms. If the parties to a commercial contract fail to specify all the operative terms of their agreements, then commercial law can act as a gap-filler, providing missing terms that should be substantially the same as those the parties would have agreed to if they had thought about the issue. In this manner, commercial law supports routine business practice and eliminates uncertainty among parties to a transaction without requiring lawyers advise the parties on each contract.

Not all commercial law issues can be resolved through the slow accumulation of business custom and practice, however. Some issues, such as consumer protection issues, are generally resolved by legislatures acting to mandate what business parties must do in order to have legally enforceable agreements or to avoid legal sanctions. Regulatory approaches to commercial law may have a shorter incubation time than "freedom of contract" approaches that defer to standards chosen by commercial parties themselves, and often have less predictable outcomes for affected businesses as a result. Regulation often works best when it corrects market failures, such as those caused by information asymmetries or unequal bargaining power in consumer transactions. The success of credit cards as a payment system for Internet retail commerce is a good example of consumer protection regulation helping a market to work better than it would in a pure freedom of contract regime, and is discussed in Section 4 below. Commercial regulation often fails when it tries to anticipate the future development of business practices. Guessing future market developments is hard enough for entrepreneurs, so the odds are generally even worse that legislators will correctly guess the outcome of current business innovations. Once an inaccurate guess about what people in business will want to do in the future is locked into a statute, the law may become simply irrelevant, or worse, may distort the development of business practice into inefficient alternatives. The 1977 revision of Uniform Commercial Code Article 8, the law governing transfers of investment securities, is a good example of failed anticipatory regulation and is discussed in Section 5 below. This analysis may also apply to current efforts to promote the use of digital signatures through legislation, but it is too soon to draw that conclusion yet.

3 Sale of Goods Transactions

A sale of goods is a very basic, very common form of commercial transaction. Under US law, a contract is generally formed by one party making an offer and the other party accepting it. Each party must offer something of value (known as consideration) to the other and there must be a meeting of the minds on what will be exchanged under the contract. Once the contract is formed by the exchange of promises, then the parties perform their obligations as defined by the contract. In a contract for the sale of goods, one party might offer goods for sale at a particular price, and the other party might accept the promise to deliver the goods, giving in exchange a promise to pay for the goods. While the theory is clear, the practice may be more ambiguous.

3.1 Signature and Writing Requirements

Contracts for the sale of goods are normally governed by Article 2 of the Uniform Commercial Code. In general, Article 2 seeks to minimize the formalities the parties must follow in order to create a binding contract so that contracts will not become unenforceable just because the parties did not comply with all manner of technical legal requirements. Even so, Article 2 cannot eliminate all uncertainty from the business contracting process about the rights and obligations of the parties. For example, it is common for a sale of goods transaction to involve the exchange of many pieces of paper between the transacting parties. These papers might include a request for a quotation, a price quote for a shipment of goods on particular terms, a purchase order, an acknowledgement of the purchase order, and an invoice. It is unclear at what point in all this exchange of papers the classic offer, acceptance and meeting of the minds occurs, especially if each of paper has boilerplate contract terms printed on it and the preprinted standard terms are mutually inconsistent. Article 2 rejects the notion that actual business practice must match classical contract law principles in order to produce a binding contract, looking instead to whether or not there is an agreement in fact between the parties as the basis for an enforceable contract (Gabriel and Rusch, 1997).

Not all provisions of Article 2 are so flexible. One rule of law governing the sale of goods is referred to as the "statute of frauds" and requires that sales of goods over a specified dollar amount must be evidenced by a writing and signed by the party against whom enforcement is sought in order to be enforceable (Gabriel and Rusch, 1997). This special rule overrides the general rule that oral contracts are just as enforceable as written contracts (although they may be so much harder to prove that the attempt to enforce an oral contract is rendered futile). The policy behind this rule is to prevent fraud such as a party claiming a contract for the sale of goods exists when in fact no such agreement exists. Although other commercial laws exist which require a signed writing for a contract to be enforceable, the UCC Article 2 statute of frauds writing requirement is one of the most commonly encountered.

The statute of frauds raises problems for electronic commerce involving sales of goods. The party seeking to enforce the contract must show that there is a signed writing stating some of the most important terms of the contract. There is no requirement that the writing state all of the terms of the contract, but it must be sufficient to indicate that a contract has in fact been made by the parties. While a court looking at the exchange of email messages between a vendor and a purchaser might find that one of the email messages could be considered a writing signed by the party against whom enforcement is sought, it is far from clear that all courts would come to that conclusion. As long as the parties cannot predict with confidence what interpretation a court would apply to their exchange of email messages, some parties will resist replacing paper forms with electronic messages even though the administrative expenses associated with paper processes are higher. The higher cost of paper-based administrative systems can be thought of as a sort of insurance premium paid to achieve more predictable legal outcomes.

3.2 EDI Trading Partner Agreements

The problem of harmonizing the exchange of email messages with the legal requirement of a signed writing was first presented in the 1980s when parties began adopting electronic data interchange contracting systems. EDI systems set up in the 1980s were often based on the use of "value added networks" (VANs) that were closed, proprietary networks with enhanced security and data integrity features. Before the exchange of electronic quotes, purchase orders, acknowledgements and invoices could begin, the parties normally had to invest considerable time and energy in reengineering their information systems to permit the exchange of messages in standardized formats to take place. In order to draw the maximum benefit from establishing an EDI trading partner relationship, each party needed to take whatever steps were necessary to permit the automated processing of standard messages. Although the parties might reach a complete meeting of the minds with regard to how different messages would be processed as a matter of information system specifications, the issue of how the exchange of messages would be interpreted by a court remained beyond the power of the parties to resolve through technical standards.

A consensus emerged among many EDI trading partners and their attorneys that the best way to reduce uncertainty about the legal status of the EDI messages they planned to exchange would be to sign a traditional contract that would set out the ground rules for interpreting the significance of the electronic messages (ABA Electronic Messaging Services Task Force, 1990). This contract, referred to as an EDI trading partner agreement, reduced the uncertainty associated with how a court would treat email messages for statute of frauds purposes, because the trading partner agreement was a writing signed by the party against whom enforcement was sought. Should litigation later arise, the court could look to the trading partner agreement for an explanation of what legal significance the parties expected their electronic messages to have. Provided that what the parties set out in their trading partner agreement was reasonable, a court could be expected to defer to the wishes of the parties. The effectiveness of a trading partner agreement is not entirely without question, however, as a court might nevertheless still expect to see a signed writing for each transaction that takes place within the trading partner relationship, not just for the relationship as a whole.

One strength of the trading partner agreement model for regulating electronic commerce is that it may eliminate the statute of frauds problem at the same time it defines the rights and obligations of the trading partners with regard to other issues as well. One weakness of this model is that it cannot govern the rights and obligations of anyone other than the two parties who signed the agreement, so each electronic contracting relationship must be governed by a separate contract. This administrative expense might not be significant in light of the large investments often required to harmonize the information systems of the trading partners. However, when the Internet made electronic contracting between strangers with no prior relationship a practical reality, the expense of having the parties meet face to face and take pen in hand to sign a paper contract would in many instances more than offset the cost savings associated with using the Internet as a communications medium.

Another weakness of the trading partner agreement model is that it might require a fair amount of work on the part of attorneys to negotiate and draw up, and many EDI trading partners simply never bothered to sign a trading partner agreement as a result. Yet there is no evidence available as to how a court would interpret an EDI trading partner relationship in the absence of a written contract. This is because there are no reported litigated cases involving EDI trading partner disputes, which is an astonishing fact in light of the enormous volume of EDI transactions taking place in the US today. There is no way to be sure why no disputes between EDI trading partners ever reached the point of litigation. It is possible that trading partner agreements provided the parties with such clear guidance as to the rights and obligations of the parties that they felt litigation was unnecessary, although that can hardly have been the case with all the relationships that were not reduced to a written agreement. It seems more likely that the parties were unwilling to write off the large investment in information system reengineering required to establish EDI trading partner relationships, since the underlying business relationship would probably be irretrievably damaged if litigation were initiated. The absence of reported legal cases may indicate that EDI trading partners tend to work hard to find acceptable compromises to keep their relationship going when disputes arise.

3.3 Technology Neutral and Technology Promoting Legislation

For a court trying to determine whether email messages sent through an EDI system can meet the requirements of the statute of frauds, two separate issues must be resolved: whether there is a signature, and whether there is a writing. The standard for what constitutes a signature under the UCC is actually not difficult to meet: any symbol executed or adopted by a party with a present intention to authenticate a writing. This definition is designed to be flexible enough to include documents marked with "X" or signed with a fingerprint, and if approached in the general spirit of flexibility that animates the UCC, can accommodate the identification of the sender on an email message. For example, courts have held that a company's printed letterhead can function as a signature for meeting a statute of frauds requirement.

What constitutes a writing is a harder problem. "Writing" is not a defined term in the UCC, but would seem to indicate that a piece of paper is required. In *In re Kaspar*, a bankruptcy case in 1997, the court held that a credit card application taken by the credit card issuer in a telephone call with the debtor did not meet the "writing" requirement of one section of the Bankruptcy Code that would have enabled the credit card issuer to prevent the debtor from discharging his obligation to pay the credit card balance in bankruptcy. The court went on to observe that if the statute required a "writing," the court was entitled to insist on a piece of paper, and did not need be concerned by the fact that so holding might prevent businesses taking advantage of more efficient new communications media.

Given that current laws do not generally treat electronic media as a functional substitute for paper documents, and that there is some uncertainty about how flexibly in fact a court will be in interpreting what constitutes a signature in electronic communication contexts, there has been considerable attention focused on the question of law reform in this area. One approach to the problem might be to enact legislation that merely authorizes a court to treat an electronic record as a writing and an electronic authentication as a signature under appropriate circumstances. Another approach might be to enact legislation that requires a court to so hold unless circumstances dictated the contrary. Such legislation, since it focuses on legal outcomes and not technical processes, can be considered "technology neutral."

This is one of the issues that has been considered at length in the context of revising the UCC to take account of new business practices. The outcome of that process will probably be a sort of global "search and replace" throughout the UCC that replaces references to "writing" with references to "record" Record is defined as information that is inscribed on a tangible medium or that is stored in an electronic or other medium and is retrievable in perceivable form. This definition is designed to be broad enough to cover both paper and electronic documents. It is unclear whether the UCC definition of signature is already broad enough to encompass electronic commerce, or whether a new defined term, such as "authenticate" should be introduced to cover both manual signatures and electronic authentication processes. As of 1998, for the most part these reforms were still being debated in the uniform law drafting process. Until the official text of the UCC is released by the ULC, state legislatures do not begin to consider the proposed revisions. Once the revised text is available for state legislatures, it may take years for it to be enacted in all 50 states.

Even if the UCC is revised along these lines, and these revisions take effect in the near future, many laws relevant to commerce are not included in the UCC. The ULC has appointed a drafting committee to work on a "Uniform Electronic Transaction Act" that is designed to update other state laws in the same manner as the UCC is currently being revised. The UETA, like the UCC revisions, is a technology neutral statute that aims to enable all electronic commerce across the board by giving courts enough flexibility to accept electronic documents and signatures where appropriate.

While the uniform law drafting process grinds on, many states have leapt into the void and enacted laws in this area (McBride, Baker & Coles, undated). The result is a bewildering variety of approaches ranging from technology neutral to technology specific. A technology specific approach identifies one electronic commerce technology and provides that its use will have certain legal consequences. This has the effect of leaving other electronic commerce technologies struggling with the current uncertainty in the law, and focusing the attention of the public on one technology as having been endorsed by the state legislature. Given the current state of rapid innovation in electronic commerce, it is not clear that a technology specific approach to legislation will help or hinder the development of electronic commerce generally. One technology that has been the beneficiary of technology-specific legislation in the US and abroad is asymmetric cryptography, which is used to produce "digital signatures" (ABA Information Security Committee, 1996).

3.4 Digital Signatures and Public Key Infrastructure

The use of the Internet for commerce changed the landscape of electronic contracting, and raised the statute of frauds problem in a new context. EDI standards and the use of VANs permitted one-to-one electronic contracting, while the Internet opened up the possibility of one-to-many contracting (Winn, 1998). In order to take advantage of the much wider market access the Internet offered, parties sought an electronic contracting model that did not depend on a written trading partner agreement signed by the transacting parties in a face to face meeting. The flip side of the greater access offered by the Internet was its lack of security infrastructure that the VANs had provided, however. For one party to have confidence that their electronic communications were in fact taking place with the correct counterparty, and that the content of the electronic communications could be trusted, the parties to Internet transactions themselves would have to take responsibility for security. Even if the parties were able to satisfy themselves that their Internet electronic contracting technology was as reliable as paper-based commerce or EDI contracting, until the UCC reforms were finalized and enacted by state legislatures, uncertainty remained as to the legal effect of such commercial practices.

One technology that seems to hold particular promise for resolving the technical problems associated with Internet contracting is asymmetric or public key cryptography (Ford and Baum, 1997). Parties interested in identifying each other over an open network can each generate a pair of matched keys, one to be kept private and one to be distributed publicly. When a message signed with a private key is tested with the associated public key, asymmetric cryptography can be used to determine with high degree of certainty that the message could not have been signed with any other private key than the one associated with that public key. However, merely establishing a strong association between a message signed with a private key with a particular public key is not very helpful for electronic commerce purposes unless the party using the public key is confident of the identify of the person in control of the private key, and confident that person's control over the key has been maintained at all times.

For public key cryptography to support electronic commerce, at a minimum a solution must be found to the problem of how to associate an online identity established through the use cryptographic keys and the identity of an actor in the material world who can be held legally responsible for performing a contract. The simplest solution is to have people meet face to face and exchange keys on floppy disks, but like the trading partner agreement, the costs associated with such a system will negate most of the benefits that the Internet can offer.

Another solution to the problem of binding real world identities with online identities that has been widely discussed is the use of "trusted third parties" to introduce parties to each other, eliminating the need for a face to face meeting between the parties. Such a trusted third party might issue a certificate attesting to the fact that a particular human being was in control of a particular private key at a particular time. The person using a cryptographic key as an online identity card might provide a new acquaintance with a copy of the public key and a certificate indicating that a trusted third party was willing to vouch for the material world identity of the holder of the private key. A trusted third party offering such services might be labeled a certificate authority, and might sell its services to parties wishing to use digital signatures to form electronic contracts with strangers. This particular solution is based on the X.509 certificate standard developed as part of the X.500 directory standard. This standard was established to promote the use of distributed directories over networked computer systems. A system for coordinating the use of digital signature certificates issued by trusted third parties to establish a system of reliable online identities is generally referred to as a public key infrastructure.

The strength of this model is the fact that it can create an environment of trust between parties with no prior relationship online or in the material world. A party considering entering into a contract based on an email communication could ask the counterparty to include an identity certificate from a trusted third party with the signed email in order to establish a reliable association between the digital signature attached to the email and a real human being that can accept legal responsibilities. If the trusted third party has reliably identified the counterparty, and the counterparty has never lost control of the private key used to sign messages, then the party considering the contract can have confidence that the signature is what it appears to be. If the only impediment to the formation of contracts over the Internet was uncertainty among the contracting parties as to their material world identities, then a public key infrastructure that distributes digital signature certificates would permit contracting to take place.

The weakness of this model is its failure to address many of the concerns that a party considering entering into an Internet transaction would have. These concerns include the need to know not simply the material world identity of the sender of a particular email, but the capacity of the sender to enter into a legally binding contract. The sender might be a minor, which creates problems because under US law contracts entered into by minors are generally voidable at the election of the minor. If the party expected to assume responsibility for a contract is a corporation or other legal entity such as a trust, then the other party needs to know whether a particular human being is duly authorized to act for the legal entity. The party considering entering into an Internet transaction also needs information about the ability of the other party to perform his or her promises. This includes the ability to deliver goods that conform to the contract terms, or to pay for the goods as agreed. The party considering whether to go forward might also want to know the jurisdiction in which the other party is located, in order to estimate the risk of being haled into court in a remote location if the transaction goes awry. A simple binding of a human being with a digital signature provides no information about any of these issues.

The most common model of a public key infrastructure and digital signature certificates was actually designed to create online directories of names and addresses equivalent to phonebooks (Feigenblum, 1998). In the material world, parties do not make the decision whether to enter into contracts based on whether someone can be found in a telephone directory, and it is unlikely that parties will begin to do business online simply based on the proffer of an online ID certificate if there is no easy way to obtain the other information needed to make a business decision about the value of the contract.

It is possible that the basic framework of a public key infrastructure and digital signature certificates can be expanded to include the rest of the information parties need before they would be willing to enter into contracts over the Internet with strangers. Just how the basic framework should be expanded is a topic of considerable debate and what, if any solutions can be found to the problem of adapting the basic model to the complex realities of electronic commerce, will not be apparent for some time (Feigenblum, 1998).

In addition to these questions surrounding the business model within which digital signatures will be used, there are also substantial unresolved question about the design of large-scale open system public key infrastructures at a technical level. For example, before relying on a digital signature certificate, a party might want to check a certificate revocation list maintained by the certificate authority to make sure that the certificate had not been revoked, but there are many unresolved issues surrounding how a certificate revocation list can be reliably maintained and made accessible in an environment in which large volumes of certificates are in use simultaneously. While digital signature certificate standards permit certificates to be adapted to specific purposes through the use of certificate policies contained in policy extension fields, it is unclear how such policies can be reliably recognized and acted upon in open network systems.

It is possible that the best application of this technology will not be in open environments in which strangers do business with strangers, but within more closed environments in which parties with prior relationships use digital signatures to permit communications to take place over insecure networks and eliminate their reliance on VANs. Many of the thorny business and technical design problems associated with creating a workable open system using digital signatures are not difficult to resolve within a more limited context.

Many entrepreneurs, technologists and lawyers have been distracted from the fact that most current proposals for establishing public key infrastructures do not address basic business issues, and have rushed to embrace the idea of digital signatures as the panacea for Internet electronic commerce. Several states, including Utah, have enacted comprehensive digital signature legislation in advance of any commercial applications of this technology on the assumption that enabling legislation will accelerate adoption of this technology. The debate surrounding how to use digital signature technology to support real commercial transactions has not yet been resolved, and may not be resolved for some time. Until that debate is resolved through actual commercial implementations of the technology, it will not be possible to judge the success of the legislative efforts to promote this technology.

3.5 Extranets and Trading Partner Agreements

In 1998, the most successful examples of Internet electronic commerce were Cisco Systems, Inc. and Dell Computer Corporation. Cisco's web revenues for 1998 were projected to be over $6 billion; Dell's web revenues were projected to be in excess of $2 billion, and unlike Amazon.com, both companies are profiting from their Internet sales. Both companies use something resembling the old EDI trading partner agreement to minimize the legal uncertainty associated with Internet commerce.

Cisco uses its website to create an extranet, permitting only authorized users to access its web-based "Cisco Connection Online" service. Parties who have entered into a contractual relationship with Cisco are allowed to designate which employees or representatives are authorized to access Cisco's website to place orders. These parties are then assigned user-IDs and passwords that they must use to log into those parts of Cisco website where product availability and prices can be checked and orders placed. These preexisting contractual relationships provide a framework, similar to that created by a trading partner agreement, within which email messages are exchanged that permit contracts to be formed for the sale of Cisco goods and services.

Dell permits credit card holders to make purchases of goods and services directly from its website. The framework of the credit card system determines the rights and obligations of the parties with regard to such possible issues as the ability of the customer to pay for the goods, liability for unauthorized use of the credit card, and the right of the customer to dispute the transaction. The Dell website uses asymmetric cryptography, not as an authentication process, but merely to establish a secure channel of communication between the Dell server and the customer's browser using the Secure SocketsLayer (SSL) protocol. Assuming the customer's browser has the certificate authority's certificate preloaded (which is true for recent releases of standard Internet browser software), then the customer's browser can download a copy of Dell's public key and determine that it has been certified by the certificate authority. The browser and the Dell server share a special cryptographic key, called a "session key" that has been encrypted with Dell's public key for security. The consumer's credit card information travels over the Internet encrypted with the session key, and so is protected from being intercepted in transit. The public key infrastructure merely reduces the risk of certain forms of fraud by third parties, while the contractual and regulatory framework of the credit card system, combined with the terms and conditions of use that Dell attaches to use of its website for electronic commerce, perform similar functions in this system as a trading partner agreement.

4 Payment Transactions

Payment systems were among the first commercial transaction systems to migrate to an electronic environment. In 1957, paper checks were first imprinted with the magnetic ink character recognition line on the bottom that permitted the check processing system to be automated. In the late 1960s, banks began experimenting with automated teller machines and secure systems for wire transfers of funds. At the same time, the use of credit cards rapidly proliferated. In 1970, in response to widespread criticism of aggressive tactics on the part of card issuers to expand rapidly the use of credit cards while at the same time severely limiting card issuer liability, Congress enacted a comprehensive scheme of consumer protections for card holders that remains in effect today. The law governing electronic funds transfers dates from 1978, when consumer protections were passed by Congress that applied to transactions such as ATM withdrawals. Outside the realm of consumer payment systems, in 1989, the ULC formalized a law governing wholesale wire transfers, UCC Article 4A, which has now been adopted in all 50 states.

In the late 1990s, all large-scale payment systems in the US had been adapted to operate within secure networked mainframe computer systems operated by regulated financial institutions. As a result, Internet-based payment systems have faced formidable competition and have not been able to establish any significant market share (Winn, 1999). Many standard developing organizations and technology vendors are competing to achieve a dominant position in the Internet payment arena, but it is unclear which, if any, of the current competitors will ultimately prevail. First Virtual, the first commercial Internet e-cash system, began operations in 1995 amid great fanfare, but ceased payment system operations in 1998 due to lack of market share. Likewise, Internet micropayment technology seemed very promising in the mid-1990s, but by 1998 commercial products such as Millicent were still not enjoying widespread acceptance. Just as it is hard to predict who will be the winners among these emerging technologies, it is also unclear how the existing large-scale mainframe-based payment systems will adapt to these new competitive forces.

4.1 Credit Card Transactions

Credit cards, used in combination with the SSL protocol supported by the end user's browser, have proven to be the payment system of choice for retail Internet electronic commerce. The SSL protocol works within a very simple public key infrastructure, and provides a secure channel for communication of information between the end user's browser and the e-commerce server. (SSL is further described in Section 3.5 above.) Early concerns over the lack of security for Internet communications led MasterCard and Visa each to begin work on designing a much more complex public key infrastructure that would provide digital signature certificates to card holders, merchants, acquiring banks and issuing banks. These projects later merged into the Secure Electronic Transaction (SET) standard. The SET standard offers a much higher level of security than the SSL standard by adding new safeguards against fraud and unauthorized use of credit card information. In order to do so, however, it will have to place heavy demands on existing credit card transaction processing infrastructure and may require the execution of complex cryptographic algorithms that exceed the processing capacity of the average end user's system. These and other problems have slowed down the rate of adoption of the SET standard and progress in further refining the standard. While work on the more sophisticated and complex SET standard has progressed slowly, the SSL protocol has become the de facto standard for security for retail Internet commerce today.

Although the SSL standard provides only minimal security for payments transactions over the Internet, the existing legal and technical framework of the credit card system supplements those protections to produce an Internet payment system that meets the current minimum requirements of merchants, end users and financial institutions. The only segment of the credit card system that uses the Internet as a medium of communication is the transmission of the cardholder's account number to the Internet merchant. From the merchant's e-commerce server, information about authorized charges are transmitted to the merchant's acquiring bank in the same manner as they would be transmitted by a telephone or mail order merchant. The rights and obligations between the merchant, the merchant's acquiring bank and the cardholder's issuing bank are set by private contracts between the parties.

Consumers considering whether to use the Internet to make purchases can limit their risk of loss due to fraud by using their credit card as a form of payment because federal regulations limit consumer liability for unauthorized charges to $50. This limit applies whether the card is used in a face-to-face transaction, in a telephone or mail order transaction, or in an Internet transaction. The Federal Reserve Board, the federal agency charged with oversight of consumer credit card regulations, has stated that merchants who accept credit card information in transactions in which the merchant does not have the opportunity to inspect the credit card cannot contest a consumer's later claim that a particular charge transaction was unauthorized. This rule was developed in the mail order and telephone order context, and applies equally to the Internet context.

A merchant considering accepting payment by credit card from an Internet retail site must first be satisfied that it has found a way to minimize the risk of fraud and error associated with credit card use, because the merchant will not be allowed to pass those costs on to the consumer, or in most cases, the merchant's acquiring bank. A merchant may decide that it nevertheless makes sense to accept credit cards as a payment device for Internet commerce given the lack of practical alternatives, the increased volume of sales that are likely to result, and the fact that the credit card issuer, not the merchant, assumes the risk of payment default by the card holder.

Consumers also enjoy access to dispute resolution services provided by credit card issuers in the event that the consumer has a dispute with the Internet merchant regarding the goods or services purchased. Under certain circumstances, federal regulations require card issuers to investigate and resolve cardholder complaints about goods and services purchased by credit card. Current business practice among card issuers has considerably expanded the use of this dispute resolution service to include more transactions than are covered by federal regulation. From the consumer perspective, the use of a credit card as a payment mechanism substantially reduces the risk of being forced either to pay for unacceptable goods or services ordered over the Internet, or to submit to the jurisdiction of a remote forum in order to dispute the value of goods and services purchased over the Internet.

4.2 Electronic Funds Transfers

If some of the new technologies for payments under development are ultimately successful, it is possible they will be outside the scope of existing laws, including consumer protection regulations. Unless and until regulators intervene, such systems would be regulated by contracts among the parties. Wholesale funds transfer systems in the US evolved largely outside of any existing regulatory framework for over a decade before a formal body of law was established to govern the rights and obligations of the parties. The law that now addresses wholesale wire transfers is UCC Article 4A. Article 4A is a very significant development in the law of electronic commerce because it was one of the first bodies of law to consider in depth how the use of electronic authentication systems should be regulated.

In the US, financial institutions operate a wholesale wire transfer system for large scale business to business funds transfers. These systems, which include the Fedwire operated by the Federal Reserve system, and the New York Clearing House for Interbank Payment Systems (CHIPS), transfer in excess of one trillion dollars per day. These systems began operations in the early 1970s, and operate largely among banks and their major corporate customers. Before the adoption of Article 4A, the only law that applied to these systems beyond private contracts among the participants were Federal Reserve Board Operating Circulars, for transfers that used the Fedwire, and the operating rules of CHIPS, for transfers that used CHIPS. Many aspects of these transactions were not covered by any organized body of law, however, and it was possible for disputes to arise between parties which were not clearly governed by any contract or operating system rule.

Banks providing wire transfer services were not particularly concerned about the lack of formal law governing the wholesale funds transfer system until some litigated cases in the 1980s raised issues that the banks found troubling. One such issue that drove the banks to the ULC to support the Article 4A drafting process was a litigated case in which a bank failed to make a funds transfer on the date requested by its customer. The court suggested that a bank making an error in handling a wire transfer might be held liable for the lost profits from any business deal the transferor lost due to the delay. Banks were unwilling to accept liability beyond the time value of the funds while they were delayed due to the error. Because a funds transfer might pass through several banks on the way from transferor to transferee, it was not possible for a bank to be certain that it would always be protected against liability by a preexisting contractual relationship with the disgruntled transferor. The only way to guarantee a limit to the bank's liability would be by statute. After considerable debate in the drafting process, the representatives of the banks' customers agreed to this limitation (Baxter and Heller, 1997).

Banks and their customers shared a commitment to keeping the price of funds transfer services low, and expanding liability for the banks would have a necessary consequence of forcing banks to raise the price of funds transfer services or to leave the market. Bank customers agreed that it was more efficient for customers to accept responsibility for monitoring the proper execution of funds transfers when large profits were at stake than to put the banks in the position of insuring all their customers against any risk of bank error in executing transfers. Many bank customers were operating at a level of sophistication that was equivalent to that of the banks themselves, and so in a context in which no consumers were involved, the customer could reasonably be expected to assume some responsibility for the operation of the system in exchange for lower prices.

Another major point of contention between the banks and their customers was how responsibility for unauthorized funds transfers should be allocated. The banks initially took the position that unauthorized funds transfers could only occur as a result of carelessness by their customers because banks had adequate security procedures in place, but their customers were unwilling to accept this analysis (Rubin, 1993). After heated debate, a complex compromise was worked out dividing liability for unauthorized funds transfers between the bank and the customer. The initial allocation of liability was on the bank, but the bank could shift the risk of liability to the customer if the bank and the customer agreed a "commercially reasonable security procedure" that would be used to initiate funds transfers. A "commercially reasonable" security procedure is one that is adapted to the customer's situation, in light of the amount, type and volume of funds transfers the customer makes, the customer's business and other factors. If the bank can prove that it complied with the security procedure agreed upon with the customer, then the bank cannot be held liable for an unauthorized funds transfer executed from the customer's account. The only exception to this rule arises in the unlikely event that the customer can prove that the unauthorized funds transfer did not originate with any person or facility under the customer's control. In that case, which would include funds transfers executed by hackers penetrating the security of the system from outside the customer's facilities, the bank must bear the risk of loss.

Article 4A takes a very different approach to liability issues than the consumer protection regulations that apply to credit card transactions. With credit cards, the consumer is presumed to be incapable of making any significant contribution to reducing the risk of loss due to unauthorized use of the card, and so is exonerated from almost all liability as a result. Card issuers, merchants and acquiring banks bear almost all risk of fraud and error, and as a result have an incentive to invest in the most sophisticated antifraud technology available. In the wholesale funds transfer environment, however, many bank customers are operating at a level of sophistication equivalent to that of the banks, and are required to be active participants in the design and maintenance of the security of the funds transfer system. Even though the loss allocation rules in each system point in opposite directions, Article 4A and the credit card system are each examples of commercial law that has been adapted very successfully to different categories of payment system.

5 Financial Asset Transactions

The depth and liquidity of US capital markets are unparalleled throughout the world today. One reason that US capital markets can operate so efficiently is that the back office clearing and settlement operations that support them is fully automated. Wall Street banks and securities firms recognized the need for automation in back office functions as early as the late1960s. The "paperwork crunch" caused by paper based settlement procedures was forcing the stock market to shut down at periodic intervals to permit back office operations to catch up with trading operations. At that time, the daily volume of stocks traded on the New York Stock Exchange was around 10 million shares, a far cry from the 1 billion shares per day trading volume that occurred in 1998. By the mid-1970s, there was a recognition in Wall Street that UCC Article 8, the law that applied to transfers of ownership interests in investment securities, would have to be revised to take account of automated processes for handling transfers of stocks and bonds.

5.1 1977 Revisions to Investment Securities Law

The ULC appointed a drafting committee to review the then-existing version of Article 8, which had been drafted in 1957, in light of changing technology in capital markets. In 1977, the drafting committee produced a new Article 8 which they hoped would promote the use of automation in securities markets. The 1977 Article 8 drew on two models: the traditional paper bond or stock certificate model drawn from the 1957 law, and a new model based on innovations occurring in the US Treasury Department with regard to government securities. The Treasury was issuing "uncertificated" securities which existed only as bookentry records in the Treasury computer system. The drafters of the 1977 revisions to Article 8 guessed that the private sector would follow the public sector's lead in automating securities transfers, and included rules governing the transfer of uncertificated securities (Rocks and Bjerre, 1997).

In fact, the private sector was not following the lead of the public sector, but was devising a different system for automating securities transfers. Private sector securities market participants increased their reliance on existing cooperative institutions such as the Depository Trust Company (DTC), a corporate custodian collectively owned by most major Wall Street banks and brokerage firms. To eliminate transfers of individual stock certificates between firms, firms agreed to maintain accounts with common intermediaries such as DTC and transfer ownership interests in stock by bookentry adjustments with the intermediary. The paper certificates were not actually eliminated from this process. Instead, the issuer of the security would provide "jumbo" certificates to the intermediary who would keep them in a secure location. The system developed in the private sector was thus a system of immobilized paper certificates combined with bookentry records of intermediaries rather a true certificateless system.

5.2 1994 Revisions to Investment Securities Law

When state legislatures considered the 1977 revisions to Article 8, many declined to enact the revisions and retained the original 1957 text of the law. Some jurisdictions enacted the 1977 revisions, doubtless unaware that the revisions did not cover the actual securities market business practices that had developed. The result was lack of uniform law throughout the US governing transfers of securities, and lack of any law corresponding to the system of indirect, immobilized securities holdings. The uncertain state of the law did not create a sense of crisis among market participants, however, until the stock market crash of 1987 and the failure of the Drexel Burnham firm in 1990. These events caused market participants to recognize that should a major market participant be unable to fulfill all of its obligations to deliver securities to other market participants, there was simply no system in place for sorting out the competing claims of ownership among all the parties with rights to the securities held by the failed firm (Smith and Shupak, 1996).

The ULC appointed a new committee to revisit the provisions of Article 8 in light of actual commercial practice in securities markets. In 1994, a revised version of Article 8 was issued. This version of Article 8 recognizes three types of investment securities: paper certificates, certificateless securities such as Treasury obligations and some mutual funds, and a "security entitlement." A security entitlement is what a customer of a brokerage firm has if the customer permits the brokerage firm to retain control of the stocks and bonds in the customer's account. The customer has a claim against the brokerage firm for the securities held at the firm. That brokerage firm may in turn not possess any stock certificates, but may have security entitlements with another firm or an intermediary such as DTC. The 1994 revised version of Article 8 includes provisions governing transfers of ownership in security entitlements, including the use of security entitlements as collateral for loans, thus resolving the uncertainty created by failure of the 1977 revisions to provide for such commercial practices.

The failure of the 1977 revisions to correctly anticipate the manner in which private sector automation occurred shows the difficulty of drafting anticipatory commercial law. The drafters of the 1977 revisions based their model on the only well established and well understood model for electronic securities transfers. Although the practice of immobilizing securities and holding through intermediaries was already taking shape in 1977, it escaped the notice of the drafters. If someone were to have suggested to the drafters of the 1977 revisions that in the future, electronic securities transfers would be possible in Wall Street because paper certificates for trillions of shares of stock would be held in vaults at DTC, the suggestion might have struck them as too ludicrous to be taken seriously. Yet that is the system that is in operation today and it is highly successful.

6 Conclusion

Existing commercial law can be adapted to new electronic commerce technologies in a manner that simplifies and supports business practice if changes are made in light of present commercial reality. There are may successful examples of technology neutral commercial law, such as the Article 4A concept of a "security procedure" and the Article 8 concept of a "security entitlement," that are flexible enough to accommodate many different forms of technology. Business practices in Internet commerce may not yet be well enough established for commercial law to capture and reflect the standard default terms the parties might expect to operate in the absence of explicit contract terms. Until a body of business practices develop to guide the direction of legislation, transacting parties should carefully consider how risks are allocated by private agreement.

If Congress and state legislatures leap in too quickly to promote promising technologies, chances are great that the result will be greater inefficiency, not less. Legislators should not be in the business of trying to guess the winners in the current competition among technologies for Internet commerce. If Congress and state legislatures cannot refrain from acting in this area, however, they should limit their intervention to protecting less sophisticated parties from possible overreaching by more sophisticated parties. The model of credit card consumer protection offers a promising model for legislation that promotes electronic commerce without dictating any technological choices. Credit card consumer protection regulations shelter less sophisticated parties from fraud and error risks they cannot control while forcing more sophisticated parties to invest in security procedures to reduce such risks as much as possible. This type of legislation can help to make the entire system operate more efficiently than it would if transactions were governed simply by standard form contracts drawn up by card issuers.

References

ABA Electronic Messaging Services Task Force, *The Commercial Use of EDI--A Report and Model Trading Partner Agreement*, Vol. 45 Business Lawyer, page1645 (1990).

ABA Information Security Committee, *ABA Digital Signature Guidelines*, Chicago, American Bar Association (1996)

Baxter, Thomas C. Jr. and Stephanie A. Heller, *The ABCs of the UCC: Article 4A: Funds Transfers*, Chicago, American Bar Association (1997)

Cisco Systems Inc., Cisco website at http://www.cisco.com/

Dell Computer Corporation, Dell website at http://www.dell.com/

Feigenblum, Joan, *Toward an Infrastructure for Authorization*, Usenix 3rd Workshop on Electronic Commerce Position Paper (1998)

Ford, Warwick and Michael Baum, *Secure Electronic Commerce*, New Jersey, Prentice Hall (1997)

Gabriel, Henry and Linda Rusch, *The ABCs of the UCC: Article 2: Sales*, Chicago, American Bar Association (1997)

McBride, Baker & Coles, *Summary of Electronic Commerce and Digital Signature Legislation* (undated) available at http://www.mbc.com/ds_sum.html

Rocks, Sandra M. and Carl S. Bjerre, *The ABCs of the UCC: Article 8: Investment Securities*, Chicago, American Bar Association (1997)

Rubin, Edward, *Thinking Like A Lawyer, Acting Like a Lobbyist: Some Notes on the Process of Revising UCC Articles 3 and 4*, Vol. 26, Loyola of Los Angeles Law Review, pg. 743 (1993).

Smith, Richard B. and Paul M. Shupak, *New York Needs a Revised Article 8*, New York Law Journal, page 1 (May 30, 1996).

Uniform Law Commission website http://www.nccusl.org

Winn, Jane K., Clash of the Titans: Regulating the Competition between Established and Emerging Electronic Payment Systems, Vol. 14, Berkeley Technology Law Journal, pg. 671 (1999).

Winn, Jane K., Open Systems, Free Markets and the Regulation of Internet Commerce, Vol. 72, Tulane Law Review, pg. 1179 (1998).

Wright, Benjamin and Jane Winn, *The Law of Electronic Commerce*, New York, Aspen Law & Business (3rd ed. 1998)

Contributors

Andrew D. Bailey, Jr.
Department of Accounting
University of Illinois at Urbana-Champaign
jabaile@uiuc.edu

John P. Baron
Department of Business Administration
University of Illinois at Urbana-Champaign
j-baron1@uiuc.edu

Martin Bichler
Fisher Center for Management and
Information Technology
Haas School of Business
University of California at Berkeley
bichler@haas.berkeley.edu

Robert W. Blanning
Owen Graduate School of Management
Vanderbilt University
bob.blanning@owen.vanderbilt.edu

Tung X. Bui
Decision Sciences
College of Business Administration
University of Hawaii at Manoa
tbui@busadm.cba.hawaii.edu

Hsinchun Chen
Management Information Systems
Department
University of Arizona
hchen@bpa.arizona.edu

Nian-Shin Chen
Department of Information Management
National Sun Yat-sen University, Taiwan
nschen@mis.nsysu.edu.tw

Ye-Sho Chen
Department of Information Systems and
Decision Sciences
E.J. Ourso College of Business
Administration
Louisiana State University
qmchen@unix1.sncc.lsu.edu

Ai-Mei Chang
Information Resources Management
College
National Defense University
chang@ndu.edu

Soon-Yong Choi
Center for Research in Electronic
Commerce,
The University of Texas at Austin
soon@mail.utexas.edu

Gina Colarelli O'Connor
Department of Management
and Technology
Rensselaer Polytechnic Institute
oconng@rpi.edu

Daniel G. Conway
Decision and Information Sciences
Warrington College of Business
University of Florida
conwaydg@ufl.edu

Michael H. Dickey
Center for Virtual Organization and
Commerce
Louisiana State University
mdickey@lsu.edu

Bill Fulkerson
CIS-Technology Integration
Deere & Company
Moline, IL
wf28155@deere.com

Dennis Galletta
Katz Graduate School of Business
University of Pittsburgh
galletta@vms.cis.pitt.edu

David M. Gardner
Department of Business Administration
University of Illinois at Urbana-Champaign
dmgardne@uiuc.edu

Paul Gray
Department of Information Science
Claremont Graduate University
Paul.Gray@cgu.edu

Clyde W. Holsapple
School of Management
Carol M. Gatton College of Business and
Economics
University of Kentucky
cwhols@pop.uky.edu

Andrea L. Houston
ISDS Department
Louisiana State University
ahoust2@lsu.edu

Thomas Huang
Beckman Institute for Advanced Science
and Technology
Department of Electrical and Computer
Engineering
University of Illinois at
Urbana-Champaign
huang@ifp.uiuc.edu

Magid Igbaria
Department of Information Science
Claremont Graduate University
Magid.Igbaria@cgu.edu

Blake Ives
Center for Virtual Organization and
Commerce
Louisiana State University
bives@lsu.edu

Nebojša Jojić
Beckman Institute for Advanced Science
and Technology
Department of Electrical and Computer
Engineering
University of Illinois at
Urbana-Champaign
jojic@ifp.uiuc.edu

Kshiti D. Joshi
School of Accounting, Information
Systems, and Business Law
Washington State University
joshi@cbe.wsu.edu

Bob Justis
Department of Management
E.J. Ourso College of Business
Administration
Louisiana State University
mgjust@unix1.sncc.lsu.edu

Alaina Kanfer
National Center for Supercomputing
Applications
University of Illinois at Urbana-
Champaign
alaina@ncsa.uiuc.edu

P. K. Kanna
Department of Marketing
The Robert H. Smith School of Business
University of Maryland
pkannan@rhsmith.umd.edu

Dave King
Comshare Inc., Ann Arbor
dking@comshare.com

Stefan Klein
Institute of Information Systems
University of Muenster, Germany
klein@wi.uni-muenster.de

Gary J. Koehler
Decision and Information Sciences
Warrington College of Business
University of Florida
koehler@ufl.edu

Kai R. Larsen
Information Science Ph.D. Program
State University of New York at Albany
klarsen@acm.org

Christoph Schlueter Langdon
Beckman Institute for Advanced Science
and Technology
Department of Electrical and Computer
Engineering
University of Illinois at
Urbana-Champaign
cschlutr@uiuc.edu

Ting-Peng Liang
Department of Information Management
National Sun Yat-sen University, Taiwan
liang@mis.nsysu.edu.tw

Alexandre Barsi Lopes
Katz Graduate School of Business
University of Pittsburgh
alopes@pitt.edu

Debbie McElroy
California State University at Long Beach
dcmcel@aol.com

Claire R. McInerney
Information Science Ph.D. Program
University of Oklahoma, School of
Library and Information Studies
cmcinerney@aol.com

Robert O'Keefe
Department of Information Systems and
Computing
Brunel University, England
bob.okeefe@brunel.ac.uk

Daniel E. O'Leary
Marshall School of Business
University of Southern California
oleary@usc.edu

C. C. Pegels
Management Science and Systems
School of Management
State University of New York at Buffalo
cpegels@acsu.buffalo.edu

Gabriele Piccoli
Center for Virtual Organization and
Commerce
Louisiana State University
gpiccol@unix1.sncc.lsu

Jaana Porra
Department of Decision and
Information Sciences
University of Houston
jaana@un.edu

H.R. Rao
Management Science and Systems
School of Management
State University of New York at Buffalo
mgmtrao@acsu.buffalo.edu

Fabrice Roghé
Department of Economics
Darmstadt University of Technology
Germany
roghe@hotmail.com

Yong Rui
Beckman Institute for Advanced Science
and Technology
Department of Electrical and Computer
Engineering
University of Illinois at
Urbana-Champaign
yrui@ifp.uiuc.edu

A.F. Salam
College of Business and Public
Administration
University of Louisville
amsala01@homer.louisville.edu

Ann Schlosser
Owen Graduate School of Management
Vanderbilt University
ann.schlosser@owen.vanderbilt.edu

Arie Segev
Fisher Center for Management and
Information Technology
Haas School of Business
University of California at Berkeley
segev@haas.berkeley.edu

Michael J. Shaw
Department of Business Administration
College of Commerce
University of Illinois at Urbana-
Champaign
m-shaw2@uiuc.edu

Michael Shank
Principal, IBM Consulting Group
New York
Shankm@us.ibm.com

Meenu Singh
Computer and Technical Sciences
Department
Kentucky State University
msingh@gwmail.kysu.edu

Troy J. Strader
Department of Management
Information Systems
Iowa State University
tstrader@iastate.edu

Chandrasekar Subramaniam
Department of Business Administration
University of Illinois at
Urbana-Champaign
csubrama@uiuc.edu

Kristin M. Tolle
Management Information Systems
Department
University of Arizona
ktolle@bpa.arizona.edu

Efraim Turban
California State University at Long Beach
and City University of Hong Kong
eturban@csulb.edu

Gek Woo Tan
Department of Business Administration
Beckman Institute for Advances Science
and Technology
University of Illinois at
Urbana-Champaign
g-tan@uiuc.edu

Edward Watson
Department of Information Systems and
Decision Sciences
E.J. Ourso College of Business
Administration
Louisiana State University
ewatson@lsu.edu

Andrew B. Whinston
Department of MSIS, Economics and
Computer Science,
The University of Texas at Austin, TX,
USA
abw@uts.cc.utexs.edu

Jane Kaufman Winn
Southern Methodist University
School of Law
jwinn@mail.smu.edu

B. Rachel Yang
Department of Business Administration
University of Illinois at
Urbana-Champaign
ryang@uiuc.edu

Yueting Zhuang
Beckman Institute for Advanced Science
Department of Electrical and Computer
Engineering
University of Illinois at Urbana-
Champaign
yzhuang@ifp.uiuc.edu

World Wide Web Sites

- **AC Nielsen**, http://www.nielsen.com
- **Advertising Age**, http://www.adage.com
- **Amazon.com**, http://www.amazon.com
- **America Online**, http://www.aol.com
- **Anything, Anywhere, Anytime - Any Questions?**, http://www.fastcompany.com/online/08/saylor.html
- **Auction Hunter**, http://www.auctionhunter.com
- **AuctionNet**, http://www.auction.net
- **Automated Systems Incident Response Capability**, http://www-nasirc.nasa.gov/nasa/index.html
- **Automated Systems Security Incident Support Team**, http://www.assist.mil/
- **Bid Find WWW Auction Search**, http://www.bidfind.com
- **BioMedNet**, http://www.biomednet.com
- **Bios Group**, http://www.biosgroup.com/
- **BizTech Network**, http://www.brint.com/
- **Bloomberg Financial Services**, http://www.bloomberg.com
- **BonusMail**, http://www.bonusmail.com
- **Brokat Infosystems AG**, http://www.brokat.com/
- **Business Researcher's Jumpstation**, http://www.brint.com/Sites.htm
- **CAD Cut**, http://www.cadcut.com/optitex.html
- **Carnegie Mellon's Computer Emergency Response Team Center**, http://www.cert.org/
- **CDNOW**, http://www.cdnow.com/
- **Center for Information Systems and Technology Management**, http://www.cba.uiuc.edu/research/centers/cistm1.html
- **Center for Research in Electronic Commerce, University of Texas at Austin**, http://cism.bus.utexas.edu/
- **Center for Technology in Government**, http://www.ctg.albany.edu/
- **Centre for Supply Chain Management Links to other Internet Resourses**, http://www.up.ac.za/academic/gsofman/logist/links.htm
- **Charles Schwab**, http://www.charlesschwab.com/
- **Charles Schwab**, http://www.eschwab.com
- **CNET**, http://www.cnet.com
- **CNN**, http://www.cnn.com
- **COAST**, http://www.cs.purdue.edu/coast/coast.html
- **Commerce Net/Nielsen**, http://www.commerce.net/research/stats/stats.html
- **CommerceNet**, http://www.commerce.net
- **Computer Design Inc.**, http://www.cdi-u4ia.com/
- **Computer Literacy**, http://www.cbooks.com
- **Computer Security Institute**, http://www.gocsi.com/csi/homepage.html
- **Computer Security Resource Clearinghouse**, http://csrc.ncsl.nist.gov/
- **Computerworld**, http://www.computerworld.com
- **Council of Logistics Management**, http://freeman.tulane.edu/faculty/faculty3.htm
- **Customer Insites**, http://www.customerinsites.com
- **CyberCash**, Inc., http://www.cybercash.com/
- **CyberGold**, http://www.cybergold.com

- **Data Warehouse Information Center**, pwp.starnetinc.com/larryg
- **Data Warehouse Institute**, http://www.dw-institute.com
- **Datamation**, http://www.datamation.com
- **Data-warehouse.com**, http://www.data-warehouse.com
- **Deere & Company**, http://www.deere.com/
- **Deja News Collection of Newsgroups Information**, http://www.dejanews.com
- **Dell Computer Corporation**, http://www.dell.com/
- **Diamond Technology Partners**, http://www.killer-apps.com/navBottom.htm
- **DigiCash: Solutions for Security and Privacy**, http://www.digicash.com/
- **Digital Library Initiatives,** http://www.dlu2.nsf.gov/
- **Carnegie Mellon University**, http://www.infomedia.cs.cmu.edu/
- **University of California at Berkley**, http://elib.cs.berkeley.edu/
- **University of California at Santa Barbara**, http://alexandria.sdc.ucsb.edu/
- **University of Illinois at Urbana-Champaign**, http://dli.grainger.uiuc.edu/
- **University of Michigan**, http://www.si.umich.edu/UMDL/
- **Stanford University**, http://walrus.standord.edu/diglib/
- **D-Lib Magazine and D-Lib Project**, http://www.dlib.org
- **DM Review**, http://www.dmreview.com
- **eBay Personal Trading**, http://www.ebay.com
- **Egghead.com**, http://www.egghead.com/
- **Eggleston firewall vendor list**, http://www.access.digex.net/~nuance/security.html
- **Electronic Commerce Canada Inc.**, http://www.ecc.ca
- **Electronic Commerce Guide**, http://e-comm.internet.com/
- **Electronic Commerce-Electronic Data Interchange at NAFTA**, http://www.nafta.net
- **Electronic Privacy Information Center**, http://www.epic.org/
- **Electronic Retailing**, http://www.zdnet.com/icom/cyberstats/1998/05/
- **Emerging Digital Economy from Dept. of Commerce**, http://www.ecommerce.gov/emerging.htm
- **Emerging Organizations and Outsourcing**, http://www.brint.com/EmergOrg.htm
- **Enterprise JavaBeans**, http://www.javasoft.com/products/ejb/index.html
- **ERIM, Center for Electronic Commerce**, http://www.erim.org/cec/
- **Etrade**, http://www.etrade.com
- **Excite**, http://live.excite.com/
- **Firefly**, http://www.firefly.net/
- **Firewall newsgroup**, http://comp.security.firewalls and http://comp.security.misc
- **Forrester Research, Inc.**, http://www.forrester.com/
- **Forum of Incident Response and Security Teams**, http://www.first.org/
- **Framework for Global Electronic Commerce**, http://www.ecommerce.gov/framework.htm
- **FTQuicken**, http://www.FTQuicken.co.uk
- **General Electric's Trading Process Network**, http://www.tpn.geis.com/
- **GeoCities**, http://www.geocities.com
- **Graphic, Visualization & Usability Center, Georgia Institute of Technology**, http://www.gvu.gatech.edu/
- **GVU Surveys**, http://www.gvu.gatech.edu/user_surveys
- **Hacker Quarterly**, http://www.hack2600.com/
- **Hoovers Company Information**, http://www.hoovers.com
- **HotMail**, http://www.hotmail.com

- **i2 Technologies, Inc.**, http://www.i2.com/
- **IBM's Data Modeling Techniques for Data Warehousing**,
  http://publib.boulder.ibm.com/cgi-bin/bookmgr/BOOKS/SG242238/COVER
- **InfoMedia**, http://www.infomedia.de
- **Institute for Operations Research and the Management Sciences**,
  http://www.informs.org/
- **Integrated Supply Chain Management Project**,
  http://www.ie.utoronto.ca/EIL/iscm-descr.html
- **International Data Warehousing Association**, http://www.idwa.org/
- **International Journal of Electronic Markets**, http://www.electronicmarkets.org
- **Internet Auction List**, http://www.usaweb.com/auction.html/
- **Internet Engineering Task Force (IETF)**, http://www.ietf.org
- **Internet Scout Project**, http://scout.cs.wisc.edu/scout/
- **Internet Society Site**, http://www.isoc.org/
- **Internet Travel Network (ITN)**, http://www.itn.net
- **Internet Trends**, http://www.genmagic.com/Internet/Trends/
- **Intranet Resource Site**, http://www.intrack.com/intranet/
- **IRI**, http://www.infores.com
- **Issue of Computer Mediated Communications**, http://jcmc.mscc.huji.ac.il/vol3/issue4/.
- **ISWORLD Net on virtual organizations**, http://www.iwi.unibe.ch/IM/virtual.html
- **Journal of Internet Banking and Commerce**, http://www.arraydev.com/commerce/JIBC/
- **Journal of Internet Purchasing**, http://www.arraydev.com/commerce/jip/
- **Juno**, http://www.juno.com
- **Kennys Bookstore**, http://www.kennys.ie/
- **LAN Times**, http://www.lantimes.com
- **Large Scale Networking group**, http://www.ccic.gov/cicrd/pca-wg/lsn.html
- **Links on Object Orientation**, http://www.rhein-neckar.de/~cetus/software.html
- **Lufthansa**, http://www.lufthansa.com
- **Malaysia Ecommerce Hub**, www.ec.com.my
- **Manugistics, Inc.**, http://www.manugistics.com/.
- **McAfee Associates, Inc.**, http://www.mcafee.com/
- **MCI Telephone Carrier**, http://www.mci.com
- **Media Motion Publications**, http://www.media-motion.com
- **Metropolitan Life Insurance Company**, http://www.metlife.com/
- **Microsoft Cinemania**, http://www.cinemania.msn.com
- **Microsoft Security Advisor**, http://www.microsoft.com/security/
- **Microsoft's COM**, http://www.microsoft.com/activex/default.asp
- **MilliCent: DIGITAL's Microcommerce System**, http://www.millicent.digital.com/
- **Monarch Design Systems**, http://www.monarchcad.com/
- **Mondex Electronic Cash**, http://www.mondex.com/
- **Music Boulevard**, http://www.musicblvd.com
- **Nasdaq Financial Services**, http://www.nasdaq.com
- **National Information Infrastructure**, http://nii.nist.gov/nii/niiinfo.html
- **National Institute of Health**, http://www.alw.nih.gov/Security/security.html
- **NetAddress**, http://www.netaddress.com
- **NetBill Central**, http://www.netbill.com/
- **NetCheque Network Payment System**,
  http://www.usc.edu/dept/Patents_Copyrights/352w.htm

- **NETIS auctionweb**, http://www.auctionweb.com/online/
- **Netscape Communications Corporation**, http://home.netscape.com/
- **Next Generation Internet Initiative**, http://www.ngi.gov/index.html.
- **NSF, Supply Chain Management in Electronic Commerce**, http://www.doce.ufl.edu/conf&sem/ElectricCommerce/index1.htm.
- **NUA Surveys**, http://www.nua.ie
- **Object Management Group**, http://www.omg.org/
- **OFFER Project**, http://haas.berkeley.edu/cmit/OFFER
- **OMG**, http://www.omg.org
- **Onsale.com**, http//www.onsale.com
- **Oracle**, http://www.oracle.com
- **Parentsplace**, http://www.parentsplace.com
- **Preview Travel**, http://www.previewtravel.com
- **Procter & Gamble**, http://www.pg.com/
- **Project 2000, Vanderbilt University**, http://www2000.ogsm.vanderbilt.edu/
- **Realtor.com**, http://www.realtor.com/
- **RelevantKnowledge**, http://www.relevantknowledge.com
- **Reuters News and Financial Information Services**, http://www.reuters.com
- **RocketMail**, http://www.rocketmail.com
- **ROI**, http;//www.research-online.com
- **Rootshell**, http://www.rootshell.com/
- **RSA Data Security**, http://www.rsa.com/
- **SAP**, http://www.sap.com/
- **Seniornet**, http://www.seniornet.org/
- **SET Secure Electronic Transaction LLC**, http://www.setco.org/
- **SGML/XML Web page**, http://www.oasis-open.org/cover/xml.html
- **Software.net**, http://www.software.net/
- **Sotheby's**, http://www.sothebys.com
- **Stanford University Supply Chain Forum**, http://www.stanford.edu/group/scforum/
- **Sun's Javabeans**, http://java.sun.com/beans/
- **Supply Chain Management Group**, http://www.uc-council.org/d42.htm
- **Supply Chain Management Research Group**, http://vlerick.rug.ac.be/rcscm/
- **Supply Chain Management Vendors**, http://www.aard.tracor.com/mfgservices/Mfg_Web_Site/lev2_links_scm.htm
- **Supply Chain Superlinks**, http://www.goldata.com.au/
- **Surflogic LLC**, http://www.surflogic.com
- **Surplus Auction**, http://www.surplusauction.com
- **SurveySite**, http://www.surveysite.com
- **Technology Review**, http://www.techreview.com/
- **Technorealism**, http://www.technorealism.org/
- **Telstra**, http://www.telstra.com.au/info/security.html
- **Thresholds, The Journal**, http://www.thresholds.com/journal/index.html
- **Toyota Motor Sales, U.S.A., Inc.**, http://www.toyota.com/
- **TPN-GEIS**, http://www.tpn.geis.com
- **Transaction Net Enabling Markets Online**, http;//www.transaction.net
- **Travelocity Travel Agent**, http://www.travelocity.com
- **TrustE**, http://www.truste.org
- **Tukaptrn, Inc.**, http://www.tukatech.com/tukaptrn.html

- **US Department of Energy**, http://ciac.llnl.gov/
- **US Library of Congress Digital Library**, http://lcweb.loc.gov/
- **USA Today**, http://www.usatoday.com/
- **Virtual Vineyards**, http://www.virtualvin.com
- **Wal-Mart**, http://www.wal-mart.com/
- **X.509 Public Key Infrastructure**,
  http://www.verisign.com/repository/ietf/draft-ietf-pkix-cmmf-00.txt
- **Yahoo! Inc.**, http://www.yahoo.com/

Index